CRUISING GUIDE TO
WESTERN FLORIDA

Other Cruising Guides from Pelican:

CRUISING GUIDE TO
WESTERN
FLORIDA

SIXTH EDITION

By Claiborne S. Young

PELICAN PUBLISHING COMPANY
GRETNA 2004

Maps customized by author
Maps typeset by Heathyr Davis
Cover photograph by author
Text photographs by author and Karen A. Young, unless otherwise indicated

ISBN 1-58980-194-6
ISSN 1097-8038

*The word "Pelican" and the depiction of a pelican are trademarks
of Pelican Publishing Company, Inc., and are registered
in the U.S. Patent and Trademark Office.*

Please note that channel conditions, depths, aids to navigation, and almost all on-the-water navigational data are subject to change at any time. While the author has been careful to verify first-hand all navigational information, on-the-water conditions may be quite different by the time of your cruise. Failure to follow current on-the-water reality, even when it differs from the instructions contained in this guide, can result in expensive and dangerous accidents. The author has worked hard to help minimize your risk, but there are potential hazards in any cruising situation for which captains, navigators, and crew are solely responsible. Information in this guidebook is based on authoritative data available at the time of printing. Prices and hours of operation of businesses listed are subject to change without notice. Readers are asked to take this into account when consulting this guide.

Pelican Publishing Company nor the author make any guarantee as to the accuracy or reliability of the information contained within this guidebook and will not accept any liability for injuries or damages caused to the reader by following this data.

Printed in the United States of America

Published by Pelican Publishing Company, Inc.
1000 Burmaster Street, Gretna, Louisiana 70053

This book is dedicated

to the memory of my dear friend

and frequent research assistant

John S. Horne.

Contents

Acknowledgments

First and foremost I want to thank my first-rate first mate, Karen Ann, without whose help as an experienced navigator, photographer, research assistant, and partner in life this book would not have been possible. I would also like to extend a warm thanks to my mother for all her encouragement and stories of Florida in the old days.

A very special thanks is extended to my research assistants, Bob Horne, Andy Lightbourne, Earle "Bud" Williams, and Kerry Horne. Without their many selfless hours spent with this writer during on-the-water research, this book would have been ever so much more difficult.

I would like to gratefully acknowledge the invaluable assistance of Morgan Stinemetz (who coauthors, along with this writer, *Cruising the Florida Keys*; Doran Cushing, founder of *Southwinds* magazine; and Janice and Jack Stevenson. Their friendship, their many nights of much-appreciated lodging, and all their good advice have been absolutely invaluable to this writer. I will be owing favors to all these dear friends for the next millennium.

A very special acknowledgment is paid to Ed Beckhorn and G. Gale Vinson of Marco Island. Ed and Gale are very active in the Marco Power Squadron and U.S. Coast Guard Auxiliary. They have done much to keep this writer informed about even the smallest change on the waters lying about Marco Island and the Ten Thousand Islands. If info like theirs was available for all the waters I cover, this job would be a snap!

I gratefully acknowledge the assistance of the many dockmasters and marina managers throughout Western Florida, who gave so much of their time and wisdom to me during my research. While they are too numerous to mention, their input was invaluable.

Finally, I would like to thank Dr. Milburn Calhoun, Nancy Calhoun, Kathleen Calhoun Nettleton, Nina Kooij, Tracey Clements, Cynthia Williams, and the rest of the staff at Pelican Publishing Company. It has been a genuine pleasure to once again work with the "Pelican bunch," and I hope our relationship will continue for many years to come.

Introduction

It has been said of Florida's western coastline that the good Lord cursed it with shallow water but then, in His wisdom, blessed the land with great beauty. This old saw is entirely apt. There is really no better summary of these memorable waters' cruising characteristics. While, to be sure, there is almost always a channel to which mariners can look for decent depths, soundings of 5 to 6 feet are considered quite respectable in Western Florida, where they might be looked at askance along the Sunshine State's eastern coastline. But, for those cruisers who find their way past the shoals and shallows, the shores that open out before them are some of the most unforgettable they will ever experience.

The vast stretches of Western Florida that have been spared the plundering hand of modern development can only be described as idyllic. I have only to close my eyes for a few moments to bring to mind the almost eerie beauty of the Little Shark River, with its tangled cypress shores reflected against brown waters and set amidst an almost palpable silence. The wide expanse of the Ten Thousand Islands, with their myriad anchorages and almost secret backwater recesses, calls to mind the adventurous outdoor yearnings in all of us. Consider for a moment the lovely waters of Pine Island Sound, with its old, stilted fishing houses that recall the days when salty men worked long and hard to harvest a life from the sea. Or you might want to reflect for a moment on serene Gasparilla Island, with its dreamlike inn, named for an infamous buccaneer whose story seems so much larger than life. Then there are the legendary man-killing turtles of

the Myakka River and the almost-shocking elegance of the Ringling estate overlooking Sarasota Bay. Still not convinced? Well, how about the singing ghosts of Manatee River and the incredible edifice of the Sunshine Skyway Bridge, spanning the entrance to Tampa Bay. And, lest we forget, there is the natural splendor of the Big Bend rivers, with names like Withlacoochee, Steinhatchee, and Suwannee, drawn from another time. While, tragically, we must acknowledge that portions of the Western Florida coastline have fallen to the bulldozer and the blight of high-rise condominiums, there is still so much that is fair and beautiful.

Cruising captains can rejoice in the many paths open to them in Western Florida that slip quietly from the hustle and bustle of mainstream, modern life and into the quiet and rewarding recesses of natural splendor. My explorations and chronicling of the waters set about Western Florida make up one of the most rewarding undertakings in my writing career. I sincerely hope that each and every one of you will have the same opportunity to experience the wonders of this storied coastline. Let's weigh anchor and get started.

The geography of Western Florida's coast is varied and sometimes complicated. Southwestern Florida lacks a protected inland waterway, and pleasure craft voyaging up the coast are relegated to the open waters of the Gulf of Mexico. Moving south to north, as we will throughout this guide, mariners cruising up from Marathon will be awed by the wild beauty of Cape Sable, the southwesternmost point of mainland Florida. This land is part of the Everglades National Park and safe from man-made changes. Two ports of call, the Park Service village of Flamingo, and the anchorages along the Little Shark and Shark rivers are well worth every cruiser's attention.

North of Cape Sable, skippers can explore the myriad backwaters and anchorages of the Ten Thousand Islands. This wild region is also little developed and offers a fascinating overview of the Everglades' coastal ecology. Everglades City is the only developed port of call in this region.

Captains cruising north of the islands to the city of Naples have two choices. You can continue your offshore voyage around the Cape Romano shoals or cut inside via a well-buoyed inland route. This latter passage features many cruising possibilities, but it is not a part of the official Western Florida ICW, and depths can be a bit thin from time to time.

Naples offers recently reduced marina and repair-yard facilities, but it's back to the open Gulf when time comes to head north again. With fair breezes or a humming engine, you will soon arrive at the port of Fort Myers Beach (featuring a very popular anchorage) and, a bit further along, San Carlos Bay and the southerly genesis of the Western Florida ICW. Here cruisers can turn aside on the combined path of the Caloosahatchee River and the Okeechobee Waterway to visit the old port town of Fort Myers before beginning their northward trek up the ICW.

The ICW soon introduces visiting cruisers to the fascinating waters of Pine Island Sound, with its rich history and enough potential havens for weeks of exploration. By all accounts, don't dare miss Cabbage Key and Gasparilla Island.

A wide body of water known as Charlotte Harbor cuts northwest from the northerly headwaters of Pine Island Sound and leads intrepid cruisers to the town of Punta Gorda and two streams of note, the Myakka and Peace rivers. A detour away from the ICW to cruise up Charlotte Harbor and its feeder rivers can be more than rewarding, particularly for sailors.

The Western Florida ICW darts north again through Lemon Bay and several sheltered land cuts on its way to Venice, one of the friendliest coastal communities in Western Florida. Another trek to the north lands pleasure craft at the southerly beginnings of this coastline's most developed region. The city of Sarasota overlooks a bay of the same name along this stretch of the Waterway and offers full facilities for visiting yachtsmen.

Soon the Waterway skips past charming Anna Maria Island on its way to sprawling Tampa Bay. Cruisers new to Florida's west coast will probably have to exercise considerable self-control to keep from gasping as the broad mouth of Tampa Bay opens out before them for the first time. The Sunshine Skyway Bridge spanning the bay's mouth is one of the most impressive structures that this writer has ever witnessed.

Tampa Bay is the largest body of inland water along the Western Florida coastline. Its waters provide ready access to the extensive marine facilities associated with the fortunate city of St. Petersburg.

The Manatee River, an important auxiliary water on southeastern Tampa Bay, leads cruisers by the hundreds to the Bradenton and Palmetto city waterfronts. Here the prolific marina facilities are supplemented by one of the most fascinating live aquatic displays that you will ever enjoy.

North of the great bay, the ICW passes

through one of the most intensely developed stretches of coastline that I have ever explored. The westerly reaches of St. Petersburg combine with the teeming city of Clearwater and a host of beachside communities to form an almost unbroken chain of condos, private homes, waterfront businesses, and docks of all descriptions. The Waterway runs through a dredged passage between heavily populated barrier islands to the west and the built-up mainland to the east.

North of Clearwater, development begins to slow its frenzied pace a bit. The village of Dunedin is a delightful port of call with out-of-this-world dining possibilities.

Finally, the Western Florida ICW ends hard by the beautifully natural shores of Anclote Key. A quick cruise up nearby Anclote River will bring fortunate mariners to the colorful town of Tarpon Springs, with its strong Greek flavor and fascinating sponge markets.

Now it's once again back to the open waters of the Gulf as mariners pass through the northernmost reaches of Western Florida on their way to the Panhandle. Look at any map of Florida and you will quickly understand why this region is called the Big Bend. While shallow water is everywhere in evidence, the various rivers along the way offer some of the most beautifully natural cruising in all of Florida. The Withlacoochee and Suwannee rivers are absolute "must-stop" ports of call in this region (always assuming your craft has a shallow enough draft).

Finally, our quick travelogue comes to an end at the snow-white lighthouse marking the entrance to the St. Marks River. This "Panhandle river" offers some marina facilities and yet another beautiful shoreline, not to mention a historic site of particular interest.

Now captains and crew must turn west on the deep and clear waters of the Florida Panhandle. A few more miles will bring you to St. George Sound, bounteous Dog Island and its excellent anchorages, the charming village of Carrabelle, and, perhaps most importantly, the easterly tip of the Northern Gulf ICW. For more information on this region and the inland and offshore waters west to New Orleans, please consult this writer's Cruising Guide to the Northern Gulf Coast.

The history of Western Florida is dotted with colorful figures and happenings like shells on a beach. It is my belief that no one can enjoy his or her cruise as he or she should without an appreciation of the heritage of the lands and waters through which he or she is traveling. For this reason, I have included a good smattering of Western Florida history throughout this guide. Wherever possible, the interested reader is referred to sources of additional information.

Weather along Western Florida is very different from what might be expected by cruisers from more northerly climes. Springs are warm to downright hot, and often humid, with relatively frequent thunderstorms. Nevertheless, this season is considered one of the best cruising times in the region. In the absence of any major storms, there is usually just enough wind for a good sail, and many days are clear and sparkling. Of course, cold fronts and other weather systems can mar this pattern of good weather, but most mariners will find spring cruising along the Western Florida coastline to be a genuine delight.

The long, hot, humid summers can leave cruisers used to cooler climates breathless from the heat. From June through September, and sometimes well into October, there are many days of calm air. Sweltering sail craft are forced to plod along under auxiliary power. As if that weren't problem enough, frequent afternoon thunderstorms can, and often do, get violent. St. Petersburg and Tampa Bay bear the unenviable moniker of "Lightning Capital of the World." Truly, summer cruising along Western Florida should be planned with a ready ear to the latest weather forecast and radar report. No matter what the weather folks say, though, if a dark cloud comes over the horizon, abandon everything and race for the nearest shelter.

The weather during the autumn months of October through December would be a serious contender with the spring season as the best cruising time on the Western Florida coast, but for the minor issue of hurricanes. The season for these great storms stretches from August through November. Any student of the region's history can readily tell you of the many, many hurricanes that have battered Florida's Gulf Coast in years past. If the weather service detects one of these giants heading your way, hole up until all that sound and fury has passed. These things are not to be taken lightly.

Winters in Western Florida are short and sweet and are usually finished by March at the latest. Rarely does any part of the coastline experience freezing temperatures, except for the occasional exception along the northerly portion of the Big Bend. Strong northerly winds are part and parcel of the Western Florida winters and cruising skippers should be alert for these strong blows. If such winds persist for several days, they can sometimes lower water levels in north-to-south-lying bodies of water below charted levels.

In this guide I have endeavored to include all the information captains may need to take full advantage of Western Florida's tremendous cruising potential. I have paid particular attention to anchorages, marina facilities, and danger areas. All navigational information necessary for a successful cruise has been included, and these data have been split apart in their own subsections and screened in gray for ready identification.

Visiting mariners should note that many, many marinas in Western Florida are currently in a state of transition. While researching this new, 2003-2004 edition, I discovered more marinas that were in the process of changing ownership, services, or some other aspect of their operation than this writer has ever noted before along this coastline. The bottom line is, "Be ready for changes."

In the past, this writer has always shied away from any listing of overnight, transient dockage rates for marinas. These sorts of charges change at such dizzying speeds that any such tabulation would be long out of date by the time the ink in this book was dry on the paper. However, for the first time, in this new edition, we are going to institute a very simple transient dockage fee-rating system. All marinas that provide overnight transient berths will be rated, "above average," "average," or "below average." Hopefully, this simple system will give you at least some idea of what to expect when it comes time to pony up your overnight dockage bill.

Each body of water covered in this guidebook has been personally visited for the very latest depth information. However, remember that bottom configurations do change. Dockside depths at marinas and inlets seem to be particularly subject to rapid variation. The cruising navigator should always be equipped with the latest charts and "Notice to Mariners" before leaving the dock.

The grayscale chart reproductions presented in the body of this text are designed to locate anchorages and facilities and give the reader a general knowledge of the coastline. They are not intended for and should never be used for navigation.

This guide is not a navigational primer, and it is written with the assumption that you have a working knowledge of piloting and coastal navigation. If you don't you should acquire these skills before tackling the coastal waters.

The waters set about the western coastline of the Sunshine State have a wide variety of navigational characteristics. As a general rule, cruisers can expect far shallower depths than those found in Eastern Florida or on the Panhandle. This exacting nature of Western Florida's waters frequently calls for careful navigation with a close watch on the sounder. Powercraft, in particular, should not be in so great a hurry to reach their intended port of call that they spend the better part of a day contemplating the value of good coastal navigation from the vantage point of a sand bar.

Tidal currents often flow swiftly along the inland waters of Western Florida. All mariners should be alert for the side-setting effects of wind and current. Sail craft, particularly when cruising under auxiliary power, and single-engine trawlers should be especially mindful of the quickly moving waters when traversing the many narrow channels so typical of this coastline.

As development has gone forward in Western Florida, many homes, modest and palatial, have been built along the banks of the ICW. Some of these have their own private docks. In order to prevent having their boats rocked and their lawns sprayed with salt water by each passing vessel, residents have petitioned for and been granted "minimum wake" and "no wake" speed restrictions in ever-increasing numbers during the last decade. I have tried to detail the major "no wake" areas, but be warned: new regulations are being put into effect constantly, and you can just about bet the old homeplace that more of these restrictive zones will be in place by the time of your visit. These regulated zones can slow your cruise considerably, particularly if you pilot a planing-hull powercraft. Be sure to allow plenty of time in your cruising itinerary to avoid frustration.

With the increasing development have also come bridges with restricted opening hours. While, again, this is not as large a problem here as on Florida's east coast, sail craft must contend with a host of regulated spans. Plan your hours around the opening times to avoid long delays. If you are forced to wait, be wary of the strong tidal currents that are often found on these waters. Stay alert and study the movements of any other vessels that might be waiting for the bridge.

Fortunately, a move is now underway by the state of Florida to replace all bridges crossing the ICW with 65-foot, fixed, high-rise spans. While it will take many years before this ambitious goal is fully realized, more and more swing and bascule bridges are disappearing. Check out our bridge listing at the beginning of each chapter to see what new high-rises are already in place. Passing cruisers should also be ready to avoid a considerable collection of construction barges and equipment wherever new bridge construction is underway. And, for the next several years at least, the list of these building projects will be anything but short.

During the last several years, other slow-speed zones have sprung up along Florida's various coastlines for a very different reason. The fascinating, gentle sea cow known as the manatee was threatened by injuries from high-speed props as the boating population of the region rose dramatically. Numerous "idle-speed" zones were established in the frequent habitats of these docile creatures. Some restrictions are in effect only from November 1 to March 31, while others are year round. Please observe all manatee signs.

Since the last edition of this guide appeared, the number and length of manatee no-wake and idle-speed zones has multiplied exponentially. Many stretch along the most traveled portions of the western Florida ICW. Power cruisers should now include extra time in their cruising itineraries for these slow-speed sections. Frankly, with this increase, even those power captains sympathetic to the plight of the manatee may be a bit frustrated. You can only grin and bear it—slow-speed manatee zones are now part and parcel of cruising all of the Floridian coastline.

Just so you are clear on the meaning of the different types of manatee slow-speed zones in Florida, here are the official definitions according to the Florida Marine Patrol. A manatee idle-speed zone is "a zone in which boats are not permitted to go any faster than necessary to be steered." A manatee slow-speed zone is "a minimum wake zone where boats must not be on a plane and must be level in the water."

There are those in the cruising community who would argue that the danger to manatees is now past, and the proliferation of manatee no-wake zones is no longer justified. We will not take a definitive stand on that issue within these pages, but I would enthusiastically refer the reader to the Web site of Standing Watch (http://www.Standing-Watch.org). These good folks have rendered great assistance by representing the cruiser's interest in the Florida state legislature (and elsewhere) and, at least in this writer's opinion, have done all of us who take to the water a great service!

Last but not least, with increasing development have come some rules this writer would prefer to describe in far saltier terms than gentility permits here. Between Naples and Clearwater, cruisers may find that anchorage is locally restricted to a 72-, 48-, or even 24-hour period. These perplexing regulations are inconsistent, in flux, and undergoing a strong and ongoing challenge by local boating groups. Check with the marinas for the latest word.

All navigators should have a well-functioning depth sounder on board before leaving the dock. This is one of the most basic safety instruments in any captain's arsenal of aids. The cruiser who does not take this elementary precaution is asking for trouble. An accurate knotmeter/log is another instrument that will prove quite useful. It is often just as important to know how far you have gone as to know what course you are following.

Western Florida skippers will find it most advantageous to keep the current chart and a pair of good binoculars in the cockpit or on the flybridge at all times. With these aids on hand, problems can be quickly resolved before you have a close encounter of the grounding kind.

The modern miracle of satellite-controlled GPS (Global Positioning System), particularly when interfaced with a laptop computer loaded with the latest digitized nautical charts, is yet another powerful navigational aid. GPS is more important when navigating the waters of Western Florida than on any other coastline that this writer has ever reviewed (with the possible exception of the Florida Keys). With the lack of a protected, well-marked, intracoastal waterway from Cape Sable to Fort Myers, and similar cruising conditions to the north along the Big Bend, a GPS suddenly becomes an invaluable, almost necessary tool that many navigators will not want to live without.

Since we have been talking about electronic navigation, this would seem a good time to announce a new feature in this guide. Approximate latitude and longitude positions of marinas and many anchorages have now been included within the body of this volume. All of these lat/lon positions are presented strictly for informational purposes; they must not be used as GPS or Loran way points!

Please also note that lat/lon positions for anchorages in this guide are given to help generally locate an overnight haven. With very few exceptions, mariners need not drop the hook at the exact location given. Within most creeks, bays, and other sheltered bodies of water appropriate for anchorage, there will likely be many places where you can rest comfortably and safely for the evening, swinging tranquilly on the hook.

With the phenomenal increase in popularity of computerized navigational software, we thought it important to begin providing this lat/lon information. For instance, this data can be plugged into Nobeltec's "Navigational Suite" or the "Cap'n" software, and the program will immediately place an icon on the digitized image of the appropriate nautical chart, almost exactly where the marina or anchorage you are making for is located.

That's a real, on-the-water advantage, but to be repetitive, please don't use this data as simple way points.

There are several reasons why. Loran C and GPS readings give mariners a straight-line distance or bearing to the intended way-point destination. Straight-line tracks do not take into account such vagaries as shoals you will need to avoid, peninsulas you will be unable to cross, or islands that just seem to get in the way.

In this guide, lighted daybeacons are always called "flashing daybeacons." I believe this is a more descriptive term than the officially correct designation "light," or the more colloquial expression "flasher." Also, to avoid confusion, daybeacons without lights are always referred to as "unlighted daybeacons." Similarly, lighted buoys are called "flashing buoys."

Things Change

If there is one constant in the world of cruising guides, it's that things change, sometimes before the ink is dry on the paper. We encourage our fellow cruisers to send us information about what comes to light as being new and different during their time on the waters of the Western Florida coastline. Have you discovered a new marina? We want to hear about it. Has there been a recent change in aids to navigation? Please let us hear from you. Are the regulations in a particular anchorage different from those we quote in the guide? Send this data our way.

Perhaps, the easiest way to send me this info is via e-mail. I can be reached at the following address:

opcom@cruisingguide.com

May we also extend an invitation to visit our

Web site at http://www.CruisingGuide.com. Here you will find not only information about our guidebooks, but also several photo galleries and a set of annotated links to every marina from North Carolina to New Orleans that has a Web site. Please check us out!

Perhaps, most important of all, we also publish an extensive, on-line, quarterly newsletter, the Salty Southeast, which allows fellow cruisers to exchange information and also helps to keep our readers updated on recent changes, modifications, and additions to the waters we cover in our guidebooks. This is a free service. All you need do to subscribe is send an e-mail to opcom@cruisingguide.com containing the word "subscribe."

So there you have it, with all its beauty, splendor, and warts too. The coastline of Western Florida from Cape Sable to the Florida Panhandle is indeed special. Cruisers of every taste and persuasion will certainly find something that strikes their fancy. It has been my privilege to help introduce these unforgettable waters to you. I sincerely hope that soon you will have the chance to experience them for yourself. Bathed by a benevolent sun and washed by the warm Gulf waters, the Sunshine State's western coastline waits to greet you. Good luck and good cruising!

CRUISING GUIDE TO
WESTERN FLORIDA

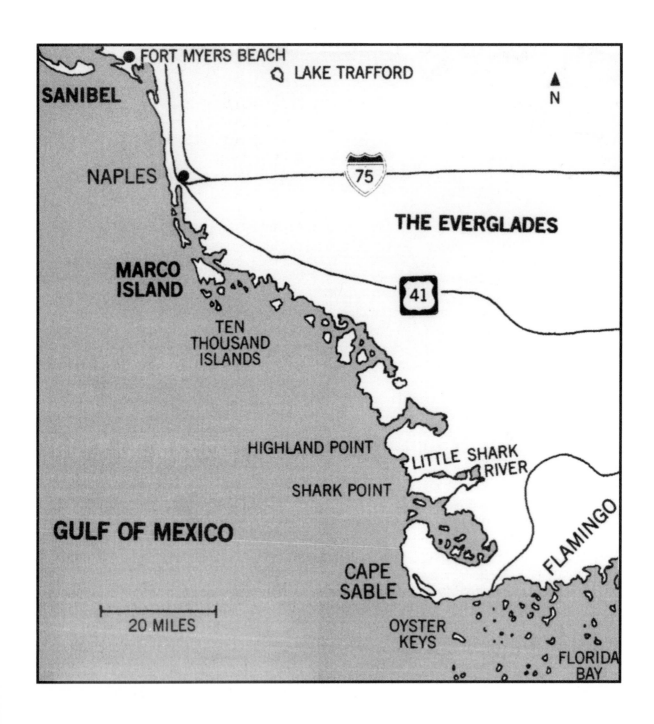

CHAPTER 1

Flamingo to Fort Myers Beach

If ever there was a single section of coastline that is a microcosm for the entire Western Florida seashore, it is most certainly that often lonely stretch of sand and vegetation between Cape Sable and Fort Myers Beach. Florida's southwesternmost coastline is a collection of varied cruising grounds that strike this writer as lands (and waters) of incredible contrasts.

Take, for instance, the almost completely undeveloped lands lying about Cape Sable, the southwestern tip of mainland Florida. This region is an integral part of the Everglades National Park and is almost completely free from human development. The waters lapping against these beautifully natural shores are almost universally shallow. There are but two ports of call to which cruising captains can look for overnight safety and security. Not to be overlooked, one of these stops comprises what may well be the most beautiful anchorage in all of Florida.

While there are significant differences between the two coastlines, the waters about Cape Sable strikingly remind this writer of Western Florida's Big Bend, north of Anclote Key and Tarpon Springs. Here, too, shallow water lies abundantly about little-disturbed shores, and only a few rivers provide deep enough entrance depths to be considered by cruisers. Also like the Big Bend, behind Cape Sable there is no protected Intracoastal Waterway maintained by the Army Corps of Engineers and to which mariners can look for safe passage. North from Cape Sable to Marco Island (at least), both pleasure and commercial craft must ply the Gulf of Mexico's open waters

while cruising north or south along the Western Florida coastline.

Above Plover Key and Lostmans River, the coastline changes radically. Suddenly skippers and crew are plunged into that fascinating portion of Western Florida known, appropriately enough, as the Ten Thousand Islands. The name says it all. There are probably ten thousand islands, or keys, at least, between Lostmans River and Marco Island. Exploration possibilities boggle the mind. The presence of but one readily accessible marina south of Marco Island and the relative lack of navigational aids, coupled with the ever-present shallow water, call for a spirit of adventure and a well-supplied vessel.

I cannot cruise the Ten Thousand Islands without musing back to my wanderings among the sparsely developed islands of Pine Island Sound, north of Fort Myers and the Caloosahatchee River. Both regions have a siren's song that speaks to the very core of the true explorer who relishes the notion that every puff of air or turn of the screw takes him or her a bit farther from civilization.

Captains cruising north through the Ten Thousand Islands must make a fundamental choice. You can continue offshore past the monumental Cape Romano shoals, or come inside these shallows and follow a marked and charted, but somewhat shallow, channel past Marco Island to the city of Naples.

Here again, the coastline, chameleon-like, takes on an entirely new character. Whether you cruise to Naples via its inland waterway (not a part of the official Western Florida ICW) or enter through the city's excellent inlet, Gordon Pass, you will find a teeming waterfront that now, surprisingly, offers only a few transient dockage berths.

Another offshore run will bring northbound cruisers to the community of Fort Myers Beach on Estero Island. The shores of this once-historic island are now fringed with a beachside honkytonk of cheap shops and motels. On a happier note, a collection of marinas and a fine anchorage wait to greet visiting cruisers.

Who could visit Naples or Estero Island and not come away feeling the kinship between this city and the shores of the ICW lying about St. Petersburg, Sarasota, and Clearwater? All of these communities represent highly developed Florida and offer services for all cruising craft.

Finally, a quick run up the Gulf from Estero will bring mariners to the southern mouth of San Carlos Bay and the official genesis of the Western Florida ICW. This latter section will be covered in the second chapter of this guide, but for now, let's push on to the exciting cruising possibilities of southwestern Florida.

Charts   Cruising navigators will need a whole bevy of NOAA charts for complete coverage of the waters from Flamingo to Fort Myers Beach.

11451—useful chart for approaching Cape Sable and Flamingo from the Florida Keys and points south

11433—principal chart for the Cape Sable and Flamingo region; cruisers planning to enter the marina at Flamingo will require this cartographical aid; also provides excellent detail of the Little Shark and Shark rivers' entrances and interior reaches

11431—large-coverage chart covering the southwestern Florida coastline from Cape Sable to the Ten Thousand Islands; this chart shows some offshore aids to navigation not pictured on the larger scale, more detailed inshore charts; most captains voyaging north along the coastline will want to have this chart

11432—a detailed chart picturing the coastline from the Little Shark River to Lostmans River that is really much more important to small craft running the Everglades National Park Wilderness Waterway than to skippers of sailboats or larger powercraft; it still might be useful to provide a more detailed look at geographic reference points as you move north along the coast; skippers with electronic navigation aboard may be able to get by with 11431 only

11430—important large-scale, detailed chart that covers all waters from Lostmans River and the Ten Thousand Islands to Naples and Wiggins Pass, including the inland Marco Island to Naples waterway; this one is a must

11429—small-scale, offshore chart covering the waters from the Ten Thousand Islands to a point north of Naples

11427—provides detailed navigational information for all inland and near-shore waters between Wiggins Pass and Fort Myers; this chart is needed by all cruisers planning to visit Fort Myers Beach, Fort Myers, or the southerly genesis of the Western Florida ICW

11426—another of those general, large-coverage offshore charts, this one detailing the waters from south of San Carlos Bay and Fort Myers to Charlotte Harbor; this chart does provide the only coverage of Charlotte Harbor, which is addressed in chapter 2

Bridges
Goodland/Highway 92 Bridge—crosses Marco Island-Naples waterway and Big Marco River north of unlighted daybeacon #12—Fixed—55 feet
Marco Island (Highway 951)/Judge S. S.

Jolley Bridge—crosses Marco Island-Naples waterway and Big Marco River west of unlighted daybeacon #26—Fixed—55 feet
Fort Myers Beach Bridge—crosses Matanzas Pass/Fort Myers Beach channel east-southeast of unlighted daybeacon #13—Fixed—65 feet

Flamingo to Lostmans River

One fine summer morning in early August of 1992, my fearless research assistant, Kerry Horne, and this writer headed out early in the morning from the marina at Flamingo, bound for the entrance to Little Shark River. As we rounded the three points of Cape Sable, we were amply rewarded for our early departure. To see the lovely white sand beaches back dropped by the mysterious cypress, brooding pines, and tall hardwoods was a very special experience indeed. Kerry described the Gulf's waters as akin to "color-tinted photographs of the Caribbean." We turned to each other and observed almost at the same moment that very few people, even frequent cruisers along Western Florida's coastline, had ever laid eyes on this magnificent sight.

In reflecting on this observation since that August morning, this writer has come to understand why so few take advantage of such a unique cruising opportunity. Skippers heading south to the Keys, or even those northbound from Marathon, are very likely to ride offshore and head for Naples or Fort Myers Beach. With only one marina (which requires a long passage off the direct north-south track to reach its docks) and a single anchorage, navigators studying chart 11433 might be excused for thinking that there is little to call them closer to shore.

What a mistake! In spite of their scarcity, the two ports of call in the Cape Sable region are worthy of attention from every single mariner cruising south of Everglades City and Marco Island.

Flamingo (25 08.505 North/080 55.407 West—Marina)

Flamingo was once one of the wildest frontier towns in all of Florida. Sadly, nothing is now left of the Flamingo of yesteryear. Today, visiting cruisers will find only a lodge, marina, and restaurant operated by a U.S. Park Service concessionaire.

It is a run of better than 12 nautical miles from the waters off the "East Cape" section of Cape Sable through the northerly waters of Florida Bay to the southerly dockage basin of Flamingo Lodge and Marina. Minimum depths on the entrance channel are about 4½ to 5 feet (found near unlighted daybeacon #16). Typically, soundings range from 5 to 9 feet. Boats drawing less than 4 feet should not have any problems. If you need more water, wait for a higher tide before attempting the passage.

Flamingo Marina has a rather unique situation. There are two dockage basins at this facility that are separated by a concrete floodgate.

1. Flamingo Marina

The harbor north of the gate is used by small craft engaged in cruising the so-called Wilderness Waterway through Everglades National Park. This shallow passage leads the adventurous small-craft skipper through the heart of the great sea of trees and grass north of Flamingo to Everglades City. The waterway is only appropriate for very small (18 feet or less), outboard-powered craft and thus will not be further discussed in this guide. The marina at Flamingo maintains a hoist that can actually lift smaller powercraft over the concrete barrier and deposit them safely in the waters to the north or south. This lift is not heavy enough for larger vessels, but as mentioned, that point is mostly moot anyway.

Of more interest to cruising-size craft is the sheltered dockage basin on the bay side of the marina, just north of unlighted daybeacon #18. Here you will find fixed wooden piers where transients may dock in 4½- to 6-foot dockside depths. Water and 30-amp power connections are available. Gasoline and diesel can be purchased at a fuel dock just south of the concrete floodgate, where you will also discover a waste pump-out service. Shoreside showers and a Laundromat are at hand beside a medium-size variety and ship's store. For those wanting to take a break from the live-aboard routine, the adjacent lodge is quite convenient. The restaurant in the complex is not open during the summer months, but you can still get pizza and sandwiches at the bar, which is in operation year round.

Flamingo Marina (239) 695-3101
  http://www.flamingolodge.com

Approach depth—4½-9 feet
Dockside depth—4½-6 feet
Accepts transients—yes
Fixed wooden piers—yes
Dockside power connections—up to 30 amp
Dockside water connections—yes
Waste pump-out—yes
Showers—yes
Laundromat—yes
Gasoline—yes
Diesel fuel—yes
Ship's and variety store—yes
Restaurant—on site

Flamingo makes an ideal base of operations for those wanting to explore Everglades National Park. Check at the lodge office concerning information about tram tours for those who arrive by water and lack landside automobile transportation. These sorts of excursions are usually offered, except during certain times of the summer. Call ahead of time to see if the park trams are operating.

We cannot leave Flamingo without a word about the mosquitoes. As a boy growing up on the North Carolina coast, I used to think the Carolinas had a mosquito problem. Boy, I did not know anything. I have never seen such bloodthirsty mosquitoes as those in the Florida Everglades. At times they swarm so thickly that it seems as if everything (and everyone) will be completely covered within a few minutes by frenzied, buzzing, biting insects the size of condors. They practically carried us off during the night and early morning one summer evening while we were docked at Flamingo. According to Park Service employees, the mosquitoes are at their worst between May and November. They really seem to come out after a rain. The more rain, the more mosquitoes. It should also be noted that calm conditions seem to encourage the little beasts. On a still summer night, or early in the morning, after a heavy rainfall it could be a battle for your life.

The Everglades' mosquitoes are not only a problem in Flamingo. The same conditions can be expected on Little Shark River and throughout the Ten Thousand Islands. The locals swear by a body lotion produced by the Avon cosmetic company called Skin-So-Soft. While it is most certainly not an insect repellent, apparently mosquitoes hate the taste of this fragrant, perfumy liquid and will not bite if you have slopped the oily concoction on your skin. By all accounts, I would have a large bottle of Skin-So-Soft on board before anchoring or tying up to the docks anywhere between Cape Sable and Marco Island.

Flamingo History   In his fascinating book *True Tales of the Everglades,* Stuart McIver comments about Flamingo's roots:

> When the settlers at the tip of Cape Sable established a post office in 1893, they were told they had to give their settlement a name. . . . They considered "End of the World." Instead, they picked a romantic, exotic name for their own personal hell-hole. They called it Flamingo. . . . In the 1890s flocks of the spectacular tropical birds were commonly seen in the Cape Sable area . . . so the name made sense. So did "End of the World," since the Cape at that time was an isolated society populated mostly by people who were running away from something— the law, civilization, or maybe their wives.

This short, quaint description tells all, and the term "hell-hole" seems particularly appropriate in view of the climate and the mosquitoes. In those early days the few residents of Flamingo made a living fishing, cultivating sugarcane, and distilling more than a few quarts of moonshine.

Apparently mosquitoes were at least as big a problem then as they are now. Each house was equipped with a room fronting the outdoors that was called a "loser." Before anyone entered a house, they were supposed to beat away or "lose" their mosquitoes with a palmetto branch in the little room.

In 1901, Flamingo received one of its most prominent early citizens, Steve Roberts. Uncle Steve, as he came to be called, migrated south from Gainesville, Florida, with "cattle rustling" rumors snapping at his heels. He raised a big family that eventually became the most prominent in the tiny settlement.

In 1908 the village's sugarcane was beset by a horde of hungry rats. Desperate to save their one cash crop, Uncle Steve's son Gene took a boat to Key West, where he advertised, "Will pay 10 cents Apiece for Every Cat." It wasn't long before he had a boat full of snarling, fighting felines. It must have been a long, trying trip back to Flamingo, but the effort was worth it. In no time at all the new swamp cats had routed out almost every rat within miles.

However, the real fame of Flamingo lies not in fishing, sugarcane, or even rats, but in the wholesale slaughter of the exotic birds which lived in the Everglades and the high-ground "hammocks" near the village. At the turn of the century, a truly unfortunate trend in fashions resulted in the stylish practice of decorating women's hats with colorful bird feathers or plumes. The demand rose so quickly that hunters in the Everglades soon could make more money than they had ever dreamed of before. At one point, egret feathers were selling for $32 an ounce, more than the price of gold at the time. The mass killings drove many of the Everglades' winged species to the brink of extinction after only a few years.

Finally, the state of Florida came to the rescue and outlawed the killing of birds for their plumage in 1901. For several years thereafter, it was a battle between the local game wardens and the plume hunters, but finally this sad trend in fashions crept into the pages of history.

In 1922 a road was pushed through the Everglades from Miami to Flamingo. Surprisingly enough, this artery of commerce was the death knell of the tiny community. As Stuart McIver comments in his other, equally fascinating book *Glimpses of South Florida History,* "People had found a way to get out." Many of the original homes were destroyed in the great hurricane of 1926 and the rest rotted away, with not a trace remaining today.

Flamingo Legend

It was during that tense period when plume hunting had been outlawed but before the fashion went out of style, that the "National Association of Audubon Societies" hired a group of wardens to enforce the new state law. Several of these heroic individuals operated out of Flamingo, and one of the most famous was Guy Bradley.

On July 8, 1905, the sounds of distant gunfire were heard over Florida Bay. Guy walked out of his front door and sighted a schooner in the distance that he recognized as the boat of Capt. Walter Smith. He had already arrested Smith twice before for plume hunting, and the gunfire left little doubt about the captain's present activities.

The intrepid warden got his gun and began rowing his small dinghy across Florida Bay. It was a trip from which he would never return. His body was found soon afterward. Guy Bradley had become the first warden to die in the defense of Florida's native bird population.

Captain Smith fled to Miami, where he managed to successfully avoid indictment through political connections. Nevertheless, the warden's sacrifice was not to be in vain. As a direct result of the anger engendered by Guy Bradley's death, new legislation was passed in both Tallahassee and Washington which was to end the plume trade within a few years once and for all.

Guy Bradley was buried on the tip of Cape Sable, and a deeply grateful Audubon Society erected a plaque over his grave. In 1960 Hurricane Donna washed the grave away, but the brave warden and his untimely but honorable death have not been forgotten. Today a notable monument has been erected to Guy Bradley's memory at the Flamingo Visitor's Center.

Flamingo and Cape Sable Anchorages (25 07.644 North/080 55.540 West)

A few boats occasionally anchor in the waters off Cape Sable during fair weather. None of the havens described below is particularly sheltered, and they should not be employed if there is a hint of foul weather in the forecast.

Captains piloting shallow-draft vessels and wanting to anchor off Flamingo, rather than tie up at the marina docks, might consider doing so in the 4- and 5-foot waters east of unlighted day-beacon #11 (near 25 07.644 North/080 55.540 West). Don't stray too far from the marked channel, or depths may deteriorate further.

In light winds, cruisers may consider anchoring in the charted 7- and 8-foot waters northwest and southeast of Middle Cape. Anchor abeam of the cape's westerly tip, either to the north or south. Do not attempt to make a closer approach to the beach except by dinghy, as depths rise quickly.

Middle Cape is surrounded by a beautiful white-sand beach backed by tall trees that look as if they have not known the hand of man since time immemorial. You explorer types might try dinghying ashore through the surf for an unforgettable visit. Just don't forget about the mosquitoes if the winds are calm.

Little Shark River and Shark River Anchorages (Various Lats/Lons—see below)

The marked entrance into the westerly mouth of Little Shark River lies some 11 nautical miles north of Middle Cape. Out of the hundreds and hundreds of anchorages that this writer has visited and reviewed, the memory of Shark River will always remain with me as one of the most beautiful and awe-inspiring of the lot. The dark waters rolling by with their strong tidal currents fitfully reflect the heavily wooded shores. Though it is well within the confines of Everglades National Park, visitors to Shark River will not see the "river of grass" for which the region is so famous. Closer to the coast, the Everglades support deep woods of cypress, pine, and a few hardwoods. The river's primeval shoreline looks as if it has been undisturbed since the days when the Timucuan Indians poled their canoes along the stream,

many hundreds of years before the first European touched the Florida shoreline. Anchoring in these rarified confines and watching the Evening Star unhindered in the clear coastal airs can quickly lead to a substantial dropping of the blood pressure. Of course, on calm nights, part of that lower reading may be courtesy of a few million mosquitoes draining you dry, but, hey, nothing's perfect.

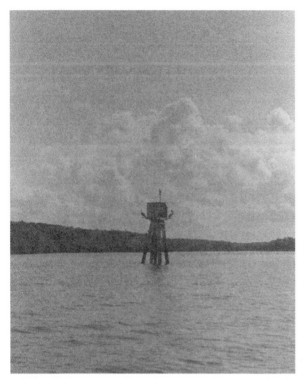

Little Shark River entrance

A complete compendium of all the places that cruising craft might anchor on the Little Shark and Shark rivers would make up a small pamphlet of its own. While a number of potential havens are outlined below, this list is by no means exhaustive. Captains with wanderlust running hot in their veins can pilot their vessels to literally dozens and dozens of overnight stopovers.

One concern when anchoring on either of the Shark rivers or their adjoining streams is the strong tidal currents that plague these waters. On-site experiments with our own

At the time of this writing, minimum low-water depths of 5½ feet can be expected in the marked entrance channel. Care must be taken to hold to these soundings at the stream's western mouth. First-time visitors should be sure to read the navigational account of Little Shark River presented in the next section of this chapter before undertaking their first entry into the stream.

East of Little Shark River's entrance, depths improve markedly, typically to better than 8 feet. While there are a few unmarked shoals to watch out for, careful cruisers piloting craft as large as 45 feet can find their way into the confines of (Big) Shark River, a few miles to the east and north. This delightful passage currently features minimum 6-foot depths.

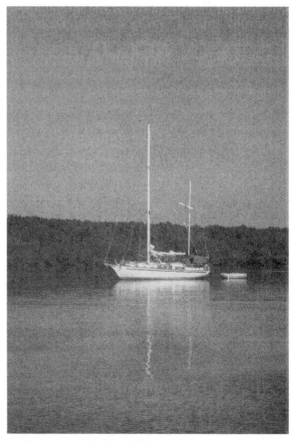

Anchored on Little Shark River

hook suggest that the holding ground is good. Nevertheless, this is one spot where you had really better take a good, long look once the anchor is down to be sure you aren't dragging before popping open a cool one (define it as you wish) to begin the evening's relaxation.

For those who want an early start the next morning, the Little Shark River offers an anchorage just east of its entrance. The charted cove northwest of unlighted daybeacon #4 (near 25 19.677 North/081 08.801 West) offers first-rate protection and depths of 5½ to 6 feet. Shallow water protrudes much farther out from the back (northwestern shores) of the cove than is indicated on chart 11432 or 11433. For best depths, anchor just inside the cove's southeastern mouth, on the center of its southwest-to-northeast axis. Protection is superb and the deeply wooded shores mentioned above are very much in the picture. Boats up to 48 feet should not have any problems with swinging room.

Notwithstanding all of this first anchorage's good qualities, I feel that bodies of water like the two Shark rivers deserve a little further upstream exploration. Believe me, you won't be sorry for the additional time spent cruising on this incredibly beautiful river.

The next anchorage (moving to the east) that you might consider is found on the river's southeasterly offshoot at unlighted daybeacon #69 (near 25 19.736 North/081 07.132 West). Good depths of 9 feet are carried to a position 100 yards north of the point where the stream splits into two southerly branches. Again, protection is superb and the shores are all one could ask for. Captains piloting boats larger than 40 feet might feel a bit cramped.

The main branch of the Little Shark River cuts northeast from unlighted daybeacon #69.

Unmarked shoals become somewhat more frequent but are still easily handled by careful cruisers. The fork of the Little Shark River that cuts back to the west-northwest, west of unlighted daybeacon #68, and leads eventually to Ponce de Leon Bay is yet another super overnight stop in most winds for all but the very largest boats. Try dropping the hook near 25 20.268 North/081 06.983 West. Depths run from 6 to 9 feet, and the shoreline is, if possible, even more magnificent. Strong westerly and northwesterly winds could blow straight into the stream from the bay and raise a chop, but otherwise, this anchorage is also well sheltered. Don't attempt to follow the stream out into Ponce de Leon Bay, where there are a host of unmarked shoals. Drop your hook well southeast of the entrance into the bay.

The marked channel in the Little Shark River cuts southeast at unlighted daybeacon #64 and eventually joins up with the Everglades Wilderness Waterway. Larger pleasure craft should avoid this passage.

It is still feasible to cut into the northerly branch of the Little Shark River just before reaching #64. After skirting around a few charted shoals, you can work your way either into the upper reaches of the Little Shark River, or through one of the deep, north-south, connecting streams into the Shark River. For those who really want a good look at the region, consider a round trip, cutting north on one of the two connecting streams southwest of charted Shark Cutoff, then east-northeast on the main body of the Shark River to the waters abeam of charted Gunboat Island. You can then retrace your steps to charted "Marker 6" and follow the upper reaches of the Little Shark River back to the

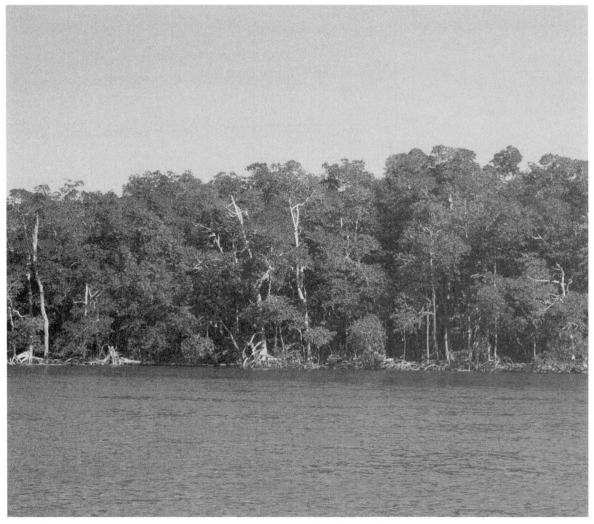

Little Shark River shoreline

stream's entrance channel. This is a magnificent trip for powerboats, albeit a bit lengthy for the sailing brethren. In any case, you don't have to undertake the entire loop. Even a portion of the passage is well worthwhile. Cruisers can anchor almost anywhere along the upper reaches of the Shark or Little Shark rivers. Just be sure that the anchor is well down and show a nighttime anchor light.

Don't attempt to follow the Shark River above Gunboat Island. Depths finally begin to deteriorate northeast of this point.

FLAMINGO TO LOSTMANS RIVER NAVIGATION

The first thing to understand about navigating the waters of extreme southwesterly Florida is the lack of any protected Intracoastal Waterway. This means that all north-to-south cruising must be accomplished by braving the waters of the open Gulf of Mexico. While this is far from a daunting prospect in fair weather, or even for sail craft in moderate breezes, the Gulf has been known to get its dander up on more than one occasion. Smaller cruising craft, in particular, *must* take the latest weather forecast into account before venturing out on these wide waters.

The second thing to remember is the almost universal shallowness of the southwestern Florida coastline. This shoaly character makes for a very long cruise between stops. Except for Flamingo and the Little Shark River, captains bound north from Marathon and the Florida Keys must cruise a good 36 nautical miles from East Cape (the southernmost of Cape Sable's three points) to the first available anchorage (shallow-draft only) at New Turkey Key. It's yet another run of better than 13 nautical miles from a position abeam of New Turkey Key to Indian Key. This isle marks the channel leading to Everglades City, the only port of call with readily accessible marina facilities in the Ten Thousand Islands region. It doesn't take a rocket scientist to understand that it's going to be a lengthy cruise from Cape Sable to Everglades City. Powerboats must be sure to have sufficient fuel aboard, and all pleasure craft should make appropriate preparations for covering such a distance without the possibility of putting into a nearby harbor.

Entrance into Flamingo   Employing either DR (dead-reckoning) navigation or GPS (preferably interfaced with a laptop computer or a chart plotter), work your way to a point south and west of East Cape. Use your binoculars to pick out unlighted daybeacon #1A, south of East Cape, and flashing daybeacon #2, 1.6 nautical miles farther to the south. For best depths, set course to come abeam of and pass #2 by about 1 nautical mile to the aid's northerly side. This wide gap will help you avoid the charted 5-foot depths north of #2.

From flashing daybeacon #2, the channel is reasonably straightforward, though there are wide gaps between the various aids to navigation along the way. Be sure to have compass/GPS courses preplotted, and faithfully follow them as you work your way along.

Pass unlighted daybeacons #6 and #8 to their northerly sides (as you would expect from the good old "red, right, returning" rule). Shallow water lies south of these aids.

At flashing daybeacon #9, the channel turns sharply north-northeast and cuts through a dredged passage into Flamingo Marina's southerly dockage basin. This is the shallowest portion of the passage to Flamingo. Expect some 5-foot (possibly 4½ at extreme low water) depths abeam of unlighted daybeacon #16.

If you should decide to anchor east of unlighted daybeacon #11, ease your way about 50 yards due east from #11. Drop the hook before proceeding any farther. A bit more to the east, soundings rise to 4-foot levels or less.

At unlighted daybeacon #16, the channel swings a bit to starboard, then cuts back north at unlighted daybeacon #18. The harbor's entrance will then be obvious dead ahead. As you cruise into the creek, the marina docks will come abeam to port.

North to Little Shark River   Cruising the gap between East Cape and Little Shark River is actually surprisingly simple in good weather. If you stay within sight of shore, both Middle and Northwest capes are quite obvious. Flashing daybeacon #4 off Northwest Cape is also valuable in determining your position.

Look at either chart 11431 or 11433 for a moment and note the "Marker" symbols. These are actually on-the-water signs that denote the boundary of Everglades National Park. You can keep up with your position by ticking these off as you go along. Thus, with the plentiful landmarks and other points of reference, even GPS-less boats should be able to find their way to Northwest Cape in good weather.

On the other hand, local cruisers have warned this writer that the "Everglades National Park" signs, mentioned above, are a real navigational hazard at night. Apparently they lack any of the reflector tape that usually allows easy detection of aids to navigation with a searchlight. Watch out for these potential obstructions if your passage through these waters takes place after sunset.

The situation changes radically north of Northwest Cape. No readily recognizable landmarks grace the shoreline between Northwest Cape and the entrance to the Shark River. There are no aids to navigation either, except for the park boundary markers. Just to make matters a bit more interesting, flashing daybeacon #1, at the western mouth of Little Shark River, is very hard to spot from the water. The 16-foot daybeacon blends right in with the tall trees along Shark River Island.

I can only recommend using your binoculars and good dead-reckoning navigation, plus a GPS, to find your way to flashing daybeacon #1. It's not always an easy process, but the reward often justifies the effort.

The Little Shark River and the Shark River The Little Shark River's entrance channel is the shallowest and most critical part of the entire passage throughout the region. Come abeam of and pass both flashing daybeacon #1 and unlighted daybeacon #3 by some 50 yards to their southeast and southerly sides. Don't get closer to the aids. The channel seems to be shoaling on its northwesterly side. By keeping off the markers, you can currently maintain minimum 5½-foot depths.

After leaving #3 behind, the river soon cuts to the north. Good depths spread out in a broad band along the centerline for some distance upstream.

If you drop the hook on the cove northwest of unlighted daybeacon #4, remember to anchor on the outer portion of the cove's mouth. Farther to the northwest, depths shelve upward with surprising rapidity at the rear of the cove.

You can easily turn into the mid-width of the river fork branching southeast from unlighted daybeacon #69. Just be sure to halt your forward progress at least 100 yards short of the split in the stream.

Cruisers seeking the more upstream anchorages and the (Big) Shark River should cut northeast between unlighted daybeacons #69 and #70. Notice that marker colors have now reversed, and upstream cruisers should begin to pass red, even-numbered aids to navigation to their (the cruisers') port side and take green beacons to starboard. The reason for this shift is that the river channel now becomes part of the Wilderness Waterway.

As you emerge from this connector stream into the wider water west of unlighted daybeacon #68, you will go through one stretch of 6-foot depths. Unlighted daybeacon #68 marks the first real shoal you need to worry with in the Little Shark River. If you are entering the anchorage northwest of #68, favor the stream's southwesterly shores to avoid the shallows. Cruising craft continuing upstream should pass #68 to its southerly side.

You can continue to follow the buoyed route to unlighted daybeacon #64. Discontinue following the markers at this point. To the east and south, the marked cut leads to the Wilderness Waterway and depths deteriorate. Those lucky captains and crew continuing on to the Shark River should probably employ the deep feeder stream just west and north of #64.

As you approach the wider waters to the northeast, the trickiest section of the passage to the Shark River will be encountered. Notice the large patch of 4-foot shoals pictured clearly on chart 11433, bounding the stream's center. To avoid this hazard, round the point, cut east, and favor the southern shores heavily until you are well past the shoal. You may then take your choice of the two north-to-south feeder streams (and enter the Shark River), or continue to track your way up the Little Shark River until intersecting the Shark River near charted "Marker 6."

On-site research did not reveal any depth problems in passing south of the island that sits at the confluence of the Little Shark and Shark rivers. Simply hold to the mid-width scrupulously as you pass the island. Good depths continue upstream to Gunboat Island. This guide's coverage of the Shark River ends at this point.

On to the Ten Thousand Islands North of the Little Shark River entrance, passing cruisers must continue on the open waters of the Gulf. This is an area where boats with GPS have a definite advantage. Some of the charted aids to navigation are actually founded in rather shallow water and the prudent mariner will pass well west of these markers. It's always possible to miss a beacon under these circumstances, and without a good dead-reckoning track or an electronic means to fix your position, it could be a white-knuckle cruise.

Shallow water is waiting to trap you on the various rivers or coves indenting the shoreline between the Little Shark River and Pavilion Key (near flashing daybeacon #10). All are quite shallow. Even Ponce de Leon Bay, just north of the Little Shark River, is riddled with unmarked shoals.

North of Lostmans River and flashing daybeacon #8, it's time to make a very basic decision. If you plan to explore the Ten Thousand Islands, or follow the inland route via Marco Island to Naples, set your course to pass east of the long, long Cape Romano shoals. Eventually, you should come abeam of flashing daybeacon #10 well to its westerly quarter. Pavilion Key heralds your entrance into the Ten Thousand Islands region. Some great cruising is just ahead.

Navigators following the offshore route should set course to pass several miles west of the Cape Romano shoals. A charted but unnumbered 18-foot flashing daybeacon marks the southerly reaches of these shallows.

Ten Thousand Islands

At the turn of the century . . . the Ten Thousand Islands, a bewildering maze of mangroves, gave cover to fugitives, derelicts and a few harmless hermits. The seven unwritten laws of that wild country, an early account says, were:

1. Suspect every man
2. Ask no questions
3. Settle your own quarrels
4. Never steal from an islander
5. Stick by him, even if you do not know him
6. Shoot quick, when your secret is in danger
7. Cover your kill

Well, since those days, the settlements in the Ten Thousand Islands have acquired a far more savory reputation. However, the rugged American individualism symbolized in this rough credo (recounted in Stuart McIver's *Glimpses of South Florida History*) is still very much part and parcel of this region where wild, untamed land is the rule, not the exception.

As we explore the Ten Thousand Islands together in the pages that follow, you will hear a few of the stories which have filtered out of the islands through the years. It's not hard to imagine how the rugged and often colorful pioneers in this land of water and islands engendered a folklore which is as rich as swampland muck, although the occasional outsider has added a bit of spice here and there as well. No less a personage than John James Audubon spent some time here while performing his early studies of birds and their habits.

And speaking of birds, those who go gently will have the opportunity to observe a bounty of winged wildlife in the islands. Great egrets, great blue herons, roseate spoonbills, wood storks, and better than a hundred other varieties of birds may be spotted as you cruise along. Practically the entire Ten Thousand Islands are within the confines of Everglades National Park. As such, these small bodies of land are some of the most prolific and varied bird sanctuaries in the United States.

Cruisers who pilot deep-draft vessels or prefer to tie up to the piers of a full-service marina with every amenity will most likely want to lay on the throttles or crank out the jib a bit more and head directly for Marco Island or Naples. But those mariners whose eyes get dreamy while contemplating the idea of backwater cruising, where few have been before them will find a wealth of rewards in cruising the Ten Thousand Islands.

The Ten Thousand Island region begins north of Lostmans River and runs to Coon Key Light. Here cruisers following the inside route can enter a sheltered but somewhat shallow passage running north to Marco Island and Naples. After exploring the Ten Thousand Islands, those captains following the outside route will have to duck back out into the Gulf well south of the Cape Romano shoals before continuing their northward trek.

Shallow water is very much commonplace in the islands. Cruisers must take extra care to stay off the bottom while trying to navigate the various anchorages and channels cutting this way and that around the islets. This process is made ever so much more difficult due to the relative lack of navigational aids. What may look quite obvious on the chart can be almost irrecognizable on the water. If you've been lucky enough to visit a particular anchorage previously and locked the location into your GPS's memory, so much the better. Otherwise, you are in for some exacting coastal navigation.

This is most certainly one portion of the Western Florida coastline where those fortunate cruisers who have a GPS chart plotter or a GPS aboard, interfaced with a laptop computer (loaded with the digitized NOAA nautical charts and appropriate navigational software such as "Navigation Suite" or the "Cap'n"), have a distinct advantage. Personally, we make it a point to have this wonderful marvel of electronic navigation aboard whenever we are cruising these waters.

With this navigational complexity in mind, the anchorages outlined below have been chosen for their relative proximity to some recognizable geographic or on-the-water point of reference. Thus, the list is by no means even close to complete. Those who simply must drop the hook where none have gone before, and are willing to risk finding the bottom, will discover many an additional overnight stop to explore and savor.

Marina facilities in the Ten Thousand Islands are meager. One old inn welcomes transient cruisers at the village of Everglades City. Good food, lodging, and supplies (not to mention good sightseeing) are close at hand, and the inn offers full fueling services. The only other marina in this region now has such a shallow entrance channel that we can no longer recommend it at all for cruising-size vessels.

The Rod and Gun Club in Everglades City is now the only realistic marina alternative for cruising vessels in the entire Ten Thousand Islands region. Better be sure those tanks are topped off and your vessel is in top condition before taking the plunge.

I cannot close without making plain my personal affection for the Ten Thousand Islands. This writer knows of no other Floridian cruising ground that offers so many gunk holes and fascinating opportunities to explore far from the remotest confines of civilization. It's truly not for everyone, but the rugged call of the islands is a song that will be hard for many to ignore.

New Turkey Key Anchorage (25 38.984 North/081 16.759 West)

Our first anchorage in the Ten Thousand

Islands will certainly not go down in history as the easiest to find. You must also travel through some definite 4-foot low-water depths to reach the haven in question. Obviously, this anchorage is restricted to those vessels drawing 3½ feet (or preferably less), with skippers who are confident in their navigational skills and who pilot boats 36 feet or smaller.

A cruise of some 5 nautical miles to the north-northwest of flashing daybeacon #8 (west of Lostmans River) will bring you abeam of Plover and North Plover keys. These twin islands, along with a third body of land, Buzzard Key, protrude fairly far out from shore and are somewhat recognizable to the careful navigator. While none of these isles offer more than light-air anchorage, a better haven awaits just to the north.

Another 1.5 nautical miles will bring you abeam of Turkey and New Turkey keys to the east-northeast. These islands tend to blend in with the shoreline, and you will have to do some yeoman's work with your binoculars to make the correct identification. After accomplishing this demanding deed, you can follow

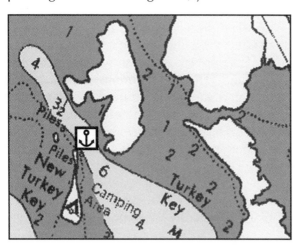

the wide band of charted 4- and 5-foot waters to the 6- and 8-foot depths off the eastern and northeastern sides of New Turkey Key. The tent symbol on chart 11430 denotes this island as an Everglades National Park campground, but we saw no evidence of this facility from the water. The shores exhibit the usual, thickly wooded growth so characteristic of these islands.

Protection is quite good from eastern and western winds but minimal in blows from the north or south. In any case, this is most assuredly not a foul-weather hidey-hole. Better-sheltered spots are found just to the north.

Pavilion Key

The large island known as Pavilion Key lies to the north of (charted) flashing daybeacon #10. I mention Pavilion Key not so much as a potential anchorage, but as a landmark and a historical location. In cruising north into the Ten Thousand Islands, Pavilion Key is quite prominent, and it is visible for several miles. As such, it can serve as an invaluable navigational point of reference.

Pavilion Key History

In 1904 the Burnham Clam factory began operating near Caxambas Pass, on the southern shores of Marco Island. A goodly portion of the clam beds that fed the hungry plant lay off Pavilion Key. In those days clams were gathered by hand, and it was back-breaking work.

Some time after 1911 Capt. Bill Collier developed the "clam dredge" at Marco which allowed clams to be harvested from deeper waters. While it led to a temporary boom for local clammers, the vast beds lying about Pavilion Key were exhausted after only a few years.

Lumber Key (25 45.627 North/081 22.835 West)

One of the most beautiful anchorages in all the Ten Thousand Islands is found off the northwestern banks of Lumber Key. Using Pavilion Key as a navigational reference, along with your binoculars, you must be careful to identify this isle from its fellows. At first, we were confused by Rabbit Key. From the water, the two islands appear to be almost joined together.

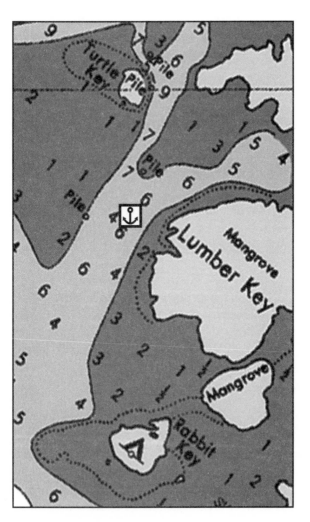

We sounded depths of mostly 6 feet while carefully cruising up the strand of deeper water northwest of the two keys. Low-tide depths of 4 feet are possible, so this anchorage is again restricted to vessels drawing 3½ feet or less. There is good protection from southern and southeasterly winds, but the anchorage is wide open to northern, northwestern, and westerly blows.

The shores of Lumber Key are fringed with a white sand beach and beg to be explored by dinghy. In the right wind and weather, this will surely be one of the most delightful spots you will ever find to swing on the hook.

Jack Daniels Key (25 47.882 North/081 25.931 West)

By the time you come abeam of Jack Daniels Key, Indian Key Pass and the marked channel to Everglades City are only 1.5 nautical miles to the northwest. You can use flashing daybeacon #1, just southwest of Indian Key, as a point of reference to help locate both of the anchorages reviewed below.

Study chart 11430 for a moment and note the unnamed, round island sitting south of Jack Daniels Key. While some shoals abut the little isle's shoreline, a band of minimum 5-foot water rings the land mass. It is quite possible to approach from the southwest side of the island through minimum 5-foot depths. You can then work your way around the southeastern quarter of the island and drop the hook off its northeastern corner. I would be uncomfortable trying this maneuver with a vessel larger than 40 feet. This spot is well sheltered from all but southerly and southeasterly winds. Small craft that draw 3 feet or less can probably circumnavigate the little island if they so desire. Vessels that need more water should probably stick to the track outlined above.

Kingston Key (25 48.005 North/081 27.011 West)

One of the navigationally simplest anchorages south of Indian Key Pass is found on the charted 7-foot waters lying off the eastern shores of Kingston Key. Using flashing daybeacon #1 as a reference to help identify Kingston Key, it then becomes an elementary matter to follow the deep water around the isle's southern and southeastern shores to the good water off the relatively straight eastern banks. Minimum entrance depths seem to be 6 feet, and you can drop the hook in 7-foot

soundings. These waters should accommodate vessels drawing 5½ feet. As usual, the scenery is all any naturalist could hope for, and you'll be sad to say you're on your way.

Indian Key Pass and the Channel to Everglades City (Various Lats/Lons —see below)

Indian Key may just be the most important of all the Ten Thousand Islands, and not just because John James Audubon once camped on its shores while drawing and studying the region's native birds. Indian Key sits astride one of only two marked passages in the Ten Thousand Islands. This channel offers not only two superb anchorages, but also reliable access to the Barron River and the village of Everglades City. This community is the only modern-day town to survive in the entire region.

Returning our attention to Indian Key for a moment, the island plays host to yet another of the official Everglades National Park campgrounds. Of more interest to cruisers, the most popular anchorage between Lostmans River and Marco Island lies just northeast of the isle near 25 48.673 North/081 27.728 West. Here, a long sandspit, not really shown on chart 11430, runs well northeast of the island proper. This bar is partially covered at high water, so be wary.

Boats of almost any size can anchor southeast of the sandspit, off Indian Key's northeasterly tip, in 6 to 10 feet of water. We have never had occasion to visit this anchorage without finding several fellow pleasure craft swinging tranquilly on the hook. Shelter is more than adequate for all but particularly strong northeasterly winds, which would blow straight down Indian Pass channel. To say that the anchorage is attractive would be akin to saying the same of, oh, Halle Berry. It would be all too easy to linger here for days on end while simply soaking up the ambiance. A dinghy trip to the all-natural shores of Indian Key is a must. It would also be a good time to break out the mask, snorkel, and fins. The waters about Indian Key are well worth an underwater exploration.

The only real disadvantage to this haven comes in the form of early morning passages by the numerous commercial fishing craft operating out of nearby Everglades City. These boats sometimes come roaring out of the channel hard by Indian Key quite early in the morning. Fellow cruisers have told this writer of being awakened as early as 3:30 A.M. by these noisy vessels.

Captains can alternately follow the charted tongue of deep water northwest of Indian Key. However, as this passage does not lead to any really sheltered spots, and depths eventually poop out as Gaskin Bay is approached, it makes sense to follow the marked passage southeast of the key.

Indian Key Pass maintains minimum 6-foot depths all the way to the Everglades City waterfront. There is one tricky spot near unlighted daybeacon #3 off Indian Key where it might be possible to briefly wander into 4 feet of water, but cautious mariners can avoid this trouble spot.

Bird-watching while cruising along Indian Key Pass is absolutely magnificent. With any luck you will observe many of the species that

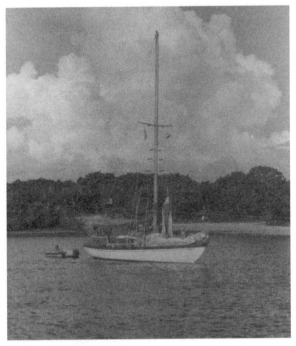

Anchored off Indian Key

originally drew John James Audubon to the region.

Southwest of flashing daybeacon #7, Russell Pass opens into the northern flank of the Indian Key-Everglades City channel. This sidewater offers yet another first-rate overnight anchorage. Cruisers must avoid a shoal at the pass's entrance, but you can quickly bypass this hazard and drop the hook in from 7 to as much as 18 feet of water. Larger vessels can anchor in the patch of charted 8- to 18-foot depths just north of the entrance, near 25 49.917 North/081 26.516 West. There's enough swinging room for the QEII.

Better protection is acquired as the stream curves to the northeast. Visiting cruisers can anchor in the 7- to 14-foot waters of the pass just short of the large, shallow cove cutting into the southeasterly banks, near 25 50.303 North/081 26.317 West. This anchorage's shelter is the finest imaginable.

If you're looking for a real hurricane hole, continue following Russell Pass to the northeast until you are 200 yards southwest of the charted split in the stream (near 25 50.542 North/081 26.019 West). Here, amidst 6 to 7 feet of water, visiting cruisers can play bridge comfortably while the winds howl overhead. This latter haven has a feeling of rare isolation, and it is highly recommended by this writer.

Returning our attention to the main Indian Key-Everglades City channel, this passage continues to track its well-outlined way to the northeast across a dredged cut through Chokoloskee Bay. Northeast of unlighted daybeacon #30, a channel runs in from the southeast. This cut serves the Everglades National Park Visitor's Center found near the Chokoloskee causeway. There are no services for private pleasure craft at the Park Service

facility and visiting cruisers are advised to avoid this cut.

Before going on to discuss the Barron River and Everglades City, let us pause a moment for a word about Chokoloskee Island. Consult chart 11430 and you will notice that Chokoloskee Island is today joined to Everglades City by a long causeway. It was not always so. Once Chokoloskee was one of the most isolated settlements in Florida. This tiny village produced some of the most colorful figures and stories in the history of the Sunshine State. We shall meet a few of these characters and hear bits of their tales in our discussion of Everglades City and Chokoloskee Island history below. Unfortunately, the accurate 2- and 3-foot soundings noted on chart 11430 in Chokoloskee Bay make it off limits for most cruising-size vessels. Even Sandfly Pass, which still serves the island's shallow-draft fishing craft, is much too tricky and uncertain for any but the local captains. If possible, try to find land transportation from Everglades City that will allow you to visit the island and its fascinating Ted Smallwood Store Museum. If only for its isolation in these days of mass transportation, the island is well worth your time.

Northeast of unlighted daybeacon #32, the marked channel cuts east into the mouth of the Barron River. Soon the development set about Everglades City will become apparent on the starboard shore. The already brisk tidal current picks up even more. Be ready for the quickly moving waters.

Everglades City

Today, Everglades City is a quiet community that still looks to the bounty of its waters for much of its livelihood. Commercial fishing boats line the city waterfront row upon row. They speak eloquently of that American spirit of individualism, which seems to be fading all too quickly into the fabric of the past.

1. Rod and Gun Club

Tourism is coming very slowly to Everglades City. The non-fishing residents of the community depend upon visitors to the Everglades National Park Visitor's Center, just to the south, for their livelihood. A few low-level modern apartments and condos have been built, but the town still looks much the same as it did fifty years ago. Be sure to take

a stroll through the center of the village and observe the old, whitewashed city hall. A tall telephone microwave tower reaches skyward in the traffic circle. It is the town's only ready link with the outside world. Barron Collier's "laundry building" still stands between the Rod and Gun Club and the microwave tower. The Everglades City Museum is now housed in this historic structure, and a stop here is highly recommended.

A visit to Everglades City and Chokoloskee always seems to have an ethereal, unreal quality, at least to this writer. It's almost as if you have found an old novel about southern Florida and turned to a yellowed picture of a village as it was in those days. If you come looking for nightlife or a glitzy restaurant, forget it. But if you seek a glimpse at an almost vanished speck of Americana, then spare no effort to visit Everglades City.

North of unlighted daybeacon #41, the old river takes a jog to starboard and flows under the obscurely charted 65-foot power line. Recently, we had a report of a catamaran, sporting an extratall mast, hitting this overhead obstruction. Sailors take note!

After rounding the turn, the cool, white exterior of the historic Rod and Gun Club will be obvious, also to starboard, near 25 51.507 North/081 23.260 West. This historic structure was built during the time when Barron Collier brought prominence to Everglades City as a sporting and timbering center. Today, the old inn maintains a long, fixed wooden face pier fronting directly onto the Barron River. Dockside depths are a good 6 to 8 feet. Power and water connections are available. Currently, the Rod and Gun Club boasts the only diesel fuel readily available for pleasure craft in all of the Ten Thousand Islands. Sail

Everglades City Hall

craft with diesel auxiliaries, take note! The Rod and Gun Club offers a single, clean shower for its transient patrons, and a Laundromat can be reached via a one-block walk.

The inn no longer rents out its rooms in the main building, but landside accommodations are available at several cabins spread about the grounds. The on-site restaurant is located just off the beautifully paneled lobby, with its huge stuffed marlin and its billiard table. Neither the lobby nor the restaurant is air conditioned, a concern during the summer and early fall months.

Those dining at the Rod and Gun Club's restaurant have the option of taking their meals on a screened porch overlooking the water. In fair, cooler weather this is a wonderful setting. We found the food very acceptable, even if not really worth writing home about.

For all the Rod and Gun Club's character, I would personally just as soon beg, borrow, or steal a ride to the Oyster House Restaurant (239-695-2073), just across the street from the entrance to the Everglades Visitor's Center. It would be quite a walk from the inn's docks, but I think you would be well rewarded for the effort. At the Oyster House you have many choices, but two are clearly outstanding. The seafood platter is legendary and is highly recommended by this writer. You simply will not find better fried shrimp, scallops, fish, or deviled crab anywhere in Florida. For the more adventurous palate, there is the Everglades platter, which features alligator meat and frog legs. *Bon appétit!*

Another good dining spot is the Oar House Restaurant (239-695-3535), located within a three-block walk of the Rod and Gun Club. While we have not yet had the good fortune to sample the fare here for ourselves, several locals have recommended this restaurant (particularly for breakfast). There are few better endorsements for any dining choice.

Rod and Gun Club (239) 695-2101

Approach depth—6-10 feet

Dockside depth—6-8 feet
Accepts transients—yes
Transient dockage rate—average
Fixed wooden dock—yes
**Dockside power connections—20 and 50 amp
    only**
Dockside water connections—yes
Showers—yes (one)
Laundromat—within 1 block
Gasoline—yes
Diesel fuel—yes
Restaurant—on site

The Barron River channel continues marked and deep for quite some distance above the Rod and Gun Club. Most of the waterfront is lined by private docks serving commercial fishing craft. Just before you

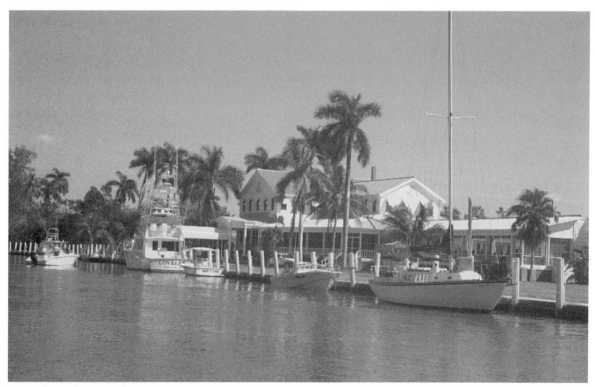

Rod and Gun Club, Everglades City

reach a low-level, fixed bridge, the Barron River Marina (239-695-3591) overlooks the southeastern banks. This facility is mostly a small-craft marina, and cruising-size vessels would probably do better to berth at the old club.

Everglades City Festival

Come the first weekend in February every year, the usually modest population of Everglades City explodes temporarily by some 70,000 hungry souls. This can only mean that it's once again time for the Everglades City Annual Seafood Festival. The downtown district is covered with local craftsmen and more than a few booths serving the best and freshest in local seafood. Visitors will also have the opportunity to learn more about this community's rich heritage. If you happen to be cruising in the water off Indian Key during early February, don't miss this festival! You'll be ever so glad to have made the extra effort.

For more information, call the Everglades City Chamber of Commerce at (239) 695-3941.

Everglades City History   During the mid-1800s, the body of water we know today as the Barron River was called Potato Creek. Local lore suggests that the Indians living along the stream grew potatoes there during the Seminole Indian Wars.

Sometime during (what the locals call) the "War of Northern Aggression," John Weeks began a vegetable-farming operation near Cape Sable. Following the war's close, Weeks moved north to Potato Creek and settled down for a short period of time.

It was not to be long before William Smith Allen, the first permanent white settler in what was to become Everglades City, arrived. Smith was a "Connecticut Yankee" who moved to Key West, along with others who were loyal to the Union, at the beginning of the Civil War. Following an abortive experiment in the cultivation of castor beans on Sanibel Island, Allen was on his way back to Key West when he put in at Potato Creek for fresh water. He was so impressed with the fertility of the land that he bought out Weeks' holdings and returned to settle on the land shortly thereafter.

Allen built a house set atop stilts on the present-day site of the Rod and Gun Club. He owned all of the land presently occupied by Everglades City from 1873 to 1889. Following this period, he returned to Key West and died shortly thereafter.

Sometime in 1881, George Shorter and his son, George Jr., arrived in Everglades (as it was then known) and began cultivating eggplants, cucumbers, and tomatoes. Following the death of the senior Shorter, George Jr. began growing sugarcane. He eventually purchased all of William Allen's holdings for a mere eight hundred dollars and vastly expanded the cultivation of his cane.

Shorter took over Allen's old house and proceeded to hold sway over the struggling community until his death in 1922. During that long reign, Allen established a post office in the small village which took the name of Everglade. The name was finally changed to Everglades in 1923, and later to Everglades City.

As the years went past, George Shorter, Jr., expanded his family home and began to take on boarders and sportsmen who came to Everglades for the magnificent hunting and fishing. As Dr. Charlton W. Tebeau writes in his informative *The Story of the Chokoloskee Bay Country*, "The Shorter House set a lavish table with all the products of that country in abundance. This was the foundation of the modern Rod and Gun Club, always famous for its cuisine. In 1898 he (Shorter) planted the great Madeira tree now growing in front of the Club."

In 1893, Everglade got its first school, only to have it demolished by a hurricane a scant year later. A new school was built and the Reverend George W. Gatewood came to Everglade soon thereafter to establish the first church.

In 1922 a man came to Everglade who was destined to change the small town forever. Barron G. Collier had made a fortune in the manufacture of New York trolley cars. He purchased nearly a million acres of land from the Southern States Land and Timber Company, including most of the swamps and hammocks set about Everglade. He also bought up Frank Shorter's holdings and set up his headquarters in Everglades. After the bright lights of Broadway, one can only assume that Collier was ready for a quieter, although not less energetic, life.

A new county was created around Everglades and named for Barron Collier. With the coming of the Tamiami Trail in 1928, linking Everglades City to Miami, Collier began logging operations in earnest. He purchased a small railway that ran from Everglades City to Deep Lake Hammock. The original engine of this tiny railroad was a modified Model T Ford. Never one to mess about, Collier changed all that over the next decade. Tons and tons of pine logs were hauled out of Deep Lake Hammock and transported by rail to Everglades City. There, they were transshipped by water to points north.

Under Barron Collier's management, the town of Everglades City became a timbering center. The local economy boomed. To better

serve his shipping operation, Collier persuaded the state of Florida to dredge the entrance to what soon came to be known as the Barron River (the former Potato Creek). Soon fishermen throughout the region began delivering their catch to the village's shores.

Sport hunting and fishing grew to be even more important. The Rod and Gun Club was built during this period, and it became known to sportsmen throughout the United States as one of the hot spots for hunting and fishing in all of Florida.

In these all-too-modern times, Barron Collier's timbering empire is but a distant memory. There is only the Rod and Gun Club to remind visitors of those days of glory. It is to the good fortune of all that the clash of a diesel truck's gears are still a rarity in Everglades City. The modern-day wanderer may yet stroll through the quiet lanes of a village that has changed little in the last sixty years. I'm sure Barron Collier, the man who fled New York for the serenity of the Everglades, would be pleased.

Chokoloskee Island History Chokoloskee Island is connected to Everglades City not only by a causeway, but by its rugged history as well. As Stuart McIver astutely comments in *Glimpses of South Florida History*, "The (Chokoloskee) island is less than 150 acres in size—yet it has seen more than its share of individualists over the years." Indeed, neither this writer nor anyone else could have said it better.

Chokoloskee Island saw its first permanent white settler arrive in the person of Capt. Dick Turner sometime around 1870. Captain Turner had been a scout during the tragic Seminole

Wars and had perhaps visited and admired the island before settling there.

In 1886 the man who was to become known as the "Sage of Chokoloskee" arrived to settle on the island. C. G. McKinney founded the settlement's first store and its first post office. He became widely known over the years as a newspaper columnist. Under his pen mosquitoes became "swamp angels" and moonshine was "low-bush lightning." In 1924 he wrote:

> Our schoolteacher . . . is going to give up her school today, it is too much for her nerves. She had a trying time here. . . . Maybe we don't need any school—we all know enough anyway. They seem to learn to chew tobacco, curse and drink booze at an early age and think their education is complete when they have these necessities ground into their topknots.

Maybe things haven't changed as much since those days as we think!

During the 1890s Ted Smallwood settled on Chokoloskee and set up what would become the island's largest retail business. Smallwood's store sat directly on Chokoloskee Bay and he soon dredged a deep-water channel to its docks. The entrepreneur invited both Indian and white settlers to visit his establishment.

In 1924 a hurricane blew the store off its foundation. Mr. Smallwood had his fill of that and raised the entire structure up on stilts. He ran this Chokoloskee Island version of the classic American country store until his death in 1943. His daughter, Thelma, continued the operation until her death in the early 1980s. The store still stands today and has been wonderfully restored as a museum by a collection of dedicated, local volunteers. Chief among

this group is Mr. Smallwood's granddaughter, Ms. Lynn Smallwood McMillian. Visitors are now welcome after paying a modest entrance fee. The store's interior has been transformed once again into a close copy of what it looked like in Ted Smallwood's day. Some of the original merchandise still adorns the shelves. Old wooden boxes, antique washing machines, classic tools, and a wide assortment of other odds and ends recalling bygone days are on display. An on-site gift shop offers books and other literature concerning the region's history.

The third Saturday in March of every year is Seminole Day at the old Ted Smallwood store. Members of the local Seminole tribe share with visitors a celebration of their Native American history, culture, and music.

Even though there is no ready waterborne access for cruising-size craft, I highly recommend a visit to the Ted Smallwood Store Museum. Sometimes, transportation can be arranged through the Rod and Gun Club, or you might try giving the museum a call at (239) 695-2989. However you get there, the museum is a joy for any who are interested in old-time Americana.

Smallwood's store also figured prominently in an event that forms the central theme of Peter Matthiesen's book *Killing Mr. Watson*. By 1900 a host of small settlements had taken root in the mangroves near Everglade (Everglades City) and Chokoloskee Island. Some of these were established by families, but others were the abodes of less savory characters who seemed to appear from nowhere. One of these latter mini-communities was known as the "Watson Place."

The principal inhabitant, Ed Watson, was known as a friendly enough man, if you did not cross him. He took up farming on the banks of the Chatham River, south of Chokoloskee. It was rumored that he paid his help little and some of the workers mysteriously disappeared around payday.

By 1910 Watson had gathered together a somewhat more permanent group of five individuals on his farm, including a woman called Hannah Smith (also known as "Big Six"), a man known as Leslie Cox, and an unidentified black man. It was during the fall of 1910 that a group of clammers from Chokoloskee found Big Six's body in a nearby swamp. Within a few days, the old black man showed up at Chokoloskee muttering about murders at the Watson Place. Soon Watson himself arrived, claiming that Cox had committed the murder.

The islanders were not convinced by Watson's story and asked the sheriff to investigate. For whatever reason, the officer delayed and Watson set out on his own, supposedly to hunt for Cox.

Within a month Watson motored back up to the Chokoloskee waterfront right in front of Smallwood's store, claiming to all who would listen that he had killed Cox. He produced the latter's hat as proof. Some of the islanders who were standing around in front of the store agreed to travel back to the Watson Place and inspect the body, but others more skeptical of Watson insisted that he first be disarmed.

According to one account, Watson became so enraged that he tried to discharge his shotgun into the assembled crowd. Both shells, apparently soaked during a recent storm, misfired. Most of the group on the docks were also carrying guns and they opened up on Watson as a man. The would-be farmer and could-be murderer fell to the dock, pierced by several dozen bullets, and his secrets died with him.

Picnic Key Anchorage (25 49.278 North/081 29.116 West)

When winds are not blowing from the west or southwest, the 4- and 5-foot waters nestled between the arms of Tiger and Stop keys, southwest of Picnic Key, make a good anchorage for boats drawing 3½ feet or less. The shores of Picnic Key are girded by a beautiful white-sand beach and are well worth breaking out the dinghy.

Faka Union River and Canal Channel and Port of the Islands Marina

Unlighted daybeacon #3 (found near 25 50.759 North/081 32.959 West) off Gomez Point marks the southwesterly genesis of the marked channel leading northeast to the Faka Union River. The marked channel southeast of Panther Key cuts a winding path generally northeast for 4 nautical miles to the mouth of Faka Union River. This body of water leads, in turn, to the arrow-straight Faka Union Canal. Another run of 2.8 nautical miles up the canal leads you to Port of the Islands Marina, flanking the northerly shores of the west-side cove just south of the U.S. 41-Tamiami Trail fixed bridge.

Within the past several years, this channel has been re-marked, but severe shoaling is still present just as the channel begins its approach to the Faka Union River. We have heard accounts of cruising craft (even those of the smaller powercraft variety) finding the bottom smack in the middle of this so-called channel. Our own on-site observations lead us to believe that low-water soundings are now considerably less than 3 feet in places. With this information in hand, we no longer recommend a visit to Faka Union Canal or Port of the Islands Marina for cruising-size craft.

If you should choose to ignore this advice, we strongly suggest that you time your entry and egress during high water. Even at high water, this cut is no longer suitable for boats drawing more than 4 feet.

As if the shoaling described above were not problem enough, tidal currents flow through the Faka River and its canal with a fierceness that this writer has seldom before witnessed. If the tide is on the ebb, it could take considerably longer to reach Port of the Islands than you might think.

It should also be noted that all of the Faka Union River and the adjoining canal are idle-speed, no-wake zones. This speed restriction is designed to protect the considerable colony of manatees that live in the area waters. We actually saw a manatee while cruising along the canal, so the restrictions are for real and quite necessary.

Port of the Islands Marina (239-642-3133) used to be an indifferently managed facility. Now, we are happy to report that new owners have taken over, and many improvements have been made, and others are on the drawing board. However, until and if this marina's approach channel via Faka Union river and canal is dredged, we cannot recommend a visit to this facility. With this stricture in mind, we will not offer any further review of Port of the Islands at this time.

TEN THOUSAND ISLANDS NAVIGATION

If it weren't for the lack of navigational markers, the abundance of shallow water, and the difficulty of telling one of the Ten Thousand Islands from the other, navigation of the waters between New Turkey Key and the Coon Key Light would be a snap.

Yes, gentle reader, that is truly tongue in cheek. There is, perhaps, no other portion of the Western Florida coastline that offers as much of a navigational challenge as the Ten Thousand Islands do. Take your time—in fact, take all the time that may be necessary to carefully identify important landmarks before plunging ahead. Maintain an eagle eye on the sounder, and if you are lucky enough to be equipped with a GPS, a GPS chart plotter, or (best yet) a GPS interfaced with a computer, make full use of these navigational wonders. The extra effort you make to avoid turning "bow" to "plow" will be more than justified by the opportunities for backwater discovery in this land that time has seemingly forgotten.

New Turkey Key Anchorage   Strangely enough, New Turkey Key can be difficult to identify from the water without the benefit of careful navigation and/or electronic positioning equipment. From a position abeam of flashing daybeacon #8 off Lostmans River (which should be passed *well* to its western side), a cruise of some 5 nautical miles will bring you abeam of Plover and North Plover keys. These two islands sit fairly far out from shore and are recognizable. Be sure to stay well to the west of the twin islands, as they are surrounded by shoal water for the most part. Continue paralleling the coastline as you cruise northwest for another 1.5 nautical miles. This should bring you abeam of New Turkey Key, which will appear to be the isle farthest from shore in the immediate area. Set a course to approach New Turkey Key by some .2 nautical miles to the south of the isle's southwestern tip. As you work your way carefully to the east, begin curving your course to the north after coming abeam of the key's northeast-to-southwest axis. Use your sounder to follow the correctly charted 6- and 8-foot depths until you are between the island's northeasterly tip and the unnamed key to the east.

Drop your hook here. *Don't* attempt to cruise north past the northeasterly tip of New Turkey Key. Depths immediately rise to 3½ feet or less.

On to Pavilion Key   Pavilion Key, west of Duck Rock, is an important body of land for navigational purposes. The key is quite prominent due to its position relatively far from the mainland. Throw in flashing daybeacon #10, lying off the islet's southwesterly tip, and it's not hard to imagine why this island and its daybeacon can serve as one of the most identifiable navigational reference points between Lostmans River and Coon Key Light.

From a position abeam of #10, many skippers will set course for Indian Key and flashing daybeacon #1. While you might also choose to cruise to flashing daybeacon #1K, well to the southwest of Indian Key,

this would seem to be a useless trek, adding several miles to your sojourn.

Before going on to detail the passage from Indian Key to Everglades City, let's pause for a moment to review the anchorages between Pavilion and Indian keys.

Lumber Key Anchorage   From flashing daybeacon #10 off Pavilion Key, use either DR (dead-reckoning) navigation or a GPS to work your way around to a point well southwest of the charted channel northwest of Lumber and Rabbit keys. Keep a close watch on your sounder as you work your way northeast along the broad tongue of deep water, northwest of the two isles. On the water, Rabbit and Lumber keys seem to be almost joined together by an interconnecting sandspit. Lumber Key will appear as the larger of the two.

Drop the hook northwest of Lumber Key as you come abeam of the island's center. You may be able to spot a small creek cutting into the island, which will help you identify this anchorage.

If you should decide to visit Lumber Key, go in by dinghy. A band of shoals abuts the island's shoreline. Be sure to scrupulously avoid the shallow bay between Lumber and Rabbit keys. Depths on this errant body of water run from ½ to 3 feet. On-site research failed to disclose the charted "pile" marking the split in the channel northeast of the just-described anchorage. Captains are strictly advised to anchor southwest of this fork!

Jack Daniels Key   It would probably be best to acquire flashing daybeacon #1 off Indian Key before attempting to enter either the anchorage adjacent to Kingston Key or the one adjacent to Jack Daniels Key. Using #1, it is a relatively simple matter to identify the Kingston isle. You should then set a course to pass this body of land by at least 300 yards to its southwesterly side before turning northeast into the anchorage. Stay well off Kingston Key and be sure to pass south of the charted marshy shoal southwest of Jack Daniels.

As you approach Jack Daniels, use your binoculars to help pick out the unnamed island south of the key. Cruise around the smaller island's southeasterly shores, keeping some 100 yards off the beach. Be on guard against the charted tongue of 3-foot water to the east.

Drop your anchor once abeam of the small island's northeastern tip. Here you will be nestled between the unnamed isle and Jack Daniels Key to the northwest.

Only very nervy skippers should attempt to continue a circumnavigation of the small island to the west and south. Shoals extend off the little island for about 50 yards on this section of the channel.

Kingston Key Anchorage Again, using flashing daybeacon #1 off Indian Key, cruise around Kingston Key's southwestern reaches, keeping several hundred yards off the beach. Turn slowly to the northeast and pass the key's southeasterly tip by at least 200 yards to your port side.

You can then bend your course yet again, this time to the north-northwest, and come abeam of the key's easterly shoreline by about 75 yards to your port side. Don't slip farther to the east, as depths climb to 4 feet or less. Drop the hook before cruising any farther to the northwest. While small craft can circumnavigate Kingston Key, depths run to 4 feet and the passage is really a little too confining for cruising-size vessels.

Indian Key Pass Channel and Anchorages
All navigators should be aware of the difficulty in spotting flashing daybeacon #1 (near 25 47.977 North/081 28.071 West), the southwesternmost aid to navigation on the marked channel off Indian Key. This very important beacon blends right in with the trees on Indian Key and can be exceedingly hard to spot, even with binoculars. Take your time and be sure to identify this aid correctly before attempting to enter the channel.

After finding #1, pass the beacon fairly close to its southeasterly side and set course to come abeam of and pass unlighted daybeacon #3 to its immediate southeasterly side. Try not to wander to the southeast between #1 and #3 or you might find the charted patch of 4-foot waters. Of course, you don't want to stray too close to Indian Key's southeasterly shoreline either.

During our last several visits to Indian Key, we tried to find this charted 4-foot shoal, but even with the aid of the GPS interfaced with a laptop computer and digitized charts, it has never appeared on our sounder. Just to be safe, though, watch out for it anyway.

Once abeam of #3, point to come abeam of flashing daybeacon #4 to its westerly quarter. As you approach #4, watch to the west, and at mid or low tide, you can spot the long (partially uncharted) sandspit running northeast from Indian Key.

Even if the tide is high and you can't find the spit, cruise west from #4 to a point at least 50 yards southeast of Indian Key's spit. If this sounds somewhat confusing, study the sketch map depicting these waters in the Ten Thousand Islands section of this chapter. You can then drop the hook in about as secure a spot as you are likely to find in the Ten Thousand Islands. If the mosquitoes and weather cooperate, your first chosen task might just be a quick breaking out of the dinghy and a trip ashore to visit Indian Key.

It is quite possible to cross to the northeast side of the Indian Key sandspit and circumnavigate the island in 6-foot minimum depths. However, since we have already found our way to the best anchorage adjacent to the key, and the southeasterly passage is marked, most cruisers will probably choose to forego this excursion.

Indian Key Pass remains broad and deep well upstream of unlighted daybeacon #6. Come abeam of this aid to its northwesterly side and continue on, pointing to come abeam of and pass flashing daybeacon #7 to its southeasterly quarter. Just before reaching #7, another excellent anchorage opportunity beckons from the north.

Successful entry into Russell Pass is complicated by the large, charted shoal thrusting into the westerly reaches of the pass's southern entrance. This hazard is easily avoided by favoring the eastern third of the entrance.

You must also take care not to approach the shoreline too closely just north of flashing daybeacon #7. A thin, but nevertheless treacherous band of shallows flanks this point.

Soon, good depths open out almost from shore to shore on Russell Pass. You need only stay within shouting distance of the centerline for good depths all the way to the split in the channel, well to the northeast at the charted "Mangrove."

Everglades City and the Barron River

East of flashing daybeacon #7, the well-marked channel follows a dredged route through the various isles to the mouth of the Barron River. Tidal currents pick up markedly and are a real concern for sail craft and single-screw trawlers. Be sure to watch over your stern as well as the course ahead to quickly note any lateral slippage.

At unlighted daybeacon #10, the cut runs hard by the southern banks and soon passes through a sharp turn to the northeast, heralded by unlighted daybeacon #11. In time past, there used to be a shoaling problem between #10 and unlighted daybeacon #13. For the moment, these shallows seem to have disappeared, but they could always reappear. Stick to the cut's mid-width between #10 and its turn to the northeast marked by unlighted daybeacons #11, #11A, and flashing daybeacon #12.

A new no-wake manatee zone stretches from the gap between unlighted daybeacon #27 and flashing daybeacon #28 to unlighted daybeacon #32. Even then, upstream of #32, you will quickly approach the Everglades City waterfront and a host of private docks. The best plan is simply to proceed at idle speed on the entire channel northeast of #27 and #28.

The channel passes between two small, rock-filled islands at unlighted daybeacons

#29 and #30. Long before reaching #29 and #30, you will spot the tall telephone microwave tower which graces the town circle in Everglades City. This antenna will be the first visible evidence that you are approaching this unique community.

Northeast of unlighted daybeacon #30, the marked channel leading southeast to the Everglades National Park Visitor's Center and Chokoloskee Bay flows into the main cut. Ignore unlighted daybeacons #1 and #2, the northwesternmost aids on this side channel, and continue straight ahead, pointing to come abeam of unlighted daybeacon #32 to your starboard side.

Unlighted daybeacon #32 marks the entrance to the Barron River. Slow down as you cruise into the river. The entire stretch between the stream's mouth and the fixed bridge well upstream is an idle-speed, no-wake zone.

At flashing daybeacon #33 the channel takes a hard jog to starboard. Soon you will pass unlighted daybeacon #34 to your starboard side. Look to port and you will sight the Ten Thousand Islands' Outward Bound program headquarters. As a cruiser, you're already enjoying many of the benefits that are provided by this organization for its participants.

Continue following the markers upstream on the Barron River under the charted 65-foot power lines. Those cruisers with extratall masts take note. The docks of the Rod and Gun Club will come abeam to starboard after rounding the turn past unlighted daybeacon #41. Farther to the north, the river's southern and southeastern banks are lined with an interesting collection of commercial fishing vessels and their attendant wharves. Eventually, the river's track is pinched by a 12-foot fixed bridge near the charted designation "Dupont."

Picnic Key Anchorage   Well, I know it's getting repetitive to say it, but again, make use of good old flashing daybeacon #1 off Indian Key to identify Stop Keys to the north-northwest. Pleasure craft that can stand some 4-foot depths can cruise into the broad swath of 4- and 5-foot waters fronting the southwestern shores of Picnic Key, sheltered between the arms of Tiger and Stop keys.

Take the greatest care to avoid the charted tongue of 1- and 2-foot waters jutting to the west from Stop Keys. On-site research revealed that this shoal has built out farther than is shown on the "current" edition of chart 11430. In fact, we once had plenty of time to contemplate the cuts in the NOAA charting budget while trying to push our grounded craft off this sand bar.

Drop anchor at least 50 yards off Picnic Key's white-sand beach. Slop on the Skin-So-Soft, blow up the old dinghy, and head ashore for some great exploration.

Faka Union River and Canal Channel
As if you weren't tired of hearing me say this, unlighted daybeacons #3 and #4, off Panther Key, are quite hard to spot from the water. Just to make matters a bit more interesting, there are no convenient geographic references nearby, either. Use your best and brightest binoculars, along with good DR or electronic navigation, to find the aids.

As mentioned repeatedly above, the

approach channel to Faka Union river and canal has shoaled badly. We have had reports of even small powercraft finding the bottom at low water. Our on-site readings confirm MLW soundings of 3 feet or less in spots.

With these problems in mind, we no longer recommend this channel for any cruising-size craft if and until the cut is dredged by the new owners of Port of the Islands Marina. As such, we will offer no further details of this passage here. If, in the future, the channel is improved, we will resume describing this cut in detail.

On to Coon Key Light   Mariners choosing to run the inside route past Marco Island to Naples should set course for the unnumbered 22-foot flashing daybeacon south-southeast of Coon Key. Depths on these waters can occasionally run to as little as 4 feet, but at most tides you can expect at least 4½ to 5 feet of water. This is the shallowest portion of the entire passage to Naples.

For best depths, come abeam of the Coon Key Light by at least 100 yards to its north-easterly side. You can then set course to the north-northwest and enter the waterway.

Coon Key to Naples

A marked inland channel leads north from Coon Key, past Marco Island and Capri Pass, to the city of Naples and its fine inlet. In recent years, this passage has been much maligned, and sailors, in particular, have abandoned it in favor of an offshore passage to Gordon Pass (Naples' inlet). For boats that draw 4 feet or less (and can clear the 55-foot, fixed Goodland and Marco Island bridges), this strategy may just be a mistake. While not a part of the official Western Florida ICW, the Marco Island-Naples channel, or waterway, as we shall dub it, maintains minimum 5-foot depths along most of its length. This passage features excellent protection from inclement weather, adequate anchorages, and good, if widely spaced, facilities. There are a few tricky spots, but if you are looking for something other than an offshore passage, the Marco Island cut is the only game in town.

The one exception to the 5-foot minimum rule on the Marco Island-Naples waterway is found at the passage's southerly entrance, near Coon Key Light. Here you may occasionally find dead low-water depths of as little as 4 feet. Boats needing 4½ to 5 feet can wait for a higher tide and run the entire route in safety.

It is also quite possible for cruisers to sail offshore to Capri Pass inlet, just north of Marco Island, and enter the inside passage through this seaward cut. This route avoids the shallower southern reaches of the waterway, but still allows mariners to visit the facilities on Marco Island, and then cruise north to Naples. This half-outside, half-inside cruising plan is an excellent alternative for boats drawing between 4½ and 5 feet. With a little caution, captains who pilot vessels of this draft can cruise inside to Naples with no problems, whereas if they tried to cruise north on the inland passage from Coon Key Light, the unhappy sound of the keel dragging bottom might just be heard.

Unfortunately for power captains, the state of Florida has seen fit to establish a whole series of extremely confusing "manatee no-wake zones" on portions of the Marco Island-Naples waterway. Some of these zones are in effect only at certain times of the day and year, and the various beginnings and endings of the restricted waters seem haphazard. As one local member of the USCG Auxiliary told this writer, "we had no idea that manatees could read the clock, the calendar, and a nautical chart." So, whatever we cruisers may think of them, these slow-speed restrictions are now a fact of life on the Marco Island-Naples waterway. Be sure to figure the delays that will be caused by these regulated waters into your cruising plans.

The Marco Island-Naples waterway begins at Coon Key Pass, skirts past the fascinating village of Goodland, and then runs down the Big Marco River past Sanctuary Sound and into East Marco Bay. Good marina facilities are available to mariners cruising along this stretch in Goodland and on Factory Bay.

Well-marked Capri Pass cuts into the Western Florida shoreline north of Marco Island. This inlet holds minimum 6- to 8-foot depths but there is now one significant shoal to avoid. As always with seaward passages, these conditions are subject to rapid change. Barring any future alterations, pleasure craft with drafts of 5 feet or less can run Capri Pass with only the usual difficulties in passing between the ocean and inland waters.

North from Capri Pass, the waterway leading north to Naples cuts in behind several

other shallow inlets. Cruisers will find a super anchorage near one of these cuts.

Most depths between Capri Pass and Naples run 6 feet or better. There is but one spot where the sounder may dip to 5-5½ foot readings.

North of Dollar Bay, the Marco Island-Naples cut intersects Gordon Pass, which serves the city of Naples. Our research has consistently shown this inlet to be well marked, adequately deep, and reasonably easy to run. Additionally, a wonderful anchorage is found just off the inlet channel.

North of Gordon Pass, the marked route follows a dead-end passage through Naples Bay to the Gordon River and the city of Naples. This teeming tourist city has been rebuilding its waterfront over the last several years, but unfortunately, only the Naples City Pier and the Naples Boat Club now offer any berths for waterborne visitors who are not members of accredited yacht clubs. Thankfully, two yacht clubs in Naples supplement this scant visitor dockage for those who are lucky enough to have appropriate reciprocal privileges.

The Gordon River passage dead-ends at the Naples waterfront, at least for cruising-size craft. Both branches of the river are pinched off by low-level fixed bridges, but the upstream reaches are quite shallow anyway. Northbound vessels must retrace their steps to Gordon Inlet and cruise offshore to Fort Myers Beach and Estero Island.

The cruising possibilities between Coon Key and Naples are varied. Let's push right on and detail the many gunk holes and ports of call along the way.

Caxambas Pass Channel

The long approach channel to Caxambas

Inlet cuts west-northwest from the unnumbered, 22-foot Coon Key Light. Depths of 5 to 6 feet are held on this cut east of unlighted daybeacon #6. The channel has shoaled between unlighted daybeacons #8 and #19, where low-water depths as thin as 3 feet can now be expected. This portion of the channel is known locally as "the picket line." Cruising craft drawing 3 feet or better must confine their explorations to the waters east of #6.

The marked approach to Caxambas Pass has also shoaled badly between unlighted daybeacon #19 and unlighted daybeacon #8. Tentative plans are in the works to define a new channel south of the current channel in this region, but unless these plans come to fruition, visiting cruisers are strictly advised to limit their explorations to the waters west of "the picket line."

The Caxambas Pass channel is not completely without merit, however. West of unlighted daybeacon #1 (west of Ramsey Key), skippers can anchor in depths of 7 to 10 feet, sheltered between Helen Key to the south and Horrs Island to the north (near 25 54.129 North/081 39.953 West). This spot is well sheltered from all but gale-force winds.

At unlighted daybeacon #19, west of Pass Key, a marked channel cuts east to Barfield Bay. This shallow passage leads to the private docks of an exclusive development on Horrs Island. There are no facilities for visiting cruisers.

Coon Key Pass Anchorage (25 54.115 North/081 38.433 West)

Back on Coon Key Pass and the principal Marco Island-Naples route, captains may consider dropping the hook with fair winds in the lee of the small, unnamed island east of Neal Key and west-northwest of unlighted

daybeacon #2. Depths of 10+ feet run to within 20 yards of the island's easterly shoreline. There should be enough elbowroom for most pleasure craft. As an additional bonus, the anchorage affords a super view of Gullivan Bay's magnificent waters to the south. You can also dinghy ashore to nearby Coon Key, which is graced with a lovely white sand beach.

Obviously, this is not a heavy-weather anchorage. Winds over 10 knots from any quarter save the west would make for a rocking evening. In calm conditions though, you simply could not choose a more beautiful setting to while away a few hours in the cockpit with a cool one in hand.

Tripod Key-Sugar Bay Anchorage (25 54.633 North/081 38.072 West)

Mariners will find an important anchorage on the charted 5-foot offshoot leading to Sugar Bay, east of unlighted daybeacon #3. This would be a great spot for captains cruising south in craft as large as 50 feet to wait out bad weather before venturing out onto the open waters of the Ten Thousand Islands. Even northbound cruisers arriving late in the day could make use of this haven before continuing on the next morning. This sidewater is well protected and has minimum depths of 5 to 6 feet. The surrounding shores are completely undeveloped and make for a real feeling of isolation.

Surprisingly enough, and contrary to soundings indicated on chart 11430, minimum 5-foot depths, with many readings in the 5- to 12-foot range, continue upstream to a point some 100 yards southwest of Sugar Bay. Be sure to anchor well short of the bay itself, as these waters are quite shoal. In heavy weather, skippers may choose to anchor in the more protected upper portion of the approach stream (southwest of

Sugar Bay) for best shelter. With fair breezes in the offing, it's a simple matter to drop the hook only 100 yards or so northeast of the main channel.

1. Goodland Bay Marina
2. Calusa Island Marina

Goodland and Associated Facilities
(Various Lats/Lons—see below)

The very special village of Goodland sits perched on the outcropping of land north and west of unlighted daybeacon #6 (on Coon Key Pass). Goodland is actually an extension of Marco Island, but it's light years different in character. Amidst all the dense development on Marco, this village survives as a rugged commercial and small-craft fishing center where the residents are still far more interested in what's biting than in what's happening on Wall Street. A small museum in the village recalls the island's early occupation by the Timucuan and Caloosa Indians.

Numbers to know in Goodland Island include

A-OK Taxi—(239) 394-1113
Yellow Cab—(239) 659-0800
Avis Rental Cars—(239)-481-1511
Hertz Rent A Car—(800) 654-3131

Goodland is noted for its superb seafood restaurants. While they may lack what some might term sophistication, the food is clearly all anyone could ask for, and the atmosphere is often festive. This writer has often been privileged to sample the bountiful fare at the Little Bar and Restaurant. This dining spot serves, without a doubt, some of the finest seafood that this writer has ever enjoyed in Western Florida.

Two marinas serve pleasure boats in Goodland. These highly competent, often crowded, and superfriendly marinas sit at a very strategic point. Much like the anchorage described above, cruisers can wait out bad weather here for the trip south or rest from their journeys through the Ten Thousand Islands, with the added benefits of full power and water connections.

Goodland Bay Marina (25 55.319 North/081 38.699 West) is located west of unlighted daybeacon #6. The dry-storage operation fronts directly onto the island's southern shores, but the principal dockage basin is located in the sheltered *T*-shaped cove just to the west.

During our last visit to this facility, in the summer of 2003, we were informed that the marina had just been sold. In keeping with our long-standing policy of only reporting on what we actually see with our own eyes, the account below is based on conditions we encountered during our last stop here. The new owners may well have made changes by the time of your arrival. Call ahead of time to check on current conditions.

Goodland Bay currently accepts transients for overnight dockage and offers berths at fixed and floating wooden piers with all power and water connections. Overnighters are usually accommodated at the floating piers. Transient space is often at a premium here, so call ahead of time to check on slip availability.

Depths at most of the marina's docks run at least 6 feet, while MLW entrance soundings are in the 5½- to 6-foot range. Some shallower soundings are found at the rear slips, but these are reserved for the exclusive use of small, shallow-draft powercraft. There is currently one very inadequate, non-climate-controlled shower on site. Gasoline (but no longer diesel fuel) is readily available, as are waste pump-out services and full mechanical repairs for both gasoline and diesel engines. An on-site 35-ton travelift readily facilitates haul-outs and full below-waterline repairs. There is also an on-site ship's/variety/tackle store, as well as extensive dry-stack storage for smaller power-craft.

The marina's on-site restaurant has been closed for several years, but it's only a quick walk to Little Bar or Stan's Idle Hour.

Goodland Bay Marina (239) 394-2797

Approach depth—5^1/$_2$ to 6 feet
Dockside depth—6 feet
Accepts transients—yes
Fixed and floating wooden piers—yes
Dockside power connections—30 and 50 amp
Dockside water connections—yes
Shower—minimal at this time
Waste pump-out—yes
Gasoline—yes
Mechanical repairs—yes
Below-waterline repairs—yes
Ship's and variety store—yes
Restaurant—several nearby

Access to Goodland's second pleasure-craft facility, Calusa Island Marina (25 55.196 North/081 39.030 West), is gained by traversing the marked entrance channel to Goodland Bay Marina and then continuing to follow the waters of charted Blue Hill Creek as they sweep to the west. First-timers should be sure to read the navigational account of this channel before attempting entry.

Calusa Island Marina actually has two dockage basins. Most resident and visiting craft are accommodated at a series of floating wooden and concrete-decked piers that front directly onto the waters of Blue Hill Creek and feature 6-foot dockside depths. A long fixed wooden face pier and the marina's fuel dock are discovered on a second harbor lining the shores of the sheltered offshoot striking north to the charted "R. Mast." Low-water depths in this harbor can run as thin as 4½ feet.

One of the marina's resident cruisers has

warned this writer against using the inner harbor piers because of the long climb necessary to reach the dock at low tide. On the other hand, no one could ask for a more sheltered spot to ride out really heavy weather.

Transients are now gladly accepted at Calusa Island Marina. In fact, the marina management has plans to add a swimming pool, chiki bar, and a cook shack (by some time in 2004) for the primary purpose of attracting cruising visitors. Yacht clubs and other nautical organizations should also note that Calusa Island is very friendly to cruising groups.

Most slips at Calusa Island feature full power, water, cable-television, and telephone hookups. Waste pump-out service is available at each berth, as are good, climate-controlled showers and an on-site Laundromat, also air conditioned. Gasoline and diesel fuel can be purchased at the inner basin fuel dock, and mechanical repairs can sometimes be arranged through independent technicians.

Calusa Island offers full haul-out, below-waterline repair services. The yard's 50-ton travelift can handle most pleasure craft.

Rounding out the marina's services are an on-site ship's and variety store as well as extensive dry-stack storage for smaller power-craft. Unfortunately, there is little in the way of provisions nearby. The closest supermarket is a good five miles away, so be sure your galley is stocked. However, all the earlier-described dining spots are even closer to Calusa Island than they are to Goodland Marina. Do your appetite a huge favor and make the two-block walk to Little Bar.

All in all, we remain impressed with Calusa Island Marina and are glad that transients are now eagerly sought after by the management.

As far as we are concerned, any night spent in Goodland is a good night.

Calusa Island Marina (239) 394-3668

Approach depth—5½ to 8 feet
Dockside depth—6 feet MLW (outer docks)
   4½-5 feet MLW (inner harbor)
Accepts transients—yes
Transient dockage rate—slightly above average
Fixed and floating wooden piers—yes
Floating concrete piers—yes
Dockside power connections—30 and 50 amp
Dockside water connections—yes
Waste pump-out—yes
Showers—yes
Laundromat—yes
Gasoline—yes
Diesel fuel—yes
Mechanical repairs—yes (independent technicians)

Below-waterline repairs—yes
Ship's and variety store—yes
Restaurant—several nearby

All three of Goodland's principal restaurants are accessible directly from the ICW, although two sport low-tide entrance and dockside depths of only 3½ feet. The fixed, wooden slips of Skeeter's Old Marco Lodge (239-642-7227) will be readily visible along the southerly flank of the Marco Island-Naples waterway principal channel between unlighted daybeacons #8 and #10. Craft as large as 35 feet should find a place to moor comfortably while dining. No overnight services are available. Depths alongside run around 5 to 6 feet at low tide.

Captains piloting vessels that can stand

Skeeter's Old Marco Lodge, Goodland

some low-tide depths of 3½ feet can opt for either a truly first-class or another funky dining experience in Goodland. The small canal, just west of Skeeter's docks (near 25 55.625 North/081 38.849 West), leads south past a host of local fishing craft to two restaurants of note.

First up is the Little Bar and Restaurant (239-394-5663), mentioned repeatedly above. This dining spot overlooks the creek's southeasterly banks and it has three small slips (3- to 3½-foot low-water depths) that should be just large enough for 28-footers.

Need more depth? Consider a stay at nearby Goodland Bay or Calusa Island marinas. It's only a short walk from either dockage basin to the Little Bar or Stan's (see below).

No matter how you get to the Little Bar, the food is wonderful. This is where many of the locals on Marco go back time and time again

for seafood. The menu is surprisingly extensive and sophisticated, but the good old fried oysters simply cannot be beat.

Stan's Idle Hour Restaurant (239-394-3041) guards the terminus of the creek. The welcome is about as warm as it gets, and the food is acceptable. Outside (as well as inside) dining is available and there is often nightly entertainment during the fall, winter, and spring months. Stan's can be the setting for some real down-home, raucous parties from time to time. The crowds on Sunday are legendary!

Several fixed, wooden slips adjoining Stan's can accommodate boats as large as 28-30 feet, although most are really meant for smaller craft. Approach and dockside depths run to 3½ feet at low tide. Be sure to take this skimpy water into account when planning a visit to Stan's.

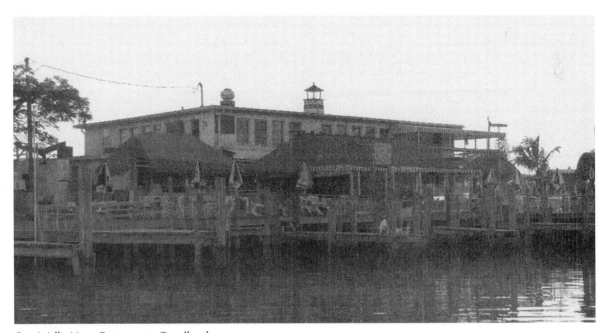

Stan's Idle Hour Restaurant, Goodland

Goodland Bay Anchorage (25 55.655 North/081 38.513 West)

Visiting captains sometimes choose to anchor in the charted patch of deeper waters northeast of unlighted daybeacon #7. Depths did not prove to be as deep as shown on the chart. Our sounder (plus the tide tables) indicated low-water depths of 5 to 6 feet. There's enough swinging room for vessels up to 45 feet in length, and good protection from eastern, southeastern, and western winds. Nevertheless, this is not a foul-weather hidey-hole. Consider the anchorage described above off Tripod Key and Sugar Bay for really heavy weather. The islands to the east, northeast, and southeast are in their natural state, while the Goodland waterfront lies just to the west. It would be only a quick dinghy trip from this anchorage to reach Skeeter's Old Marco Lodge, the Little Bar and Restaurant, or Stan's Idle Hour Restaurant (see above).

Big Marco River

From Goodland, the Marco Island-Naples channel cuts first north and then northwest through the Big Marco River. The channel passes under the Goodland fixed bridge north of unlighted daybeacon #12. Immediately north of this span, a marked channel cuts west to Moran's Barge Restaurant, Marina, and Motel (239-642-1920). This cut holds 4½-foot low-water depths. A visit in the summer of 2003 found this establishment undergoing a transition. The restaurant was "closed for the summer," while the marina only appeared to be in nominal operation. The local rumor is that a condo project may start on this site within the next year or so. The management had previously informed this writer than no transient dockage was available.

Between unlighted daybeacons #16 and #17, the river's track is deep almost from shore to shore. While there is most certainly some tidal current, the river offers more than enough protection and swinging room for overnight anchorage by most sizes of pleasure craft. This stretch of the channel is mostly free from commercial traffic, but you should still anchor well away from the mid-width and show a bright anchor light just in case some fishing craft happens along during the night.

Northwest of unlighted daybeacon #24, the channel runs past Sanctuary Sound. This portion of the passage is subject to shoaling and navigation becomes more than slightly tricky. Be sure to read the navigational account of the Marco Island channel presented later in this chapter before running this stretch for the first time.

Addison Bay Channel

East of the Marco Island (Highway 951)/Judge S. S. Jolley Bridge, chart 11430 correctly notes a broad stretch of deep water running toward Three Island Cove and Addison Bay. This cut has recently been marked by the county, and, would you believe, the (as yet uncharted) green markers denote the "starboard" side of the cut for inbound vessels. I guess Collier County never heard of "red, right, returning." In any case, we do not suggest that cruising-size craft attempt to make use of this cut. It eventually leads to the shallower waters of Addison Bay, which, while they are of great interest to local fishing folk, are not sufficiently deep for cruising vessels.

Marco Island and Associated Facilities (Various Lats/Lons—see below)

Marco Island was once considered the northernmost of the Ten Thousand Islands.

Well, it doesn't seem that way any longer. It now looks as if some unwanted corner of Fort Lauderdale or Clearwater has been dropped from the sky upon this body of land. To say that portions of Marco are intensely developed falls short of the mark. High- and low-rise condominiums dot the landscape, set beside far more attractive single-dwelling neighborhoods that sprawl like grains of sand on a beach. To find all of this so close to the natural world of the Ten Thousand Islands and the mostly undeveloped passage south from Naples is a real shock.

By the way, if you find yourself on or near Marco Island and in need of outboard or I/O repairs, you're in luck. Call Mike Polly at Intercoastal Marine (754 E Elkcam Street, 239-642-0067).

Numbers to know on Marco Island include

A-OK Taxi—(239) 394-1113
Patron Transportation—(239) 394-6179
Yellow Cab—(239) 659-0800
Avis Rental Cars—(239) 481-1511
Enterprise Rent-A-Car—(239) 642-4488
Hertz Rent A Car—(800) 654-3131

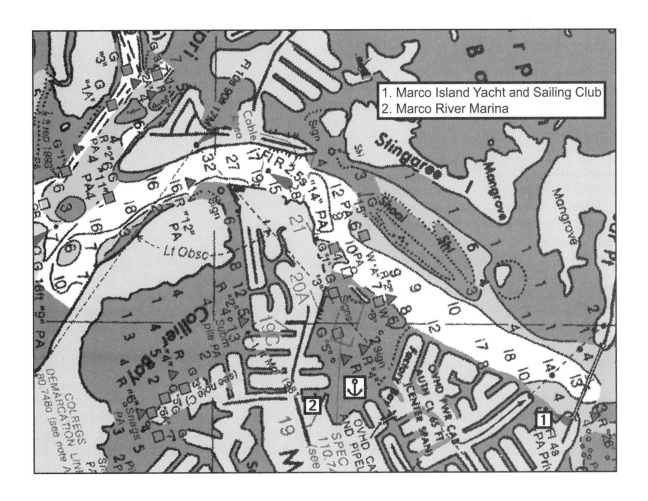

1. Marco Island Yacht and Sailing Club
2. Marco River Marina

Marco Island's easternmost pleasure-craft facility graces the waterway's southerly banks, immediately west of the high-rise, fixed Marco Island bridge (itself west of unlighted daybeacon #26, near 25 57.649 North/081 42.738 West). Marco Island Yacht and Sailing Club is a sumptuous development, set amidst an ultrasheltered harbor and beautifully manicured grounds. A large, luxurious clubhouse overlooks the dockage basin's northwesterly tip and is prominently visible from the water. Thankfully, in spite of its "yacht club" moniker, the dockmaster has informed this writer that transients are readily accepted without the need for reciprocal arrangements with other yacht clubs.

Dockage is afforded at the latest version of concrete-decked, floating piers featuring 30- to 50-amp power, freshwater, and cable-television connections. A few slips have 100-amp hookups as well. Depths alongside run to some 6 feet or better at low water. There are also a few fixed, wooden slips in the basin.

A single shoreside shower is open to visitors, but it's a long walk to its location at the harbor's northwesterly tip (near the large clubhouse). We are happy to report that construction will soon begin on a new "dockmaster's building" that will contain four first-class, climate-controlled showers. When this unit is complete, it will add immeasurably to an already excellent facility.

Waste pump-out service is available, but you will have to look elsewhere for fuel. Transient visitors are allowed to satisfy their appetite at the club's memorable dining room one night. Otherwise, those cruisers not wishing to prepare a meal aboard will probably want to call a taxi and visit one of the many restaurants on Marco Island or Goodland.

It's a hefty walk of some five blocks to a supermarket and Eckerd Drugs. Ask the friendly dockmaster or any of his staff for directions. Many will probably want to take a taxi rather than undertake this prodigious hike (check above for taxi numbers).

Marco Island Yacht and Sailing Club deserves every cruiser's consideration. If you seek a fully appointed marina with all the amenities of a stopover in Fort Lauderdale, this is the spot.

Marco Island Yacht and Sailing Club
   (239) 642-2531
   http://www.marcoislandyachtclub.net

Approach depth—6-10 feet
Dockside depth—6+ feet
Accepts transients—yes
Transient dockage rate—above average
Floating concrete and fixed wooden piers—yes
**Dockside power connections—30, 50, and some
   100 amp**
Dockside water connections—yes
Waste pump-out—yes
Showers—yes (one)
**Restaurant—one on site and several accessible
   by taxi**

Marco Island's other first-class marina is found on the southerly banks of Factory Bay, south-southwest of unlighted daybeacon #15, near 25 57.750 North/081 43.640 West. Though you would probably never know it from looking at chart 11430, two channels actually serve the bay. The easternmost of the two passages (marked by three, red, unlighted daybeacons) cuts through the bay's waters and leads to Marco River Marina. Entrance depths range from 6 to 8 feet, while you will find 7 to 8 feet of water at the well-sheltered docks. Transients are eagerly accepted for overnight or temporary dockage at (mostly) fixed wooden piers sporting every conceivable power and water connection. There is also a whole raft of smaller, floating, concrete-decked piers that have obviously been designed for smaller powercraft.

Complete mechanical and haul-out services (using either of two travelifts rated at 15- and 35-ton capacities, respectively) are readily available. If you need it fixed, this is the place to be.

Gasoline, diesel fuel, and waste pump-out services are on hand, as is a very impressive, full-line ship's, clothing, and variety store, plus a large parts department. Adequate, climate-controlled shoreside showers are available, and a Laundromat is located some two miles away from the harbor. Smaller powercraft will find plentiful dry-stack storage.

Cruisers needing to restock their larders will find a supermarket and large drugstore within a half- to three-quarter-mile walk. If this is a bit too much of a hike, call one of the taxi services listed above.

The on-site Jack's Lookout Restaurant (239-394-5944) serves sandwiches, hamburgers, and hot dogs. For more substantive fare, several other restaurants, including the Windjammer (239-643-6880) and Snook Inn (239-394-3313), are within walking distance. These two restaurants will also provide complimentary transportation and a free drink to all patrons of Marco River Marina. If you are looking for a large, full-service marina, Marco River is certainly one of the best bets on the island waters.

Marco River Marina (239) 394-2502
http://www.marcoriver.com

Approach depth—6-8 feet
Dockside depth—7-8 feet
Accepts transients—yes

Transient dockage rate—above average
Fixed wooden and floating concrete pier and slips—yes
Dockside power connections—up to 50 amp
Dockside water connections—yes
Waste pump-out—yes
Showers—yes
Laundromat—two miles away
Gasoline—yes
Diesel fuel—yes
Mechanical repairs—full service
Below-waterline repairs—full service
Ship's and variety store—yes (large)
Restaurant—one on site and several more nearby

A good anchorage is found on the southern shores of Factory Bay, southwest of unlighted daybeacon #6 (near 25 57.773 North/081 43.447 West). Minimum 5½-foot depths hold to within 100 yards of a shoreline that is overlooked by dense high-rise condo development. This is not the spot to be caught in strong northern or northeasterly winds, but it does feature good shelter when the fickle breezes are blowing from other quarters.

A second marina used to flank Factory Bay's western shoreline. The old Factory Bay Marina is now closed and is rapidly being replaced by a high-rise condominium.

Coconut Island

West of flashing daybeacon #14, the Marco Island-Naples waterway runs quickly on to an important intersection with Big Marco Pass and Capri Pass. Big Marco Pass is impassable by all but smaller, very shallow draft local powercraft. Capri Pass is quite a different story.

Coconut Island sits squarely at the confluence of the two inlets. In earlier editions of this guidebook, I used to recommend anchoring off the isle's eastern and southeastern shores, south of flashing daybeacon #9. However, as part of its continuing effort to remove non-native trees from the state of Florida, the government in Tallahassee has cut down all the once-beautiful Australian pines that once guarded the shoreline. Perhaps, someone might want to point out to the powers that be in the Florida state government that those peoples of European extraction are not native to the state either. Somehow, I don't think this would lead to the removal of all but Native Americans from Florida, however.

Anyway, as you've probably guessed, the removal of its vegetation has led to the radical erosion of this small isle. It is now no more than a bump in the water, and to make an already lengthy story just a shade shorter, we no longer recommend that anyone try to anchor east of what's left of Coconut Island.

Capri Pass

Capri Pass is the only reasonably safe inlet for cruising-size craft between Coon Key Light and Gordon Pass. This inlet currently holds minimum 6- to 8-foot depths and is well marked. Be sure to read the navigational section on Capri Pass later in this chapter before attempting first-time entry.

As mentioned earlier, boats drawing a bit too much for comfortable passage through Coon Key Pass and the Big Marco River can run offshore to Capri Pass and then put in to the deeper section of the Marco Island-Naples waterway. You can then either turn south to take advantage of the marina facilities on Marco Island or north to Gordon Pass and Naples along the protected inside passage.

Johnson Bay Anchorage (25 59.952 North/081 44.569 West)

North of Capri Pass, the inland channel to

Naples skirts through a dredged cut in Johnson Bay. Cruisers will find an anchorage near unlighted daybeacon #14 for boats up to 40 feet. The charted deep water west-northwest of #14 makes a good spot to spend the night if winds do not exceed 20 knots. Depths of 8 to 12 feet hold to within 75 yards of the western banks. You will be subject to the wake of all passing vessels, but otherwise protection is pretty good. Don't forget to show an anchor light.

The current configuration of the deep water adjacent to this anchorage is now different than that pictured on the present edition of chart 11430. Read the navigational account of this anchorage in the next section before visiting this haven.

Little Marco Island Anchorage (26 00.305 North/081 45.539 West)

North-northwest of unlighted daybeacon #29, the waterway to Naples enters a superbly sheltered land cut that extends north to Dollar

Bay. At unlighted daybeacon #33, the main passage intersects a deep channel running back south beside Little Marco Island to Hurricane Pass (also known as Little Marco Pass). The southern two-thirds of the creek leading to Hurricane Pass can serve as a near ideal heavy-weather anchorage. While there are a few unmarked shoals to avoid, the cautious skipper should be able to hold minimum 6½- to 7-foot low-water depths north of the stream's intersection with Hurricane Pass.

Until a few years ago, cruisers could watch for a large stand of Australian pines overlooking the westerly banks, and drop the hook abeam of this delightful foliage in 8 to 10 feet of water. These pines have now been removed (as at Coconut Island—see above) by the state of Florida. Now, your best bet is to watch the sounder. As soon as depths improve to 8 feet or better, select any likely spot to drop the hook.

The Little Marco Island channel eventually swings south to Hurricane Pass. While chart 11430 would suggest shoal water on the interior portion of the inlet, on-site research revealed a very different situation. As a matter of fact, the southern tip of the peninsula lining the channel's western flank is undoubtedly one of the most popular stopovers for local weekend (smaller) powercraft.

During an earlier visit to the pass, it looked as if all of Florida had their small powerboats pulled up onto the beaches. Pleasure craft of almost any size can anchor off the point in minimum 7-foot depths. Protection is fair from all but southern and southwesterly winds, but insufficient for strong blows. For my money, I would choose the interior anchorage sandwiched between the beach and Little Marco Island every time.

Cruising craft should not attempt to run

Hurricane or Little Marco passes, no matter what the size or draft of their vessel might be. While we observed a few local outboarders running the inlet, unmarked shoals are rife and there are absolutely no markers on the pass.

Rookery Bay Anchorage (26 02.546 North/081 46.456 West)

Take a look at the current edition of chart 11430 and note the charted 5-foot offshoot leading to shallow Rookery Bay, opposite unlighted daybeacon #47. Boats up to 38 feet can drop anchor in 5 to 8 feet of water on the westernmost hundred yards of this passage. Protection is wonderful and should be sufficient for anything short of a hurricane. Rookery Bay itself is quite shallow and is part of a huge wildlife refuge. Exploration by dinghy would be worthwhile. If you do visit the bay, go quietly and don't disturb any nesting birds.

Gordon Pass Inlet

Immediately north of unlighted daybeacon #73, the markings on the Marco Island-Naples waterway come to an end. To the north, a set of beacons leads to Naples, while the well-outlined path to Gordon Pass inlet cuts to the west. Gordon Inlet offers just about everything any mariner might ever hope for from a pass. The channel is clearly outlined by

numerous aids to navigation and features minimum 10-foot depths. There is even a super anchorage on the cut's interior reaches. If you want more than that from an inlet, then you are hard to please.

Gordon Pass Anchorage (26 06.200 North/081 47.675 West)

Northwest of flashing daybeacon #13 on Gordon Pass, minimum depths of 5 feet can be held through the mid-width of the charted channel that leads to a series of canals lined by sumptuous homes. This passage allows ready access to a most fortunate anchorage. Cruisers can safely wait for fair breezes before venturing out Gordon Pass, or those who arrive late in the day from points offshore can spend the night in peace and security before heading up to Naples or down to Marco Island the next morning.

While it would otherwise be possible for a boat of any size to anchor in the first baylike area north of the entrance, chart 11430 designates these waters as a cable area. Heed this warning unless the notion of a high-voltage anchor appeals.

Instead, cut east on the first offshoot to starboard, north of the entrance. You can then cruise through minimum 9-foot depths until the stream turns again to the north. Here the waters open out into another wide bay with excellent 7- to 9-foot depths. There is enough room for a small ocean freighter to swing easily on the hook near 26 06.200 North/081 47.675 West, and there is immaculate protection from all winds. It is not an exaggeration to contend that you should be safe in any blow under 50 knots. The surrounding shores are heavily lined by some of the most expensive private homes that you are likely to see in all of Western Florida. Be sure to foster good relations between cruisers and property owners by not trespassing on any of this very private property.

Port Royal Anchorage (Various Lats/Lons —see below)

North of Gordon Pass, it's as if someone has flipped a light switch connected with residential development. Gone are the undeveloped shores to the south. Passing cruisers are now engulfed in a mass of palatial homes, beginning first on the western banks. This development is the harbinger of the city of Naples to the north. Before visiting with this fascinating city, we need to review one anchorage, a repair yard, and a marina that lie between Gordon Inlet and the principal Naples waterfront.

North of unlighted daybeacon #21, a $5\frac{1}{2}$- to 7-foot channel cuts into the western banks and leads to a Y-shaped series of canals. There are two unmarked shoals to avoid at the entrance, but good navigators should be able to make it through with the usual caution.

Once the pesky entrance is left behind, there are at least three spots where pleasure craft can drop the hook in peace and security. The first refuge is found abeam of the toe of charted 7-foot water cutting to the southwest, near 26 06.318 North/081 47.421 West. You can drop the Danforth (or the plow) into waters of $6\frac{1}{2}$ to 7 feet of depth with excellent protection from inclement weather.

During a really heavy blow, it is quite feasible to ease down into the southwesterly offshoot a bit for even more shelter. Try dropping the hook near 26 06.239 North/081 47.468 West. As is the case with all three of these anchorages, the shoreline is covered with affluent private homes.

The next potential anchorage is discovered south of the split in the canal, near 26 06.514 North/081 47.473 West. Here the waters broaden out enough to give plenty of swinging room, but there is still good shelter. Depths run from 6 to 7 feet. To my mind, this is an even better spot than the first anchorage described above. There is a bit more protection, and it's still quite close to the main channel.

Just about any captain could find what he might be looking for in the way of superior anchorage in these first three havens, but for those who like to explore, you may also follow the westerly branch of the canal until it broadens out into a lakelike area (where it dead-ends near 26 07.060 North/081 47.771 West). Skippers will find good depths ranging from 7 to 10 feet and the splendid protection so characteristic of this entire region.

Southpointe Yacht Club (26 06.298 North/081 47.059 West)

South of unlighted daybeacon #22, one marina graces the eastern shores of the Naples channel. Southpointe Yacht Club (239-774-6392) is part of a large condo and townhouse development.

Mariners visiting Southpointe must enter through a strangely marked entrance (be sure to read the navigational account on the marina later in this chapter) and then cruise up a long canal to reach the super-protected harbor. Minimum low-water entrance depths run from 6 to 7 feet, while excellent soundings of 8 to 9 feet are exhibited dockside.

Unfortunately, Southpointe Yacht Club no longer accepts transients or live-aboards. Cruisers must now bypass this facility unless they are lucky enough to own property in the development.

Royal Yacht Services

At unlighted daybeacon #25, a short hop north of the just-discussed Port Royal anchorage, a marked channel strikes off to the north-northeast. This shallow cut leads to Royal Yacht Services (239-775-0117). With the demise of Turner Marine and Boat Haven (see below), this is one of the few repair yards left in Naples that caters to pleasure craft.

On the other hand, let it be known loud and clear that the only word to describe this yard's approach channel is "shallow." Depths are all but nil at low tide, and even at high water, you can't count on any more than 5 feet. Clearly, this facility is limited to boats drawing less than 5 feet, and even then, most vessels must time their entrance and egress for high tide.

If you successfully traverse the entrance cut, you will find a friendly repair yard offering full below-waterline, haul-out repairs courtesy of a 60-ton travelift. Complete mechanical servicing for both diesel and gasoline power plants is also available. Some do-it-yourself work is still allowed here—a real rarity in modern-day Florida.

Always assuming you can negotiate the tricky entrance channel, we recommend this facility to our fellow cruisers. Wise captains will call ahead to check on the latest depths and the time of high tide.

Naples

No one without seriously impaired vision would ever characterize Naples as a village. It is a genuine city in every sense of the word. During recent visits, this writer could not help but be reminded of the likes of Fort Lauderdale or even Clearwater. While I have always found Naples to be a delightful vacation and tourist city, there is no doubt that development has reached an evermore-frenzied pace here over just the past several years.

Naples is famous for its long city pier (on the Gulfside beach) and its fabulous sunsets over the Gulf. The *T*-shaped pier was originally built in 1888 and extends 600 feet out into the Gulf. In spite of having to be rebuilt following a hurricane in 1910, a fire in 1922, and a hurricane in 1960, this venerable structure survives intact.

During one visit to Naples, we were privileged to observe one of the city's famous late-day displays of natural pyrotechnics. I can truthfully tell you that these spectacular sunsets are not just a creation of the local chamber of commerce. Another point of interest in Naples is the Palm Cottage Museum (137 12th Avenue South, 239-261-8164). Palm Cottage has been preserved to appear just as it did upon its construction in 1895, when Naples was just a quiet fishing village. The old homeplace is one of the last surviving tabbie homes in southwest Florida.

What is tabbie, you may ask? For those of you who don't know, tabbie was an early building material used in coastal sections of the southeast United States. It was formed by burning limestone and shells together. The secret of its making has now been lost.

Cruisers will need a taxi or rental car to visit Palm Cottage. It is a bit too far for walking from the city waterfront.

Cruisers lucky enough to tie up in Naples between May 3 and 19 will find themselves smack in the middle of the Tropicool Fest. This celebration of art exhibits, concerts, food, and sporting events is becoming larger and larger with each new season.

Numbers to know in Naples include

Yellow Cab—(239) 659-0800
Avis Rental Cars—(239) 643-0900
Budget Rent A Car—(239) 643-2212
Hertz Rent A Car—(239) 643-1515
Boat/U S Marine Center—(239) 774-3233

West Marine—(239) 793-7722
Chamber of Commerce—(239) 262-6376

Naples Anchorages and Facilities
(Various Lats/Lons—see below)

North of flashing daybeacon #34, cruisers will observe the Naples City Pier and the city's largest yacht club along the western shores. North of flashing daybeacon #40, the waters split at the mouth of the Gordon River. The second of the Naples yacht clubs guards the tip of land lying between the two branches of Gordon River here. Tidal currents are absolutely fierce along this stretch. Both forks of the Gordon River are soon blocked by low-level fixed bridges. Passage above the bridges is not recommended for cruising-size craft and is not further commented upon in this guide.

As we shall see in the account below, transient-slip dockage may soon become an endangered species in Naples. In fact, the Naples City Pier and the Naples Boat Club now offer the only non-yacht-club transient berths in this region. Fortunately, for those who are members of yacht clubs with appropriate reciprocal privileges, there are two notable clubs in Naples that supplement this dearth of visitor dockage. Wise captains should now be sure to make advance reservations rather than arrive late in the day, only to find no room at the inn.

We begin our trek along the Naples waterfront at unlighted daybeacon #35. West of #35, cruisers will find Naples Yacht Club (26 07.804 North/081 47.728 West), the southernmost of two side-by-side facilities on Crayton Cove. This yacht club is one of two such organizations in the Naples region. Entrance depths run between 7 and 13 feet.

1. Naples Yacht Club
2. Naples City Dock
3. Naples Boat Club
4. Port of Call Marina
5. Naples Sailing & Yacht Club

Most of the slips have 7 to 8 feet of water, with a few 6-foot soundings on the inner piers.

Members of accredited yacht clubs with

reciprocal agreements are accepted for transient dockage only with advance arrangements. Be sure to call well ahead of time to work out your dockage needs. The club dockmaster is on duty daily from 8 A.M. to 4:30 P.M. Berths are provided at fixed wooden piers with full power and water connections. Gasoline and diesel fuel are available to members and club guests only. Showers and ice are available in the clubhouse. The club also features a swimming pool at which accredited guests are welcome. The dining room serves lunch and dinner daily, but reservations are requested. Coat and tie are required after 6 P.M.

Naples Yacht Club (239) 262-6647 (clubhouse)
(239) 262-7301 (dockmaster)

Approach depth—7-13 feet
Dockside depth—6 to 8 feet
Accepts transients—members of clubs with
reciprocal agreements only with advance arrangements
Fixed wooden piers—yes
Dockside power connections—30 and 50 amp
Dockside water connections—yes
Showers—yes
Gasoline—yes (members and club guests only)
Diesel fuel—yes (members and club guests only)
Restaurant—on site

The city of Naples has installed a six-buoy mooring field on the waters between the Naples Yacht Club and the Naples City Pier near 26 07.908 North/081 47.605 West. Plans are in the works to add eight more moorings to this field, but the culmination of this scheme, or lack thereof, will depend on the future ownership of the city facility (see below). For the moment, visiting cruisers can pick up a mooring buoy (if they are lucky enough to find one empty) for $10 per day, plus tax. That fee also entitles you to make use

Naples mooring field

of the showers and Laundromat at the nearby city pier as well. A small dinghy dock is now located on the south side of the Naples City Pier, just beside the shower building, to facilitate visits to this facility by those anchored in the mooring field. This is a very nice addition indeed!

As you enter the mooring field, a sign warns all captains to check in with the city dockmaster. Skippers who have not already arranged for a mooring buoy ahead of time may want to make their first stop at the outermost face (fuel dock) of the Naples City Dock to sign up with the dockmaster and get their mooring buoy assignment.

Within the mooring field, low-water depths of 6 to 8 feet can be expected. Shelter is quite good from all but fresh northeasterly breezes. The surrounding shores are, as you would expect, heavily developed.

The Naples City Dock (near 26 07.967 North/ 081 47.607 West) is found just north of the Naples Yacht Club and to the west of unlighted daybeacon #36. Before going on to describe this city facility, it must be noted that big changes may or may not be in the offing here by the fall of 2003. During my last visit, in the summer of 2003, the city dockmasters were very forthright in telling me that there was a "50/50 chance" the entire marina would be leased out to a private company later in the year. If this does come to pass, only time will tell whether this will be a positive or a negative change for the cruising community. The report below is based on my visit to Naples City Pier as a municipally owned facility. Should private forces take over, things could be very different by the time of your arrival.

At the moment Naples City Pier accepts transients at fixed wooden piers with freshwater hookups and power connections of the 30-,

50-, and a few 100-amp varieties. Good entrance depths of 7 to 12 feet are complemented by similar dockside soundings. Just as you would expect, the deeper slips are found on the outer docks. Gasoline and diesel fuel are dispensed at the outermost section of the fixed, wooden, T-shaped pier. Fuel prices are some of the best in the region. The marina also features good, air-conditioned showers. The on-site Laundromat is covered but open to the weather on one side. Free waste pump-out service is available as well.

Naples City Dock (239) 434-4693

Approach depth—7-12 feet
Dockside depth—7-12 feet
Accepts transients—yes
Transient dockage rate—above average
Fixed wooden piers—yes
Dockside power connections—30 and 50 amp (and a few 100 amp)
Dockside water connections—yes
Waste pump-out—yes
Showers—yes
Laundromat—yes
Gasoline—yes
Diesel fuel—yes
Ship's store—nearby
Restaurant—on site

An interesting complex of shops and restaurants is found just behind the city docks. The Dock at Crayton Cove Restaurant (239-263-9940) sits immediately north of the city pier. This fine eatery features open-air dining and some of the most delectable cold seafood salads that you will ever enjoy. In season, the stone crab claws are nothing to sneeze at either. Just watch out for the price of imported beer. Crayton Cove has its own small, C-shaped dock to which small powercraft are free to moor. Dockside depths run 5 to 6 feet.

Naples City Dock

Dock at Crayton Cove Restaurant, Naples

Now, as if all that were not enough, there is a whole series of shops located behind the restaurant. One of these, the Naples Ship's Store (830 12th Avenue South, 239-649-0899), will be of great interest to visiting and resident cruisers alike. This well-managed establishment features an extensive selection of nautical gear, clothing, and marine publications. Take a few moments to browse the teeming shelves. Anyone interested in things nautical will find more than a little to engage him. Tell Eric we sent you!

Napoli on the Bay Restaurant (239-649-7337) sits just beside the Naples Ship's Store. This firm boasts super pizza and other Italian delicacies, as well as scoop ice cream.

Cruisers seeking fresh fruit will want to set a course for Crayton Cove Gourmet and Fruit Shipper (800 12th Avenue South, 239-262-4362), a few doors up from Napoli on the Bay. This is a great place to restock the galley with a few specialty items.

Those whose tastes run to French-style cuisine will want to make every effort to check out the Bleu Provence (1234 8th Street South, 239-261-8239), just across the street from Crayton Cove Gourmet. We have not had a chance to sample the fare here, but judging from this restaurant's popularity, the food must be spectacular. Be sure to call for reservations on weekends to avoid long waits.

Visiting cruisers up for a five-block walk (or a short bicycle or taxi ride) can visit another couture-style Naples shopping district. Stroll west on 12th Avenue. Eventually you will come to 3rd Street. An elegant collection of specialty shops, art galleries, and sophisticated restaurants stretches along this byway for several blocks.

In this latter category, Tommy Bahamas Tropical Café (1220 3rd Street South, 239-643-6889) is clearly one of the most popular, with plentiful outdoor seating. Anyone up for a visit to jolly old England should be sure to check out the Old Naples Pub (255 13th Avenue South, 239-649-8200). Superb Continental-style dining is readily available at Campiello Restaurant (1177 3rd Street South, 239-435-1166). Try to get a table in the delightful courtyard.

One of the most tempting dining spots, at least to our palates, is the Ridgeway Bar and Grill (1300 3rd Street South, 239-262-5500). Check it out!

Turning now to Naples' other, suddenly meager, on-the-water facilities, the docks of Cove Inn Hotel and Marina (239-262-7161) lie immediately north of the city pier and share the same cove. As its name implies, this facility features a large hotel with a line of docks out back. All of the facility's slips are privately owned and no transient dockage is currently available.

On the other hand, the small coffee shop in the Cove Inn Hotel may just serve the best breakfast in Naples. It's a quick walk of only two blocks from the Naples City Dock to this notable dining spot, so if you're up for some great eggs or scrumptious hot cakes, give this restaurant your immediate attention.

Just north of the Cove Inn, passing cruisers will note the Naples Coast Guard Auxiliary headquarters on the western banks. There are no facilities at the clubhouse for visiting craft, but it's a comfort to know that the squadron is on the job in Naples.

A large cove indents the western banks above the Coast Guard Auxiliary headquarters. There is a local launching ramp for small craft here, but depths of as little as 3 feet render this water inappropriate for anchorage by larger vessels.

Cruisers who have not visited Naples for the last two years will be surprised to spot a huge collection of condos west of flashing daybeacon #40 at the one-time site of Old Naples Seaport. As you will see, this is the way things are going in Naples.

For many years, resident and transient cruisers alike looked forward to a visit with Turner Marine of Naples, guarding the western banks, north of flashing daybeacon 40. This property was purchased some three years ago and has been radically transformed into the Naples Boat Club (26 08.260 North/081 47.500 West). Now, visitors will be awed by the truly huge dry-stack storage building, sitting cheek by jowl with quite a collection of on-site, luxury condos. This impressive facility has chosen to accept transient cruisers on a space-available basis. Actually, all the available slips have been sold to permanent owners, but the helpful dockmaster has informed this writer that there are almost always some slips open for visitors. Be advised that transient dockage rates are well above average. Smart skippers will call ahead of time to check on slip availability.

Berths at the Naples Boat Club consist mostly of floating, concrete-decked piers, though there are some fixed wooden structures in place as well. Depths alongside run at least 6 feet. Freshwater and 30-, 50-, and 100-amp power connections are in the offing (plus dockside cable-television hookups), as well as gasoline, diesel fuel, and waste pump-out service. Shoreside, visitors will discover air-conditioned showers, a Laundromat, swimming pool, plus a small variety store hard by the fuel dock. Those in need of repairs will

want to make the acquaintance of the on-site repair yard, Allied Marine (http://www.allied-marine.com/services/naples/index.cfm, 239-262-6500). Mechanical repairs are available for both gasoline and diesel power plants. The yard's travelift is rated at 70 tons.

All in all, Naples Boat Club presents an impressive array of services and amenities for visiting and resident mariners alike. Just hold onto your wallet when it comes time to pay your overnight dockage fee.

Naples Boat Club (239) 263-2774
http://www.naplesboatclub.net

Approach depth—7-12 feet
Dockside depth—6+ feet
Accepts transients—yes
Transient dockage fee—above average
Floating concrete docks—mostly
Fixed wooden piers—some
Dockside power connections—30, 50, and
**   100 amp**
Dockside freshwater connections—yes
Waste pump-out—yes
Showers—yes
Laundromat—yes
Gasoline—yes
Diesel fuel—yes
Mechanical repairs—yes
Below-waterline repairs—yes
Variety story—small
Restaurant—easy walking distance

Naples Sailing and Yacht Club (26 08.280 North/081 47.342 West) maintains a floating breakwater-enclosed harbor on the point of land separating the two branches of the

Gordon River. This club is glad to accept members of other yacht clubs with reciprocal privileges for overnight or temporary dockage. Berths are cheerfully provided at first-class, floating concrete-decked piers with full power and water connections. Low-tide dockside depths range from 4½ to 6 feet. The club's dockmaster is in attendance daily from 8:00 A.M. until 4:00 P.M. Call ahead to make advance arrangements if you plan to arrive at any other time. Showers are available in the clubhouse.

The on-site dining room is open for lunch and dinner Tuesday through Saturday, and there is also a Sunday midday brunch. Reservations are requested but not required. A host of other restaurants is close at hand, including the famed Kelly's Fish House.

This writer has always been impressed by the friendliness of this organization during his several brief contacts with the club membership. It is highly recommended.

Naples Sailing and Yacht Club
  (239) 774-0424
  (239) 774-2649 (dockmaster)

Approach depth—6 feet
Dockside depth—4½-6 feet
Accepts transients—members of other yacht clubs with reciprocal privileges
Fixed and floating docks—yes
Dockside power connections—30 and 50 amp
Dockside water connections—yes
Showers—yes
Restaurant—on site and several others nearby

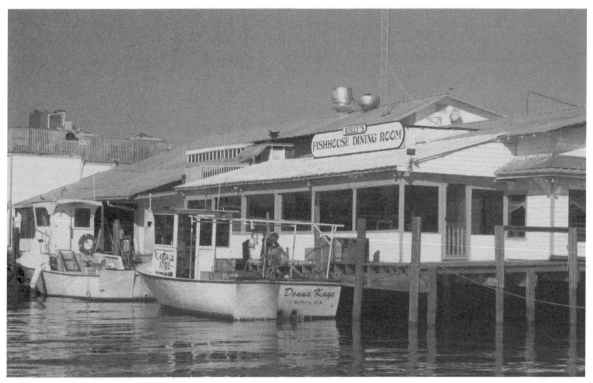

Kelly's Fish House, Naples

Turning our attention now to the deeper, western branch of the Gordon River, passing cruisers will first come upon a stream making its way in from the western banks that serve both Marine Max and the Naples Powerboat Marina (239-261-8878). This latter facility maintains a host of covered slips set back in a protected *L*-shaped cove. All dockage is strictly reserved for resident craft and signs warn against entry into the slips by visiting boats.

Marine Max (239-262-6137) is a full-service repair facility offering complete mechanical and below-waterline, haul-out repairs. The yard's travelift is rated at 70 tons. You will spot Marine Max's docks to starboard as you enter the westerly stream. This firm is part of a chain that we will meet throughout our remaining journey north along the Sunshine State's western coastline. This location caters particularly to the needs of larger pleasure craft. All wet-slip dockage is reserved for service customers.

Continuing up the west-side branch, the western shores are flanked by a portion of the so-called Tin City shopping center. This complex series of gift shops, restaurants, and retail businesses of all descriptions are grouped under (you guessed it) tin-roofed buildings. One of the largest of these structures fronts directly onto the water.

On the eastern shore, visiting cruisers will spy newly minted Port-O-Call Marina. This is a dry-stack storage facility for powercraft. No services other than gasoline are available for transients.

Immediately south of the fixed bridge, Kelly's Fish House (239-774-0494) lines the eastern banks. While the available dockage is taken up by the restaurant's own fishing vessels, visiting cruisers should make every effort to visit this outstanding dining spot. Locals and this writer agree that Kelly's serves the finest fried (and a few broiled items) seafood in Naples, bar none. The restaurant is within walking distance of Boat Haven Marine.

Let us now turn our attention briefly to the easterly branch of the Gordon River below the fixed bridges. This track is much shallower than its western counterpart. Low-tide depths of 4 to $4\frac{1}{2}$ feet are not uncommon. Only boats drawing less than 4 feet should attempt to visit the facilities along this stream.

Besides, there is now no real reason to visit this eastern branch, anyway. In years past, this was the route to reach Boat Haven Marine Supply. Some transient dockage was available, but the real attraction was the excellent on-site marine and nautical-clothing store. Now, the store is closed, and the remaining wet slips are only rented out on a month-to-month basis, The on-site, new, boat-sales operation is still very much an ongoing concern, however.

There is a strong local rumor—which, let me hasten to add, I've been unable to confirm—that this entire property is set for major redevelopment, possibly as yet another condo project. Only the future will tell.

COON KEY TO NAPLES NAVIGATION

Cruising captains voyaging north from the Ten Thousand Islands to Naples have

three different routes to choose from. Sailors, in particular, might decide to skirt well west of the Cape Romano shoals and follow the open waters of the Gulf north to Gordon Pass. While this route serves up nothing in the way of protection, there are certainly no depth problems.

A second alternative is to split your passage between the offshore and inland routes. Those choosing this alternative can cruise offshore to a point just north of Marco Island and then come inside via mostly deep and well-marked Capri Pass. You can then turn briefly south to visit Marco Island's marinas, or cruise north through minimum 5½-foot depths (with typical depths from 6 to 10 feet) all the way to Gordon Pass and Naples. Obviously this passage has some of the best of both worlds (and it avoids the 55-foot Goodland Bridge) and should be a serious consideration, particularly for sailors.

This writer's personal favorite, though, is the full inside channel from Coon Key Light, past Goodland, Marco Island, and then on to Naples. Of course, sailors should take the 55-foot vertical clearance of the fixed, Goodland Bridge into account. Otherwise, in spite of its problems, there is a backwater feeling to the waterway south of Marco Island that will appeal to the heart of any true cruiser.

Skippers setting out upon the Marco Island-Naples waterway from Coon Key must contend with the possibility of encountering a few low-tide depths of 4½ feet. Only boats drawing 4 feet or preferably less can cruise this waterway in safety. On a rising tide, you might consider taking a boat needing 4½ or even 5 feet of water through the passage, but this is a bit risky. A few portions of the waterway south of Marco Island are not really as well marked as they should be, and the channel is subject to shoaling.

Let me also once again mention the complex manatee no-wake zones that have been set up along the Marco Island-Naples waterway. Be *sure* to read the various signs along the way, even if you have to use your binoculars to make out the small print. You won't believe how the speed limits change back and forth at certain times of the day and certain months of the year.

Whatever route you choose, this is a pleasant section of the Western Florida coastline. With the exception of the heavy development on portions of Marco Island, most of the coastline, both inside and outside, is undeveloped. Good coastal navigation must be practiced on all three passages, so stay alert, and don't concentrate so much on the scenery that you become a fixed part of it.

The Offshore Route   Any cruiser worth his or her salt knows that it's not a very swift idea to undertake a 25-nautical-mile offshore passage if foul weather is in the offing. If you decide to cruise offshore to Capri Pass or Naples (Gordon Pass), it would be very wise to wait for fair breezes before undertaking the passage.

Study chart 11429 and note the miles and miles of shoals extending south from Cape Romano. Boats that try to cut this corner obviously do so at their own considerable peril. For safety's sake, you should set your course to pass well south and west of the unnumbered 18-foot flashing daybeacon marking the shoal's southerly limits. Cruise west from the 18-foot daybeacon for a good 4 nautical miles before making your turn to the north. This maneuver will assure a safe passage past these deadly shallows.

For the next 18 nautical miles you're on your own. There are no aids to navigation between the unnumbered 18-foot flashing daybeacon and flashing daybeacon #2 off Capri Pass. Fortunately, except in the vicinity of Big Marco Pass, good depths run reasonably close to the Gulf beaches. This relatively deep water allows navigators to keep the shoreline in sight during daylight and fair weather as they work their way north. Nevertheless, all mariners should follow careful compass courses on this long run and maintain an accurate dead-reckoning track. Of course, a Loran or GPS would be most helpful as well.

Be sure that you are *at least 1.5 nautical miles offshore* as you approach Big Marco Pass, at the northern end of Marco Island. Extensive shoals run well west from this unusable passage.

East of flashing daybeacon #2, you can now switch to chart 11430 for a more detailed picture of the pass. Further navigational information on Capri Pass will be presented in our review of the Marco Island-Naples waterway.

It's another cruise of slightly better than 7 nautical miles from #2 to flashing daybeacon #1 off Gordon Pass. Again, you can follow the shoreline. In the absence of strong winds, this is a relatively simple and quite delightful passage. From #1, it's a straight shot east into the inlet's interior reaches. Don't drift too far to the north. A partially

submerged jetty extends for several hundred yards out into the Gulf from the pass's north-western point. For more information, consult the navigational account of Gordon Pass presented later in this chapter as a part of the inland route's coverage.

Caxambas Pass Channel Returning now to Coon Key Light, east of Cape Romano, let us turn our attention briefly to the channel leading first northwest and then west to Caxambas Pass. Remember that depths of 5 to 6 feet are held only as far west as unlighted daybeacon #6. West of #6, the channel turns briefly north and runs through a shoal-ravaged section with low-water soundings of 3 feet or less. Obviously, cruising-size craft should halt their forward progress well east of #6.

Also, as noted earlier in this chapter, extensive shoaling has taken place west of unlighted daybeacon #19, in and around the waters denoted by unlighted daybeacons #8 and #10. Unless a new channel is marked at some future point by the county authorities, these shallows are even more reason for visiting cruisers to confine their explorations to the waters east of #6.

To enter the channel, set course from Coon Key Light to come abeam of unlighted daybeacon #2, well south of Neal Key, to its immediate northeasterly side. Do not drift to the south as you approach #2. Chart 11430 correctly forecasts depths of 1 to 3 feet in that quarter.

Continue on by pointing to pass unlighted daybeacon #4 fairly close to its northerly quarter. Northwest of #4, deep water spreads out in a broader passage.

Note that marker colors now reverse for

no good reason that I can see. Point to come abeam of unlighted daybeacon #1 to its immediate northeasterly quarter.

At #1, the channel swings around the northeasterly tip of Helen Key and plunges west. Between #1 and unlighted daybeacon #3, cruisers will find the best place to drop the hook.

Coon Key Pass

Let us now return to a review of the principal Marco Island-Naples waterway via Coon Key Pass. One of the shallowest portions of this passage is found between Coon Key Light and Coon Key. Despite the 4-foot soundings noted on chart 11430, we did not find any low-water readings of less than 5 feet in this region. Boats drawing more than 4 feet should, nevertheless, proceed with the greatest caution and probably wait for a rising tide.

From Coon Key Light, set a northerly course to pass the easterly shores of Coon Key by some 200 yards off your port side. Point to eventually come abeam of and pass unlighted daybeacon #2 by about 100 yards to its westerly quarter. By the time you are abeam of Coon Key's white sand enshrouded, northerly tip, good depths of 6 feet or better will return and be with you for some time.

As you approach #2, be mindful of the shallower water running off Coon Key's northerly tip. North of #2, you may choose to throw out the anchor just east of the small, unnamed island east of Neal Key. Good depths run to within an amazing 20 yards of the island's eastern shoreline.

To continue on the main channel, set a course to come abeam of and pass unlighted daybeacon #3 to its easterly side. Just before reaching #3, a superb anchorage possibility opens out to the east.

Tripod Key-Sugar Bay Anchorage   Enter the broad stream leading northeast to Sugar Bay on its centerline. Drop the hook well short (southwest) of Sugar Bay. This body of water is quite shoal and should only be entered by dinghy.

On Coon Key Pass   North of unlighted daybeacon #4, Coon Key Pass skirts around the point of land occupied by the village of Goodland. On-site research did reveal the charted 3-foot depths immediately adjacent to unlighted daybeacon #6. Happily, we sounded nothing less than 5 feet by staying at least 25 yards west of #6. As you pass #6, the dry-stack storage building associated with Goodland Bay Marina will be visible to the west.

Goodland Bay and Calusa Island Marinas To access both these marina facilities, continue on the main channel past unlighted daybeacon #6 until you are some 50 yards short of Goodland's southeasterly point. Cut sharply to the west and favor the northerly shores heavily as you work your way along. You will spy several pilings outlining the southerly side of the channel, with arrow pointers atop the piles indicating that they should be passed to their (the pilings') northern sides. Stay at least 40 yards north of these aids to navigation for best depths.

Soon you will pass the dry-stack storage

and a few floating docks to starboard. This is not the principal Goodland Bay Marina dockage area. Continue cruising west and the charted *T*-shaped cove will open out to the north. Enter on the mid-width. The marina docks and buildings will be sighted on the cove's easterly banks.

To continue on to Calusa Island Marina, bypass the northerly turn into Goodland Bay. Cruise west on the waters of Blue Hill Creek, favoring the northerly shoreline. Soon you will round a point with a private, fixed wooden dock, backed by a sumptuous homeplace. Hug the outer edge of the private dock for best depths.

Continue favoring the northerly banks, and soon you will spot Calusa Island's outer dockage basin lining the creek's northerly banks. Be sure to hug the outer face of these piers as you cruise to your assigned slip. Even a small jog to the south may well land you in 4 feet of water.

The entrance into Calusa Island's inner harbor basin will open out to the north, just as you sight the outer docks ahead. Here you will find the fuel dock, but remember that low-water soundings can run as skinny as 4½ to 5 feet. Captains piloting vessels drawing better than 4½ feet would do well to fuel up at mid- or high tide.

On the Coon Key Channel   North of unlighted daybeacon #6, slow-speed regulations are in effect to unlighted daybeacon #10, with an associated no-wake zone running from #10 to unlighted beacon #15. At unlighted daybeacon #7, the channel turns sharply west and skirts the southerly reaches of otherwise shallow Goodland Bay.

Goodland Bay Anchorage   To make good your entry into the tongue of deeper waters northeast of unlighted daybeacon #7, abandon the main channel as you come abeam of #7 on it easterly side. Work your way carefully to the north for some 25 yards, and then cut to the northeast. Drop the hook as soon as you are clear of the channel and any fellow cruisers that you might find in this haven. Farther to the northeast, depths deteriorate quickly.

On to Big Marco River   Watch the southern shores as you cruise west between unlighted daybeacons #8 and #10. The slips associated with Skeeter's Old Marco Lodge will be readily visible along the banks.

Captains seeking to visit Stan's Idle Hour Restaurant and the Little Bar and Restaurant should cut into the mid-width of the southward-running canal, immediately west of Skeeter's. Follow the canal's centerline to its southern terminus. Stan's will be spotted on the southeastern corner of the stream's southerly tip. Remember, low-water soundings in this small stream run as little as 3½ feet. If you need more depth, consider a stop at nearby Goodland Bay or Calusa Island Marina.

Don't slip to the north as you approach unlighted daybeacon #8. A huge patch of shallows flanks the channel in this quarter.

North of unlighted daybeacon #12, the waterway meets up with the 55-foot fixed Goodland Bridge. This pesky span and its Marco Island-Judge S. S. Jolley counterpart to the northwest is a limiting factor for many sail craft!

Immediately north of Goodland Bridge, a marked and charted channel cuts sharply west to Moran's Barge Marina. Enter on the mid-width and expect low-water soundings of some 4½ feet. Remember, no transient dockage is available.

Chart 11430 pictures an offshoot of 7-foot water just north of the bridge on the eastern banks. Our research showed that this small sidewater has almost shoaled in entirely. It is still possible to barely get off the main channel, should you be desperate to drop the hook, but you cannot cruise more than 25 yards or so to the east before depths begin to rise.

Unlighted daybeacon #15 introduces visiting cruisers to Big Marco River, running first north and then northwest to unlighted daybeacon #17. This portion of the stream is deep almost from bank to bank and is well sheltered. If you should decide to drop the hook here, ease your way off the main channel and remember to show an anchor light.

West of unlighted daybeacon #20, the channel cuts south of a small island even though chart 11430 would suggest that the best water runs north of this isle. Our soundings showed up nothing less than 5 feet through the buoyed section; however, so keep the faith with the marked passage.

Be sure to stick to the marked channel between unlighted daybeacons #20 and #22. Shoal water waits to greet the unwary outside the buoyed cut.

By the time you approach unlighted daybeacon #24 to its southerly side, the high-rise development on Marco Island will be glaring at you in the distance. Hold on for a minute—there is still one trouble spot to negotiate.

Perhaps the shallowest and trickiest portion of the entire run from Coon Key Pass to Capri Pass is found between unlighted daybeacon #25 and the fixed, 55-foot Marco Island (Highway 951)/Judge S. S. Jolley Bridge. This portion of the channel calls for the greatest caution.

From #25, you must set course to come abeam of unlighted daybeacon #26 to its immediate *southerly* side. On the water, this looks all wrong. You will be headed away from the bridge's very visible pass-through, and you will be tempted to adjust course to the north. *Don't do it!* This maneuver will land you in 2 to 3 feet of water.

Just to make matters a bit more complicated, it's a fairly lengthy run of almost 1 nautical mile between #25 and #26. My best advice is to run a careful compass (or GPS) course and monitor your depth sounder continuously. After coming abeam of #26 hard by its southerly quarter, you should curl around the aid and cruise north-northeast until coming abeam of the bridge's central pass-through. Cut west to pass under the bridge.

The mostly unmarked (but reasonably easy to follow) entrance to Marco Island Yacht and Sailing Club strikes to the southwest, between the western face of the Marco Island/Judge S. S. Jolley Bridge and the charted power lines crossing the main channel farther to the northwest. Look for the canal that allows entrance to the harbor, and cut directly in from the main channel toward the canal's mid-width. Along the way, you will spot two signs north of your course that warn of a shoal impinging on this flank of the approach cut. Obviously it would not bode well to slip to the north. Once into the canal, the marina and yacht club will be quite visible to port.

Marco Island and Factory Bay Anchorage

North and west of the Marco Island/Judge S. S. Jolley Bridge, the color configuration for aids to navigation reverses. Northbound craft should now pass red beacons to port and green markers to starboard. This scheme holds as far as Capri Pass, and actually continues out to sea on the inlet.

A wide swath of deep water opens out past the 55-foot fixed bridge. You should not have any difficulty in cruising to a point abeam of Factory Bay, which is southwest of the main channel. Remember that Factory Bay is served by two channels. Most cruisers will want to contend with the easterly (or central) passage only, as it leads to the bay's principal marina and the earlier-reviewed anchorage.

Captains cruising north on the waterway will first come upon the well-marked cut leading through the bay's easterly section. The three, red, unlighted daybeacons outlining this cut make a cruise down this channel to Marco River Marina a snap. Be sure to pass unlighted daybeacons #2, #4, and #6 to your starboard side.

Cruisers looking to drop the hook in the anchorage along the southern shores of Factory Bay should depart the marked east-side channel abeam of unlighted daybeacon #6. Ease your way a bit to the south-south-east, feeling your way along with the sounder. Drop the hook before approaching to within less than 100 yards of the heavily developed banks.

The second channel skirts along Factory Bay's western banks and calls for caution. Should you choose to ignore our advice, and explore this cut, abandon the main channel some 50 yards northwest of unlighted daybeacon #15 and cut to the south. Watch for the first aid to navigation on the westerly cut, unlighted daybeacon #1. Pass this marker fairly close to your port side. From #1, use your binoculars to pick out the westerly channel's next aid to navigation, unlighted daybeacon #3. Between #1 and #3, you will most likely spy a whole series of piles and signs east of your course line. All these structures mark a large shoal running along the midsection of Factory Bay. Stay well away from these markers and point to pass #3 to your port side. From #3 point to come abeam of #5, also to your port side.

Capri Pass and Coconut Island Anchorage

West of Factory Bay deep water opens out almost from bank to bank on the Marco Island-Naples waterway, moving toward Big Marco and Capri passes.

North and west of unlighted daybeacon #15, power cruisers will have to contend with yet another manatee no-wake zone until reaching unlighted daybeacon #11. To me, this regulated zone seems especially ludicrous, as the waters are wide and the currents move swiftly—seemingly not a good place for manatees to hang out. Oh well, who understands the Florida Department of Natural Resources anyway?

West of flashing daybeacon #14, passing cruisers may note a small channel cutting south into Collier Bay. We cruised through this cut and found no facilities or room for anchorage. Collier Bay itself is quite shallow, with depths less than 3 feet as the norm.

Southwest of unlighted daybeacon #11, the northerly shores drop away. The channel continues west-southwest toward Coconut Island, skirting a long shoal building west-southwest from the north-side point of land. Set course to eventually come abeam of flashing daybeacon #9 to its fairly immediate southerly side. At this point, the channel cuts sharply to the north-northwest.

To continue north along the Marco Island-Naples waterway to Capri Pass, cut north-northwest from flashing daybeacon #9 and pass to the west of unlighted junction daybeacon #C. The main body of Capri Pass will then lie to the west, while the channel to Naples cuts to the northeast.

As with all inlets, bottom configurations are subject to change on Capri Pass, and aids to navigation are often moved to follow the shifting sands. Don't be too surprised to find a somewhat different configuration of markers by the time you visit than the one outlined below or on chart 11430.

To enter Capri Pass, set course from #C to pass to the south of unlighted daybeacon #7 and continue out to sea, keeping (as you would expect) green markers to your starboard side and red beacons to port. Just be sure to stay inside the marked passage. Shoal water waits to greet your keel both south and north of the channel.

Cruisers entering Capri Pass from the Gulf of Mexico must be sure to pass to the west of #C if they are turning south-southeast to Marco Island.

Don't attempt to run Big Marco Pass south of flashing daybeacon #9. This passage is shoal and dangerous, even for small powercraft.

Waterway to Naples Mariners continuing north to Naples and Gordon Pass must now contend with some shallows flanking the channel running inland from Capri Pass. Shoaling on the channel's northern tier prompted the Coast Guard to relocate unlighted daybeacon #1 farther to the south several years ago. This scheme of aids to navigation still seems to have solved the problem, but be on the alert for new intrusions of shallow water as you pass through this tricky passage.

Be sure to pass unlighted daybeacon #C to its northwesterly side to avoid the long tongue of charted shallow water east and northeast of this aid. Only then should you swing to the northeast and point to pass unlighted daybeacon #1 to its southeastern quarter. Take your time and watch the sounder carefully during this difficult passage between #C and #1.

After rounding the turn at unlighted daybeacon #C, the color configuration of the local aids to navigation changes yet again. From Capri Pass to the intersection with the Gordon Pass channel, northbound captains should pass green aids to their (the cruisers') port side and take red markers to starboard.

As you make the turn from #C, you may spy a few weekend boats pulled up onto the beach inside charted Cannon Channel, north of unlighted daybeacon #7. Cruising boats should not attempt to enter this offshoot. Depths run less than 4 feet.

After passing between #2A and #3A, the Naples waterway channel takes a sharp jog to the north and enters a more sheltered passage. A marked, but mostly uncharted, local channel makes off to the northeast from #2A into the "Isles of Capri." Visiting cruisers should probably ignore this cut and follow the principal Marco Island-Naples waterway channel by pointing to pass unlighted daybeacon #5 to its easterly side. Between #5 and #12, favor the western shore slightly, just as the markers would indicate, to avoid the correctly charted band of shallows flanking the eastern banks.

From #12, the channel turns east and follows a dredged cut through the lower reaches of shallow Johnson Bay. Stick strictly to the marked channel throughout this stretch.

Johnson Bay Anchorage   To visit this haven, come abeam of unlighted daybeacon #14 and then cut directly in toward the northwestern banks. Drop the hook before approaching to within less than 75 yards of shore. Do not drift to the south toward unlighted daybeacon #13. In spite of what chart 11430 would lead you to believe, some shoaling has apparently occurred near #13.

On to Little Marco Island   The Naples waterway leaves Johnson Bay near unlighted daybeacon #25. Don't be tempted to try the tiny charted offshoot of deeper water north of #25. Shoaling has reduced the depth in this sidewater to 3 feet or less. At unlighted daybeacon #27, the waters running inland from Hurricane Pass

briefly intersect the Naples waterway. This passage is now very shoal. Even small powercraft will find the bottom if they stray onto these waters.

Unlighted daybeacon #28A heralds a turn to the northwest through a dredged cut. Pay close attention to the markers as you pass out into the waters north of Little Marco Island. A long shoal is building out from this island's northerly tip. Pass between unlighted daybeacons #33 and #34, favoring #34 slightly.

Little Marco Island Channel and Anchorage
To enter this lovely sidewater, be sure you are at least 50 yards north of unlighted daybeacon #34. Enter the side channel by favoring the western shores. Continue favoring the western banks as you cruise downstream for the next .5 nautical miles to avoid the correctly charted 4-foot shallows abutting the eastern shoreline. South of this point, good depths open out almost from shore to shore. Pick any likely spot to drop the hook.

If you should decide to continue on to Hurricane Pass, hold to the mid-width until you intersect the wide waters to the south. If you are really brave, you can partially round the westside point, keeping some 25 yards or so off the beach. I would seriously suggest discontinuing your explorations once abeam of this point. To the south and west, depths are uncertain at best.

Rookery Bay Anchorage   The charted offshoot leading to Rookery Bay is located abeam of unlighted daybeacon #47. Enter on the centerline and drop the hook before proceeding more than 75 yards upstream. Visit Rookery Bay strictly by dinghy.

On the Naples Channel   North of unlighted daybeacon #47, the waterway leading north to Naples and Gordon Pass enters a sheltered land cut for some 2.3 nautical miles. Another no-wake, manatee zone holds sway on the waters between #47 and unlighted daybeacon #52. Slow down and enjoy the sights.

After passing between unlighted daybeacons #64 and #65, the channel leads out into shallow Dollar Bay. Again, stay to the marked passage and you should not have any difficulty.

North of unlighted daybeacon #71, the Naples waterway rushes on toward an intersection with Gordon Pass and the marked channel running north through Naples Bay. Watch for shoaling and additional markers at this intersection. At the current time, you should pass unlighted daybeacon #73 to its fairly immediate easterly side. Then, look for unlighted junction daybeacon #G. If you are cruising north, pass this aid to its easterly quarter and come abeam of flashing daybeacon #20 to its westerly quarter. Just north of #G, you can easily turn west into the Gordon Pass channel.

Gordon Pass   Be sure to pass to the north of unlighted junction daybeacon #G when making your initial approach to Gordon Pass. After coming abeam of #G, point to initially pass unlighted daybeacon #18 to its northerly side and continue seaward by passing all subsequent red markers to your port side and all green beacons to starboard. At unlighted daybeacon #10, an idle-speed, no-wake zone begins and stretches west to unlighted daybeacon #7A.

At flashing daybeacon #9, the channel takes a temporary turn to the south and then curves back sharply to the west at unlighted daybeacon #7A. Between #7A and the next aid to navigation, unlighted daybeacon #7, a dramatic shoal encroaches on the northern side of the Gordon Pass channel. Be sure to stay south of #7A and #7. Follow the remaining markers out to sea. For best depths, don't cut either north or south from the inlet channel until you reach flashing daybeacon #1, the outermost marker on this passage. Some shallow water lies south, and particularly north, of the cut's outer reaches between unlighted daybeacon #7 and flashing daybeacon #1.

Gordon Pass Anchorage   To enter the excellent anchorage making into the northern shores of the Gordon Inlet channel, depart the main cut directly abeam of unlighted daybeacon #13 and cruise north-northwest into the canal's mouth, favoring the west-side banks slightly. Follow the centerline as the main branch of the canal turns to the east and then opens out to the north.

On the Naples Channel   North of Gordon Pass, the numbering scheme on the aids to navigation lining the channel to Naples changes one last time (in order to keep pace with the configuration of marker numbers on

Gordon Pass), but the color configuration remains the same. North of unlighted daybeacon #21, cruisers will find a good anchorage to the west and a private marina to the east.

Port Royal Anchorage North of unlighted daybeacon #21, identify the canal entrance cutting into the western banks. Enter the mouth by favoring the southerly banks. This maneuver will help you to avoid the charted patch of 3-foot shallows to the north.

Once past the bothersome entrance, all you need to do is stay just slightly off any of the banks for good depths all the way to the upstream limits on both arms of the canal.

Southpointe Yacht Club Two privately maintained aids to navigation associated with Southpointe Yacht Club will be spotted east of the main channel just north of unlighted daybeacon #21. To enter the marina, pass between unlighted daybeacon #2 and an unnumbered warning beacon (to your port side). You will find this to be a strange maneuver, as these aids will point you south of the entrance canal. Be assured, however, that a shoal guards the mid-width of the canal's entrance. After cruising between the two aids, work your way carefully to the northeast and enter the canal. Yes, I know this sounds strange, but an on-site check and a conversation with the marina dockmaster confirmed that this is the correct procedure.

On to Naples As you pass between flashing daybeacon #24 and unlighted daybeacon #25, you will spy the marked channel cutting north-northeast to Royal Yacht Services. Remember that low-tide depths are nil, and even at high water, depths run only about 5 feet. Good luck!

North-northwest of flashing daybeacon #27, you will pass out into the main body of Naples Bay. Tidal currents begin to pick up and reach a crescendo as you approach the Gordon River.

After passing between unlighted daybeacon #33 and flashing daybeacon #32, cruisers should slow to idle speed. No-wake regulations are in effect for all the waters of Naples Bay and Gordon River north of #33 and #32.

North of unlighted daybeacon #33, Crayton Cove opens out on the western banks. Continue following the main channel and pass between unlighted daybeacon #35 and flashing daybeacon #34. You can then cut west to the Naples Yacht Club, and the adjacent mooring field.

The Naples Yacht Club and the adjacent city mooring field have their own combined marked entry channel outlined by small unlighted daybeacons. When leaving the main channel to visit either facility, pass (you guessed it) green markers to your vessel's port side and take red beacons to starboard. Cruisers intent on a visit to the mooring field can cut to the north and pick up a buoy immediately after passing west of unlighted daybeacon #4.

Visitors to the Naples City Dock should turn northwest after passing between #34 and #35 and head for the outer fuel dock. Here you will find the dockmaster's office and your slip assignment.

To continue cruising north to the Tin City shopping center, set course to pass just west of unlighted daybeacon #36. Between #36 and unlighted daybeacon #39, unlighted daybeacon #38 denotes the channel's easterly edge. Pass #38 to its westerly side.

North of flashing daybeacon #40, you will spy the enclosed harbor of Naples Sailing and Yacht Club bordering the point between the two branches of the Gordon River. To reach Marine Max and the Tin City shopping area, cut into the mid-width of the west-side fork. Be prepared for some of the strongest tidal currents that you have ever seen. Marine

Max will come up first on the western shores, followed by the Tin City complex. Kelly's Fish House lines the eastern shore.

Those few captains who choose to enter the eastern fork of the Gordon River should pass just south of the Naples Sailing and Yacht Club docks, north of flashing daybeacon #40. While you may see local small craft entering and exiting this fork via a straighter course, trust me when I say that you can hold best depths by following the above maneuver.

Gordon Pass to Fort Myers Beach

North of Naples there is no inland passage leading to Fort Myers Beach and San Carlos Bay, gateway to the official Western Florida ICW. Mariners must, by necessity, cruise offshore through the Gulf's open waters. In fair weather, this can be a truly enjoyable passage, particularly for sail craft. If winds exceed 20 knots and the all-too-usual summer thunderstorms are present, it could be a very different story.

South of San Carlos Bay there are really only two ports of call that might interest cruising captains, and both of these are now marginal.

In times past, some boats used to take shelter in Doctors Pass, about 5 miles north of Gordon Pass. Unfortunately, this channel is subject to periodic shoaling. A local group known as the Save the Bays Association has been working with the city of Naples to keep the channel open. We wish the association well in its efforts, but until the channel is completely stabilized, we still suggest visiting cruisers consider this channel a bit risky.

Wiggins Pass, 12 nautical miles above

Gordon Pass, was, until recently, a more realistic alternative. However, this cut has always been very subject to periodic shoaling, and the number-one facility of interest on these waters for pleasure cruisers is now only a memory.

The teeming resort community of Fort Myers Beach on Estero Island represents a very different sort of port. An offshore run of 12.7 nautical miles north of Wiggins Pass will lead cruising craft to Matanzas Pass. This inlet, immediately north of Estero, is a deep and reliable channel that pleasure craft of all descriptions can use with confidence. The inlet leads, in turn, to a whole series of channels east and northeast of the island. No fewer than ten marinas and boatyards, plus one super anchorage, are adjacent to Fort Myers Beach.

Wild-eyed captains may even consider following the marked but ill-charted track southeast to Big Carlos Pass. While there are some 4- to 5-foot low-tide depths along the way, there is also one marina and a few remote anchorages.

So let's push on to explore these last waters south of the Western Florida ICW. With any luck at all, we should find more than a little to interest us along the way.

Wiggins Pass

The first thing to understand about Wiggins Pass is that the entrance channel is mercurial. At times, maintenance dredging deepens soundings to 12-foot MLW levels. The problem is that by the time the dredge disappears over the horizon the sands are silting back in at a prodigious pace. Within six months, visiting captains may look in some alarm at 4-foot readings on their depth sounders. Smart captains will give Pelican Isle Yacht Club a quick call to check on present conditions before attempting to enter the inlet.

After negotiating the entrance, depths improve to 6 feet or better. One passage cuts off to the south along the course of the Cocohatchee River, but this stream leads only to some private docks grouped around a development near the charted 25-foot fixed bridge. Visiting cruisers making for Pelican Yacht Club should continue on to the east along a cut between several undeveloped mangrove islands. It used to be that, in times past, a passage cut off to port here and led to Marco River Marina-Wiggins Pass Division. This marina is now closed, and this writer has been told that yet another high-rise condo will soon rear its head high above the waters on this property.

A mammoth high-rise condo and marina complex known as Pelican Isle Yacht Club looms over the southern point of land flanking the one-time approach channel to Marco River Marina. From as few as two to as many as a dozen slips are kept open for visitors with appropriate reciprocity agreements through the Register of American Yacht Clubs. If you should have the necessary affiliation and space is available (be sure to call before your arrival), you will find berths at both fixed and floating wooden decked piers featuring all power and water connections. The harbor is well sheltered from inclement weather. Depths alongside run 6 feet or better. Some shoreside showers are available as well.

Pelican Isle Yacht Club (239) 566-1606

Approach depth—6+ feet (if dredging completed)
Dockside depths—6+ feet
Accepts transients—limited
Fixed and floating wooden piers—yes
Dockside power connections—30 and 50 amp
Dockside water connections—yes
Showers—yes

In times past this writer recommended anchorage on the waters west of the charted, 14-foot fixed bridge. Both banks are now lined so heavily with private docks that it is impractical to spend an evening here swinging on the hook.

Big Carlos Pass

Big Carlos Pass cuts between the southeastern tip of Estero Island and Black Island. Don't even think about trying this seaward cut. It is completely unmarked and shoals flank the so-called channel from every quarter. Again, as at Doctors Pass, local small-craft skippers may tell you that they use Big Carlos all the time. Just remember, they don't have your size or draft, and it's a lot easier for them to extricate themselves from the bottom.

Matanzas Pass

Matanzas Pass Inlet cuts in from the southeastern foot of San Carlos Bay and runs behind Estero Island. This passage holds minimum depths of 9 feet, with most soundings being much deeper. It is a relatively simple matter to follow this well-defined channel southeast to the 65-foot fixed bridge connecting Estero with San Carlos Island. A host of facilities associated with Fort Myers Beach line both banks east and west of the fixed span.

Alternate Channel

A charted and well-buoyed channel cuts east from flashing daybeacon #9 on the Matanzas Pass channel and leads to one small repair facility on the sheltered waters northwest of the 6-foot fixed bridge connecting the mainland with San Carlos Island. Minimum depths are 5½ feet, but the interior portion of the channel can be confusing for first-timers, and this cut no longer leads to any active facilities serving cruising visitors. We now suggest you bypass this errant side trip.

Fort Myers Beach

The community of Fort Myers Beach sits on one of the most intensely developed strips of land in Western Florida. Quite frankly, not all of this development can be accurately described as attractive. Strip-type shopping centers line both sides of the main road. While some are becoming, obviously well-managed operations, others look as if they are about to collapse. During the winter tourist season, visitors to Fort Myers Beach can be counted in the thousands. During my last visit, in July 2003, the beach was, shall we say, jumping.

While Fort Myers Beach may not be all that the naturalistically inclined among us might ask for, there is no denying its wonderful pleasure craft facilities and its popularity among the cruising crowd. Sailboats from far

Fort Myers Beach Anchorage

and wide regularly take advantage of the large, well-sheltered anchorage adjacent to the town waterfront. Bolstered by no fewer than ten marinas and boatyards, visiting cruisers have a plateful of choices.

Mariners in need of supplies should be able to find whatever they might desire at Fort Myers Beach. While it may be a bit of a walk (or you might bum a ride with a friendly local), groceries, personal items, and marine supplies are all available within a mile or so of the waterfront.

Numbers to know in Fort Myers Beach include

Apple Taxi—(239) 482-1200
Locomotion Taxi—(239) 463-4111
Royal Palm Transportation—(239) 765-6669
Avis Rental Cars—(239) 768-2121
Budget Rent A Car—(239) 549-7755
Enterprise Rent-A-Car—(239) 772-5565
Chamber of Commerce—(239) 454-7500

The Koreshans of Estero Island

In 1894 one of the strangest religious groups in the long and varied history of Florida came south to settle along the shores of Estero Island. Dr. Cyrus Read Teed, a Chicago physician, developed a cosmology known as Koreshan Unity. He was described by a contemporary as "an undersized, smooth-shaven man whose brown, restless eyes glow and burn like live coals." Dr. Teed contended that the universe was a hollow sphere with a circumference of 25,000 miles. Mankind lived on the interior portion of the shell that comprised the universe's limits, and the sun was at the center.

Along with 200 of his followers, Teed arrived on Estero Island in 1894 and founded "New Jerusalem." He planned a city of eight million inhabitants with streets 400 feet wide.

In 1896 Dr. Teed presented a demonstration south of the Naples Pier. He conducted what were described as "geodetic surveys," which, he claimed, proved his theory that the earth was concave-shaped. As Stuart McIver comments in *Glimpses of South Florida History*, "His survey . . . convinced his followers, who already believed. Outsiders were unimpressed."

Members of the Koreshan sect were required to sign over all their worldly goods to the community. Neither coffee, tea, nor alcohol was permitted. In an even more bizarre twist, Dr. Teed insisted on total celibacy among the commune's members. Men and women were housed in separate dormitories. Like the earlier Shakers, no one ever seemed to address the question of how the community was supposed to continue into the next generation.

By all accounts the Koreshans became highly competent farmers and bakers. For a time they published an agricultural newspaper known as *The American Eagle*. Copies are now rare collector's items.

In spite of his declaration that he was immortal, Dr. Teed died suddenly in 1908. His faithful followers kept watch over his body for a week, convinced he would rise from the dead. Finally, the county authorities insisted that he be buried. As Stuart McIver again comments, "So Teed's body was placed in a bathtub and sealed in a brick-and-concrete tomb at the east end of Estero Island. In 1921, a hurricane washed his tomb away." Oh, how the mighty have fallen!

After Dr. Teed's death, the Koreshan community broke up. The last four members deeded the remaining property to the state of Florida as a historical site in 1961. Three of the original buildings have been preserved, including the "planetary court," art hall, and bakery. The site is now open to the public daily from 9 A.M. to 4 P.M. Guided tours are conducted at 10:30 A.M. and 2:30 P.M. You will need motorized land transportation to access this attraction from the Fort Myers Beach marinas.

Fort Myers Beach Facilities and Anchorage (Various Lats/Lons—see below)

Moving west to east, the first Fort Myers Beach facility that you will encounter on the southern shoreline is Moss Marine (26 27.440

North/081 57.405 West, south of unlighted daybeacon #13). In the last edition of this guide, I was very critical of Moss Marine because of a large gambling ship's permanent presence at this facility. Well, the floating gambling casino is still here, but the marina people have made it clear to me (and I believe them) that they do their own thing, while the gambling folks do theirs. Of course, cruisers will still have to put up with the crowds of win, lose, or draw patrons, and the marina's parking lots are generally almost full of the gamblers' automobiles. Nevertheless, I was

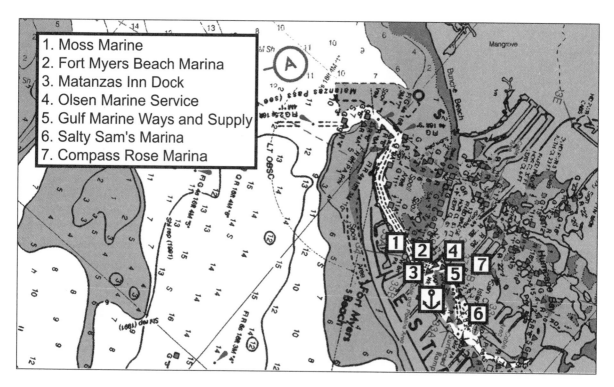

1. Moss Marine
2. Fort Myers Beach Marina
3. Matanzas Inn Dock
4. Olsen Marine Service
5. Gulf Marine Ways and Supply
6. Salty Sam's Marina
7. Compass Rose Marina

impressed with Moss Marine's air-conditioned cruiser's lounge, complete with a color television, newspapers, and a paperback exchange library. New showers and a Laundromat, immediately adjacent to this lounge, are also climate controlled and quite nice. Clearly Moss Marine is making a real effort to accommodate the cruising community, and we applaud their efforts. Only you can decide whether these positive attributes offset the hubbub associated with the gambling ship.

Moss Marine accepts transients at fixed wooden piers with water hookups and up to 50-amp power connections. Gasoline, diesel fuel, and waste pump-out services are available. The marina has some dry-stack storage for smaller powercraft, and there is also a small ship's and variety store on the premises. A host of good seafood restaurants are within walking distance.

Moss Marine (239) 765-6677
  http://www.mossmarine.com

Approach depth—8 feet (minimum)
Dockside depth—7-10 feet
Accepts transients—yes
Transient dockage rate—average
Fixed wooden piers—yes
Dockside power connections—30 and 50 amp
Dockside water connections—yes
Waste pump-out—yes
Showers—yes
Laundromat—yes
Gasoline—yes
Diesel fuel—yes
Ship's and variety store—yes
Restaurant—several nearby

Snug Harbor Restaurant (239-463-8077) guards the southern banks just east of Moss Marine. While no docking is allowed next to the restaurant itself, the facility does maintain a T-shaped pier on the southern banks, just short of the bridge. Restaurant patrons are free to moor to this pier in depths of $5\frac{1}{2}$ to 8 feet.

Fort Myers Beach Marina (26 27.503 North/081 57.236 West) occupies the northern banks opposite the Snug Harbor docks (still west of the bridge). This ultrafriendly facility was in the process of changing hands during our last visit, in July of 2003. If the sale goes through, it is likely that many improvements to this already good facility will be in the cards. However, as we can only report on what we see, the account below is based on what we found here during our last on-site inspection. Call Joe prior to your arrival to check on any late-breaking enhancements.

Currently, Fort Myers Beach Marina welcomes not only transients but also live-aboards, a true rarity in the present-day Florida marine community. Berths are cheerfully provided at modern, fixed wooden piers with all power, water, cable-television, and telephone connections. Depths at the outer slips are an impressive 8 to 20 feet, dropping to about 6 feet at the inner berths. A fuel dock fronting onto the main channel offers both gasoline and diesel fuel. Waste pump-out service is available at the fuel pier.

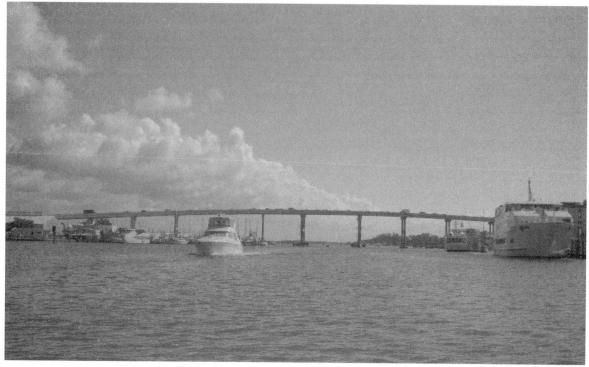

Fort Myers Beach high-rise bridge

Shoreside, visiting cruisers will find showers and a ship's store. Full mechanical repairs are featured for both gasoline and diesel engines. While the marina does not have a travelift or railway, smaller boats can be hauled out with the forklift that usually serves the facility's dry-stack storage customers. A host of dining spots is within an easy step, including the notable Bridge Restaurant (see below). For breakfast or lunch, though, we heartily recommend that you check out Kristine's Island Cafe (751 Fisherman's Wharf, 239-765-8988), a scant block and a half from the docks. The cuisine can accurately be described as down-home, but trust us, it doesn't get better than this.

This writer has always found Fort Myers Beach Marina to be an unusually friendly establishment ready to go that extra mile to meet any and all needs of visiting cruisers. It is highly recommended.

Fort Myers Beach Marina (239) 463-9552

Approach depth—8 feet (minimum)
Dockside depth—6-20 feet
Accepts transients—yes
Transient dockage rate—slightly above average
Fixed wooden piers—yes
Dockside power connections—30 and 50 amp
Dockside water connections—yes
Waste pump-out—yes
Showers—yes
Gasoline—yes

Diesel fuel—yes
Mechanical repairs—yes
Ship's store—yes
Restaurant—many nearby

East of the 65-foot fixed bridge, the mid-width of the wide waters stretching to the east plays host to a large shoal. Deep channels run north and south of these shallows. First-time visitors who aren't aware of the centerline shoal can be confused by the markers.

Immediately east of the fixed span, Matanzas Inn (26 27.381 North/081 57.213 West, 239-463-9258) offers a single, fixed wooden pier along the southern shore. The piers have 30- and 50-amp power hookups and freshwater connections. Depths vary widely, ranging from 8 to 12 feet at the outer docks to 5 to 6 feet nearer shore. A Laundromat and a refreshing swimming pool are available to transients at the adjacent motel. This would also be a convenient spot to take a break from the live-aboard routine if you have recently braved one too many waves. The on-site restaurant serves superb seafood, particularly of the broiled variety.

Considering the limited number of available transient slips, advance reservations would be an excellent precaution.

Matanzas Inn Dock (239) 463-6345

Approach depth—8 feet (minimum)
Dockside depth—5-12 feet
Accepts transients—yes (3 to 5 slips usually open for transients)
Transient dockage rate—below average
Fixed wooden pier—yes
Dockside power connections—30 and 50 amp
Dockside water connections—yes
Laundromat—yes
Restaurant—on site

Moving east of the 65-foot fixed bridge, deep water runs along the southern banks in a fairly broad band. The stretch east-southeast of unlighted daybeacon #18 (near 26 27.360 North/081 57.021 West) is a very popular anchorage for both sail craft and powerboats. Depths range from 7 to 12 feet, with the deeper soundings to the west. Protection is excellent and anchored visitors should be able to play a round or two of cards in peace as long as winds don't exceed forty knots. Skippers will find plenty of swinging room, unless the anchorage happens to be very crowded, and then larger vessels may be a bit cramped. Should you encounter this state of affairs, try a Bahamian-style mooring to minimize your swinging room.

Courtesy of a local cruising enthusiast, dinghy dockage is available along the anchorage's southerly shores at a private pier. Look for a snow-white house with a short, fixed wooden pier stretching out from a green lawn. You will probably spy several other dinghies already tied to this structure. All the owner asks is that visiting cruisers complete his informal registration process. Wow, what a service! We salute him for his thoughtfulness.

The markers can be confusing along this stretch for newcomers. This, coupled with the proximity of the large shoal occupying the center of the bay, means it would be more than slightly prudent to consult the navigational account of Fort Myers Beach (below) before entering Matanzas Pass.

The well-marked channel flanking the northern banks, east of the 65-foot bridge, maintains minimum depths of 8 feet, with typical soundings of 10 to 12 feet. As you enter this cut at unlighted daybeacon #18, picturesque Dixie Fish Company will be spotted to

Dixie Fish Company, Fort Myers Beach

port as you cruise north. There are no facilities for pleasure craft at Dixie, but diplomatic cruisers might be able to purchase some of the freshest seafood to prepare aboard.

A quick jog north on the channel will bring you abeam of Gulf Star Marina and the Bridge Restaurant (239-765-0050). Gulf Star (239-765-1956) is in the dry-stack storage business for smaller powercraft. No regular transient services other than gasoline are available. The marina does have one L-shaped dock fronting onto its shoreside facilities, and patrons of the Bridge Restaurant are free to tie up while dining. During the winter tourist season, much of this dock is occupied by a large tour boat. Dockage space is a bit skimpy during these periods.

Near unlighted daybeacon #20, the channel swings sharply to the east. As you are passing through this turn, Olsen Marine Service (26 27.616 North/081 57.079 West, 239-463-6750) will come abeam on the northern banks. This yard offers full mechanical and below-waterline, haul-out repairs. According to a conversation with the yard personnel, all wet-slip dockage is now occupied by resident craft and service customers.

The yard's travelift is rated at 37 tons.

The monstrous travelift belonging to Gulf Marine Ways and Supply boatyard (26 27.594 North/081 57.040 West, 239-463-6166) will become quite apparent as you come abeam of unlighted daybeacon #22. This writer has seldom before beheld such a mammoth lift. It is rated at 150 tons. This may just be one of the only yards in the country that could haul the infamous *Trump Princess*. Gulf Marine specializes in repairs to large pleasure craft. If you are lucky enough to own a boat larger than 45 feet, and it is in need of repairs, this is clearly the place to be between Cape Sable and St. Petersburg!

Salty Sam's Marina (formerly Palm Grove Marina) is found on the northern banks, northeast of unlighted daybeacon #28, near 26 27.425 North/081 56.613 West. Transient berths are cheerfully provided at first-rate, all-floating (wooden-decked) docks. Depths at most of the marina's piers range from 9 to 10 feet, but a few slips near the eastern end of the complex have only 6 to 7 feet of water. Water hookups and power connections up to 50 amp are at hand, as are gasoline, diesel fuel, and waste pump-out services.

Those cruisers who have not visited Salty Sam's for a year or two are in for a surprise. The entire shoreside complex has been rebuilt. This series of buildings now includes the dockmaster's office, ship's and variety store, air-conditioned showers, a climate-controlled Laundromat, and a popular restaurant known as Parrott Key (239-463-3257). Mechanical repairs for gasoline power plants are available on-site, and some limited diesel servicing is also in the offing.

Salty Sam's Marina (239) 463-7333
http://www.saltysamsmarina.com

Approach depth—8-11 feet

Dockside depth—9-10 feet (mostly)
Accepts transients—yes
Transient dockage rate—slightly below average
Floating wooden docks—yes
Dockside power connections—30 and 50 amp
Dockside water connections—yes
Waste pump-out—yes
Showers—yes
Laundromat—yes
Gasoline—yes
Diesel fuel—yes
Mechanical repairs—yes (mostly gasoline engines)
Below-waterline repairs—haul-out up to 27 feet with forklift
Ship's and variety store—yes
Restaurant—on-site

Hurricane Bay Channel and Facilities

East of unlighted daybeacon #28, the marked channel follows the northeastern shores of Estero Island and continues on to the east and southeast. At unlighted junction daybeacon #A, the channel leading to Hurricane Bay opens to the northeast. This cut is reasonably well marked with small, privately maintained daybeacons and it is fairly easy to follow during daylight.

Minimum depths of 5 feet are held moving first northeast and then northwest on the Hurricane Bay passage as far as the canal serving Compass Rose Marina. A few low-water soundings as shallow as 4½ feet are encountered between the marina canal and the low-level fixed bridge.

Compass Rose Marina (239-463-2400) sits perched on the southern headwaters of the canal that makes into the northern shores of San Carlos Island, south of unlighted daybeacon #24, near 26 27.678 North/081 56.880 West. This facility is one of the best live-aboard marinas in all of western Florida, but no temporary transient dockage is available. That's due to the fact that there is a long, long waiting list of live-aboards who want to take up residence at Compass Rose (a. k. a. "The Dead End Canal Yacht Club").

This marina provides many services for its patrons, including a wonderful cruiser's lounge and paperback exchange library. Most every day you will find a "community lunch" in progress midday at the marina lounge. The feeling of community is tangible.

Compass Rose berths are set amid fixed wooden piers with water hookups and 30-amp power connections. Typical depths alongside run 6 to 7 feet. Adequate showers and a Laundromat are found on the premises. Waste pump-out is also available.

All cruisers can count on full mechanical and below-waterline, haul-out repairs at Compass Rose. Compass Rose seems to specialize in repairs to sail craft, judging from the number of sailing vessels in its slips. The yard's travelift is rated at 40 tons. Gasoline (but no diesel fuel) can be purchased, but the on-site ship's store has been pretty well phased out.

West of the Compass Rose Canal, Channelmark Waterfront Restaurant (19001 San Carlos Boulevard, 239-463-9127) features dockage for its patrons on the southern flank of the low-level, fixed bridge. While you must traverse some 4½-foot depths to reach the restaurant, pierside depths are in the 5- to 8-foot range. No overnight accommodations are available.

Channel to Big Carlos Pass

There are two schools of thought about the marked channel leading southeast from Fort Myers Beach, past the northeastern shores of Estero Island, to Big Carlos Pass. On the one

hand, local powercraft and pontoon boats use this cut regularly without mishap. On the other, visiting cruisers should know that they must contend with a few patches of 4- to 4½-foot depths in the winding, often-confusing channel. To this writer's way of thinking, the channel is clearly only for boats under 36 feet in length, drawing less than 4 feet, and piloted by captains with wanderlust in their souls and hair on their chests (women included).

For those who brave the passage, there are some potential rewards. Mid-Island Beach Marina (26 26.304 North/081 55.129 West) guards the banks of Estero Island, southwest of unlighted daybeacon #29. This friendly firm is located, as its name implies, at about the midpoint of the island's southeast-to-northwest axis. While the marina is glad to accept transients for overnight or temporary dockage at its modern, fixed wooden piers (with all power and water connections), the management has informed this writer that few have hitherto made it this far. Dockside depths are a very respectable 7 to 8 feet. Another plus is that the shallowest portion of the channel to Big Carlos Pass seems to lie southeast of the marina. It should be possible to traverse the cut from Fort Myers Beach to this marina with minimum depths of 5 feet.

Mid-Island offers full services, including gasoline, diesel fuel, and mechanical and haul-out repairs (35-ton travelift), plus a ship's and variety store. The adjacent Fernando's of Martha's Vineyard restaurant is well worth your time. A large, Publix supermarket sits just behind the marina.

Mid-Island Beach Marina (239) 765-4371
  http://www.midislandbeachmarina.com

Approach depth—5-8 feet

Dockside depth—7-8 feet
Accepts transients—yes
Transient dockage rate—above average
Fixed wooden piers—yes
Dockside power connections—30 and 50 amp
Dockside water connections—yes
Waste pump-out—yes
Gasoline—yes
Diesel fuel—yes
Mechanical repairs—yes
Below-waterline repairs—yes
Ship's and variety store—yes
Restaurant—nearby

Southeast of Mid-Island Marina, the channel twists and winds its way to the waters northeast of Big Carlos Pass. The cut can be confusing and low-water depths occasionally drop to 4½ feet.

As mentioned earlier, Big Carlos Pass is completely unmarked and surrounded by shoal water. While the interior portion of the inlet north of the bascule bridge is deep, this would be a terribly exposed spot to anchor, and the tidal currents are expectedly swift.

It is possible for those who simply must anchor where none have gone before to follow a few markers into the correctly charted deeper waters northeast of Black Island (itself southeast of Big Carlos Inlet). The best spot to drop the hook is found abeam of the first small offshoot, which runs to the southwest (near 26 24.070 North/081 52.122 West). While this small stream is quite shallow, the channel east and northeast of the creek is broad and should provide enough swinging room for any vessel, even a large one, brave enough to make it this far. Protection is good to fair, and the shoreline is undeveloped. In fact, it is part of a park. Those few who find their way to this haven will have the satisfaction of knowing that they have successfully navigated waters that have known little else but small fishing skiffs for many years.

GORDON PASS TO FORT MYERS BEACH NAVIGATION

Captains accustomed to mostly inland cruising along sheltered waterways may be a bit daunted by cruising offshore to Matanzas Pass and Estero Island. Sailors used to offshore passages will hardly be bothered.

With winds under 15 knots, almost all mariners will find the cruise north along the Gulf to be pleasant. In foul weather, all but larger sail craft should deeply consider staying in port and putting on another pot of coffee.

As with the outside route north from Cape Romano to Gordon Pass, there are no offshore aids to navigation with which skippers can tick off their progress. Again, though, good depths run to within a mile of the shoreline. It's reasonably easy to follow the coast and duck in at the appropriate spot.

Those of you who hunger for a little inland cruising with gunk holes aplenty nearby, hang on a bit longer. Just to the north, the official Western Florida ICW begins and the siren's song of Pine Island Sound Charlotte Harbor calls to the explorers among us. Just be sure to get through this last offshore route safely, and then you'll be ready for the exciting waters ahead.

Gordon Pass to Wiggins Pass   It is a run of some 12 nautical miles from flashing daybeacon #1, at the western terminus of the Gordon Pass Channel, to Wiggins Pass. As discussed above, there are no aids to navigation along the way, except the few markers associated with shallow Doctors Pass, but you can follow the beaches, staying at least 1 nautical mile offshore. Keep a good dead-reckoning or GPS track. Don't mistake the markers of shallow Doctors Pass for Wiggins Pass.

Use your binoculars to pick out flashing daybeacon #WP, the westernmost aid to navigation on the Wiggins Pass channel. Even if you don't plan to put into the pass, this beacon can serve to fix your position.

Wiggins Pass   As reported earlier in this chapter, the outer portion of Wiggins Pass is very subject to periodic shoaling. It makes no sense to report the soundings from our last visit, because, by the time you arrive, water depths could be anywhere from 3 to 12 feet, depending on when the latest dredging has or has not occurred. Proceed with extreme caution. Better yet, call up the dockmaster at Pelican Isle Yacht Club and inquire about the latest channel conditions.

After passing through the outer, shoal-prone section of the channel, cruisers will spot the southeastward-running course of the Cocohatchee River, marked by a pair of daybeacons, as they near green, unlighted daybeacon #11. This sidewater is not suggested for visitors. Instead, continue dead ahead between the mangrove islands.

Soon you will spy a whole series of teeming docks ahead. These belong to Pelican Isle Yacht Club. Remember that the longtime nautical anchor for these waters, Marco River Marina-Wiggins Pass Division, is now closed.

Please also recall that this writer no longer recommends anchoring on the waters west of the charted 14-foot fixed bridge. One look at all the vessels berthed on both sides of this channel will tell you in short order the reason for this change of heart.

On to Matanzas Pass   It's a run of 12.7 nautical miles north from Wiggins Pass to Matanzas Pass, at the northwestern tip of Estero Island. Keep at least a mile offshore as you pass Wiggins, to avoid the shoals running off the inlet's northerly flank.

Increase your offshore clearance to at least 1.5 nautical miles as you cruise past Big Carlos Pass. This maneuver will serve to avoid the considerable offshore shoals surrounding the seaward side of this errant cut.

Use your best DR skills or electronic navigation to locate flashing daybeacon #SC, south-southwest of the Estero Island microwave tower (near 26 25.133 North/ 081 57.547 West). This is the southernmost aid marking the broad passage of deep water between the incredibly long shoals running southeast from Point Ybel on Sanibel Island and a second set of shallows abutting the western shores of Estero Island. By all means, stay east and northeast of #SC, unlighted daybeacon #1, and flashing daybeacon #3. West and southwest of these markers, you could wander into the Point Ybel shoals.

From a position abeam of flashing daybeacon #SC, cruise directly between the next two pairs of beacons, unlighted daybeacon #1 and flashing daybeacon #2. It's a run of almost 1 nautical mile between #SC and the gap between #1 and #2. It might be a good idea to follow a compass/GPS course through this section of the channel.

As you come between the next set of aids to navigation, flashing daybeacons #3 and #4, it's decision time. You can either continue on into San Carlos Bay to the northwest or swing sharply northeast into the Matanzas Pass channel.

Flashing daybeacon #1 is the westernmost aid in the Matanzas cut. Anybody who remembers his or her good old "red, right, returning" rule will know to pass #1 to his or her port side when making his or her way into the inlet.

East of #1, tidal currents pick up, as expected, but the channel is well marked and reasonably simple to follow in good weather. Unlighted daybeacon #4B marks the northwestern point of Estero Island. Give this aid a wide berth, as the adjacent point seems to be building outward.

At flashing daybeacon #7, the channel begins a hairpin curve to the south-southeast. Be sure to come abeam of flashing daybeacon #9 to its southwesterly side. At #9, an alternate channel makes off to the east.

Alternate Channel   Remember that the alternate channel leading from #9 no longer leads to any facilities for visiting cruising craft. Most mariners would be better served to continue cruising upstream on the main cut.

If you do run the alternate channel in spite of this advice, depart the inlet passage at flashing daybeacon #9. Immediately you are faced with a choice. The principal alternate channel runs to the east, while a second, uncharted but marked cut makes off to the east-northeast. Choose the starboard (easternmost cut), and enter this channel by cruising between unlighted daybeacons #1 and #2.

Follow the prolific markers to the east into the mouth of the canal off the northwesterly end of San Carlos Island. As you pass into the canal, watch for a marked channel running to the north. Ignore this cut—it leads to a series of private docks associated with area homes and a condo complex. Continue up the main canal, holding to the center as you approach the low-level fixed bridge.

On to Fort Myers Beach   A slow-speed, no-wake zone begins at flashing daybeacon #10 and remains in effect throughout the waters surrounding Fort Myers Beach. All vessels should slow to idle speed.

Continue following the markers as they lead you along the deep water abutting the northern and northeastern banks of Estero Island. Some .2 nautical miles east-southeast of flashing daybeacon #15, Moss Marine will come abeam on the southern banks, followed by Snug Harbor Restaurant. Fort Myers Beach Marina will come abeam to the north, just short of the fixed bridge.

Fort Myers Beach Waters and Anchorage   The 65-foot fixed bridge heralds your entrance into the waters lying about the resort community of Fort Myers. As you pass under the bridge, it might be a good time to virtually stop and sort out the markers. They can be quite confusing for first-timers.

It's best to think of the channel east of the fixed bridge as an irregular circle built around an oval-shaped shoal, occupying the middle of the bay. Unlighted daybeacon #18 is a key aid, marking the southwestern foot of the shoal. If you plan to follow the channel skirting along the northerly shore, cut north soon after passing through the bridge, and pass #18 to its westerly side. At unlighted daybeacon #20, the channel begins a turn to the east, paralleling the northern shore. The remainder of the channel is marked by red beacons, which should all be passed to your starboard side.

You will first pass the Bridge Restaurant and Gulf Star Marina, followed by Olsen Marine Service and Gulf Marine Ways and Supply. Salty Sam's Marina will be spotted northeast of unlighted daybeacon #28.

Unlighted daybeacon #28 marks the intersection of the cut running along the northerly banks with the channel skirting the southerly shore. Let us now turn our attention to this passage.

As you pass under the 65-foot fixed bridge, you will undoubtedly see a host of anchored vessels dead ahead. These craft occupy the deep-water anchorage along the southerly banks, south of the mid-width shoal. To enter this channel safely, pass unlighted daybeacon #18 to its southerly side. Yes, I know this seems wrong by the color, but trust me, this is the way to do it.

As you cruise east, continue favoring the southerly shore. Unlighted daybeacon #28 marks the easterly reaches of this southside channel. Pass #28 also to its southerly side and continue cruising east.

The channel remains well marked east and southeast of #28. Cruisers wanting to visit Compass Rose Marina should continue following the markers, passing red beacons to your starboard side and green markers to port, until encountering unlighted junction daybeacon #A. Cut to the northeast and pass #A to your starboard side as you enter the Hurricane Bay Channel.

Hurricane Bay Channel Captains and crew bound northeast and then northwest on the Hurricane Bay Channel should pass red beacons to their (the cruisers') starboard side and take green markers to port.

The cut skirts first to the northeast, passing around the easterly tip of San Carlos Island, and then turns northwest. The canal cutting south to Compass Rose Marina comes up just west of unlighted daybeacon #24.

A 6-foot fixed bridge spans the water just west of unlighted daybeacon #28. All but very small craft will be forced to retrace their steps to the east.

Channel to Big Carlos Pass It would take page upon page upon page to even begin to describe all the twists and turns in the marked passage leading to Big Carlos Pass, and the markers would probably be different by the time you arrive anyway. Suffice it to say that the channel can be confusing and as shallow as 4½ feet in places. Passage in the dark would be nothing short of a nightmare. Southeast-bound vessels should take red beacons to their (the cruisers') starboard side and green markers to port.

At unlighted daybeacon #12, a no-wake zone begins and stretches southeast for 2 miles. Mid-Island Beach Marina is found abeam of unlighted daybeacon #29 on these waters.

The portion of the channel between Fort Myers Beach and Mid-Island Beach Marina is certainly the deeper part of this cut. Boats drawing 4 feet or less should be able to reach the marina with proper caution. Southeast of this facility, the channel is far more winding and treacherous.

The southeasterly running passage eventually encounters Big Carlos Pass after passing between unlighted daybeacons #67 and #68. We suggest that you continue straight across the inlet, pointing for the northeasterly corner of Black Island. You will spot a high-rise Days Inn on the northwestern shores of Black Island, near the inlet bridge.

Watch for unlighted daybeacon #2 off Black Island. Pass this beacon by some 15 yards to your starboard side. Continue following the shores of Black Island to the east and southeast. Several more red markers help you keep to the good water.

Eventually, you will spy the first offshoot cutting to the southwest, south-southeast of unlighted daybeacon #10. You can recognize this little sidewater by its low-level, fixed bridge. Anchor abeam of this stream, but don't try to enter the creek. It is quite shoal.

CHAPTER 2

Fort Myers to Gasparilla Island

While researching the various marinas and boatyards around Fort Myers, I came across the story of a couple from Vermont who chartered a sailboat at nearby Burnt Store Marina and set out for a week's cruise of Pine Island Sound. The charter operator told the cruising duo to give him a call on the VHF if they encountered any problems. After six days or so, the charterer had not heard a peep and decided to give the couple a call. His radio broadcast found them sitting in a snug anchorage alongside Chino Island. When he inquired about when they were going to come home, the captain replied, "We are home." Within a few months husband and wife had moved their own boat to Fort Myers and were happily living aboard.

Now, while it would certainly be a bit of an exaggeration to claim that every cruiser who explores Pine Island Sound, Charlotte Harbor, the Caloosahatchee River, and Fort Myers decides to move there, this little tale does serve to point out the incredible appeal these waters have for mariners. You could literally spend weeks exploring Pine Island Sound alone and still not exhaust all the possibilities. Secluded anchorages, good marinas, historic inns with fabulous dining, deserted, white-sand beaches, beautiful state parks . . . well, the list could go on and on, but perhaps you are beginning to get the idea. There is perhaps no other portion of the Western Florida coastline that combines, in such delightful measure, the fortunate qualities of ready accessibility and rich, often-unpopulated cruising grounds as does the stretch between the Caloosahatchee River and

Gasparilla Island! Get ready for a genuine cruising treat!

Cruising captains arriving from points south will be pleased to learn that the official genesis of the Western Florida ICW begins near the mouth of the Caloosahatchee and runs north from San Carlos Bay through Pine Island Sound. Skippers may also alternately choose to cruise up the Caloosahatchee to Fort Myers. This river boasts a host of fine marinas and several anchorages.

Before continuing our geography lesson, let us pause for a moment to note that the Caloosahatchee is the westerly genesis of the Okeechobee Waterway. This most useful route allows cruisers ready, prompt, and enjoyable access between the Sunshine State's eastern and western coastlines (for boats that can clear one 49-foot bridge). For additional information, please consult this writer's *Cruising Guide to Eastern Florida*, a quite pleasant and totally comprehensive work that can, like this book, be had at your local bookstore or marine-supply dealer for a mere fraction of its true value.

From San Carlos Bay, the ICW flows north and northwest into enchanting Pine Island Sound. As already alluded to above, this water body is a mecca for cruising craft, with a siren's call that may require lashing yourself to the mast.

The western reaches of Pine Island Sound are bordered by a series of barrier islands that all have their own unique appeal. Sanibel, Captiva, Cayo Costa, Cabbage Key and, most particularly, Gasparilla Island are ports of call that are well known and loved by every cruiser plying Western Florida's coastal waters.

The northwestern arm of these waters is known as Gasparilla Sound. The ICW cuts briefly through the sound before rushing beyond this chapter's coverage at the long Gasparilla Island causeway bridge.

North of Pine Island Sound, the vast bay known as Charlotte Harbor opens out to the northeast. Abandoned by the ICW, the harbor offers many miles of good cruising grounds, with marina facilities available at the old port town of Punta Gorda. Charlotte Harbor's two feeder streams, the Myakka and Peace rivers, offer power-craft captains additional opportunities for gunk-holing and overnight anchorage.

Northbound skippers and crew must bid a fond goodbye to this region of delightful waters north of Gasparilla Island as the ICW enters Placida Harbor. This writer would be willing to wager that even with all the fine waters to the north, many dyed-in-the-wool cruisers will look back with a glance of sad longing in their eyes.

Charts   Navigators must purchase three NOAA charts for a complete picture of all the waters between Fort Myers Beach and Gasparilla Island, including Charlotte Harbor. **11427**—a most important chart; provides complete coverage of the approaches to San Carlos Bay, the Caloosahatchee River to Fort Myers, Pine Island Sound, and the ICW's southerly section **11425**—large-scale, detailed chart that picks up the Western Florida ICW at Boca Grande Pass, just south of Gasparilla Island, and runs north all the way to Tampa Bay; another must for anyone traveling this section of the coastline **11426**—a general chart good for showing the offshore entrances to San Carlos Bay and Pine Island Sound; its principal use, however, is its coverage of the upper reaches of Charlotte Harbor, including the Myakka and Peace rivers

---

Bridges
Sanibel Island Causeway Bridge, southwestern span—crosses Sanibel Island channel northwest of Point Ybel and flashing daybeacon #2—Fixed—26 feet
Sanibel Island Causeway, eastern span—crosses San Carlos Bay channel leading north from the Gulf to mile 0 of Western Florida ICW and western mouth of the Caloosahatchee River—Bascule—26 feet (closed)—opens on the hour and every 15 minutes thereafter 7:00 A.M. to 7:00 P.M.; at other times of day opens on demand
Pine Island/Matlacha Pass Bridge—crosses

Matlacha Pass channel north of unlighted daybeacon #55—Bascule—9 feet (closed)—opens on demand 8:00 A.M. to 7:00 P.M.; closed overnight
Cape Coral Bridge—crosses Caloosahatchee at Standard Mile 142 of Okeechobee Waterway, northeast of flashing daybeacon #70—Fixed—55 feet
Mid-Point Bridge—crosses Caloosahatchee at Standard Mile 138 of Okeechobee Waterway, northeast of unlighted daybeacon #62—Fixed—55 feet
Caloosahatchee/Highway 41 Bypass Bridge—crosses Caloosahatchee at Standard Mile

135 of Okeechobee Waterway, east-northeast of flashing daybeacon #49—Fixed—55 feet

Edison Memorial Bridge—crosses Caloosahatchee at Standard Mile 134.5, west of unlighted daybeacon #41—Fixed—56 feet—incorrectly charted on 11427, it actually forms a Y and appears to be two separate bridges

Boca Grande Bayou Bridge—crosses Boca Grande Bayou (and canal), north of Gasparilla Island basin anchorage—Fixed—13 feet

Boca Grande Causeway Bridge—crosses ICW at Standard Mile 34.5, northwest of unlighted daybacon #21—Swing bridge—9 feet (closed)—January through May, opens on the hour and every 15 minutes thereafter 10:00 A.M. to 5:00 P.M.; at other times of day and year opens on demand

Myakka River/El Jobean Bridge—crosses Myakka River at charted location of El Jobean—Fixed—24 feet

Live Oak Point/Punta Gorda (Highway 41) Twin Bridges—cross foot of Peace River northeast of unlighted daybeacon #4 near Punta Gorda waterfront—Fixed—45 feet

Peace River/Interstate 95 Twin Bridges—crosses Peace River east of unlighted daybeacon #12—Fixed—45 feet

San Carlos Bay

The wide, sometimes shallow inner reaches of San Carlos Bay introduce cruising skippers to the southerly beginnings of the Western Florida ICW and the mouth of the Caloosahatchee River highway to Fort Myers and the Okeechobee Waterway. This interior section of the bay is enclosed by Sanibel Island to the west and southwest and the Florida mainland to the east. A very long shoal, discussed in the last chapter, stretches southeast from Point Ybel on Sanibel Island. There is a smaller but still worrisome patch of shallows southeast of Punta Rassa on the mainland side, while the mid-width of the bay above the Sanibel Island bridge is rife with shoals. Fortunately, there are deep, marked passages around all these hazards.

Entry from the Gulf of Mexico

Once the long shoal stretching southeast from Point Ybel on Sanibel Island (see preceding chapter) is safely in your wake, there are actually two viable channels that powercraft can use to enter San Carlos Bay. The westerly passage, paralleling the southeasterly reaches of Sanibel Island, is deep and reasonably well marked, but it does pass under a fixed bridge with only 26 feet of vertical clearance. Obviously, for most sail craft this route is not a viable option. Happily for cruisers, Sanibel Island's one full-service marina is found southeast of this span and is accessible to all types of pleasure craft.

Many mariners, particularly those piloting sail craft, will choose the primary entrance into San Carlos Bay by way of the marked channel skirting the southwesterly reaches of Punta Rassa. This passage passes under a bascule bridge and soon leads to both the mouth of the Caloosahatchee and the southerly entrance to the Western Florida ICW. Along the way, there are at least two anchorages worthy of consideration.

Let us now turn our attention to the Sanibel Island channel, and then return to a review of the principal Punta Rassa Cut.

Sanibel Island

Even though a goodly portion of Sanibel Island actually fronts onto Pine Island Sound, as opposed to San Carlos Bay, the island's one marina facility catering to cruising-size craft is found in the latter region. We will therefore take a moment to review its history and characteristics here.

Strong archeological evidence suggests that Sanibel Island was occupied by Caloosa Indians long before the first white man ever gazed upon its shores. The highly organized Caloosa culture survived through the 1700s, but by 1801 the Indians had been decimated by disease, slave traders, and other hostile tribes.

Historical rumors link Sanibel with the pirates that operated along the Western Florida coastline during the early 1800s. Jose Gaspar was the most famous of these buccaneers. It is said that he stopped at Sanibel from time to time. Who knows—maybe a portion of his treasure still lies in the island's soil, waiting for some enterprising young explorer to come along with shovel and pail.

In 1833, a New York investment company established the town of "Sanybel" near the island's southerly tip. This was a short-lived community and within a few years all the settlers had left the island.

In 1884 construction began on a lighthouse to mark the eastern tip of Sanibel. This aid to navigation was needed by the numerous cattle transports voyaging to and from nearby Punta Rassa. The light's foundation was actually pre-built in New York and shipped by water to Sanibel. Within a mile of the island,

the transport ship sank, but most of the structure was eventually salvaged. New parts were manufactured to replace those that were lost, and the light shone out over San Carlos Bay within a few months thereafter.

The Sanibel Lighthouse remains in operation to the present day. A park has been built around the old light, and the original keeper's quarters have been preserved. Visitors with automobile transportation will find parking within a few hundred yards of the lighthouse. Cruising craft can anchor for an hour or two behind Point Ybel and dinghy ashore in fair weather *only!!!!!* However you get there, be sure to take the opportunity to visit this old

Sanibel Island Lighthouse

sentinel that speaks so eloquently of those rugged, uniquely American days of men and tall ships that will never come again.

Sanibel Island was opened for homesteading in 1888. Within a few years a successful agricultural community had been established in the "Wulfert area." The first schoolhouse was built in 1892 at a cost of $75.

In 1894 the Bailey family opened a general store under the name of the Sanibel Packing Company. This family firm has survived for almost a hundred years and today is doing business as Bailey's General Store (2477 Perwinkle Way, 239-472-1516).

The great hurricanes of 1921 and, particularly, 1926 all but wiped out the farmers on Sanibel. Shortly after this latter storm, regular ferry service was established with the mainland, allowing the island to be visited by more and more tourists.

This trend toward tourism was forever established as the island's future when a bridge was built from Punta Rassa to Sanibel in 1964. Since that time a portion of the island has been intensely developed, while other regions have been set aside as all-natural areas. Sanibel was incorporated as a city in 1974 and community leaders have striven to protect their island from overpopulation through strict zoning regulation. These efforts have met with some success, though it must be said that gunk-holers seeking a remote island paradise may find a bit too much hustle and bustle for their tastes.

The largest and most accessible undeveloped portion of Sanibel Island is the 5,000-acre J. N. ("Ding") Darling National Wildlife Refuge. The sanctuary is named for Mr. J. N. Darling, a famous political cartoonist who served as head of the U.S. Biological Survey. Under his supervision at least 330 wildlife refuges were established across the country.

Today, visitors to the Ding Darling refuge can take a quiet five-mile drive through the grounds and observe many of the birds and other wildlife that thrive in the region. There is also a visitor's center that gives a fascinating overview of the island's ecological character.

Two other island attractions are worth every visitor's attention. The Sanibel Island Visitor's Center (239-472-1080, 1159 Causeway Road) sits just to the right of the main highway, a short distance west of the Punta Rassa bridge. Here newcomers can pick up all sorts of information about the island, its facilities, and its attractions. The Visitor's Center can be accessed via a long walk from Sanibel Island Marina (see below).

Visiting cruisers will probably need ground transportation to reach the Island Historical Museum (950 Dunlop Road, 239-472-4648). The charming island home that houses the museum is made from hard Florida pine and peppered with "Cracker furniture." Beaded woodwork, bronze water fixtures, and large, old, glass windows add to the appeal and allow visitors to gain a sure impression of how the early islanders lived. The museum is open from 10 A.M. to 1 P.M., Wednesday through Saturday.

Sanibel Island is the site of many festivals and annual events. One of the most notable is the Sanibel Shell Fair, usually held in early March. The fair is centered around a colorful shell exhibit competition. Needless to say, there are a host of other activities in which sporting competitions and food figure prominently.

Speaking of the Shell Fair, we would be remiss in our review of Sanibel if we left without mentioning the fabulous shell hunting for which the island is so famous. Because of the way Sanibel thrusts out into the Gulf, every new tide brings fresh treasures to the island's exposed beaches. Many a cruiser has dinghied ashore day after day to search for these colorful offerings from the sea.

So there you have it—the collection of the historic and the latter-day spirit that makes up modern Sanibel Island. While it is undoubtedly the most developed part of Pine Island Sound, many of Sanibel's charms most assuredly endure.

Numbers to know on Sanibel Island include

> Airport Trans]portation—(239) 472-0007
> Apple Taxi—(239) 482-1200
> Sanibel Taxi—(239) 472-4160
> Enterprise Rent-A-Car—(239) 454-0770
> Sanibel Island Visitor's Center—(239) 472-1080

Point Ybel Anchorage

For many years, this writer and any number of other cruising authors recommended anchoring in the shelter of Point Ybel, southeast of flashing daybeacon #2. However, several years ago, boats began dragging anchors while taking shelter in this haven during foul weather. Some of these unfortunate craft ended up stuck on the bridge just to the northwest. Severe damage to the vessels and the bridge was often the unhappy result. For this reason, cruisers should bypass this one-time anchorage unless it is used for a very quick trip ashore to visit Sanibel Lighthouse and, even then, only if there is not even a hint of windy weather in the forecast.

Sanibel Island Marina (26 27.060 North/082 01.876 West)

Southwest of flashing daybeacon #2, a single pair of daybeacons marks the entrance into Sanibel Island Marina. As you cruise between unlighted daybeacon #2 and unlighted daybeacon #1, the canal leading to the marina will be spotted dead ahead. This cut holds 5- to 7-foot depths if and only if you can avoid a flanking shoal. Check out our navigational account of Sanibel Island Marina below to discover how best to keep to the good water. After traversing the entrance cut, the marina will be spotted on the canal's southerly face.

This facility gladly accepts transients and offers protected dockage at fixed wooden piers featuring freshwater and 30- and 50-amp power connections. The piers are relatively new and are quite nice. In the mornings, the cheerful staff delivers muffins and the local newspaper to all guest craft.

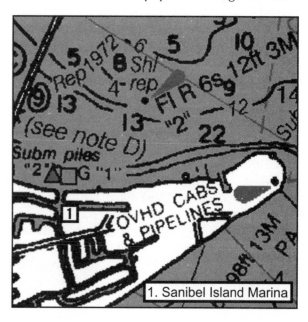

1. Sanibel Island Marina

How's that for great service? The fuel dock fronts onto the canal, but most of the dockage is found in a covelike basin just to the south. Minimum dockside depths run around 5½ feet, but many slips in the harbor boast 6 to 8 feet of water. Gasoline and diesel fuel are readily available, as are adequate, non-climate-controlled shoreside showers and a Laundromat. The marina offers full mechanical repairs for both gasoline and diesel power plants. The on-site ship's and variety store is worth a perusal.

Immediately behind the docks, famished cruisers will find the famous Gramma-Dot's Restaurant (239-472-8138). Named for a woman who fell in love with cruising Pine Island Sound, this famous dining spot features open-air dining and marvelous Western Florida seafood. The fried grouper sandwiches have to be experienced to be believed. To be succinct, don't miss it!

Sanibel Island Marina (239) 472-2723

Approach depth—5-7 feet
Dockside depth—5½-8 feet
Accepts transients—yes
Transient dockage rate—above average
Fixed wooden piers—yes
Dockside power connections—30 and 50 amp
Dockside water connections—yes
Showers—yes
Laundromat—yes
Gasoline—yes
Diesel fuel—yes
Mechanical repairs—yes
Ship's and variety store—yes
Restaurant—on site

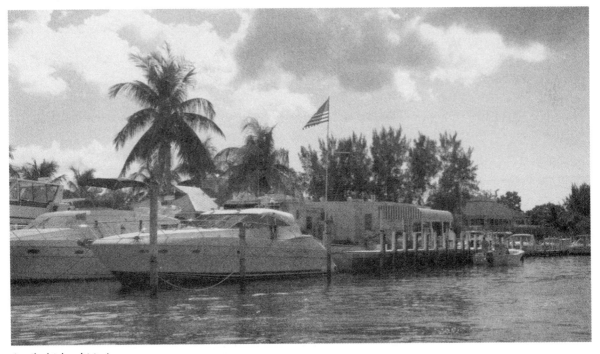

Sanibel Island Marina

Tarpon Bay Channel

Northwest of the 26-foot (vertical clearance) section of the Sanibel Island bridge, passing cruisers may note a pile-marked channel cutting southwest (well northwest of unlighted daybeacon #4) to shallow Tarpon Bay. In spite of the "7 ft rep 2000" notation on chart 11427, this passage is quite shoal and fit only for dinghies and large to mid-size wading birds. A few captains occasionally choose to anchor in the deeper waters of the main channel during fair weather and dinghy into Tarpon Bay through this cut. However, it would be far more convenient for cruising-size craft to berth at Sanibel Island Marina. You can then rent bikes easily enough at the marina or several other commissaries to visit the remainder of the island, including the Ding Darling wildlife refuge to the north.

Dixie Beach Anchorage (26 28.000 North/082 03.101 West)

In fair weather and light winds, some boats occasionally anchor off charted Dixie Beach, flanking the southwesterly shoreline between unlighted daybeacon #4 and flashing daybeacon #5. Depths of 8 feet or better stretch to within 200 yards (only) of shore. Care must be exercised to avoid the charted 2- and 3-foot shallows lying to the northwest. This haven offers some protection from southern and southwesterly winds that don't exceed 10 knots, but it is wide open to breezes from all other directions. Obviously, this is not a foul weather hidey-hole. The surrounding shore is peppered with moderate, but not unattractive residential development.

Like the anchorage behind Point Ybel (see above), the holding ground adjacent to Dixie Beach is suspect. Be sure your hook is well

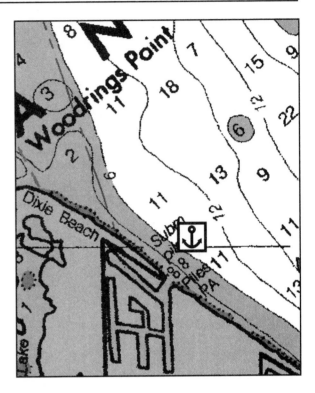

set, and check for dragging periodically. Again, in a like vein to the Point Ybel haven, the Sanibel Island city government imposes a 48-hour-stay limit for this anchorage.

Punta Rassa Anchorage (26 28.785 North/082 00.098 West)

Let us now return our attention to the principal entrance into San Carlos Bay, southwest of charted Punta Rassa. Cruisers can anchor in the charted deep water northeast of flashing daybeacon #6. You must avoid the long tongue of shallows north and east of #6, but with careful navigation, minimum depths of 6 to 7 feet can be held to within 300 yards of the northeasterly banks. Closer to shore soundings rise to 4- and 5-foot levels. Protection is good from northern and eastern breezes, but nil when winds are blowing from the south or west. This is not a heavy-weather anchorage and should not be used if a stormy forecast is in the offing. The immediate shoreline is delightfully in its natural state, but several tall, high-rise condo buildings at Punta Rassa are visible to the northwest.

Punta Rassa

The bascule bridge stretching from the high-rise Jimmy Connors tennis complex at old Punta Rassa to Sanibel Island serves as a landmark for what was one of the most unexpectedly important ports of call in early Florida. Following the conclusion of that dark conflict known as the War Between the States, semi-wild cattle wandered the marshes and hammocks of North Central Florida. Some were strays that had wandered off from ranches, while others had escaped from both Confederate and Union troops during the war.

A few enterprising individuals began rounding up these beasts and forming small cattle ranches. As a fortunate coincidence, it was just about this same time that Spanish authorities came to Florida from nearby Cuba searching for a ready source of beef. The Spaniards set up headquarters at the tiny village of Punta Rassa, and offered gold coins for every cow delivered. Soon cattle drives were in progress all across Northern Central Florida, headed for Punta Rassa. The bewildered owners of the small ranches suddenly found more hard money in their pockets than they had expected to see during their entire life. They bought clothes, guns, and furniture before heading home to begin the process anew.

These Florida cowboys used long, rawhide whips to keep the cattle together. All accounts agree that they could pop and crack the whips with an explosion of sound that would subdue even the most reluctant steer. As the years went by, these cowboys became known as "Florida Crackers." Though this term was later used to describe poor farmers throughout the South, it had its origins with the Florida cattle drivers who traveled to and from Punta Rassa.

With the coming of Cuban independence, the trade at Punta Rassa dried up, though cattle raising has remained a part of Central Florida's economy to the present day. If you would like to learn more about the Florida cowboys, Patrick D. Smith's wonderful novel *A Land Remembered* is highly recommended. It is a "must read" for anyone interested in Floridian history.

Meanwhile, a prominent citizen of the small coastal village, George Shultz by name, had begun a business that presaged modern-day Punta Rassa. Shultz took over an old army barracks that was sitting practically out over the water and proceeded to open a hotel that drew the likes of no less than Pres. Grover Cleveland, Thomas Edison, the Duke of Sutherland, and John Jamison, the famous distiller of Irish whiskey. The clever operator and promoter ran off the snakes and rats and set up a fine restaurant. He did little else to improve his building, however, and the old walls remained unpainted. According to Stuart McIver, writing in *Glimpses of South Florida History*, "Instead of deriding him for not painting the place, Shultz's guests praised him for not tampering with its primitive charms. Instead of calling the hotel run-down, they called it unique." In this writer's opinion, whatever the modern-day promoters of the Jimmy Connors Tennis Center may have up their sleeves, they have nothing on Mr. Shultz.

The unique hotel burned in 1906 and is now but a distant memory.

Kitchel-Miguel Key Anchorage (26 29.960 North/082 01.297 West)

North of the Punta Rassa-Sanibel Island span, chart 11427 correctly notes a channel of deep water cutting northwest from the main channel (near unlighted daybeacon #11) to the southwesterly tip of Kitchel and Miguel keys. This route is unmarked and navigationally challenging and there is certainly some danger of slipping into the surrounding shoals, but good navigation and cautious cruising may bring you through minimum 7-foot depths to an anchorage just off the southwestern point of the two keys. Boats up to 36 feet should have ample room. The two keys, as well as the other nearby islands, are completely undeveloped mangroves. This natural character produces a feeling of enjoyable isolation, which is altogether welcome.

On the water, Kitchel and Miguel keys appear as one solid mass of land and trees, very different from the nebulous structure pictured on chart 11427. Don't be fooled by this contradiction.

This is not a good anchorage for riding out a heavy blow. The two islands provide shelter to the east and northeast, and Big Island and Fisherman Key give some protection to the south and west. Nevertheless, winds over 15 knots, particularly from the northwest or southeast, clearly call for a different plan.

Punta Rassa Cove Anchorage (26 30.271 North/082 00.654 West)

Some cruisers occasionally anchor in the deep water east of the gap between flashing daybeacons #13 and #14, bordering on the western reaches of shallow Punta Rassa Cove. Clearly this is a fair-weather refuge at best. It is open to all but easterly winds and is regularly scoured by the strong tidal currents present throughout this entire area. Minimum 6-foot depths are held to within 150 yards of the eastern banks.

Port Sanibel Marina (26 29.413 North/081 59.434 West)

East of unlighted daybeacon #11, a 5½-foot marked channel cuts through the otherwise shallow waters of Punta Rassa Cove to a large, well-sheltered facility that goes under the moniker of Port Sanibel Marina (239-472-8443). Even though this facility's Web site lists transient dockage among the marina's services, the office manager has, on two widely separated occasions, firmly informed this writer that all slip space is currently rented strictly on an annual basis.

Resident craft are berthed at fixed wooden piers in about as sheltered a harbor as you are ever likely to find. Annual patrons will discover full power and water connections, waste pump-out, extensive dry-stack storage, plus full fueling services (gasoline and diesel). Depths alongside run 6+ feet. Shoreside, both showers and a Laundromat are available. The on-site Lighthouse Restaurant is ever so handy.

Major Intersection

North of the gap between flashing daybeacon #14 and unlighted daybeacon #15, the northward-running channel through San Carlos Bay runs headlong into a very crucial intersection. Mile 0 of the Western Florida ICW is found just west-southwest of flashing daybeacon #101 and a short hop east-northeast of unlighted can buoy #1. The Waterway runs west-southwest from this point across the so-called Miserable Mile until it begins to turn north at flashing daybeacon #11 into the southerly reaches of Pine Island Sound.

Flashing daybeacon #101 marks the beginning of the Caloosahatchee River channel and the Okeechobee Waterway. We will first briefly review the initial section of the ICW and then follow the Caloosahatchee to Fort Myers in a separate section.

The Miserable Mile

For a Waterway that can boast of so many delightful sights and cruisable waters, the Western Florida ICW's beginning is far from auspicious. The problem stems from the north-to-south set of the prevailing tidal currents which regularly boil out of Pine Island Sound, Matlacha Pass, and the Caloosahatchee River. This initial portion of the ICW runs east to west, thereby ensuring that currents run across the Waterway. This 90-degree current can lead to rapid shoaling of the Waterway channel. While the Corps of Engineers can usually be relied upon to keep the passage open, it's a good idea to hold strictly to the middle of the channel. This is not the sort of place to test the ICW's limits.

In addition to the shoaling problems comes the real possibility of lateral leeway. All pleasure vessels, not just sail craft and single-screw trawlers, must keep just as vigilant a watch over their sterns as on the course ahead to quickly note any slippage. Failure to follow this commonsense practice can quickly result in a call to Sea Tow.

Fortunately, the Miserable Mile is very well marked and most captains will come through with nothing worse than tense shoulders. Markers are frequently added, taken away, and shifted, so don't be surprised to find a different configuration of aids to navigation than those pictured on chart 11427 or discussed in the navigational account below.

Picnic Island Anchorage (26 29.469 North/082 02.931 West)

Believe it or else, there is actually a fair-weather anchorage available to cruising craft along the Miserable Mile. Study chart 11427 for a moment and note Picnic Island, southeast of unlighted daybeacon #8. The charted deep water east and northeast of the island makes a good anchorage in light airs or when winds are blowing from the southwest. Good depths of 12 feet hold to within 50 yards or so of the island's northeastern shores. Don't attempt to circumnavigate the island. There is very shoal water to the south and west.

Picnic Island is completely in its natural state, with white, sandy beaches backed by scrub growth and a few smaller trees. It is apparently a popular weekend destination for local cruisers. During a research trip several years ago, we spotted a party in progress amidst a remote broadcast by a local radio station.

SAN CARLOS BAY NAVIGATION

Navigation of the various San Carlos Bay channels would be pretty simple stuff if it were not for the all-too-pervasive tidal currents. Even so, most skippers need only be on guard against excessive leeway and follow elementary compass/GPS courses between the various aids to navigation.

Entry from Gulf of Mexico   After avoiding the long shoal stretching southeast from Point Ybel (see preceding chapter), point to come abeam of flashing daybeacon #6 to its southwesterly side. Once abeam of #6 you can explore the anchorage to the northeast, follow the Sanibel Island channel to the southwest, or cut up the main San Carlos Bay passage to the northwest.

Punta Rassa Anchorage   To enter the anchorage southeast of Punta Rassa, sweep widely around flashing daybeacon #6 to the southeast. This maneuver will help to avoid the large, charted tongue of shallows running southeast from Punta Rassa. Once you are within some 300 to 400 yards of the northeastern banks, begin feeling your way carefully to the northwest with your sounder. Minimum depths of 6 to 7 feet extend for almost .7 nautical miles to the northwest. If soundings rise above 6 feet, you have gone too far. Retreat a bit to the southeast for better depths. Good water runs to within 300 yards of the northeastern shoreline, short of the charted shallows to the northwest.

Sanibel Island Channel   Remember that the upper reaches of the Sanibel Island channel are spanned by a fixed bridge with 26 feet of vertical clearance. Cruisers can visit the island's only full-service marina without having to pass through this span.

From flashing daybeacon #6, set a careful compass course to come abeam of flashing daybeacon #2, northwest of Point Ybel, by some 100 yards to its southerly side. It's a fairly lengthy run of 1.5 nautical miles between #6 and #2. Stay on course and watch for leeway.

Ignore unlighted daybeacon #1, which you may sight northwest of your track when cruising between #6 and #2. This aid marks an old center channel in San Carlos Bay that is now shoal and dangerous.

Point Ybel Anchorage   As you approach flashing daybeacon #2, the one-time anchorage adjacent to the shores of Sanibel Island will come abeam to the south. Due to the poor holding ground, please remember that we no longer recommend anchoring on these waters, unless you are planning a quick dinghy ashore to visit the lighthouse. Even then, don't even think about trying this in anything but the fairest of weather.

Should you ignore this strong advice and decide to enter this treacherous haven, simply cruise in behind (to the west of) the shelter of Point Ybel, which you will recognize courtesy of its tall Australian pines, and drop the hook within 100 yards of the shoreline. Watch out for a dragging anchor!!!

Sanibel Island Marina   Once abeam of flashing daybeacon #2, point directly for the southernmost pass-through of the long Sanibel Island bridge, which you will sight dead ahead. Soon you will come abeam of the entrance to Sanibel Island Marina to the south.

Watch the southern shore for a single pair of daybeacons, unlighted #1 and #2. Continue cruising on the main channel until the gap between these aids is directly abeam to the south. Then turn sharply south and pass between #1 and #2 into the mouth of the canal dead ahead.

As you cruise through the connecting canal, favor the westerly (starboard) banks. A shoal seems to be building out from the canal's easterly flank.

Soon additional canals will open out to port and starboard. Ignore these side streams and continue straight ahead. You will soon spy the marina's fuel docks to port.

On the Sanibel Channel   Northwest of flashing daybeacon #2, the wide Sanibel Island channel soon meets the 26-foot fixed, southernmost span of the bridge connecting Punta Rassa and the island. Cruise through the bridge and point to pass unlighted daybeacon #3 to its northeasterly side. Use your binoculars to pick out unlighted daybeacon #4 ahead. As you would expect, pass this aid to its southwesterly quarter.

It's a cruise of another 1.2 nautical miles or so before you reach the next aid on the Sanibel channel, flashing daybeacon #5. Fortunately, the passage remains wide and mostly deep. Be sure to pass #5 by at least 50 yards to its northeasterly side. This beacon marks a shoal building into the channel from the southwest.

Dixie Beach Anchorage   To make good your entry into the open anchorage lying southwest of the gap between unlighted daybeacon #4 and flashing daybeacon #5, point for the deeper waters just northwest of the charted local canals immediately southeast of Dixie Beach. Don't approach the canals themselves as they are rather shallow. Also, take extra care to avoid the correctly charted, broad tongue of shoal water stretching north-northeast from Woodrings Point. Remember, this anchorage is only recommended in fair weather and light breezes.

On to the ICW   From #5 it's a quick run to intersect the ICW at flashing daybeacon #11. At #11 the Waterway cuts west and northwest into the southerly foot of Pine Island Sound.

Main San Carlos Bay Channel   Let us now return to flashing daybeacon #6, southeast of Punta Rassa, where our discussion of the Sanibel Island channel began. The principal bay channel continues straight ahead from #6 until eventually reaching flashing daybeacon #10.

Once abeam of #10, you may spot flashing daybeacon #3 well southwest of your course. Do not attempt to cruise toward this aid—it is founded in shoal water.

Instead, turn north-northwest from #10

and point for the easternmost, bascule section of the long Sanibel Island bridge. Be mindful of the correctly charted shallows to the east between #10 and the bridge.

The Punta Rassa span (of the Sanibel Island bridge) has a closed vertical clearance of 26 feet. Cruisers whose craft can't clear this height must contend with a restrictive opening schedule. This span opens on the hour and every 15 minutes thereafter from 7:00 A.M. to 7:00 P.M., seven days a week, year round. At all other times of the day, the bridge opens on demand.

On the Bay Channel   North of the Punta Rassa-Sanibel Island span, the tall towers of the Jimmy Connors Tennis Center will be sighted to the east. The channel bends farther to the north at this point and skirts the eastern shores along a broad band of deep water. Point to eventually pass unlighted daybeacon #11 to its easterly quarter. Just before reaching #11, adventurous mariners may choose to anchor abeam of Miguel and Kitchel keys to the northwest.

Kitchel-Miguel Key Anchorage   Here's a novel way to find the deep-water channel leading to the anchorage southwest of Kitchel and Miguel keys. Look at the five high-rise buildings along the Punta Rassa shoreline. Note the center and largest of the structures. If you align your stern with this building and set course for a point just southwest of the twin keys, you will hopefully be in good water all the way. Of course, more buildings could go up in the future in the Punta Rassa complex, so take these instructions with a grain of salt.

Better yet, try out your new chart plotter or GPS interfaced with a laptop computer while running this unmarked cut. These electronic wonders will greatly simplify this otherwise tricky process.

In any case, depart the main channel well south of unlighted daybeacon #11 to avoid the charted shoal building south from the aid. You can then follow the channel past the northeastern tip of Fisherman Key until coming abeam of Miguel and Kitchel keys (which will appear as one solid land mass) by some 30 yards to your starboard side.

Don't attempt to cruise farther to the northwest. Very shallow water guards the approaches to the ICW northwest of the twin keys.

Punta Rassa Cove Anchorage   Simply cruise northeast from the gap between flashing daybeacons #13 and #14 toward the shoreline. Drop the hook before approaching to within less than 150 yards of the banks. Don't attempt to enter either charted Punta Rassa Cove or Shell Creek. They may look good, but on-site research revealed that depths quickly rise to less than 3 feet on both bodies of water.

On to the Intersection   North of flashing daybeacon #13, point to pass between flashing daybeacon #14 and unlighted daybeacon #15. After passing #15, powercraft should slow down and all vessels should proceed with caution. The intersections with the ICW and the Caloosahatchee channel are just ahead.

Watch for flashing daybeacon #101, to the northeast, and unlighted can buoy #1 to the northwest. Cruise directly between these markers.

Now you must choose whether to cut northeast into the Caloosahatchee River, or west-southwest to follow the Waterway.

On the Miserable Mile   Pass unlighted can buoy #1 to its fairly immediate northwesterly side and continue cruising to the west-southwest to follow the Waterway. Northbound craft should pass all red markers to their (the cruisers') starboard sides and take green beacons to their port. Watch for strong currents sweeping across the channel and be ready for leeway corrections.

Just before passing unlighted daybeacon #8 to its northerly side, passing cruisers may spy unlighted daybeacon #1 to the northwest. This is the first aid on the Matlacha Pass channel, which is reviewed later in this chapter. Navigators following the ICW's track should ignore #1 and take care not to mistake this aid to navigation as a Waterway maker.

Captains may also choose to cruise to the anchorage off Picnic Island between unlighted can buoy #7 and unlighted daybeacon #8.

Picnic Island Anchorage   Simply depart the Waterway about halfway between unlighted can buoy #7 and unlighted daybeacon #8, and cruise carefully toward the northeastern banks of Picnic Island. Drop the hook within 50 yards (no closer) of the shoreline and break out the old dinghy.

Remember, this is not a foul-weather anchorage. If a thunderstorm appears along the horizon, better head for more secure shelter.

On the ICW   At unlighted daybeacon #10, the Miserable Mile ends as the ICW comes under the shelter of Pine Island to the northwest. Flashing daybeacon #11 introduces northbound ICW cruisers to the southern reaches of Pine Island Sound.

We will now turn our attention to a brief discussion of Matlacha Pass, followed by a more extensive review of the Caloosahatchee River to Fort Myers. Continued coverage of the Western Florida ICW will resume in the Pine Island subsection, later in this chapter.

Matlacha Pass

Many captains traversing the so-called Miserable Mile have probably looked at the markers running northwest from unlighted daybeacon #1 and wondered about the charted passage east of Pine Island known as Matlacha Pass. Due to a lack of reliable information, few have heretofore been willing to try this cut. Below you will find the details needed to explore this little-frequented passage, but let it be known that this channel has more than its share of problems, particularly along its southern reaches. It is only appropriate for wild-eyed skippers piloting smaller craft, drawing 4 feet or less and able to clear a *32-foot power line!*

Matlacha Pass cuts through the broad but mostly shallow body of water that separates the Florida mainland from Pine Island. This island has long been the refuge of commercial fishermen and small villages. While some modern development is beginning to be evidenced on Pine Island, it is still for the most part delightfully devoid of tourists and intensive land use.

The pass channel is a winding, twisting route that has some low-water depths of as little as 4½ to 5 feet. Typical soundings range from 6 to as much as 15 feet. The cut must be navigated with extreme caution. Nighttime passage is strictly not recommended.

There are no real facilities for cruising vessels on Matlacha Pass, and there are only two anchorages.

Pine Island History In 1513 Pine Island was visited by none other than Ponce de Leon, the founder of St. Augustine. By this time, he had probably given up on the fountain of youth and was exploring Western Florida in the hopes of founding a Spanish outpost on the western shores of the Florida peninsula. The explorer left a stone marker behind, and was killed nearby soon afterward in an attack by hostile Indians. Speculation persists that had Ponce lived, another St. Augustine might have arisen near the shores of Pine Island.

Givney Key Anchorage (26 30.750 North/082 03.132 West)

Matlacha Pass's first anchorage, moving south to north, is found southeast of Givney Key in the charted deep water north-northeast

of unlighted daybeacon #3. The questionable haven is located conveniently near the Miserable Mile portion of the Western Florida ICW and well south of the annoying 32-foot power lines. This fortunate position renders the refuge accessible to most pleasure craft of either the sail or powered persuasion that draw 5 feet or less (always assuming that you can successfully navigation the unmarked approach passage).

Minimum depths of 6 feet are held between #3 and a position 250 yards southeast of Givney Key. The key gives good protection from northerly winds, while Pine Island to the west and the mainland to the northeast provide some shelter when it's blowing from either of these quarters. The anchorage is wide open to southerly blows.

This is clearly not a foul-weather stop. On the other hand, if fair breezes are in the forecast, it is a lovely overnight refuge. The undeveloped shores of Givney Island to the northwest are hard to stay away from. The Pine Island banks to the west are also delightfully in their natural state. During our first cruise of Matlacha Pass, almost fifteen years ago, we observed a 30-foot sailboat tucked snugly for the night in this anchorage.

Pine Island Bridge and Anchorage (26 37.892 North/082 03.987 West)

North of unlighted daybeacon #55, the Matlacha Pass channel ducks under a 9-foot (closed vertical clearance) bascule bridge that links Pine Island with the mainland. This span is known locally as "the fishingest bridge in the world." Chances are that passing cruisers will spot a host of anglers fishing from the span at any time of the day or night.

A few low-key docks are found on either

side of this bridge. A small restaurant fronts the channel on its southwestern banks, just southeast of the span. While it would not appear to be standard operating procedure, one thirty-footer could probably tie to the pier in 5- to 6-foot depths. On the opposite shore, a small gift and novelty shop has a dock boasting 9 feet of water. Besides a public launching ramp, these are really the only facilities along this portion of Pine Island for all but small powercraft.

It is possible to anchor just east of the main channel, immediately south of the bridge in 6½ to 10 feet of water. Protection is good from all but particularly strong southern and southeasterly blows. Once the hook is down, the diplomatic cruisers among us should be able to dinghy ashore and find a place to tie off temporarily. Two restaurants and some low-key, convenience-type variety stores are within walking distance.

The 56-foot charted power line immediately north of the bridge was raised to 75 feet of vertical clearance several years ago. Wonder when the NOAA charting folks will catch on? Sailors cruising south from Pine Island Sound can take advantage of this anchorage without having to contend with the 35-foot power line to the south or the more tortuous southerly portion of the Matlacha Pass channel.

MATLACHA PASS NAVIGATION

Matlacha Pass winds, twists, and squirms its way north from San Carlos Bay to Charlotte Harbor and Pine Island Sound. Remember that a few soundings show waters as thin as 4½ to 5 feet (though typically depths are much better), and the passage is spanned at one point by a 32-foot power line. Only maneuverable vessels drawing 4 feet or less should attempt this passage.

Waters outside of the marked channel have consistent depths of 3 feet or less. This is most assuredly not the place to go exploring off the buoyed track.

The southerly reaches of the pass are best navigated using chart 11427. This cartographical aid's minute detail makes for much easier identification of the cut's winding path. North of unlighted daybeacon #25, you must switch to chart 11426. Unfortunately, no larger-scale chart covers the northerly section of Matlacha Pass.

Be advised that all the waters of Matlacha Pass, from its southerly genesis, just north of the Miserable Mile, to unlighted daybeacon #77, north of the Pine Island bridge, have now been declared a year-round, manatee, slow-speed zone. Don't ask me, folks!

Leaving the Miserable Mile   Continue cruising west-southwest on the Waterway channel until you are some 100 yards to the east-northeast of unlighted daybeacon #8. Watch to the northwest for unlighted daybeacon #1. This is the first aid on the Matlacha Pass channel, and it closely borders the Waterway passage. Cut off the ICW and pass #1 fairly close to its northeastern side. Then, set a new course to come abeam of unlighted daybeacon #2 to your starboard side (its southwesterly quarter). From this point on, cruisers northbound on Matlacha Pass should take all subsequent red beacons to their (the cruisers') starboard side and pass all green markers to port. This rule holds true on the pass all the way north to unlighted daybeacon #95, off Pine Island's northern tip, bordering the southern reaches of Charlotte Harbor.

Givney Key Anchorage   For best depths, leave the main channel immediately after passing unlighted daybeacon #3. Point directly for the center of Givney Key, which you will spot well to the north. Drop the hook before approaching to less than 250 yards of the small key. Closer in, depths rise above 5 feet. Do your explorations by dinghy. Retrace your track back to #3 when departing the anchorage.

On Matlacha Pass   It would take more pages than I can count to try and delineate every twist and turn of the Matlacha Pass channel. A few of the more obvious bends are described below, but be ready for quick course changes at all times, and watch over your stern for leeway.

Between unlighted daybeacons #3 and #4, the channel takes a hard jog to the northwest. Set course to pass unlighted daybeacon #5 to your port side and continue on, pointing to pass between unlighted daybeacons #6 and #7. This is one of the shallowest stretches of Matlacha Pass. Be ready for some 4½- to 5-foot depths.

Adjust course sharply north after passing between #6 and #7 and point to come abeam of and pass unlighted daybeacon #8 to your fairly immediate starboard side.

At unlighted daybeacon #17, northbound skippers must follow a hairpin to

port, followed by another turn to starboard at unlighted daybeacon #18.

Watch the western shores at unlighted daybeacon #24 and you will catch sight of Masters Lodge on the Pine Island shoreline. No services are available for cruising craft, but the buildings make for an interesting view from the water.

North of unlighted daybeacon #29, the channel greets an overhead power line with a measly 32 feet of vertical clearance. Sail craft—take note of this very real hazard!

Northbound mariners will sight the Pine Island-Matlacha Pass Bridge after passing unlighted daybeacon #55. This span has a closed vertical clearance of 9 feet. It opens on demand from 8:00 A.M. to 7:00 P.M., but is closed entirely during the evening and nighttime hours.

To anchor south of the bridge, simply ease your way off the channel a bit to the east and drop the hook. Be sure to show an anchor light!

The 56-foot charted power line immediately north of the bridge has been raised to 75 feet of vertical clearance.

North and northwest of the bridge, the two shorelines exhibit even less development and are absolutely beautiful. Minimum depths of 7½ feet continue on to the end of the pass, with most soundings being much deeper.

At unlighted daybeacon #79 the Matlacha Pass channel begins a very lazy turn to the west, skirting the northern tip of Pine Island. The passage ends at unlighted daybeacon #95, north of Bokeelia Island, which is an offshoot of its larger sister, Pine Island.

A marked and charted channel continues south down the easterly reaches of Pine

Island Sound. This route will be reviewed in the discussion of Pine Island Sound presented later in this chapter. For now, we need only note that marker colors reverse after leaving the Matlacha Pass route and entering the southbound channel.

Caloosahatchee River to Fort Myers

Few Western Florida rivers can lay claim to as delightful a port of call as the Caloosahatchee has in Fort Myers. Many captains cruising the Western Florida coastline may want to take a day or two out of their schedules to experience the delights of this colorful city, with its excellent marina (and yacht club) facilities, a beautifully restored downtown business district, and more than its share of historic attractions.

Of course, the Caloosahatchee (which translates to "river of the Caloosa") also serves as the westernmost link in the exciting Okeechobee Waterway. This reliable route not only provides ready access between Florida's two coastlines, it also allows cruisers to experience the "other Florida" of cowboy ranches, small villages, and mighty lakes. Sadly, we can only explore a small portion of this enticing route in this guide. East of Fort Myers, please consult my *Cruising Guide to Eastern Florida* for a minutely detailed account of the Okeechobee Waterway.

The Caloosahatchee below (west of) Fort Myers offers a few anchorages and good marina facilities. At least one of these anchordown spots is sufficient for heavy weather.

The banks of the Caloosahatchee range the full gamut from very heavy, high-rise type development to all-natural stretches. The cruising is certainly not dull from a visual perspective.

All in all, this writer heartily recommends a cruise up the Caloosahatchee to Fort Myers. In fair weather, it's a delightful sojourn, and a night or two spent in Thomas Edison's adopted city is sure to yield cruising memories to be cherished for many years to come.

Shell Point Anchorage (Okeechobee Standard Mile 148, 26 31.389 North/082 00.413 West)

Boats drawing less than 5 feet and in need of immediate anchorage might consider the charted deep water on the cove east and south of flashing daybeacon #96. You must avoid several unmarked shoals, but it is possible to get off the main channel and drop the anchor in some 5 to 6 feet of water near the cove's mouth. Farther to the south, water levels rise to 4 feet or less in spite of the soundings shown on 11427. Protection is fairly good from southern and southeasterly winds, but the anchorage is wide open to blows from any other direction. This is not a poor-weather haven. The surrounding shores are in their natural state and are quite attractive.

Tarpon Point Marina and Glover Bight Anchorage (Okeechobee Standard Mile 146.5—Various Lats/Lons—see below)

A marked channel leads cruisers from the Caloosahatchee River's unlighted daybeacon

#92 past Cattle Dock Point and finally to a first-class marina on the charted offshoot making into the northwestern shores of Glover Bight.

Big changes are now underway at Tarpon Point Marina (26 32.366 North/082 00.010 West). Fortunately, all the upcoming improvements will benefit the cruising community. Over the next several years, a huge complex of condominiums, retail shops, restaurants, and at least one hotel will arise behind the Tarpon Point dockage basin. Construction was just getting underway dur-

ing our last visit to these climes in July 2003. The old dockmaster's building had already been transformed into a sales office, while the marina staff was relegated to a trailer out in the parking lot.

We are happy to report that even with all these big changes in the offing, transients will still be accepted for overnight dockage at Tarpon Point Marina. In fact, the dockmaster informed this writer that the development's permit from the state of Florida requires the marina to continue accepting

1. Tarpon Point Marina

overnight visitors in perpetuity. See, the state of Florida occasionally does something right.

For now, Tarpon Point continues to feature ultramodern, fixed wooden docks and slips in a very well-protected harbor. Transients are accepted at berths with all power and water connections. Minimum entrance depths are 7 feet, with typical soundings ranging up to 15 feet. Dockside, visiting cruisers will find at least 7½ to 12 feet of water. We did sound some 6½-foot depths directly against the seawall, but almost all of the marina's other 175 slips have much better water.

Fully climate-controlled showers and waste pump-out service are both readily available. Gasoline and diesel fuel can be purchased at a separate fuel pier near the marina's entrance. A Boat/US towboat makes its home at Tarpon Point as well. About the only services you will not find at Tarpon Point are a Laundromat, repairs, and a restaurant. Of course, that may well change with all the new construction. Stay tuned!

Tarpon Point Marina (239) 549-4900
   http://www.tarponpointmarina.com (Web
   site currently under construction)

Approach depth—7-15 feet

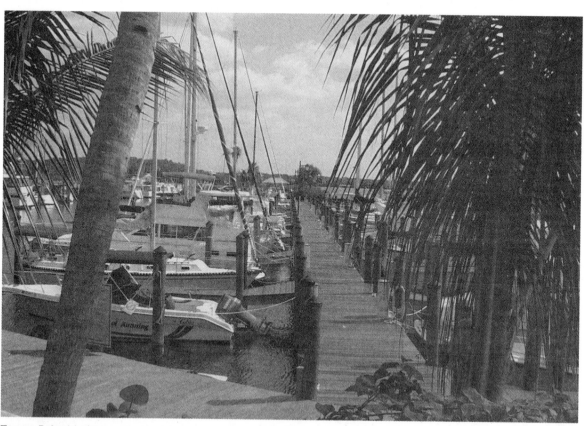

Tarpon Point Marina

Dockside depth—7½-12 feet (many slips much
   deeper)
Accepts transients—yes
Transient dockage rate—average
Fixed wooden piers—yes
Dockside power connections—30 and 50 amp
Dockside water connections—yes
Waste pump-out—yes
Showers—yes
Gasoline—yes
Diesel fuel—yes

The charted channel traversing Glover Bight
continues west past the marina and eventually
leads to a series of canals, mostly lined by private
homes. There are no facilities or enough anchor
room for visiting cruisers on these waters.

On the other hand, mariners may well
choose to anchor on the northeasterly reaches
of Glover Bight, northeast of unlighted daybeacon #9, near 26 32.282 North/081 59.820
West. Depths of 7 to 14 feet extend to within
200 yards of the rear of the cove, but there is
an unmarked shoal to the southeast that must
be avoided. There is good shelter from all but
strong southwesterly blows. The surrounding
shores are delightfully undeveloped.

St. Charles Yacht Club (Okeechobee Standard Mile 146, 26 30.635 North/081 58.849 West)

A well-appointed yacht club guards the
Caloosahatchee's southerly banks between
flashing daybeacon #89 and unlighted daybeacon #86. The club's basin is designated as
facility #16A on chart 11427.

St. Charles Yacht Club is glad to welcome
guests from other yacht clubs with the appropriate reciprocal agreements. The well-
marked entrance cut carries at least 6 feet of
water, and skippers will discover 6½- to 7-foot
dockside soundings.

All berths are provided at modern, fixed
wooden piers featuring freshwater connections
and 30- and 50-amp power hookups. Gasoline,
diesel fuel, and waste pump-out services are
available for members and official club guests
only. Showers and a full Laundromat are on
hand shoreside, in the clubhouse.

The club dockmaster is on duty 8:00 A.M. to
5:00 P.M., seven days a week. He suggests that

1. St. Charles Yacht Club

visitors make advance arrangements by telephone. Call (239) 466-4935.

Lunch is served in the club dining room 11:30 to 2:30 Wednesday through Saturday, and the evening meal is available between 6:00 and 8:30 Wednesday through Saturday. There are no other restaurants within easy walking distance.

On the other hand, cruisers with the fever to purchase something can hike one mile to the Sanbel Factory Outlets center. Here you will find 55 shops waiting to take your money. Just be sure it's a real bargain before you lay out the cold cash.

All in all, we have always been very impressed with St. Charles Yacht Club. I have had the good fortune to visit with and speak to this organization's membership on two occasions, and the warm greeting will always remain with me as a fond memory. St. Charles' location is very advantageous for those with the appropriate reciprocal agreements who don't want to stray as far upstream as Fort Myers. We suggest that you give these good folks a look-see.

St. Charles Yacht Club (239) 466-2007

Approach depth—6 feet MLW
Dockside depth—6½-7 feet MLW
Accepts transients—members of other yacht
   clubs with reciprocal privileges only
Fixed wooden piers—yes
Dockside power connections—30 and 50 amp
Dockside water connections—yes
Waste pump-out—members and official guests
   only
Showers—yes
Laundromat—yes
Gasoline—members and official guests only
Diesel fuel—members and official guests only
Restaurant—club dining room on site

Bimini Basin Anchorage (Okeechobee Standard Mile 145, 26 33.624 North/081 57.869 West)

East of unlighted daybeacon #83, a well-marked channel maintaining 6-foot depths leads into the northern banks. By easing west-southwest along this shoreline, you can find your way to the charted northward-running canal that eventually leads to a large bay-like body of water correctly charted as Bimini Basin on 11427. Depths hold in the 6- to 8-foot region all the way into this super-protected anchorage. The surrounding shores are guarded by a dense collection of residential, and some high-rise, development.

There is the opportunity to dinghy ashore in this anchorage. Use your binoculars to pick out a city park along the northeasterly shoreline. You can temporarily moor your dinghy adjacent to this park while hiking a short distance to a convenience store, bank, bakery, hardware, or grocery store. Ask any local for directions.

Cape Coral Yacht Basin (Okeechobee Standard Mile 144, 26 32.630 North/081 57.076 West)

Another good marina is found north-northwest of unlighted daybeacon #78 in a sheltered canal and dockage basin behind Redfish Point. City-owned Cape Coral Yacht Basin has minimum entrance depths of 5½ to 8 feet, with 5½ to 10 feet of water dockside. The entrance channel can be a bit confusing for first-time visitors, but a little explanation, courtesy of the navigational data presented in the next section of this chapter, should see you through.

The friendly dockmaster gladly accepts transients at fixed wooden piers with water connections and power connections up to 50 amps. There are usually 6 to 10 slips open for transients. Given this limitation, advance reservations would be a wise precaution. Two fair, non-climate-controlled showers (one per sex), a tiny, non-air-conditioned Laundromat, and waste pump-out service are available. The city of Cape Coral leases out a fuel dock (gasoline and diesel fuel) alongside a small open-air snack bar that flanks the western side of the canal leading from the river to the dockage basin.

This city marina is set within the boundaries of a delightful city park. For a nominal fee visitors can make use of tennis courts and a large, heated swimming pool.

Cruisers can hike nine lo-o-ong blocks or, better yet, make use of the marina's free bike rentals or the city bus service to access a Publix supermarket, Eckerd Drugs, and liquor store in the main Cape Coral business district astride Cape Coral Parkway. You can also take a taxi (see below).

In this same business district, hungry visitors should make every effort to find their way to Mr. C's Restaurant (850 W Lafayette, 239-542-2001) or Sal's Just Pizza (910 Cape Coral Parkway, 239-540-7373). Both of these dining spots have been recommended to this writer by the city dockmaster.

Clearly the Cape Coral Yacht Basin has a lot to offer, particularly for a municipal facility. You can scarcely do better anywhere on this portion of the Caloosahatchee. Tell Paul we sent you!

Cape Coral Yacht Basin (239) 574-0809

Approach depth—5½-8 feet
Dockside depth—5½-10 feet
Accepts transients—yes
Transient dockage rate—above average (with electrical connections)
Fixed wooden piers—yes
Dockside power connections—30 and 50 amp
Dockside water connections—yes
Waste pump-out—yes
Showers—yes
Laundromat—yes
Gasoline—yes
Diesel fuel—yes
Restaurant—long walk, medium bike ride, or quick taxi away

Numbers to know in Cape Coral include:

Lou's Airport Service—(239) 549-5272
Yellow Cab—(239) 495-3200
Budget Car Rentals—(239) 772-1672
Chamber of Commerce—(239) 549-6900

Gulf Harbour Yacht and Country Club (Okeechobee Standard Mile 143.5, 26 31.948 North/081 56.302 West)

An impressive marina, condo complex, and golf club known as Gulf Harbour Yacht and Country Club (239-437-0881) overlooks the Caloosahatchee's southeasterly shoreline,

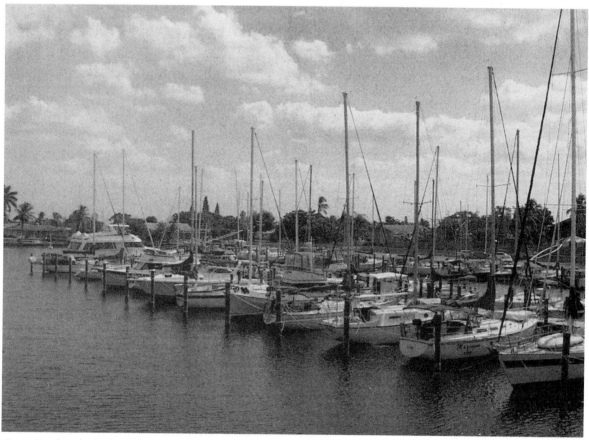

Cape Coral Yacht Basin

south-southeast of unlighted daybeacon #74. The marina's well-marked entrance channel runs south off the main Caloosahatchee cut between unlighted daybeacon #74 and flashing daybeacon #73. This cut carries 6½- to 8-foot depths at MLW, and the passage is denoted by a tall, square "lighthouse," which displays a white light at night.

There have been definite changes at this facility since the last edition of this guidebook appeared. Now, the marina's ownership and management have been taken over by the complex's owner's association. At least for the moment, transients are no longer accepted, and all slips are leased for a minimum stay of 30 days. After telling you all that, however, the dockmaster has informed this writer that he and his staff hope to change this policy in the future and once again begin accepting cruising craft for a night or two or three. Only the future will tell. With this uncertain situation in mind, we strongly suggest that you call well in advance of your arrival to check on whether any visitor wet-slip space is available.

Gulf Harbour's dockage basin has been

1. Gulf Harbour Yacht & Country Club
2. Cape Coral Yacht Basin
3. Deep Lagoon Boat Club

dredged out behind a barrier island that separates the harbor from the main body of the Caloosahatchee. This arrangement affords excellent protection from foul weather for all vessels moored in this marina. The mainland shores are overlooked by a vast array of medium-rise condos.

Should you be lucky enough to land a berth at Gulf Harbour, your boat will be berthed at excellent floating, concrete-decked piers, featuring freshwater and 30-, 50-, and 100-amp power hookups, as well as telephone and cable-television connections. Depths alongside run some 6½ feet at MLW. Each and every slip boasts its own waste pump-out connection.

Both gasoline and diesel fuel are available at a fueling pier located in the heart of the dockage complex. Light mechanical servicing can be arranged through local, independent technicians by the friendly dockmaster and his staff.

First-class showers and a full Laundromat are available shoreside in their own building overlooking the harbor. The dockmaster's office doubles as an extensive ship's and variety store.

Cruising visitors, even of the seasonal variety, are no longer welcome at the complex's club house, dining room, golf course, or tennis courts. Guess the property owners want to keep all these goodies to themselves.

Deep Lagoon Boat Club (Okeechobee Standard Mile 143.5, 26 32.272 North/081 55.288 West)

Cruisers seeking entry to Deep Lagoon can break off from the main river channel between flashing daybeacons #73 and #72 and follow a rather confusing channel east and then south into the interior reaches of Deep Lagoon.

Since 1964, this body of water has played host to a small pleasure-craft dockage facility and repair yard known as Deep Lagoon Marina. This facility, renamed the Deep Lagoon Boat Club (239-545-2628) is now in the midst of a confusing transition, and the eventual shape of all these changes is much in doubt. Several years ago, this marina and its adjoining property were purchased by the same folks who eventually developed the Naples Boat Club (see chapter 1). Plans called for a complex of condos, wet slips, and dry-stack storage buildings to be built very similar in character to the Naples development. However, objections were raised to this plan, and the upstart is that virtually no new construction has occurred. As we've said, just what the future will bring is very uncertain. We were told during our last visit, that it was also still very much up in the proverbial air as to whether cruising visitors would be accepted in the new complex, if it ever does indeed become a reality.

With all this confusion, we suggest that visiting cruisers make use of Naples Boat Club as a repair stop only. Of course, local captains might still want to utilize the marina's wet slips and dry-stack storage.

The Landings Yacht Club (Okeechobee Standard Mile 142.5, 26 33.105 North/081 55.446 West)

The charted channel southeast of flashing daybeacon #70 serves the private dockage basin of the Landings Yacht Club (239-481-7181). This facility is associated with a huge condo development and does not accept visiting craft for dockage. The adjacent ship's (and variety) store and fuel dock (gas and diesel fuel) are open to the public. Entrance depths run around 6 feet with 5- to 6-foot soundings dockside.

Cape Coral

Northeast of flashing daybeacon #70, captains and crew cruising up the Caloosahatchee will soon exchange greetings with the Cape Coral Bridge. Forty years ago, there was not even a small village at the modern-day site of Cape Coral. Today, the community numbers 48,000 citizens, making it the largest city on the Caloosahatchee. As you might have guessed, Cape Coral is the product of a development company which promoted the town as a "planned city" beginning in 1954.

In the fascinating book *The Rivers of Florida* (edited by Del and Marty Marth), George Lane, Jr., recalls the days before the coming of Cape Coral as seen through the eyes of an old fisherman: ". . . the fish once were so thick that you could nearly walk across their backs in the river. . . . Downriver (opposite Cape Coral) we'd see redfish feeding, and it would look like a hundred square yards of fish tails in the air." Sadly, those days are gone in the wake of rampant development.

Whiskey Creek Anchorage (Okeechobee Standard Mile 140, 26 34.644 North/081 53.915 West)

Captains piloting boats less than 34 feet in length and drawing 4 feet or less will find an obscure anchorage on Whiskey Creek, southeast of unlighted daybeacon #66. While the channel is well marked with small, unlighted daybeacons, depths run as thin as 4½ feet.

Eventually, the stream takes a sharp swing to starboard and is soon crossed by a low-level, fixed bridge. Between the starboard turn and the bridge, visiting cruisers can anchor in 4½ feet of water amidst fairly numerous, but quite seemly private homes on both shores. Protection is excellent from all winds and should be sufficient for anything short of a full gale. The skimpy swinging room may call for a Bahamian mooring or even a stern anchor.

Paradise Yacht Club (Okeechobee Standard Mile 137, 26 37.686 North/081 55.054 West)

Captains will discover Paradise Yacht Club (formerly Harbour Village Marina) along the Caloosahatchee's westerly banks, in the well-sheltered harbor to the west-northwest of unlighted daybeacon #58. This marina is now a 100 percent live-aboard facility with a waiting list. Transients are sometimes accepted if space happens to be available, but clearly the vast majority of all the available wet slips are rented out on a seasonable basis. Call well ahead of time to see if any overnight berths happen to be available.

There are not many marinas left in all of Florida friendly to live-aboards, much less a facility that is populated almost exclusively with cruisers of this ilk. If you are seeking a good spot to spend a life on the water, get your name on the waiting list here right away. You could scarcely make a better choice than Paradise Yacht Club.

The yacht club's docks are composed of first-class, fixed wooden piers with good power and water connections. Minimum entrance depths now run in the 5-foot range,

with dockside soundings in the 5½- to 7-foot region. The marina features new, adequate, climate-controlled showers and a small, non-air-conditioned Laundromat. Waste pump-out services are also available. The marina's dockmaster has now been installed in a new building, and the old headquarters (just next door) has been converted into a small, air-conditioned, captain's lounge, complete with color television. The only restaurant within walking distance is located at the adjacent, public golf course (see below). This establishment is open for breakfast and lunch and some evenings. Check with the friendly dockmaster. Of course, you could always take a taxi into nearby Cape Coral for your evening repast.

Just across the street, patrons of Paradise Yacht Club may make use of a public golf course, a refreshing swimming pool, and several tennis courts. This is yet another great advantage for live-aboards and visitors berthing at this facility.

It's unfortunate that slip-space limitations will keep many cruisers from experiencing the delights of Paradise Yacht Club. On the other hand, if you are looking for a marina in which to live aboard for an extended period of time, this is "the" place in the Fort Myers, Caloosahatchee region.

Paradise Yacht Club (239) 997-1603

Approach depth—5 feet
Dockside depth—5½-7 feet
Accepts transients—limited (space-available basis)
Transient dockage rate—average
Fixed wooden piers—yes
Dockside power connections—30 and 50 amp
Dockside water connections—yes
Waste pump-out—yes
Showers—yes
Laundromat—yes

1. Paradise Yacht Club
2. Caloosa Isle Marina

Caloosa Isle Marina (Okeechobee Standard Mile 136.5, 26 38.331 North/081 54.470 West)

Caloosa Isle Marina, yet another of the Caloosahatchee, Fort Myers facilities, is found at the western terminus of the charted channel west of (32-foot) flashing daybeacon #C. Mechanical repairs for both diesel and gasoline engines and haul-outs via a 30-ton travelift are available.

Caloosa Isle is known for having a decent selection of parts at its ship's and variety store. A few transient berths might possibly be available at the facility's smaller, fixed wooden piers, but the number of wet slips is very limited, and clearly transient dockage is not the

focus of this marina. Calling ahead of time would be a very good idea, indeed. Power connections of the 30- and 50-amp variety and freshwater hookups are found at each berth. Entrance depths run a meager 4 to 5 feet with 4-foot low-water dockside depths. Obviously, dockage at Caloosa Isle is pretty much confined to shallow-draft vessels. Gasoline is readily available, as is dry storage for smaller powercraft. The on-site Shucker's and Company Crabhouse (239-995-7001) is open for all three meals of the day, and it seems popular with the local crowd.

Caloosa Isle Marina (239) 656-1700

Approach depth—4-5 feet
Dockside depth—4 feet
Accepts transients—limited
Transient dockage rate—average
Fixed wooden piers—yes
Dockside power connections—30 and 50 amp
Dockside water connections—yes
Showers—yes
Laundromat—yes
Gasoline—yes
Mechanical repairs—yes
Below-waterline repairs—yes
Ship's and variety store—yes
Restaurant—on site

Royal Palm Yacht Club (Okeechobee Standard Mile 135.5, 26 38.197 North/081 52.906 West)

The channel leading to the breakwater-enclosed harbor of Royal Palm Yacht Club cuts southeast between flashing daybeacon #54 and unlighted daybeacon #52. Good entrance depths of 7 to 8 feet lead to an occluded entrance marked by arrows painted on the breakwater. Inside the harbor, cruisers will find depths of 6 to 7 feet at fixed wooden slips (some set against the concrete breakwater). Members of other yacht clubs with reciprocal privileges are gladly accepted for guest dockage. The dockmaster is on duty from 8:00 A.M. to 4:00 P.M. Tuesday through Saturday and from 8:00 A.M. to 3:00 P.M. Sundays. The club's slips feature both 30- and 50-amp power connections, as well as water connections. Shoreside, visitors will discover good showers in the clubhouse. Lunch and dinner are served in the club dining room Tuesday through Saturday. A convenience store is located two blocks to the north on McGregor Boulevard. Joe's Crab House restaurant (239-332-1881) can be reached by a three-block walk.

This writer gained the swift and sure impression that Royal Palm is an active club that is friendly to visiting cruisers from other clubs. If you are lucky enough to have the appropriate credentials, then by all means give this facility your most serious consideration.

Royal Palm Yacht Club (239) 334-2176
  http://www.rpyc.org

Approach depth—7-8 feet
Dockside depth—6-7 feet
Accepts transients—members of other yacht
  clubs with reciprocal privileges only
Fixed wooden piers—yes
Dockside power connections—30 and 50 amp
Dockside water connections—yes
Showers—yes
Restaurant—on site and nearby

Marina Town Yacht Club (Okeechobee Standard Mile 135.5, 26 39.573 North/081 53.421 West)

The long, charted channel leading northwest

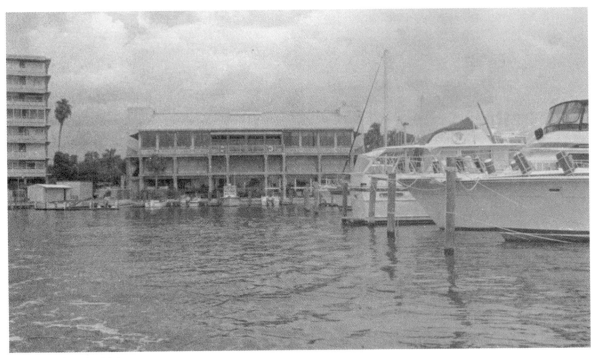

Royal Palm Yacht Club, Fort Myers

from unlighted daybeacon #52 to Hancock Creek serves Marina Town Yacht Club. This facility eagerly accepts transients at fixed wooden piers and slips, set against a concrete seawall, with water connections and power connections up to 100 amps! Currently only two slips are kept open full time for transients, but the dockmaster has informed this writer that three of four other resident boats are almost always absent, and visitors can be accommodated in these berths as well. Call ahead of time to check on berth availability.

Marina Town's harbor is very well protected and would be a good place to ride out heavy weather before venturing out into the open Gulf. Minimum entrance and dockside depths run around 5 feet, with many soundings ranging from 6 to 8 feet. Adequate, newly climate-controlled showers and an on-site Laundromat are readily available, as is a waste pump-out facility. Mechanical repairs of both the gas and diesel varieties are readily available on-site by way of Gulf Coast Yacht Services (239-997-8822). This firm also maintains a small ship's store in the complex just behind the docks. Still not enough for you? Well, let's throw in a cooling swimming pool and tennis courts. Several supermarkets, drugstores, and motels are all within a three-block walk.

OK, so now you want to stay awhile. You're in luck. Surprisingly enough, Marina Town caters to live-aboards, which is an all-too-occasional rarity along the present-day Western Florida coastline.

When it comes time to slake a healthy appetite, Marina Town features three (soon to be four) dockside restaurants. Hurricane Harry's Bar and Restaurant (239-997-8300) is a lively establishment that features extensive and very informal dining. Wally's Waterfront Restaurant (239-997-7110) and the Dancing Water Piano Bar offer more elegant cuisine. By the time this account finds its way into your hands, a fourth dining alternative will most likely be operating on the premises as well.

Cruisers intent on chartering a sail or powercraft to explore the Western Florida coastline can do themselves a *huge* favor by contacting Southwest Florida Yachts (800-262-7939), based at Marina Town Yacht Club. The firm's fleet of first-class trawlers is located at this facility, while a selection of sail craft is maintained at Burnt Store Marina on Charlotte Harbor (see below). Tell Captains Vic or Barb that we sent you.

Marina Town Yacht Club (239) 997-2767
   http://www.pegan.net/marinatown
Approach depth—5-8 feet
Dockside depth—5-6 feet
Accepts transients—yes
Transient dockage rate—below average
Fixed wooden slips—yes
Dockside power connections—up to 100 amp
Dockside water connections—yes
Waste pump-out—yes
Showers—yes
Laundromat—yes
Mechanical repairs—yes
Ship's store—yes
Restaurant—3 on site

Hancock Creek Anchorage (Okeechobee Standard Mile 135.5, 26 39.334 North/081 53.712 West)

Skippers piloting boats 34 feet and (preferably) smaller, which draw less than 4½ feet, can track their way to a small but very secure anchorage on Hancock Creek, within shouting distance of Marina Town. At unlighted daybeacon #26, the Marina Town approach channel swings sharply to the north. Cruisers looking to anchor off can instead swing to the south-southwest and enter the small, charted cove indenting Hancock Creek's southerly banks. Low-water depths do run as thin as 4½ to 5 feet, and swinging room is somewhat limited. On the other hand, you won't find better shelter anywhere. A few private homes overlook the rear section of the cove, but their lush green lawns stretching down to the water only add to this haven's appeal.

The best place to anchor is found on the rear (southwesterly) third of the cove's length. There is a bit more swinging room here than at the creek's entrance. If you can fit the somewhat stringent size and draft requirements, this is a great place to spend the evening.

Centennial Harbour Marina (Okeechobee Standard Mile 135.5, 26 38.505 North/081 52.574 West)

The enclosed, well-protected dockage basin of Fort Myers' newest pleasure-craft facility guards the Caloosahatchee's southeasterly banks, southeast of flashing daybeacon #49. Centennial Harbour Marina has been completed since the last edition of this guide. When last we reported on this facility, only a portion of its dockage basin was in place. Now, the entire harbor is protected by a long breakwater, and there are many more wet slips.

The marina's scantily marked entrance channel carries 7 to 8 feet of water, while soundings of 6½ to 8 feet are typical in the breakwater-enclosed dockage basin. Transients are eagerly accepted, as well as large cruising groups. Full power and water connections are readily available dockside, as is waste pump-out service. Diesel fuel delivery can be arranged by way of a shoreside fuel truck for vessels requiring a goodly amount of petrol in the tank.

Nice, climate-controlled showers and an adjacent, air-conditioned Laundromat are located in the dockmaster's building just behind the basin. Here you will also find a welcome e-mail hookup. On-line cruisers, and that's now most of us, will be ever so glad of this feature. Joe's Crab Shack (239-332-1881), mentioned above, is located immediately adjacent to this marina, while Tucan Charlie's restaurant (2220 W First Street, 239-334-2727) is a scant two blocks away. The entire Fort Myers business district is easily accessible by foot or a very quick taxi ride.

There can be no argument that Centennial Harbour is a wonderful addition to the Fort Myers cruising scene. With its plentiful dockage (now breakwater protected) combined with the municipal marina's prodigious wet-slip space (see below), transient berth availability in and near downtown Fort Myers is quite impressive indeed.

Centennial Harbour Marina (239) 461-0775

Approach depth—7-8 feet
Dockside depth—6½-8 feet
Accepts transients—yes
Transient dockage rate—average
Floating concrete piers—yes
Dockside power connections—30 and 50 amp
Dockside water connections—yes
Waste pump-out—yes
Showers—yes
Laundromat—yes
Variety store—small
Restaurant—next door and several nearby

Fort Myers Yacht Basin (Okeechobee Standard Mile 135, 26 38.870 North/081 52.180 West)

Three bridges span the Caloosahatchee northeast of the Marina Town channel. Well,

1. Royal Palm Yacht Club
2. Marina Town Yacht Club
3. Centennial Harbour Marina
4. Fort Myers Yacht Basin

at least on the water it looks like three bridges. Fort Myers Yacht Basin guards the southeasterly banks between the first and second (moving west to east) river bridges. The marina actually

encompasses two protected dockage basins, as well as a long face dock fronting directly onto the river. This facility features 276 slips. While extensive space is always reserved for transients, advance reservations might be a wise course of action.

Visitors will find just about every type of dockage imaginable. Some slips are composed of wooden pilings set out from the concrete breakwater, while the eastern basin features a set of concrete floating docks reserved for smaller craft. All are absolutely first-rate berths with 30-, 50-, and some 100-amp power hookups and water connections. While especially large pleasure craft sometimes have to be moored to the outer face dock, the two breakwater-enclosed basins provide better protection and are much to be preferred. Dockside depths in the east basin run about 7 feet, with soundings of 6 to 7 feet encountered in the west-side harbor. The outer face dock boasts at least 10 feet of water.

The marina ship's store, dockmaster's office, superb air-conditioned showers, clean bathrooms, and semi open-air Laundromat occupy a good-sized building set between the two dockage basins. The ship's store at Fort Myers Yacht Basin (239-334-6446) is privately leased and well stocked with not only nautical but convenience-store-type food items as well.

Gasoline (both 89 and 93 octane grades available) and diesel fuel can be purchased at a fuel pier on the Caloosahatchee immediately in front of the dockmaster's building (between the two dockage basins). Free waste pump-out service is now offered at most every slip in the marina.

Visitors to Fort Myers Yacht Basin will find themselves a short step from the many attractions of downtown Fort Myers (see discussion below). A host of hotels, car-rental agencies, and other shoreside businesses of all descriptions are a short stroll or taxi ride away.

Joe's Crab Shack (2024 W First Street, 312-332-1881) is also within walking distance, as is the French Connection (2288 First Street, 239-332-4443), both recommended by the local marina staff. Tucan Charlie's restaurant (2220 W First Street, 312-334-2727) is close by too. There is no longer a downtown grocery store accessible by foot, but you can easily take a taxi to and from one of the local supermarkets.

Fort Myers Yacht Basin (239) 334-8271

Approach depth—8-10 feet
Dockside depth—10 feet (fuel and face dock)
                                       7 feet (east basin)
                                       6-7 feet (west basin)
Accepts transients—yes
Transient dockage rate—below average
Fixed wooden and concrete docks—yes
Floating concrete docks—yes
Dockside power connections—up to 100 amp
Dockside water connections—yes
Waste pump-out—yes
Showers—yes
Laundromat—yes
Gasoline—yes
Diesel fuel—yes
Mechanical repairs—arranged through local

Fort Myers Yacht Basin

independent contractors
Ship's and variety store—yes
Restaurant—several nearby

Lofton Island Mooring Field and Anchorage (Okeechobee Standard Mile 135, 26 39.118 North/081 52.412 West)

Several years ago the city of Fort Myers began sanctioning an official city anchorage behind charted Lofton Island. This small body of land lies along the charted channel's northerly flank, opposite Fort Myers Yacht Basin. Since that time, the city has added a sail-craft only, 25-buoy, fee-charging mooring field on these same waters. Fort Myers hopes to add another 25 mooring buoys in the future. A dinghy dock is available for those who pay for a mooring in the east basin of the Fort Myers city facility.

By the way, the city dockmaster has informed this writer that it was not Fort Myers' notion to restrict these moorings to sailing vessels. Rather, this was a requirement by the state of Florida. Fortunately, powercraft can still anchor on these waters with their own hook!

After traversing its unmarked entrance cut

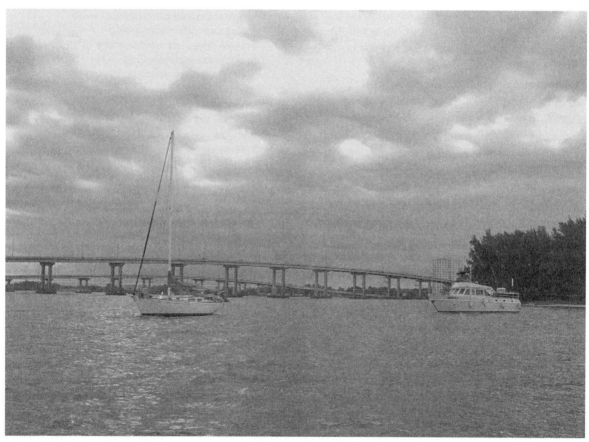

Lofton Island anchorage, Fort Myers

(see our navigational account of this anchorage below), cruising craft can curl around behind (north and northwest of) Lofton Island on the broad, correctly charted patch of 7- and 8-foot waters. Here you can pick up a mooring buoy or anchor. For maximum shelter, drop anchor as the body of Lofton Island comes abeam to the south and be sure to leave plenty of swinging room between your vessel and any other pleasure craft that have picked up a mooring. Stay at least 50 yards off the isle's shoreline.

Protection is good from southerly blows, courtesy of the lee afforded by Lofton Island, and there is some shelter to the north from the mainland shores. This is most certainly, however, not a foul-weather hidey-hole. Nevertheless, when winds aren't too ornery, this is a good spot to spend the evening, and it has the distinct advantage of being within shouting distance of downtown Fort Myers.

Downtown Fort Myers

Numbers to know in Fort Myers include

Bluebird Cab—(239) 275-8294
Preferred Taxi—(239) -334-0000
Yellow Cab of Fort Myers—(239) 332-1055
Avis Rental Cars—(239) 768-2022
Budget Rent A Car—(239) 768-1500
Hertz Rent A Car—(239) 768-3100
Boat/US Marine Center—(239) 481-7447
West Marine—(239) 275-6077
Chamber of Commerce—(239) 332-3624

Within the last decade Fort Myers has done a good job renovating its downtown waterfront. Where once old wharves and crumbling warehouses stood, cruising visitors will now find a lovely green park, an arts center, a convention complex, and the local Chamber of Commerce. All of these attractions are located within walking distance of the city marina on

Edwards Drive. You might also take the time to stroll down First Street through the main downtown business district. It will soon be obvious that business is returning to this section of the city.

One cannot visit Fort Myers without getting the deep impression of a warm welcome and a general air of friendliness. It's no secret among my friends that Fort Myers is one of this writer's favorite cities in Western Florida. I hope you too will have the opportunity to make the acquaintance of this unique town that Thomas Edison adopted.

Fort Myers History

Fort Myers was established along the banks of the Caloosahatchee after the Seminole Indian wars in 1850. It was abandoned shortly thereafter, but again saw service during the Civil War. With the river serving as a ready source of transportation and commerce, the village of Fort Myers began growing about 1868, and the town was finally incorporated in 1911.

Beginning in the late 1800s Fort Myers played host to three giants of American science and industry. Thomas Alva Edison, perhaps America's greatest scientist, came south to the city by the Caloosahatchee searching for a healthful winter climate. He fell in love with Fort Myers and returned every winter for the rest of his days.

The energetic scientist soon bought a lot by the river and began to design his winter residence. The house was built in sections in Fairfield, Maine. The various components were then transported by two sailing schooners to Fort Myers, where they were assembled in 1886. This was one of the first prefabricated homes in the United States.

An extensive laboratory was added so that Edison could continue his scientific work while in residence. A swimming pool was built, braced with native bamboo rather than the usual steel rods. It was filled by an artesian well that was 1,100 feet deep.

Before long Edison managed to convince his friends Henry Ford and Harvey Firestone to share his winter quarters in Fort Myers. Ford eventually built a home next door to Edison, and the two remained fast friends until the great scientist's death.

While wintering in Fort Myers, Edison dreamed up the notion of manufacturing synthetic rubber from Florida's native goldenrod weed. With the financial backing of both Ford and Firestone, Edison managed to produce a new strain of the weed which grew to an astonishing 14 feet in height. History suggests that these experiments led to the modern-day production of synthetic rubber, without which automobile transportation would be impractical at best.

Thomas Edison loved tropical plants and was interested in the by-products that might be derived from them. Over the years he established an elaborate botanical garden at his Fort Myers home containing more than 1,000 plants from around the world. In one instance he planted a 2-inch (diameter) banyan tree that Harvey Firestone brought him from India. That same tree survives to this day and the circumference of its trunk has increased to 400 feet.

Edison loved automobiles. In 1907, Henry Ford presented a gift of a prototype Model T Ford to his neighbor. For the next twenty years, Ford had his engineers add the latest updates to the car every twelve months. Edison refused to part with the original model for a newer version.

Today, both the Thomas Edison and Henry Ford homes (2350 McGregor Boulevard, 239-334-3614) have been preserved and are open to the public. The scientist's homeplace has been left just as it was upon Edison's death. The rooms are filled with memorabilia, including the phonographs, brass lamps, and carbon-filament light bulbs designed by Edison himself. The old laboratory is still intact and immensely impressive. A collection of antique cars is also on display, including Edison's 1908 Cadillac Opera Coupe, prototype Model T Ford, and a 1936 Brewster limousine.

CALOOSAHATCHEE RIVER NAVIGATION

All cruising and landlubber visitors to Fort Myers should make every effort to tour these two historic homes for themselves. They are open from 9:00 A.M. to 4:00 P.M. weekdays, and Sunday afternoons as well.

Navigation of the Caloosahatchee can certainly not be described as a proverbial piece of cake. Unlike many Floridian rivers, shoal water is rife on the Caloosahatchee, often abutting the marked channel. Cruising navigators, particularly those visiting this stream for the first time, must proceed with due caution and deliberation. Keep chart 11427 and the information contained in this account handy at all times to quickly resolve any confusion. Maintain a closer than usual watch on the sounder, and you should catch sight of the soaring towers of Fort Myers with good water still under your keel.

It would serve little purpose to outline every single shoal near the river's main channel in the account below. It would require page after page, and you can certainly read chart 11427 as well as this writer. We will therefore only review those waters of critical concern and the instances where my on-site research showed the chart to be in error.

Sidewaters along the Caloosahatchee are usually well marked. Even so, the channels often wind and intersect other cuts. Care is again called for when navigating the various gunk holes along the way.

The prolific markers denoting the river's various side channels can give rise to unexpected difficulties when cruising the main body of the Caloosahatchee. It's often all too easy to mistake some of the markers on these alternate cuts for those stretched along the main channel. Have your binoculars ready to help sort out any confusion.

While we are discussing side channels, it should be noted that a majority of the charted cuts appearing on chart 11427 serve only private docks in residential neighborhoods. Most of these passages are only of the most minimal interest to visiting cruisers.

All captains should take careful note of the fact that the waters adjacent to both banks of the Caloosahatchee River are now year-round, official, manatee, slow-speed zones. Clearly this is not the place to go charging into one of the river's side channels at full bore, unless, of course, an on-the-water speeding ticket is to your liking.

Well, let's push on up the Caloosahatchee's appealing path to Fort Myers. There are more than a few sights for us to enjoy along the way.

Entry into the Caloosahatchee River   Come abeam of flashing daybeacon #101 at the river's mouth to its northwesterly side. Cut to the northeast and point to come abeam of and pass unlighted daybeacon #99 to its northwesterly side. From this point on, skippers cruising upstream (eastbound) on the Caloosahatchee should take all green markers to their (the cruisers') starboard side and all red beacons to port.

From #101 to #99, captains can make use of the charted range. The forward marker is found north-northeast of #99. Westbound mariners can also use a similar range anchored with flashing daybeacon #96 as its forward marker.

At #99 passing cruisers should take note of an idle-speed, no-wake zone that extends upstream for 1.4 miles. This restriction comes to an end near flashing daybeacon #89. The regulation is apparently in place to protect manatees, though the speed-limit signs lack the usual manatee designations. There are certainly no docks or private property on these waters to worry with.

Northeast of unlighted daybeacon #99, the river channel is flanked by two long islands to the northwest and the Punta Rassa mainland to the southeast. This is a sheltered portion of the Waterway, but the channel is narrow, and currents can run quite swiftly. Stay alert and watch for leeway.

East-northeast of flashing daybeacon #96, the river's first anchorage opportunity, albeit a limited one, will come abeam to the south.

Shell Point Anchorage   Entry into the anchorage west of Shell Point is complicated by the unmarked (but charted) underwater rock flanking the westerly side of the entrance and the tongue of 1-foot water to the east. To avoid these treacherous hazards, continue cruising upstream (east) past flashing daybeacon #96 on the main river channel for some 200 yards. Then cut sharply to the south and cruise into the mouth of the cove. Be sure to drop the hook at the cove's entrance. Farther to the south, depths rise markedly.

On the Caloosahatchee River   East of flashing daybeacon #96, the river channel cuts a bit to the east-northeast and heads past unlighted daybeacon #94 near Shell Point. East-northeast of #94, a whole collection of markers impinges upon the main cut. The daybeacons ranging to the south serve local craft, while the marked channel cutting northwest into Glover Bight, past Cattle Dock Point, serves a first-class marina and an excellent anchorage.

Cruisers following the main river channel should point to pass unlighted can buoy #93A and flashing daybeacon #93 to their northerly sides. Past #93, use your binoculars to pick out unlighted daybeacon #92 ahead. This aid marks a sunken wreck. Favor the southerly side of the channel when passing #92.

Tarpon Point Marina and Glover Bight Anchorage   Be sure to pass east of unlighted

daybeacon #92 before turning into the Glover Bight channel. Turn hard to the northwest and point to pass the channel's first aid, unlighted daybeacon #1, to port. From this point on, follow the old, faithful red, right, returning rule into the marina.

Continue on, pointing to pass unlighted daybeacon #2 to starboard. This portion of the track will bring you pretty close to the shores of Cattle Dock Point. Don't worry—good depths seem to run quite close to this shoreline.

The entire Glover Bight channel is now a minimum-wake zone. Power captains should slow to non-planing speed all the way in to the marina docks.

Continue following the markers outlining the winding channel until you are abeam of unlighted daybeacon #9. At this point, break off from the marked track and set course to the north-northeast for the marina entrance, which will be spied dead ahead. As you cruise into the marina, watch to your starboard side for the fuel dock. The marina office is located at the rear of the harbor.

To anchor on the northeasterly waters of Glover Bight, depart the marina entrance channel once abeam of unlighted daybeacon #9. Work your way carefully to the northeast, favoring the northerly shores slightly. This maneuver will serve to avoid the correctly charted shallows abutting the southern and southeasterly shoreline. Be sure to drop the hook before cruising to within less than 200 yards of the cove's northeasterly tip.

The charted markers continue past Glover Bight hard by the northern shoreline into a series of canals. There are no facilities, and there really isn't even room to anchor on these small streams. Those intrepid explorers who just have to see it all should be sure to follow the starboard cut at the first *T*-intersection in the canals. The port branch is quite shoal.

St. Charles Yacht Club Channel   The partially charted channel leading to the protected St. Charles Yacht Club dockage basin breaks off to the south about halfway between flashing daybeacon #89 and unlighted daybeacon #86. A sign at the northern head of this passage identifies the channel as the St. Charles Yacht Club cut. There are actually far more markers outlining this channel than are depicted on the latest edition of chart 11427. The presence of these numerous aids renders navigation of this cut a snap. Just pass all red markers to your starboard side and take green, odd-numbered beacons to port. What could be simpler?

Eventually the channel will swing sharply to starboard as you enter the inner basin. Soon the yacht club's docks will come abeam to port.

On the Caloosahatchee River   East of flashing daybeacon #89, the river channel bypasses two shoals flanking both sides of the cut by cutting south of unlighted daybeacon #86 and just north of unlighted #85. The channel running to the north abeam of #86 is one of the local cuts servicing resident craft.

Bimini Basin Anchorage   To visit the sheltered anchorage in Bimini Basin, break off from the main Caloosahatchee channel

east of unlighted daybeacons #83 and #84. Follow the marked (and charted) channel to the north. As you would expect, take all red beacons to your starboard side and green markers to port. After passing the last of the south-to-north markers, you will approach the northerly banks and sight a broad entrance to a series of canals. This is not the route to Bimini Basin.

Instead, turn to the west (don't cut this corner too sharply) and keeping the charted, unlighted red daybeacons off your *port* side, work your way around the shore until coming abeam of unlighted daybeacon #16. You should then cut north into the canal that is (almost) abeam of this aid.

Continue following the main canal, ignoring all the various side branches, until the main stream turns slightly to the north-northeast. At this point the canal splits in a *Y* intersection. Follow the northeasterly branch to the basin.

Study chart 11427 for a moment and these seemingly complex maneuvers will seem far clearer. Drop the hook anywhere you choose in the basin. Do not attempt to land anywhere except along the shores of the public park.

We specifically do *not* suggest making use of the marked and charted channel running south from the canal's mouth (opening onto the Caloosahatchee) and unlighted daybeacon #16. This passage is very shoaly. Leave it to local outboarders.

On the Caloosahatchee River   The Caloosahatchee channel between unlighted daybeacon #86 and flashing daybeacon #72 is rife with shoals abutting the channel.

Chart 11427 even warns of "Rocks" near unlighted daybeacon #86. This writer didn't try to find them, but conversations with local captains indicate they are indeed down there. Slow down and be absolutely sure of the proper course before cruising ahead.

A charted range south of unlighted daybeacon #78 may help navigators keep to the channel, which runs south of unlighted daybeacon #80. At #80, the channel turns ever so slightly to the north.

Between unlighted daybeacons #80 and #78, unlighted daybeacon #78A has been placed along the channel's northwesterly edge. Be sure to pass #78A to its fairly immediate southeasterly side. Don't stray too far to the south or southeast, or you could wander into the charted shallows south of #78.

Cape Coral Yacht Basin   Enter Cape Coral Yacht Basin by abandoning the river channel some 25 to 50 yards southwest of unlighted daybeacon #78. Set course for the mid-width of the canal west of Redfish Point. Along the way you will pass between unlighted daybeacons #1 and #2, then between #3 and #4. After you leave #3 and #4 in your wake, the long Cape Coral fishing pier will come abeam to port. At this point marked channels serving local docks cut to the east and west. Ignore these cuts and cruise into the mid-width of the canal dead ahead.

As you enter the canal, the fuel dock will come abeam to port, followed by the main harbor farther upstream in the charted, squared-off cove also to port.

On the Caloosahatchee River   Flashing daybeacon #73 denotes the channel's southeastern edge between unlighted daybeacon #74 and flashing daybeacon #72. This aid to navigation marks the charted tongue of 4-foot shallows abutting the channel. Obviously, you should pass northwest of #73.

Watch for the charted 2-foot shoal south and southeast of flashing daybeacon #72. Be sure to pass #72 close by its southeasterly side. Cruisers may choose to enter the channel leading to Deep Lagoon short of #72.

Gulf Harbour Yacht and Country Club   The marked entrance channel leading to the Gulf Harbour dockage basin cuts southeast between unlighted daybeacon #74 and flashing daybeacon #73. Use your binoculars to pick out the outermost channel markers, flashing daybeacons #1 and #2. Should you have any trouble (and you probably won't) locating this channel, look for a tall, beige, square-towered "lighthouse" towering over the southeastern shoreline. This tower guards the harbor entrance's southwesterly flank and displays a white light at night.

Set a course from the main river channel, designed to cruise directly between #1 and #2. After leaving these markers in your wake, pick out unlighted daybeacons #3 and #4 ahead. As you pass between #3 and #4, your course will lead you between the arms of twin stone breakwaters. Soon this track will pass into a sheltered harbor behind a barrier island. A long series of small, red unlighted daybeacons denotes a shelf of shallow water jutting out for a short distance from the shore of the barrier island. Pass all these aids to navigation by at least 10 yards to your starboard side.

Continue cruising into the heart of the basin. The dockmaster's office overlooks the harbor's southeasterly shores in the middle of the complex.

Deep Lagoon This channel is complicated by the presence of several local side cuts that do not appear on the current edition of chart 11427. To enter, break off from the Caloosahatchee some 300 yards southwest of flashing daybeacon #72. Set course to pass between the westernmost aids on the Deep Lagoon channel, unlighted daybeacons #1 and #2. Continue cruising straight ahead. Soon you will spot a small channel cutting off to starboard. Ignore this local passage and maintain your course to the east.

After cruising a bit farther into the stream's mouth, watch for a red and green junction daybeacon. Channels radiate out to port and starboard, as well as straight ahead, from this aid. To reach Deep Lagoon Boat Club, pass the junction daybeacon to your port side and cut sharply into the starboard-side (southward-running) channel. A group of mostly uncharted aids will bring you abeam of the new complex.

On the Caloosahatchee River The main river channel begins its approach to the Cape Coral fixed bridge northeast of flashing daybeacon #72. As you cruise to flashing daybeacon #70, the marked channel to the Landings will be passed southeast of your course, while a host of local channels may be spied to the northwest.

The Cape Coral span has a vertical clear-ance of 55 feet. Sail craft that need more height must forego visiting Fort Myers and cruising the remainder of the Okeechobee Waterway (which, incidentally, has one bridge east of Lake Okeechobee with a vertical clearance of only 49 feet).

Northeast of the Cape Coral bridge, the channel remains straightforward, with nothing but local cuts flanking the river as far as unlighted daybeacon #68. From this aid, captains who pilot vessels drawing 4 feet or less may choose to enter and anchor in Whiskey Creek on the southeastern shore.

Whiskey Creek Anchorage Set course from unlighted daybeacon #68 to pass between the outermost set of markers on the Whiskey Creek channel, unlighted daybeacons #1 and #2. This entire cut is an idle-speed, manatee zone. All craft should proceed strictly at slow speed.

After passing the last red daybeacon to your starboard side (did you remember "red, right, returning"?), the creek cuts sharply to starboard. You will spy the charted, low-level fixed bridge dead ahead. Anchor on the mid-width between the starboard turn and the bridge.

On the Caloosahatchee River Shallow water flanks the main channel to the northwest between unlighted daybeacons #68 and #64. East and northeast of this point, good water opens out on both sides of the passage for the most part to unlighted daybeacon #60.

The Caloosahatchee's newest, fixed high-rise bridge spans the river northeast of unlighted daybeacon #62. This span has a vertical clearance of 55 feet.

Cruisers choosing to visit Paradise Yacht Club can depart the main channel at unlighted daybeacon #58 and follow the marina's markers to the western banks. The harbor entrance lies immediately northwest of the innermost markers, unlighted daybeacons #18 and #19.

North-northeast of unlighted daybeacon #60, shallow water abuts a goodly portion of the river channel's westerly flank. Watch for leeway. You can use the charted range (both of its markers are charted as "#C") to help avoid the shallows.

Cruisers heading for Caloosa Isle Marina should leave the river channel just north of unlighted daybeacon #58 and set course to pass between the approach channel's outer markers, unlighted daybeacons #1 and #2. Once on this prolifically marked passage, favor the southwesterly side of the marked cut. This channel seems to be shoaling on its northern and northeasterly sides.

At flashing daybeacon #54, the main river channel begins to bend around to the northeast and heads on toward the Caloosahatchee fixed bridge. Short of the span, cruisers can access Royal Palm Yacht Club by the easy-to-follow channel cutting southeast, visit Marina Town to the northwest, or check out Centennial Harbour Marina guarding the southeasterly banks at flashing daybeacon #49.

Marina Town Yacht Club and Hancock Creek   The southeasternmost markers on the Marina Town-Hancock Creek channel sit close by the Caloosahatchee channel's northwestern flank, just northeast of unlighted daybeacon #52. The multitude of markers will carry you safely across the charted bar and in toward the northwestern banks. Close to shore, the channel takes a hard jog to starboard and eventually leads into the interior reaches of Hancock Creek.

To make good your entry into Marina Town Yacht Club, continue following the marked cut and watch for a broad offshoot cutting off to the north at unlighted daybeacons #25 and #26. Enter this stream by passing between #25 and #26. Continue along its mid-width as the canal flows through a sharp turn to the east. The marina docks will soon be obvious on the port-side shore.

Cruisers who choose to anchor in the small cove south-southwest of unlighted daybeacons #25 and #26 should depart the marked channel before passing between these two markers. Instead, cut sharply to the south-southwest and enter the mid-line of the small cove that you will sight dead ahead. For maximum swinging room, continue on the centerline into the rear third of the cove's waters. Remember, depths can run as thin as 4½ to 5 feet in this anchorage.

Centennial Harbour Marina   The breakwater-enclosed dockage basin of Centennial Harbour Marina guards the Caloosahatchee's southeasterly banks between flashing daybeacon #49 and the Caloosahatchee fixed bridge. The basin's entrance is found along its upstream (northeasterly) side.

On to Fort Myers   East- and westbound skippers alike should take great care while cruising along the channel southwest of the Caloosahatchee fixed bridge. Shallow water abuts the cut on its northwestern side, and it's pretty doggone easy to confuse the markers on the Marina Town passage with the main channel's aids to navigation. Be sure to come abeam of and pass unlighted daybeacon #52 to its southeasterly side and continue on straight to the bridge's central pass-through, favoring the southeastern side of the channel. Along the way, pass flashing daybeacon #49 to its fairly immediate northwesterly side.

As you approach this fixed span, slow down. Numerous signs warn that the entire stretch between the three Fort Myers bridges is an idle-speed, no-wake zone. The Florida Marine Patrol is known for its vigilance on these waters. All vessels should proceed strictly at slow speed.

The Caloosahatchee/Highway 41 Bypass fixed bridge has a vertical clearance of 55 feet. After leaving the span behind, you will observe a cool, airy park on the southeastern shores, followed by the Fort Myers Yacht Basin.

Fort Myers Bridges   As stated earlier, there are three bridges across the main Caloosahatchee channel adjacent to the downtown Fort Myers waterfront. Both spans of the Edison bridge are fixed structures and feature 56 feet of vertical clearance.

Thankfully, the NOAA charting folks have at last caught on to this on-the-water reality. The bridges are correctly depicted on the latest version of chart 11427!

On the Caloosahatchee   This chapter's coverage of the Caloosahatchee River ends at the Edison bridges. A continuing account of the upper Caloosahatchee and the Okeechobee Waterway can be found in my *Cruising Guide to Eastern Florida*.

Lofton Island Anchorage and Mooring Field
For best depths, cruisers should depart the main river channel immediately west of the westerly span of the Edison bridge. Cruise to the north-northwest, keeping the bridge about 25 yards off your starboard side. Shallower water lies off Lofton Island's easterly shoreline, so best depths can be maintained by heavily favoring the bridge's westerly face. Similarly, soundings off the western shores of Lofton Island are quite thin.

Eventually, after tracking your way north-northwest just off the Edison bridge's westerly face, you will come abeam of the correctly charted, broad ribbon of deeper water that stretches to the southwest. Turn to port and follow these good depths to a point some 50 yards off Lofton Island's northerly banks. Here you will find room to anchor, or those captains who pilot a sail craft can pick up one of the city-provided mooring buoys. Chances are that you will already find several fellow craft ensconced in this haven.

Pine Island Sound

If it weren't for the difference in the color and depth of the water, the lack of island vegetation and stilted houses along the shores, this writer could almost think of a cruise through Pine Island Sound as a sojourn amidst the northern Abaco chain in the Bahamas. Even with all the obvious differences, there is that same feel of adventure mixed with myriad gunk-holing and anchorage possibilities. As the story of our cruising couple at the beginning of this chapter points out, it's an easy place on which to wander off and forget that the rest of the world is out there. In short, Pine Island Sound comprises some of the most wonderful cruising grounds in Western Florida.

Pine Island Sound's southern reaches are bordered to the west by the long body of Sanibel Island. This isle was reviewed in the first section of this chapter. To the east, the lightly developed shores of Pine Island are a delight, as well as a reminder of a colorful past.

North of Sanibel, Captiva and North Captiva islands offer marina facilities and a few possible overnight anchorages. The various passes between these islands are unmarked and tricky for strangers.

Cayo Costa is completely in its natural state and will be preserved in the foreseeable future as a state park. Cruisers should make every effort to visit this wonderland of white-sand beaches, lush scrub growth, and maritime forests. There are at least two anchorages along its length, and the fabulous inn at Cabbage Key is also within striking distance.

In addition to these larger bodies of land, Pine Island Sound is peppered with many smaller islands. The majority (though not all) of these islets are wildlife preserves, and landing is not permitted. Many species of birds use these small islands as nesting grounds. The hundreds of birds and dozens of species present are truly magnificent. The National Park Service requests that cruising craft stay at least 50 yards offshore from these protected beaches. It's just possible that a closer approach could scare nesting birds violently out of their nests, possibly causing injury to their young.

Feel free to look from a safer distance, however. Have your binoculars ready! Pine Island Sound is a mecca for bird watchers by all accounts.

We will now rejoin the Western Florida ICW where we left it at the western terminus of the Miserable Mile, earlier in this chapter. The Waterway darts north through the heart of Pine Island Sound, past deep and reliable Boca Grande inlet, before flowing north into the upper reaches of Pine Island Sound, which is known appropriately enough as Gasparilla Sound. This body of water is bordered to the west by wonderful Gasparilla Island. With its beautiful Victorian inn, two lighthouses, quaint downtown, and a plenitude of wonderful restaurants, this isle should be on every cruiser's list of must-stop ports of call.

The ICW takes its leave of Gasparilla Sound at the long bridge and causeway connecting the Florida mainland to Gasparilla Island. Continued coverage of the Waterway will be presented in the next chapter.

St. James City Channel (Standard Mile 4)

St. James City is a residential community occupying the southern tip of Pine Island, which displays a strong bent toward sportfishing. A marked and charted channel leads northwest from the ICW's flashing daybeacon #13 to an intricate series of canals serving St. James City and southern Pine Island. On-site research reveals that this passage has low-water depths as thin as 4 feet.

York IslandAnchorage (Standard Mile 5, 26 29.038 North/082 05.731 West)

In northwestern or northerly breezes, cruising captains can anchor in minimum 7-foot depths off the southern shores of York Island, well northwest of the ICW's flashing daybeacon #13. Good water runs to within 100 yards of the all-natural banks. This anchorage is quite open to winds blowing from any other quarter. Unless light airs or northerly winds are definitely in the forecast, it would be better to consider the haven described below.

Be sure to anchor well east of the Waterway's flashing daybeacon #20. This aid marks the southwesterly tip of a prohibited sea-grass flat. Anchoring on these waters is a real no-no.

Ding Darling Anchorage (Standard Mile 5.5, 26 27.495 North/082 05.532 West)

The wide and mostly deep cove south of flashing daybeacon #16 is an absolutely enchanting anchorage for any size pleasure craft. The shores are part of the J. N. ("Ding") Darling National Wildlife Refuge and are magnificently in their natural state. Good depths of 5½ to mostly 6 feet run to within 200 yards of the banks. Protection is excellent from all but northerly winds. This is a superior anchorage that this writer highly recommends to his fellow cruisers.

Unfortunately, the local government on adjacent Sanibel Island now limits stays in this anchorage to 48 hours. Go figure.

Chino Island Anchorage (Standard Mile 8, 26 30.086 North/082 07.718 West)

Northeast of unlighted daybeacon #24, visiting cruisers can carry a good 7½ to 8 feet of water to within 75 yards of the Chino Island shoreline. During any number of visits to these waters, we have often observed any number of large sail craft anchored in the lee of this isle. The anchorage is well protected from northern and northeasterly blows but growth resembling mangrove. Chino Island is privately owned, and landing by dinghy is not permitted. If the weather forecast is cooperative, this is yet another in the long list of wonderful overnight stops on Pine Island Sound.

Wulfert Channel

An indifferently marked, dead-end channel runs west from flashing daybeacon #26 to Wulfert Channel and a tiny, now-closed inlet that used to be called Blind Pass. As this channel is shallow, and now, with the inlet's closing, leads pretty much nowhere, we strongly suggest that captains avoid this cut entirely.

Captiva Island

Captiva Island sits directly north of Sanibel and is joined to the latter body of land by a

wide open to breezes blowing from any other direction. The island's shores are completely undeveloped and are enshrouded with thick fixed highway bridge. In many ways, Captiva is a carbon copy of Sanibel, except that it lacks large wildlife refuges and is, for the most part, a bit less crowded.

Captiva is five miles in length but seldom more than a half-mile wide. In earlier times, Captiva served as a "lime plantation." In this sort of agricultural enterprise, plants are grown in the rich limestone (hence the name) soil. The original owner, a man named Chadwick, planted hundreds of palm trees under which modern visitors still enjoy a pleasant shade. The great hurricane of 1926 blew so much salt water over the island that the land was "ruined for agriculture."

By 1938 tourists had begun arriving by mailboat and the island has been developed as a resort colony ever since. Today, the South Seas Plantation development occupies 330 acres on Captiva's northern tip.

Roosevelt Channel Facilities and Anchorage (Standard Mile 13, Various Lats/Lons—see below)

Minimum depths of 5 feet lead from unlighted daybeacon #38 down a surprisingly well-outlined passage into Roosevelt channel, running between Captiva Island and Buck Key. Two marinas and one anchorage serving Captiva Island are both found along this passage.

Moving north to south, the first facility, Jensen's Twin Palms Marina (239-472-5800), lies west of unlighted daybeacon #13. This is a strictly small-craft, albeit superfriendly, facility that offers only gasoline and a bait-and-tackle store. Low-water depths at the fuel dock run 6 feet or so.

Between Jensen's and Tween Waters, veteran Western Florida cruisers will note several docks associated with the Green Flash

1. Tween Waters Marina

Restaurant (239-472-3337). These fixed wooden piers sport soundings of 5 feet or better. There should be enough room for vessels as large as 36 feet. We have not had the opportunity to review the bill of fare at this dining attraction. Please let us know your experiences by e-mailing us at opcom@cruisingguide.com.

Green Flash restaurant, Captiva Island

The larger Tween Waters Marina (26 30.640 North/082 11.353 West) is found a good distance to the south on the Captiva Island shoreline, southwest of unlighted day-beacon #19. This facility is associated with a large inn and three on-site restaurants. The marina accepts transients, but space is somewhat limited at its two wooden, fixed piers. Mean low-water dockside soundings are some 6 feet for the outer berths, while the inner slips have soundings around 5 feet. Full power and water connections are supplemented by gasoline, diesel fuel, waste pump-out service, and a variety store. The air-conditioned showers are in good shape, and there is also a non-climate-controlled Laundromat on site. Mechanical repairs can sometimes be arranged through independent contractors.

Tween Waters Inn features a host of excellent rooms, a newly opened fitness center, hot tubs, tennis courts, and a swimming pool with an outside bar. A three-mile-long, pristine public beach is found just across the street. If you need a day or two off the water

with solid ground under your feet, this resort is very convenient.

When it comes time to satisfy the old appetite, I highly suggest the on-site Old Captiva House restaurant. Housed in a "conchlike" building recalling the Florida of yesteryear, it delights diners with baked grouper, plus other seafood entrées, as well as excellent steaks. There are also two other on-site restaurants, plus two bars and the waterside Kayak Deli.

How's that for a full-service resort!

Tween Waters Marina (239) 472-5161
http://www.tween-waters.com

Approach depth—6 feet (minimum)
Dockside depth—5-6 feet (MLW)
Accepts transients—yes
Transient dockage rate—average
Fixed wooden pier—yes
Dockside power connections—30 and 50 amp
Dockside water connections—yes
Waste pump-out—yes
Showers—yes
Laundromat—yes
Gasoline—yes
Diesel fuel—yes
Variety store—yes
Restaurant and snack bar—three on site (plus one bar)

A popular anchorage is found just off the Roosevelt Channel, near unlighted daybeacon #20. Depths vary widely in this anchorage, ranging from as little as 5 to as much as 14 feet of water. Shelter is not adequate for heavy weather, and the anchorage is wide open to northern and northeasterly blows. The shores of Captiva Island display moderate to heavy residential and condo development, while Buck Key to the east is completely in its natural state.

Note that there is no more dinghy dockage at Tween Waters Marina. In times past, cruisers anchored in this haven could easily dinghy ashore at Tween Waters, but apparently, some few abused this privilege, and now it has spoiled the scene for everyone.

South Seas Plantation Marina (Standard Mile 13.5, 26 32.912 North/082 11.791 West)

One of the best-known marinas in Pine Island Sound is found near the western foot of the marked and charted channel running west from the ICW's flashing daybeacon #39. South Seas Plantation Marina is part of a huge condo and private-home development near the northern tip of Captiva Island. The facility offers very protected dockage for transient and resident craft alike at both fixed wooden and concrete piers in the charted basin northwest of unlighted daybeacon #21.

Before pushing on to discuss the many positive attributes of South Seas Plantation, we must spend a few minutes exploring its entrance-channel woes. This facility has gained something of a reputation due to these problems over the past several years, but we found that the highly competent dockmaster staff is doing all in its power to minimize these worries. In fact, we were very, very impressed with the honesty and helpfulness of the assistant dockmaster during out last visit.

The problem stems from currents courtesy of nearby Redfish Pass. These swiftly moving waters continue to push a shoal into the northern flank of the South Seas approach channel near unlighted daybeacon #16. The cut was dredged in 2002, and for the moment, it holds 5½ to 6 feet of water.

However, barring any future dredging, these soundings will deteriorate over time.

Recognizing this problem, the county has marked an alternate (but currently uncharted) channel flowing southwest and eventually west from the ICW's flashing daybeacon #39. For the moment, neither the South Seas dockmasters nor this writer suggest that cruising-size craft make use of this alternate passage. Rather, we suggest the main, charted channel. This situation could, however, change over time, and the day may (or may not) come when the alternate channel will be the best way to gain access to South Seas Plantation. We *strongly* suggest that all cruisers make contact with the dockmasters at South Seas Plantation well before their arrival and seek information as to the best plan of access. If past experience is any guide (and it usually is), these good folks will tell you how to get through with nary a scratch.

Once the pesky entrance channel is behind you, the South Seas' ultrasheltered dockage basin will open out northwest of unlighted daybeacon #21. This basin has typical soundings of 6 to 8 feet, but a few of the innermost slips carry only 5 feet of water.

Full power (including a few 100-amp services) and water connections are readily available at each berth. The docks also have cable-television and telephone hookups. The marina maintains spotless, climate-controlled bathrooms and showers, plus a non-air-conditioned Laundromat. There is also an on-site variety store with an extensive deli. Gasoline, diesel fuel, and free waste pump-out service are offered as well.

Transients can enjoy a cooling dip at the swimming pool a short stroll away or a rousing game of tennis at any of several nearby courts. If golf is more your thing, there is a

1. South Seas Plantation Marina

PGA-certified nine-hole course in the complex, and visiting cruisers are welcome to use it.

When it's time for dinner, you have four restaurants, a pool bar, and a pizzeria to choose from. This writer can confidently recommend the King's Crown, a "formal gourmet restaurant." Better dig out your last clean shirt for this one. Those wanting a more informal atmosphere will find the freshest of seafood and (optional) open-air dining at Captain Al's to be delightful. Free trolley service is provided throughout the spacious South Seas Plantation complex, and you might use this novel method of transportation to visit Chadwick Restaurant, some 1½ miles from the docks. Captain Al's and King's Crown can be reached through the main South Seas switchboard, while Chadwick can be direct-dialed at (239) 472-7575.

Many cruisers with a sweet tooth (like this writer) frequent Uncle Bob's Ice Cream Emporium. It's open late into the evening. Yuuummm!

Cruisers who want to do a little dry-ground exploration can take advantage of the on-site Enterprise Rent A Car office. Ask any of the friendly marina staff to make contact for you.

Speaking of the trolley, visiting cruisers may very well want to take a trolley ride to the complex's southern gate. Just beyond, you will find a nice strip shopping area with a host of gift shops and CW's Market and Deli (239-472-5111), a most useful specialty grocery store. A walk of four or five additional blocks holds even more promise.

If you don't take heed to any of this writer's other dining recommendations in this guide, please listen to this one. The (no kidding) Mucky Duck Restaurant (239-472-3434) fronts onto the Gulf-side beach, just a quick walk from South Seas Plantation's southern gateway. Ask any local for directions. The hamburgers are absolutely scrumptious and the fried-grouper sandwiches, well—words just fail me. There is nothing on the menu that isn't good, and the atmosphere is wonderful—sort of a British-style pub with the waves crashing in the background. Every time we visit Captiva, we feel it is mandatory to re-review this restaurant, just to be sure the quality hasn't suffered, you understand.

Another superb Captiva Island dining attraction is the Bubble Room Restaurant (15001 Captiva Drive, 239-472-5558). Visitors up for a walk of three blocks or so from the South Seas gate can track their way to this memorable restaurant. The name is derived from the old-style Christmas bubble lights that are sprinkled throughout the dining room. There are no bubbles in the cuisine, however. It's first rate!

South Seas Plantation Marina can accurately be described as having some of the finest amenities and services on Pine Island Sound. Cruisers can rely on a warm and knowledgeable welcome, and the amenities are truly world class.

South Seas Plantation Marina (239) 472-5111

Approach depth—5½-6 feet minimum (low tide)
Dockside depth—5-8 feet
Accepts transients—yes
Transient dockage rate—above average
Fixed wooden and concrete piers—yes
Dockside power connections—up to 100 amp
Dockside water connections—yes
Waste pump-out—yes
Showers—yes
Laundromat—yes
Gasoline—yes
Diesel fuel—yes
Ship's and variety store—yes
Restaurant—four in complex and others nearby

South Seas Plantation Marina, Captiva Island

Redfish Pass (Standard Mile 13.5)

After traversing the channel leading to South Seas Plantation Marina as far west as unlighted daybeacons #19 and #20, it is possible to break off to the north and follow a fairly broad but mostly unmarked track to the inlet known as Redfish Pass. By paralleling the western shoreline, 6-foot depths can be carried into the interior reaches of the pass.

This inlet separates Captiva Island, to the south, from North Captiva Island. No bridge as yet crosses the pass, and it is hoped none ever will.

At the moment there seems to be a fairly deep and reliable channel through this seaward cut. County-sponsored markings outline Redfish Pass's seaward channel, and currently minimum 6-foot depths can be expected. Of course, on-the-water conditions may be very different by the time of your arrival. Most of the channel markers are not charted, and they are frequently shifted and changed to follow the ever-moving sands. Nevertheless, for the moment at least, local captains seem to be making good use of this outlet to the briny blue.

North Captiva Island

North Captiva still enjoys what one writer has termed as "true island status." You must still travel by water to reach its shores, and landlubbers can only look longingly across the waters of Redfish Pass.

Once upon a day, intrepid Pine Island fishermen maintained an on-again, off-again occupancy in a small village set on the shores of North Captiva's Safety Harbor. With the demise of large-scale commercial fishing on the sound, the old buildings fell into disrepair. Until just a few years ago, cruisers with shallow-draft vessels could anchor abeam of the one-time settlement and dinghy ashore for exploration.

The last remnants of the Safety Harbor village were destroyed with the development of a private club around the shores of the harbor. Today's visitors will find only modern buildings overlooking the water, with one interesting exception. One of the old stilted fishing houses remains on the northeastern point of Safety Harbor. This historic structure has now been restored as a private home, and speaks to passing mariners of those rugged, simple days of the Pine Island Sound commercial fisherman, which are now gone forever.

Safety Harbor and Anchorage (Standard Mile 17, 26 36.340 North/082 13.064 West—Anchorage)

During fair weather (only!), cruisers might choose to anchor off the southern flank of Captiva Pass, north of the charted channel leading to Safety Harbor and behind the easterly banks of the northernmost point of North Captiva Island. The channel leading from the ICW's unlighted daybeacon #48 to Safety Harbor and this anchorage is more than slightly confusing and sometimes frustrating

(see below), but many navigators will be able to track their way to this overnight haven and maintain minimum 6-foot depths.

Once behind North Captiva's northerly point, cruisers can anchor in some 6 to 12 feet of water. There is good protection to the west and southwest and some minimal shelter for light breezes blowing from the northwest. Otherwise, this anchorage is wide open. It is most definitely not the place to spend the evening in high winds or thunderstormy conditions. The adjacent North Captiva shoreline exhibits moderate residential development.

Safety Harbor itself is accessed by way of an indifferently marked, but charted, channel that leads south from the deep water abutting the southeasterly reaches of Captiva Pass to a large, almost landlocked lagoon. This once-secret refuge used to house an abandoned fishing village. Those times are unfortunately in the past, and the land is now intensively developed as a housing and condo complex known as the Safety Harbour Club.

The channel itself is tricky and currently exhibits minimum 4- to 4½-foot depths. We do not recommend this passage for any craft larger than 34 feet, and most certainly it is not for vessels drawing 4 feet or more.

At one point, just when making the turn into the main body of Safety Harbor, you will pass one of the old stilted fishing houses. Captains straying just a mite too far to the east will find themselves in 1 to 2 feet of water.

If you do find your way through the Safety Harbor channel, you can tie off temporarily to a fixed wooden pier, abeam of unlighted daybeacon #17. This dock is associated with the adjacent Barnacle Phil's Restaurant. Dining patrons are free to moor here while sampling the restaurant's delights, but overnight stays

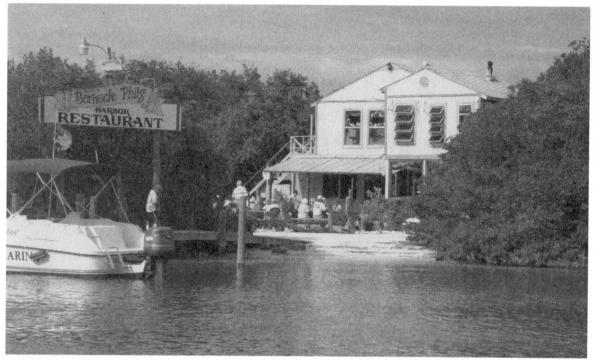

Barnacle Phil's Restaurant, Safety Harbor

are not allowed. Judging from the huge crowds we witnessed at Barnacle Phil's during a recent visit, this place must be doing something right. Many dining patrons were seated at long, family-style tables in the open air and within easy sight of the water. A very good time seemed to be had by all.

While docked at the Barnacle Phil's pier, you might also ask directions for the Island Market Place Deli and Groceries. Galley restocking was never so easy.

There is no transient dockage available in Safety Harbor at the current time. All the many piers and slips you will spy are part of the very private Safety Harbor Club. So, except for the restaurant dock and its culinary attractions, visiting cruisers need only traverse

the difficult Safety Harbor channel for sight-seeing purposes.

Captiva Pass and Anchorage (Standard Mile 18.5, 26 36.785 North/082 13.266 West)

The inlet cutting between North Captiva Island and Cayo Costa (island) is a mixed bag for cruisers. On the one hand, the pass's seaward passage is anything but straightforward. Even the channel from the ICW is flanked by unmarked shoals. On the other hand, the interior reaches of Captiva Pass are deep and provide one of the most delightful fair-weather anchorages in Pine Island Sound. During weekends a fleet of local craft about the size of the Spanish Armada descend on the pass and anchor just behind (east of) the southern tip of Cayo Costa. This island is part of a state park (see below) and is almost entirely in its natural state. The inlet is overlooked by tall Australian pines from the shores of Cayo Costa, with a beautiful beach a short step away to the northwest.

Minimum 8-foot depths run to within 50 yards (or sometimes closer) of the eastern side of Cayo Costa's southern tip (just where you would expect good depths from a study of chart 11427). For best shelter, try anchoring amidst the charted 10- to 11-foot depths just north of the pass. Here you will be sheltered from western and northwestern winds. Strong breezes from any other quarter call for a different choice of overnight stops.

Tidal currents, as you would expect, run quite swiftly through the pass. Be sure the hook is well set before breaking out the dinghy and heading ashore.

The Stilted Fish Houses of Pine Island Sound

East of flashing daybeacon #52, passing cruisers can still see some of the houses built on stilts which are so much part and parcel of Pine Island Sound's colorful history. While some of these structures have sadly fallen victim to the passage of the years, many have survived and some have now been renovated as private vacation homes and even permanent residences.

The history of Pine Island Sound's stilted houses began in 1897 with the development of the Punta Gorda Fish Company. To accommodate the booming trade in commercial fishing which soon materialized on the sound's waters, the company built a whole series of houses raised atop stilts directly on the water. The intrepid Pine Island anglers would live for weeks at a time in these primitive structures while harvesting mullet from the sound. Other stilted buildings were used as "ice houses." Writing in the April 1989 issue of *Southern Boating* magazine, Jane T. Adams described something of the life of the Pine Island fisherpeople:

> The fisherman's job was arduous. . . . The gill netters and seine fishermen often worked together. Mr. Quednau recalls that he . . . and two crew members caught 33,000 pounds of mullet in 10 days. . . . On occasion, 40,000 to 60,000 pounds were caught at a time. The gill netters would then take their catches to the ice houses to be kept cold until the run boats could transport them to the Punta Gorda wharf. . . . Since refrigeration was so important to the welfare of the industry, it was quickly discovered that the ice houses could be moved. . . . Two barges would flank the building at low tide and slide large beams underneath it. At high tide, the barges and beams lifted the building off its pilings. The barges then moved the structure to another location.

While, tragically, some of the old stilted houses have been wantonly destroyed, others are now being preserved as a reminder of those early days of Florida's commercial fishing trade. Mariners should take every opportunity to observe these vanishing pieces of Americana for themselves.

Alternate Pine Island Sound Channel (Standard Mile 19.5)

A wide channel strikes north-northeast from flashing daybeacon #52 (on the ICW) and eventually leads past Useppa Island until finally passing into Charlotte Harbor hard by the northwestern tip of Pine Island (charted as Bokeelia Island). While the southerly portion of this route is unmarked, the broad width of the channel allows most navigators (particularly those with chart plotters) to keep to good depths with careful attention to the surrounding landmarks. Minimum depths run around 6 feet on this passage, but most soundings are better than 8 feet.

Nervy skippers might consider working their way carefully to the east from a position north of flashing daybeacon #52 on the alternate channel, toward the charted stilted houses. Be on guard against the charted shallows.

South of unlighted daybeacons #5 and #6, the alternate channel skirts Useppa Island to the west. This island, its facilities, and its adjacent anchorage will be reviewed below in the discussion concerning the Pine Island Section of the ICW.

A reliable, marked channel north of Useppa Island allows mariners ready access from the ICW to the alternate Pine Island Sound channel and vice versa. Minimum depths are 7 feet in this cut, with most sections boasting at least 8 feet of water.

As you are traversing this connecting cut, look north to charted Mondongo Island. This body of land features a beautiful private home. Boy, talk about getting away from it all.

Back on the alternate Pine Island Sound Channel, it would be possible in fair weather (only) for captains to anchor off the southeastern shores of Patricio Island, between unlighted daybeacons #6 and #7 (near 26 40.653 North/082 12.041 West). You will be protected only from northern breezes, but in light airs, this is a delightful place to spend an evening, overlooked by the isle's wild shores.

Jug Creek and Four Winds Marina

The alternate Pine Island Sound channel eventually intersects a marked cut leading into Jug Creek, southwest of flashing daybeacon #8. Jug Creek lies between Pine Island to the south and Bokeelia Island to the (you guessed it) north. The stream winds through a series of mangrove stands and, after much twisting and turning, eventually leads to a marina facility. The channel is shallow, with low-tide depths of only 3½ feet. Clearly, this limits the passage and its associated facilities to boats drawing less than 3½ feet.

Four Winds Marina is found on the most upstream section of the Bokeelia Island channel, past unlighted daybeacon #39. This is a surprisingly complete and extra-friendly, down-home-type marina. The facility's obvious drawback is its 3½-foot entrance depth on the Jug Creek channel. If your draft can squeak through this thin water (and the 4-foot low-water dockside depths at the marina), then you should not hesitate to make use of this fine facility.

Four Winds gladly accepts transients and provides overnight berths at fixed wooden piers replete with water hookups and 30-amp (or less) power connections. The harbor is extremely well sheltered and would be a good spot to ride out heavy weather. Gasoline and diesel fuel are on hand, as are clean showers and a full-line ship's and variety store. Mechanical repairs are available for both gasoline- and diesel-powered craft, and boats up to 30 feet can be hauled out via a forklift. The marina also features dry-stack storage for smaller powercraft. An on-site restaurant, the Lazy Flamingo (239-283-5959), makes for convenient dining. Seperate boat slips are available for restaurant customers (while dining), without the necessity of obtaining a berth at the marina.

All in all, this writer could not help but like Four Winds Marina, in spite of its skimpy water and the long cruise necessary to reach its docks from the ICW. If you're not in a hurry, and your craft draws less than 4 feet, give this facility a try for a different cruising experience.

Four Winds Marina (239) 283-0250
http://www.fourwindsmarina.com

Approach depth—3½ feet (minimum, low water)
Dockside depth—4 feet (minimum, low water)
Accepts transients—yes
Transient dockage rate—average
Fixed wooden piers—yes
Dockside power connections—30 amp
Dockside water connections—yes
Showers—yes
Gasoline—yes
Diesel fuel—yes
Mechanical repairs—yes
Ship's and variety store—yes
Restaurant—on site

Cabbage Key (Standard Mile 21.5, 26 39.402 North/082 13.350 West)

Let us now return to the ICW route and review the Pine Island Sound facilities and anchorages between flashing daybeacon #52, where our discussion of the alternate channel (above) began, and Gasparilla Island.

North of flashing daybeacon #60, a charted channel cuts sharply west to an interesting port of call. Cabbage Key is home to an inn of the same name, and its history is more than fascinating. The rambling, venerable house that today houses Cabbage Key Inn was built in 1938 as a winter home for Alan Rinehart, son of American mystery writer Mary Roberts Rinehart. It is said that Ms. Rinehart actually penned some of her most famous stories while visiting with her son, possibly including the famous *The Circular Staircase*.

Alan bought Cabbage Key for $2,500 and spent another $125,000 on his house. The walls are painted a cool white with green trim, and guests are cooled by large ceiling fans. The private-home-turned-inn sits perched atop a huge shell mound left over from the days of the Caloosa Indians.

The house was first opened as an inn in 1942 and has been operated continuously as a hostelry and restaurant ever since. It does not require any imagination on this writer's part to understand why patrons are attracted to this lovely, peaceful isle. Oh, yes—the inn's "nature walk" among the island's tropical blend of palms, royal poincianas, and cabbage palms is not to be missed, either.

Another unique aspect of Cabbage Key Inn is the wallpaper adorning its dining room. This room is papered with genuine one-dollar bills donated and autographed by the inn's guests. According to Laura Stewart and Suzanne Hupp, writing in their absolutely fascinating book, *Florida Historic Homes*, "the practice began years ago when a pessimistic patron tacked a dollar on the wall with his name on it. That way, or so the story goes, even if he lost everything, he could still come back to the pleasant island for a drink."

Unfortunately, we must report that the interior of Cabbage Key Inn seems darker and a bit dingier to us than in times past. It looked as if the whole place could use a good cleaning.

It should also be noted that the luncheon crowd carried out to Cabbage Key from the mainland has grown considerably. The midday meal has, quite frankly, become rather touristy in character. To experience the full charms of Cabbage Key dining, this writer now suggests that you pay the inn an evening visit.

Cabbage Key can only be reached by water. Cruisers can, of course, find their way to the inn's docks with ease.

The marina associated with Cabbage Key Inn is found at the western terminus of the marked channel. While transients are readily accepted, be prepared to be greeted by an abrupt dockmaster who will likely inquire forcibly whether you are there to stay overnight or to have a meal. If the answer is no to both questions, you will be asked to move along immediately.

Visiting vessels will find berths at somewhat

Cabbage Key Inn (rear view)

sparse fixed wooden piers with full water and power connections. Dockage for boats larger than 40 feet is somewhat limited. All skippers would be well advised to make advance dockage reservations. Entrance depths are an impressive 6 to 8 feet, with similar soundings dockside. While no fuel or repairs are available, the marina does feature fair showers and a Laundromat.

Cabbage Key Inn Marina (239) 283-2278
  http://www.cabbagekey.com

Approach depth—6-8 feet
Dockside depth—6½-8 feet
Accepts transients—yes
Transient dockage rate—average
Fixed wooden piers—yes
Dockside power connections—30 and 50 amp
Dockside water connections—yes
Showers—yes
Laundromat—yes
Restaurant—on site

Useppa Island and Associated Anchorages (Standard Mile 21.5, Various Lats/Lons—see below)

Like Cabbage Key, Useppa Island can only be reached by water. This body of land is home to an ultra-exclusive resort known as the Useppa Club. The development's fine homes set on huge lots can be seen peeping out from the well-vegetated shores of Useppa Island from the water. The houses make for an attractive view, to say the least. The club's marina (239-283-5005) is found at the eastern terminus of the marked channel that heads off from the Waterway's eastern flank between flashing daybeacons #63 and #64. Sadly enough, transients are not accepted at this facility, though the dockmaster has informed this writer that "prospective members" are

Useppa Club, Useppa Island

allowed a trial visit. Better hold on to your wallet.

Even those of us who do not qualify financially to be considered "prospective members" can visit Useppa's waters courtesy of two good anchorages adjacent to the island shores. The most easily accessible of the two is found just off the ICW, east and northeast of unlighted daybeacon #61 and opposite the Cabbage Key Inn Channel (near 26 39.504 North/082 12.935 West). Here boats can get off the Waterway and hold minimum 6-foot depths to within 75 yards of the island shoreline. A bit farther out from shore, soundings improve to 9 feet or so. Protection is excellent from eastern, northeastern, and southeastern

1. Cabbage Key Inn

breezes and there is even some shelter from westerly airs. Strong winds from the south or (particularly) the north would be a problem.

In fair weather, it's a quick dinghy trip from this anchorage across the ICW to the docks of Cabbage Key Inn. Unless you have some fresh Florida lobster in the galley, I would suggest taking this dinghy ride for your evening's repast.

Useppa Island's other anchorage is accessed by first traveling the deep, marked channel north of the island that we met in our discussion of the Pine Island alternate channel. At unlighted daybeacon #4, you can curve around to the south and follow the correctly charted band of deep water abutting the island's eastern beaches. Here boats can anchor (near 26 39.954 North/082 12.555 West) in 7- to 8-foot depths with plenty of protection from westerly winds. There is little protection from strong breezes blowing from any other direction. While this is certainly a fair-weather anchorage, Useppa's attractive shoreline may well draw many skippers to this spot during appropriate weather conditions.

Of course, it goes almost without saying that you should not attempt to dinghy ashore from either of the Useppa Island anchorages described above. The entire island is very private.

Point Blanco Anchorages (Standard Mile 23, Various Lats/Lons—see below)

In westerly winds cruising craft of any description can anchor just off the ICW in 8-foot depths along the deep waters off Point Blanco, north of flashing daybeacon #64, near 26 40.681 North/082 13.488 West. Drop the hook off the point's eastern flank. Here the beautifully green shore is overlooked by tall Australian pines that sigh in the wind and lull you to sleep. You will be open to the wake of vessels passing by on the ICW, and protection is minimal for heavy weather.

Wild-eyed captains piloting vessels that can stand some 4-foot soundings might choose to carefully follow a difficult, unmarked channel to the charted deeper water behind Point Blanco. By following the shores as they cut first north, then east behind the point, you can find your way into a super-sheltered basin with wonderful protection from even the most foul weather, near 26 40.673 North/082 13.616 West. Depths in the basin itself run 5 to 9 feet, but again, you will have to plow through some thin 4-foot waters to get there, and one mistake can land you in about 12 inches of water. The encompassing shores are well wooded and completely in their natural state. Be sure to read the navigational account of this anchorage in the next section of this chapter before attempting entry. Even with these specific instructions, you may need a touch of luck to stay off the bottom.

Pelican Bay Anchorage and Cayo Costa State Park (Standard Mile 25, 26 41.184 North/082 14.570 West)

The last refuge adjacent to the ICW on Pine Island Sound south of Boca Grande Pass is found on the waters of broad Pelican Bay, west-southwest of unlighted daybeacon #74 (the former position of unlighted daybeacon #72). If you can stand the 4- to (mostly) 4½-foot MLW entrance depths, this is one of the best anchorages on Pine Island Sound. The bay is surrounded by the magnificently undeveloped shores of Punta Blanca Island to the east and Cayo Costa to the west. Cayo Costa State Park maintains a fixed wooden dock on the bay's western shore (near 26 41.156 North/082 14.697 West). While overnight slips (lacking any power and water connections) can be rented for $10, these berths are really only appropriate for small craft. Depths at the outer piers run 5 to 6 feet, while only 3 to 4 feet of water is found at the inner slips. Most boats should anchor in the bay and dinghy in to the docks.

This park dock is a very fortunate find for cruisers, as it provides ready access to the island and its park. Cayo Costa is owned entirely by the state of Florida and it remains the largest undeveloped barrier island along

1. Cayo Costa State Park Dock

the western shores of the Sunshine State. The park rangers run a shuttle from time to time between the docks and the Gulf-side beaches. Here, visitors will discover a campground, picnic area, and bathrooms. Please note that trash collection at the park docks is no longer offered as it was in years past.

For the truly adventurous among us, it's possible to take a long, long dinghy ride south to charted Murdock Bayou (south of charted Primo Island). Study chart 11427 and note that the westerly branch of the bayou cuts back to the north and eventually leads to a shallow, lakelike body of water. The passage from the main bayou to the lake cuts between (and under) dense, overhanging mangroves. It resembles nothing so much as a tunnel set amidst lush vegetation. This is one of the most unique cruising experiences in Western Florida, but please remember that approach depths are quite shallow. Perform your explorations strictly by dinghy.

Cayo Costa was once inhabited by the Caloosa Indians, as is evidenced by the many shell mounds archeologists have identified on the island. In later years there was a small fishing village on the isle's shores, but today the only human residents are the park rangers.

Well, they may be the only human residents, but Cayo Costa is a treasure chest of local wildlife. The island features such diverse terrain as pine forests, oak-palm hammocks, and mangrove swamps. Amidst this varied landscape, quiet visitors may observe ospreys, bald eagles, and the magnificent frigate birds. These creatures have the largest wingspan for their body size of any bird in the world. In addition, one of the state's largest colonies of white and brown pelicans resides on Cayo Costa. If you are into bird watching, it would be easy to linger on this timeless isle for weeks at a time.

An early morning walk on the nearby deserted beaches of Cayo Costa is something that must be experienced to be understood. Walking along the wet sand, with the sun just beginning to peep over the isle's easterly reaches, this writer was struck with the thought that once all of Western Florida was just like this. How fortunate that we in the cruising community plying the waters of this coastline still have the opportunity for such an intensely isolated and personal experience.

The entrance into Pelican Bay is known appropriately enough as Pelican Pass. This passage carries meager depths of 4 to 4½ feet at low water, though we have often observed sail craft drawing better than 4 feet entering and leaving the bay during high and mid-tide. Be sure to read the navigational account of Pelican Pass below before attempting first-time entry.

Once on Pelican Bay's interior reaches, depths improve to 5½ feet or better along a broad band. Consider dropping the hook once abeam of the park docks to the west (near 26 41.183 North/082 14.570 West) amidst 5½ MLW depths. While a legion of local craft regularly cruise the waters south of this point, there are many unmarked shoals to worry with.

If you prefer to anchor a bit in somewhat deeper waters (6 feet MLW or better), and do not really care about proximity to the park docks, consider dropping the hook farther to the north, near 26 41.495 North/082 14.595 West. This anchor-down spot is far closer to the Pelican Pass entrance and is very convenient for mariners who want to make an early morning getaway.

Pelican Bay is sheltered enough for light to moderate airs, but it is not the sort of spot where this writer would want to ride out a full gale. Check the forecast and pick a sunny day of fair breezes for your visit.

The Meeting of the Waters

North of flashing daybeacon #75, the ICW skirts out into a broad body of water which charts 11427 and 11425 label as Charlotte Harbor. Personally, I think of these waters as the northern reaches of Pine Island Sound, with the foot of broad Charlotte Harbor found to the east and northeast. Whatever you call it, it can be bit of a shock for mariners to find themselves on such an open section of the ICW where the waters seem to go on and on in almost every direction. To the west lies reliable Boca Grande Inlet. The Waterway cuts north into Gasparilla Sound past the island of the same name, with its many facilities and lovely Victorian inn.

Boca Grande Pass (Standard Mile 26.5)

The inlet lying between Cayo Costa and Gasparilla Island boasts the deepest naturally occurring seaward channel in all of Western Florida. Boca Grande Pass has minimum 18-foot depths, with soundings up to 50 feet in a few spots. The passage is well marked and relatively easy to run during daylight. Clearly, this is the best path to and from the open Gulf between Fort Myers and Venice.

In spite of all these fortunate characteristics, however, cruisers should be aware of several significant shoals flanking the inlet channel. During one of our many visits to Gasparilla Island, we once observed a large sail craft that had tried to enter Boca Grande at night and run aground amidst breaking water on the inlet's southern shoal. Fortunately, the craft was later able to extricate itself without major damage, but that must have been some night to endure on those rolling waters.

Northbound captains can take advantage of the charted swash channel cutting north along the western banks of Gasparilla Island's southerly tip (immediately west of the charted lighthouse). This cut is unmarked, but an old pier will help you to keep to the good water (see below). Currently, this channel holds at least 6 to 7 feet of water at low tide, and, in fair weather, during daylight, it is reasonably easy to run. Don't try it at night or during stormy conditions. Please read the navigation account in the next section of this chapter for additional details.

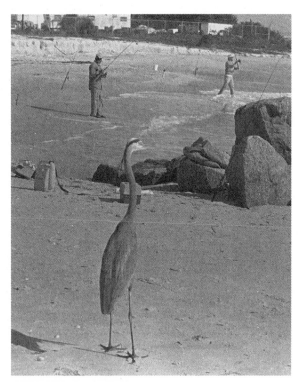

Gasparilla Island shore

Passing cruisers cannot help but notice a lovely, cottage-style lighthouse overlooking the northern banks of Boca Grande Pass. This old sentinel of the sea began operation in 1890. After some years of disuse in the late 1960s and early 1970s, it has now been fully restored and lighted once again. Please check out our account of Gasparilla Island history below for the full story.

Gasparilla Island

What can I say about a Gulf barrier island that has provided some of the best times this writer and his first-rate first mate have ever enjoyed? Well, you might say that if a barrier island is not going to be left in its natural state, Gasparilla is a shining example of how it should be developed. You could also say that the island serves as the home for one of the most beautiful and delightful Victorian inns in all of America, or you might mention the quiet delights of the isle's one village, Boca Grande. Whatever this writer or anyone else says about Gasparilla Island in the way of both cruising and shoreside delights, it will probably fall short of the mark. Perhaps it's not really going too far to say that those who have not visited Gasparilla have not really seen the best Western Florida has to offer. To be certain, Gasparilla Island deserves a heavy red circle on every cruiser's chart and several days of his or her cruising itinerary.

Gasparilla Island has benefited from the exclusivity of its visitors since the early 1900s. Wealthy Northerners by the hundreds came to Gasparilla during the Roaring Twenties and thereafter to hide from the harsh northeastern winters amidst the rambling confines of the island's famous inn. While a few small condos have been built near the island's northerly tip, most development has taken the form of lovely residential neighborhoods punctuated by beautifully kept lawns and large, clapboard homes painted in pastel shades.

A bike path made from the old roadbed of the Gasparilla railroad runs the length of the island. Bicycles are for rent everywhere. A pedaling excursion down this path from Boca Grande to the old Gasparilla Lighthouse and its new museum allows visitors an intimate view of the island homes, as well as some of the more undeveloped regions. A stroll along the beaches bordering Boca Grande inlet within sight of the lighthouse is an experience to be savored like a fine, claret wine.

Within the last several years, the Barrier Island Park Society, in cooperation with the Florida Park Service, have opened the Boca Grande Lighthouse Museum and Visitors Center in the old Boca Grande Lighthouse keeper's quarters. There are four display rooms dedicated respectively to "Native Americans, the Spanish and the Fishing Industry," "Port Boca Grande," "the Railroad and Two Lighthouses," "Boca Grande and Tarpon Fishing" and "Natural History." A fifth room houses an interesting gift shop. We highly recommend that visiting mariners rent bikes or an electric golf cart and visit this wonderful attraction. Call (941) 964-0375 for more information!

You might also choose to visit the second of Gasparilla Island's lighthouses, a short hop from downtown Boca Grande. A small park around the base of this sentinel is interesting for its plaques with explanations about Boca Grande Inlet and the lighthouses.

A third site well worth your time is Banyan Street. Here a canopy of stately but twisted trees planted by Peter Bradley in 1914 has

formed a roof over the street. Biking down the road, it almost appears as if you are cycling through a tunnel.

The quaint village of Boca Grande has long served as the center of activity on Gasparilla Island. Today, visitors will still find brick streets and walking paths flanked by cooling palm and banyan trees. The old train station has been converted into a complex of shops, including an ice cream stand and restaurant. Interesting shops and quaint dining attractions pepper Boca Grande like grains of sand on a beach. None of these is large enough to be intrusive upon the idyllic scene. Rather, these gift shops, drugstores, and clothing boutiques add to the island's charm.

Downtown Boca Grande is within easy walking distance of all the marina facilities discussed below. This is indeed fortunate, as all cruising visitors will have the opportunity to experience the delightful atmosphere of this island village for themselves.

Cruisers looking to resupply their larders should track their way to Hudson's Grocery (417 Park Avenue, 941-964-2621) in the heart of downtown Boca Grande. This small but surprisingly full line market is a Gasparilla tradition. Here you will find fresh produce, good meats, and even roasted chickens. It's a five-block walk from Millers Marina or a four-block hike from Inn Marina to Hudson's. If you have trouble with this distance and know exactly what you need, this market does offer dockside delivery for phone orders of $25 or more.

For a great breakfast, hike the short distance from Millers Marina (or a much longer walk from the Inn Marina) to Loons on a Limb (corner of Third Street and E Railroad Avenue, 941-964-0155). This is where all the locals go to break their morning fast, and there are few better recommendations for any dining establishment. Take our word for it, both the pancakes and omelets are memorable. For an offbeat dining experience with scads of local color, give Loons on a Limb a try.

Come lunch or dinner, track your way to the Loose Caboose (Fourth Street and Park Avenue, 941-964-0440). This delectable little restaurant is located on the south side of the old depot and features outdoor dining during fair weather. The bill of fare here is surprisingly sophisticated. The evening meals feature true Continental-style cuisine. Fortunately, the good old cheeseburgers and milkshakes for which this dining spot has long been famous are still available at lunch (and as good as they ever were). The Loose Caboose also has its own ice cream stand. Of course, you may hear your arteries stopping up after a lunch like this, but hey, it's only now and then, right?

The best coffee, cappuccino, pastries, and delectable homemade breads on the island are found at the Boca Grande Bakery (941-964-2234, 384 E Railroad Avenue). Several

Loose Caboose restaurant

outside tables are available for sidewalk dining. You will undoubtedly discover a host of locals taking advantage of this outstanding dining attraction. It also wouldn't be a bad idea to take a fresh-baked loaf of bread back to the galley. Ummm, I can smell the wonderful aroma now.

The Pink Elephant Restaurant (Bayou Avenue, 941-964-0100) overlooks the Gasparilla Island anchorage basin (see below) just to the west. This restaurant is under the same ownership as Gasparilla Inn (see below). It rivals the inn's dining room, and visitors can be assured of finding the highest-quality cuisine while dining in an airy atmosphere of large, plate-glass windows. Downstairs there is a delightful English-style pub, which is a perfect spot to unwind after a long day on the water.

If you are in the market for anything in the way of outdoor clothing, check out Boca Grande Outfitters (375 Park Avenue, 941-964-2445). While there, be sure to visit the real boss of the outfit, Sophie. Of course, any reply to your questions will probably be a bark, as Sophie is a friendly yellow Labrador retriever. Sophie has become such a hit among Boca Grande regulars that the shop has had special T-shirts printed with the pooch's likeness. How's that for a popular pet? Give Sophie a pat for us!

Summertime cruisers should note that activities are curtailed on Gasparilla Island from June through September. Some of the restaurants and shops close, and there is a general exodus of the seasonal population.

Boca Grande is a village built around an inn. Since 1911 faithful visitors have flocked to the pastel-shrouded Victorian mansion known as Gasparilla Inn (941-964-2201). This delightfully rambling behemoth of a hostelry is open to guests every year from mid-December to mid-June. Some new, limited services are now available between Thanksgiving and the inn's official opening in December. Surprisingly enough, the main inn and its dining room (but not the associated marina) are closed during other times of the year, though some of the separate cottages can still be rented.

Gasparilla Inn also owns a nearby, far less formal hostelry known as the Innlet. This facility is open year round and features a small,

on-site restaurant open for breakfast and lunch. To check on room availability or make reservations at the Innlet, call (941) 964-2294.

The main inn building and its various smaller companions are painted a pale yellow. The large lobby and common room are decorated with shades of white, green, and pink set atop a natural wood floor. White wicker furniture is everywhere in evidence and tea is served in the afternoon at 4:00 P.M. Sitting there sipping our tea, my first mate and I would not have been too surprised to see Zelda and F. Scott Fitzgerald or his favorite

Gasparilla Inn (main entrance)

character, Jay Gatsby, come strolling by in a white linen suit. Gasparilla Inn is just the sort of place where dreams seem to become reality.

The inn also features a billiard room, a backgammon room, and a lovely bar. All the rooms look as if they have just stepped out of the 1920s.

An eighteen-hole golf course and spectacular clubhouse serve as the inn's backyard. Linksters visiting the golf club will ascend a tall, rounded bridge spanning the island's main canal. Power cruisers may have their first real view of the inn's facilities while cruising under this unique bridge.

Guests of Gasparilla Inn never go wanting for fine dining. Your room fee includes *all three daily meals*. Few who sample the quality of Chef Alfons' cuisine will want to miss any of these repasts. Breakfast and dinner are served in the massive main dining room, just off the lobby. Guests may choose to have their lunch either in the dining room or at the nearby beach club. Lunch at the beach club features an unforgettable buffet line replete with everything from fine hamburgers to an incredible selection of cold salads (the crab and lobster salad is our favorite) to the freshest of crab cakes and other hot, daily specials.

Gasparilla Inn is now looking to attract non-inn guests to their evening meal in the main dining room (with advance reservations *only*. For a little less than $50 per person, visiting cruisers who cannot quite cough up the hefty room tariff can still experience the inn's inimitable dining experience. Be warned, though, coat and tie are required (except during the May Tarpon season) in the inn after 6:00 P.M. Trust me, this is one time when it's really worth it to bring along a navy blazer

and a "sailboat" tie. Call (941) 964-2201 for reservations.

Gasparilla Inn offers lodging both in the main building and in separate cottages, many of which have their own porches. While we have stayed in one of these latter units, I would actually suggest a room in the main inn for your first stay. The Victorian ambiance is even more pronounced in this intimate setting.

During our first stay at Gasparilla Inn, none other than the prominent actor Harrison Ford and his entire family occupied the table next to us. The inn's air of sumptuous relaxation must have been a very welcome respite from the hustle, bustle, and daily demands of Hollywood.

To state the obvious, cruisers or landlubbers desiring to stay at Gasparilla Inn should make reservations early! It should also be noted that the rates will never be described as inexpensive, but considering the timeless memories you will take away with you, the price seems reasonable to this writer.

Well, as you have probably surmised, I could go on and on and on singing the praises of Boca Grande and Gasparilla Inn, but for now, let us push on to a quick look at the island's fascinating history, followed by an overview of the region's marine facilities.

Gasparilla Island History

History suggests that Spanish explorers had established a Catholic mission on Gasparilla Island as early as 1565. This small settlement was part of the ongoing Spanish attempt to bring the local Indian population under European sway through religion. Even though hundreds of missions once dotted the Florida landscape from St. Augustine to Key West, the program ended in failure even before Florida was ceded to the English following the Seven Years' War.

Sometime during the 1700s, legend has it that the infamous pirate Jose Gaspar established his headquarters on Gasparilla Island. Tall tales speak of his warehouse of treasures and ill-gotten booty. By all accounts, Gaspar was a real ladies' man. His reputation for the treatment of female prisoners is unsavory, to say the least.

One story often told of Gaspar tells of his capturing a lovely Spanish princess named Josefa in the latter stages of his buccaneering career. For the first time in his life, the pirate was smitten with true love and begged for the young lady's hand in marriage. When she proudly refused, Gaspar was so incensed that he is supposed to have drawn his sword and decapitated her on the spot. Overcome with remorse, Jose buried her body on the island shores but, as a reminder, kept her head preserved in a glass jar on his ship.

In 1890 construction began on a "cottage-style" lighthouse overlooking deep Boca Grande (meaning "Big Mouth") Inlet. Boca Grande Lighthouse shone its light out over the Gulf for the first time December 31, 1890, and storm-tossed sailors breathed a sigh of relief. In 1927 a second lighthouse was built on Gasparilla to serve as a rear range marker for the older light. This tall, white, skeletal structure still sits hard by the Gulf beaches near the village of Boca Grande.

Boca Grande Lighthouse was abandoned

Boca Grande Lighthouse

by the Coast Guard in 1967 and quickly fell victim to vandals and the salt air. In an effort to save the old light, the local citizens of Gasparilla persuaded the federal government to transfer ownership of the light to the islanders in 1972. The lighthouse was placed on the National Register of Historic places in 1980. Beginning in 1985, a local group, the Gasparilla Island Conservation and Improvement Association, has worked diligently to restore the lighthouse and its various outbuildings. The effort has been an unqualified success and modern visitors will find the venerable lighthouse, once again with its immaculate white clapboard walls, relighted and gazing out over its inlet. The lands about the light are now part of the 135-acre Gasparilla Island State Recreation Area. As described above, a new visitor's center and museum is now housed in the old keeper's quarters.

In 1894 Peter Bradley, a successful Boston business leader, acquired a large interest in the phosphate mining operation on the Peace River to the north. He correctly foresaw that the only way for the company to prosper was the establishment of a deep-water shipping port. The obvious choice was naturally deep Boca Grande Inlet. Within a year, Bradley, along with James Gifford, president of the Charlotte Harbor and Northern Railroad, had successfully completed a railroad running from Punta Gorda to the southern tip of Gasparilla Island. Soon tons and tons of phosphate were being loaded onto oceangoing vessels, and in later years, the port was used for the shipping and receiving of oil. (The old terminal has been abandoned, and the old site now plays host to a huge group of luxury condos and town houses.

Anyway, Bradley soon began to realize that the true value of Gasparilla lay not so much in phosphate shipping as in tourism. He founded the town of Boca Grande and, as Sara Bird Wright comments in her exemplary book, *Islands of the South and Southeastern United States*, "the town was built with gracious boulevards lined with casuarina (Australian pine) and banyan trees. . . . The Gasparilla Inn was completed in 1912, along with a casino, bathhouse, boat house, and marina. Affluent patrons then began coming down; the island even lured people away from Palm Beach, which was becoming overcrowded."

"Affluent" is certainly the operative word in Ms. Wright's description. None other than the likes of the Morgans, Cabots, and DuPonts journeyed to Gasparilla Inn in their luxurious private railway cars. The famous tycoon J. P. Morgan died while vacationing in Boca Grande, and John Jacob Astor used to go shark fishing here.

The course of Gasparilla Island and the village of Boca Grande had been set. Today, the isle is still mercifully free of high-rise condos, fast-food restaurants, and honky-tonk night clubs. The old inn still brings in the rich and famous, as well as humbler guests. Katharine Hepburn is a frequent visitor and the Levi Strauss family owns a private residence on the island.

The 1,500 year-round residents of Gasparilla Island and Boca Grande are working hard through their island conservation association to preserve their unique corner of paradise from the rampant commercial development which has overtaken so many other regions of Florida. So far, they have succeeded admirably, and it is hoped the future will remain much as the past. With its rich history, ranging from Spanish missions to pirates to phosphate shipping, and its natural beauty, Gasparilla today remains one of the brightest and truest gems on the Western Florida coastline. Perhaps even the old pirate himself would be pleased.

Gasparilla Island Facilities and Anchorage (Standard Mile 28.5, Various Lats/Lons—see below)

Most of Gasparilla Island's marina facilities are found off the charted passage west of unlighted daybeacon #2. Minimum depths on this channel are about 6 feet, but there are a few unmarked shoals to avoid. After coming abeam of flashing daybeacon #7, visiting cruisers must make a choice. A turn to the south-southwest will lead you down a broad creek to Gasparilla Island's principal marina and a smaller second facility.

A cut to the north provides access through a narrow passage into a wide basin that serves as a popular anchorage (near 26 45.084 North/082 15.404 West). Minimum 5- to 5½-foot depths are initially encountered on the passage from the main channel to the anchorage, deepening to 6 feet or better on the basin itself.

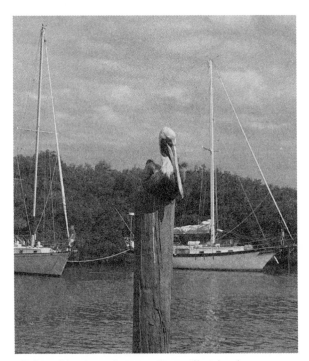

Sheltered basin anchorage, Gasparilla Island

1. Millers Marina
2. Inn Marina

This is a superbly protected overnight haven that boasts good shelter no matter from which quarter the fickle winds choose to blow. You won't find a better foul-weather hidey-hole anywhere.

Anchor in the Gasparilla basin near its midline and then back down toward the easterly banks. To minimize swinging room, consider setting a stern anchor toward this shoreline. Some captains actually tie off their sterns to the mangrove shoreline, but this is a decidedly bad idea, as this sort of shoreside growth is protected by law.

Gasparilla Inn and the Pink Elephant Restaurant maintain a few docks on this harbor's western shores. The northernmost five slips in this small complex are under county control. When it comes time to break out the dinghy, you can usually find a spot to tie off on one of these five berths. Depths in all these slips run to 4 feet or less at low water. Only dinghies and smaller power vessels need apply. The five south-side slips are reserved for patrons of the adjacent Pink Elephant Restaurant.

The one exception to this happy state of dinghy dockage occurs during the tarpon-fishing season in April through July. During this time, all the shoreside slips are reserved for the use of local fishing craft. Tying a dinghy off even for a few moments in any one of these berths will likely result in a ticket. On the other hand, the northernmost slip is quite shallow (1 foot at MLW), and most local fishermen do not make use of this space. You may be able to temporarily moor your dinghy here during tarpon season, but then again, you might still be greeted with a ticket.

Gasparilla Inn's principal boating facility is found farther upstream on the canal (charted as Boca Grande Bayou), making off to the north-northwest from the basin anchorage (see below). Smaller craft that can clear a 13-foot fixed bridge can continue cruising up Boca Grande Bayou to these docks. Sailing and other vessels needing more clearance must enter via the southernmost of the canal's two northern entrances, making off from the Waterway's unlighted daybeacon #3.

Let's now turn our attention to the two marinas on the southwestern arm of the entrance channel. The first up is Millers Marina (26 44.835 North/082 15.365 West), overlooking the northwestern banks. This facility offers the only real transient dockage for cruising-size craft in Boca Grande. And, happily, it has changed ownership since the last edition of this guide. We have been most impressed with the fresh management, and future plans call for a sure and steady improvement to this important facility.

There was serious discussion as to whether the name "Millers Marina" would be retained by the new owners. However, as of August 2003, we have been told that, for continuity's sake, the moniker will remain as is.

Millers is a medium-size establishment that happily accepts transients at its fixed wooden piers, with 30- and 50-amp power hookups and freshwater connections. Depths at the outer slips are an impressive 7 to 8 feet, and 5½ feet of water can be carried at the inner docks. Boats up to 100 feet can be accommodated, though there is only room for a few craft at the larger end of this spectrum. Note that fuel can no longer be purchased at this marina. Two barely adequate but air-conditioned showers are found on site. There is good reason to believe that these showers will be upgraded and expanded in the future. Electric and gas golf carts are cheerfully provided for visiting cruisers to facilitate a visit to nearby downtown Boca Grande.

At the time of this writing, the new ownership is in the process of thoroughly renovating the building just behind the dockage basin. A new fishing-tackle shop has already been installed, and a new restaurant (possibly known as "Anglers Grill") will be opened upstairs by mid-October 2003.

Not to be repetitive, but this writer found the current incarnation of Millers to be a friendly marina that does all in its power to meet the needs of visiting cruisers and resident boat owners alike. Please stop by and tell Aaron we sent you!

Millers Marina (941) 964-2100

Approach depth—7-9 feet
Dockside depth—7-8 feet (outer slips)
   5½ feet (inner docks)
Accepts transients—yes
Transient dockage rate—average
Fixed wooden piers—yes
Dockside power connections—up to 50 amp
Dockside water connections—yes
Showers—yes
Variety and tackle store—yes
Restaurant—on site

The few small docks of Whidden's Marina (941-964-2878) are also found on the northwestern banks a bit farther upstream from Millers Marina. This is a truly low key facility. Virtually all of the scanty wet-slip dockage is occupied by rental powercraft. The dingy on-site variety store opens out into a dim-lit pool hall. That should give you some idea of what's going on here. Just behind the docks, visitors will discover a motley collection of caged animals, including Ziggy the pot-bellied pig. You don't see marinas like this much anymore. That's a good thing!

Moving north-northwest past the basin anchorage discussed above, Boca Grande Bayou is soon spanned by a bridge leading to the Gasparilla Inn golf club. Powerboats that can clear this span's 13 feet of vertical clearance can continue upstream to the island's other marina facility. Larger craft and wind-powered vessels must make use of the northside entrance to the canal.

Another several hundred yards of upstream cruising will bring cruisers abeam of the Inn Marina (941-964-2777) on the western banks. This facility was acquired by Gasparilla Inn in late 1990. Unfortunately, all this facility's fixed wooden pier slip space is now occupied exclusively by long-term, resident craft. Transients are no longer accepted due to the space limitations. Gasoline and diesel fuel can still be purchased dockside, and a small ship's store is located just behind the docks. The Inn Marina also features an enlarged dry-stack storage building.

Boca Grande Bayou eventually splits. One branch passes through a hard turn to the east and heads out for the open water of southern Gasparilla Sound. This passage out to the Waterway features a bit of a navigational challenge, but it is decidedly the route of choice for cruising-size craft. Be sure to read the navigational information presented later in this chapter concerning this channel before running this cut.

Study chart 11425 for a moment and notice the broad, semicircular cove, just northeast of the cut's outer limits, described above, and hard by charted Jack Point. Boats drawing less

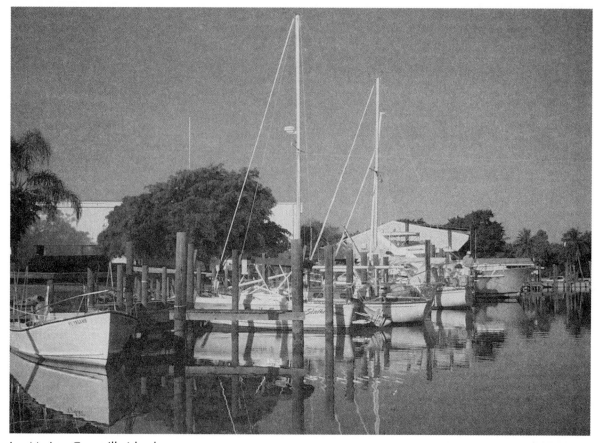

Inn Marina, Gasparilla Island

than 4½ feet can anchor on this cove, near 26 45.792 North/082 15.196 West, with good protection in northerly and westerly winds. There is absolutely no shelter from southerly breezes and little to be had when winds blow briskly from the east. Depths of 4½ to 6 feet hold to within 150 yards of the northwesterly shoreline. This cove's northern and western shorelines are guarded by a thick belt of opulent homeplaces, but the east-side banks remain essentially in their natural state.

Study chart 11425 for a moment, and notice that a newly charted channel stretches north from the intersection where we first met up with the easterly passage from the Boca Grande Bayou to the ICW, outlined just above. There are two serious limitations in regards to this cut for cruising-size craft. First, this route passes under a low-level, fixed bridge with a bare 14 feet of vertical clearance. Secondly, the marked channel is quite narrow in places and runs hard by the shores of Gasparilla Island here and there. While local outboarders can and do make use of this channel almost every day, for the reasons specified above, it is not a serious consideration for cruisers, and thus will not be further described in these pages.

Peekins Ranch Cove Anchorage (Standard Mile 32, 26 47.842 North/082 16.168 West)

1. Uncle Henry's Marina Resort

Let us now return to the ICW as it knifes its way through mostly shallow Gasparilla Sound. In westerly breezes, skippers may choose to anchor in Peekins Ranch Cove, west of flashing daybeacon #13. There are some unmarked shoals to avoid, but careful navigation should see you safely inside the cove and anchored in 6 feet (or better) of water. The shoreside is partially in its natural state, with several fine-looking homes breaking the landscape here and there. This is definitely not the spot to drop the hook in fresh easterly winds, as my mate and I discovered one fine sunny day in January. It should also be mentioned that there is no opportunity to dinghy ashore from this anchorage to sample the delights of Gasparilla Island.

Gasparilla Marina (Standard Mile 34, 26 50.089 North/082 15.634 West)

Gasparilla Marina provides superbly sheltered dockage at modern, fixed wooden piers. The charted entrance channel cuts northeast from flashing daybeacon #20, just southeast of the old Gasparilla Island railway bridge. Entrance depths run between 8 and 9 feet, with a good 6 to 6½ feet of low-tide depths dockside. Transients are welcome. All berths feature full power and water connections. Gasparilla Marina's harbor is very well protected. You should be able to hunker down snugly in your slip with any but hurricane-force winds in the offing.

Cruising visitors will also discover gasoline and diesel fuel at a new, swanky fuel pier guarding the western side of the passage into the inner portion of the dockage basin. Some variety and fishing-tackle-type items are found in a small store just behind the fuel dock. Additionally, waste pump-out service and extensive dry-stack storage are provided. The two on-site showers have been refurbished and are now air conditioned, but they were not as clean as they should have been during our last visit. There is also a climate-controlled

Laundromat on the marina grounds. Depending on where your berth is located, it can be a bit of a trek to the showers and laundry.

Mechanical repairs for outboards and I/Os are available from the on-site repair firm of Ingman Marine (941-697-1000). Haul-outs can be accomplished by yet another local firm, Gasparilla Marine Services (941-698-1144). Their travelift is rated at 70 tons.

The nearby Fishery Restaurant (see below) is spoken of with longing by local residents. The Fishery features a seafood market as well. It's ever so nice to just hike a very short distance and then bring the freshest catch of the day back to your galley.

All in all, Gasparilla Marina is a friendly marina facility that this writer recommends to all cruisers who don't need a first-class shoreside shower.

Gasparilla Marina (941) 697-2280
http://www.gasparillamarina.com

Approach depth—8-9 feet
Dockside depth—6-6½ feet (low-water)
Accepts transients—yes
Transient dockage rate—average
Fixed wooden piers—yes
Dockside power connections—30 and 50 amp
Dockside water connections—yes
Waste pump-out—yes
Showers—yes
Laundromat—yes
Gasoline—yes
Diesel fuel—yes
Mechanical repairs—yes
Below-waterline repairs—yes
Variety store—small
Restaurant—one nearby

Fishery Restaurant (Standard Mile 34, 26 49.860 North/082 15.919 West)

Study chart 11425 for a moment and note the channel cutting to the north-northeast, between unlighted daybeacon #21 and the old Gasparilla Island railway span. This minimum 6½-foot cut leads to a long, fixed wooden pier associated with the Fishery Restaurant (941-697-2451), mentioned above. Depths alongside run some 6 to 8 feet, but you must be sure to moor only to the dock's southern face. Dining patrons are welcome to tie up while patronizing the adjacent restaurant or seafood market, but no overnight stays are allowed.

The restaurant and fresh seafood market are both wonderful. Now, cruisers can decide whether to stoke up their bellies in the restaurant or take something fresh back to the galley to be prepared aboard. Seldom will cruisers find such a convenient dining attraction, particularly one with such good dockage facilities.

1. Gasparilla Marina
2. Fishery Restaurant

Uncle Henry's Marina Resort (Standard Mile 34, 26 48.227 North/082 16.510 West)

This large, ultramodern marina is found at the terminus of the long, southward-flowing channel that cuts off from the ICW between the old railway span and the Gasparilla Island causeway bridge. The passage is narrow in places, but it is well marked. Minimum low-water depths seem to be about 6 feet. Meanwhile dockside soundings run at least 6 to 7 feet.

The entrance channel leads to the fixed concrete docks of Uncle Henry's Marina Resort. The dockage basin is well sheltered from all but unusually strong northerly winds. Full dockside power, water, telephone, and cable-television hookups are available at every slip. Transients are eagerly accepted for overnight dockage or a longer stay. Gasoline and diesel fuel are available, as are adequate, climate-controlled shoreside showers and a Laundromat (with paperback exchange library). The friendly and very knowledgeable dockmaster can usually make arrangements through local independent technicians for boats that need mechanical servicing. Waste pump-out service is offered dockside.

A shopping and motel complex is located immediately behind the marina. Here visiting cruisers will find Choo Choo Boys restaurant (941-964-6437) on the second floor of the complex. The dining room features a great view of the harbor.

The retail complex also includes a flower shop, a beauty salon, the Boca Grande Chamber of Commerce (941-964-0568), and a surprisingly well-supplied and sophisticated food store, Gill's Grocery and Deli Market (941-964-2506). Gill's features imported foods, a full-service deli, and dockside deliveries for phone orders of $25 or more. How's that for shoreside amenities?

While the many delights of downtown Boca Grande are a bit too far for comfortable walking, Uncle Henry's rents golf carts.

All in all, Uncle Henry's offers just about every imaginable service except repairs. Advance reservations are recommended, particularly during the winter and spring tourist seasons.

**Uncle Henry's Marina Resort (941) 964-2300
http://www.bocagrande.com/marina.htm**

Approach depth—6-15 feet
Dockside depth—6-7 feet (minimum)
Accepts transients—yes
Transient dockage rate—above average
Fixed concrete piers—yes
Dockside power connections—30 and 50 amp
Dockside water connections—yes
Waste pump-out—yes
Showers—yes
Laundromat—yes
Gasoline—yes
Diesel fuel—yes
Mechanical repairs—arranged through local independent contractors
Variety store—yes
Restaurant—on site

Gasparilla Pass

The inlet lying north of Gasparilla Island is known, appropriately enough, as Gasparilla Pass. This evil cut is shoal and should not be attempted by any pleasure craft. Two of its three entrances are cut off by low-level fixed bridges. The third has depths of as little as 3 feet. The passage out into the open Gulf is shoaly and breakers are very much in evidence. Don't let them do any breaking for you.

PINE ISLAND SOUND NAVIGATION

Probably the largest impediment to good navigation on Pine Island Sound is the beautiful scenery. It's not uncommon to become enraptured with the all-natural isles and stilted fishing houses and not watch where you are going. Scraping the barnacles off the bottom of your craft is a time-honored maritime practice, but this writer suggests you have it done in a yard and not on a sand bar.

For the most part, successful fair-weather navigation of Pine Island Sound is a delight. While shallow water is present, the channel is usually fairly broad and forgiving. Sidewaters and the various anchorages along the way require a more cautious approach.

All navigators should take note of the fact that the Army Corps of Engineers changed the Waterway markers on Pine Island Sound between flashing daybeacon #69 and Boca Grande Pass in 2002. This has led to monumental confusion, but thankfully, the latest edition of charts 11427 and 11425 now depict the correct scheme of aids to navigation. Will wonders never cease! Be *sure* you have the latest versions of these charts aboard before beginning your cruise of Pine Island Sound. Older editions can run you aground in a hurry on these waters, particularly if you are making for the anchorage on Pelican Bay.

When winds exceed 15 knots and storms are in the forecast, Pine Island Sound can have a decidedly different look. Winds have more than enough fetch to stir up a wicked chop. Skippers of smaller cruising craft should deeply consider waiting for a day of light airs to undertake passage through the sound.

Those used to traversing more open inland waters will find no unusual navigational problems on Pine Island Sound. Captains accustomed to sheltered passages may, on the other hand, be a bit daunted by the wide water. Take heart—with charts 11427 and 11425 in hand, plus a GPS and the information below, you should come through with no problems.

On the ICW   Our account of the passage through Pine Island Sound begins abeam of flashing daybeacon #11 (to its northwesterly side). While some may consider the waters to the west to be a part of San Carlos Bay, for our purposes we will think of this area as the southern foot of Pine Island Sound.

From #11, the ICW swings sharply west-northwest and passes flashing daybeacon #12 to its southern side. At #12 an underwater power line passes under the ICW. The line reemerges on either side of the Waterway and continues its path set atop 26-foot towers. Sail craft that somehow miss the channel on these waters could be in for a shocking experience.

Another swing, this time to the southwest, leads cruisers past flashing daybeacon #13 and unlighted daybeacon #13A. Very shallow water is found south and southeast of #13 and #13A. Be sure to stay to the north and northwest of these aids.

Past #13A, northbound cruisers will follow a lazy turn to the northwest. Unlighted daybeacon #14 and flashing daybeacons #16 and #18 warn of shallows abutting the Waterway's north and northeastern flank.

York Island Anchorage   To make good your entrance into the anchorage off the southeastern shores of York Island, depart the ICW about half-way between flashing daybeacon #13 and unlighted daybeacon #13A. Cruise to the northwest, pointing to end up some 100 yards off the island's southeasternmost point.

Be sure to retrace your steps when it comes time to leave. Shoals lie to the west and south separating this anchorage from the ICW channel.

Ding Darling Anchorage   From flashing daybeacon #16, set course for the mid-width of the broad cove to the south. As you cruise into the interior reaches of this water body, watch ahead for some small signs set atop equally petite pilings. These markers denote the boundaries of the Ding Darling Wildlife Refuge. For best depths, be sure to set the hook north of the signs.

On the ICW   The Waterway flows northwest along a broad path of deep water through the heart of southern Pine Island Sound. Flashing daybeacon #20 and unlighted daybeacon #22 mark shallows to the northeast. Stay well to the southwest of these aids.

After leaving #22 behind, set course to come abeam of flashing daybeacon #23 to its northeasterly side. A huge power line with 85 feet of vertical clearance spans Pine Island Sound from northeast to southwest near #23. It could certainly lead to confusion during nighttime passages. There is also shoal water west and southwest of #23. Be sure to pass this aid well to its northeastern side. Soon you will come abeam of unlighted daybeacon #24 and another anchorage opportunity.

Chino Island Anchorage

Simply cruise northeast from unlighted daybeacon #24 toward the northwest-to-southeast centerline of Chino Island. Good depths persist to within 75 yards of the island's shores. Be sure to drop the hook far enough from the banks so that you will not swing into the shallows immediately adjacent to the shoreline.

On the ICW   Do not attempt the charted passage west of flashing daybeacon #26. Not only is this cut shoal and treacherous, but Blind Pass has now closed completely.

North-northwest of the gap between flashing daybeacon #32 and unlighted daybeacon #31, the ICW channel passes through an improved cut. Numerous unlighted aids help keep you to the proper course. At unlighted daybeacon #37, good water again broadens out in a wide band to the north.

Captiva Island-Roosevelt Channel and Anchorage   Cruisers running the Roosevelt channel, which serves two of Captiva Island's marinas and one anchorage, should set course from unlighted daybeacon #38 for the cut's northeasternmost marker, flashing daybeacon #2. The channel angles southwest from #2. All you really need do is remember your "red, right, returning."

Jensen's Twin Palms Marina lines the western shores near unlighted daybeacon #13. Tween Waters Marina is considerably farther to the south, near unlighted daybeacon #19, also on the western banks.

Be careful if you attempt to drop the hook inside the anchorage on the eastern side of the channel between unlighted daybeacons #20 and #21. Even though you will most likely find a host of local craft moored here, on-site research shows that it ain't too difficult to wander into 5-foot depths. The best water seems to be found nearer to #21.

Do not cruise south of unlighted daybeacon #22. Depths begin to rise thereafter.

South Seas Plantation and Redfish Pass
May we be so bold as to reiterate our strong suggestion that you make contact with the helpful dockmasters at South Seas Plantation *before* attempting to run the marina's entrance cut. These good folks can quickly give you advice about the channel conditions and direct you through the best possible passage, depending on what the nearby sand and shoals have been doing lately.

The well-outlined channel leading to South Seas Plantation Marina and Redfish Pass cuts sharply west from flashing daybeacon #39. As you would expect, simply pass all red, even-numbered markers to your starboard side, and take green beacons to port.

While cruising west from #39 for the gap between the South Seas' outermost markers, unlighted daybeacons #1 and #2, you may well spy a series of PVC markers cutting off to the southwest. These "county" aids to navigation mark the alternate channel described above. Again, for the moment, neither this writer nor the dockmasters at

South Seas suggest that cruising-size craft make use of this cut. Should this situation change in the future, your best source of information will once again be an advance call to the South Seas harbormasters.

The South Seas entrance channel doglegs slightly at unlighted daybeacons #15 and #16. As described earlier, there is a potential for the passage to shoal from the north at #16. For the moment, we suggest you favor #15 slightly, but, and I know this is getting repetitive, let the South Seas dockmasters be your guide.

West of the gap between flashing (currently charted as unlighted) daybeacon #20 and unlighted daybeacon #19, it's a pretty straight shot into the South Seas harbor entrance. After making your way past unlighted daybeacon #21 into the entrance canal, the fuel dock and the first rank of piers will soon open out to starboard.

Captains making for Redfish Pass from Pine Island Sound should follow the South Seas channel to a point just west of the gap between unlighted daybeacons #17 and #18. At this point, turn to the north-northwest and cruise carefully along, parallel to the eastern shores of Captiva Island's northern tip. Stay some 75 to 100 yards off the beach, and you can follow the channel into the inlet's interior reaches. Be on guard against the correctly charted finger of 2-foot waters to the east.

While the inner portion of Redfish Pass between Captiva and North Captiva islands is quite deep, the passage out to sea is flanked by extensive shoals to the north and south. This seaward cut is marked and can often be run successfully in fair weather. As always, though, it would be best to investigate local knowledge before attempting the cut. Check with the good people at South Seas Plantation Marina for the latest information.

Pine Island Channel   An indifferently marked channel well east of unlighted daybeacon #42 runs into the western shores of Pine Island. This cut is used regularly by local fishermen piloting small outboard craft. It is much too winding and shallow for safe cruising by larger vessels.

Safety Harbor and Anchorage   Skippers bound for either the Safety Harbor channel or the anchorage behind the northern tip of North Captiva Island can depart the ICW at unlighted daybeacon #48. Run a careful compass/GPS course from #48 to a point some 100 yards north of flashing daybeacon #1 and unlighted daybeacon #2, the outermost aids to navigation on the Safety Harbor channel.

Once abeam of #1 and #2, captains choosing to drop the hook can break off to the northwest. Be mindful of the correctly charted shallows west and northwest of #2. Be sure to keep east of #2 as you work your way to the northwest. Eventually, this shoal will be left behind, and good depths begin to run to within 100 yards of the westerly shoreline. Anchor well before coming abeam of the main Captiva Pass outlet to the Gulf.

The Safety Harbor channel cuts south-southwest between flashing daybeacon #1 and unlighted daybeacon #2. This cut is a bit better marked than in times past, and virtually all the various aids to navigation

are now charted. Remember, though, this channel is rather shallow in spots and is not appropriate for vessels drawing more than 4½ feet.

Take all red markers to your starboard side and green beacons to port. After passing between unlighted daybeacons #3 and #4, you will be confronted by one of the old stilted fishing houses dead ahead.

All vessels must pass hard by the eastern tip of the old stilted house and then curl around to the west and follow the markers into the interior of Safety Harbor. Hapless navigators who wander even a speck too far to the east when passing the stilted house will find themselves aground in 1 foot of water. Even when passing the old house closely as you should, low-tide depths of 4 feet can be expected.

Soon the single fixed wooden pier of Barnacle Phil's Restaurant will come abeam to starboard. The channel continues on and eventually curls around the rear portion of Safety Harbor. This portion of the passage leads to a large collection of private docks, but no accommodations are available for visitors. Most transient cruisers will want to cease their explorations at the restaurant dock.

Captiva Pass Anchorage   Captiva Pass offers a fine fair-weather anchorage. The waters east of Captiva Pass are occupied by a huge shoal, with depths running to 3 feet. You must pass either north or south of these shallows to find your way into the inlet's interior.

From the south, you might choose to set course from unlighted daybeacon #48 to bypass the shoal on its southern flank. Work your way along the broad band of charted deep water abutting the eastern shores of North Captiva Island's northerly tip. Eventually, you can swing to the west and enter the inlet.

Many cruisers choose to enter Captiva Pass via its northerly passage. This cut is nearer and more convenient to the good anchorage off Cayo Costa. Leave the Waterway some 100 yards north of flashing daybeacon #51 by curling back around slowly to the west. This maneuver will help to avoid the charted shoal southwest of #51.

As the eastern banks of southern Cayo Costa come abeam, break off from the inlet channel and track your way north, paralleling the island's easterly shoreline. Stay some 50 to 75 yards off the beach. Good water continues for some distance to the north, but eventually the charted shoals begin to shelve out from the shore. To be on the safe side, drop anchor after proceeding no more than 200 yards north of the inlet's passage.

Alternate Pine Island Channel At flashing daybeacon #52, the alternate channel leading to the southern reaches of Charlotte Harbor breaks off to the north-northeast. Much of the southerly section of this cut is unmarked, but the channel is quite broad. By using a GPS (hopefully interfaced with a laptop), plus chart 11427 and identifying the various landmarks along the way, most navigators will be able to find their way to a point abeam of Useppa Island with little difficulty.

After cruising north from #52 for some .4 nautical miles, cruisers whose craft draws less than 5 feet can work their way carefully to the east-southeast for another .6 nautical miles for a close view of the stilted fish houses near Captiva Rocks. Don't approach to within less than 300 feet of the houses, as they are anchored in shoal water.

As you cruise the gap between Part Island to the east and Useppa Island to the west, you will soon catch sight of unlighted daybeacon #5. From this point to the end of the channel off Bokeelia Island, northbound craft should pass all green beacons to their (the cruisers') port side and take red markers to starboard.

Unlighted daybeacon #5 serves the dual purpose of marking the western tier of the alternate channel and as the easternmost aid to navigation on the passage connecting with the ICW north of Useppa Island. This cut will be covered in the discussion of Useppa Island below.

Unlighted daybeacons #6 and #7 help skippers run the gap between Patricio and Broken islands. It's then a long run of some 1.5 nautical miles from #7 to flashing daybeacon #8 off Jug Creek. Point to come abeam of #8 to its westerly quarter.

Jug Creek/Bokeelia Island

South of flashing daybeacon #8, the Jug Creek channel begins its twisting and winding path to the east-southeast. The prolific markers follow the usual "red, right, returning" strategy.

The channel has so many hairpin curves that collision with a powercraft traveling at high speed around one of the blind turns is a very real concern. This writer suggests that you proceed at a wary speed while running this cut.

At unlighted daybeacon #30 the channel to Four Winds Marina takes a hard jog to starboard and passes through a narrow cut. Don't miss this turn. It's easy to overlook.

On to Charlotte Harbor via Alternate Channel From flashing daybeacon #8, set course to pass unlighted daybeacons #9 and #11 fairly close to their southeastern sides. This is the shallowest portion of the alternate channel, with some low-tide soundings in the 6-foot range or slightly less. Good water soon opens out again to the north.

If, by some chance, you should be continuing around Pine Island into Matlacha Pass, be aware that beacon colors reverse at unlighted daybeacon #95. Southbound cruisers navigating the pass should now begin to take green beacons to their (the cruisers') starboard side and red to port.

Back to the ICW North of flashing daybeacon #52, the ICW cuts through another dredged cut until finding deeper water at flashing daybeacon #57. At this point, the Waterway darts briefly northeast and then cuts north again between Cabbage Key and Useppa Island. North of flashing daybeacon #60, the easy-to-follow Cabbage Key channel strikes to the west.

Useppa Island and Associated Anchorages At unlighted daybeacon #61, mariners can cut into the western shores of Useppa Island to the previously described anchorage, once abeam of the Cabbage Key channel to the west. Good depths continue to within 100 yards of shore. Cruisers entering the cove may spy a small, marked channel

to the north. This cut is used by local property owners on Useppa Island and is of no interest to visiting cruisers.

The channel to the private Useppa Club Marina runs off to the southeast between flashing daybeacons #63 and #64. The prolific markers are obvious.

Chart 11427 correctly forecasts a small channel running from the Useppa Club harbor hard by the island's northerly tip. On-site research found this cut passable, but most larger vessels should probably opt for the wider, marked channel a bit farther to the north, discussed below. If you should try this first cut anyway, watch out for a stone jetty abutting the island's shoreline. Give this hazard a wide berth when passing.

Note the marked channel running east to west between the ICW and the alternate Pine Island Sound channel, north of Useppa Island. Its westerly entrance is found a short distance south of the Waterway's flashing daybeacon #64. Captains cruising this cut from the ICW to the alternate channel should pass red beacons to their (the markers') northerly sides and green markers to their southern quarter.

You can enter the anchorage bordering on Useppa Island's eastern shores by continuing to cruise east on the connecting channel for some 50 yards past unlighted daybeacon #4. Then, cut sharply to the south and, keeping the island shoreline some 150 yards to your westerly side, you will find good water between #4 and the first point on the island. Farther to the south, depths rise somewhat.

Point Blanco Anchorages To access the outer anchorage adjacent to Point Blanco, begin easing west of the Waterway channel as the southeastern portion of the point comes abeam, west of your course, between unlighted daybeacons #65 and #67. Good water runs to within 75 yards or so of the shores, which are lined by tall Australian pines.

Brave captains who attempt to enter the anchorage behind Point Blanco should follow the charted deeper waters striking west, south of the point. Set a course designed to keep your craft off the banks by some 25 yards or so. Proceed at idle speed and keep a close watch on the sounder. Soon you will pass between a large patch of old pilings to port and a smaller, motley collection of piles striking out from the Point Blanco shoreline.

Eventually the channel cuts around the western side of Point Blanco. Maintain your 25 yards' clearance with the shoreline until the waters open out to the east behind (north of) the point. This is, without a doubt, the most critical part of this difficult passage, and even careful navigators can come to grief.

For best depths, hug the southerly banks as soon as you swing to the east and begin to enter the sheltered anchorage. Eventually, if you are lucky enough to make it this far, the channel opens out a bit at the rear of the cove. Even so, set the hook so as to favor the southerly shoreline.

On the ICW   Shallow water abuts the eastern and northeastern sides of the ICW between unlighted daybeacons #72 and #74. Favor the westerly side of the channel to avoid this hazard.

As mentioned earlier, the Waterway markers between flashing daybeacon #69 and Boca Grande Pass were changed in 2002. Thankfully, the latest edition of charts 11427 and 11425 now depict the correct scheme of aids to navigation. Be *sure* you have the latest versions of these charts aboard before beginning your cruise of Pine Island Sound. Older editions can run you aground in a hurry on these waters, particularly if you are making for the anchorage on Pelican Bay.

Pelican Bay and Cayo Costa Anchorage
Come abeam of unlighted daybeacon #74 and set a careful course that will carry you into the northwestern third of Pelican Pass's northerly mouth, thereby favoring the Cayo Costa shoreline. Be on guard against the correctly charted finger of 3-foot waters stretching out from Punta Blanca Island to the southeast. These shoals seem to be forever building outward.

Curve slowly around to the south and enter the main body of Pelican Bay on its mid-width. Consider dropping the hook either just south of the pass or as the park service docks come abeam on the western shoreline. Farther to the south, depths become much more uncertain.

On to Boca Grande Pass   Flashing daybeacon #76 is the last aid to navigation on the ICW south of Boca Grande Inlet. Switch from chart 11427 to 11425 at this point for continued detail of the Waterway to points north.

It's a run of slightly less than 2 nautical miles from #76 to flashing daybeacon #1, the first marker north of Boca Grande. While this track does not border on any shoals, you can expect chop and current to pick up as you traverse the waters east of Boca Grande Pass.

Boca Grande Pass and Swash Channel It truly doesn't get much easier than this on those often-unstable tracks between inland waters and the open Gulf. Boca Grande Pass is wide and its seaward passage is well marked. Nevertheless, there are a few potential problems about which cruisers should be informed.

The inlet's waters between Cayo Costa and the southerly tip of Gasparilla Island are deep almost from shore to shore. The situation changes somewhat as you move seaward. Favor the northerly and north-western side of the channel slightly as you move out to sea from the two islands. This maneuver will help to avoid charted Johnson Shoal off Cayo Costa.

A long, thin band of shoals also flanks the northern and northwestern side of Boca Grande Pass for a goodly distance out to sea. Use the charted channel markers to avoid this hazard. Come abeam of and pass flashing buoys #12 and #10 close to their northerly sides. Too wide a berth to the north or northwest could land the luckless navigator in the aforementioned shallows.

To run the swash channel cutting into Boca Grande's northerly flank, cut to the north after passing the southern tip of Gasparilla Island, defined by its charming cottage-style lighthouse. Keep the easterly banks some 50 yards off your starboard side. Be very, very mindful of the correctly

charted shoals to the west. Soon you will spot a long, dilapidated concrete pier striking out from the easterly banks. Pass this old structure by some 20 yards to your starboard side. Eventually, good water will open out to the north and northwest.

Please remember, this swash passage is totally unmarked and borders on very shoal, breaker-tossed water to the west. We specifically do not recommend this passage during foul weather or at night. Even in the bright sunshine and the best of conditions, please proceed with more than the usual caution.

Gasparilla Island Facilities and Anchorage The principal entrance to the anchorage and facilities grouped about the village of Boca Grande on Gasparilla Island will be spied west-northwest of unlighted daybeacon #2. The channel is straightforward until coming abeam of flashing daybeacon #7. Be sure to come abeam of #7 to its northern side (your port side). On the water, #7 will appear to be much farther from the southerly entrance point than chart 11425 would lead you to believe. A shoal is building out from this promontory and is beginning to encroach on #7. Once abeam of #7, take a few moments to assess the situation.

The stream to the southwest leads to Millers and Whidden's marinas, while a cut into the canal to the north will bring the visiting cruiser to a basinlike anchorage and the docks just behind the Pink Elephant Restaurant.

All craft should proceed at idle, no-wake speed past #7, no matter which course they may choose. These speed restrictions remain in place throughout the northside canal and southwestern creek.

If you choose to continue down the southwesterly passage to Millers or Whidden's marinas, favor the northwesterly shores heavily as you cruise upstream to the two marinas. Inviting as it may look, the southeastern side of the creek is quite shallow. It might appear as if there's enough room for anchorage, but the shallows are far closer than you might think. While we have often observed a few small sail craft swinging on the hook just south of Whidden's Marina, most larger vessels would do better to make use of the marina facilities.

To access the basin anchorage or the Inn Marina, enter the north-running canal (charted as Boca Grande Bayou) on its centerline. The Gasparilla Inn golf course will be prominent to starboard. Soon you will pass into the broad basin, where you will undoubtedly observe many fellow cruising craft at anchor. Remember, swinging room is at a premium, so use a Bahamian moor or a stern anchor. The docks behind the Pink Elephant will be sighted to the north on the western banks.

Boats that can clear a 13-foot fixed bridge can continue on up Boca Grande Bayou, holding to the middle. Eventually the docks of the Inn Marina will come abeam to port.

Eventually a charted branch of the bayou turns sharply to the east and begins its trek out into the open waters of southern Gasparilla Sound. Don't attempt to enter either of the two coves lining the northerly banks between the easterly turn and the canal's exodus into the sound. Both are quite shoal.

If you would like to anchor on the broad, semicircular cove east and north of the canal's exodus into Gasparilla Sound, continue cruising dead ahead from the mouth of the east-flowing canal for some 200 yards. You can then turn into the northerly banks and feel your way in with the sounder.

The channel from this easterly running arm of Boca Grande Bayou back to the ICW is a bit tricky, but as described earlier, it is the only game in town for cruising-size craft. After exiting the canal, continue cruising straight ahead (to the east) for 200 yards or so. Then turn sharply to the southeast and set a compass course directly for unlighted daybeacon #3. Good depths of 6 feet or better are carried by following this procedure.

On the Waterway   The Western Florida ICW knifes its way through Gasparilla Sound via a dredged channel. Shallow water is very much in evidence outside of the Waterway. This is not the place for haphazard exploration. Take your time and stay on course.

Peekins Ranch Cove Anchorage   Entry into this anchorage is complicated by the long tongue of charted but unmarked 3-foot (or less) water that stretches far to the east, north of Peekins Ranch Cove. To avoid these shoals, set a careful compass/GPS course from flashing daybeacon #13 into the cove's interior section, bypassing the shallows well north of your course. If depths should start to rise, try giving way to the south and see if your soundings improve. Once past the shoal, drop anchor before closing to within less than 200 yards of the westerly shores.

On to the Gasparilla Causeway   As you pass unlighted daybeacon #14, you may catch sight of two green, unlighted daybeacons to the west and northwest. Ignore these aids. They mark a shortcut through the old railway bridge. This passage is somewhat shallow and poorly marked. Only shallow-draft outboards and I/O-powered craft should attempt it.

At flashing daybeacon #20, the marked channel to Gasparilla Marina breaks off to the northeast, while the Waterway turns to the northwest and soon passes through the old Gasparilla Railroad bridge. The center span has been removed on this now unused bridge, and it no longer poses a barrier, but be advised that this pass-through is a bit on the narrow side.

The charted channel leading to the Fishery Restaurant runs north-northeast immediately southeast of the Gasparilla Railway bridge. As usual, pass red markers to your starboard side and take green beacons to port. Eventually, the restaurant's one, long face dock will come abeam to port. Be sure to moor to the southern face of this pier only!

The waters between the railway span and the Gasparilla Causeway (highway) bridge can be a busy place. To the north, two deep coves make off from the Waterway. The eastern offshoot is used for the dumping of treated waste water and would be a truly lousy place to anchor. The western stream used to lead to a huge Mercury outboard and I/O testing facility. This entire complex has now been sold, and rumors abound as to some type of condo or convention facility that may arise on this property.

The well-marked passage to Uncle Henry's Marina cuts in from the south between the two bridges. Keep all red markers to starboard and all green to port. Stay in the channel. Shoal water with less than 1-foot depths borders a portion of this cut.

Gasparilla Pass   Absolutely no cruising-size craft should attempt to run Gasparilla Pass. The waters are shoal and two of the three entrances into the pass are spanned by fairly low-level fixed bridges.

Charlotte Harbor

Cruisers reading this account who have had occasion to cruise North Carolina's Pamlico Sound will already have a pretty good notion of just what Charlotte Harbor is really like. While it cannot lay claim to the Pamlico's breadth, this is also a large body of water with two impressive feeder rivers. Charlotte Harbor has very few protected anchorages and only a single marina, south of Punta Gorda, which services cruising craft.

Unlike Pamlico Sound, Charlotte Harbor can boast of one good-sized city along its banks. Punta Gorda, a name for many years synonymous with commercial fishing in Western Florida, is today a quiet, but by no means small, residential community that usually offers one full-service marina, two yacht clubs, and several anchorages.

The Myakka and Peace rivers feed into Charlotte Harbor's northerly reaches. The Myakka suffers from some shallow depths, and neither stream provides what could really be described as first-rate anchorages, though adventurous captains will discover several spots worthy of consideration.

In spite of these somewhat negative characteristics, this writer could not help but like Charlotte Harbor, and I recommend it to my fellow cruisers. There are few other spots in Western Florida where mariners can experience such wide waters bounded by such little-developed shores. Sailors, in particular, will find Charlotte Harbor well suited for a good day of cruising. So, don't be in such a hurry while passing by on the ICW that you miss the considerable charms of this lovely water.

Lower Charlotte Harbor

For once, the story can be told in a few words. Charlotte Harbor south of Punta Gorda lacks any really protected anchorages and sports only one (albeit a fine one) marina. While it makes for a wonderful sailing ground, when evening approaches, it's time to head for either Burnt Store Marina or one of the marinas, yacht clubs, or anchorages to the north at Punta Gorda.

Burnt Store Marina and Country Club (26 45.581 North/082 03.455 West)

Charlotte Harbor has only one marina facility that is located outside of Punta Gorda, but it

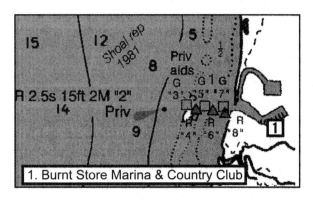

1. Burnt Store Marina & Country Club

is a good one. The charted channel running to the east, east of flashing daybeacon #6, leads to the sheltered dockage basin of Burnt Store Marina. The approach cut carries 6½ feet (more likely 7 feet) of water. Depths in the dockage basin run around 7 feet at low water. The marina is set in the middle of a large condo and resort housing project. In fact, the best way to spot the entrance channel is to watch for a line of three-story condos and/or a six-story condo tower overlooking the shoreline.

Burnt Store harbor is home to an unusually large collection of manatees. In fact, a live manatee birth that took place in the waters of the dockage basin was featured on a local television broadcast in 1998. Power captains should be ultrasure to proceed strictly at idle speed when cruising to and from their slips. This is the sort of place where even a small wake could be a real problem.

Burnt Store features full services. Transients are accepted at (mostly) fixed wooden piers. The marina boasts 525 slips in all! Full water and power connections are readily available, as are gasoline, diesel fuel, and waste pump-out services. Full mechanical servicing for both diesel- and gasoline-powered plants is now offered Monday through Friday. Vessels can also be hauled out via the marina's 40-ton hydraulic trailer. Extensive dry-stack storage for powercraft is now available at Burnt Store as well.

Shoreside, cruisers will find fair, climate-controlled showers and a tiny, non-air-conditioned Laundromat, alongside a full-line ship's, variety, and grocery store (including deli and snack bar). Transients may also make use of the complex's swimming pool, 27-hole golf course, athletic club (with sauna), and tennis courts. Bicycle rentals are also available. Portobello's at Latitudes Restaurant (open for lunch and dinner, 941-639-3650) is found immediately adjacent to the docks and offers the freshest in fried and broiled seafood.

Incidentally, cruisers looking to charter cruising craft on Florida's western coastline need look no further than Burnt Store Marina. Several charter services make their home in the marina's dockage basin. One of the largest

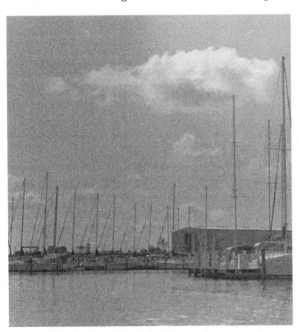

Burnt Store Marina, Charlotte Harbor

is operated by Southwest Florida Yachts (800-262-7939). While this firm's home offices are found at Marina Town Yacht Club in north Fort Myers, their impressive sail-craft fleet is housed at Burnt Store.

Another well-respected charter operation based at Burnt Store Marina is Yachting Vacations (800-447-0080). Boasting a sail-craft fleet of 16 vessels, this agency was declared (several years ago) the best charter agency in the world by *Cruising World* magazine!

**Burnt Store Marina (941) 637-0083
http://www.burntstoremarina.com**

**Approach depth—6½-7 feet (minimum)
Dockside depth—7 feet (minimum)
Accepts transients—yes
Transient dockage rate—average
Floating docks—one
Fixed wooden and concrete piers—yes (mostly
   wooden)
Dockside power connections—30 and 50 amp
Dockside water connections—yes
Waste pump-out—yes
Showers—yes
Laundromat—yes
Gasoline—yes
Diesel fuel—yes
Mechanical repairs—yes
Below-waterline repairs—yes
Ship's and variety store—yes
Restaurant—on site**

Cotton Key Channel

The charted channel north of Key Point that cuts east to Pirate Harbor serves a series of private docks built along a huge complex of canals. There are no facilities for visitors, nor is there enough room to anchor. Most cruisers, except those fortunate enough to own a home in this development, will want to continue north to Punta Gorda or the Myakka and Peace rivers.

LOWER CHARLOTTE HARBOR NAVIGATION

Entry into Charlotte Harbor from the northerly reaches of Pine Island Sound is facilitated by good markings at the large bay's southern mouth. These aids are rather widely placed, however, and wise captains will lay out compass and/or GPS courses well ahead of time and follow them religiously while on the water. North of Burnt Store Marina, there are no more aids to navigation short of Punta Gorda and the entrance to the Myakka. Fortunately, there are no shoals, save a narrow band of shallows directly abutting the shoreline, to worry with.

Entering Charlotte Harbor Come abeam of and pass flashing daybeacon #4, well south of Cape Haze, by some 100 yards to its northerly side. You need not be too cautious. There is no shallow water for several miles in either direction.

Set a new, semicircular course to pass between flashing daybeacons #5 and #6. Stay away from #5. This aid marks a large shoal building out from Cape Haze.

The channel cutting east to Burnt Store Marina will be found east of flashing daybeacon #6. You will most likely sight the development's six-story condo tower looking out over the marina entrance long before you are able to pick out the outermost aids to navigation. Remember the good, old "red, right, returning" axiom and you will have no difficulty.

North of flashing daybeacon #6, you need only keep anywhere vaguely near the mid-width of Charlotte Harbor for excellent depths. If your destination is Punta Gorda, point to eventually find flashing daybeacon #1, west of Mangrove Point. If the Myakka is your intended destination, follow a course to meet up with unlighted daybeacon #7, well south of Hog Island.

The Myakka River

Killer turtles swoop from overhanging trees, the Myakka's river people claim, and a sea monster once lurked in the waters near the pit where Jose Gaspar buried his doubloons. But beneath the hype and legend, the amber river flows through some of Florida's most treasured wilderness and through history as real as mastodons, Ponce de Leon and the Indian and Civil Wars.

You will seldom read a better description of the Myakka than the one presented above from Del and Marty Marth's magnificent book

The Rivers of Florida. The chapter on the Myakka, written by Tim Dorsey and Rick Barry, is typical of this "must-read" study of the Sunshine State's great waterways.

Indeed, few will ever contest the claim that the Myakka is one of the most beautiful and historic streams in all of Florida. Years ago this writer wandered happily through the confines of Myakka State Park, many miles upstream from Charlotte Harbor, and came away with the memory of breathtaking river banks, tall cypress trees crowned with black ravens, and a bridge to nowhere disappearing into the lush foliage.

There is, unfortunately, some bad news for those of us who pilot cruising craft. While, to be sure, there is still the opportunity to anchor amidst wonderfully natural shores, it must also be noted that depths in the river channel fall to 4-foot levels after cruising a mere 8 miles from the river's juncture with Charlotte Harbor. This is far short of the river's most beautiful sections, many miles farther to the north.

Adding insult to injury, the Myakka is spanned by two new fixed bridges with only 24 feet of vertical clearance a mere 3 nautical miles from Charlotte Harbor. Although in fair breezes sail craft could conceivably anchor below this span, the fair upper reaches of the river are clearly off limits for most wind-powered vessels.

Equally clear is the lack of protected sidewaters along the stretch of the river accessible to cruisers. Those desiring to spend the night swinging on the hook amidst the Myakka's storied waters must anchor in the river itself. While such a strategy is fine in light to lower, moderate winds, this is not the place to be caught out in anything approaching heavy weather.

Some soundings of 5 feet will be encountered along the course of the Myakka channel, well short of the 4-foot region described above. Along with the height restriction imposed by the bridge, this thin water pretty well restricts a river cruise to boats drawing less than 4½ feet (preferably less than 4 feet).

So check the forecast, assess your boat's draft and vertical clearance requirements, and make your plans accordingly. Even with all its restrictions for larger craft, few will forget a trip up this timeless river, where life seems to have ebbed by, much as the river's current, leaving behind little change for the last hundred years.

Myakka River Anchorages (Various Lats/Lons—see below)

Remember that all the anchorages described below are only appropriate for light winds. During stormy times, head for one of the marinas or anchorages at Punta Gorda or Peace River and visit the Myakka another day.

Any pleasure boat drawing less than 4½ feet may consider anchoring on the charted patch of 7- and 10-foot water south of the small, charted channel leading north to El Jobean, near 26 57.365 North/082 12.174 West. The river waters abeam of the side channel make for a truly wide-open anchorage. Some development is still apparent along the river's banks, particularly to the north.

Skippers may also consider dropping the hook along the river between unlighted daybeacons #A and #B, near 26 58.693 North/082 14.333 West. These nondescript aids are not easy to spot on the water. This anchorage affords a good view of the Myakka's undisturbed easterly shore. In fair weather, it would be easy to linger here for a day or two just drinking in the magnificent scenery like fine wine.

There is a third, far more protected anchorage a few miles farther upriver, but you must be able to stand some 3½- to 4-foot depths to reach this haven. North of unlighted daybeacon #22, soundings deteriorate to the 4-foot, and possibly an occasional 3½-foot, mark. There is an unmarked shoal to avoid, but north of unlighted (and uncharted) daybeacon #23, the river narrows and depths deepen to between 5 and 9 feet. Cruising craft can anchor abeam of charted Tarpon Point, near 27 01.165 North/082 16.327 West, in about 6 feet of water with good protection from western and eastern breezes. There is even some shelter to the north. With its depth requirements, this anchorage can only be recommended for somewhat wild-eyed captains piloting smaller powercraft.

MYAKKA RIVER NAVIGATION

As delightful as the Myakka truly is, one must acknowledge the presence of shallow water along much of its length. Navigators who wander from their intended track could find themselves in 4-foot waters before they know what is happening. You must pay strict attention to business while cruising this river. When the scenery gets to be too much for you, drop anchor and kick back for an hour or two. Of course, don't forget you must be able to clear the 24-foot fixed bridges spanning the Myakka at the charted location of El Jobean to even visit the upper portion of the river.

Approach from Charlotte Harbor   From the main body of Charlotte Harbor, point to pass unlighted daybeacon #7, well south of Hog Island and Locust Point, to its fairly immediate northeasterly side. You can then curve your track to the northwest and set course to pass unlighted daybeacon #8, south of Shoal Point, by at least 100 yards to its westerly quarter. As the name of the point implies, the shoal to the northeast is building out into the river.

From #8, it is a run of 2.5 nautical miles upriver to the next aid, unlighted daybeacon #9. Stick to the river's mid-width. A broad band of shoals extends out from both banks of the river. Come abeam of and pass #9 by at least 100 yards to its eastern side.

Past #9, you must follow a markerless stretch of the river to the 24-foot fixed bridges stretching between Charlotte Beach and El Jobean. Again, stick to the centerline. You can expect some 5-foot depths, possibly even less, between #9 and the bridge.

Upstream on the Myakka River   The newly reconstructed Myakka fixed bridges have a vertical clearance of 24 feet. Immediately after passing under these spans you will catch sight of an old railroad bridge. This venerable span has been left in place (though it is long since unused) with its center section swung permanently open. The horizontal clearance through the span is only 30 feet, a rather narrow passage for some larger powercraft.

After leaving the two bridges behind, the Myakka begins a long, slow turn to the north. Stick to the centerline and watch carefully for unlighted daybeacon #A. This is a rather nondescript aid to navigation consisting of a small piling with some sort of strange round daymark atop it. Pass #A to its westerly side and continue upriver on the centerline looking for unlighted daybeacon #B. This latter aid is of the same sort as #A. Now, I know it doesn't make sense from the color, but pass #B to its immediate easterly side. From this point, the color scheme returns to the usual pattern. Pass red beacons to your starboard side and green markers to port as you cruise upstream.

Depths begin to fall off to 4 feet, possibly a little less, near unlighted daybeacon #20. If you can take these soundings, it's possible to continue cruising northwest past unlighted daybeacon #22. Upstream of this aid, favor the western banks to avoid the charted shoal abutting the eastern shoreline. Once past this hazard, you can drop the hook in 5- to 6-foot depths.

Don't attempt to cruise upstream past the intersection with Big Slough. The river narrows considerably and depths become much too uncertain for cruising-size craft.

Punta Gorda

Modern Punta Gorda is a prosperous residential/retirement community that guards the intersection of the Peace River and Charlotte Harbor. One cannot visit this thriving city without coming away with the sure and certain conviction that the town is undergoing a boom in housing. The incredible series of charted canals southwest of the principal waterfront serves a growing metropolis of expensive homes, many with their own private docks. If the fishermen of yesteryear could see Punta Gorda today, they would scarcely recognize the town they once knew.

Visiting cruisers will find two yacht clubs, one good marina (currently under reconstruction), and four anchorages to serve their needs in Punta Gorda. Shopping facilities of all descriptions are within walking distance or, at most, a cab ride from all the area facilities. Punta Gorda makes a fine restocking depot for pleasure craft cruising between Fort Myers and Venice.

The town of Port Charlotte sits across the southerly mouth of the Peace River from Punta Gorda. The two communities are so alike that they can almost be thought of as one town by visiting cruisers.

It doesn't take a genius to see why more and more people are being drawn to Punta Gorda and the town of Port Charlotte during their retirement years. The fine waters set about beautiful shores and quiet, often palatial residential neighborhoods, not to mention the nearly ideal climate, are enough to set anyone to musing on a property purchase in this fortunate community.

Numbers to known in Punta Gorda include

Astor Cab—(941) 624-4554
Charlotte Shuttle and Transporation—
  (941) 627-8922
Budget Rent A Car—(941) 625-6696
Enterprise Rent-A-Car—(941) 575-4200
West Marine—(941) 637-0000
Chamber of Commerce—(941) 639-222

Punta Gorda History   Punta Gorda was a quiet fishing village until the arrival of the Florida Southern Railroad in 1886. This new mode of transportation at last provided a ready outlet for Charlotte Harbor and Pine Island Sound's rich seafood bounty. For many years it looked as if the northeastern United States was determined to consume all the aquatic life in these waters.

A large ice plant was soon built and the Punta Gorda Fish Company was formed. Within a few months, this well-organized operation undertook construction of the stilted fishing houses on Pine Island Sound that we considered earlier in this chapter.

By 1897 more than 230 people worked the offshore fisheries, with another several dozen plying the sound and bay. These intrepid fishermen accomplished their hardy tasks aboard 140 different vessels. Gill netting for mullet was the most profitable activity. The northern markets simply could not seem to get enough of this seaborne delicacy. Spanish mackerel, oysters, and channel bass were also harvested in quantity.

As the twentieth century progressed, the phenomenal catches lessened. The boom days of the Punta Gorda commercial fisherman now live only in the memory of the town's older residents. Well, gone they may be, but those who listen carefully along the waterfront during a quiet night may still hear, in their mind's ear at least, the groan of the nets or the cry of the fisherman as he returns from a successful catch. The lore and history of the Punta Gorda fisherpeople are part and parcel of this town, and they will never be entirely forgotten.

Riviera Marina (26 53.316 North/082 03.213 West)

The charted, *L*-shaped channel south of Mangrove Point provides access to Alligator Creek and what must be described as one of the seediest marinas and repair yards that this writer has ever visited. Honestly, folks, you kind of have to see this one to believe it. The fixed wooden docks are not in the best of repair and some of the covered slips are truly dilapidated.

Riviera Marina claims to offer both mechanical and haul-out repairs, but the travelift looks as if it may have just been the original experiment in the product. The management has informed this writer that transients are accepted, and it is quite possible that you might find a slip for the evening, assuming you can beat off the seemingly hundreds of stray cats that frequent the piers. Gasoline is available, and there is a small variety store on site.

In spite of the negative characteristics noted above, we did note a large number of hauled craft sitting on cradles undergoing work by their owners. It was also equally obvious that Riviera Marina is used by many local fishermen. For all this, though, most visiting cruisers, particularly sail craft, will probably want to choose one of the other facilities farther to the north.

Surprisingly enough, the adjacent Riviera Oyster Bar Restaurant (941-639-2633) is absolutely first rate! It is under entirely different management from the marina. I was very taken with my fried seafood platter, as was my mate with her deviled crabmeat. By all accounts, this is a memorable dining spot. If you should happen to find a slip in Riviera, then, by all means, visit the Oyster Bar.

Riviera Marina (941) 639-2008

Approach depth—4½-5 feet (minimum)
Dockside depth—5 feet (low water)
Accepts transients—limited
Fixed wooden slips—yes (some not in the best of condition)
Dockside power connections—20 amp only
Dockside water connections—yes
Gasoline—yes
Mechanical repairs—limited
Below-waterline repairs—yes
Variety store—yes
Restaurant—on site

Punta Gorda Canals

The charted passage north of Mangrove Point skirts by a small park and public launching ramp, and eventually enters the maze of canals to the east. While good depths of 6 feet or better are carried well into the canals, we could not find enough swinging room anywhere for a vessel over 26 feet to anchor. The local residents might take a dim view of this practice in any case.

Punta Gorda-Port Charlotte Anchorages (Various Lats/Lons—see below)

East of unlighted daybeacon #3, the marked channel leads into the southern mouth of Peace River and directly between the Punta Gorda and Port Charlotte waterfronts. There are at least four spots that visiting cruisers might consider dropping anchor along this populated portion of Peace River.

First up, boats drawing less than 4½ feet can break off from the main channel just east of unlighted daybeacon #3 and track their way almost due north to the westernmost of the three charted and marked channels, west of Live Oak Point. Point for the gap between the outermost markers, flashing daybeacon #1 and unlighted daybeacon #2. Study chart 11426 for a moment and notice that the canal north of #1 and #2 leads to a fairly large basin known (but not charted) as Edgewater Lake. The entrance and approach channel carries at least 5 feet of water, while soundings on Edgewater Lake run from 6½ to 8 feet.

Once past the entrance, track your way directly up the connecting canal to Edgewater Lake. Anchor anywhere near the basin's mid-width (near 26 57.801 North/082 05.594 West). This refuge is wonderfully sheltered from all winds—in fact, it's the only really sheltered anchorage along the Punta Gorda-Port Charlotte waterfronts. The shoreline is, as you would expect, pocked by very heavy residential development. Do not try to dinghy ashore in Edgewater Lake. All the banks are privately owned.

With fair winds or moderate breezes from the north or northwest, you might consider anchoring northeast of #3 in the correctly charted 5- and 6-foot depths southwest of Live Oak Point (near 26 57.073 North/082 04.228 West). This is obviously not the place to ride out foul weather, but with fair breezes in the offing, it will serve as an acceptable overnight haven. Cruisers needing to go ashore can dinghy to the northeastern side of the Peace River bridges (see below) and come ashore on the east side of Live Oak Point at a public beach.

Southeast of unlighted daybeacon #4 (near 26 56.233 North/082 03.720 West), just short of the high-rise Peace River bridges, skippers might choose to drop the hook in the 5-foot waters abutting the southeastern banks. Some shelter is afforded from southern and southeastern airs, but this anchorage is wide open to blows from all other quarters. Again, this is not the place to hunker down when bad weather shows up in the NOAA forecast. Cruisers visiting this anchorage can dinghy ashore at Gilchrest Park. Watch for a pink gazebo overlooking the southeastern shoreline. Pull your dink up on a sandy beach that you will spot close by. The city of Punta Gorda, which used to limit stays in this anchorage to 24 hours, now allows cruising craft to anchor here for 5 days (out of any 30 days).

Finally, cruising craft that can clear the 45-foot fixed twin bridges northeast of unlighted daybeacon #4 can anchor on the charted 7- and 8-foot waters behind (northeast of) Live Oak Point, near 26 57.096 North/082 03.498 West. Depths quickly rise to 4 and 5 feet as you track your way west and northwest toward the shoreline. Boats drawing more than 4 feet should anchor just far enough behind the point for effective shelter and stay well off the southwesterly banks.

Live Oak Point does provide a lee when the fickle breezes are blowing from the west and southwest. Well, you guessed it—this overnight stop is wide open from all other directions. The shores are guarded by a fairly thick collection of commercial development.

The northeasterly banks behind (northwest of) Live Oak Point (adjacent to the just described anchorage) are flanked by two small restaurants with petite docks. One is a raw bar while the other is associated with an adjacent motel. Both the piers are too shallow and small for cruising-size craft, but mariners looking to dine here can tie off their dinghies temporarily while patronizing the restaurants. You may also land your dinghy on the narrow, sandy beach south of the raw bar. This is a publicly owned strip of land.

Isles Yacht Club (26 55.452 North/082 04.335 West)

One of Punta Gorda's two yacht clubs is found south and east of unlighted daybeacon #3A. The yacht club channel is actually the easternmost of the three marked and charted cuts south of #3A.

After cruising south on the well-marked channel past unlighted daybeacon #11, the passage enters a sheltered, southward-running canal. Cruisers making for Isles Yacht Club should hang a turn to port off this stream onto the first eastward-running canal. The yacht club will come up at the easterly end of this stream. Minimum low-water soundings on the approach channel and canal are 6½ feet.

Isles Yacht Club is one of the best and friendliest clubs in this land of fine yacht clubs. A member of the staff once took the time to help this writer find a nearby launching ramp during our research, and at a later time, the club membership gave this writer more than one warm reception following several speaking engagements with the membership.

Cruisers who are members of clubs with appropriate reciprocal privileges are gladly accepted for guest dockage at mostly fixed wooden piers. Some slips consist of wooden pilings set out from a concrete seawall. Minimum dockside depths are a very impressive 8 feet. The harbor is very well sheltered and should be more than sufficient for a snug stay in really nasty weather. Full dockside power and water connections are available, and both gasoline and diesel fuel can be purchased by members and club guests only (except on Mondays, when the club is closed). Dockage is free for the first 24 hours to members of FCYC yacht clubs. Reservations are requested, and they must be cancelled at least 48 hours in advance. The marina is staffed from 8:30 A.M. to 4:00 P.M. Tuesday through Saturday, and 8:30 A.M. to 3:00 P.M. on Sundays. Shoreside, visitors will find a swimming pool, tennis courts, and showers. The club dining room is open for lunch from 11:30 A.M. to 2:00 P.M., and dinner is served from 5:00 P.M. to 9:30 P.M. every day except Sunday and Monday. The club closes on Sundays at noon (after serving breakfast). Visiting cruisers will most definitely want to take advantage of this sumptuous dining opportunity.

> **Isles Yacht Club (941) 639-1369**
>   **http://www.islesyachtclub.com**
>
> **Approach depth—6½-11 feet**
> **Dockside depth—8 feet**
> **Accepts transients—members of yacht clubs**
>   **with reciprocal privileges**
> **Fixed wooden piers—yes**
> **Dockside power connections—30 and 50 amp**
> **Dockside water connections—yes**
> **Gasoline—yes (members and guests only)**
> **Diesel fuel—yes (members and guests only)**
> **Showers—yes**
> **Restaurant—on site**

Fishermen's Village Yacht Basin (26 55.745 North/082 03.800 West)

The mostly breakwater-enclosed, well-protected harbor of Fishermen's Village Yacht Basin is found at the southeastern foot of the well-buoyed channel near flashing daybeacon #2.

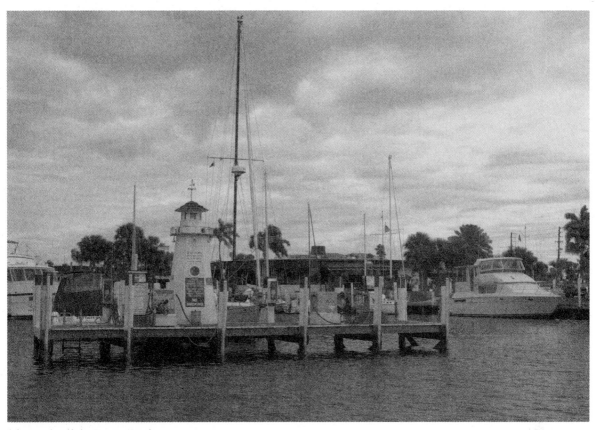

Isles Yacht Club, Punta Gorda

For many years, this facility has been "the" marina in Punta Gorda. However, at the time of this writing, the marina is mostly closed down, pending a full reconstruction and (likely) dredging of the dockage basin. The new incarnation of Fishermen's Village will undoubtedly be even better than ever upon completion. Sticking with our long-standing policy of not commenting on any facility until we can actually see it with our own eyes, we will not speculate any further at this time as to just what form the marina will be in and what services will be available in the new Fishermen's Village.

Unfortunately, a call to the marina management as late as August 2003 did not yield a time line for the completion of construction. Call (941) 575-3000 for updated information.

When cruising craft are once again accepted for dockage in Fishermen's Village, captain and crew entering the harbor will quickly spy a huge enclosed shopping and dining complex southwest of the dockage basin. This unique collection includes 7 restaurants and 33 shops of all descriptions. For steak and prime rib, you can't beat the Captain's Table (941-637-1177). Those up for the best catch of the day should spare no

Peace River shoreline

pains to make their way to the Village Fish Market (941-639-7959). Not only can you dine on the freshest of seafood here, but there is also a retail counter where you can purchase all types of sea creatures and take them back to your own galley for preparation. Finally, those with a taste of Italy simply can't do better than the Bella Luna Italian Restaurant (941-575-4544).

Charlotte Harbor Yacht Club (26 57.557 North/082 04.740 West)

Charlotte Harbor Yacht Club maintains good dockage in a protected basin along the northerly shores of the lower Peace River, directly across from the Punta Gorda waterfront. The yacht club channel is the first marked and charted cut west of Live Oak Point.

Members of other yacht clubs with appropriate reciprocal arrangements are accepted for guest dockage at fixed piers and slips. Low-water entrance depths run to 6½ feet, while cruisers will find a good 7 feet of water dockside. The club's dockmaster is on duty from 8:00 A.M. to 3:30 P.M., Tuesday through Saturday. The club is closed on Mondays, and there are no dockside attendants on Sunday. Full power and water connections are readily available at every slip, and members and guests (only) can purchase gasoline and diesel fuel dockside. Showers are available in the clubhouse, and accredited visitors can make use of several on-site tennis courts. The club's impressive dining room is open for lunch and dinner Tuesday through Saturday, with a Sunday brunch from 11:00 A.M. to 2:00 P.M.

Charlotte Harbor Yacht Club (941) 629-5131
  http://www.thechyc.com

Approach depth—6½-8 feet
Dockside depth—7 feet
Accepts transients—members of other yacht
  clubs with reciprocal privileges
Fixed wooden piers—yes
Dockside power connections—30 amp
Dockside water connections—yes
Showers—yes
Gasoline—yes (members and guests only)
Diesel fuel—yes (members and guests only)
Restaurant—on site

Other Punta Gorda and Port Charlotte Facilities

Just northeast of the fixed bridge, the city of Punta Gorda maintains a city park with a launching ramp and some piers along the southeasterly banks. This small facility is being reconstructed at the time of this writing, but there is some reason to believe that even when completed, the wet-slip emphasis will remain focused on local commercial fishing craft, as has been true in times past.

On the opposite shore, across from the small city marina, a restaurant and a motel (with restaurant) maintain two small, low-level docks overlooking the eastern side of Live Oak Point. Both of these piers have very thin water, running to only 3 feet. Also, the piers are so low that they can really only accommodate small, runabout-type power-craft. Again, cruising craft larger than 24 feet should seek dockage and shelter at some more appropriate location.

PUNTA GORDA AND CHARLOTTE HARBOR NAVIGATION

Everything is pretty much straightforward in navigating the waters lying about the southerly mouth of the Peace River and the Punta Gorda-Port Charlotte waterfront. Just be sure to take enough time to correctly identify all markers before going ahead. At times, it's easy to confuse the main channel markings with some of the side cuts' aids to navigation.

Alligator Creek and Riviera Marina Vessels cruising to this rather different marina should pass between the first two western-most markers, flashing daybeacon #1 and unlighted daybeacon #2. A host of uncharted markers will then lead you through an *L*-shaped channel into the mouth of Alligator Creek. Pass red markers to your starboard side and take green beacons to port.

Once inside the creek's boundaries, hold to the mid-width as you work your way upstream. The marina will eventually come up on the port-side banks.

On to Punta Gorda and Charlotte Harbor Set course to come abeam of flashing daybeacon #2, well east of Locust Point, to its northwesterly side. While you could actually pass #2 on either side, its color dictates the west and northerly passage as preferred.

Flashing daybeacon #2 marks your entry into the southerly mouth of the Peace River.

The upper reaches of this stream will be covered in the next section of this chapter, but for now, let us review the Punta Gorda and Port Charlotte waterfront and their various facilities.

From #2, set course to come abeam of unlighted daybeacon #3 to its fairly immediate southerly side. While there are no shoals other than a thin strip of shallows abutting the shoreline in the immediate vicinity, the preferred channel takes a turn to the southeast. Look to the southeast and use your binoculars to pick out unlighted daybeacon #3A and the markers leading to Isles Yacht Club. Come abeam of #3A to its immediate southerly side.

Isles Yacht Club   At unlighted daybeacon #3A, the channel to Isles Yacht Club will be obvious to the south. There are actually many more markers on this cut than those indicated on chart 11426. Follow the markers into the mouth of the sheltered canal dead ahead. Take the first canal that opens up to your port side. Follow the mid-width of this stream east to the yacht club docks.

Lower Port Charlotte Anchorages   From unlighted #3, mariners have access to two anchorages on the Port Charlotte (northern) side of Peace River. To reach the sheltered refuge on Edgewater Lake, set a northerly course from a position just east of #3 for the gap between flashing daybeacon #1 and unlighted daybeacon #2. These aids are the outermost (southernmost) markers on the westernmost of the three charted channels west of Live Oak Point. Once between #1

and #2, continue dead ahead for the westernmost of the three canals that you will spy ahead.

Enter the canal on its mid-width and track your way upstream to Edgewater Lake. Drop the hook anywhere within shouting distance of the lake's mid-section.

You might also choose to spend the evening anchored southwest of Live Oak Point. Set course from #3 for the charted 5- and 6-foot waters southeast of the easternmost of the three sets of markers leading into the northern banks. Don't approach to within less than 250 yards of the banks and be on guard against the correctly charted 2- and 3-foot shoals a bit farther to the east. These shallows surround the point and the shoreline just to the north and northeast. Be sure to drop the hook well west and south of this thin water.

Charlotte Harbor Yacht Club   You can gain access from unlighted daybeacon #3 to Charlotte Harbor Yacht Club on the northern banks. Set course from #3 for the easternmost of the charted channels, west of Live Oak Point.

Don't be fooled. From the river you can only see a portion of the dockage harbor. Keep the faith. Follow the markers in and the basin will eventually open out to starboard, while the clubhouse will be prominent to port.

On Peace River Channel

From unlighted daybeacon #3A, come abeam of and pass unlighted daybeacon #2X and flashing daybeacon #2 to their northerly sides. It's easy to confuse #2 with the markers leading southeast to Fishermen's Village Yacht Basin. This latter cut is easily followed into the marina's sheltered harbor.

Upstream from flashing daybeacon #2, the channel narrows a bit. Pass unlighted daybeacon #4 to its immediate northerly side and then point directly for the pass-through of the 45-foot fixed twin bridge dead ahead. After passing under both spans, you should spot the small city marina to the southeast, and a line of power-cable towers breaking the water in a northwest-to-southeast line across the breadth of the river. Chart 11426 warns of submerged ruins on these waters. Continue straight ahead and put this hazard behind you.

Punta Gorda Anchorage Depart the main channel at unlighted daybeacon #4, itself a short hop southwest of the twin fixed bridges. Ease your way toward the southeastern banks, feeling your way along with the sounder. For best depths stay at least 200 yards off the shoreline.

Live Oak Point Anchorage After passing under the twin, fixed high-rise Peace River bridges, continue straight ahead under the charted 75-foot power lines. After leaving these hazards well behind, curl around to the northwest and point for the charted 7- and 8-foot waters east of Live Oak Point's southeasterly tip. Watch your sounder carefully as you approach a position abeam of the point. If depths start to rise, retreat to the southeast. Drop anchor as soon as the point comes abeam southwest of your course line. Stay well off the southwesterly, Live Oak Point shoreline. Depths of 3 and 4 feet await your keel just a stone's throw farther to the west and northwest.

The Peace River

The Peace River is actually named for the wild peas that once grew profusely along its banks. In fact, the stream was originally named "Pease River." The spelling was apparently changed after Florida became a part of the young United States in the 1840s.

Today, while the river suffers to some extent from decades of phosphate mining along its banks, the upper reaches of this river are known as a canoeing paradise. Unfortunately, these idyllic waters are far beyond the practical cruising limits for larger pleasure craft.

The lower Peace River boasts a shoreline ranging from all-natural terrain to stretches where a few private homes show through here and there. Most of the banks are composed of marsh grass and are, frankly, not as attractive as those of the Peace's sister stream, the Myakka.

Not that the Peace River lacks for gunk holes. There are myriad opportunities to anchor well off the beaten track, sometimes with nary a house or building within sight. The anchorages discussed below are only a portion of the possible havens along the river's lower reaches. Imaginative and adventurous captains can take chart 11426 and carefully cruise to many additional overnight or lunch stops.

There are practically no marina facilities on the course of the Peace River. One boatyard near Punta Gorda offers repairs, but no dockage.

Only boats drawing 5 feet or, preferably, less should attempt to cruise the Peace River. In a few spots, 5-foot depths could be a problem for longer-legged craft.

Sailors must also take the twin Live Oak Point/Punta Gorda and I-75 bridges into account. All these spans have a vertical clearance of 45 feet. Larger sail craft must forego the cruising charms of the Peace River in light of these height restrictions.

In summation, this writer cannot say that the Peace River was his favorite body of water in Western Florida. Nor was it the worst. I would place the river somewhere in the middle.

Punta Gorda Marina (26 56.612 North/082 02.193 West)

West of the 45-foot Highway 41 fixed bridge, a relatively shallow, poorly charted channel along the southerly banks leads through a narrow, tree-enveloped opening to Punta Gorda Marina (941-639-2750). Low-tide entrance and dockside depths of only 4½ feet could be a problem for some boats.

Punta Gorda Marina does not offer any transient dockage, but they do feature full mechanical and below-waterline, haul-out repairs. Their travelift can haul any boat up to 35 tons.

Cleveland Anchorage (26 57.662 North/081 59.860 West)

After swinging under the twin I-75 bridges,

Entrance to Punta Gorda Marina

the Peace River channel cuts over to the southeastern shores near the charted village of Cleveland. Actually, only a few homes overlook the river—not much of a village really, but still quite aesthetically appealing from the water.

Good depths of 6 feet or better run to within 25 yards of the banks northeast of unlighted daybeacon #19. There should be enough swinging room for boats up to 45 feet. Protection is quite good for all but strong southwesterly winds. There is some river current in evidence, so make sure the anchor is well set before heading below.

NOTE Q
The daybeacons are
private and positions
are approximate.

Harbour
Heights

Shell Pt

OVHD CABS

FIXED BRIDGE
HOR CL 60 FT
VERT CL 10 FT

OVHD CABS

OVHD CABS

Long
Island

Mangrove

Marsh

Shell Cr

Marsh

Marsh

Bird
Key

(see note Q)

Cleveland

Piling

Piles

OVHD CAB

Coon
Key

Mangrove

Solana

FIXED BRIDGE
HOR CL 75 FT
VERT CL 45 FT

Subm pile

Ramp

Mkrs

Subm
piles

Mangrove

1. Punta Gorda Marina

1

OVHD CAB

SSRR

Long Island Anchorage (26 58.223 North/081 59.769 West)

North of unlighted daybeacon #21, boats can anchor just off the river channel in the correctly charted 5-foot waters. Protection is good from all winds and vessels up to 38 feet should have enough elbowroom. Be sure to show an anchor light at night. While there is little in the way of commercial traffic on the Peace River, there is always the possibility that someone could happen along during the evening hours.

Harbor Heights Anchorage (26 59.714 North/081 59.339 West)

North-northeast of unlighted daybeacon #24, a broad channel of deep water rushes on to a parting of the river below Hunter Creek. This guide's coverage of the Peace River ends at this division of the waters. You can anchor south of the forks in 8 to 12 feet of water with plenty of swinging room and superb protection. Again, it would be a very good idea to show a bright anchor light.

PEACE RIVER NAVIGATION

Trust me when I tell you that the Peace River is not the sort of place to go cruising ahead at full bore with an occasional visual reference to the various aids to navigation along the way. The river channel wanders this way and that, and not all the markers are visible from the preceding aid. Depths do run to 5 feet in one or two spots, but most of the channel is far deeper. Remember that the 45-foot height of the two fixed bridges sets the overhead clearance for boats cruising the Peace River.

On the Peace River   After passing under the twin spans of the Live Oak Point/Punta Gorda (Highway 41) fixed bridge (45 feet of vertical clearance), continue straight ahead until you are at least 100 yards northeast of the (75-foot) power line. At this point, the channel swings sharply north, but should you be seeking Punta Gorda Marina, your course will be different.

Punta Gorda Marina   Follow the charted deep water off the southeasterly banks. Be sure to stay well away from the 1- and 2-foot shoal lying well off the shoreline. Watch for a series of markers running on a west-to-east line out from the southeastern shore. Ease your way into the channel and expect some 4½-foot depths.

On the Peace River   Be sure to use the "Continuation of Peace River" section of chart 11426 for all your upstream navigation on this body of water. This portion of the chart gives excellent detail of the river well upstream past this guide's coverage.

After leaving the power lines behind, turn to the north and point to come abeam of unlighted daybeacon #6 to its westerly side. Curve around #6 and head east. Set your course to come abeam of and pass unlighted daybeacon #8 to its northerly side.

Now the channel follows yet another turn, this time to the southeast. From #8 you must point to come abeam of unlighted daybeacon #9 to its southerly side. Be on guard against the charted 3-foot shoal lying to the southwest between #8 and #9.

North and east of unlighted daybeacon #9 the channel narrows but becomes better marked. Vessels bound upstream should pass green markers to their (the cruisers') port side and take red beacons to starboard.

East of unlighted daybeacon #12, the river channel passes under the twin I-75 fixed bridges. Vertical clearance is set at 45 feet.

At the time of this writing, construction is underway on a new expansion of this bridge. Watch out for barges and construction equipment when passing.

East of the I-75 bridge, be sure to pass unlighted daybeacon #15 to its southerly side. Don't get too close to #15, as a shoal seems to be building around the aid from the north.

Cleveland Anchorage   Once abeam of unlighted daybeacon #19 to its southeasterly side, begin feeling your way to the northeast with your sounder. Drop the hook before you are less than 25 yards from the shore. Be sure your anchor is set so as not to swing closer to the banks.

On the Peace River   At unlighted daybeacon #19, the Peace River channel begins a lazy turn to the north. Point to eventually pass unlighted daybeacon #21 to its easterly side. Between #21 and the next upstream aid, unlighted daybeacon #22, you can drop the hook just off the river's mid-width, providing you show a prominent anchor light at night.

The most difficult (and shallowest) portion of the upstream Peace River channel lies between unlighted daybeacons #22 and #24. Even by following the instructions outlined below, you will more than likely find your vessel tracking its way through 5-foot soundings.

To maintain the best depths possible, curve around to the northeast after leaving #22 behind, and point to come abeam of #24 to its immediate northwesterly side. This track will run you close to the marshy southeastern shoreline. As soon as you pass #24, cruise quickly to the northwest out into the mid-width of the river and the correctly charted broad band of deeper water.

North-northeast of unlighted daybeacon #24, mariners may again choose to drop the hook on the river's centerline. Don't forget the anchor light.

This guide's coverage of the Peace River ends where Hunter Creek breaks off to the northeast. Farther upstream, unmarked shoals become frequent—not much of a problem for canoes, but a very different situation for cruising vessels.

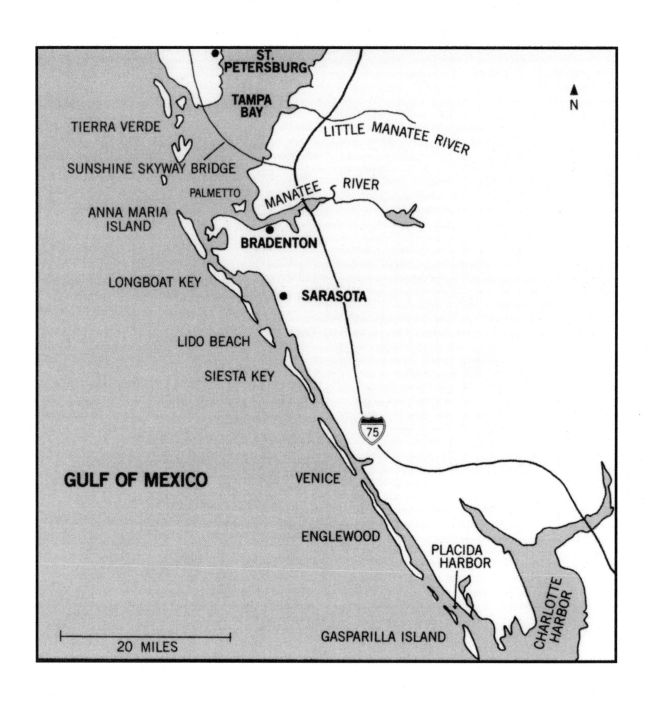

ST. PETERSBURG

TAMPA BAY

TIERRA VERDE

SUNSHINE SKYWAY BRIDGE

LITTLE MANATEE RIVER

PALMETTO

MANATEE RIVER

ANNA MARIA ISLAND

BRADENTON

LONGBOAT KEY

SARASOTA

LIDO BEACH

SIESTA KEY

75

GULF OF MEXICO

VENICE

ENGLEWOOD

PLACIDA HARBOR

CHARLOTTE HARBOR

20 MILES

GASPARILLA ISLAND

N

CHAPTER 3

Placida Harbor to Anna Maria Island

The Western Florida ICW between Placida Harbor and Anna Maria Island comprises some of the most intriguing waters on the Sunshine State's western coast. While the region may lack some of the scope, grandeur, and adventure of Pine Island Sound and Charlotte Harbor, gunk holes and anchorages abound on this stretch of the Waterway.

From Placida Harbor, north of the Gasparilla Island Bridge, the ICW runs between the Western Florida mainland and a whole series of barrier islands to the west. With a few exceptions, this geographic arrangement makes for a sheltered passage, which power captains will dearly love. Sailors will be less happy to learn that most of the passage south of Sarasota is relatively narrow. After all those great sails on the wide waters to the south, it's once again time to crank up the iron gennie and join your powered brethren in cruising with the screw.

The Waterway's sheltered nature is most certainly not all bad news, though. It takes really rough weather to churn up a nasty chop along much of this section. Lemon and Sarasota bays are two notable exceptions to this generally forgiving character. Winds over 15 knots can make for a rough ride on these two wider bodies of water, particularly in the Sarasota region.

If you should somehow dislike anchoring off, or just need to spend a night or two moored to a marina's dock, don't be concerned. A host of facilities serves up all the services that cruisers might require. Another rather prolific group of marine firms along this stretch caters mostly to smaller powercraft and their dry-storage needs. Read the data below and make your selection accordingly.

Two major communities demand any cruiser's attention along this stretch. Moving south to north, the first of these is the delightful town of Venice. Boasting good, if not prolific, marina facilities, Venice is a friendly community with a far slower lifestyle than that of the metropolitan regions farther to the north. Sarasota is a major city with a whole bevy of marinas, yacht clubs, waterside restaurants, and a fine collection of anchorages.

Only two inlets currently offer reliable access to and from the open Gulf north of Gasparilla Island. Venice Inlet can be used with confidence by most craft. At Sarasota, both Big Pass and New Pass have serious problems. Big Pass is now virtually unusable as an outlet to the Gulf of Mexico, and New Pass cannot be currently recommended without serious reservations.

Moving to the north, the next inlet encountered by cruisers will be Longboat Pass. This seaward cut can now be considered a reasonable navigational risk.

In between these cuts are various other, mostly smaller seaward channels, which some locals use regularly. Unfortunately, without specific up-to-date local knowledge, visiting cruisers must traverse these passages at their own risk.

Most mariners will find their sojourn between Placida and Anna Maria Island to be a real cruising delight. Few will want to rush blindly north to Tampa Bay without sampling the various gunk holes and other watery delights along the way. This writer strongly suggests that you include plenty of time in your cruising itinerary to fully enjoy these memorable waters.

Charts   Most navigators can get by with but a single chart along this section of the coastline, though offshore sailors may want a second.
11425—covers all inland waters and inlets between Gasparilla Island Causeway and Placida Harbor to Anna Maria Island and the ICW's southerly entrance into Tampa Bay
11424—offshore chart that covers pretty much the same area as 11425 with considerably less detail; it would be useful for offshore cruisers approaching the coastline

Bridges
Englewood Bridge—crosses ICW at Standard Mile 43.5, northwest of flashing daybeacon #22—Bascule—26 feet (closed)—opens on demand
Manasota Bridge—crosses ICW at Standard Mile 50, northwest of flashing daybeacon #42—Bascule—26 feet (closed)—opens on demand
South Venice/Tamiami Trail Bridge—crosses ICW at Standard Mile 55—Bascule—25 feet (closed)—opens on demand
Venice Avenue Bridge—crosses ICW at Standard Mile 56.5—Bascule—30 feet (closed)—opens 10, 30, and 50 minutes after the hour weekdays 7:00 A.M. to 4:30 P.M.—does not open at all 4:35 P.M. to 5:35 P.M.—at all other times opens on demand—New, high-rise bridge currently under construction at this location
Hatchett Creek Bridge—crosses ICW at Standard Mile 57, southwest of flashing daybeacon #5—Bascule—16 feet (closed)—opens on the hour and every 20 minutes thereafter weekdays 7:00 A.M. to 4:20 P.M. but does not open at all 4:25 P.M. to 5:25 P.M.—opens every 15 minutes weekends 7:30 A.M. to 6:00 P.M.—at all other times opens on demand—Construction associated with bridge expansion currently underway at this location

Casey Key Bridge—crosses ICW at Standard Mile 59, north of flashing daybeacon #9—Bascule—14 feet (closed)—opens on demand
Blackburn Bridge—crosses ICW at Standard Mile 63, north of unlighted daybeacon #32—Swing bridge—9 feet (closed)—opens on demand
Stickney Point Bridge—crosses ICW at Standard Mile 69, northwest of unlighted daybeacon #62—Bascule—18 feet (closed)—opens on demand
Siesta Key Bridge—crosses ICW at Standard Mile 71.5—Bascule—25 feet (closed)—opens on the hour and every 20 minutes thereafter 11:00 A.M. to 6:00 P.M.
Ringling Bridge—crosses ICW at Standard Mile 73.5, northwest of flashing daybeacon #10—Bascule—22 feet (closed)—opens on the hour and half-hour 7:00 A.M. to 6:00 P.M.—at all other times opens on demand—New, high-rise bridge currently under construction at this location
New Pass Inlet Bridge—crosses New Pass Inlet west-southwest of unlighted daybeacon #11—Bascule—23 feet (closed)—opens on the hour and every 20 minutes thereafter 7:00 A.M. to 6:00 P.M.

Longboat Pass Bridge—crosses Longboat Pass Inlet west of unlighted daybeacon #4—Bascule—17 feet (closed)—opens on demand 6:00 A.M. to 10:00 P.M.—at all other times requires three hours' notice

Cortez Bridge—crosses ICW at Standard Mile 87.5, north of unlighted daybeacon #49—Bascule—22 feet (closed)—opens on the hour and every 20 minutes thereafter 7:00 A.M. to 6:00 P.M.

Anna Maria Island Bridge—crosses ICW at Standard Mile 89, northeast of unlighted daybeacon #52—Bascule—24 feet (closed)—opens on the hour and every 20 minutes thereafter 7:00 A.M. to 6:00 P.M.—at all other times opens on demand

Gasparilla Island Bridge to Alligator Creek

North of the Gasparilla Island causeway, the ICW flows into Placida Harbor. While the harbor is a good-sized body of water in its own right, northbound cruisers leaving Pine Island Sound or Charlotte Harbor behind will quickly note its relatively narrower width. Soon the Waterway follows a canal to Lemon Bay. This impressive body of water runs north for some 10 nautical miles but narrows as it approaches another canal near Alligator Creek, leading to Venice. Lemon Bay's average width is better than half a nautical mile and strong winds can kick up a chop. Most of the bay's waters are shallow, and with a few notable exceptions, cruisers should stick to the Waterway channel. Even this formalized cut is known to experience shoaling along its edges.

This portion of the ICW is characterized by beautiful, lightly developed shores. Lemon Bay is absolutely lovely. Seen from the cockpit in the warm sunshine of a late summer afternoon, with the blue waters stretching out to the green, well-wooded shores—well, you'll just have to experience it for yourself to know what I mean.

Marina facilities are adequate on Placida Harbor and Lemon Bay, but they could not be described as prolific. At least four marinas provide good overnight dockage along this 18-statute-mile run. Slow-moving craft should take these distances into account if night is fast approaching.

Excellent anchorages abound and seem to be everywhere. Most offer good shelter for even heavy weather. If you should happen to fall short of a marina and a moonlight cruise is not to your liking, there is almost certainly a good place to drop the hook nearby.

Your cruise south of Venice is typical of the entire run to Anna Marina Island. While there are still great waters ahead, they offer little else save simpler navigation than the cruising grounds on Lemon Bay.

Placida Harbor Anchorage (Standard Mile 34.5, 26 49.812 North/082 16.715 West)

Captains whose craft draw less than 4½ feet can leave the ICW between unlighted daybeacon #24 and #24A and feel their way west for 100 yards or so in minimum 5-foot low-water depths. This is strictly a fair-weather anchorage. The only real protection is provided by the causeway to the south. Frankly, there are far better refuges close at hand, so unless you just have to stop here, consider one of the anchor-down spots described below.

Cape Haze Anchorage (Standard Mile 36, 26 50.706 North/082 17.184 West)

It's almost as if some omniscient marine architect decided to start things off right just north of Gasparilla with a really first-class anchorage. The large cove cutting into the Waterway's northeastern banks northwest of unlighted daybeacon #30 offers minimum 8-foot depths and super shelter from all winds.

The bottom of this cove has been dredged in years past, and the holding ground is a bit suspect, though neither we nor our neighbors have had any problems with dragging anchors during our several stays. There is enough swinging room for anything smaller than the *Exxon Valdez*. The shores are overlooked by moderate to heavy residential development. While many among us would prefer a natural shoreline, it must be noted that the homes are not unattractive and the many private docks with vessels lying beside them make for a true nautical atmosphere. Seldom will cruising mariners find such a well-sheltered and easily entered anchorage so close to the ICW.

Cove Anchorage (Standard Mile 36.5, 26 51.061 North/082 17.831 West)

Note the large cove indenting the northeastern banks at unlighted daybeacon #35. While not as large, nor quite so sheltered, as the Cape Haze anchorage, this water does provide good protection and features minimum 7-foot depths. The main body of the cove provides enough elbowroom for a 48-footer to swing comfortably. Cruisers dropping the hook in this cove will again have the opportunity to view the heavy but comely shoreside residential development. The cove eventually leads to a small canal lined with private docks. There are no facilities and no room to anchor along this stream.

Don Pedro Island Anchorage (Standard Mile 37, 26 51.181 North/082 18.197 West)

North of unlighted daybeacon #5 the Waterway quickly begins its approach to the sheltered canal which provides a conduit into Lemon Bay. There is one additional opportunity for snug overnight anchorage before entering the canal.

This haven is found on the charted 7-foot waters west-southwest of unlighted daybeacon #4. Boats drawing 5 feet or less can leave the ditch and cruise to within 25 yards of the western banks. Minimum depths are in the 5-foot range. Craft needing more water can drop the hook within 25 yards of the Waterway channel in 6 to 7 feet of water. Protection is good for all but the heaviest weather. Strong northerly blows would cause the most problems.

This is a delightful anchorage. The Don Pedro Island shoreline to the southwest is an all-natural collection of leafy green banks with taller trees farther to the west. A few private homes overlook the shoreline northeast of the Waterway. You will have to contend with the wake of any passing powercraft, but otherwise your stay should be one punctuated by peace and security.

Palm Island Marina/MarineMax (Standard Mile 38, 26 52.267 North/082 18.716 West)

One of the best marina facilities between Placida Harbor and Venice sits at the southern foot of Lemon Bay, northwest of unlighted daybeacon #7. We have been repeatedly impressed with the can-do attitude of Palm Island Marina's dockmaster and his staff. Visiting cruisers can now be assured of receiving a warm and knowledgeable welcome.

Good entrance and dockside depths of 6 to 6½ feet will be plenty for most vessels. Transients are accommodated at fixed wooden slips featuring full power, water, and cable-television connections. Gasoline or diesel fuel can also be purchased (at good prices), while shoreside amenities include

1.Palm Island Marina
2. Cape Haze Marina Bay

good, air-conditioned showers and a climate-controlled Laundromat. Waste pump-out service and extensive dry-stack storage for powercraft are available as well.

Palm Island Marina features a refreshing on-site swimming pool, where transients are welcome. An adjacent kitchen facility is open for free use by all visiting cruisers.

While a ferry still leaves the Palm Island Marina docks regularly for Rum Bay Restaurant on nearby Knight Island (see below), we now recommend that cruisers bent on a night of landside dining check out the on-site Johnny Leverocks Seafood House (941-698-6900).

A local branch of the ubiquitous MarineMax chain (941-697-2161) leases the rear portion of the Palm Island dockage basin and offers

Palm Island Marina

dry storage for smaller powercraft, mechanical repairs, haul-outs by way of a new 50 ton travelift, and a ship's store.

Palm Island Marina (941) 697-4356
http://www.palmislandmarina.com
MarineMax (941) 697-2161

Approach depth—6 feet minimum
Dockside depth—6-6½ feet
Accepts transients—yes
Transient dockage rate—average
Fixed wooden slips—yes
Dockside power connections—up to 50 amp
Dockside water connections—yes
Waste pump-out—yes
Showers—yes
Laundromat—yes
Gasoline—yes
Diesel fuel—yes
Mechanical repairs—yes (at MarineMax)
Below-waterline repairs—yes (at MarineMax)
Ship's store—yes (at MarineMax)
Restaurant—on site

Cape Haze Marina Bay (Standard Mile 38.5, 26 52.462 North/082 18.803 West)

An indifferently charted channel cuts east off the ICW, south of unlighted daybeacon #9, to a marina that has recently changed ownership. Cape Haze Marina Bay (formerly Cape Haze Yacht and Beach Club) offers transient dockage at very attractive rates. Berths are provided at fixed wooden piers set in a fairly sheltered harbor. Minimum entrance and dockside depths run about 5½ feet, with many slips having 6- to 7-foot soundings. Full power and water connections are offered, as are waste pump-out service, extensive dry-stack storage, and mechanical repairs for gasoline engines (only). Gasoline and diesel fuel can be purchased at the marina fuel dock. The on-

site, adequate, air-conditioned showers are now located in a trailer, behind the dry-stack storage building. There is also a new cabana bar, featuring a Laundromat, Jacuzzi, and swimming pool, plus propane grills that can be used by visitors.

The once-decrepit on-site Ship's Lantern restaurant has finally bitten the proverbial dust. There are two other dining spots within walking distance, including Johnny Leverocks (see above) and the Pix-Sea. We have not had the opportunity to review either dining spot.

Cape Haze Marina Bay (941) 698-1110
(800) 544-2436

Approach depth—5½-6½ feet minimum
Dockside depth—5½-7 feet minimum
Accepts transients—yes
Transient dockage rate—below average
Fixed wooden piers—yes
Dockside power connections—up to 50 amp
Dockside water connections—yes
Waste pump-out—yes
Showers—yes
Laundromat—yes
Gasoline—yes
Diesel fuel—yes
Mechanical repairs—gasoline engines only
Restaurant—within walking distance

Lemon Bay

North of unlighted daybeacon #8 the ICW flows out into the wider waters of Lemon Bay. Cruisers lucky enough to sight the bay's waters for the first time during fair weather will never forget the experience. To be succinct, Lemon Bay is gorgeous.

Lemon Bay often reminds me of author Mike Greenwald's description of the Mediterranean. The bay can be "a bit like the girl with green eyes. There can be a surprise behind her smile." So it is with this body of

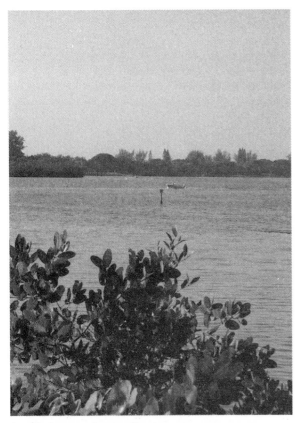

Looking out on Lemon Bay

water. While serving up a true aesthetic feast for the eyes, much of the bay is shallow and the ICW channel itself often shoals along its margins. While there are side trips, gunk holes, and anchorages galore, depths of as little as half a foot wait to greet the keel of the unwary.

So enjoy the sights, take your time, and have a safe cruise. Just remember that most of us can't stay on Lemon Bay forever. I know it's hard, but *c'est la vie*.

Rum Bay Restaurant on Knight Pass (Standard Mile 39.5)

North-northwest of unlighted daybeacon #9, unlighted daybeacon #9A marks the intersection of the Waterway and the passage running west and north into old Knight Pass channel. The inlet that gave rise to this stream has long been closed, but Rum Bay Restaurant (941-697-0566) maintains a marked and dredged channel from the ICW into the old cut. This passage leads to two sets of wooden piers where Rum Bay patrons are free to tie while dining. The restaurant also operates a ferry from the mainland to allow for visits by landlubbers. Channel and dockside depths are around 5½ to possibly 6 feet. While a sign on the docks advertises slips for boats up to 40 feet, they appeared to this writer to be more appropriate for craft under 36 feet. No overnight accommodations are available.

Stump Pass (Standard Mile 41)

The Stump Pass channel makes into the Waterway's southwestern flank immediately southeast of unlighted daybeacon #17A. The buoyed passage leads to a locally controversial passage.

Stump Pass is one of those inlets that the locals are constantly agitating to have dredged, but Mother Nature has another idea. Put another way, it's shoaling constantly, and captains of cruising-size craft should think long and hard before attempting to cruise through or anchor alongside this cut. You should, at the very least, check at one of the nearby marinas or with some local captains before making the attempt. Even then, don't be surprised if the bottom says hello to your keel.

For the moment (and that moment would be as of August 2003), MLW soundings of 6 feet can be expected if and only if you keep to the marked cut. Outside of the channel, depths run in inches. Stump Pass was dredged

1. Fish Tail Marina at Stump Pass

a little better than a year ago, and these depths are obviously the by-product of that project.

Navigators who do venture onto the waters of Stump Pass will find far more aids to navigation than what are pictured on the current edition of chart 11425. Precious few of these markers are lighted; however, and nighttime entry would be a quick study in foolhardiness.

There is one possible anchorage on the interior reaches of Stump Pass for smaller cruising-size craft. Note the cut running between the northern banks of Thornton Key and the unnamed island, northeast of charted, unlighted daybeacon #4. Entry into this stream is not nearly so easy as the chart would lead you to believe. A finger of very shallow water has built across most of the westerly entrance. Skippers must carefully skirt these shallows by hugging the stream's southerly shoreline.

If you can find your way past the entrance shoal, it is possible to drop the hook at 26 53.922 North/082 20.233 West, near where chart 11425 notes a 7-foot sounding. Indeed, we discovered MLW depths of 7 feet on these waters, but again, things could be *very* different by the time of your visit. The charted shoal to the north (southeast of unlighted daybeacon #4), stretching out from the unnamed island, is for real and greatly restricts swinging room in this anchorage. We don't suggest this haven for any craft larger than 32 feet.

In earlier editions of this guidebook, we used to recommend anchoring on the stream that lies along Stump Pass's northwestern flank, between Peterson Key and the beachside barrier island. However, we sounded low-water depths as thin as 2½ feet on this errant cut during our last visit. We strongly suggest bypassing this stream.

The seaward side of Stump Pass now bears little resemblance to what is pictured on chart 11425. The shoreline of Thornton Key, in particular, is now much altered. Passing cruisers will note a large, uncharted cove running off to the southeast, just inside the inlet's southeastern-side entrance point. While you may see a host of local, small craft anchored or pulled up onto the beach inside this cove, low-water soundings of as little as 2½ feet suggest that larger vessels should keep clear.

Stump Pass's exodus channel out into the Gulf of Mexico was carrying minimum 8-foot depths as of August 2003, and it was reasonably well marked. Daylight passage should not prove to be too taxing, as long as these depths hold. Not to be repetitive, but things could be very different in the future.

Fish Tail Marina at Stump Pass (Standard Mile 41, 26 54.354 North/082 19.695 West)

The well-marked entry channel leading to Fish Tail Marina (formerly Stump Pass Marina) cuts to the northeast abeam of unlighted daybeacon #17A. You can't miss the marina, courtesy of a lighthouse-like tower perched over the ship's store and fuel dock.

Fish Tail provides limited wet-slip dockage in an enclosed, well-protected harbor. Low-water entrance depths run a somewhat thin 4½ to 5 feet, with 5-foot low-water soundings in the enclosed basin. Transients are accepted, but clearly the forte here now runs far more to dry-stack storage of smaller powercraft rather than overnight dockage. In fact, the dockmaster has informed this writer that the marina usually only sees transients on the weekends. Berths at Fish Tail consist of wooden pilings set out from a concrete seawall. Dockside power connections run the gamut from 30 to 50 amps. Shoreside, cruisers will find a swimming pool, one semi-open-air shower, and a hot-tub spa. Other marine services include gasoline and diesel fuel. The on-site service and sales firm known as Dockside Marine (941-697-3600) offers some mechanical repairs for outboards and I/Os.

A ship's and variety store overlooks the entrance cut just behind the fuel dock. This pier fronts directly onto the bay and is not breakwater protected as the remainder of the marina's slips are. The poolside, semi-open-air Marker 17A Cafe (941-697-0241) is open for lunch daily and serves dinner Tuesday through Saturday.

Fish Tail Marina at Stump Pass (941) 697-2206

Approach depth—4½-5 feet (MLW)
Dockside depth—5 feet (MLW)
Accepts transients—limited
Transient dockage rate—average
Fixed wooden slips—yes
Dockside power connections—up to 50 amp
Dockside water connections—yes
Showers—yes
Gasoline—yes
Diesel fuel—yes
Mechanical repairs—outboards and I/Os
Ship's and variety store—yes
Restaurant—on site

Rock Creek (Standard Mile 43)

Captains cruising north-northwest of unlighted daybeacon #21A on the ICW may notice a locally marked channel cutting east-northeast to charted Rock Creek. Unless you pilot a shallow-draft outboard or I/O-powered craft, don't enter this cut. Low-water depths run to as little as 4 feet. If you should happen to fit these requirements, there are several small-scale marinas on the creek near the 9-foot fixed bridge. Gasoline and some low-key mechanical repairs can usually be had.

Englewood Beach Anchorage (Standard Mile 43.5, 26 55.191 North/082 21.268 West)

Study chart 11425 for a moment and notice the broad ribbon of deep water that stretches southwest, northwest of flashing daybeacon

#22 (immediately southeast of the 26-foot bascule bridge). Skippers with a flair for taking a chance can find good anchorage along this stretch of water. The channel (which eventually leads to Englewood Beach) is unmarked and surrounded by shoal water, so enter with caution and be ready for the unexpected. By keeping to the channel, 6-foot minimum depths can be maintained for quite some distance upstream, though not as far as 11425 would lead you to believe.

Cruisers following the Englewood Beach channel to the southwest will encounter a side cut running to the west-northwest just as the main passage swings to the southeast. With a great deal of navigational caution (see below), minimum 6-foot depths can be carried on this side channel. The stream eventually dead-ends at a restaurant called the White Elephant Pub (941-475-6801). The food is reportedly much improved here under the present owners. This dining spot has its own docks, which patrons are free to use while dining. Low-water depths alongside run around 5 feet.

Englewood Beach's best anchorage is found southeast of the just discussed side channel, on the charted 8-foot waters. This spot has excellent protection, courtesy of the adjoining southwestern (beach-side) banks and the charted shallows and islands to the northeast. It would take some seriously heavy weather to bother you in this haven. As you would expect, the small islands and shoals to the northeast are undeveloped, while the southwestern banks are populated by pleasant residential neighborhoods.

Do not try to continue following the Englewood Beach channel to the southeast. While the stream eventually rejoins Stump Pass, depths run out far sooner than chart 11425 would lead you to believe.

Englewood Anchorage (Standard Mile 44.5, 26 56.964 North/082 21.627 West)

Between unlighted daybeacons #25 and #26, skippers can safely depart the ICW and cruise east-northeast through 6-foot waters to within 200 yards of the banks. This shoreline is part of the mainland community of Englewood—not to be confused with Englewood Beach, which occupies the barrier island to the southeast. In fair weather, these waters make for a fine anchorage with a super view of Lemon Bay's wide expanse. The northeastern shoreline gives some protection when breezes are blowing from the north or northeast, but otherwise the anchorage is pretty open. Overnighters must also contend with the wake of any vessels passing by on the Waterway, but hopefully most power captains will be respectful. During one visit, we spotted at least four sail craft bedded

1. Royal Palm Marina

down in this refuge. One can only conclude that it is a popular stopover with the local sailing crowd. Captain and crew stopping in this anchorage can dinghy ashore northeast of unlighted daybeacon #28 at a public park which will be spied along the eastern banks.

Royal Palm Marina (Standard Mile 46.5, 26 57.893 North/082 22.093 West)

Royal Palm Marina's entrance channel breaks off from the ICW to the east-southeast, just northwest of unlighted daybeacon #30. This facility is friendly to transients and stays up to 10 days are allowed. Depths on much of the entrance cut run from 5 to 6 feet, but one lump places the minimum MLW soundings at 4½ feet. Dockside, 7- to 8-foot soundings can be expected. Transients are berthed at fixed concrete piers featuring a full array of power and water connections. With winds blowing directly across Lemon Bay, boats docked at Royal Palm may experience a fair amount of chop. According to the marina management, this effect is minimized by the shallows southwest of the docks.

Gasoline and diesel fuel are readily available, as are full-service mechanical and below-waterline, haul-out repairs. The marina's travelift is rated at a 50-ton capacity.

Shoreside amenities include clean, non-climate-controlled showers, a small combination ship's and variety store, and a Laundromat. An on-site Tiki Bar Restaurant is now under construction, and may well be open by the time this account finds its way into your hands.

The Old Englewood Diner (498 Dearborn Street W, 941-473-1858) and Café on Dearborn (470 Dearborn Street W, 941-474-3333) are all found within a fairly long walk from the dockage basin. Ask any of the marina staff for directions.

Royal Palm Marina Yacht Basin (941) 475-6882
http://www.royalpalmmarina.com

Approach depth—4½-6 feet
Dockside depth—7-8 feet
Accepts transients—yes
Transient dockage rate—below average
Fixed concrete piers—yes
Dockside power connections—up to 50 amp
Dockside water connections—yes
Showers—yes
Laundromat—yes
Gasoline—yes
Diesel fuel—yes
Mechanical repairs—yes
Below-waterline repairs—yes
Ship's and variety store—yes
Restaurant—several nearby

GASPARILLA ISLAND BRIDGE TO ALLIGATOR CREEK NAVIGATION

Let's make this simple. Except for the side trips outlined below, stick to the Waterway. In most cases, if you make an unplanned deviation from the ditch, it's time to either get out and push or find out what Sea Tow is doing at the moment.

Watch your stern as well as your forward progress to quickly note any leeway. Stick to the centerline of the ICW channel. Keep your binoculars handy to help pick out markers in Lemon Bay. For some reason, many of these aids seem to blend in with the shoreline. Stay alert, watch the sounder, and you will reach Venice without scrapes.

Gunk holes and anchorages along this portion of the ICW run the full gamut, ranging from those where you would just about have to be asleep to find the bottom, to others where even the careful mariner can stir some mud.

North through Placida Harbor After leaving the Gasparilla Island Bridge behind, the Western Florida ICW follows a bit of a winding path through the waters of Placida Harbor. At flashing daybeacon #23, the Waterway takes a swing to the north-north-west. Come abeam of unlighted daybeacon #24 to its westerly side and point to pass unlighted daybeacon #24A to the same quarter. Between #24 and #24A, the Placida Harbor anchorage will come abeam to the southwest.

Placida Harbor Anchorage Leave the Waterway about halfway between unlighted daybeacons #24 and #24A, and feel your way to the west at idle speed for a hundred yards or so. Watch the sounder. Farther to the west and southwest depths deteriorate to 4 feet or even less.

On the ICW At flashing daybeacon #26, the Waterway again changes its track. This time cruisers must follow a bend to the northwest. A minimum-wake zone begins at unlighted daybeacon #28 and runs north to unlighted daybeacon #4. This regulation apparently protects the many private docks that line the Waterway along the northeastern banks.

Just to keep life interesting, you must again cut back to the north-northwest at flashing daybeacon #29. Northwest of unlighted daybeacon #30, one of the best anchorages on the entire run from Placida Harbor to Venice comes up on the north-eastern banks.

Cape Haze Anchorage Simply enter this cove on the mid-width of its broad mouth. Drop anchor anywhere so as not to swing to within less than 25 yards of the surrounding shores and settle down for a night of peace and security. The adjoining canal retains fair depths, but it is too narrow for effective anchorage. Visiting cruisers should probably avoid this stream.

Cove Anchorage Favor the southeastern shoreline slightly as you enter the cove northeast of unlighted daybeacon #35. Anchor anywhere near the cove's mid-width. Don't attempt to enter the canal heading off to the east if your craft is larger than 30 feet.

On the ICW Northwest and north of unlighted daybeacon #2, the Waterway enters a sheltered passage known as "The Cutoff." This ribbon of deep water ushers cruising craft into the bright confines of Lemon Bay.

Don Pedro Island Anchorage Once abeam of unlighted daybeacon #4, swing 90 degrees to the west-southwest and follow the deep waters in toward the shoreline. Good depths of 6 to 7 feet are found within 25 yards of the Waterway channel. Skippers will find 5 feet of water almost to the banks. If you draw 4½ feet or less, it's quite possible to loop the anchorage to the south and east, and rejoin the Waterway just southeast of flashing daybeacon #3.

On the Waterway Boats drawing 3 feet or better should not attempt to enter the unnamed sidewater northwest of unlighted daybeacon #5. In spite of the "6-foot" soundings shown on chart 11425 at the stream's entrance, on-site research revealed that depths have risen to at least 4-foot levels.

Northwest of unlighted daybeacon #7, powercraft captains should slow to no-wake speed to protect the two marinas along the northeastern banks. Both have marked entrances that are visible from the Waterway.

At unlighted daybeacon #8, the ICW at last passes out into the wider waters of Lemon Bay. Unless winds exceed 15 knots, it should be a merry meeting.

Northwest of unlighted daybeacon #9, passing cruisers will note unlighted daybeacon #9A. A marked channel leads west and then northwest from #9A into old Knight Pass and the Rum Bay Restaurant dock. Cruisers continuing north or south on the ICW must take care to separate the Waterway markers from the beacons on this side cut.

Knight Pass/Rum Bay Restaurant Channel
The channel is well outlined from #9A and reasonably easy to follow into the old pass's interior reaches. The restaurant docks will come up on the port shore. The first set of piers is used by the ferry running from the mainland to the restaurant. Visiting mariners may want to consider the more upstream set of docks. Here you won't be bothered by the ferry.

Cruising farther upstream past the second set of restaurant docks is not recommended. Depths quickly decline as you begin to approach the now closed pass.

On the ICW The Waterway takes a sharp cut to the north at flashing daybeacon #11 and heads toward Lemon Bay's eastern banks. This can be an unexpected turn for those not following the ICW's track on chart 11425. Be ready for it.

Use your binoculars to help pick out unlighted daybeacon #13 to the north. At #13 the Waterway begins to bend back to the northwest. You will have completed this turn by the time you pass flashing daybeacon #14. North of #14 the ICW channel runs straight for the Venice approach canal, with only a few minor angles here and there.

The charted channel east of unlighted daybeacon #17 leads to a private dockage area. There are no services for transients, nor is there room to anchor.

Take care as you approach unlighted daybeacon #17A. The Stump Pass channel departs from this marker and cuts west. Similarly, the marked route to Fish Tail Marina runs northeast from #17A. Be sure to sort out the bevy of markers and pass #17A to its easterly side. Northbound cruisers should then point to pass unlighted daybeacon #18 to its southwesterly quarter.

Stump Pass The Stump Pass channel cuts to the west, just southeast of the ICW's unlighted daybeacon #17A. As mentioned above, this entire passage is very subject to shoaling, and visiting cruisers would be well advised to bypass any exploration of these waters.

Should you choose to ignore this advice, cut to the west, and point to pass all subsequent red, even-numbered aids to navigation to your port side, and take green markers to starboard. What a surprise!

It would serve no purpose here to recount all the daybeacon numbers, plus twists and turns, we encountered during our last visit in the channel. There will undoubtedly be any number of differences by the time you arrive. This is one place where the local aids to navigation are practically your only means of staying off the bottom.

Mariners who decide to anchor between Thornton Key and the unnamed island, northeast of charted, unlighted daybeacon #4, will have to contend with a long finger of shallow water that has built across most of this stream's western mouth. To (hopefully) avoid this hazard, approach the cut by heavily favoring the south-side (Thornton Key) banks. After cruising east-southeast for some 25 to 30 yards, you can edge just a bit to the north and drop the hook. Be mindful of the correctly charted shallows abutting the unnamed island, just a short jog farther to the north. Set your anchor so that your craft will not swing into these shallows.

Captains and crew continuing through Stump Pass out to the Gulf will spot an uncharted cove flanking the southeastern side of the cut's seaward mouth. Even though you may see some small craft anchored on these waters, low-water depths of ½ feet or less demand that larger vessels keep on trucking.

The seaward portion of Stump Pass is currently well outlined with aids to navigation. Just continue passing all aids to navigation to their appropriate side (depending on their color). Eventually, a rather funky hexagonal-shaped daybeacon, #SP, denotes the outermost limit of the Stump Pass channel. Those who've made it safely this far can breathe a welcome sigh of relief.

On the ICW   The Waterway continues to be straight and reasonably easy to follow from the Stump Pass intersection to flashing daybeacon #22. Some of the runs between the various daybeacons are rather lengthy, so you may want to use your binoculars to help pick out the next aid. Just northwest of #22, an anchorage opportunity will come abeam to the west and south.

Englewood Beach Channel and Anchorage
The channel leading to Englewood Beach is not as simple to traverse as it might appear from a casual study of chart 11425. The route is entirely unmarked, and it borders on shoals to the east and west. While the deep water extends south-southwest (and then southeast) in a wide band, it's all too easy to wander away from the good depths. Proceed slowly and detail a crew member to keep a constant watch on the sounder. If depths rise to less than 5½ feet, you are encroaching on the surrounding shallows. Stop and make corrections at once before grounding depths are reached. Better yet, try out your new chart plotter on these waters, and sing praises to the wonders of modern, electronic navigation!

Depart the Waterway about halfway

between flashing daybeacon #22 and the Englewood Bridge (to the northwest). Cut sharply south-southwest and point to eventually come abeam of (what I call) the "Subm pile" island by some 30 to 50 yards to your port side. A shallow spoil bank shelves out from the westerly shoreline along this portion of the channel, and there is also very shallow water north of the submerged pile island, lying east of your initial passage from the ICW to the waters west of the island. If all this sounds confusing (and I know it does), follow along on chart 11425 with me and all will become clear. Well, clearer.

Continue favoring the island shores slightly as you cruise to the south. Eventually, you will pass by the southern tip of the island, east of your course. Continue holding to the same track until you are within 25 yards or so of the barrier island banks lying to the south-southwest.

You may then choose to cut back to the west-northwest and enter the charted cove, overlooked by the White Elephant Pub. Skippers following this cut must heavily favor the southern shoreline to bypass the correctly charted, broad band of shallows to the north.

The main Englewood Beach channel cuts sharply southeast at the intersection with the restaurant cove. Favor the southwestern banks as you cruise along. Eventually, the channel takes a jog to the south. Halt your forward progress before reaching this southerly turn. As suggested by the "Shl rep 1983" designation on chart 11425, our research revealed that depths have risen to 4 feet or less in the body of the southerly turn. Drop the hook well northwest of this unhappy obstruction.

On the ICW Northwest of flashing daybeacon #22, the ICW passes through the Englewood Beach bascule bridge. This span has a closed vertical clearance of 26 feet and currently opens on demand.

After passing through the bridge, cruisers will spy a collection of boats docked and anchored to the southwest. After a whole series of attempts to find an anchorage on these waters, we have always hit 4-foot depths every time. Obviously the locals know something we don't, but, equally obvious, it would be difficult if not impossible for first-time visitors to find the good water without local help. Navigators lacking this sort of specific information are advised to bypass this potential haven entirely.

North of the Englewood Beach span, cruisers will pass flashing daybeacon #24 to its southwestern side. Just northwest of #24, you may spy a channel running into the northeastern banks. This cut serves Travis Boating Center (941-475-7100), a dry-stack storage facility for smaller powercraft. No significant transient services are available.

Between the next two (moving north) aids, unlighted daybeacons #25 and #26, captains may choose to enter an open but deep anchorage to the northeast.

Englewood Anchorage Simply depart the Waterway about halfway between unlighted daybeacons #25 and #26, and cruise toward the northeasterly banks. Good depths persist to within 200 yards of the banks. This good water actually runs well to the southeast and is bounded by the Travis Boating Center channel, described above.

On the ICW Don't attempt to explore the charted but unmarked channel running off to the west-southwest, southeast of unlighted daybeacon #29. Our soundings showed that this one-time cut has shoaled to 4-foot depths. There is also no protection to speak of for overnight anchorage.

The marked entrance to Royal Palm Marina will come up just northwest of unlighted daybeacon #30. The passage is well marked and reasonably easy to follow.

Northwest of the gap between flashing daybeacon #32 and unlighted daybeacon #33, Lemon Bay begins to narrow as it runs on toward its connecting canal near Alligator Creek. Depths outside of the ICW channel rise significantly. Take all precautions to keep to the Waterway.

The small, charted channel northeast of unlighted daybeacon #36 leads to a few private docks. There are no services for transients and no room to anchor.

Similarly, the channel leading to Forked Creek, northeast of unlighted daybeacon #38, holds 5-foot depths, but the stream offers no facilities nor anchorage possibilities.

Northwest of unlighted daybeacon #41, the Waterway markers seem to be a bit easier to pick out from the surrounding shoreline. Perhaps the narrower width of the water helps in these observations. At any rate, you will not need to use your binoculars with quite so much regularity, but keep them close at hand just in case.

The Manasota bascule bridge with 26 feet of closed vertical clearance crosses the Waterway northwest of flashing daybeacon #42 and unlighted daybeacon #43. Wonder of wonders, this span opens on demand for vessels that need more clearance.

Northwest of unlighted daybeacon #50, all boats should slow to idle speed. A pontoon ferry crosses the Waterway here to provide access to the Gulfside beaches. Continue at idle speed until reaching the "Resume Safe Operation" sign.

Flashing daybeacon #51 and the shallow mouth of Alligator Creek (on the northeastern banks) herald the Waterway's entrance into the Venice Canal. Hang on, there is yet more great cruising ahead.

Venice to Little Sarasota Bay

While performing the original research for the first edition of this guidebook in 1992 on the waters lying about the charming community of Venice, this writer had occasion to spend a bit of time with one of the local marina managers one hot, summer afternoon. After we got to know each other, he inquired as to where my research had taken me before coming to Venice. I related my lengthy cruises on Tampa Bay and the surrounding waters. The manager looked at me for a few moments out of the corner of his eye and finally said, "Please don't tell them we're here."

While it would take the rosiest-colored glasses to look at Venice as if it were a small, backwater village, there is no denying that a calmer, more tranquil lifestyle is found here than at some of the metropolitan centers to the north. Venetians, many of whom are retired folks, seem intent on enjoying their lives in the Florida sunshine and simply taking it easy. They are happy to welcome cruising visitors, and their town provides marina facilities and at least one anchorage.

With its fine inlet, wonderful waterside restaurants, and good marinas alone, Venice deserves any cruiser's full attention. Factor in the town's innate friendliness and you have a must stop for every vessel cruising the Western Florida ICW.

North of Venice, the ICW soon tracks through the somewhat wide reaches of Blackburn Bay, and then spills into the larger confines of Little Sarasota Bay. Marina facilities continue to be prolific and there are two decent Gulf-side anchorages on Little Sarasota Bay.

Enough said—let's explore these marvelous waters together. Some of the best cruising in all of Western Florida awaits.

Venice Attractions

Believe it or else, Venice is known as the "shark's tooth capital of the world." These old teeth are remnants of the hundreds of thousands of sharks who have died in the Gulf of Mexico. The teeth survive and some are eventually washed to shore. The local Chamber of Commerce actually gives away a small bag of shark's teeth gathered by local residents to any visitor for the asking.

The week of July 4 brings the Venice downtown festival. An extravaganza of arts, crafts, and food, this notable event also features a fascinating sandcastle-building contest. This sandy competition has attracted the attention

of the national press and it has been featured on the ABC show "Good Morning America."

The largest special event of the year is the Venice Sun Fiesta in October. This weeklong celebration includes a parade, musical entertainment, and a community fair. Of course, no Floridian festival would be worth its salt without copious quantities of good seafood, not to mention an old-fashioned beauty contest.

A host of other events augments these two major happenings. No matter when you cruise into Venetian waters, there's a good chance that you will find something going on out of the ordinary.

Numbers to know in Venice include

Yellow Cab—(941) 480-9222
Avis Rental Cars—(941) 484-2227
Budget Rent A Car—(800) 763-2999
Enterprise Rent-A-Car—(941) 485-2774
Chamber of Commerce—(941) 488-2236

Venice History   Following the close of the Civil War, the state of Florida made an earnest bid to attract settlers to its western coastline. One hundred and sixty acres were free for the asking to anyone who would agree to settle and develop his tract.

In 1868 a group arrived from Georgia and points north to settle around the inlet that we would one day come to know as Venice Pass. These early pioneers included some of the oldest family names in Venetian history, including Webb, Roberts, Blackburn, and Higel.

The small village's first post office was established by Frank Higel in 1888. The original name given to the new town was "Horse and Chaise."

The modern history of the town we call Venice really began in 1911 when Ms. Potter

Palmer purchased 140,000 acres of land in Western Florida, much of which comprised the site of the modern-day town. Ms. Palmer had inherited a sizable fortune from her late husband, who owned the Chicago Palmer House Hotel. With her encouragement, both moral and financial, the railroad reached Venice in 1911. Transportation was further enhanced by the completion of a hard-surface road to Sarasota in 1916.

The Roaring Twenties saw a construction boom that was to transform the village into the town of Venice. Some years earlier a New York physician, Dr. Fred Albee, came to town with the idea of planning a model community. His blueprints languished for a decade but were eventually undertaken by the Brotherhood of Locomotive Engineers as a retirement community for their members. Soon a whole series of canals graced by houses of Northern Italian architecture had been built. Someone suggested that the town change its name to Venice to acknowledge its striking resemblance to that Italian city. The idea took root and today visitors will find a uniquely American version of the city of canals.

With the opening of the Western Florida ICW in the 1960s, pleasure-boating traffic increased by leaps and bounds.

Today Venice boasts 78,000 year-round residents, with many more seasonal visitors. The community is still a lovely mix of Italian and American architecture which draws more retirees year after year. Even in these days of rapid change and progress, those gallant pioneers who settled so long ago by the small inlet are not forgotten. Their names are indelibly etched on such landmarks as Roberts Bay, Blackburn Point, and Higel Park. Without

their efforts, the bright and shining city that is today's Venice might never have come to pass.

MarineMax of Venice (Standard Mile 55, 27 04.838 North/082 25.881 West)

Look at chart 11425 for a moment and notice the L-shaped offshoot coming off the Waterway's western shore just north of Standard Mile 55. This water plays host to the first of Venice's several marina facilities. MarineMax of Venice (formerly Gulfwind Marine) features transient dockage in a well-sheltered harbor. Berths are found at fixed wooden piers with full power and water connections. Depths run from 7 to 8 feet. Mechanical repairs for both gasoline and diesel power plants are offered, as are gasoline, diesel fuel, and below-waterline repair services (40-ton travelift). The on-site restaurant is now closed, and those cruisers in search of shoreside dining will probably want to take a taxi into downtown Venice. A small motel is still located on the premises.

MarineMax of Venice (941) 485-3388

Approach depth—6½-8 feet
Dockside depth—7-8 feet

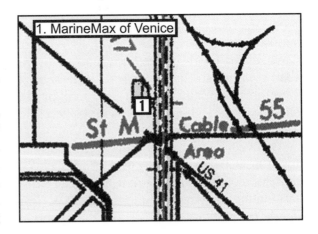

Accepts transients—yes
Transient dockage rate—above average
Fixed wooden piers—yes
Dockside power connections—up to 50 amp
Dockside water connections—yes
Gasoline—yes
Diesel fuel—yes
Mechanical repairs—yes
Below-waterline repairs—yes
Restaurant—taxi ride necessary

Fisherman's Wharf Marina (Standard Mile 57, 27 06.260 North/082 26.712 West)

Follow the Venice canal on chart 11425 until it flows out into wider waters just north of the Hatchett Creek Bridge. East of unlighted daybeacon #4, the second of Venice's pleasure-craft stops will come abeam.

Fisherman's Wharf Marina (941-484-9246) is clearly a facility in the throws of some sort of transition at the time of this writing. During my last visit in August 2003, the slips fronting onto the northern side of the marina were shut down, as was the large, on-site restaurant just behind the docks. Construction equipment and building materials were stacked around the parking lot in a seemingly haphazard fashion. The on-site dockmaster informed me curtly that he didn't know "when anything is going to be finished" nor what form the eventual construction might take.

This writer has been told by some knowledgeable locals that the property owner had planned to erect a condo project here and had actually started construction, but, at least

MarineMax of Venice

for the moment, the necessary local permits have not been obtained. Of course, we can't take these "rumors" as hard fact, but it would seem to explain a lot of what I saw.

For the moment, some vessels are still being docked at the long, fixed, wooden face pier fronting onto the Waterway's northeastern flank, but frankly, we would strongly suggest that most cruisers push on to the Crows Nest (see below) until the situation at Fisherman's Wharf Marina stabilizes.

Should you decide to visit Fisherman's Wharf anyway, cruisers must avoid an obscurely charted shoal. This tongue of shallows has grown over the last several years, and it is now more of a problem than once it

was. Please read the navigational information on this marina, presented below, before attempting first-time entry. Your keel will be ever so much happier for the effort.

By successfully avoiding the above-mentioned shoal, 5½ MLW depths can be carried on the approach to Fisherman's Wharf. Dockside there is some 5½ to 6½ feet of water at low tide.

Venice Yacht Club (Standard Mile 58, 27 06.533 North/082 27.667 West)

After traversing the shallow reaches of Roberts Bay, the ICW turns sharply northwest at flashing daybeacon #13. As you approach the next northerly aid, unlighted daybeacon

Venice Yacht Club

#14, a very well-marked channel breaks off to the west-southwest and leads to the docks of the Venice Yacht Club. Excellent depths of 7½ feet or better are held in this channel.

The club's formidable dockage basin and clubhouse overlook the western shores of the wide swath of waters spanning the gap between Roberts and Donna bays, near the mouth of the southernmost of the three charted canals. Some additional slips are located on this stream. Dockside soundings range from 7 to 8 feet. Transients who are members of yacht clubs with appropriate reciprocal privileges are accepted for guest dockage with advance reservations (only). The club maintains a full-time dockmaster on duty from 8:30 A.M. to 4:00 P.M. Mondays and from 8:30 A.M. to 5:00 P.M. Tuesday through Sunday. The fixed slips feature all power and water connections and (unusual for a yacht club) gasoline and diesel fuel can be purchased by members and accredited guests (only) while the dockmaster is on duty. Shoreside, visiting cruisers will find good, air-conditioned showers and excellent dining facilities. Lunch and dinner are served Monday through Saturday, and there is also a super Sunday brunch. There is a refreshing swimming pool for those needing to cool off after a hot day on the water. Downtown Venice is found within a very long walk, or you might choose to take a taxi. Here you will find several additional restaurants and good shopping.

Venice Yacht Club (941) 488-7708
    http://www.veniceyachtclub.com

Approach depth—7½-10 feet
Dockside depth—7-8 feet
Accepts transients—members of yacht clubs
    with reciprocal privileges
Fixed wooden piers—yes

Dockside power connections—30 and 50 amp
Dockside water connections-yes
Showers—yes
Gasoline—yes (members and accredited guests
    only)
Diesel fuel—yes (members and accredited
    guests only)
Restaurant—on site

Donna Bay (Standard Mile 58)

The southwestern mouth of Donna Bay fronts onto the ICW's flank between unlighted daybeacon #14 and flashing daybeacon #1. While some local outboarders regularly cruise this body of water, depths of 2 to 4 feet are all too common. Cruising captains are advised to avoid this shallow trap.

Venice Anchorages and Higel Park Facilities (Standard Mile 58.5, Various Lats/Lons—see below)

The best anchorage on the waters lying about Venice is found on the charted ribbon of deep water south of the ICW's unlighted daybeacon #17. This haven changed a few years ago. At that time, the city of Venice marked the channel from its northernmost aid to navigation, unlighted can buoy #1, to the Venice Yacht Club. This cut runs hard by the seawall that flanks the channel to the west. There is still space to anchor on the eastern third of the charted deep water (near 27 06.642 North/082 27.601 West), but clearly swinging space was reduced. Be sure to anchor east of the marked channel. Cruisers dropping the hook in the channel may well be asked to move along by a local water cop.

Many skippers wisely choose a Bahamian-style mooring in this reduced-space anchorage. Minimum depths run around 7 feet, but you must take care to avoid the correctly

1. Venice Yacht Club
2. Fisherman's Wharf Marina
3. Crows Nest Marina

charted shoal farther to the east. The westerly banks provide excellent protection when winds are blowing from this quarter and there is also fair shelter for moderate breezes from the north or south. Easterly winds over 15 knots could make for a bumpy evening.

Good water runs all the way from #1 to a position abeam of the Venice Yacht Club. With its ample markings, this passage can even be used as an alternate entrance to the club's docks.

Shallow-draft vessels sometimes anchor south of the Venice Yacht Club, opposite the charted southernmost, blunt-ended cove (near 27 06.509 North/082 27.652 West), which chart 11425 (Venice inset) denotes with a sounding of 6 feet. You can now count on finding 6 feet of water in this haven, but thinner depths lie just to the east. There is good protection from western, southwestern, and northwestern winds, but shelter is nil to the east, northeast, and none too good to the southeast. The flanking shoreside development is prolific, to say the least.

Cruisers dropping anchor in either of these two spots can dinghy ashore at Higel Park (near 27 06.480 North/082 27.678 West). The public park is perched on the southern shores of the blunt-tipped cove, just west of the second anchorage reviewed above. Cruisers will find bathrooms, telephones, and trash disposals in the park. Restaurants (including the Crows Nest—see below) and shopping are within a walk of several blocks. Ask any local for directions.

Another feature at Higel Park is a fixed, wooden face dock that lines the southerly banks of the cove. A public launching ramp guards the innermost reaches. Stays up to 18 hours (once each 10 days) are allowed at this pier, and low-water depths alongside run about 5½ feet. We saw two large sailing vessels moored here temporarily during our last visit in the summer of 2003.

Venice Inlet (Standard Mile 58.5)

Between unlighted daybeacon #17 and flashing daybeacon #1, the ICW intersects the easterly reaches of reliable Venice Inlet. This well-defined cut is a popular passage to and from the waters of the open Gulf. At the present time, cruisers can expect minimum depths of 10 feet in the channel. Tidal currents do run quite swiftly, however. These swiftly moving waters seem to keep the inlet in optimal condition, so, at least for the foreseeable future, cruisers can use this seaward passage with a goodly amount of confidence.

Crows Nest Marina (Standard Mile 58.5, 27 06.720 North/082 27.825 West)

Crows Nest Marina maintains a line of slips on the southern shores of Venice Pass inlet, southeast of unlighted daybeacon #5. This is, perhaps, the friendliest and best of the marinas in Venice that accept transients. Overnight berths are provided at fixed wooden (and, would you believe, recycled plastic) decked slips featuring all power, water, and cable-television connections. Gasoline and diesel fuel are available, as are good, air-conditioned shoreside showers alongside a climate-controlled Laundromat. Most of Crows Nest's slips have depths of 6 to 7 feet, with 12 to 15 feet of water at the outermost face docks and a few berths with soundings as thin as 4 feet. Swift tidal currents can make docking tricky, so have all hands stand by with your largest fenders. The marina dockmaster is very helpful in minimizing this problem.

While the Crows Nest dockage basin is relatively well sheltered, it must be noted that this would not be a good spot to get caught in a gale. The chop in the inlet could build to prodigious proportions, and the marina is bound to get some of this backwash.

During our last visit, a new dockmaster headquarters building was under construction just behind the fuel dock. It will undoubtedly be in full operation before this account even makes its way to the printers. Reportedly, this new building will also contain a tiny ship's store. By the way, the old dockmaster's office is being turned into a wine cellar for the on-site restaurant (see below).

The real star at Crows Nest is the on-site restaurant of the same name. This dining spot is divided into upper and lower floors, each with its own distinctive character. The first level is a pub-type atmosphere with a nautical, raw bar and a grill. The upper story is what we in the South used to call a "sit-down" restaurant, with an expansive view of Venice Inlet from its large, plate-glass windows. The food upstairs is simply superb. The seafood bisque appetizer remains some of the best I have ever enjoyed, and the broiled red snapper entrée is enough all on its own to bring this writer back time and time again. Crows Nest Restaurant has also been presented with an Award of Excellence by *Wine Spectator* magazine. To be succinct, this is just about as good as it gets.

Crows Nest Marina and Restaurant
(941) 484-7661
(941) 484-9551 (Restaurant)
http://www.crowsnest-venice.com

Approach depth—10-foot minimum

Dockside depth—4-15 feet
Accepts transients—yes
Transient dockage rate—average
Fixed wooden slips—yes
Dockside power connections—yes
Dockside water connections—yes
Showers—yes
Laundromat—yes
Gasoline—yes
Diesel fuel—yes
Restaurant—on site

Lyons Bay (Standard Mile 59)

A marked channel makes off to the north from the ICW at flashing daybeacon #4 into the waters of Lyons Bay. Low-water depths on this cut can run to as little as 4 feet. Add to this the lack of swinging room for cruising-size vessels and you have two good reasons to bypass this body of water entirely.

Crows Nest Marina, Venice

Casey Key Bridge Facilities (Standard Mile 59.5)

North of flashing daybeacon #5, the Waterway leaves the principal Venice waterfront and begins its northward trek to the Casey Key Bridge. Two waterfront restaurants with dockage and a large, dry-stack-oriented marina line the eastern banks just south of this span (north of unlighted daybeacon #10).

The fixed, wooden face dock associated with the Sunset Grill (941-488-2941) comes up first, moving south to north. This pier fronts directly onto the Waterway and features 6 feet of water at low tide. As with all the facilities along this stretch, docking can be tricky, as tidal currents run quite swiftly indeed. During one visit, it looked as if a 3-knot ebb tide was boiling through the bridge!

Gulf Harbor Marina (941-488-7734) maintains a fuel dock north of Sunset Grill. This facility specializes in dry storage of small powercraft, as evidenced by its mammoth, twin, dry-stack storage buildings. However, this facility also offers some services of interest to transients. Gasoline and diesel fuel can be purchased at a fuel dock (depths alongside are 5½-6 feet) fronting directly onto the waterway. A ship's and variety store is found just behind the fuel pier. While no transient wet slips are available, the marina does offer covered slips for resident craft. Some mechanical repairs are offered, mostly for outboards and I/Os, and boats can be hauled out on the marina's 20-ton travelift.

Pelican Alley Restaurant (941-485-1893) sits hard by the southern side of the Casey Key Bridge. It has a hundred-foot, fixed face dock with good depths of 7 to 8 feet.

Now, listen up. If you haven't eaten at Pelican Alley, you have missed one of the real treats in Western Florida. Do yourself a big favor and stop here. Everything is wonderful, from the sandwiches to "Shrimp and Scallops Marie," a delightful blend of diced tomatoes, onions, peppers, olives, and mushrooms in a very tasty tomato sauce. Well, there goes my diet again!

Blackburn Bay Anchorage (Standard Mile 61.5, 27 09.240 North/082 28.886 West)

North of the Casey Key Bridge the ICW soon enters the marginally wider waters of Blackburn Bay. While much of the bay outside of the Waterway is shallow, there is one pretty good spot to anchor for boats drawing 4½ feet or less. Depths of 5 feet or so swing in toward the bay's western shores between unlighted daybeacons #20 and #21. Good water holds to within 50 yards of shore and there is superior protection from all but strong northerlies. On the negative side, the bottom is mud, so anchoring is not carefree, and you may be rolled around a good deal by the wake of passing vessels. The western shores are populated by heavy residential development, but the landscaped yards alongside the palm and palmetto trees make for an eye-pleasing combination.

Blackburn Bridge Facilities (Standard Mile 63, Various Lats/Lons—see below)

North of unlighted daybeacon #32, the Western Florida ICW takes its leave of Blackburn Bay after passing under a decrepit 9-foot swing bridge. Some marina facilities are found both north and south of this span.

Blackburn Point Marina (27 10.780 North/082 29.738 West, 941-966-3735) is a small operation guarding the western shores immediately south of the Blackburn Bridge. This marina does not offer any transient dockage at its less-than-stellar, fixed wooden piers.

On the plus side, the on-site restaurant, known as the Casey Key Fish House, must clearly be doing something right. Its screened-in dining room remains well populated every time we pay a visit. Unfortunately, as alluded to above, wet-slip dockage is rented out on a month-to-month basis, so it is doubtful if there will be any room for those who just want to dock long enough to partake of the restaurant's delights. Of course, you could always secure a slip at nearby Casey Key Marina (see below) and take the short walk back across the Blackburn Bridge. It might just be worth it.

North of the Blackburn span, a channel leading east to no fewer than three pleasure-craft-oriented facilities is outlined by low-level, privately maintained unlighted daybeacons. Entrance depths run between 5 and 6 feet, while 4½ to 6 feet of water is found at most of the interior piers and slips.

First up is Casey Key Marina on the southern banks (near 27 10.862 North/082 29.521 West). While the marina's slips are not terribly numerous, transients are sometimes accepted for overnight dockage on a space-available basis. Berths are found at fixed wooden piers with good power and water connections. Advance reservations would be almost mandatory at Casey Key. Gasoline can be purchased at the fuel dock and modest, non-climate-controlled showers and a Laundromat are on hand as well.

The Flying Bridge restaurant (941-966-7431) is located on the upper floor of the Casey Key complex. The downstairs location is now occupied by Caroline's on the Bay (941-966-4822) restaurant. While this writer has never had the opportunity to sample the fare at either dining spot, the impressive population of cars in the parking lot for the midday meal certainly gives good cause to believe that these restaurants are popular with the local crowd.

Casey Key Marina (941) 966-1730

Approach depth—5-6 feet
Dockside depth—4½-6 feet
Accepts transients—yes
Transient dockage rate—below average
Fixed wooden piers—yes
Dockside power connections—up to 50 amp
Dockside water connections—yes
Showers—yes
Laundromat—yes
Gasoline—yes
Restaurant—on site

Mariners in need of repairs should continue cruising east past Casey Key to Bob's Boatyard (27 10.875 North/082 29.452 West, 941-966-2552), formerly John Holmes Boatyard. This impressive facility will be spotted overlooking the northern banks. Bob's has a reputation among local mariners for providing quality mechanical (gasoline- and diesel-powered

1. Blackburn Point Marina
2. Casey Key Marina
3. Bob's Boatyard

Dockside Marina

plants) and haul-out repair services. As one of the yard managers put it recently to this writer, "We can do everything!"

Bob's boasts an impressive 80-ton travelift. All available wet-slip dockage is reserved for the use of service customers. Skippers needing repairs north of Venice need look no further.

Dockside Marine (941-966-5657) lines the eastern terminus of the canal directly across from Lighthouse Boatyard. This small firm's primary concern is small-craft dry storage, but gasoline, a ship's and variety store, and some outboard and I/O mechanical repairs are also offered.

Little Sarasota Bay (Standard Mile 63)

North of Blackburn Bridge, the Western

Florida ICW breaks out into the wider waters of Little Sarasota Bay. Your passage should still be reasonably smooth unless some really strong winds are in the offing. Most of the bay is quite shallow, and, as usual, you should stick to the Waterway except for the gunk holes outlined below.

A portion of Little Sarasota Bay's western shoreline is protected as part of the Jim Neville Preserve. The incredibly green, all-natural shores are a striking sight from the water.

Midnight Pass Inlet (Standard Mile 65)

Under present conditions, cruisers should not even consider trying to make a "midnight run." The channel, such as it ever was, lies west of the gap between the ICW's flashing day-beacon #41 and unlighted daybeacon #41A, but it has shoaled and now sports shallow patches with only a few feet of depth.

Midnight Pass Facilities (Standard Mile 66)

South of unlighted daybeacon #48, a pile-marked channel leads cruisers who can stand some 4½-foot depths west-southwest to a single marina and several restaurants, two of which offer waterside dockage. The channel markings lack any daybeacons, or even arrow markers, so you must approach this cut with care and keep an eye glued to the sounder.

As you begin your approach to the south-westerly banks, the channel divides. The northside fork leads to Turtle Beach Marina, while the southerly branch provides water-borne access to Ophelia's on the Bay restaurant. Let us first review the marina.

Turtle Beach Marina (941-349-9449, formerly Midnight Pass Marina) is a small facility that does not offer overnight, transient dockage. The marina does have a travelift and can haul pleasure craft up to at least 40 feet. Some low-key mechanical repairs (to gasoline engines only) and gasoline are available. Low-water approach and dockside depths run in the 4½- to 5-foot range. Turtle Beach Pub is located just in front of the marina. Free dockage is afforded to patrons of this establishment.

The channel cutting south to Ophelia's on the Bay restaurant (941-349-2212) carries depths of as little as 4 feet. Water levels dockside deepen to 5 and 6 feet. Skippers whose craft draw less than 4 feet can thank their shallow keels for affording them a unique dining experience. If you are about to grow gills and are just a bit tired of the fresh catch of the day, then Ophelia's on the Bay is just the ticket. Offering Continental-style cuisine, this dining spot is one of the most elegant in the region, and certainly the best of its type available from the water.

Little Sarasota Bay Anchorage (Standard Mile 67, 27 14.122 North/082 31.270 West)

Cruising craft can anchor within 100 yards of the southwestern banks at unlighted day-beacon #51 in minimum 5½-foot depths. Typical soundings are around 6 feet. There is little in the way of protection from winds over 10 knots unless the breezes in question are blowing from the west or southwest. The southwestern banks are flanked by heavy and not so attractive residential development. Passing powercraft may throw you a goodly amount of wake.

White Beach Anchorage (Standard Mile 67.5, 27 14.726 North/082 31.567 West)

A much-improved anchorage (better than the one reviewed above) is available to cruisers south and west of unlighted daybeacon #57. A sharp point of land to the south forms a shel-tered cove. Minimum depths of 5½ feet run to within 100 yards of the banks. There is good protection from southern, southwestern, and western breezes, but very little from northerly or easterly blows. The banks are overlooked by the usual private homes. The houses to the south are particularly attractive. Again, you will have to deal with the wake of passing vessels, but it is hoped that this won't be too much of a problem during the evening hours.

Stickney Point Bridge Facilities (Standard Mile 69)

Two radically different facilities are located

on the northeast and southwest shores of the ICW, southeast of the Stickney Point Bridge (northwest of unlighted daybeacon #62). Dockside Marina (941-349-8880) guards the southwestern banks and offers dry storage. This firm is primarily a dry-stack storage facility for smaller powercraft. No other transient services save a hard-to-reach gas pump and a ship's store are offered.

A large complex of retail shops and one restaurant overlook the northeastern shores. Coasters Restaurant (941-925-0300) fronts directly onto the Waterway, but the other shops border a man-made basin lying to the southeast. Coasters has a few extremely shallow slips fronting onto the Waterway, while additional docks line the northern side of the basin.

Very skimpy entrance and (interior basin) dockside depths of a mere 2½ to 4½ feet will limit the accessibility of this stop for almost all cruising-size vessels. We once ran aground on the docks fronting directly onto the Waterway in a 19-foot I/O-powered craft. These slips are virtually useless at low tide.

Coasters Restaurant

VENICE TO LITTLE SARASOTA BAY NAVIGATION

While there are very few navigational concerns in running the Venice Canal portion of the ICW, it's a different story while cruising through the waters about the city of Venice and its inlet. This is most certainly not the place for powercraft to go charging ahead at planing speeds. For one thing, there are many private docks to consider. Even more importantly, the markers on the various Venice-side channels, coupled with more than a few twists and turns in the Waterway channel, demand caution. Have the Venice inset portion of chart 11425 close at hand and be ready to sort out any confusion over aids to navigation before you actually reach the beacons in question.

Tidal currents run swiftly on the Venetian waters, courtesy of the nearby inlet. Sail craft and single-screw trawlers should be on the alert for leeway. All vessels need to take this rapid water movement into account when docking or anchoring.

North of Venice, the tidal currents continue for a few miles, but eventually the Waterway widens a bit while traversing Blackburn and Little Sarasota bays. Fortunately, it would take a really strong wind to make things uncomfortable on this portion of the Waterway.

While the ICW remains well marked throughout the two bays, most of the waters outside the channel are shoal. As per standard operating procedure along this section of the Western Florida coastline, stick to the marked Waterway channel or risk running aground.

Navigators should also take into account several long, no-wake zones outlined below. Trust me, they will affect your arrival time in Sarasota if you pilot a powercraft.

Venice Canal   North-northwest of unlighted daybeacon #52, the ICW enters a protected canal that runs generally north for some 3.8 miles until emptying into wider waters adjoining the Hatchett Creek Bridge. At flashing daybeacon #53, the canal swings sharply to the northeast. All markers cease north of #53 until you leave the Hatchett Creek span behind.

With one exception, there is little development along the canal and power cruisers can make good time. If you happen to meet or overtake a sailor or slower craft, please slow down and watch your wake when passing. Tall wakes can be a real problem in this relatively narrow channel.

Cruisers will pass under the 25-foot South Venice/Tamiami Trail bascule bridge near Standard Mile 55. This span opens on demand. At the time of this writing, a new, high-rise bridge is under construction at this location. Passing cruisers should proceed with maximum caution for the next year or so until this mammoth project is complete.

Immediately north of the South Venice bridge (northeast of charted Venice Municipal Airport), powercraft skippers must slow to idle speed when passing MarineMax of Venice. This facility is found on the *L*-shaped cove and is designated as facility #17 on chart 11425. Official no-wake signs warn both north- and south-bound vessels of this regulation. Please pay attention to this stricture. Unthinking captains who power by at planing speed can severely rock boats docked in the basin.

As you cruise between MarineMax and the Venice Avenue Bridge, watch the western banks. You will catch sight of the Venice High School football stadium. I can't recall offhand another location on the ICW where you can see such a sports center from the water.

Another 1.4 nautical miles brings north-bound cruisers to the Venice Avenue bascule bridge, with 30 feet of closed vertical clearance. This span has restricted opening hours. From 7:00 A.M. to 4:30 P.M., Monday through Friday, the bridge opens 10 minutes, 30 minutes, and 50 minutes after the hour, except it does not open at all between 4:35 P.M. and 5:35 P.M. At all other times of the day or night and on weekends, the bridge opens on demand. Sail craft should do everything possible to coordinate their arrival with this complicated schedule. There is little room to maneuver in the land cut while waiting for the bridge to open.

Switch to the Venice inset section of chart 11425 as you approach the Hatchett Creek Bridge. The minute detail of this inset will give you a much clearer picture of the sometimes complicated Venetian waters.

Adding insult to injury, the Hatchett

Creek-U.S. 41 Highway Bridge comes up soon after the Venice Avenue span. With the bridge's closed clearance of only 16 feet, most cruising captains will have to contend with the regulated opening schedule. Currently, the bridge opens on the hour and each 20 minutes thereafter from 7:00 A.M. to 4:20 P.M., Monday through Friday, except that it does not open at all from 4:25 P.M. to 5:25 P.M. On Saturdays, Sundays, and legal holidays, the bridge deigns to open for us peon cruisers on the hour and each quarter hour from 7:30 A.M. to 6:00 P.M. At all other times (if you can figure out when those might be) the bridge opens on demand. Don't look at me, folks. I didn't make up the schedule.

Captains should again note the presence of new bridge construction adjacent to the Hatchet Creek span. It appeared to this writer that another bridge of the same height was simply being added, as opposed to the installation of a high-rise span. In any case, watch out for barges and construction equipment as you pass through.

Cruise northwest at idle speed once through the Hatchett Creek span. An official no-wake zone runs from the bridge to flashing daybeacon #10. This prohibition protects Fisherman's Wharf Marina, which will come up to the northeast at unlighted daybeacon #4.

Fisherman's Wharf Marina   Entry into Fisherman's Wharf Marina is complicated by a shoal flanking the Waterway to the northeast, between unlighted daybeacons #4 and #6. This patch of shallows has grown to the southeast over the past several years, and it is now more of a problem. Nevertheless, this hazard can be avoided if you know it's there. The shortest passage for northbound cruisers is a bit more problematic. Leave the Waterway soon after passing under the Hatchett Creek Bridge, and begin hugging the outer face of the marina dock that fronts directly onto the ICW.

Captains cruising south on the ICW or piloting deep-draft vessels should depart the Waterway some 25 yards southeast of unlighted daybeacon #8 and begin heavily favoring the port-side banks as you cruise southeast to Fisherman's Wharf. The trick is to stay well away from the patch of water lying northeast of the gap between #6 and #4.

On the ICW   Northwest of Fisherman's Wharf, the waters about the ICW spread out and the passage becomes far more complicated. Continue to cruise at idle speed at least until reaching flashing daybeacon #10. There are many private docks on these waters, and a large wake could damage any number of vessels. In fact, it would be a good policy to cruise at minimal speed through the entire Venice region. Not only will this wise practice reduce wake, but it will also give you a chance to sort out the markers.

At flashing daybeacon #10, the ICW channel takes a sharp turn to the west. Don't miss this turn! The shallow waters of Roberts Bay lie to the east and north waiting to trap the unwary. Point to pass unlighted daybeacon #11 to its fairly immediate northerly quarter.

At flashing daybeacon #13, the Waterway again swerves sharply, this time to the north-northwest. Make the cut just before reaching #13 and point to come abeam of unlighted daybeacon #14 to its southwesterly side.

As you are cruising between #13 and #14, you will undoubtedly spot the prolific markers stretching west from #14 to the Venice Yacht Club. Don't let these charted aids confuse you. Use your binoculars to positively identify #14 before cruising on to this aid.

Venice Yacht Club Channel and Anchorage The Venice Yacht Club channel stretches west-southwest from unlighted daybeacon #14 on a well-marked, slightly curved path to the club's dockage basin. The clubhouse will be obvious.

If you wish to anchor off the yacht club, drop the hook just east of the southern-most, blunt-tipped cove, indenting the westerly banks. Although you will see some boats anchored farther to the south and southeast, on-site research revealed that these vessels were in 4-foot waters. Higel Park is found on the southern shores of the blunt-tipped cove.

On the ICW From unlighted daybeacon #14, the Waterway continues straight on until coming abeam of flashing daybeacon #16 to its southwesterly side. At #16 the channel cuts farther to the northwest and the daybeacon numbering sequence begins anew. At unlighted daybeacon #17, cruisers can enter the northernmost of the two Venice anchorages.

Venice Anchorage Enter the wide swath of deep waters abutting the western banks by cutting sharply south and passing just east of unlighted daybeacon #17. Point to then pass west of unlighted can buoy #1. If you continue cruising to the south, be sure to also pass west of unlighted can buoy #3. These latter two aids define a channel running hard by the west-side seawall that eventually leads to the Venice Yacht Club. To anchor, ease a bit to the east of the marked cut, but take care to avoid the correctly charted 1-foot shoal farther to the east.

On to Venice Inlet Cruisers northbound on the ICW, or those seeking Venice Inlet, should pass unlighted daybeacon #17 to its northeasterly side and point to come abeam of flashing daybeacon #1 to its northeasterly quarter. Daybeacon #1 lies just northwest of a strategic intersection between the ICW and Venice Inlet.

Venice Inlet Enter Venice Inlet by turning sharply southwest about halfway between unlighted daybeacon #17 and flashing daybeacon #1. Pass #1 well to your starboard side.

Be on the alert for strong tidal currents as you cruise through Venice Inlet. The surge will surprise you at full ebb tide.

Between Venice Inlet's unlighted daybeacons #7 and #5, you will quickly spot Crows Nest Marina flanking the south-side banks. With the possible exception of a few problems courtesy of the strong tidal currents, this marina is easily entered.

West of unlighted daybeacons #2A and #3, the inlet channel runs between twin stone jetties. The channel is obvious. Continue straight on out into the Gulf. Next stop . . . Carrabelle?

On the Waterway   Cruisers continuing north on the ICW past Venice Inlet should set their course to pass between flashing daybeacon #4 and unlighted daybeacon #3. Then, continue on by pointing to run the gap between flashing daybeacon #5 and unlighted daybeacon #4A. Between #3 and #5, the charted shoal flanking the Waterway's southwestern margin has been known to build into the Waterway's flank. Watch your sounder as you cruise through this section, and if depths begin to rise, favor the northeastern side of the channel slightly.

Just before reaching #4A, the marked cut to Lyons Bay heads off to the north. As this side trip is not recommended for strangers, it will not be further reviewed here.

The Waterway takes its last major turn in the Venice area at flashing daybeacon #5 and unlighted daybeacon #4A. After passing between #5 and #4A, turn to the north-northwest to follow the ICW.

The route remains straightforward until reaching flashing daybeacon #9. North of this aid, all vessels should slow to idle speed to protect the marina and restaurant docks lining the eastern banks.

Soon the Waterway is spanned by the 14-foot Casey Key/Albee Road bascule bridge. It is fortunate that this bridge opens on demand. The tidal current boiling through this portion of the ICW on the ebb and flood is something to see. We estimated its speed at 3 knots plus. All vessels should proceed at maximum alert when docking or passing through the bridge.

At unlighted daybeacon #14, the Waterway is pinched between two prominent shoals as it passes out into Blackburn Bay. Favor the western side of the channel slightly between #14 and flashing daybeacon #16. At #16, the channel turns a bit to the north-northwest.

Blackburn Bay is another portion of the Western Florida ICW where it is almost mandatory to keep strictly to the marked channel. For much of its run through Blackburn Bay, the Waterway borders on significant shoals to the east and west.

North-northwest of unlighted daybeacon #20, mariners will encounter the first good anchorage after leaving Venice behind.

Blackburn Bay Anchorage   Depart the Waterway some 100 yards southeast of unlighted daybeacon #21. Cut in sharply toward the southwestern banks. Good depths run to within 50 yards of shore. Retrace your steps to the northeast when it's time to leave.

North on the ICW   A long slow-speed manatee zone begins at flashing daybeacon #23 and unlighted daybeacon #22, and stretches north to unlighted daybeacon #29. Just grin and bear it.

North-northwest of unlighted daybeacon #29A, powercraft skippers should again slow to minimal speed to protect the docks of South Bay Yacht and Racket Club to the northeast. Continue at idle speed to unlighted daybeacon #35, north of Blackburn Bridge.

North of unlighted daybeacon #32, the Waterway hurries on toward the Blackburn Point swing bridge. You may spot some boats anchored east of the channel, south of the bridge. Don't be tempted! Our research revealed that these vessels were moored in less than 4 feet of water.

The relic known as the Blackburn Point bridge has a closed vertical clearance of only 9 feet, but it does open on demand. Just before passing under the bridge, you will spot Blackburn Point Marina to the west. Similarly, the privately maintained, unlighted daybeacons leading to Casey Key Marina, Bob's Boatyard, and Dockside Marine cut off to the east, north of the span.

North of the Blackburn Point span, the ICW passes out into the wider waters of Little Sarasota Bay. Chop should still not be a problem unless winds exceed 20 knots. No side trips are available on the bay until reaching flashing daybeacon #41.

Midnight Pass   Brave captains whose craft draw less than 3 feet may consider entering the easterly portion of the Midnight Pass channel as an interesting gunk hole. The passage is unmarked, and the seaward channel is unusable by strangers.

If you should make the attempt, leave the ICW north of flashing daybeacon #41 and enter the channel by favoring the port-side banks. Don't get right up next to the beach. Stay some 20 yards off the sands for best depths.

Watch ahead for a sandy beach, also on the port banks. It would be best to drop the hook once abeam of this spot. On weekends, local power cruisers often beach small craft here.

Turtle Beach Marina and Ophelia's on the Bay Channel   The pile-marked channel to Turtle Beach Marina and Ophelia's restaurant takes off from the west-southwestern flank of the ICW between unlighted daybeacons #47 and #48. Take the first two red-topped piles to starboard. As you approach the third pile, the channel splits. Boats visiting Turtle Beach Marina can follow the northern fork, while diners putting into Ophelia's should follow the channel cutting to the southwest. Remember—depths on both these cuts run as thin as 4 feet.

Little Sarasota Bay Anchorage   The deep waters west of unlighted daybeacon #51 actually present a wide prospect. It is quite possible to leave the Waterway just southeast of #51 and make a broad loop in toward the southwestern banks, rejoining the ICW 200 yards southeast of unlighted daybeacon #53, all with 5-foot minimum depths. Drop the hook anywhere you choose on these waters. Be sure to anchor so as not to swing closer than 100 yards to the southwesterly banks, where depths finally deteriorate.

White Beach Anchorage   Best depths are maintained by cutting in toward the southwestern banks some 100 yards northwest of unlighted daybeacon #57. While boats drawing 4 feet or less can cruise a goodly distance to the southeast, some 5-foot soundings will be encountered on this corner of the cove. Good water runs to within 100 yards or so of shore. Watch out for the correctly charted finger of 3-foot waters to the west.

On the ICW   Powerboats should slow down north of flashing daybeacon #60 as they begin their approach to the Stickney Point Bridge in order to protect the craft berthed at the facilities south of the span.

The Stickney Point Bridge has a closed vertical clearance of 18 feet, but it does open on demand.

North of the Stickney Point span, no-wake regulations are in effect to unlighted daybeacon #72. This is yet another of those seemingly interminable slow-speed zones for powercraft.

Sarasota Bay to Anna Maria Island

Picture a tall, bright city shimmering against the clear waters of a wide bay in the hazy summer sunshine. Now throw in plenty of protected waters glutted with anchorages (albeit restricted ones) and a more-than-adequate selection of marina facilities and yacht clubs. Add a host of waterside restaurants with their own dockage. Well, my friend, we have just managed to conjure up a mental picture of Sarasota Bay and the city for which it's named. Add all these fortunate qualities to the Gulf-side islands known as St. Armands Key, Longboat Key, and Anna Maria Island, three of the most popular, though partly unspoiled, barrier islands in Western Florida, and you have the formula that brings cruisers back time and time again to the waters lying about the city of Sarasota.

On the negative side, Sarasota is one of the only cities in Western Florida that continues to impose what this writer considers illegal anchorage limits. Cruisers dropping the hook on the waters surrounding Sarasota are restricted to no more than a 48-hour stay. Go figure!

Vessels cruising in from the Gulf or sailors ready to make the offshore jump will have to contend with serious navigational problems that plague both of Sarasota's inlets. Even though New Pass is regularly dredged, the shoals seem to reappear by the time the dredge disappears over the horizon. Even worse, all the outer aids to navigation have recently been removed from Big Sarasota Pass. The U.S. Coast Guard has determined that it is just not possible to maintain a reliable channel on these waters.

The ICW enters Roberts Bay north of the Stickney Point Bridge and follows this water body's ever-widening shores until it passes through the Ringling Bridge near Standard Mile 74. Cruisers used to the sheltered waters running north from Fort Myers are in for quite a shock. The wide reaches of Sarasota Bay stretch before you to the north, while the city of Sarasota rears its high-rise buildings to the east and New Pass Inlet eventually makes off to the southwest. After a memorable, though sometimes choppy, transit of Sarasota Bay, the Waterway crosses south to north through Anna Maria Sound and finally meets the mighty waters of Tampa Bay.

This is a generally pleasant section of the Western Florida ICW, with good anchorages and warm, friendly marinas. Don't be in such a hurry to explore the wonders of Tampa Bay that you pass Sarasota's many charms too quickly.

Phillippi Creek (Standard Mile 70)

North of Stickney Point Bridge, the ICW follows a short land cut into the southern reaches of Roberts Bay. Along the way, mariners will pass the confusing, multiple mouths of Phillippi Creek along the eastern shore near unlighted daybeacon #72. While a few local runabouts sometimes go upstream to a restaurant with a small-craft rental agency, the creek's depths are totally inadequate for cruising-size craft. Cheer up! Better things are not far ahead.

Roberts Bay Anchorage (Standard Mile 71)

The first anchorage and yacht club you will encounter north of Stickney Point will be discovered near unlighted daybeacon #78. Notice the charted "Spoil" west of #78. This feature is actually a rather substantial, well-wooded body of land, and it is much more prominent in reality than it appears from a careless study of chart 11425. Boats drawing 4 feet or less can cruise around the entire island keeping some 25 to 30 yards off the (island) shores and rejoin the Waterway near unlighted daybeacon #80. In good weather, you can drop the hook amidst ample swinging room for most pleasure boats between #78 and the island's eastern banks. This spot has 5 feet of water, but only minimal protection. With strong breezes in the offing, boats as large as 48 feet and drawing less than 4½ feet can cruise carefully behind the isle or drop the hook off either of its points, depending on wind direction, for good shelter. As you would expect, the island sports no development, while a few private homes peep out from the Siesta Key shoreline to the west. This is a particularly attractive anchorage, and it is still highly recommended by this writer.

Unfortunately, during the last several years, local water skiers and jet skis (which we cruisers call "water maggots") have begun using the waters west of the spoil island as a kind of competition course. Hopefully, this won't be a problem during your visit, but at least we've warned you. Be sure to read the navigational information presented later in this chapter before beginning your first circuit around the island.

The Field Club (Standard Mile 71, 27 17.208 North/082 32.442 West)

Passing cruisers cannot help but note the elegant Field Club headquarters. Housed in the former Florida homeplace of Marshall Fields, this is one of the most exclusive yacht clubs in all of Florida. The clubhouse is actually built over an arm of its entrance stream. A moatlike opening allows water to flow under the clubhouse.

1. Field Club

The club's marked channel cuts east off the ICW just south of unlighted daybeacon #78 and maintains depths of 5½ feet. A few docks (including the fuel pier) are found on the southern shore of the creek leading to the clubhouse, but most of the club's piers are enclosed in a well-protected basin cutting into the stream's southern banks. Dockside soundings range from 6 to 6½ feet at the fuel pier and other docks on the creek leading to the clubhouse and as little as 5 feet (MLW) in the protected dockage basin. Members of yacht clubs with appropriate reciprocal arrangements are accepted for guest dockage at the club's fixed wooden piers featuring full power and water connections. The club has a dockmaster on duty from 9:00 A.M. to 5:00 P.M. Tuesday through Friday and from 8:30 A.M. to 5:30 P.M. weekends. The docks are unattended on Mondays. While the dockmaster is on duty, club members and accredited visitors (only) can purchase gasoline and diesel fuel.

Upon going ashore, visiting cruisers will find showers, a swimming pool (open from June through Labor Day), and tennis courts. The Field Club offers good dining, with lunch served Tuesday through Friday; the evening meal, Tuesday through Sunday; and a Sunday brunch. Reservations are required! No other restaurants are within walking distance, but a short taxi ride can take you into nearby Sarasota, where the dining and shopping choices are practically unlimited.

The Field Club has some special rules for cruising visitors, and we quote from the *Florida Council of Yacht Clubs' Guide:*"No outdoor cooking allowed. No laundry or towels to be hung on boats. Leashed pets allowed in marina area only. Owners responsible for clean-up. All food & beverages consumed on club grounds must be purchased on club grounds."

The Field Club is perched amidst a lovely setting with beautifully green shores and palatial homes. Captains and crew who enjoy the quieter side of cruising, as opposed to the bustling facilities along the principal Sarasota waterfront, and have the necessary club affiliation, should give the Field Club their most serious consideration. Call well ahead of time to make advance arrangements.

Before leaving the Field Club behind, this writer would like to note that he has had the good fortune to visit with and make presentations to this wonderful organization on three occasions. In 23 years of speaking engagements, I have never enjoyed a warmer greeting. Thanks to one and all!

> **The Field Club (941) 924-1201**
>   **http://www.thefieldclub.com**
>
> **Approach depth—5½ feet MLW**
> **Dockside depth—6-6½ feet fuel dock MLW**
>   **5 feet minimum MLW—dockage harbor**
> **Accepts transients—members of clubs with**
>   **reciprocal agreements**
> **Fixed wooden piers—yes**
> **Dockside power connections—yes**
> **Dockside water connections—yes**
> **Showers—yes**
> **Gasoline—yes (members and accredited guests**
>   **only)**
> **Diesel fuel—yes (members and accredited**
>   **guests only)**
> **Restaurant—on site**

Siesta Key Bridge Anchorages (Standard Mile 71.5, Various Lats/Lons—see below)

Two additional anchorages are found east and west of the Waterway respectively, just south of the Siesta Key bascule bridge (north

The Field Club

of flashing daybeacon #82). The west-side haven has everything except an all-natural shoreline. Good depths of 6 to (mostly) 8 feet lead you into a lakelike bay where you can drop the hook in 8 to 9 feet of water (near 27 18.059 North/082 33.180 West). Protection is sufficient for anything short of a full gale. There is enough swinging room for Benny Goodman. The surrounding shores are overlooked by an attractive residential neighborhood.

Boats as large as 36 feet and drawing *less than* 4 feet can find a real hurricane hidey-hole on the eastern anchorage (near 27 18.056 North/082 32.429 West). The cove is shaped like an inverted C. Depths at the difficult entrance run a bare 4 feet, but improve to 7- and 9-foot levels at the rear, protected portion of the cove. The shores are bordered by a concrete seawall and are lined by private docks set beside a dense collection of expensive homes. If you need to duck the weather, it doesn't get much better than this.

Spoil Anchorage (Standard Mile 72, 27 18.848 North/082 32.523 West)

In easterly winds or light airs, boats that are not bothered by a cruise through 4-foot depths can skirt the charted spoil northeast of flashing daybeacon #2 and anchor within 75 yards of shore in some 6 feet of water. You must be careful to avoid the spoil, which is marked with a concrete pile and sign indicating the presence of an artificial underwater reef. Skippers who successfully leave this hazard behind can drop the hook within 50 yards of the eastern banks in 5 to 6 feet of water. Shelter is good for easterlies and fair for breezes from the north or south. Winds over 10 knots blowing from the west would make this anchorage most uncomfortable.

Big Sarasota Pass (Standard Mile 72.5)

The wide, marked channel cutting southwest to Big Sarasota Pass makes into the Waterway northwest of flashing daybeacon #6 and unlighted daybeacon #7. As alluded to earlier, the United States Coast Guard has now designated Big Pass as a "Dangerous Inlet" and has washed its hands of trying to maintain a reliable channel and of maintaining the channel's aids to navigation. Originally, all the outer aids to navigation were to be removed, but then local government stepped in and took over maintenance of all markers north of unlighted daybeacon #9. Southwest of #9, the remaining markers have been withdrawn. We *strongly* recommend that no craft—large, small, or indifferent—attempt to use Big Pass for a passage out to the Gulf or from the briny blue into the inland waters of Sarasota Bay.

The interior reaches of Big Pass do not suffer from the same shallow water and shoaling problems as does the cut's outer section. Generally, minimum 6-foot depths can be expected on the inner portion of the channel. Study chart 11425 for a moment and notice that the inlet's inner, west-side flank is composed of Lido Key. As long as you stay north of the point of land formed by the southeasterly tip of Lido Key, all should be well.

This is a happy situation, as cruisers can find their way to a good, fair-weather anchorage off Lido Key, south of the marked entrance to the side channel flowing north-northwest to the Sarasota Yacht Club (see below).

Big Sarasota Pass Anchorage (27 18.015 North/082 33.887 West)

Minimum depths of 7 feet run almost into the western shores southwest of unlighted daybeacon #15 (on the Big Sarasota Pass channel). Typical soundings run in the 10- to 17-foot region. This is a very popular stopover for local pleasure craft. During weekends, you will undoubtedly be joined by a host of fellow cruisers.

This anchorage is set against a local park and the beautiful, all-natural western shores are overlooked by tall Australian pines. It's terribly tempting to break out the dinghy and head ashore to explore the nearby beaches. In fact, with fair winds in the offing, I recommend it heartily.

Obviously, this is not an anchorage fit for strong or really even moderate winds. You may even want to think long and hard before committing to an overnight stay. While it's a great spot to while away a warm fall afternoon, the awakening might be rude should an unexpected thunderstorm blow up during the night. Another drawback is the strong currents that regularly sweep through these waters. Don't try to swim ashore!

Sarasota Yacht Club Channel and Associated Anchorages (Various Lats/Lons—see below)

The broad channel running north-northwest to the Sarasota Yacht Club breaks off from the flank of Big Sarasota Pass abeam of unlighted daybeacon #15. The stream runs between Bird Key to the east and the shoals outlying Otter, St. Armands, and Lido keys to the west. The passage is eventually blocked to the north by a 10-foot fixed bridge.

This cut provides access not only to the club's docks, but also to two anchorages as well. While fairly well marked, this channel definitely requires caution on the part of visiting cruisers. Be sure to read the navigation data for this passage, presented later in this chapter, before making your first attempt.

Minimum depths on the channel are about 6½ feet. However, the charted marsh flats west of the cut cover at high and mid-tide. It's altogether too easy to wander into 3 feet of water. Cruisers should also be warned that the aids to navigation on this cut are rather small and can be hard to spot from the main body of Big Sarasota Pass.

The first spot that you might consider dropping the hook lies west of unlighted daybeacon #7. A small but relatively deep channel makes in from the west just south of Otter Key. This stream leads to a wonderful overnight haven, which will be reviewed separately below.

North of unlighted daybeacon #10 a difficult, mostly unmarked channel cuts east-northeast and eventually leads through a small canal and a 7-foot fixed bridge to the docks of the Bird Key Yacht Club. As most cruising vessels will use this club's primary entrance off the ICW, we shall review this facility later in this chapter.

For now we need only note that the square cove west of the small Bird Key canal makes a good anchorage (near 27 19.192 North/082 33.768 West). While extra caution must be exercised to bypass several shoals bordering the channel's entrance, once past these hazards, good depths of 7 feet or better are found on the cove's broad interior reaches. Boats anchoring here would be protected from all winds except those blowing west across the main body of the yacht club channel. Vessels as large as 40 feet will find plenty of room to swing gracefully on the hook. Be sure to read the navigational account of this anchorage below before trying it for the first time.

The dockage basin adjoining the Sarasota Yacht Club is found on the channel's western shores, just south of the 10-foot fixed bridge, pretty much abeam of unlighted daybeacon #12 (near 27 19.315 North/082 34.053 West). This friendly club maintains a full-time dockmaster seven days a week, 8:30 A.M. to 5:00 P.M. Transients from all clubs with appropriate reciprocal privileges are accepted for guest dockage at fixed concrete piers with all power and water connections. Depths at the outer docks are an impressive 10 feet or better. The innermost slips against the seawall have only 5 feet of water, but these soundings are clearly the exception. Most boats will find plenty of water at this club's piers.

The club maintains a fuel dock featuring gasoline and diesel fuel. This service is provided for members and accredited guests only, and it's not open to the general public. Ashore, transients will find showers, a swimming pool, and excellent dining facilities. Lunch and dinner are served seven days a week. A host of other nearby restaurants is accessible by foot or a short taxi ride. The St. Armands Key shopping area is also within walking distance, but unfortunately there is not a grocery store in the immediate vicinity.

Sarasota Yacht Club (941) 365-1908

Approach depth—8-18 feet
Dockside depth—5-10 feet (most slips in the deeper part of this range)

Accepts transients—members of clubs, with
    reciprocal privileges
Fixed concrete piers—yes
Dockside power connections—yes
Dockside water connections—yes

Showers—yes
Gasoline—yes (members and guests only)
Diesel fuel—yes (members and guests only)
Restaurant—on site and several others nearby

1. Sarasota Yacht Club
2. Bird Key Yacht Club

All cruisers without very specific local knowledge are discouraged from an attempt to explore the waters north of the 10-foot fixed bridge. The numerous shoals are unmarked, and it's a cinch to run aground, even when you are trying to proceed with care.

Otter-Lido Key Anchorage (27 18.852 North/082 34.353 West)

What must surely be the best, though not the navigationally easiest, anchorage anywhere near the Sarasota Yacht Club and Big Sarasota Pass is found by following the 5-foot (minimum depth) channel south of Otter Key. Anchorage on these waters is restricted to a 48-hour stay courtesy of the Sarasota city government. Fortunately, this time period will not bother many mariners, but it is a wholly needless restriction nevertheless.

After you cruise west-southwest from unlighted daybeacon #7, deep waters eventually open out before you in a broad pool. The offshoot directly southwest of the entrance is surrounded by high-class residential development and affords excellent protection from all but strong easterly winds. Unfortunately, there is only enough elbowroom for vessels up to 32 feet.

The correctly charted, 9- to 13-foot waters southwest of Otter Key are far roomier and still well protected. The dredged bottom strata are a bit suspect for holding, but we have not had any troubles of this type during our several visits. Otherwise, this is a super anchorage and comes highly recommended by this author. There is plenty of swinging room, but the entrance's narrow mouth (from the yacht club channel) might be a bit tricky for vessels exceeding 42 feet in length.

The Otter Key banks to the northeast are undeveloped, but Lido Key's shores to the southwest are lined by what my friend and research assistant Andy Lightbourne once termed "millionaire's row." The houses are simply enormous and quite impressive. Surrounded by manicured lawns that look as if each blade of grass has been individually clipped, many have swimming pools and private docks. It is a very special treat to spend an evening tucked snugly amidst such luxury without a single worry about the next mortgage payment.

As the Otter Key channel flows placidly on to the northwest, the stream eventually splits and wraps enfolding arms around St. Armands Key. In spite of depths shown on chart 11425, we found less than 4 feet of water on the northeastern fork. The westerly arm is spanned by a fixed bridge with only 7 feet of vertical clearance. Skippers of all but small craft should confine their explorations to the waters southeast of the split.

St. Armands Key History   This delightful island is named in honor of its first permanent European resident, Charles St. Amand. Somehow the extra r has appeared over the years with nary an explanation.

According to legend, John Ringling won Lido and St. Armands keys in a poker game before establishing the winter headquarters for his famous circus in Sarasota during the late 1920s. Ringling dreamed of making St. Armands into an exclusive shopping district surrounded by palatial homes. Canals were dredged, rose-colored sidewalks took shape, and roads were pushed this way and that on the island. Hundreds of Australian pines were imported to line the streets.

To allow ready access to his island paradise, Ringling built a causeway across the water from Sarasota. In 1926 the new roadway was opened with great ceremony. A parade marched across the bridge and a band from the circus played on a bandstand in the island's traffic circle. Opening-day sales of lots exceeded one million dollars.

A scant year later Ringling presented the causeway to the city of Sarasota as a gift. Soon the Depression hit, and the once graceful avenues and traffic circle languished in obscurity. The bandstand rotted away and it seemed as if a century had passed since the triumphal opening-day parade.

Finally, development again returned to St. Armands in the 1950s and continued through the 1960s. In 1972, the "circle" was redeveloped as a lavish shopping center with fine Continental restaurants. While it may have come some fifty years later than planned, Ringling's dream has at last become a reality.

Sarasota (Standard Mile 73)

The modern-day city of Sarasota has grown by leaps and bounds since the days when John Ringling first brought his circus to its winter home in the small town. Today, huge glass-and-steel skyscrapers gaze benevolently over the waters of Sarasota Bay. Traffic is thick on the streets, but there is still something of Old Florida about this city.

There are so many things to see and do in modern Sarasota that it would be a simple task to fill an entire book with activities for visitors. Only a few of the stand-out attractions can be mentioned in the course of this account.

Auto buffs will be more than fascinated by the Sarasota Classic Car Museum (5500 Tamiami Trail N, 941-355-6228). Visitors can examine an unbelievable collection of 175 restored antique automobiles, including Rolls

Royces, Pierce Arrows, and many others. The museum is located at 5500 North U.S. 41. Cruising visitors will need a rental car or a taxi to reach this attraction.

The Sarasota Jungle Gardens (3701 Bayshore Road, 941-355-5305) is a 10-acre extravaganza of lush tropical growth, waterfowl, and beautiful sculpture. A petting zoo, bird show, and a shell and butterfly museum round out the attractions.

One of Sarasota's premier architectural landmarks is the Van Wezel Performing Arts Hall. Its lavender seashell shape is easily visible from the bay. Many a cruiser has probably passed by and wondered at this unusual structure.

The shoppers among us will want to set their course for the antique shops and art galleries of historic Palm Avenue. During the 1920s Sarasota's most affluent citizens, including the Ringling family, shopped in this district. This district deteriorated during the Great Depression, but it has now been rebuilt. Today, modern buildings sit side by side with restored edifices dating to the Roaring Twenties.

Even though the circus has moved its winter headquarters elsewhere, its one-time owner, John Ringling, left behind a huge art museum and one of the most fascinating houses in the United States. The John and Mable Ringling Museum of Art (5401 Bayshore Road, 941-359-5700) was created in 1927 by John Ringling for the people of Florida. After making millions through his far-flung business enterprises, Ringling "amassed an art collection of over 600 paintings, numerous statues, and decorative arts, including approximately 27 tapestries." Ringling and his wife assembled their amazing collection between 1924 and 1931.

The museum is housed in a whole series of buildings on the former Ringling estate. The entire property, along with all its assembled artwork, was deeded to the state of Florida upon John Ringling's death in 1936. It is now open to the public. The museum is an absolute "must see" for every visitor to Sarasota. You must also be sure to see the circus museum and the Asolo Theater, the "Official State Theater of Florida."

John Ringling and his wife, Mable, did more with their time in Sarasota than just putting together a world-class art collection. They also built one of the most unique homeplaces in America.

The Ringlings originally came to Sarasota seeking a winter home in 1912. The circus's winter headquarters was established in the city much later. In 1924 John and Mable began construction of their winter homeplace. They called it "Ca'd'Zan," which means "House of John." Writing in their wonderful book, *Florida Historic Homes,* Laura Stewart and Susanne Hupp describe Ca'd'Zan as "one of Florida's grandest homes. Completed in 1926 at a cost of about $1.5 million, the structure combined architectural elements drawn from two of Mrs. Ringling's favorites—the facade of the Doge's Palace in Venice and the tower of the old Madison Square Garden in New York, where her husband's circus regularly appeared."

Well, you can understand that this writer could go on and on describing this unbelievable estate. Fortunately for your eyes and my fingers, Ca'd'Zan is also open to the public. Guests by the hundreds gawk and wonder at the Ringling home's almost bizarre opulence daily. Cruisers not only have the opportunity to tour Ca'd'Zan by land—they may also choose to anchor within sight of its tiled walls. Out of the hundreds of points of interest in Sarasota, if I had to pick but one, the magnif-

icent Ringling estate and Ca'd'Zan would most certainly be my choice. Again, cruisers will need some form of motorized transportation to visit the grounds. There are no dockage facilities on the bay.

Phone numbers to know in Sarasota:

> Courtesy Transportation—(941) 954-1970
> Yellow Cab—(941) 955-3341
> Alamo Car Rentals—(941) 359-5540
> Avis Rental Cars—(941) 359-5240
> Budget Rent A Car—(800) 763-2999
> Boat/US Marine Center—(941) 755-9670
> West Marine—(941) 924-6777
> Chamber of Commerce—(941) 955-8187

Marina Operations and Marina Jack's Restaurant (Standard Mile 73, 27 19.988 North/082 32.771 West)

Returning now to the ICW's principal south-north track, the first of mainland Sarasota's principal facilities comes up on the east-northeastern shores, to the northeast of red, unlighted daybeacon #8A. A marked, deep channel leads the fortunate cruiser to one of the largest marinas in Western Florida, a super restaurant, and a popular anchorage. Think it might just be worth your time?

Study inset 2 on chart 11425 for a quick moment and locate the facility known as Marina Operations. This marina is designated as facility #43 on 11425, and it is found in the semi-enclosed basin east of Golden Gate Point. Believe you me, on the water, the marina's location will be readily apparent.

While you might expect Marina Operations to be a publicly owned facility, it is actually a friendly commercial operation that eagerly accepts transients for overnight or temporary dockage. The marina maintains prolific transient dockage at fixed, concrete piers with every conceivable power, water, and cable-television connection. The marina management is now in the permitting process to add a whole collection of new floating docks. When and if this project reaches completion, these new structures will add to this already first-class marina's usefulness. Courtesy of the hook-shaped peninsula to the south, protection is good for all but the heaviest weather. Gasoline, diesel fuel, waste pump-out service, adequate, (but slightly cramped) air-conditioned showers, and a semi-open-air Laundromat complete the facility's non-dining

amenities. New showers are slated for construction in 2004. Some mechanical repairs can occasionally be arranged through independent local contractors. Entrance and dockside depths are better than 8 feet, with typical soundings ranging from 10 to as much as 12 feet.

If you happen to arrive at Marina Operations during the lunch or dinner hour, a lucky star must be shining over your vessel. The on-site restaurant, Marina Jack's (941-365-4232), sits out over the piers and provides its patrons with a fine view of the harbor and the western skies at sunset. The interior of Marina Jack's

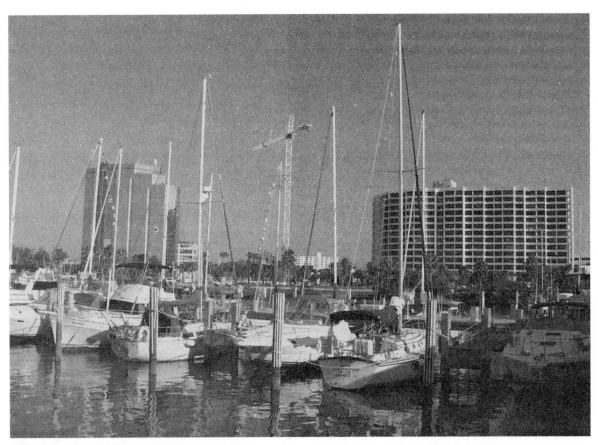

Marina Operations, Sarasota

features attractive décor. Downstairs you will find a large open-air bar, which is great for lunch or evening cocktails. Serious diners will want to head upstairs to the main dining room. Here patrons will find an unbelievably extensive menu ranging from Scallops Elyse to Fillet Florentine to grilled rib-eye steaks served in a Madeira sauce. While not exactly inexpensive, the prices are reasonable for the quality of food you will enjoy at this house of gastronomic pleasure.

As you would imagine, a bevy of shoreside shopping opportunities are available by foot from Marina Operations. This facility is located in the heart of downtown Sarasota. Those needing to reprovision will need a taxi to reach a supermarket or ship's store, but otherwise there is plenty to do and see close at hand. An impressive collection of glass-and-steel high-rise buildings overlook Marina Operations to the east, while idyllic Bayfront Park occupies the tongue of land to the south that helps to enclose the dockage basin.

Marina Operations (941) 955-9488
  http://www.marinajacks.com

Approach depth—10-12 feet
Dockside depth—8-12 feet
Accepts transients—yes (extensive)
Transient dockage rate—above average
Fixed concrete piers—yes
Fixed wooden piers—a few
Floating docks—a few
**Dockside power connections—up to 100 amp
  (in case you need to run your elevator)**
Dockside water connections—yes
Waste pump-out—yes
Showers—yes
Laundromat—yesGasoline—yes
Diesel fuel—yes
**Mechanical repairs—arranged through
  independent contractors**
Restaurant—on site and several nearby

Sarasota Anchorage (Standard Mile 73, 27 19.834 North/082 32.801 West)

Cruisers who prefer to anchor off have not been forgotten in the scheme of mainland Sarasota. The charted 8- to 12-foot waters west and south of Bayfront Park's hooklike peninsula bordering Marina Operations' southerly flank regularly play host to several dozen anchored vessels. Some local craft are hooked to mooring buoys, but there is plenty of swinging room for almost any craft to drop anchor. There is good protection from easterly breezes and some shelter from northerly or southerly blows. Strong winds blowing across the Waterway from the west could make for a bumpy evening.

This anchorage is quite pleasing to the eye. The all-natural shores of Bayfront Park are backed by Sarasota's high-rise downtown buildings. In the absence of strong westerlies, you could scarcely do better when anchoring in the Sarasota region.

Anchorage is officially limited to a maximum stay of 72 hours in this city-sanctioned haven (as opposed to 48 hours on all other Sarasota area waters). In practice, however, it has been our experience that this 72-hour limit is seldom enforced. Things could have changed by the time of your visit, however.

Dinghies are no longer accommodated at Marina Operations, and dinghy landing at Bayfront Park is now restricted to the beach in front of O'Leary's Water Sports and Grill (941-953-7505). This small facility is located on the southeastern corner of Bayfront Park, on the land hook's southerly shore. Once pulled up on O'Leary's beach, you will find public rest rooms and telephones within walking distance.

Golden Gate Point Anchorage (Standard Mile 73, 27 20.056 North/082 33.145 West)

Some boats occasionally anchor in the charted 12-foot waters west of Golden Gate Point. Here you will find a cove formed between the arms of the point and the causeway leading to the eastern genesis of the Ringling Bridge. You must be sure to anchor well in toward the rear of the cove to avoid the charted cable area. Boats as large as 40 feet should find plenty of swinging room and good protection from all but strong southerly and westerly winds in 7- to 9-foot depths. The causeway shores play host to a public launching ramp and a jet ski rental shop. The Golden Gate shores are flanked by extremely heavy, high-rise condo development. With the headlights and noise of passing automobiles, this could not exactly be described as a particularly peaceful overnight haven.

Bird Key Yacht Club (Standard Mile 73, 27 19.237 North/082 33.609 West)

West-southwest of flashing daybeacon #10, itself just southeast of the Ringling Bridge, cruising vessels can follow a well-marked channel to the docks of the Bird Key Yacht Club. You will see a sign denoting the club channel near unlighted daybeacon #2, the first aid on the cut. The channel carries 9 to 12 feet of water and dockside depths are a good 8 to 10 feet in the principal basin in front of the clubhouse. A few of the smaller slips located around on the canal carry only 5 to 6 feet of water.

Bird Key Yacht Club accepts cruising visitors who are members of other clubs with reciprocal privileges. Advance reservations are required by the club management. As guest slip space is somewhat limited, make your arrangements well in advance. Dockage is at fixed wooden piers with full power, water, and cable-television connections. Gasoline and diesel fuel can be purchased by members and accredited guests only—not the public. Showers (but no laundry facilities) to wash away the day's salt are available in the clubhouse. The club is closed Tuesdays. Lunch and dinner are served daily (except Tuesdays) in the on-site dining facilities. The club boasts a swimming pool (also closed on Tuesdays) and several tennis courts.

Bird Key Yacht Club (941) 953-4455
http://www.birdkeyyc.com

Approach depth—9-12 feet
Dockside depth—8-10 feet (main basin)
Accepts transients—members of clubs, with
   reciprocal privileges (advance reservations
   required)
Fixed wooden piers—yes
Dockside power connections—up to 50 amp
Dockside water connections—yes
Showers—yes
Gasoline—yes (members and guests only)
Diesel fuel—yes (members and guests only)
Restaurant—on site

Sarasota Bay

Sarasota Bay (also known as Big Sarasota Bay) stretches for a length of some 9 nautical miles on its southeast-to-northwest axis from the Ringling Bridge to Longboat Pass, west of Tidy Island. The southern two-thirds of the bay is deep and quite broad, with an average width of almost 3 nautical miles. The mainland shores to the east exhibit surprisingly light development north of downtown Sarasota and make for a good view from the water. Some smaller facilities, including one good boatyard and several marinas accepting transients, are available. You also have the opportunity to anchor within sight of one of the most famous houses in all of Florida.

The western banks of Sarasota Bay are comprised of the long, thin island known as Longboat Key. This body of land was actually used by the Timucuan Indians as a vacation spot long before the first Europeans touched the shores of Western Florida. Today, the isle has been intensely developed, but the condos and private homes are still interspaced with some natural stretches. This writer could not help but like Longboat Key, if only for the memory of becoming hopelessly lost on its much less developed roads during my high-school years.

One large marina and several other smaller facilities beckon cruisers on Longboat Key. There are also several notable waterside restaurants with their own docks and one particularly good anchorage south of Longboat Pass.

The Quay (Standard Mile 73.5)

The L-shaped cove east of flashing daybeacon #12 is definitely worth a look. Most navigators will be able to find their way to the cove's interior reaches with minimum 5-foot depths. As you enter the cove and follow its sharp turn to the north, a huge, peach-colored building will be prominent on the eastern banks. This complex is known as the Quay. It is occupied by offices, retail shops, and several restaurants. Dockage is plentiful at a privately maintained wooden face pier in front of the complex. Visitors are free to dock here while patronizing any of the Quay's businesses. Depths at the pier run 5 to 7 feet. There are no overnight accommodations.

Among the Quay's restaurants is Michael's Mediterranean Grill (941-951-2467). Also, the Boathouse Restaurant (941-363-2628), associated with the Sarasota Hyatt, maintains its own docks on the cove's northeastern corner. Depths of 6 to 7 feet can be expected at its fixed wooden face docks. The restaurant is built out over the water and is quite prominent, though the only sign is a very small affair. In good weather outside dining is available.

Payne Terminal (Standard Mile 74.5)

The eastward extension of the New Pass Inlet channel (reviewed below) crosses the southern foot of Sarasota Bay and leads to a rectangular cove on the mainland shore charted as Payne Terminal. Apparently, this stream was once used as an oil loading and offloading terminal. That era has now passed and present-day visitors will find only a public launching ramp and the headquarters of the Sarasota Coast Guard Auxiliary (on the cove's southern banks). There are no services for transients, nor is there enough swinging room to anchor. Most visiting cruisers will wisely choose to bypass this errant sidewater.

Whitaker Bayou (Standard Mile 75)

Whitaker Bayou cuts into the mainland (eastern) shore of Sarasota Bay northeast of flashing daybeacon #13. The bayou plays host to one of Sarasota's premier repair facilities, The Yacht Center (941-365-1770). This facility is located on the stream's southern banks. The yard offers full-service mechanical (gas and diesel) and below-waterline, haul-out repairs. The on-site travelift is rated at 70 tons.

Surprisingly, the entrance to Whitaker Bayou is somewhat indifferently marked with white PVC pipes. Even more surprising, low-water entrance depths are a meager 4 to 4½ feet, and these soundings continue on into the boatyard docks. If you need more water, make your approach at high tide.

New Pass Inlet (Standard Mile 74.5)

The channel leading southwest to New Pass Inlet breaks off from the ICW at unlighted daybeacon #NP, on the southern reaches of Sarasota Bay. Shoaling on this seaward cut is a bit on the legendary side. The sands wash in just about as fast as the Army Corps can pump them out. We sounded minimum 6-foot depths on the channel in early August 2003.

However, we also noted a sunken ketch that had recently foundered on the shoals just south of the inlet's outer channel. Depths could be far worse by the time of your arrival, or, if dredging has just occurred, then soundings could be temporarily better.

If anyone thinks this is an easy or generally reliable seaward passage, think again! Captains not intimately familiar with New Pass's condition on a week-to-week basis should continue tracking their way northward to Longboat Pass (see below) or even the Tampa Bay entrance before making that often difficult jump from inland to offshore waters (or vice versa). By all accounts, don't even think about attempting New Pass Inlet at night or in anything approaching foul weather. If you think I'm being too conservative, look at the photo of the sunken ketch on these pages!

New Pass is spanned by a bascule bridge

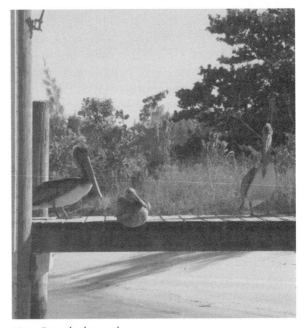

New Pass dock watchers

with 23 feet of closed vertical clearance. I'm sorry to say that this span has a regulated opening schedule. Because of the strong current, this bridge is more than a casual cause for concern.

A few low-key facilities are found on the pass's southeasterly banks, northeast of the 23-foot bridge. None cater to larger cruising craft. First up is the friendly bunch at the Sarasota Sailing Squadron (27 20.241 North/082 34.409 West, 941-388-2355). A host of small sailing craft belonging to the club's members anchor off the point southeast of flashing daybeacon #13, near the charted WSPB radio tower. The club does not have much in the way of dockage and there does not seem to be anything in the way of services for transients.

Moving farther toward the Gulf, MarineMax (941-388-4411) comes up next. This marina caters almost exclusively to smaller powercraft and there are no services for transients except gasoline and a ship's store. Old Salty Dog Restaurant (941-349-0158) does have a dock adjacent to MarineMax to which patrons are free to tie while dining. Depths are a very impressive 10 feet at dockside, but the fierce tidal currents can make for a hazardous approach to the pier.

Just short of the bascule bridge, mariners will find a small convenience and tackle store with its own dock guarding the southeastern banks. Dockside depths run 9 to 10 feet and there should be enough room for one 40-footer to tie up temporarily. Again, the current is a cause for genuine concern and caution.

We are sorry to report that the entrance to the once-popular anchorage on the charted cove indenting New Pass's northwestern banks, southwest of the bridge, shoaled badly several years ago, and things have not improved. While the interior waters remain

deep, no craft larger than a skiff can now enter this sidewater safely.

Quick Point Channel

A marked channel breaks off from the northwestern flank of New Pass and curves around Quick Point. While the initial portion of this passage lacks any beacons, the channel northwest of Quick Point is well outlined with red, unlighted daybeacons. The cut eventually rejoins the deeper waters of Sarasota Bay at unlighted daybeacon #18. The vast majority of this channel holds 10 to 13 feet of water, but there is one exception. Near unlighted daybeacon #2, hard by Quick Point, water depths rise to some 5½ to 6 feet. Deep-draft vessels that might have a problem with these depths can enter and leave the cut by way of its deeper, easier-to-follow northwesterly entrance.

Quick Point channel leads to one small facility abeam of unlighted daybeacon #8. Spindrift Yacht Services (941-383-7781) offers dry-stack storage, gasoline, and a well-stocked ship's store.

Ringling Mansion (Standard Mile 77.5, 27 22.978 North/082 34.137 West)

Let us now turn our attention to the various sidewaters, facilities, and anchorages along Sarasota Bay's northeastern flank between Whitaker Bayou and Long Bar Point (north of the ICW's flashing daybeacon #18). The first point of interest worthy of our attention is the fabulous Ringling mansion, Ca'd'Zan, east of flashing daybeacon #15. This attraction is noted as a "Cupola" on chart 11425.

The old mansion sits directly on the bay's banks and makes a truly striking sight from the water. Depths of 5 feet or better run to within .2 nautical miles of the house. There are no provisions for dockage by pleasure craft, but in good weather you can anchor abeam of the homeplace for an evening which will not soon be forgotten.

Even if an overnight stop is not in your plans, please take a few minutes to depart from the Waterway for a closer look at this unique attraction. Your voyage will be far richer for the extra effort.

Bowlees Creek and the Holiday Inn Marina (Standard Mile 78.5, 27 24.816 North/082 34.452 West)

A pile-lined channel cuts the northeastern shores of Sarasota Bay northeast of unlighted daybeacon #16 and leads to a good facility on Bowlees Creek. Low-water entrance depths on the stream's interior reaches run as little as $4^1/_2$ to 5 feet. Vessels drawing $4^1/_2$ feet or less should not have any undue difficulty.

Bowlees Creek splits into two branches some 100 yards upstream from its mouth. The southeasterly fork leads to the Holiday Inn-Sarasota/Bradenton Airport Marina. This facility is nestled in the sheltered upstream terminus of Bowlees Creek and should make a great spot to ride out heavy weather. Transients are accepted for dockage at fixed wooden piers. Resident craft are moored to floating concrete piers. Power connections up to 30 amp, water hookups, gasoline, and diesel fuel are available. Visiting cruisers can even connect to cable television and the pier-side telephone system. Captains and crew will also discover clean shoreside showers, a Laundromat, and a swimming pool perfect for cooling off in after a hot day on Sarasota Bay. If you should wish to spend a night or two away from the live-aboard routine, the adjacent Holiday Inn is quite convenient. The motel also maintains a restaurant, which the dockmaster described to this writer as "elegant." A lunchtime snack bar, serving hamburgers and other sandwiches, is available poolside. This is the only facility offering transient dockage on the mainland shores of Sarasota Bay north of the Ringling Bridge.

Holiday Inn-Sarasota Airport Marina (941) 355-2781)

Approach depth—$4^1/_2$-5 feet (mean low water)
Dockside depth—$4^1/_2$-5 feet (mean low water)
Accepts transients—yes
Transient dockage rate—average
Fixed wooden piers—for transient use
Floating concrete docks—for resident craft
Dockside power connections—up to 30 amp
Dockside water connections—yes
Showers—yes
Laundromat—yes
Gasoline—yes
Diesel fuel—yes
Mechanical repairs—independent contractors
Restaurant—on site

Longboat Key Moorings (Standard Mile 77.5, 27 22.089 North/082 37.119 West)

Turning our attention back to Sarasota Bay's southwesterly shoreline, one of finest facilities on the bay is found at the foot of the charted channel south of Bishops Point and west of the ICW's flashing daybeacon #15. The dockage basin is denoted as facility designation #54A on chart 11425.

Longboat Key Moorings is a huge dockage facility enclosed in a protected basin and associated with an adjacent housing and condo development. It would take a serious gale to bother pleasure craft berthed snugly in this harbor.

While many of the marina's entrance-cut markers remain uncharted after many years

1. Longboat Key Moorings

television connections. Gasoline and diesel fuel are available, as well as waste pump-out services and a complete Laundromat. The marina's large collection of shoreside showers is one of the finest on the Western Florida coastline, and it is fully climate controlled. Mechanical repairs for both gasoline- and diesel-powered plants, plus refrigeration and electrical service, are now available through an on-site repair firm. Make arrangements through the accommodating dockmasters.

Longboat Key Moorings features a most impressive complex of shops and restaurants along the harbor's southerly shores. Housed in these buildings is a well-outfitted ship's store (and harbormaster's office), rubbing elbows with a full-line deli. The friendly staff will even make deliveries from the deli directly to your slip. For larger orders, a Publix supermarket and Eckerd drugstore are found within easy walking distance. Bike rentals are also available and courtesy van transportation can be arranged to the St. Armands shopping center.

When it comes time to slake a healthy appetite ashore, the Cafe on the Bay (941-383-0440), also located in the same complex, is a good choice. This is a sophisticated dining attraction with Continental-style cuisine. Shorts and T-shirts, while tolerated, are not exactly the preferred uniform of the day. If your attitude needs some adjustment beforehand, don't overlook the Marker 15 Lounge.

Other shoreside amenities include a heated swimming pool, tennis court, and a hot tub. A golf course is found a stone's throw from the marina grounds.

Well, if you know of a marina with more complete services, then, by all means, stay there. For my money, if you are in the market for a large, resort-type marina, then don't miss

(where are you, NOAA?), the Moorings' approach channel is actually quite well defined with a host of mostly unlighted daybeacons (the outermost pair of aids to navigation are now lighted and charted). Once you spot this collection of markers, it's an easy task to enter the harbor with good water. Minimum entrance soundings run around 6½ feet with a generous 9 to 20 feet of water dockside.

Transients piloting boats 35 feet and larger are accepted at Longboat Key for overnight berths at ultramodern, fixed PVC-decked, concrete pile piers featuring 30-, 50-, and 100-amp power connections, water hookups, and cable-the chance to berth at Longboat Key Moorings.

Longboat Key Moorings (941) 383-8383
http://www.longboatkeymarina.com

Approach depth—6½+ feet
Dockside depth—9-20 feet
Accepts transients—yes
Transient dockage rate—above average
Fixed concrete and wooden piers—yes
Dockside power connections—30, 50, and some
  100 amp
Dockside water connections—yes
Waste pump-out—yes
Showers—yes
Laundromat—yes
Gasoline—yes
Diesel fuel—yes
Mechanical repairs—yes
Ship's and variety store—yes (large)
Restaurant—on site and several nearby

Whale Key-Buttonwood Harbor Channel (Standard Mile 81)

South-southwest of unlighted daybeacon #19, cruisers can follow the marked and charted channel to a restaurant with dockage. Most of the cut holds minimum 6½-foot depths, but it climbs to 4½ feet as you approach the restaurant docks.

The Buttonwood Harbor Channel splits at unlighted daybeacon #12. Take the right-hand, or northwestern, arm of the channel to visit Pattigeorge's Marina Restaurant (941-383-5111). This fine dining spot has the deserved reputation of serving some of the most imaginative, Oriental-flair cuisine on the Western Florida ICW. Believe you me, if your craft fits the size and draft requirements, this is a must stop for those in search of waterside epicurean pleasures.

Unfortunately, Pattigeorge's docks did not

appear adequate to this writer to serve vessels larger than 30 feet. Also, remember those 4½-foot dockside depths.

Whitney Beach Channel (Standard Mile 83.5)

Northwest of flashing daybeacon #23, Sarasota Bay begins to narrow as the Waterway rushes on to the southern foot of Anna Maria Sound. In times past, cruisers could cut southeast at unlighted daybeacon #33 on what this writer terms the "Whitney Beach Channel" and visit a large marina and restaurant known as the Buccaneer. The restaurant is now closed, and apparently the marina is only in a bare-bones state of operation. We found no dockmaster in attendance during a visit in early August 2003, and several phone calls have not yielded an answer or even an answering machine. For the moment at least, we suggest that cruisers not count on being able to find a berth at Buccaneer Marina.

The Whitney Beach Channel does still provide access to a small-craft facility. Cruisers can access Cannons Marina (941-383-1311) by cutting southeast at unlighted daybeacon #11, and then turning west into the first canal. After a fairly lengthy cruise down this stream, Cannons will be spotted dead ahead. This small facility has gasoline, a ship's store, and mechanical repairs for outboards. There is no overnight dockage and no other services for transients. Depths on the approach channel run 5½ to 7 feet, with 5½- to 6-foot soundings dockside.

Longbeach-Jewfish Key Anchorage and Associated Restaurants (Standard Mile 85, Various Lats/Lons—see below)

One of the best and most popular anchorages between Placida Harbor and Tampa Bay is found on the wide swath of deep water stretching west from the gap between unlighted can buoy #39 and unlighted day-beacon #40. Minimum 9-foot depths, excellent shelter, and easy access to and from the ICW have combined to make this refuge one of the most-used havens on or near Sarasota Bay. As if all that were not quite enough to attract you, consider the presence of not one but two restaurants with their own docks bordering the southerly portion of the anchorage. This was all enough reason for me to tarry here for a while; you do what you want.

The deep-water channel eventually rejoins Longboat Pass (see below) to the west. However, the northwestern portion of this passage is quite shoal, and we strongly suggest that cruising craft make exclusive use of the entrance from the ICW.

Two spots provide excellent shelter. Choose the one that is best sheltered from the prevailing winds. The first is found on the tongue of charted 13-foot water stretching south into a cove hard by the village of Longbeach (near 27 26.215 North/082 40.799 West). Minimum depths of 9 feet are held to within 75 yards of the western banks and even closer to the northwestern shores. There is some shallow water to the south and southeast, but boats up to 50 feet will find plenty of swinging room with excellent protection from all but northeasterly winds. If you find this anchorage crowded, it might be a good idea to use a Bahamian-style mooring to

Moore's Stone Crab Restaurant, Longbeach

avoid swinging into your neighbor during the night. The surrounding shores are only lightly developed and are quite attractive.

So, you think the haven described above sounds pretty good. Well, hold on to your captain's hat—the best is yet to come. No fewer than two fine restaurants flank the cove's northwesterly banks. Moore's Stone Crab Restaurant (941-383-1748) is readily visible near the cove's northeasterly point. The docks stretch out well into the water. Vessels as large as 45 feet can tie to the outer pier, where skippers will find 6 to 8 feet of water. Depths on the smaller inner piers run to 5 feet. Restaurant patrons are welcome to spend the night at this dock without further charge, but no power or water connections are available.

Put simply, Moore's is one of this writer's favorite Western Florida restaurants. The atmosphere of simpler days has been preserved here and the pace is delightfully relaxed. Do you like fresh seafood? (If you don't, shame on you.) Moore's has its own fishing fleet. The catch of the day is unloaded out of the boats and straight into the kitchen, which tends to make it fresh. Moore's is open seven days a week.

Mar-Vista Dockside Restaurant (941-383-2391) guards the cove's southwesterly corner. The restaurant dock is a rather small affair that has only 4 feet of water at low tide. Cruising-size boats would do well to anchor out and dinghy ashore. Mar-Vista features a warm, convivial atmosphere. The al-fresco dining is very popular. My first mate and I enjoyed an idle time over excellent drinks sitting at the long bar and looking out over the many boats anchored in the cove. Sandwiches and fresh seafood are served along with the copious drinks. The local favorite seems to be the grouper.

The second spot where you should consider anchoring, particularly if the winds are blowing strongly from the north or northeast, is found on the deep water behind (to the southwest of) the long, private island southwest of flashing daybeacon #41, known as Jewfish Key (near 27 26.386 North/082 40.754 West). Minimum depths are again 9 feet, and there is almost enough swinging room for a small freighter. Some tidal current is present in this cut, so make sure the anchor is well set and there is plenty of room between you and your neighbors. The island to the northeast sports a single house and private pier, but is otherwise in its natural state. The mainland shores are lightly developed. This is an attractive anchorage that most cruisers will want to visit time and time again. The two coveside restaurants are still only a short dinghy ride away.

Mariners in need of galley supplies, and up for a very long dinghy ride, can work their way south to the charted mouth of Bishop Bayou. By following this stream as it cuts to the northwest, you will eventually come up behind a shopping center. Here you will find a few cleats set off a concrete seawall where you can tie your dinghy off temporarily.

Longboat Pass (Standard Mile 86)

The channel leading to Longboat Pass breaks off from the ICW between unlighted daybeacon #45 and flashing daybeacon #47. This is a narrow inlet through which tidal currents often boil. The seaward cut is spanned by a 17-foot bascule bridge that opens on demand from 6:00 A.M. to 10:00 P.M. Minimum depths of 8 feet can now be expected in the marked cut. Of course, future shoaling could eventually erode these happy

1. Moore's Stone Crab Restaurant
2. Mar-Vista Dockside Restaurant

soundings. Considering the current and the 17-foot horizontal clearance of the bascule bridge, I would not attempt to bring anything larger than a 45-footer in through this inlet. If you should make the attempt, proceed with caution.

Cortez Bridge Facilities (Standard Mile 87, Various Lats/Lons—see below)

Two marinas are ready to serve cruising craft hard by the Cortez Bridge, north of unlighted daybeacon #49. Moving south to north, the first of the two facilities is found at the terminus of its charted, *L*-shaped channel cutting in from the

bridge's southwestern corner. Bradenton Beach Marina (27 28.090 North/082 41.809 West) is a medium-size establishment that features a huge dry-stack storage building flanking the harbor's southerly side. The dockmaster's office resides behind the principal wet-slip dockage pier. An on-site restaurant is scheduled to be open by the time this account finds its way into your hands.

The marina's entrance channel is a little curvy for first-timers, but it carries minimum 5½- to 6-foot depths. Check out our navigational account of this facility below for channel advice.

1. Bradenton Beach Marina
2. Seafood Shack Restaurant and Marina

Bradenton Beach gladly accepts transients at its fixed wooden piers, equipped with 30- and 50-amp power hookups and freshwater connections. The outer docks carry some 10 to 11 feet of water, while 5½ to 6 feet is encountered on the innermost slips. Neither this marina nor the Seafood Shack (reviewed below) is particularly well sheltered for really nasty weather. Gasoline, diesel fuel, waste pump-out service, and full mechanical (gas and diesel engines) plus haul-out repairs are available. The new on-site travelift is rated at an impressive 77 tons. Adequate, non-air-conditioned showers are accessible via a long walk from the wet slips, and there is also a semi-open-air Laundromat on the premises. Several restaurants, including the Bridge Tender Inn (see below), are only a few steps away.

Bradenton Beach Marina (941) 778-2288
http://www.bradentonbeachmarina.com

Approach depth—5½-6 feet (minimum)
Dockside depth—10-11 feet (outer docks)
    5½-6 feet (innermost slips)
Accepts transients—yes
Transient dockage rate—slightly above average
Fixed wooden piers—yes
Dockside power connections—30 and 50 amp
Dockside water connections—yes
Showers—yes
Laundromat—yes
Waste pump-out service—yes
Gasoline—yes
Diesel fuel—yes
Mechanical repairs—yes
Below-waterline repairs—yes
Restaurant—several nearby

While running the approach cut leading to Bradenton Beach Marina, cruisers will be led hard by the outermost tip of the Bradenton Beach Historic Pier. It is quite possible for boats drawing 4 feet or less to break off first to the west and then southwest and follow a channel indifferently outlined by white PVC pipes to a small pier that fronts the Bridge Tender Inn (135 Bay Street, 941-778-4849). Consult the navigational account later in this chapter for more complete navigational instructions.

Slips are for the use of dining patrons only—no overnight stays are allowed. Depths in the white-PVC-pipe-outlined channel run around at least 4½ to 5 feet at mean low water, with 5-foot soundings dockside.

The Seafood Shack Restaurant and Marina is found on the ICW's easterly banks, just north of Cortez Bridge, near 27 28.256 North/082 41.419 West. Berths are provided by the friendly dockmaster for both resident and visiting craft at fixed wooden piers with

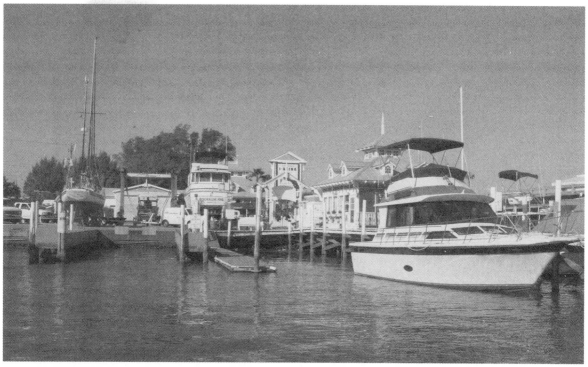

Bradenton Beach Marina

water and 30- to 50-amp power connections. These berths are not particularly well sheltered from foul weather. The marina's unmarked entrance channel carries at least 7 feet of water, with typical soundings in the 9 to 10 foot region. Dockside depths run a very respectable 8 to 10 feet on the outermost piers but fall off to only some 5 feet of water on the inner sections of the harbor. After tying up, cruisers going ashore will find good, air-conditioned showers and a Laundromat, located cheek by jowl with a small cruiser's lounge on the second floor of the building flanking the harbor's easterly shores. The adjacent Seafood Shack restaurant serves the freshest of Florida seafood. There is an excellent view of the Waterway from the upstairs dining room. Ask for a table by the large windows. Don't miss the Seafood au Gratin, a tempting combination of shrimp and fresh fish served in a tangy cheddar cheese sauce. Ah, I can taste it now!

**Seafood Shack Restaurant and Marina
(941) 794-1235**

**Approach depth—7-10 feet
Dockside depth—8-10 feet (outermost dock)
  5-6 feet (inner slips)
Accepts transients—yes
Transient dockage rate—below average
Fixed wooden piers—yes
Dockside power connections—30 and 50 amp
Dockside water connections—yes
Showers—yes
Laundromat—yes
Mechanical repairs—independent contractors
Restaurant—on site**

Anna Maria Sound

North of the Cortez Bridge, the Western Florida ICW begins its trek through Anna Maria Sound. This body of water can get as rough as a cob when winds are blowing from the north, off Tampa Bay and down the sound's full length. Most of Anna Maria's waters are quite shallow. Stick to the Waterway unless you plan to try one of the somewhat questionable sidewaters reviewed below.

Palma Sola Bay (Standard Mile 87.5)

The marked channel cutting east to Palma Sola Bay intersects the ICW near unlighted daybeacon #50. If you have followed this writer's account from Flamingo, you know that I'm not bashful about recommending gunk holes. However, Palma Sola may be one body of water that you might want to consider bypassing. Depths in the often-confusing channel run as little as 4½ feet. There are currently no facilities for cruisers available on the bay. Most of the charted side channels serve condos and private dockage areas. There is certainly no room for anchorage on any of these cuts.

Fearless skippers piloting boats that draw 4 feet or less can, if they are willing to undertake a long cruise, find one anchorage on upper Palma Sola Bay. Study chart 11425 and notice that the bay's northerly lobe is pinched off by a 10-foot fixed bridge. In spite of the soundings shown on chart 11425, depths of 5 feet or better run quite close to the westerly banks, south of the bridge (near 27 29.722 North/082 39.496 West). You can throw out the hook in 5 to 7 feet of water with good protection from northerly and westerly winds. This anchorage provides little shelter from strong southern breezes. The causeway lying to the north is made up of a white sand beach which the locals often use for fishing. Traffic noise and lights from the adjacent highway could disturb your esteemed repose.

Anna Maria Island

North of Cortez Bridge, the Western Florida ICW begins to border Anna Maria Island along its western flank. This body of land continues to pace the Waterway all the way north to TampaBay.

Anna Maria Island has one of the most delightful climates in Western Florida. The surrounding waters tend to mitigate both very hot or unusually cold weather. It is said that frost has appeared only once in the last ten years.

This writer has come across two accounts of how the island came by its name. The first, found in Sarah Bird Wright's Islands of the South and Southeastern United States, asserts that the name is a contraction of "Ana-Maria-Cay," named in honor of Mary, the mother of Christ, and Mary's mother, Ann. An article written by Paul Winder in the November 1988 edition of Southern Boating magazine contends that "in the early 1500s, Hernando de Soto named the island for the wife of Charles II of Spain. . . ." Readers may take their pick.

Anna Maria Island has a long history of tourism. At the turn of the century, Rurick Cobb built the isle's first resort, which was known as the Oar House. This venerable hostelry survived until 1980 when, tragically, it burned to the ground.

The residents of Anna Maria remain a close-knit bunch. The local citizens are bound together by the common purpose of preserving those qualities that drew visitors to their isle in the first place. In the past several years the town council has dealt successfully with nonresident parking on the beach and the dumping of toxic wastes by the Army Corps of Engineers.

The island has three communities. Anna Maria City is perched on the shores to the north, with Holmes Beach in the middle and Bradenton Beach to the south.

Amidst much modern construction, many old-style Floridian homes remain on Anna Maria Island. It seems altogether fitting and proper that these structures are still present. In this land where the locals are fighting tooth and nail to preserve the past from the ravages of the present, the old Floridian island dwellers would be proud.

Perico Harbour and Johnny Leverocks Restaurant (Standard Mile 89)

Northeast of unlighted daybeacon #52, the ICW flows under the Anna Maria Island Bridge. Immediately after passing through this span, a marked channel leads east and then northeast to a small marina and a restaurant. Entrance depths into Perico Harbour's dockage basin are a scant 4 feet at low tide. Obviously, this facility is confined to vessels drawing less than 4 feet. Gasoline and diesel fuel are available dockside and there is a shoreside ship's store plus extensive dry-stack storage. No other transient services are available.

Yet another branch of the fine Johnny Leverocks Restaurant chain (941-342-8865) is located just south of the dockage basin. Patrons of this seafood restaurant can dock in 4 feet of water at a floating pier while dining. Skippers of larger cruising craft will not want to attempt entry into this harbor.

Holmes Beach Facilities (Standard Mile 91)

Boats drawing less than 4 feet can (but probably should not) carefully follow a channel with 4 to 4½ depths west and southwest of flashing daybeacon #62. This cut leads to two small-craft marinas.

The pile-marked channel can be hard to follow, as it skirts first southwest and then west to a split near unlighted daybeacon #18. The south-side branch leads to Holmes Beach Marina (27 30.330 North/082 42.663 West, http://www.holmesbeachmarina.com, 941-778-2255). This medium-size firm is concerned mostly with dry storage of small powercraft. Dockside depths are a meager 4½ feet, and the marina's few wet slips are open to rough water. Gasoline (but no diesel fuel) and mechanical repairs to outboards, I/Os, and some inboard gasoline engines are offered.

The northerly branch of the channel leads careful cruisers to a sheltered canal that again splits on its interior reaches. Approach depths at the canal's entrance run as thin as 4½ feet at low water. The northerly arm is home to Captain's Marina (941-778-1977). This facility is yet another of those small powercraft-type marinas so prevalent in this region. One or two slips are sometimes available for small-craft transients, but this writer would certainly not recommend this dockage for any craft larger than 26 feet. Gasoline can be purchased, and mechanical repairs to outboards and I/Os are offered. There is a combination ship's and tackle store on the marina grounds.

Galati's Yacht Basin (Standard Mile 92, 27 31.599 North/082 43.279 West)

North of unlighted daybeacon #63, the ICW cuts to the north-northeast and follows a dredged cut through "the Bulkhead," which is the rather imaginative name for a large shoal blocking the northern mouth of Anna Maria Sound. Just short of the sound's terminus, cruisers have a last opportunity to visit a combination friendly marina, super-service facility, and great restaurant. Lying west of unlighted daybeacon #63, a marked channel makes its way in from Bimini Bay, home of Galati's Yacht Basin.

Big changes are underway and almost complete, at the time of this writing, at Galati's Yacht Basin. As one of the dockmasters put it to this writer in August 2003, "We are in the process of becoming a big boat marina." Indeed, we were most impressed with the wide array of modern, fixed wooden piers that were in place and almost ready to open during our last visit. Gone are the old, cramped covered slips and limited dockage.

As part of this expansion project, the approach channel and harbor have been duly dredged. Captains can now expect minimum 6-foot soundings at mean low water.

After cruising into the mouth of Bimini Bay, the expanded piers of Galati's will be spotted to the northwest. Look for a series of uncharted and unlighted daybeacons marking the channel into the docks.

The new incarnation of Galati's is happy to accept transients at their fixed wooden docks featuring freshwater hookups and new, ultra-modern 30- to 50-amp power connections. The superfriendly dockmaster will be glad to direct you to the fuel dock, where you can purchase gasoline or diesel fuel. Waste pump-out service is available as well. Clean, but slightly cramped, climate-controlled showers and a non-air-conditioned Laundromat are found just behind the basin. There is also a ship's store on site. Galati's Yacht Basin is highly recommended by this writer to his fellow cruisers.

Skippers in search of service work need

1. Galati's Yacht Basin

look no further than the adjacent Galati's Marine repair yard. Extensive mechanical repairs for both gasoline- and diesel-powered plants, plus haul-out, below-waterline services by way of a 55-ton travelift, are very much in the offing. Judging from the number of craft that we always observed hauled up on the dry, this yard must enjoy a sure and certain reputation with local skippers.

If you are lucky enough to arrive at Galati's at or even near mealtime, a lucky star is shining over your cruise. The on-site dining attraction at this marina is known (inappropriately enough) as Rotten Ralph's Restaurant (941-778-3953). Let's not mince words with this one: in spite of its somewhat less-than-appealing name, the seafood is fabulous—some of the best you will enjoy along this coastline. During fair weather, open-air, dockside dining is available with a wonderful view of the harbor and the nearby boat slips. Even during times of less-than-ideal climate, the dining room's plate-glass windows usually give a more than satisfactory view of the water. The adjacent bar is a local gathering spot for the cruising and fishing crowd and a great place to meet up with some fellow mariners. What more could you want from a marina restaurant? Don't miss this one!

Galati's Yacht Basin and Galati's Marine
  (941) 778-0755
  http://www.galatiyachts.com

Approach depth—6 feet MLW
Dockside depth—6 feet MLW
Accepts transients—yes
Transient dockage rate—above average
Fixed wooden piers—yes
Dockside power connections—30 and 50 amp
Dockside water connections—yes
Waste pump-out—yes
Showers—yes
Laundromat—yes
Gasoline—yes
Diesel fuel—yes
Mechanical repairs—yes (extensive)
Below-waterline repairs—yes (extensive)
Ship's store—yes
Restaurant—on site

Rotten Ralph's Restaurant

SARASOTA BAY TO ANNA MARIA SOUND NAVIGATION

Successful navigation of Sarasota Bay and Anna Maria Sound is sometimes complicated by the relative width of these two bodies of water. Winds over 10, and certainly 15, knots have more than enough fetch to raise a teeth-chattering chop. Also, tidal currents in and around Big Sarasota Pass, New Pass, and Longboat Pass can be formidable. On Sarasota Bay, some of the Waterway markers are spaced so widely that it's a good idea to run compass and/or GPS courses between the beacons. In short, this is not a stretch of the ICW to be taken lightly. Make good preparations beforehand and try to pick a sunny day with light airs, and you should eventually find your way to the mighty waters of Tampa Bay without any unhappy incidents.

On to Roberts Bay   North of the Stickney Point Bridge, the ICW runs through a dredged land cut for some 1.7 nautical miles before emptying into the relatively wider waters of Roberts Bay near unlighted daybeacon #75. A substantial portion of this cut is lined by private docks with vessels moored to the piers. No-wake regulations are now in effect from the Stickney Point Bridge to Roberts Bay.

Don't attempt to enter the cove indenting the northeasterly banks at flashing daybeacon #64. It may look inviting, but on-site research revealed depths of 4 feet or less.

Only very shallow-draft boats with specific local knowledge should attempt to enter the southwestern mouth of Phillippi Creek, near unlighted daybeacon #72. We

have always encountered 4-foot depths when trying to enter this stream.

North of unlighted daybeacon #75, the ICW passes out into Roberts Bay. Continue following the well-marked channel until coming abeam of unlighted daybeacon #78 to its westerly quarter. Two excellent side trips are available from this aid to navigation.

The Field Club   Fortunate cruisers visiting the Field Club, east of unlighted daybeacon #78, should turn into the well-marked channel just south of #78. For best depths, do not try to enter the channel from flashing daybeacon #79 as chart 11425 would tend to suggest.

Roberts Bay Anchorage   To enter the anchorage in and around the spoil island west of unlighted daybeacon #78, cut almost due west from #78 and point toward the center of the substantial island dead ahead. In good weather, you can drop the hook some 50 to 75 yards offshore.

For better protection, you can cut to the north and track your way around the spoil island's northerly tip, keeping some 25 to 50 yards offshore. Turn to the south and cruise behind the island, keeping about the same distance offshore. Drop anchor once the mid-width of the island comes abeam to the east. Vessels drawing 4 feet or less can actually circumnavigate the island.

Siesta Key Bridge Anchorages   The westside anchorage, south of the Siesta Key Bridge, is entered by abandoning the

Waterway some 50 yards south of the span and cutting into the broad entrance which you will spot to the west. Favor the sea-walled starboard banks as you enter the stream. Soon the cove forks. Don't attempt the left-hand (southerly) branch. It is shoal with 4-foot depths. The principal right-side (northerly) fork leads into a lagoonlike body of water with excellent depths. A canal comes off the northwestern corner of the lagoon, but there is no room for anchorage on this offshoot.

The easterly anchorage has a tricky entrance and should only be attempted by boats drawing less than 4 feet. The best water is found hard by the cove's southerly entrance point. Here you should spy two unadorned pilings. Pass between these piles, favoring the southern side heavily. Even with this procedure, expect some 4- to 4½-foot depths at low tide. After leaving the entrance behind, cruise back into the mid-width and follow the cove as it swings to the south and then back to the north in a classic C-shape. The best depths and protection are found on the wider upstream section of the cove.

On the ICW   North of flashing daybeacon #82, the ICW says hello to the Siesta Key bascule bridge. This bridge has a closed vertical clearance of 25 feet and sports a restricted opening schedule. The bridge opens on the hour and every 20 minutes thereafter from 11:00 A.M. to 6:00 P.M., year round, seven days a week.

Spoil Anchorage   Depart the ICW at unlighted daybeacon #1 and set course to

enter the cove to the northeast, favoring the southerly and easterly banks. As you enter the anchorage, you may spy a concrete piling with a diamond-shaped yellow sign to the north. Don't approach these waters. The sign warns of an artificial reef. After passing this obstacle to your port, you can begin a slow, lazy turn to the north and anchor along the cove's south-to-north centerline. Return to the Waterway by retracing your steps. A straight course back out to the ICW would land the hapless (clueless?) navigator right on the artificial reef.

On the ICW   The Waterway cuts a tiny bit farther to the west at flashing daybeacon #2. This is a narrow portion of the channel, and you must be sure to pick out the various aids to navigation before proceeding. Tidal currents pick up markedly, courtesy of nearby Big Sarasota Pass inlet. Watch your stern for excessive leeway. Eventually you will pass between flashing daybeacon #6, to its westerly side, and unlighted daybeacons #5 and #7 to their easterly quarters. North and northwest of #7, the channel broadens and Big Sarasota Pass lies to the southwest.

Big Sarasota Pass   Please recall our earlier discussion about Big Sarasota Pass, and allow us to once again mention that *all* aids to navigation south and west of charted unlighted daybeacon #9 have been removed. We now *strongly* suggest that all vessels confine their exploration of these waters to a point *north* of the southeasterly tip of Lido Key and flashing daybeacon #14! If you keep to this stricture, minimum 6-foot soundings can be expected at MLW.

To enter the interior reaches of Big Pass, continue cruising on the ICW for some 100 yards northwest of unlighted daybeacon #7. Then turn sharply to the southwest and point to come abeam of and pass flashing daybeacon #19 by at least 50 yards to its southeasterly quarter. Point to pass unlighted daybeacon #17 to the same side.

Eventually you will pass flashing daybeacon #16 by some 50 yards to its northwesterly side. Opposite #16, pass unlighted daybeacon #15A fairly close to its southeasterly quarter.

The charted channel swinging east around Fishery Point near flashing daybeacon #16 carries good 12- to 13-foot depths, but it is a narrow cut that borders on shoal water. There is certainly not enough room for a cruising boat to anchor. This small passage is best left to local small craft.

From #16, set course to come abeam of and pass unlighted daybeacon #15 fairly close to its southeasterly side. From #15, you can enter the Sarasota Yacht Club channel (see below) or visit the delightful anchorage along the southern shores of Lido Key, to the west.

If you decide to anchor off Lido Key, continue following the Big Sarasota Pass channel past #15 for some .1 nautical miles, as if you were putting out to sea (but *don't*). You can then cut directly in toward the western shores with excellent depths almost into the beach. Remember the strong tidal currents that regularly scour this anchorage. Be absolutely sure the hook is well set before you leave the helm.

As mentioned repeatedly above (but let's do it one more time for good measure), *stop* your cruising north of Lido Key's southeasterly tip and flashing daybeacon #14. Past this position, not only are you likely to run aground, but you could also lose your boat and your life as well.

Sarasota Yacht Club Channel   Navigation of this channel is complicated by two persistent problems. Note the long shoal correctly charted on 11425 striking out from the entrance's northeastern point. This hazard can quickly trap the unwary, particularly at high tide. Also, remember that the mud flats west and southwest of unlighted daybeacons #2 and #4 are covered at high tide. This stretch of water looks very different than what you might expect from the chart.

Just to make matters a little more interesting, the initial daybeacons on this cut are very hard to spot from the main body of Big Pass. Be sure to use your binoculars to help pick out #1, #2, and #4.

For best depths, cut north some 100 yards southwest of unlighted daybeacon #15 (on the Big Sarasota Pass Channel) and point to pass between the first two aids to navigation on the yacht club channel, unlighted daybeacons #1 and #2.

Once between #1 and #2, you need only pass all the subsequent red markers by some 25 yards to your starboard side for good depths to the yacht club docks. North of unlighted daybeacon #10, the channel swings a bit to the northeast. The deep water still extends in a broad stretch before you. Just be mindful of the charted shoal abutting the eastern banks. Pass unlighted daybeacon #11 to its easterly side and favor the western shores to avoid this hazard.

Extra care must be exercised should you choose to anchor in the cove east of unlighted daybeacon #10. This side cut is mostly unmarked and can only be described as difficult. Very shoal water of 2 feet or even less flanks the entrance channel to the north and, particularly, the south. To find the deeper water, continue on the main yacht club channel, north of #10. Watch for two "No Wake" signs. Cut to the east, and pass just *south* of these signs. Of course, the two signs in question may just have been removed by the time you arrive, which would render successful entry into this anchorage very difficult indeed. Once the second "No Wake" sign is (hopefully) in your wake, continue more or less straight into the cove, favoring the northerly banks.

Don't venture to the south until you are well into the cove's interior reaches. Only very small craft that can clear the 7-foot fixed bridge may make use of the cut-through to Bird Key Channel.

Otter/Lido Key Anchorage   Watch along the southwestern banks for unlighted daybeacon #7. Depart the main channel immediately south of #7 and point to enter the passage running south of Otter Key by favoring the undeveloped, mangrove-lined northerly banks. Soon the main channel will cut to the northwest, while the smaller, southwesterly-side arm will be spotted almost dead ahead.

Ignore two pilings that you may spy near the shoreline to the southwest, immediately southeast of the smaller (southwesterly) arm of water. These piles are founded in very shallow water.

After you swing northwest on the main cut, good water spreads out almost from shore to shore, but to be on the safe side hold to the waters at least somewhat near the mid-width. Don't attempt to enter the waters surrounding St. Armands Key to the northwest. In spite of soundings shown on chart 11425, shoals are immediately encountered.

Back on the ICW   Captains navigating along the Sarasota waterfront between flashing daybeacon #6 and the Ringling Bridge (plus the eastern banks of Sarasota Bay, north of the Ringling span) should switch to inset #2 of chart 11425. Its greater detail simplifies an understanding of the area.

From flashing daybeacon #6, cruisers northbound on the ICW should set course to come abeam of flashing daybeacon #8 to its westerly side. It's then a simple hop to unlighted daybeacon #8A. The deep channel to Marina Operations and its adjacent anchorage cuts east-northeast, to the north of #8A.

Marina Operations and Anchorage   To visit Marina Operations, Marina Jack's Restaurant, and/or the adjacent anchorage, continue on the Waterway until you are about halfway between #8A and flashing daybeacon #10. Watch to the east-northeast for unlighted daybeacons #2 and #3. Once these aids are abeam, simply alter course to the east-northeast and cruise between #2 and #3. The remainder of the passage into the marina is quite broad and deep.

If you decide to anchor, follow the marina entrance channel past Golden Gate Point. Watch to the southeast and you will undoubtedly observe a host of anchored vessels. Depart the marina cut some 100 yards southwest of the hook-shaped point which encloses the dockage basin. Cruise to the southeast and pick out any likely spot. Remember to leave plenty of room between your craft and any neighbors you might find already secure in the anchorage.

Golden Gate Anchorage   From flashing daybeacon #10, set course for the northeastern corner of the cove that lies west of Golden Gate Point. Be sure you are well past the charted cable area before dropping the hook. Note the correctly charted shoal abutting the northwestern banks on the cove's southwesterly reaches.

On the ICW   Northwest of flashing daybeacon #10, the Waterway exchanges greetings with one of the busiest bridges on the entire Western Florida ICW. The Ringling causeway span has a closed vertical clearance of 22 feet and a restrictive opening schedule. Currently, the Ringling Bridge opens only on the hour and half-hour, daily, from 7:00 A.M. to 6:00 P.M., year round. During the evening and nighttime hours the bridge opens on demand. Plan your cruise around these regulations to avoid long delays.

Well, you probably have already guessed this. A mammoth project is underway, as this account is being tapped out on the keyboard, to replace the present Ringling Bridge with a fixed, high-rise span. Construction is proceeding nicely on this impressive new bridge, and it may well be complete by early 2004.

Once through the Ringling span, set course to come abeam of flashing daybeacon #12 by some 50 yards to its westerly quarter. You have now crossed into the southern reaches of broad Sarasota Bay. Expect increased chop courtesy of the long wind fetch. From #12, several side trips are found on the bay's easterly shores.

The Quay   Skippers who choose to visit the waters adjacent to the Quay shopping center should depart the Waterway some .1 nautical miles southeast of flashing daybeacon #12. Point for the broad opening of the *L*-shaped cove on the northeastern corner of the causeway leading to the Ringling Bridge. In spite of soundings shown on 11425, you can expect minimum 5-foot depths between the Waterway and the cove's entrance.

Enter the cove on its centerline and follow it as the water swerves sharply to the north. After making the turn, the Quay will be obvious to starboard and the Boathouse Restaurant will be dead ahead.

Payne Terminal   If for some unexpected reason you should decide to cruise into Payne terminal, cut east-northeast just north of unlighted junction daybeacon #NP. Several unlighted daybeacons will lead you in. Be aware that unlighted daybeacon #23 is found well north of the stream's entrance, and there is shallow water east of this aid. Favor unlighted daybeacon #22 and cruise into the entrance on its mid-width.

Whitaker Bayou and the Yacht Center Vessels bound for Whitaker Bayou, home of the Yacht Center, should set a course from flashing daybeacon #13 for the stream's westerly mouth. Enter the creek on its mid-width and be ready for some low-tide depths of 4 feet.

New Pass Inlet Remember that depths on New Pass Inlet are subject to rapid shoaling. The seaward side of the channel is also frequently ringed by breakers, and it can be more than slightly intimidating. We strongly caution all navigators to check on current conditions at one of the nearby marinas or yacht clubs before attempting this difficult passage. Lacking the completion of some future dredging project or specific, up-to-date local knowledge, visiting cruisers might do better to make use of Longboat Pass to the north or even the Tampa Bay entrance channel.

North of flashing daybeacon #12, the ICW quickly rushes on to an intersection with the New Pass Inlet channel at unlighted junction daybeacon #NP. To run the inlet, cut sharply west-southwest at #NP and point to pass between flashing daybeacon #16 and unlighted daybeacon #17. You are now heading toward the open sea, so take all green markers to your starboard side and all red beacons to port. Be ready for sharp tidal currents. Watch your stern carefully for lateral leeway.

For reasons that fall well beyond this writer's understanding, the New Pass approach channel between #16 (and #17) and the bascule bridge crossing the inlet is now an official no-wake zone. Once again, go figure!

As you span the gap between unlighted daybeacon #15 and flashing daybeacon #13, watch to the south for anchored sail craft associated with the Sarasota Sailing Squadron.

While many local boats follow the charted belt of 7-foot waters east of the point occupied by the Sailing Squadron's headquarters (and the charted WSPB radio tower) to the south and then back to the west, this trip is not recommended for strangers. The entire passage is unmarked and borders on very shoal water.

West-southwest of flashing daybeacon #13, the inlet channel comes under the lee of Lido Key to the south. Between unlighted daybeacon #11 and the bascule bridge, MarineMax will be spotted on the southeastern banks, followed by a bait and tackle store with its own dock.

Just before reaching the bascule span, cruisers can cut back to the north and enter the Quick Point channel. This passage will be reviewed in detail below, but for now we need only note that entry into the cut from this quarter is complicated by the absence of any aids to navigation south of Quick Point. If you do attempt to enter this channel from New Pass, take it slow and glue your eyes to the sounder.

The New Pass bascule bridge, west-southwest of unlighted daybeacon #11, has a closed vertical clearance of only 23 feet and a highly restricted opening schedule. Seven days a week, from 7:00 A.M. to 6:00 P.M., the bridge opens on the hour and then every 20 minutes thereafter. In light of the strong tidal currents which regularly scour the inlet, this span can be a real cause for concern during its regulated waiting periods.

If you have to wait, stop well back from the bridge and mark time in the channel as best you can, making sure to leave plenty of room between yourself and any other vessels which happen to be waiting.

Please remember that we no longer recommend entry into the one-time Sands Point-Longboat Key anchorage lining New Pass's northwesterly shore, just southwest of the bascule bridge. The entrance to this cut has now shoaled to MLW soundings of only 2½ feet, even on its eastern and western flanks, where the good water used to be.

Passage west of the New Pass bridge gets far more problematic. West of flashing daybeacon #7, the passage cuts out into the Gulf, with a huge shoal flanking the inlet just to the north. During our last visit, this outer portion of the channel was poorly marked by small, hard-to-see floating aids to navigation. Take great care; this portion of the channel is treacherous and most definitely not for the faint of heart.

Quick Point Channel   Many captains will wisely choose to enter Quick Point Channel from its easy-to-follow northerly entrance rather than the passage from New Pass. To reach the northerly entrance, cruise northwest from the ICW's flashing daybeacon #13 for .9 nautical miles. Then, set a new compass course for unlighted daybeacon #18 on the southwestern banks. This aid marks the northerly entrance to Quick Point Channel. Pass #18 and all the other red daybeacons on this channel to your port side.

From #18 the channel runs southwest past unlighted daybeacon #16. At unlighted daybeacon #14, the channel swings sharply to the northeast. Stay well to the west and southwest of all the red markers and you can follow the cut as far as Quick Point with little difficulty. Spindrift Yacht Services will come up on the southwesterly banks at unlighted daybeacon #8.

On the ICW   It's a long run between the four daybeacons which mark the Waterway's passage along the southeast-to-northwest axis of Sarasota Bay. It would be a good idea to plot compass and/or GPS courses between these aids to navigation long before your visit to the bay. There is little in the way of shallow water to worry with for almost a mile to either side of the ICW's track. Nevertheless, if you're like this writer, it is always comforting to have some idea of where you are. Follow the courses/way points you have laid out carefully and tick off the markers on 11425 as they come up.

From flashing daybeacon #13, it is a long run of 2.3 nautical miles to the next northerly aid, flashing daybeacon #15. While it makes little difference, officially you're supposed to pass #15 to its northeasterly side. From #15, mariners may choose to cruise to the Ringling Estate on the northeastern shore.

Ringling Estate Anchorage   The Ringling Mansion is noted on chart 11425 north of Stephens Point, by the "Cupola" notation. Boats that can stand some 5-foot depths can cruise directly from flashing daybeacon #15 for the charted location. Skippers piloting craft that need a bit more water should approach the estate from the north, thereby bypassing the long, correctly charted shoal stretching out from Stephens Point. If you plan to anchor, be sure to drop the hook before approaching to less than .2 nautical miles of the shore. Closer in, depths rise to 4 feet or less.

On the ICW   It's a run of 1 nautical mile between flashing daybeacon #15 and unlighted daybeacon #16 on the ICW. West of #15, one of the finest facilities on Sarasota Bay guards the Gulf-side banks.

Longboat Key Moorings   A large collection of (mostly) unlighted and uncharted daybeacons outlines the entrance to Longboat Key Moorings' sheltered dockage basin, south of charted Bishops Point. Use your binoculars to pick out the various pairs of markers as you approach the westerly shoreline. Be mindful of the shallows stretching well out from Bishops Point to the north as you make your approach.

Cruise between the outermost set of lighted daybeacons, and continue straight ahead between the various markers into the harbor. Note that the outermost pair of aids to navigation, flashing daybeacons #1 and #2, are now lighted and charted.

After entering the harbor, look toward the basin's southern banks. The dockmaster's office is found in the complex of buildings that overlook this shoreline.

Bowlees Creek Channel   Northeast of unlighted daybeacon #16, mariners can cruise to a variety of sidewaters in the Whitfield Estates/Bayshore Gardens region.

The only facility catering to cruising craft is found on Bowlees Creek.

The Bowlees Creek entrance channel is outlined by small, privately maintained daybeacons. The channel's southwesterly entrance is denoted by a sign advertising Holiday Inn Marina. Cruise between the various markers until coming abeam of the small, charted island lining the channel's southeastern flank near the creek's mouth. Favor the starboard side of the channel as you pass the island's northeastern tip and enter the creek. Once past the stream's mouth, immediately cruise back to the mid-width.

Soon the creek splits. The southerly (starboard) branch leads directly to Holiday Inn Marina.

On the ICW   From unlighted daybeacon #16, it's a 1.3-nautical-mile run to flashing daybeacon #17. Come abeam of #17 to its northeasterly side. The Waterway takes a sharp turn west at #17. Follow the well-marked channel until it again swings to the northwest at flashing daybeacon #23.

After leaving flashing daybeacon #21 behind, northbound cruisers will pass into a stretch of the Waterway where shoal water begins to line a goodly portion of the ICW channel. Gone for the most part are the deep waters of Sarasota Bay. Stick to the Waterway and you should not have any difficulty.

Before entering the stretch reviewed above, captains and crew have a last opportunity for dockside dining on the wider reaches of Sarasota Bay.

Buttonwood Harbor Channel and Pattigeorge's Restaurant   Most mariners will want to cruise into the Buttonwood Harbor Channel strictly for dining at Pattigeorge's. The southerly branch of the channel leads only to a condo dock.

Leave the Waterway at unlighted daybeacon #19 and set a compass course for the red-and-white junction daybeacon #A. Pass this aid closely to its northwesterly side. Continue on the same course, pointing to pass between the first two aids on the Buttonwood Harbor Channel, unlighted daybeacons #1 and #2.

Remember your "red, right, returning" rule as the cut skirts to the northwest of Whale Key. At unlighted daybeacon #11, the channel splits. To visit the restaurant, cut to the west-northwest and follow the red markers to the restaurant docks. No-wake regulations are in force throughout these waters.

On the ICW   Northbound skippers on the Western Florida ICW will follow an almost arrow-straight track from flashing daybeacon #23, northwest through the shoaling reaches of upper Sarasota Bay. The charted markers southwest of unlighted daybeacon #25 lead to a series of private docks and are of little interest to visiting cruisers.

At unlighted daybeacon #33, a charted channel cuts sharply to the south and then swerves to the west. This cut used to serve Buccaneer Marina and Restaurant, but as the dining spot is now closed, and the marina in an uncertain state, we suggest bypassing this facility.

Should you be seeking small-craft-oriented Cannons Marina, run the well-marked channel that cuts to the south

immediately to the southeast of unlighted daybeacon #33. Enter the channel by passing between the first two unlighted daybeacons, #1 and #2. The cut remains straightforward until passing between the innermost set of unadorned pilings. At this point, depart the marked channel by cutting sharply to port. Follow the southwestern shoreline until you spot the first canal running toward the Gulf. Turn into this stream on its mid-width. Cannons Marina will eventually be encountered on the western terminus of the canal.

Longbeach Anchorage   Between unlighted can buoy #39 and unlighted daybeacon #40, a wide channel sweeps off to the west and provides wonderful anchorage. To enter this haven, depart the Waterway some 75 yards south of #40. Do not get too close to #39. There is some shoal water west of this aid.

Slowly curl back around to the west-northwest by keeping the undeveloped Jewfish Key shoreline to your starboard side. Soon you will spy a deep cove to the southwest which is lined by the two restaurants described earlier. If you decide to anchor here, favor the western shores. While good depths extend out from this shore in a broad band, notice the charted shallows to the south and southeast.

You may also anchor behind "Jewfish Key." Drop the hook at any likely spot well short of the channel's approach to the Longboat Pass Bridge.

The passage to Longboat Pass via this channel is not recommended. A shoal coming in from the northeast pins the cut almost directly against the bascule bridge crossing the inlet. Even by hugging the bridge, some 4-foot depths (or possibly less) can be encountered.

On the ICW   Slow down after passing between unlighted daybeacons #43 and #44. The markers to the north can be quite confusing. It's all too easy to scramble the aids to navigation denoting the channel to Longboat Pass with the Waterway beacons. Point to pass between flashing daybeacon #46 and unlighted daybeacon #45. If you do not plan to enter Longboat Pass, continue on course, pointing to pass flashing daybeacon #47 to its easterly side. Southbound captains should observe the same precautions. Use your binoculars to help differentiate the various aids to navigation.

Be prepared for strong tidal currents as you pass through the intersection between the ICW and the Longboat Pass channel. Single-screw trawlers and sail craft should be particularly alert for side-setting currents.

Longboat Pass   The swiftly moving channel leading to Longboat Pass cuts into the ICW's western flank between unlighted daybeacons #45 and #47. The inlet passage cuts back sharply to the southwest. Initially you should pass unlighted daybeacon #9 to its fairly immediate southeasterly side. You are now heading seaward, so pass all subsequent red markers to your port side and all green aids to your starboard as you continue toward the inlet. Be ready for a different configuration of aids to navigation than those shown on chart 11425 or discussed below. With the swift current, this is a changeable channel and markers are frequently shifted.

Visiting cruisers can pretty much ignore the side channel cutting back to the northwest between unlighted daybeacons #8 and #6 on the Longboat Pass channel. This uninteresting cut leads to a launching ramp and some private docks.

Nonetheless, for purely personal reasons I will never forget this little passage. While performing our original research on these waters, we observed a fisherman "catch a seagull." The angler in question threw out his bait, only to have it snatched up by an alert seagull. Unfortunately, the creature became hooked. The fisherman was able to reel in the bird and detach his hook, apparently without injury to the gull. That was one lucky bird to be able to fly on his way.

At unlighted daybeacon #4, the pass channel turns sharply to the west-southwest and hurries on toward the 17-foot (closed vertical clearance) bascule bridge crossing the inlet. Favor the eastern side of the inlet channel slightly as you approach #4. Some shoaling seems to have encroached on the cut's western quarter in this region.

Fortunately, the bascule bridge spanning Longboat Pass opens on demand during the daylight and evening hours (6:00 A.M. to 10:00 P.M.). During the night and early morning, the span only opens with three hours' notice. Even then, I wouldn't hold my breath.

West of the bascule bridge, follow all markers carefully out into the Gulf. A long shoal extends out from the inlet's northwestern point and flanks the channel for some distance out to sea.

On the ICW   North-northwest of flashing

daybeacon #47, it is sometimes hard to pick out the next northward aid to navigation, flashing daybeacon #48. Use your binoculars to identify #48 and set course to come abeam of and pass this aid to its westerly quarter.

North of #48, the ICW begins its approach to the Cortez bascule bridge. North of unlighted daybeacon #49, no-wake regulations are in effect on both sides of the Cortez span. Powercraft take note. Slow to idle speed or risk the gift of a ticket from the Florida Marine Patrol.

Bradenton Beach Marina and Bridge Tender Inn Directly north of unlighted daybeacon #49, the *L*-shaped channel leading to Bradenton Beach Marina cuts off to the west. As you cruise the initial stretch of this cut, you will come hard by the outer tip of the Bradenton Beach Historic Pier. This structure makes for a striking sight from the water.

Boats bound for the dining delights of the Bridge Tender Inn should leave the Bradenton Beach Marina channel once abeam of the historic pier, pass the pier's outer tip, and then cut to the southwest, passing the length of the historic dock to your starboard side. Watch for several white PVC pipes lining the channel. Some have been painted with green tops—obviously you should pass these close by your port side. Eventually, the Bridge Tender Inn pier will be spied dead ahead.

Conversely, the Bradenton Beach Marina channel cuts north past the large pier. Soon the marina docks will be obvious to port.

On the ICW The Cortez bascule bridge has a closed vertical clearance of 22 feet. It has a restricted opening schedule year round. From 7:00 A.M. to 6:00 P.M. daily, the span opens only on the hour and every 20 minutes thereafter. Oh well, one more delay!

Once through the Cortez Bridge, you will spot the Seafood Shack Marina and Restaurant on the eastern banks. Continue at idle speed until well past this facility.

Favor the eastern side of the channel slightly between the Cortez Bridge and unlighted daybeacon #50. Chart 11425 correctly indicates a wide band of shoal water abutting the western banks. The two small, charted channels opening into the western shores between the Cortez Bridge and #50 serve private docks and are best bypassed by cruising craft.

Just short of unlighted daybeacon #50, especially adventurous mariners may decide to explore Palma Sola Bay to the east.

Palma Sola Bay Don't forget that there are currently no marina facilities available to visiting cruisers on Palma Sola Bay and the only good bay anchorage requires a long cruise from the Waterway. The channel is also more than slightly confusing. But for those of you who simply have to anchor where no man (or woman, for that matter) has dropped the hook before, a navigational account of the bay is presented below.

Leave the Waterway some .2 nautical miles south of unlighted daybeacon #50 and set course to come abeam of unlighted daybeacon #1, southwest of Prices Key, by some 20 yards to its southerly side. Be mindful of the tongue of 3-foot shallows east of #50 and the shelf of 2-foot water flanking the Cortez peninsula. Unlighted daybeacons #3, #5, and #7 lead east to a very confusing intersection.

Near unlighted daybeacon #9, three channels converge and the markers are as mixed up a collection of aids to navigation as you will ever see. The southern channel leads to some private docks. Depths are more than slightly suspect. The north-side cut is far deeper, but it serves a series of private docks associated with a condo development on the bay's northern banks. Unless you happen to have a friend in this development, there are no services to be had.

All but local skippers will want to continue east on the main Palma Sola Bay channel. To achieve this objective, find unlighted daybeacons #9 and #10 amidst all the clutter, and continue cruising east by passing between these two aids.

The channel then becomes much easier to follow. East and north of unlighted daybeacon #24, a broad section of deeper water opens out before you. Ignore the charted channel on the easterly shores at Palma Sola Park. This small stream is crossed by a low-level fixed bridge and leads to a small-craft launching ramp.

Instead, set course for the westerly end of the 10-foot bridge that pinches off the bay's northerly reaches. As you approach the bridge, drop anchor.

On the ICW Aids to navigation are a bit few and far between from unlighted daybeacon #50 to the Anna Maria Island Bridge. The Waterway is not particularly narrow along this stretch, but it does border

on shoal water to the east and west. Observe all aids carefully and watch for leeway.

Be sure to come abeam of and pass unlighted daybeacon #52 to its westerly side. Only after passing #52 should you adjust course to the north-northeast and point for the Anna Maria Island Bridge's pass-through. This bascule bridge has a closed vertical clearance of 24 feet and restricted opening times. The span is regulated year round, seven days a week, 7:00 A.M. to 6:00 P.M. During these times the bridge opens only on the hour and every 20 minutes thereafter. At all other times of the day, the span opens on demand. Look, don't blame me—write your congressman.

North of the Anna Maria span, a C-shaped channel cuts to the west. This small cut serves a small-craft launching area. Besides the fact that it is hard to follow, there are no facilities nor anchorage opportunities for cruising-size vessels.

The shallow channel to Perico Harbour and Johnny Leverocks Restaurant makes off to the east, just north of the bridge. If you decide to make the attempt, proceed with the greatest caution.

From the Anna Maria bridge, the ICW cuts to the northeast. Be sure to pick up the markers. The hapless navigator cruising due north will land in 2 to 3 feet of water. Set course to pass flashing daybeacon #54 to its westerly side. Continue on course, pointing to pass between flashing daybeacon #56 and unlighted daybeacon #55.

The channel now begins a slow turn back to the north-northwest. Again, take care to pick out the markers. Very shoal water flanks both sides of the Waterway.

Near unlighted daybeacon #59, a charted range helps southbound vessels keep to the Waterway from flashing daybeacon #62 to #59. The channel is quite narrow in this section. Keep an eagle eye on the sounder. If depths start to rise, make corrections at once before grounding depths are reached. At flashing daybeacon #62, skippers whose craft can stand 4½-foot depths can break off to the southwest and visit Holmes Beach Marina and Captain's Marina.

Holmes Beach Channel and Facilities South of flashing daybeacon #62, a sign advertises Captain's Marina. The channel is outlined by small but fairly numerous green and red unlighted daybeacons as well as unadorned pilings. The channel winds quite a bit, and you must take great care to keep to the marked cut. Eventually the channel splits near unlighted daybeacon #18. To visit Holmes Beach Marina, cut south after passing #18. Follow the markers in to the dock.

The canal to Captain's Marina is entered by striking north immediately after passing #18 and setting a course to cruise between #20 and #21. Once between these aids, curve your course around to the west and enter the canal on its mid-width. As you enter the stream, watch for a single upright piling. Be sure to stay away from this faceless marker and pass it to your port side.

Soon the canal splits. Cruisers seeking Captain's Marina should follow the northerly fork.

On the ICW The charted spoil island east-northeast of unlighted daybeacon #59 will appear far closer to the channel than might be expected by northbound navigators. After making the turn at flashing daybeacon #58 (the forward, red, flashing range marker), it will be obvious that this is an optical illusion.

From flashing daybeacon #62, the Waterway skips along to unlighted daybeacons #62A and #63 and flashing daybeacon #64. Study chart 11425 for a moment. Notice the 4-foot shoal south of #64. These shallows are for real and are now marked by #62A. Be sure to pass #62A to its westerly quarter, and come abeam of #63 to its immediate easterly side. From #63, the ICW cuts to the north-northeast. Point to pass flashing daybeacon #64 to its fairly immediate westerly side.

Just before making your final run from Anna Maria Sound into Tampa Bay, you may decide to visit one last facility to the west.

Galati's Yacht Basin Cruisers may enter Bimini Bay to visit Galati's Yacht Basin by either of two different routes. The deeper approach is by way of Tampa Bay. From the bay's deeper waters, you must point to pass flashing daybeacon #1, west of the Bulkhead, to its westerly quarter. Then, set a course to pass between unlighted daybeacons #1 and #2, the northeasternmost aids to navigation on the Bimini Bay entrance channel.

Mariners cruising north on the ICW will find the passage described above to be a bit out of their way. All but especially deep draft vessels can cut sharply west-northwest at a point about halfway between unlighted daybeacon #63 and flashing daybeacon #64 and point to come abeam of flashing daybeacon

#1 by some 25 yards to its southerly side. Be mindful of the 2- and 4-foot depths found on the Bulkhead to the north during this run and, equally daunting, the correctly charted 4- to 5-foot waters west of #63. Once abeam of flashing daybeacon #1, turn again, this time to the south, and point to pass between unlighted daybeacons #1 and #2.

South of #1 and #2, a series of uncharted but nevertheless prolific markers leads cruisers into Bimini Bay. The newly dredged channel eventually turns to the northwest toward Galati's Yacht Basin. As you would expect, pass red markers to your starboard side and green aids to your port.

On to Tampa Bay Flashing daybeacon #64 marks the southerly genesis of a dredged channel running through the formidable shoal known as "the Bulkhead" that lies along the northern mouth of Anna Maria Sound. This stretch of the Waterway is subject to shoaling. Don't be surprised to find different markers than those shown on chart 11425.

For the moment, the channel seems to be holding good depths and it is well marked. North-northeast of flashing daybeacon #67 and unlighted daybeacon #68, the wide and deep waters of mighty Tampa Bay beckon.

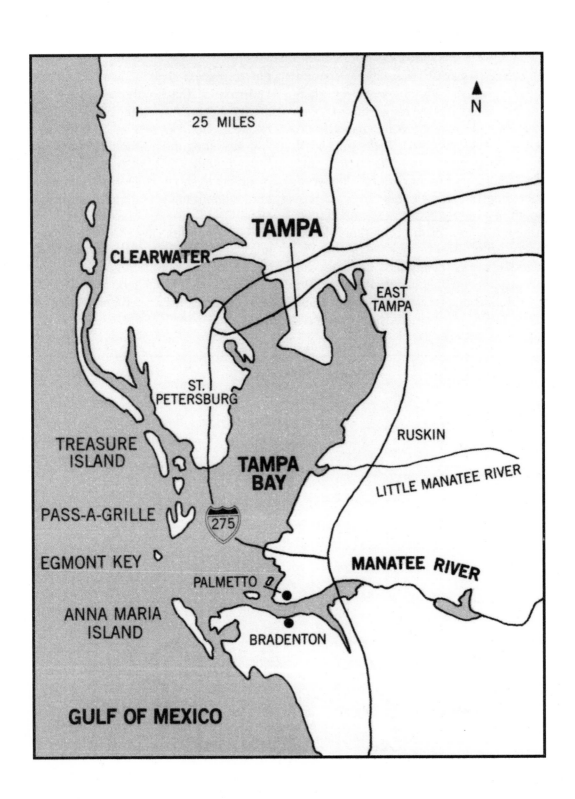

CHAPTER 4

Tampa Bay

Look at any map of Florida's western coastline and you will undoubtedly note that the most prominent geographic feature on the chart is a body of water which resembles a short, fat-bodied alligator with a curved tail and wide, gaping jaws. This imposing landmark is none other than Tampa Bay, described by some as the liquid heart of Western Florida. Since the times of earliest European colonization (and before that vis-à-vis the local native Americans), ships and boats of every size and description have set their course to this vast bay. Modern-day pleasure craft skippers are following in the footsteps of their nautical ancestors by the thousands. This writer's heart is with that happy horde. The beautifully natural shores set amidst bright, shining cities and isolated anchorages comprise a siren's call that mariners cannot and must not ignore.

Tampa Bay's yawning mouth thrusts west into the Gulf of Mexico. Several small barrier islands bisect the entrance, principal among them being Egmont Key. In fair weather, this magnificently undeveloped island beckons to be explored and enjoyed.

A host of channels darts between these various land masses and allows for ready access to and from the open Gulf. The extremely well marked large ship's channel cuts between Egmont and Mullet keys. Heavily used by oceangoing ships, this passage can be confidently relied upon by pleasure-boat skippers.

The Western Florida ICW cuts across the bay's mouth south to north. While some deep-draft pleasure craft drawing better than 5½ feet may want to follow the magenta line and turn east into the bay before tracking back to the

north, most cruisers will be able to follow the Sunshine Skyway Channel straight across the lower bay. This memorable route parallels the huge Sunshine Skyway Bridge. Believe you me, this colossal structure makes for a sight from the water which you will not soon forget.

The Manatee River (the "alligator's" curved tail) cuts into Tampa Bay's southeastern flank. This deep stream is easily navigated to a host of anchorages and marina facilities, most of which are associated with the thriving cities of Bradenton and Palmetto.

The two shorelines of lower Tampa Bay exhibit strikingly different characters and must be considered separately in any discussion of cruising on the bay. To the west, the magnificent city of St. Petersburg guards the shoreline, with its wealth of beautiful green parks, a successfully restored downtown section, and one of the largest municipal marinas that this writer has ever visited. The lower bay's eastern banks are only lightly developed, and are quite eye-pleasing from the water. Several small rivers and lesser streams lead to an adequate selection of marinas and more than a few anchorages.

Farther to the north, Tampa Bay is bisected by the so-called Interbay Peninsula. The large lobe of water striking to the northwest is known as Old Tampa Bay, while the smaller body of water to the east is named Hillsborough Bay. While much of Old Tampa Bay is off limits to larger sail craft, there are still a few marinas and repair yards, plus some well off-the-beaten-path anchorages for power cruisers to consider.

Hillsborough Bay is dominated by the city

of Tampa. This metropolitan area seems bent on moving into the twenty-first century with a real bang. Sadly, marina facilities catering to visiting pleasure craft in Tampa are now all but nonexistent. Fortunately, two first rate yacht clubs are ready to serve Tampa's cruising visitors who have the appropriate reciprocal agreements.

In our review of Tampa Bay, we will first explore the Manatee River, followed by a discussion of the bay's western mouth and the ICW passage across this body of water. This account will be followed by a detailing of lower Tampa Bay's western shoreline, then the eastern banks. Finally, we will explore Old Tampa and Hillsborough bays. There's a lot of water to cover, so bend on the jib and let's forge ahead.

Charts   Most captains will find the second and third charts listed below sufficient for navigational coverage of Tampa Bay. Those who want to see everything may choose to acquire all five.

11425—provides somewhat more detailed coverage of the Manatee River (over much of its track) than is available on 11414

11414—large-scale chart giving good coverage of Lower Tampa Bay, including the inlet channels and passages through the Sunshine Skyway; also details a portion of the upper Manatee River not covered on 11425; this chart is a must have for anyone cruising Tampa Bay, as is the one listed below

11413—covers upper Tampa Bay, Old Tampa Bay, and Hillsborough Bay, including the channels and approaches to Tampa

11412—a general, small-scale chart whose chief purpose for many cruisers may be to give a good overview of the coastal waters between the Manatee River and Tarpon Springs

11411—detailed ICW chart that follows the Waterway across the mouth of Tampa Bay into Boca Ciega Bay; it includes detailed coverage of the Sunshine Skyway Channel; oddly enough, if you follow the magenta line course of the ICW, which briefly darts east of the Sunshine Skyway, you will need chart 11414 in addition to 11411 in order to follow the Tampa Bay portion of the Waterway

Bridges
Sunshine Skyway Bridge, central span—crosses mouth of Tampa Bay, east of flashing buoy #1A—Fixed—175 feet
Sunshine Skyway Bridge, northern, ICW span—crosses mouth of Tampa Bay hard by ICW-Sunshine Skyway Channel intersection, east of unlighted daybeacon #13A—Fixed—65 feet
Snead Island Bridge—crosses small canal connecting Manatee River and Terra Ceia Bay—Fixed—13 feet

Bradenton/Highway 41 Business Bridge—crosses Manatee River hard by Bradenton waterfront, east of unlighted daybeacons #21A and #22A—Fixed—41 feet
Bradenton/Palmetto Railway Bridge—crosses Manatee River hard by Bradenton waterfront—Bascule—5 feet (closed)—usually open unless a train is due
Bradenton/Highway 41 Bypass Bridge—crosses Manatee River west of unlighted daybeacons #23 and #24—Fixed—40 feet
Interstate 75/Manatee River Bridges—cross

Manatee River northeast of unlighted daybeacon #31, near Ellenton—Fixed—40 feet

Alafia River/Highway 41 Bridge—crosses Alafia River east of turning basin and unlighted daybeacon #18—Fixed—28 feet

22nd Street Causeway Bridge—crosses passage between East Bay and McKay Bay near commercial port of Tampa—Fixed—40 feet

Platt Street Bridge—crosses Hillsborough River in downtown Tampa—Bascule—15 feet (closed)—opens only on the hour and half-hour 9:00 A.M. to 4:30 P.M. weekdays and 8:00 a.m. to 6:00 P.M. weekends and legal holidays

Leroy Selman/Highway 618 Bridge—crosses Hillsborough River in downtown Tampa—Fixed—40 feet

Brorein Bridge—crosses Hillsborough River in downtown Tampa—Bascule—15 feet (closed)—opens only on the hour and half-hour 9:00 A.M. to 4:30 P.M. weekdays and 8:00 A.M. to 6:00 P.M. weekends and legal holidays

John F. Kennedy Boulevard Bridge—crosses Hillsborough River in downtown Tampa—Bascule—11 feet (closed)—opens only on the hour and half-hour 9:00 A.M. to 4:30 P.M. weekdays and 8:00 A.M. to 6:00 P.M. weekends and legal holidays

Gandy Bridge—crosses southerly mouth of Old Tampa Bay, well north of unlighted can buoy #11K—Fixed—43 feet

W. Howard Franklin/Interstate 275 Bridge—crosses Old Tampa Bay north of Gandy Bridge—Fixed—44 feet

Courtney Campbell Parkway Bridge—crosses Old Tampa Bay north-northeast of flashing daybeacon #A—Fixed—40 feet

The Manatee River

Mariners making the 5-nautical-mile upstream cruise to Bradenton and Palmetto on the Manatee River will experience one of the most delightful waterborne treks in Western Florida. Much of the shoreline is undeveloped and begs to be explored by dinghy. Good overnight anchorages abound, though most must be chosen with a ready ear to the forecast wind speed and direction. Marina facilities are available along the river's entire course, but the best spots are found adjacent to the Bradenton and Palmetto waterfronts.

While there are certainly some shoals to watch for, most sailors can cruise a goodly portion of the waters between the river's westerly reaches and Bradenton. The entrance channel itself is narrow and usually calls for firing up the auxiliary.

Farther upstream, a marked channel continues east and northeast for another 3 nautical miles to the twin Interstate 75 bridges near Ellenton. A new, glittering power-craft-oriented marina is located along this stretch, but otherwise, this portion of the Manatee River is much too open for anchorage in all but the lightest of airs.

Legend of the "Singing River"

While gathering my original research for the Manatee River, this writer was already aware of the local lore that speaks of the Manatee as a "singing river." What took me by surprise were the many sober residents who informed me that after living by the river's banks for many years, "you get so used to hearing the singing that it doesn't bother you anymore." Even on a warm summer morning that statement left a bit of chill in the air.

The so-called singing has been described as an "intense, melodic humming." Several tall tales purport to explain the unearthly melody that wafts its way down the riverbanks from time to time. One story speaks of two competing Indian tribes that lived on opposite shores of the Manatee River. The son of one tribal chief fell in love with the daughter of the opposing band's leader. Forbidden to marry or even meet, the couple stole away one night and rendezvoused at modern-day DeSoto Point. When the lovers met face to face at last, they heard a ghostly singing on the water. Soon, the two tribes were united following a great battle. The estranged couple were then allowed to marry and their offspring became the tribe's future leaders.

Another tale tells of the ghost of a woman who was imprisoned by a pirate, and forever after would wail for her freedom. Others believe that the sounds come from the ghost of a dog who was mysteriously killed with his owner while walking along the river's banks.

Whatever the cause may be, natural or supernatural, don't be overly concerned should you hear the "humming" while anchored along the quiet river shores. The spirits, whoever they are, seem to be friendly.

Boca Del Rio Marina (27 31.306 North/082 39.025 West)

Navigators studying charts 11425 or 11414 will note the partially breakwater-enclosed harbor of Boca Del Rio Marina (941-792-9610), south of unlighted daybeacon #9. This is perhaps the funkiest little marina and repair yard operation left on this portion of the Western Florida

coastline. Don't try to find your way to Boca Del Rio by land. It is stuck smack in a residential neighborhood, just where you would least expect to find any sort of pleasure-craft facility.

Boca Del Rio features a U-shaped harbor, which is sheltered only on its western flank. Strong northerly or easterly blows funnel directly into the harbor and can make for a bumpy evening. Entrance depths run from 7 to 9 feet, while 6 to 7½ feet of water can be expected dockside. All wet-slip dockage at Boca Del Rio is now rented out on a month-to-month basis (plus service customers), with no provisions for overnight transients.

The repair yard here features a 35-ton travelift and full mechanical repairs for both gasoline and diesel power plants. More than a few local captains seem to take advantage of these services. While clearly not offering the resources of Snead Island Boat Works (see below), Boca Del Rio is one of those vanishing breed of mom and pop yards. Give them a look-see if your servicing problems are not too broad ranging.

DeSoto Point Anchorage (27 31.380 North/082 38.462 West)

While it's certainly not the simplest anchorage on Manatee River, local cruisers often choose to drop anchor in the pocket of 6-foot water just inside the shelter of DeSoto Point, south and east of flashing daybeacon #12. Great care must be taken to avoid the correctly charted shoals to the south, and a similar patch of 4-foot shallows guarding the point. Captains circumventing these hazards will find themselves in a cove protected from western and southerly blows. The very best spot to anchor is found on the waters west of the charted 4-foot shallows, but, of course, you must avoid all the surrounding thin water to get there safely. There is scant shelter for winds blowing from the east or north. The surrounding shores are almost entirely in their natural state and are generally quite attractive. The rear of the cove is now overlooked by a huge, white cross, a part of the national memorial (see below).

It is quite possible to dinghy in to shore and leave your tender pulled up on the beach while visiting the highly recommended DeSoto National Memorial. The park offers a 20-minute orientation film, which describes the landing of Hernando DeSoto (supposedly)

on the waters of Manatee River in 1539. There is also a museum and a nature walk for visitors to enjoy. Every spring DeSoto's landing is reenacted as part of a weeklong festival.

Snead Island Anchorage (27 31.826 North/082 37.974 West)

One of the finest anchorages on the Manatee River is easily found along the broad band of deep water northeast of unlighted daybeacon #11. Good minimum depths of 6 feet or more run to within 75 yards of the northern banks. The shoreline is entirely undeveloped and challenges the angler to try

1. Boca Del Rio Marina
2. Snead Island Boat Works
3. Bradenton Yacht Club
4. Cut's Edge Harbor Marina

out his rod and reel. The banks are well wooded, with many trees set out into the water. This setting reminded me of a coastal river along my native North Carolina shores.

In northerly winds, the protection is excellent, though the anchorage is wide open to blows across the river from the south. There is some shelter to the east and west courtesy of Emerson and McKay points. For this writer's money, mariners cruising on the Manatee's friendly waters should give this anchorage their most serious consideration.

Snead Island Boat Works (27 31.427 North/082 37.224 West)

One of the biggest surprises on the Manatee River comes up just to the east of McKay Point (north of flashing daybeacon #14) on the charted harbor indenting the northern banks. What would appear when first seen from the river to be only a large repair operation turns out to be a wet-slip facility as well, with a full-blown dockage basin. Snead Island Boat Works' (941-722-2400) deep-water harbor is actually far larger and more sheltered than a quick study of chart 11425 would lead you to believe. Covered slips are very much in evidence, though there is open dockage as well. Unfortunately, all available wet-slip space is now taken up by resident pleasure craft and service customers. Depths in the basin range from 7½ to 10 feet, while some 6 to 7 feet of water will be found at the fuel dock. Gasoline and diesel fuel are readily available at a separate fuel pier fronting directly onto the river's banks. Snead Island Boat Works (including the fuel pier) is closed Saturdays and Sundays.

Snead Island Boat Works, Manatee River

As you would expect, the firm's mechanical and haul-out repair capability is quite extensive, to say the least. Snead Island's marine railway is complemented by two travelifts (50 and 60 tons, respectively). If you can't get it fixed here, better find out how new boat sales have been doing lately. The yard also maintains a well-stocked ship's and parts store just behind the fuel dock. One of the truly fine marine firms on the Manatee River, Snead Island Boat Works is most certainly an integral cog in the region's excellent pleasure-craft-oriented facilities.

Bradenton Yacht Club (27 31.512 North/082 36.701 West)

Between flashing daybeacons #14 and #15, passing cruisers will observe the charted channel along the northern banks leading to Terra Ceia Bay. Bradenton Yacht Club guards the western banks of this small cut's southerly mouth and is readily recognized by the bright blue roof of its mammoth clubhouse. This large, obviously well-financed operation accepts members of other accredited yacht clubs with reciprocal agreements. Most of the club's fixed wooden piers (with all power and water connections) are found in a concrete breakwater-protected harbor immediately adjacent to the clubhouse. A few additional berths are found on a face dock fronting onto the canal. The club dockmaster is on duty daily from 8:30 A.M. to 4:00 P.M. Gasoline and diesel fuel can be purchased by club members and accredited guests when the dockmaster is on duty. Waste pump-out is also available.

Ashore, fortunate visitors will find full dining

Bradenton Yacht Club

and bar services from Tuesday through Sunday. The club is closed on Mondays. There is also a large swimming pool and two tennis courts, plus invigorating showers.

Bradenton Yacht Club (941) 748-7930
  (941) 722-5936
  http://www.bradenton-yacht-club.org

Approach depth—7½-9 feet
Dockside depth—7-9 feet
Accepts transients—members of clubs with
  reciprocal agreements
Fixed wooden piers—yes
Dockside power connections—up to 50 amp
Dockside water connections—yes
Showers—yes
Waste pump-out—yes
Gasoline—yes (members and accredited guests
  only)
Diesel fuel—yes (members and accredited
  guests only)
Restaurant—on site

McKay Point Anchorage (27 31.382 North/082 36.910 West)

Study chart 11425 or 11414 for a moment and notice the "Special Anchorage" north-northeast of flashing daybeacon #14. Pleasure-craft skippers are welcome to make use of this haven. Depths of 5 to 9 feet can be held to within 100 yards of shore along a (more or less) centerline between McKay Point to the west and the docks of Bradenton Yacht Club to the east. There is good shelter from northern, north-easterly, and northwesterly blows, but the anchorage is wide open to winds from the south, southeast, or southwest. The surrounding shores are interspaced with sparse and very attractive residential development.

Terra Ceia Bay

The small canal leading northeast from Bradenton Yacht Club to Terra Ceia Bay plays host to several other interesting pleasure-craft facilities. However, to reach these yards and marinas directly from the Manatee River, cruisers would need to pass under a 13-foot fixed bridge. On the other hand, it is quite possible to make a bridge-less approach from Terra Ceia Bay. Thus, we shall review these facilities as part of our look at Terra Ceia in the next section of this chapter.

Hooker Point Anchorage (27 30.944 North/082 36.107 West)

On many occasions, this writer has found anchorages on the water which are far better than they first appear on a nautical chart. The patch of deeper water east of Hooker Point (northeast of flashing daybeacon #15) is a study in the opposite case. During our several visits to these waters, we have consistently discovered that you can only cruise a short distance behind the actual land mass of the point before the shallower water to the north intrudes upon your course. The charted marsh south of the point was barely visible and gives no protection to speak about. Nevertheless, careful skippers can pilot their way into minimum 6-foot waters just east of the point with good protection from western and northern winds. This is definitely not the place to spend the night if breezes are blowing from the south unless you want to imitate a Mexican jumping bean. The surrounding shores are overlooked by light to moderate residential development. Be sure to read the navigational information presented later in this chapter before making your first attempt to enter this haven.

Wares Creek Anchorage (27 30.123 North/082 35.230 West)

Skippers who mind their navigational p's

and q's (or, better yet, have a GPS interfaced with a laptop computer containing the latest digitized charts) can take advantage of the patch of charted deep water north and west of Wares Creek, well southwest of unlighted daybeacon #16. In southerly winds, this is a good anchorage, and there is also some protection from easterly blows, courtesy of nearby Point Pleasant. Minimum depths of 6 feet can be maintained by staying in the unmarked cut. Two sets of dilapidated pilings actually help you to keep to the good water, but there are no formal aids to navigation. Be sure to read the Wares Creek navigational information presented later in this chapter before attempting your first entry.

The best spot to drop the hook is found northeast of a private dock which you will spot at the southern foot of the entrance channel, where chart 11425 indicates that the deep water swings to the southeast and heads for the creek's mouth. On-the-water research revealed that, in spite of what 11425 indicates, good depths deteriorate soon thereafter. There should be enough swinging room for boats as large as 36 feet, short of the shallower water. The southerly shoreline is overlooked by moderate residential development.

Bradenton and Palmetto

Bradenton is the dominant city on the Manatee River. It is only appropriate that a river as beautiful as the Manatee should have a community such as Bradenton, which seems to exude an atmosphere of class and graciousness. This writer found has always found Bradenton to be one of the most likable cities in Western Florida. To be sure, this is no village, but the atmosphere of a smaller town has somehow been preserved. Life clearly moves a bit slower in Bradenton than the frenzied pace of Tampa or Clearwater to the north. Cruising visitors are the delighted beneficiaries of this genteel atmosphere.

The city of Palmetto, on the other hand, guards the Manatee's northerly banks opposite Bradenton and offers one fascinating historical attraction and good provisioning. Cruisers berthing at Regatta Pointe Marina will want to make the acquaintance of this community.

Cruisers docking at either Twin Dolphin Marina or Regatta Pointe (or anchoring nearby) can easily walk to a potpourri of local sights and attractions. The Manatee County Chamber of Commerce (222 10th Street, 941-748-3411) is only a quick two-block walk from Twin Dolphin Marina. This is a great place to begin your visit in Bradenton. The chamber provides several excellent pamphlets and maps which will help to ensure that you get the most from your time in the city.

After leaving the chamber, your next stop should probably be the South Florida Museum and Parker Manatee Aquarium (201 10th Street W, 941-746-4131). Here you will find the South Florida Museum, which gives a thorough overview of southwestern Florida's natural history.

However, as wonderful as the naturalistic exhibits at the museum are, the star attraction is "Snooty," the oldest living manatee in captivity. He was born in captivity and transported from the Miami Seaquarium to Bradenton in 1949. He has been delighting crowds of children and adults alike for the last half-century.

This manatee has it made. He is fed a huge quantity of the finest lettuce, carrots, and apples every day, which probably contributes to his weight, which is currently 1,100 pounds.

If he thinks someone is watching, this ham disguised as a manatee will roll over on his back and lie just below the surface of the water. His keeper will then throw the food on his stomach, and he will sweep it into his mouth via his flippers.

In 1999, Snooty was joined by a "teenage" manatee (five years of age) named Mo. Mo weighs better than 900 pounds, and we have been told by their handler that the two manatees are now eating almost 200 pounds of food a day. Boy, that's some serious groceries.

Another Bradenton attraction worthy of your attention is the Manatee Village Historical Park (604 15th Street E, 941-741-4075). The park features a restored historical courthouse, church, general shore, and furnished "cracker-style" house. The park is open 9:00 A.M. to 5:00 P.M., Monday through Friday, and 2:00 P.M. to 5:00 P.M. on Sunday. Cruisers will need a taxi to get there.

The Gamble Plantation Mansion, located in nearby Ellenton (3708 Patton Avenue, 941-723-4536), is the only surviving antebellum mansion in Western Florida. Constructed between 1843 and 1850, it was built by Maj. Robert Gamble, a member of an Old Virginia plantation family and veteran of the Seminole Indian Wars. The house features Greek Revival architecture and walls of tabby and brick that are two feet thick. The front verandah is adorned with eighteen 25-foot columns. The house originally presided over a 3,500-acre estate where massive quantities of sugarcane were grown. Over 1,500 acres of this land were under cultivation in 1851, worked by 151 slaves.

During the last sad days of the War Between the States, Confederate secretary of state Judah P. Benjamin fled south on an odyssey that would eventually take him to England. Major Gamble hid the Confederate official for several weeks on his plantation until transportation to Cuba could be arranged.

Today, the Gamble mansion has been restored and outfitted with period furnishings. It is open to the public from 9:00 A.M. to 4:00 P.M. daily, except Tuesday and Wednesday. Again, you will need a taxi or rental car to reach the plantation. Don't miss this example of Floridian plantation life.

Bradenton features many other attractions and points of interest, but we must hurry on to take a quick look at this community's colorful history and then return to our account of the Manatee River. Check in at the Chamber of Commerce for more touring suggestions.

Numbers to know in Bradenton include

> Bruce's Taxi Service—(941) 755-6070
> Checker Cab of Bradenton—(941) 755-9339
> Yellow Cab—(941) 748-4800
> Avis Rental Cars—(941) 359-5240
> Hertz Rent A Car—(941) 355-8848
> Boat/US Marine Center—(941) 925-7361

Bradenton History   Sometime during 1521, Ponce de Leon explored the central section of Florida's western coastline. It is likely that he visited the Manatee River, but hostile Indian attacks soon forced his withdrawal.

The Manatee enjoyed almost 300 years of isolation until the arrival of Josiah Gates in 1842. He was followed by two brothers, Hector and Joseph Braden. These two successful professional men came south after the 1837 collapse of Union Bank in Tallahassee. They eventually settled much of the land around present-day Braden Creek.

Bradenton was largely spared the pains of battle during the Civil War, but it struggled through Reconstruction, as did the rest of the South. The first post office was founded in 1878 and named "Braidentown." The spelling was later changed to conform to the pioneer brothers' family name.

By the early 1900s, Bradenton's future had been assured by the arrival of the Seaboard Railroad. A bridge was built across the river to the community of Manatee, and Bradenton was incorporated in 1903.

Following World War II, tourists and people seeking a warmer climate have been arriving by droves. It seems likely that this bright picture will continue in the future.

Regatta Pointe Marina (27 30.624 North/082 34.589 West)

Northeast of flashing daybeacon #19, one of the finest marinas in Western Florida graces the Manatee River's northerly banks. A marked channel leads visiting cruisers and resident captains alike to fabulous Regatta Pointe Marina. Anyone visiting this facility is sure to agree that here is a first-class operation that simply exudes friendliness and competency.

The marina's dockage basin is almost completely enclosed by a concrete riprap breakwater that gives good protection from all but the strongest storms. Transient dockage is eagerly provided at fixed wooden piers with water hookups and power connections to 100 amps. The central pier is a fixed concrete structure.

Entrance depths fall between 6½ and 9 feet. While the approach cut is well marked, there can be some confusion for first-timers attempting to reach the easternmost piers. Dockside depths run from 6 to 8 feet.

Visiting cruisers now have access to two climate-controlled shower facilities. Eight good showers are found on the first floor of the large building occupying the southerly tip of the central pier (which, on and off, plays host to a restaurant on the second floor). A new, second shower building has recently been opened on the northwest side of the harbor, This is ever sooo much more convenient for cruisers typing up in this portion of the basin. There is also an air-conditioned Laundromat on site. A small paperback exchange library is found in the Laundromat.

Gasoline and diesel fuel are readily available at a fuel dock that is accessed through the central entrance channel. Mechanical repairs can be arranged through a plentiful supply of independent contractors. A small ship's and variety store is located in the dockmaster's office just behind the fuel pier. The marina dockmasters have done a commendable job in stocking this relatively small space with an impressive assortment of marine essentials.

One of the most impressive features at Regatta Pointe is the presence of waste pumpout connections at every slip. According to my experience, there are only a handful of marinas anywhere else in the world that offer this novel and most-useful service.

Regatta Pointe features a refreshing swimming pool and hot tub that are open to all waterborne visitors. The adjacent Tiki Hut bar serves basic sandwiches, a few salads, and cold beverages.

Regatta Pointe boasts 350 wet slips. Several years ago, the available dockage was vastly expanded. With all the additional berths, this already-impressive facility is now a real nautical showplace.

The large, two-story building that occupies the southerly tip of Regatta Pointe's central pier has played host to a dizzying array of short-lived restaurants over the years. It's been very difficult for this writer to keep up with all the openings and closings. During our last visit, in August 2003, the operation located here was in the process of closing. Another may have taken its place by the time your prow finds its way into this harbor, but then again, who knows?

Not to worry though, for many years now, Regatta Pointe has hosted what is, in our collective opinion, one of the best restaurants on the Western Florida coastline. Riverside Café (941-729-4402) is a medium-size restaurant located on the harbor's northeastern corner. Open for all three meals of the day, Tuesday through Saturday (Sunday and Monday, breakfast and lunch only till 3:00 P.M.), the cafe offers food that can only be described as

wonderful. This writer and his first-rate first mate are forever dreaming of the excellent grouper sandwiches and Bleu cheese burgers at Riverside. Trust me, don't miss this one!

Cruisers who are in need of galley restocking will find a convenience store within two blocks and a supermarket about one-half mile away. You may want to take a taxi to the grocery store. Ask one of the friendly dockmasters to call a cab for you.

If you happen to be in the market for a new boat, several brokerage firms are based in the office complex flanking Regatta Pointe to the north. Be sure to stop by Massey Yacht Sales (941-723-1610) and say hello to Ed Massey, one of the largest yacht dealers in Western Florida. Tell him we sent you. My good friend

Regatta Pointe Marina

Andy Lightbourne, to whom my Cruising Guide to the Northern Gulf Coast is dedicated, purchased his proud Pearson 35 here.

Regatta Pointe Marina (941) 729-6021
  http://www.regattapointemarina.com

Approach depth—6½-9 feet
Dockside depth—6-8 feet
Accepts transients—yes
Transient dockage rate—average
Fixed wooden and concrete piers—yes
Floating docks—a few in the outer area
Dockside power connections—up to 100 amp
Dockside water connections—yes
Waste pump-out—yes (at every slip)

Showers—yes
Laundromat—yes
Gasoline—yes
Diesel fuel—yes
Mechanical repairs—independent local
  contractors
Ship's and variety store—yes (small)
Restaurant—on site

J. A. Lamb House

Just a stone's throw west of Regatta Pointe Marina, the venerable J. A. Lamb House (circa 1899) looks out proudly over the Manatee River's northern banks. Constructed for Julius Lamb, the son of Palmetto's founder, S. S.

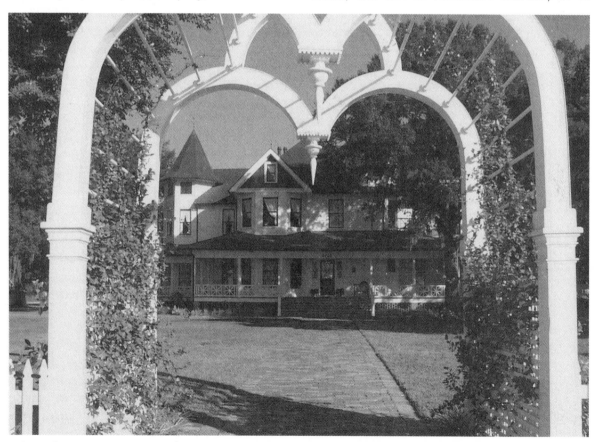

J. A. Lamb House, Manatee River

Lamb, the house was extensively renovated and restored in 1996. It now presents a peaceful, snow-white, but striking facade to Riverside Drive. While privately owned and not open to the public, the house is nevertheless well worth the two-block walk from your slip at Regatta Pointe. Take the camera along.

The J. A. Lamb House consists of three floors with heart pine as the major construction timber. The most notable features are the octagonal turret towers and handsome columned porches. Leaded, beveled-glass windows are placed throughout the residence. The interior is arranged on a classic central-hall plan with 20 major rooms and four fireplaces. The woodwork is highly detailed with deep stepped baseboards and casings. Tidewater red cypress was utilized for the solid doors and heart pine for the flooring. How's that for impressive construction?

Twin Dolphin Marina (27 29.972 North/082 34.329 West)

One of the most improved marinas on the entire Western Florida coastline overlooks the Bradenton waterfront along the Manatee River's southerly banks, south of unlighted daybeacon #22A. Twin Dolphin Marina has always been a good place to moor your craft, but the rub was always the unprotected nature of the facility's twin dockage basins. All that has now changed in a big way with the addition of a major new breakwater that protects the two harbors about as well as could be imagined. What a great improvement!

Twin Dolphin Marina is absolutely first rate in all other respects as well. It boasts both eastern and western dockage basins with 8 to 14 feet of water. The east-side basin features fixed concrete piers, with concrete-decked floating piers in the newer, western harbor. All slips feature full 30- and 50-amp power connections and freshwater hookups. As you've probably guessed by now, transients are eagerly accepted.

Still not enough for you? Well, check on the marina's heated swimming pool, open to all visiting cruisers. It is perched above the eastern dockage basin, with a commanding view of the river. There is also a twin gas grill adjacent to the pool, free for the use of all mariners, and a Jacuzzi.

Gasoline and diesel fuel can be purchased dockside. Some mechanical repairs can be arranged through local, independent technicians. Waste pump-out service is offered at each slip. How's that for topnotch?

The dockmaster's building is located immediately behind the swimming pool, itself just to the rear of the east-side dockage basin. Housed here is a good ship's and variety store, plus very good, air-conditioned showers and a full Laundromat. During our last visit, we were impressed to observe paperback exchange libraries in the Laundromat and outside the shower facilities.

When it comes time to slake a healthy appetite, your choices are many. The on-site Twin Dolphin Marina Grill (941-748-8087) is worth considering, but it is a bit pricey. The restored downtown Bradenton business district on 12th Street is within walking distance, or you might choose to get there by way of Twin Dolphin's convenient bike rentals. On 12th Street you will discover Fisherman Joe's Restaurant (440 12th Street W, 941-746-3077), open for lunch and dinner, as well as Robin's Restaurant (428 12th Street W, 941-747-8899), where you can get a good breakfast or lunch. Of course, you could always take a quick taxi ride over the bridge and visit the Riverside Cafe at Regatta Pointe (see above). That would be a good choice indeed!

Twin Dolphin Marina is located hard by the Bradenton library. The South Florida Museum (reviewed above) is only a short step from the marina docks. Twin Dolphin has also just added wireless, high-speed Internet service. This service is available in both harbors and is a real advantage for cruisers who are equipped to take advantage of this cutting-edge technology. The hits just keep on coming!

Wow, are you as tired out from reading about all Twin Dolphin has to offer as I am from typing? If so, put a red circle around the Bradenton waterfront and be sure to check out Twin Dolphin Marina the very next time your waterborne travels take you to the Manatee River.

With the cross-river presence of Regatta Pointe and Twin Dolphin, Bradenton and the Manatee River can now claim two world-class marina facilities, second to none. See you there!

Twin Dolphin Marina (941) 747-8300
   http://www.twindolphinmarina.com

Approach depth—8-14 feet
Dockside depth—8-12 feet
Accepts transients—yes
Transient dockage rate—below average
Fixed concrete fixed piers—yes (east basin)
Floating concrete floating piers—yes (west basin)
Dockside power connections—30 and 50 amp
Dockside water connections—yes
Waste pump-out—yes
Showers—yes
Laundromat—yes
Gasoline—yes
Diesel fuel—yes
Mechanical repairs—independent local contractors
Ship's and variety store—yes
Restaurant—one on site and several nearby

Bradenton-Palmetto Anchorages (Various Lats/Lons—see below)

With no major storms in the forecast, there are two anchorages just short of the Bradenton-Palmetto (Highway 41 Business) bridge that cruisers might consider. If winds are blowing from the north, northeast, or northwest, captains whose craft draw less than 5 feet and are no more than 38 feet in length might drop the hook northeast of unlighted daybeacon #20, in the shelter of the east-side point jutting out to the bridge (near 27 30.549 North/082 34.416 West). This haven, featuring 5-foot MLW depths, is found between the Regatta Pointe dockage basin and the point. Care must be taken to avoid the charted but unmarked 2- to 4-foot patch of shallows south and a bit east of Regatta Pointe Marina when entering this anchorage. Skippers visiting this refuge for the first time may be surprised to discover an unlighted daybeacon #1, seemingly in the middle of the anchorage. This aid marks a small channel leading to a local launching area and Regatta Pointe's northeastern slips. Anchor well south of #1 for best protection and depths. Closer to shore, the correctly charted 3-foot shallows wait to trap deeper draft vessels. The bridge automobile traffic can be a bit of an annoyance during the evening and early morning. The eastern point of land comprises a small, but highly restful local park. Visiting cruisers can probably find a place to moor temporarily at the adjacent launching ramp. Bathrooms are found in the park, and a walk of several blocks north into Palmetto will lead you to grocery stores and several restaurants. You might also consider the short hike to nearby Regatta Pointe for dining at one of their fine restaurants.

1. Regatta Point Marina
2. Twin Dolphin Marina

MANATE

Pt Ogden

Ruins TR

Q G 15ft 3M "19"

Piles rep

4   6   2   6"   3   3   2
10   G
                                          Pil   5
11   10   6   4
R "16"   3   G "R "2"   "1"
        10   12"1"   4   SO Cable
R "18"   8   7   Area
Obstn   7   8   (see note)   6   4
Fish Haven   10   6   5
(auth min 9 ft)   8   R   G
        9   "20"   G "21"   6   6
Pile   6   "21A"   1
2   Piles   2   3   2 Tky.   R "22"   "2"   6   5
        8   5   5   R "22A"
3   3   3   7
        8   4   4   R   7   8
3   Pu   5   "A"   7
                                        7   5   12
3   3   R TR   2
                4   Pt Pleasant   F R LTS
BRADENTON   WTRL F P
                Wares Cr   1490 kHz
        4   4
                4
        TOWER   GRE

BASCULE HOR CL 75 VERT CL 5

Be warned that space in this anchorage can be a bit cramped courtesy of Regatta Pointe's dockage complex to the west. There's still room for a few boats but not nearly so much as once there was. Many veteran cruisers are now anchoring farther to the south (out into the main body of the river) for increased swinging room. Of course, there is less shelter, but you also won't have to worry about bumping into your neighbor during the night. Be sure to show an anchor light!

A slightly deeper but more open anchorage is found on the opposite shore of Manatee River, south of unlighted daybeacon #22 (near 27 30.056 North/082 34.476 West). Visiting cruisers can anchor off the prominent point of land, occupied by Twin Dolphin Marina Grill restaurant, just west of Twin Dolphin Marina. Depths run to some 6 feet and protection is fair for southern and southwesterly breezes, but the anchorage is open on all other sides. This is most definitely not a spot for foul weather. The adjacent shoreline is surprisingly pleasant, flanked by a developing riverfront park. Dinghy landing is not allowed at Twin Dolphin Marina, and getting ashore from this anchorage can be more than slightly challenging.

Riviera Dunes Marina Resort (27 30.696 North/082 33.570 West)

The Manatee River's newest pleasure-craft facility occupies a mostly uncharted harbor along the stream's northern banks, just east of the easternmost of three bridges crossing the river at Bradenton and Palmetto (near charted Craig Point). Because vessels must pass under both the 41-foot Highway 41 Business and the 40-foot Highway 41 Bypass bridges to reach Riviera Dunes, this facility is pretty much relegated to powercraft.

However, depths will never be a problem here. The dockage basin was once a rock quarry, and low-water depths run 15 feet or better. The marked, newly dredged entrance channel, making in from the southeastern side of the basin, carries 8 feet of water. Anyone got a power vessel drawing more than that?

Riviera Dunes is still very much a work in progress at the time of this writing. The marina is complete, as is one building overlooking the harbor's westerly flank. Here you will find the dockmaster's office, the on-site climate-controlled showers, plus Laundromat and sales office. Eventually, if all goes well, a whole complex of buildings will rise on the extensive property surrounding the dockage basin. Only time will tell for sure what form all this projected construction will take.

For the moment, mariners can count on finding transient dockage at fixed wooden piers with 50-amp power and freshwater connections. Gasoline and diesel fuel can be purchased, and waste pump-out service is available.

Come mealtime, most cruisers not content to stay in their galley will want to take a taxi to any of Bradenton's or Palmetto's dining attractions described above. The same holds true for provisions.

We will try to keep our readers apprised of future developments at Rivera Dunes by way of our on-line newsletter, the *Salty Southeast*. Remember, all you need do to subscribe to this free service is to send an e-mail to opcom@cruisingguide.com, containing the word "subscribe."

Riviera Dunes Marina Resort 941-723-9595
  http://www.rdmarina.com
Approach depth—8 feet MLW
Dockside Depth—15+ feet MLW
Accepts transients—yes

Transient dockage rate—average
Fixed wooden piers—yes
Dockside power connections—50 amp
Dockside water connections—yes
Showers—yes
Laundromat—yes
Waste pump-out—yes
Gasoline—yes
Diesel fuel—yes

The Upper Manatee River

The upper reaches of the Manatee River, east of the Bradenton-Palmetto (Highway 41 Business) bridge, make for an interesting and aesthetically pleasing cruise, but there are no good anchorages. Minimum depths of 6½ feet, with most soundings showing better water, can be held on the river's marked channel to a point just short of the I-75 bridges.

The various coves are uniformly shallow and your only anchoring option is to drop the hook almost in mid-river. While this might be fine for light airs, you wouldn't catch this writer swinging out there in any breeze of 10 knots or better.

Much of the shoreline on the Manatee's upper reaches is less developed than the banks to the west. Private homes peep out here and there, while heavier residential development is in evidence near the charted site of Ellenton on the northern banks.

Eventually, mariners will encounter the twin, high-rise I-75 bridges. East of these spans, depths quickly rise and cruising craft are advised to stay clear.

The Braden River

The wide but shallow mouth of the Braden River makes into the Manatee's southern flank south-southeast of unlighted daybeacon #26. While chart 11414 indicates a shallow channel, on-site research failed to discover this cut. All but small, shallow-draft outboard-powered boats are advised to bypass this stream.

MANATEE RIVER NAVIGATION

With the exception of its entrance, the Manatee River is a joy to navigate. Good markings are amply supplemented with usually deep water. The few exceptions to this forgiving nature are noted below.

As mentioned, the Manatee's entrance is one of these exceptions. While well marked, it is a narrow cut where navigators must watch carefully for leeway and pay close attention to business. Sail craft should proceed under auxiliary power, and all captains should affix an eye to the sounder.

The various sidewaters and anchorages noted below are also of a generally forgiving

nature. While shallows do abut a goodly portion of the river's shoreline, this shoal band is rather narrow and is usually easily avoided.

Take your time, keep charts 11414 and 11425 at hand, and review the information below. These simple precautions will allow you to enjoy this magnificent river as it should be appreciated, cruising gaily up and down its track rather than heeled over on a sand bar.

Entrance into the Manatee River   As discussed above, the Manatee River's westerly mouth is the most complicated portion of the stream's passage. Study chart 11425 carefully and coordinate it with the information below before making your attempt. This cartographical aid gives much better resolution than its sister, 11414, does.

Northbound cruisers on the Western Florida ICW can set their course from unlighted daybeacon #68, immediately north of "the Bulkhead," to flashing daybeacon #2, the northwesternmost aid on the Manatee River channel. Some 1.3 nautical miles of deep and open water separate #68 and #2. Cruisers voyaging south on the Waterway can set course from flashing daybeacon #70, the first ICW aid south of Mullet Key Channel, for #2. This is a longer run of some 1.9 nautical miles. Intrepid skippers entering Tampa Bay from the open Gulf should probably also use #70 as a point of reference. Be sure to read the navigational information on the bay's various inlets and the ICW's passage across its mouth in the next section of this chapter for more details.

Come abeam of flashing daybeacon #2 to its fairly immediate northeasterly side and look southeast to catch sight of a pair of range markers. Line up on this range and begin cruising toward the forward marker. Some 30 yards before reaching this beacon, alter course slightly to pass it to your starboard side. As you pass, you may well be surprised to see that this forward range marker is actually flashing daybeacon #4. In a very unusual arrangement, there is a sign pointing northwest on the aid that designates it as "#A," while the "#4" sign points to the southeast.

At any rate, abandon the range before reaching #4 (or #A) and set course to come abeam of flashing daybeacon #6 to its fairly immediate northerly side. Be sure to pick out #6 with your binoculars. Do not mistake the tall, rear range markers as #6. Flashing daybeacon #6 is only 17 feet tall and it will be found a bit farther to the east. Be on guard against the correctly charted shallows north of your course. At low water this hazard is quite visible, but during rough conditions or higher water levels, it can take you by surprise.

At #6 the Manatee River entrance channel takes a jog to the east. Set a careful compass course to come between flashing daybeacon #7 and unlighted daybeacon #8. Again, you must guard against the large shoal to the north. The run between #6 and #8 is the narrowest in the entrance channel. Take your time, watch for leeway, and have the chart ready to quickly resolve questions which might arise.

Once between #7 and #8, bend your course to the southeast and point to pass unlighted daybeacon #9 to its immediate southwesterly side. There is shallow water of 4 feet or less east-northeast of #9, but otherwise good depths open out before you almost all the way to Bradenton. There is still one other trouble spot to worry with, though.

Skippers choosing to visit Boca Del Rio Marina will want to depart the river entrance channel at #9 and set a careful compass/GPS course for the harbor's entrance to the south-southwest. If you pilot a fixed-keel, deep-draft sail craft, watch out for the finger of 5-foot water to the west.

Back on the main river channel, from #9, point to pass unlighted daybeacon #10 to starboard and unlighted daybeacon #11 to port, soon followed by flashing daybeacon #12, hard by DeSoto Point. Take #12 by some 15 to 20 yards to your starboard side.

Unlighted daybeacon #10 marks a patch of 3-foot shoals building northwest from DeSoto Point. Favor the northeastern side of the channel when passing #10. From flashing daybeacon #12, pleasure boats of most drafts will find excellent water all the way east to the Bradenton-Palmetto (Highway 41 Business) bridge. The few hazards along the way are noted below.

DeSoto Point Anchorage   The anchorage east of DeSoto Point is not recommended for boats drawing more than 4½ feet due to the surrounding shallows. While 6-foot minimum depths can be maintained, it's a breeze to wander into 4-foot soundings.

To enter the anchorage, continue past flashing daybeacon #12 for another 100 yards as if you were heading for Bradenton. Then turn sharply south and come behind DeSoto Point, leaving the land 100 yards or so to your northwestern side. The trick is to avoid the 2-foot shoals surrounding the point and stay west of the charted 4-foot shoal. This can be a whole lot easier said than done. Eventually, though, if you successfully avoid both hazards, you can drop the hook in the bubble of deep water west of the 4-foot patch of shallows.

To say the least, it would be hazardous for strangers to attempt to find the narrow, unmarked channel between the point shoals and the 4-foot shallows.

A far easier passage, particularly for deep-draft vessels, is to continue cruising on the main river channel until you are east of the charted 4-foot shoal. You can then cut in toward the southerly banks and drop the hook well short of (north of) the correctly charted band of shallows abutting the shoreline. Then, you can explore the waters to the west behind DeSoto Point by dinghy.

Snead Island Anchorage   From either unlighted daybeacon #11 or flashing daybeacon #12, you can set course for the deeper water running to within 75 yards of the northeastern banks. Simply stay at least 75 yards from shore and avoid the charted shallows well to the east and west for minimum depths of 6 feet. Boats needing 7 or 8 feet of water need only drop the hook a bit farther out into the river.

East on the Manatee River   The charted sidewater east of Bishop Point holds 5-foot depths, but it is too narrow for anchorage by cruising-size boats. While the stream plays host to any number of local craft docked at private piers, visiting cruisers would be well advised to avoid this stream.

Be sure to pass well to the north of flashing daybeacon #14. This aid marks a large shoal building out into the river's flank from McNeil Point.

As you pass #14, Snead Island Boat Works will be visible to the north. Remember that you can only see the fuel dock and a small portion of the available dockage from the river.

Both Warner West Bayou and Warner East Bayou, southeast of #14, are crossed by low-level fixed bridges. This, coupled with some relatively shallow soundings, means that these streams are off limits for larger boats.

McKay Point Anchorage   To enter the anchorage north-northeast of flashing day-beacon #14, cut in toward the northerly banks, pointing for the waters west of the Bradenton Yacht Club dockage basin. Drop the hook before approaching to within less than 100 yards of the shoreline. You can depend on 6-foot depths in this area, drop-ping off to 4½ to 5 feet moving east closer to the yacht club.

Passage to Bradenton Yacht Club   Cruisers making for the Bradenton Yacht Club should set course from the main channel as if they intend to enter the small canal leading from the Manatee River to Terra Ceia Bay. Set course from a position abeam of flashing daybeacon #14 to come abeam of unlighted #2 to its immediate westerly side. From this point, you need only cruise dead ahead into the mid-width of the canal's southerly entrance. Be ready for the swift tidal currents which regularly plague this cut.

As you enter the canal, Bradenton Yacht Club's entrance will be obvious to port.

Additional navigational information on Terra Ceia Bay will be presented later in this chapter as a part of our review of lower Tampa Bay's eastern shores.

On the Manatee River   Flashing daybea-con #15 marks another long, building shoal that runs southwest from Hooker Point. Be sure to pass well south of #15 to avoid these shallows. East of #15, captains may decide to take a stab at the anchorage upstream from Hooker Point.

Hooker Point Anchorage   Remember that you cannot actually get in very far behind the protection of Hooker Point (to the west) before depths begin to deteriorate. Set your course for the first of the several private homes you will spot fronting onto the west-ern shores north of the point. As the main body of Hooker Point comes abeam to the west, drop the hooker. Farther to the north, 4-foot depths are soon encountered.

Wares Creek Anchorage   Entry into the charted deep water leading to the mouth of otherwise shallow Wares Creek is facili-tated by the presence of two dilapidated groups of pilings. There are unmarked shoals with 1- and 2-foot depths on both sides of the cut, so this haven is pretty well relegated to the adventurous among us.

The first set of pilings is well charted and serves to mark the shallows on the entrance's eastern flank. Pass the piles by some 15 yards to their westerly sides, and head straight in toward the southern banks.

The second group of pilings is charted as a single "pile" on 11425, but there are actually quite a few just visible above the water's sur-face. Stay about the same distance to the east of these derelicts and point for a private dock you will see on the shore.

You can drop the hook some 30 yards before reaching the private dock, or more devil-may-care captains can feel their way carefully to the southeast for a short dis-tance. Be warned that the good depths do not extend as far southeast as chart 11425 would lead you to believe. Those who push their luck a bit too far will wind up in 4-foot waters.

On to Bradenton and Palmetto   A series of shoals, most likely spoil islands, pepper the mid-width of the Manatee River just west of the Bradenton and Palmetto waterfront. To avoid these traps, simply follow the prolific markers.

Swing a bit to the north and point to pass unlighted daybeacons #16 and #18 to their fairly immediate northerly sides and come abeam of flashing daybeacon #19 to its southerly quarter. Your course then shifts sharply to the south-southeast. Point to come abeam of and pass unlighted daybeacon #20 to its easterly side and continue on course until you pass between unlighted daybeacons #22 and #21. Another sharp turn, this time to the east, leads you between unlighted daybeacons #21A and #22A. The pass-through of the Bradenton/ Highway 41 Business Bridge will then be dead ahead.

Bradenton-Palmetto Marinas   Wise captains who decide to do themselves a big favor and visit Regatta Pointe Marina should depart the track outlined above at flashing daybeacon #19. Two sets of unlighted, privately maintained daybeacons lead you into the central entrance without undue difficulty.

The easternmost slips at Regatta Pointe are not accessible via the main entrance after you have passed through the breakwater. Instead, skippers looking to find these

(eastern) slips should depart the approach channel shortly before passing through the main entrance and follow the breakwater to the east. The restaurant building will be to your port side. Don't slip too far to the south. The charted bubble of 3- and 4-foot waters awaits cruisers who make this unhappy maneuver. Curl around the easternmost tip of the piers and follow the boat ramp markers (beginning with unlighted daybeacon #1) to the northeastern slips.

Captains making for the twin, breakwater-protected dockage basins of Twin Dolphin Marina will sight the side-by-side entrances south of the gap between unlighted daybeacons #21 and #22. Cruise through the entrance of whichever basin wherein lies your assigned slip. Be mindful of the correctly charted 4-foot shallows to the west.

Bradenton-Palmetto Anchorages   Mariners choosing to drop anchor in the refuge adjacent to Regatta Pointe, along the river's northerly shoreline, should depart the marked channel at unlighted daybeacon #20. Cut toward the northeast, giving the waters fronting onto Regatta Pointe a wide berth. This maneuver will serve to avoid the correctly charted bubble of 2- to 4-foot waters just south and a bit east of the dockage basin. Eventually you will slip into the gap between Regatta Pointe and the eastern point of land. Watch for unlighted daybeacon #1 dead ahead. Anchor well south of this aid for best depths.

The anchorage along the opposite shoreline is found by continuing to follow the Manatee River's well-marked channel until passing between unlighted daybeacons #21 and #22. You can then cut almost due south toward the large building and point of land that will be so obvious along the shoreline. Drop anchor before approaching to within less than 50 yards of the point. Charts 11425 and 11414 warn of a sunken wreck immediately adjacent to the banks.

On the Manatee River East of unlighted daybeacons #21A and #22A, the river's track soon flows under the Highway 41 Business fixed bridge. Twin Dolphin Marina is easily accessible south of #21A and #22A.

Except for those mariners making for newly minted Riviera Dunes Marina Resort, many will choose to discontinue their upstream explorations at this point. The first Highway 41 Business span has a vertical clearance of 41 feet, followed closely by a railway bridge with only 5 feet of closed vertical height. Fortunately, this span is usually open unless a train is due.

From the railway span, head straight for the third, Highway 41 Bypass bridge's pass-through (vertical clearance 40 feet). Shallow water impinges on the channel to the north and south, east of the third span. Be on guard for leeway.

Once through this bridge, you need only follow the markers to unlighted daybeacon #31, abeam of Ellenton. Farther upstream, there are no additional aids to navigation, and depths drop off quickly east of the twin I-75 bridges.

The newly marked but currently uncharted channel leading to Riviera Dunes Marina Resort will be spotted along the northern bank as you come abeam of unlighted daybeacon #24A. Don't try to access the harbor by cruising north from unlighted daybeacon #23. A 2-foot shoal waits greedily for the keel of any skipper who tries this foolhardy maneuver.

Instead, curl back to the northwest from #24A, and point for the gap between the outermost marina entrance channel markers. Just remember good, old, "red, right, returning," and all should be well.

Tampa Bay Entrance and the ICW

The gaping westerly mouth of Tampa Bay reaches out into the open waters of the Gulf of Mexico by way of three deep passages. To the south, the bay's mouth is bordered by Anna Maria Island, while to the north a whole series of sandspits and barrier islands associated with Mullet Key make up an often indistinct barrier where it is all too easy for visiting cruisers to become confused and disoriented. Don't commit this error; the waters around Mullet Key and its lovely county park are mostly cheats and blinds waiting quietly to trap the incautious mariner.

Southernmost of Tampa Bay's three seaward cuts is Passage Key Inlet. This passage, along with Southwest Channel to the north, is deep but not well marked. The principal inlet is known as Egmont Channel on its westward reaches and Mullet Key Channel farther inland. This route is used by large, oceangoing ships, which regularly ply the bay to Tampa's commercial docks. It is, as you would expect, extensively marked with lighted aids to navigation. Strangers (particularly those without benefit of electronic navigation) are advised to make this passage their inlet of choice.

Two barrier islands divide Tampa Bay's three inlets. Passage Key is a small, uninhabited sandspit lying between Anna Maria Island and Egmont Key. Egmont Key, farther to the north, is a more substantial body of land and boasts a lighthouse alongside a possible anchorage.

The Western Florida ICW leaves the protected reaches of Anna Maria Sound and darts north via a sparsely marked passage to Mullet Key Channel. From this point the magenta line cuts eastward under the magnificent Sunshine Skyway fixed bridge. The Waterway follows a C-shaped path and eventually crosses back under the northerly spans of the Sunshine Skyway on the southern reaches of Boca Ciega Bay. Cruisers who pilot vessels drawing 5 feet or less and plan to forego a visit to the interior reaches of Tampa Bay, including the waterfronts of St. Petersburg and Tampa, may ignore this complicated route and follow the well-marked Sunshine Skyway Channel directly north to Boca Ciega.

It is only fair to observe that Tampa Bay's entrance can become more than slightly choppy with even moderate breezes. Many a captain and crew have breathed a sigh of relief when coming under the welcome protection of the shallows east of Mullet Key.

It is unfortunate that this reputation for wind and wicked wave has blinded many visiting cruisers to the fair-weather charms of this most westerly region of Tampa Bay. In appropriate conditions, mariners should seriously consider leaving a bit of time in their schedules to appreciate this unique region. A Native American evidently felt long ago that there could not be a fairer place than Egmont Key anywhere else in the world. This writer urges his fellow cruisers to experience these delights for themselves.

Passage Key Inlet

Passage Key Inlet lies between Anna Maria Island and Passage Key. While it is mostly deep, the pass lacks any aids to navigation and is surrounded by unmarked shoals. It is the least desirable of the three inlets serving Tampa Bay. Although fair-weather daylight navigation of the pass is possible, most cruising visitors will wisely choose either Southwest or Egmont channels to the north.

Passage Key Anchorage (27 33.446 North/082 44.428 West)

Passage Key is a small, oblong island guarding the waters north of Bean Point. From the cockpit, this isle appears to be little more than a sand bar at high tide. In light breezes and fair weather, cruisers may consider anchoring in the 7- and 8-foot waters east of the key. Do not approach to within less than 300 yards of the shores for best depths. If a thunderstorm appears over the horizon, all anchored craft should skedaddle as soon as possible.

Passage Key is a bird sanctuary and is home to gulls, skimmers, terns, and mallard ducks. Landings are strictly prohibited. Numerous signs posted on the island shores reinforce this prohibition.

Southwest Channel

The Tampa Bay inlet known as Southwest Channel consists of a broad ribbon of deep water lying between Passage and Egmont keys. While there are really only two aids to navigation along the cut, this inlet is actually quite simple to run in all but foul-weather, low-visibility conditions. Minimum depths are currently an impressive 15 feet, with soundings up to 30 feet in evidence.

Egmont Key

During the 1840s Florida became a new territory of the young United States and Americans began streaming south to this new land with a tropical climate. It was not long before these vigorous settlers came into conflict with the Seminole Indians, ushering in one of the saddest chapters in American history.

The Seminoles were actually not native to the Florida peninsula. The original Timucuan and Calusa Indians had mostly died out by the mid-1800s from disease. Several branches of the Creek Indian nation began moving into Florida during the early 1800s and took on the name of Seminoles.

There were actually three Seminole Indian

wars. The first two were inconclusive conflicts which were destined from the start to be repeated. The third war saw a change in the strategy of government forces. Rather than try to exterminate the Seminoles, the emphasis shifted to capturing and then deporting them to Oklahoma, which was then known as Indian territory.

As the third Seminole Indian war drew to an unhappy close, a host of the Native Americans were temporarily imprisoned on Egmont Key before being sent west. One of the Seminole chieftains, Tigertail, looked about at the lovely cabbage palms and sea oats set amidst the sugar white beaches of Egmont Key and decided to remain forever in his beloved land. According to legend, Tigertail swallowed powdered glass and lay down one last time upon his blanket set under the swaying palms. The young chief could not have picked a more beautiful place for his bones to rest.

Egmont Key retains its haunting loveliness to this very day. The 300-acre island is now a state park and it is protected from development. Tall palm trees reflect in the clear, glistening waters, and cruising couples stroll along the white beaches without a care. The old lighthouse guarding the key's northerly tip still winks at passing vessels as it has for the last 140 years. Truly, Egmont is a wondrous place that every cruiser should visit without fail.

Unfortunately, during the last decade, the county park authorities have seen fit to close more and more of Egmont Key to protect nesting birds. As it currently stands, the southern two-thirds of the island is now closed to landside visits. Fortunately, the northern section, including Egmont's fascinating lighthouse, remains friendly to human visitors. Numerous signs warn cruisers away from the closed portion of the key. Be sure to land your dinghy on a signless portion of the shoreline.

Besides the solitary beaches and swaying palms, cruisers also land on Egmont for its shelling. There are far fewer shell hunters here than on Sanibel or Captiva islands to the south. This writer's conversations with local cruisers indicates that Egmont now boasts the best shelling in all of Western Florida.

Snorkelers and scuba divers may want to explore the ruins of old Fort Dade, which once guarded Egmont Channel on the island's northern tip. This old stockade was built in the late 1800s during the Spanish-American War and, as far as this writer has been able to learn, never fired a shot in anger. Today, the fort's ruins are quickly being washed away into the waters of Egmont Channel.

Don't overlook the old lighthouse near the island's northeastern point. After checking at

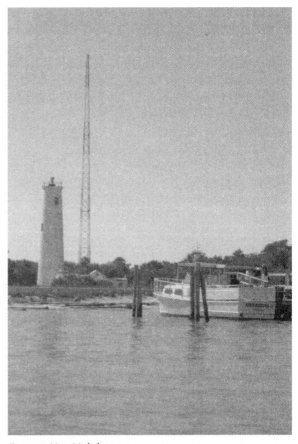

Egmont Key Lighthouse

the Coast Guard station, visitors can climb up to the top of the 85-foot lighthouse for a breathtaking view of Tampa Bay and Egmont Key.

The best place to anchor is found off the charted pilot boat dock along the isle's easterly shores (near 27 35.134 North/082 45.547 West). This location is noted as "Pilot Lookout" on the current edition of chart 11411. The pier has been leased by the Tampa Bay Pilot Association since 1912. Pleasure craft are not allowed to moor here, but you can certainly drop the hook east and south of the dock. Minimum depths of 10 feet run within 50 yards of the beach. This anchorage is well protected from westerlies, and the hooked southside tip of the island gives some protection when winds are blowing from this quarter. Strong blows from the east or northeast call for a delay in your visit.

A second pier lying off Egmont's northerly point is known as the "coal dock." At the turn of the century, coal and other supplies were offloaded at Egmont from ocean freighters and temporarily stored before being ferried to the mainland by shallow-draft vessels. A ferry boat carries passengers from the mainland to this pier. As far as I have been able to learn, pleasure craft are still not allowed to tie up here, but, again, you could anchor off in good weather and dinghy ashore.

Egmont Channel

This cut is also known as Tampa Bay Channel, and rightly so. It is through this channel that dozens and dozens of oceangoing ships enter and leave Tampa Bay every week. With this sort of deep-draft traffic, it's not difficult to imagine that the passage is exceedingly well marked with lighted aids to navigation. While, as with all inlets, the chop

Pilot boat dock, Egmont Key

can be more than a bit daunting at times, you would have a tough time getting lost in Egmont Channel. By all accounts, this is the best passage into and from Tampa Bay, particularly during inclement weather.

Mullet Key and Fort DeSoto Park

Mullet Key guards the northerly flank of Egmont and Mullet channels. Along with its sister islands, Madelaine, St. Jean, St. Christopher, and Bonne Fortune keys, Mullet Key remains one of the only undeveloped pieces of land left on the barrier islands lying off St. Petersburg and Clearwater. This region has been designated a county park and named after the old fort which has been partially preserved on Mullet Key's southwestern point.

Mullet Key is a historically significant body of land. It is thought that Ponce de Leon anchored off the isle in 1513 while exploring

Western Florida. Indian attacks forced him to use his ship's cannon for defense. During this engagement one of the Spanish sailors was killed. His was the first known death of a European soldier in North America.

Ponce returned to Mullet Key in 1521 and again fought with the local Indians. The old explorer received a mortal wound and died upon returning to Havana.

In February of 1849 a young army engineer named Lt. Col. Robert E. Lee visited Mullet Key. After surveying both Mullet and Egmont keys, Lee recommended that forts be established on both islands.

It was not until long after the Civil War, in 1898, that Lee's plans were put into practice. Construction of Fort DeSoto began in the fall of that year and was completed some twenty-four months later. The fort was armed with 12-inch mortars which, as at Fort Dade, were never actually put to use in military action.

During World War II, Mullet Key was used as an Air Force gunnery and bombing training center. In 1948 Pinellas County took possession of the island and its surroundings fellows with the express intention of creating a county recreational park. A road was finally completed in 1962 and the park officially opened in 1963.

Unfortunately, there are no reliable means for larger cruising vessels to visit the county park and historic fort. Consult the review of Bunces Pass Channel below for more information.

Sunshine Skyway Bridge

The mammoth Sunshine Skyway Bridge and causeway stretch across the mouth of Tampa Bay for almost 11 statute miles. This huge span is one of the longest bridges and causeways in the world, and it is certainly one of the most impressive.

The bridge cruisers see today spanning Tampa Bay is actually the second Sunshine Skyway. The original bridge was struck by a ship in 1980 during foul weather. The center portion of the west-side span was completely swept away and several vehicles, including one tourist bus, tragically plummeted into the waters below.

It was decided not to rebuild the old bridge but to construct an entirely new span. This newer structure was in use for several years before the older bridge was removed completely. Small, shallow, spoil islands have been placed around the new bridge's central supporting pillars. Now barges and ships should run aground before striking the bridge a death blow.

Sunshine Skyway Channel

At flashing buoy #26, chart 11411 shows the magenta-line ICW passage cutting east-north-east under the Sunshine Skyway. Eventually this passage curls back around to the west and rejoins the Waterway's trek to the north, just off the northernmost section of the Sunshine Skyway (known as the Misner Bridge). While this route is fine (but lengthy), any boat drawing less than 5 feet should not have a problem following the more direct Sunshine Skyway Channel paralleling the bridge's (and causeway's) western flank. This cut rejoins the official Waterway channel on Boca Ciega Bay.

However, passing cruisers should know that within the past several years the southern tip of the Sunshine Skyway Channel has been shoaling. In August 2003, we sounded MLW depths of only 5 feet between unlighted day-beacons #2 and #3. It is possible that an especially low tide might even bring on a 4½-foot soundings. Captains should access their vessel's draft with a critical eye and make their decisions accordingly.

Sunshine Skyway Bridge over Tampa Bay, photo courtesy Florida Department of Commerce

One alternative, should your vessel's draft be on the borderline, would be to simply time your passage for mid- or high tide. This would give you an extra 1 to 2½ feet of depth. Otherwise, you must take the much longer, official, ICW route outlined by the magenta line, passing under the Sunshine Skyway and then back through the northernmost passage of this long bridge and causeway.

By the time you cruise several hundred yards north-northwest of #2 and #3, depths greatly improve on the Sunshine Skyway Channel, and for the remainder of its well-marked passage, minimum 7-foot soundings can be expected. This is a far more sheltered cut than the official ICW passage, and unless the shoaly depths near #2 and #3 are a problem for your vessel, this is the route of choice.

Bunces Pass (Various Lats/Lons—see below)

The well-marked channel to Bunces Pass breaks off to the west between unlighted day-beacons #11 and #13 (on the Sunshine Skyway Channel). This cut is a very interesting side trip for powercraft. Why powercraft? you may ask. Well, that's because the channel from the Sunshine Skyway cut to the interior reaches of Bunces Pass (where all the visual interest lies) flows under a 19-foot fixed bridge. Only the very smallest sail craft could clear this span.

Perhaps, you might think that sailboats could approach Bunces Pass from the Gulf of Mexico. Wrong! The seaward side of this passage carries a mere 3 feet at MLW, and it twists and turns its

way between a whole raft of unmarked shoals. We strongly suggest that no cruising-size craft even think about attempting this outermost section of Bunces Pass.

So, with all that out of the way, powercraft can expect minimum 7-foot depths on the run from the Sunshine Skyway Channel to the 19-foot bridge, with most soundings being in the 10+-foot region. Once the bridge is in your wake, things get really interesting. The surrounding shores are part of Fort DeSoto Park and are beautifully in their natural state. In fact, seldom will you find a more visually elegant place to drop the hook. While I would not want to be caught anchored on these waters during really foul weather, under normal conditions, there are few better spots on this section of the Western Florida coastline to spend some time.

There are at least two anchorages to consider. Moving east to west, the first spot is easy to find, but less private. Shortly after passing under the fixed, 19-foot bridged discussed above, passing cruisers will sight a large public launching-ramp facility on the southern banks. It is quite possible to anchor off this section of the banks, near 27 38.834 North/082 43.149 West, in some 7 to 8 feet of water at low tide. Of course, you may be bothered by all the coming and going from the launching ramps, but this activity will fall off after sunset. There is good protection from southern and southeastern winds, but woe be unto you if fresh breezes are wafting from the east or west.

Our favorite overnight haven on Bunces Pass is found on the waters just northwest of the charted offshoot in the southerly banks, between charted and unlighted daybeacons #4 and #2 (near 27 38.703 North/082 44.184 West). Here, good depths of 8 feet or better run to within 75 yards of the southerly banks. Closer to shore, soundings rise rapidly. Be sure to set your anchor so as not to swing into these shallows. Again, there is excellent shelter from southern, southeastern, and southwestern winds, but very little to the east and west.

By the way, while anchored on this haven during our last visit, we noticed a sign on shore that warned against swimming on these waters, due to strong currents. We heartily suggest that you heed this stricture.

TAMPA BAY ENTRANCE AND ICW NAVIGATION

Many sailors rejoice when leaving the more constricted waters of Anna Maria Sound behind and passing out into the wide mouth of Tampa Bay. At last, you can cut the iron gennie and let out the sails. Just remember that this region can become exceedingly rough when wind speeds exceed 10 knots from any quarter. In really heavy weather, it would be far wiser to put back into port for a day or two and await fair breezes before crossing the bay.

Cruisers interested in running one of Tampa Bay's three inlets, or anchoring off either Passage or Egmont keys, can safely abandon the Waterway and approach either of these islands from the deep waters off their easterly shores.

Aids to navigation on the ICW's southerly run across Tampa Bay are very widely spaced. Be sure to preplot your compass/GPS courses and follow them faithfully on the water.

At flashing buoy #26, vessels drawing more than 5 feet should cut east-northeast through the Sunshine Skyway into the heart of lower Tampa Bay. You must then follow a 10-nautical-mile semicircular route to rejoin the Waterway's trek to the north in Boca Ciega Bay. Most other pleasure-craft skippers will opt for the shorter, sheltered Sunshine Skyway Channel, but just remember those new 5-foot soundings along this passage's southernmost section.

The Bulkhead to Mullet Channel From flashing daybeacon #67 and unlighted daybeacon #68, set a careful compass/GPS course for flashing daybeacon #70 to the north-northeast. It's a run of 2.4 nautical miles between #68 and #70. Fortunately, the track does not stray near any shoals.

Come abeam of #70 to its westerly quarter and continue on, pointing to come abeam of flashing buoy #26 to its westerly side. At #26, you must choose whether to turn east into lower Tampa Bay, west into Egmont Channel and the Gulf of Mexico, or follow the Sunshine Skyway Channel to the north.

As you approach #70, the tilted, round top of the St. Petersburg Thunder Dome will be visible on the Pinellas peninsula to the north. We shall learn more about this unusual entertainment facility in our discussion of St. Petersburg. Let's pause for a moment in our account of the ICW to address navigating Tampa Bay's three inlets and its two barrier islands.

Passage Key Inlet Successful navigation of Passage Key Inlet, the narrowest of Tampa Bay's three seaward passages, is complicated by the long, unmarked shoal building out from Passage Key's (the island's) southwesterly point. To avoid this hazard, favor the Bean Point (southerly) side of the channel slightly when passing out into the Gulf. Notice that there are also significant shoals lying southwest of Bean Point. These shallows are equally unmarked. My best advice is to continue cruising to the west between these two shoals and hope for the best (or make use of a GPS interfaced with a laptop computer). Frankly, this writer suggests using the Southwest or Egmont channels instead, but so many local captains seem to make use of Passage Key Inlet that I have always felt obligated to present the navigational information above.

Passage Key Anchorage Approach Passage Key off its eastern shores from the deeper waters of Tampa Bay. Point for the waters lying east of the isle's northern section. Drop the hook before approaching to within less than 300 yards of the beach. Remember that Passage Key is a nesting bird sanctuary and landing is not permitted.

Southwest Channel All you need do to find your way through Southwest Channel is to avoid the small shoals off southern Egmont Key and stay well north of the long tier of shoals slashing west from Passage Key.

To enter the channel, come abeam of flashing buoy #3, well off Egmont Key's southeastern point, by .3 nautical miles to its southerly side. Set course to pass out into the Gulf, leaving Egmont's southern tip at least .3 nautical miles to your northerly side.

Stay several hundred yards (at least) north of Passage Key.

Egmont Key   Approach Egmont Key on its eastern banks from Tampa Bay. Use your binoculars to pick out the charted pilot boat dock on the southern half of the east-side beaches. Head directly for this pier.

As you approach to within 100 yards of the pilot boat dock, break off to the south and select your anchorage. Good depths run to within 50 yards of shore.

Alternately, you can follow the deep water north, keeping at least 200 yards off Egmont Key, to Egmont Channel. Deep water runs hard by Egmont's northerly point. You should spot the coal dock and lighthouse as this point comes abeam.

Egmont Channel   Flashing buoy #26 marks the intersection of the Western Florida ICW and Mullet Key Channel. This latter cut leads west to Egmont Channel which, in turn, provides super-reliable access to the open Gulf. It doesn't get much simpler than this, gang. Both Mullet Key and Egmont channels are lit up like Christmas trees.

As you pass by Egmont Key's northerly point, use your binoculars to try and pick out the ruins of Fort Dade. They may have already washed away by the time you arrive.

ICW Route through Lower Tampa Bay   If you pilot a deep-draft vessel (drawing more than 5 feet) and choose to follow the semi-circular, C-shaped ICW passage through lower Tampa Bay rather than the Sunshine Skyway Channel, turn east-northeast at flashing buoy #26 and head under the

Sunshine Skyway's central pass-through. Vertical clearance is set at 175 feet, so most masts should clear it.

Once past the span, follow the well-marked Cut A Channel to flashing buoy #3B on the Cut B Channel. Between #3B and the next northeasterly aid to navigation, flashing buoy #6B, the ICW track breaks off to the north. Abandon the Cut B Channel about halfway between #3B and #6B and set course to pass between flashing daybeacon #1 and unlighted daybeacon #2.

Let's pause for a moment to mention the potential confusion about the numbering system on the aids to navigation in these waters. As will be seen in the discussion below, there are two flashing daybeacon #1's along this stretch of the Waterway and another on the Sunshine Skyway Channel. Follow along carefully on charts 11414 and 11411 to avoid confusion.

Once between the (first) #1 and #2, continue almost due north, pointing to pass between flashing daybeacon #4 and unlighted daybeacon #3. Hold your course for another hundred yards or so, and then cut sharply west and point to pass the second flashing daybeacon #1 to its fairly immediate northerly side. A well-outlined track will now open out before you, leading west to the Sunshine Skyway's northerly span. Consult the discussion of Tampa Bay's western shore presented later in this chapter for a review of facilities along this portion of the channel.

West of unlighted daybeacon #13, the Waterway meets up with twin fixed spans that have 65 feet of vertical clearance. The channel is narrow between #13 and the bridge. Come abeam of #13 to its fairly immediate northerly side and continue straight ahead to the span's pass-through. Watch for leeway.

After leaving the twin bridges behind, point to pass unlighted daybeacon #13A to its northerly side. You will now find yourself at a critical intersection. The Sunshine Skyway Channel makes in from the south, while the Waterway sweeps to the west and an alternate channel cuts to the north. These various passages will be covered in the next chapter.

Sunshine Skyway Channel   Don't forget that soundings have shelved up to 5-foot MLW levels on the southernmost section of the Sunshine Skyway Channel near unlighted daybeacons #2 and #3. If your vessel draws 5 to 5½ feet, either use the ICW official route described above or wait for high tide. If your boat needs more than 5½ feet to stay off the bottom, use the ICW passage by all accounts.

Captains who choose the Sunshine Skyway Channel should cruise from flashing buoy #26 by turning east-northeast as if they intended to pass under the Sunshine Skyway. Point to pass flashing buoy #1A to its southerly side and continue on toward the bridge for another hundred yards or so. Then, cut sharply to the north-northwest and point to come abeam of the Sunshine Skyway's southernmost aid to navigation, flashing daybeacon #1, to its easterly quarter. Again, don't confuse this flashing daybeacon #1 with the two other flashing daybeacons bearing the same number on the ICW passage through lower Tampa Bay, discussed above.

From #1, set course to pass between unlighted daybeacons #2 and #3. As mentioned almost ad nauseam above, some 5-foot depths at MLW will be encountered near #2 and #3. After cruising north-northwest for about 200 yards, depths deepen considerably, and you need worry with no other shallows on this marked passage.

The remainder of the Sunshine Skyway Channel is unusually well marked all the way into Boca Ciega Bay. You will intersect the Waterway immediately after passing flashing daybeacon #26. Slow down. All the markers can be quite confusing. Be sure to correctly identify your intended track before forging ahead.

Bunces Pass   Remember that the passage from the Sunshine Skyway Channel to the interior reaches of Bunces Pass is a powerboat-only club, courtesy of the 19-foot fixed bridge crossing the channel. Otherwise, captains will find the section between the Skyway channel and the bridge well marked with unlighted daybeacons. As you've probably guessed already, pass red beacons to your port side and take green beacons to starboard.

Don't stray from the marked route. While this channel could never be accurately considered narrow, depths of as little as ½ foot lie just to the north and south. Cruisers who wander into these waters will surely have a close encounter of the grounding variety.

West-southwest of the gap between unlighted daybeacons #9 and #10, the Bunces Pass channel exchanges greetings with the aforementioned 19-foot fixed bridge. Captains whose craft cannot clear this span must retrace their steps.

After cruising under the 19-foot bridge, look toward the southern banks, and you should spot the public launching ramps mentioned above. If you choose, it's easy to anchor off this section of shoreline. Just watch out for the crazies.

To continue cruising west into the heart of Bunces Pass, set course to pass some 25 to 50 yards south of unlighted daybeacon #5. Before reaching #5, you may spot some small, floating markers making off to the south. These informal aids to navigation outline a small, outboard-only channel. Similarly, there is another one of these tiny cuts to the southwest of #5. Cruising-size craft should strictly avoid both of these petite channels.

To drop anchor at the recommended haven between unlighted daybeacons #4 and #2, watch the southern banks for a small stream cutting off to the south. Ease into the waters west of this offshoot, and drop the anchor before approaching to within less than 75 yards of the shoreline. Closer to shore, depths rise dramatically!

Don't even think about cruising west of the gap between unlighted daybeacons #1 and #2 toward the open waters of the Gulf. Not only are there 3-foot MLW depths waiting farther to the west, but the channel, such as it is, convulses this way and that between killer shoals, which could do in your boat for good. Confine your explorations to the interior waters of Bunces Pass, and your vessel will live to cruise another day!

Lower Tampa Bay—Western Shore

The western shoreline of Tampa Bay, south of Interbay Peninsula, can be summed up by two words: "St. Petersburg." This shining city dominates the banks with its beautifully restored downtown, excellent marina facilities, and myriad green parks. Cruisers may be surprised to learn that there are also any number of opportunities to anchor, often within sight of attractive residential neighborhoods. Vessels in need of repairs are not forgotten, either. The yards on Salt Creek are second to none. In short, mariners will find everything and anything they might ever need for an enjoyable and productive stay in this region of Tampa Bay, no matter what their cruising tastes.

While lower Tampa Bay's easterly banks may be a bit less developed, there is no denying this writer's fondness for the western shoreline. St. Petersburg simply seems to radiate a warm welcome for the visiting cruiser and I, for one, advise my fellow skippers to pack it in.

Sunshine Skyway Anchorage (27 42.260 North/082 40.621 West)

Some mariners occasionally anchor in the

1. Holiday Inn/Annapolis Sailing School Marina

lee of the northernmost section of the Sunshine Skyway causeway, north-northwest of unlighted daybeacon #13. In all but light airs or westerly winds, this is a very open haven and it is certainly not recommended for anything approaching heavy weather. Minimum depths are around 7 feet, but there is one shoal which must be avoided. The surrounding shoreline is overlooked by heavy, high-rise condo development that is not particularly attractive.

Holiday Inn/Annapolis Sailing School Marina (27 42.398 North/082 40.655 West)

Cruisers will discover a sheltered harbor and dockage basin just north of the anchorage discussed above in the charted, water-tank-shaped bay. This marina is associated with an adjacent Holiday Inn and is home to the Annapolis Sailing School (727-867-8102),

which also uses the docks for its vessels. Let me say here and now that if you are looking for a good introduction to sailing, you simply can't go wrong by selecting this school of instruction.

The marina itself is a somewhat low-key but friendly operation that welcomes transients at its well-sheltered, fixed wooden and concrete piers. We have been warned that this operation gets very busy on weekends, so be sure to call ahead for reservations. Mean low-water entrance depths are about 5 feet, and dockside soundings range from 6 to as much as 8 feet. Full dockside power, freshwater, and cable-television connections are complemented by one, non-climate-controlled shoreside shower (at the pool) and a Laundromat. Transient cruisers receive a discounted dockage fee if they also rent a shoreside room. The adjacent Holiday Inn features a very simple restaurant.

Holiday Inn/Annapolis Sailing School Marina
(727) 867-1151, ext. 562
http://holiday-inn.com/marinacove-ss

Approach depth—5 feet (mean low water)
Dockside depth—6-8 feet
Accepts transients—yes
Transient dockage rate—average
Fixed concrete and wooden piers—yes
Dockside power connections—30 and 50 amp
Dockside water connections—yes
Showers—yes
Laundromat—yes
Restaurant—on site

Little Bayou (Various Lats/Lons—see below)

North of unlighted daybeacon #3 and flashing daybeacon #4, the official ICW passage cuts sharply west, as outlined in the preceding section of this chapter. A second, well-marked channel runs on to the north and provides reliable access to Little Bayou, Big Bayou, Salt Creek, and the various St. Petersburg marina facilities. We shall call this passage the western Tampa Bay channel.

The marked cut leading to Little Bayou lies west of the mid-point between the western Tampa Bay channel's unlighted can buoys #5 and #7. The Little Bayou cut maintains minimum 6-foot depths and eventually leads to two anchorages for boats that draw 4½ feet or less.

One fair spot is found near 27 43.325 North/082 37.903 West, hard by unlighted daybeacon #17. Drop anchor immediately west of the channel. Just a hair's breadth farther to the west, the bottom shelves up sharply. If you avoid these shallows, MLW soundings of 4½ to 5 feet can be expected. We found two sail craft comfortably riding on the hook at this spot during our last visit to Little Bayou, in August 2003. This haven affords good shelter from northern and northeastern winds, but there is less protection to the south and west.

A better spot will be discovered immediately southeast of unlighted daybeacon #21, near 27 43.455 North/082 37.952 West. Here low-tide soundings of 5 to 5½ feet can be expected, with good shelter to the north, northwest, and (to a lesser extent) east. Just don't be caught here in fresh southerlies.

The Little Bayou shoreline supports moderate to heavy residential development and is exclusively private property. Please respect the local homeowners, and do not attempt to dinghy ashore.

The Little Bayou entrance channel is no picnic, courtesy of a side channel cutting south at unlighted junction daybeacon #A. Be sure to read the navigational account of Little Bayou presented later in this chapter before attempting this cut.

Little Bayou is joined to Big Bayou (see below) by a mostly deep canal, which, at one point near the mid-point of its passage between the two bayous, opens out into a deep, sheltered bay. Unfortunately, both the northern and southern ends of the connecting canal are crossed by 9-foot (vertical clearance) fixed bridges that bar this useful short-cut for all but small powercraft. If you should happen to power one of these feisty runabouts, don't overlook the opportunity to drop anchor in the interim bay west of Coquina Key.

Big Bayou (27 44.358 North/082 38.129 West)

The often-confusing entrance channel to Big Bayou cuts into the western shores of Tampa Bay, west of unlighted nun buoy #10. If you can keep to marked cut (a not inconsiderable accomplishment), 5-foot MLW depths can be maintained, but it's an incredibly simple proposition to wander into 2 and 3 feet of water, even when you are trying to be careful.

The inner waters of Big Bayou play host to a rather motley collection of anchored sail craft. Some of these vessels look as if they have not moved in a long time and aren't going anywhere in the near future, while others are trim and bright, ready for a day's sail.

It is quite possible to anchor amidst these local craft, but be warned that some seem to be anchored in only a few feet of water at low tide. Don't assume just because you see another boat anchored near a particular spot that the waters are deep.

One good anchorage seems to lie about mid-way between unlighted daybeacons #14 and #16, near 27 44.358 North/082 38.129 West. We found good depths of 7 feet or better on these waters, but only a short step away, we were sweating out a shallow bottom.

The good news about anchoring in Big Bayou is that it's quite possible to dinghy ashore for a good meal. A public launching ramp overlooks Big Bayou's western banks, near unlighted daybeacon #16. You can dinghy in to the piers associated with this facility, tie off temporarily, and walk one block south to Munch's Restaurant (727-896-5972). Both breakfast and lunch (open 7:00 A.M. to 3:00 P.M.) are terrific.

All in all, there are certainly other anchorages along lower Tampa Bay's westerly shoreline that are far less complicated than Big Bayou. Perhaps, first-timers may want to consider one of these more accessible havens. But, for those who must see it all, a navigational account is presented later in this chapter.

St. Petersburg

North of Big Bayou, the western shores of lower Tampa Bay border upon the central St. Petersburg waterfront, which hosts the city's many marinas and repair yards. St. Petersburg was quite a surprise for this writer when I performed my original research on these waters back in the early 1990s. At the time, for some reason I expected a carbon copy of Clearwater, to the north, and I could not have been more mistaken. What this writer found instead was a vital, active city that has not forgotten what drew people to it in the first place. While, to be sure, the St. Petersburg waterfront is highly developed, the various buildings are now part of a rehabilitated downtown with impressive architecture and many, many attractions for residents and visitors alike. The number of city parks is quite impressive and long, luscious green grass is everywhere in evidence. Frankly, this writer was startled by the delightful contrast between this lovely community and its neighbors to the north.

In the space of this account, we can only begin to enumerate St. Petersburg's many attractions. You should make use of the material below as a starting point in coming to know this impressive community. If you plan a longer stay, it might be a good idea to contact the St. Petersburg—Clearwater Convention and Visitors Bureau at (727) 464-7200 or the

St. Petersburg Chamber of Commerce at (727) 821-4069. Either of these fine organizations can provide enough information to fill weeks of your time with fresh new activities.

Every visitor to St. Petersburg should begin his or her stay with a trip to the St. Petersburg Historical Museum (727-894-1052). This fascinating collection of St. Petersburg memorabilia is found at the entrance to The Pier (see below). Such things as the nation's first commercial flight, the Orange Belt Railroad, and the famous "Green Bench" of St. Petersburg are recalled in the museum's display. The museum is within an easy walk of the large St. Pete municipal marina (see below).

Also within walking distance is the Bayfront Center, at 400 First Street S. The Bayfront Center is the site for numerous concerts, opera, and local theater. Check at the ticket office (727-892-5700) for the latest offerings.

The Museum of Fine Arts (255 Beach Drive NE, 727-896-2667) boasts a most impressive collection of French impressionist paintings as well as European, American, Pre-Columbian, and Far Eastern art. Anyone interested in art will find the displays well worth his or her time. You will need a taxi to find your way comfortably to this attraction.

For a more offbeat look at the world of art, try the Salvador Dali Museum at 1000 Third Street S (727-823-3767) next door to the Harborage at Bayboro Marina. Here you will find the world's largest display of the controversial artist's paintings and graphics. As the museum's own pamphlet states, "Salvador Dali created images which will captivate the mind and imagination of the world forever. The images he created perplex, confound, enlighten, and intrigue everyone who

encounters them." There is really nothing else to add to that.

Every March sees the appearance of the St. Louis Cardinals baseball team in St. Petersburg's Al Lang Stadium. Fans thrill to open practices and exhibition games. Of course, St. Petersburg (and the entire Tampa Bay region) now have their very own professional baseball team: the Tampa Bay Devil Rays. Catching a game at the nearby Thunderdome is a worthy experience for baseball fans.

Only in a city such as St. Petersburg which is so sensitive to its natural environment will you find a park like the Boyd Hill Nature Trail (1101 Country Club Way). Six trails wind peacefully through 216 acres of all-natural forests, marshes, and swamps. A multitude of wildlife is always present.

St. Petersburg, as you can readily imagine, plays host to an impressive group of seasonal activities that ought to provide something for just about everybody. March brings the SPIFFS International Folk Festival to town, with traditional ethnic foods, costumes, entertainment, and crafts from more than 40 countries, as well as The Festival of States, in which marching bands from throughout the United States compete.

Well, if by now you've decided that there's more to do and see in St. Petersburg than could be accounted for in an entire book, you are on the right track. Cruising and landlubber visitors alike should plan to give this rare jewel sitting beside Tampa Bay a hefty slice of their time.

Numbers to know in St. Petersburg include

Independence Taxi—(727) 327-3444
Yellow Cab—(727) 821-7777
Avis Rental Cars—(727) 536-8026

Budget Rent A Car—(800) 527-7000

West Marine—(727) 867-5700

Chamber of Commerce—(727) 821-4069

St. Petersburg—Clearwater Convention and
Visitors Bureau—(727) 464-7200

St. Petersburg History The modern city of St. Petersburg sits perched on the southern tip of what has come be known as the Pinellas Peninsula. Recent archaeological evidence suggests that Pinellas was visited by both Narvaez and DeSoto during their explorations of Western Florida.

The first settler on the peninsula is thought to have been Antonio Maximo, who arrived in 1823. By this time Florida had passed from its second era of Spanish rule and was now a part of the young United States. Maximo had fought in the Seminole wars and secured a land grant in recognition of this service. He was joined by another individual named William Bunce, and the two partners established a "fish ranche" which did a lively business in supplying seafood to Cuba. A strong hurricane in 1848 completely obliterated the enterprise and both Maximo and Bunce left the area, never to be heard from again.

Within the next several years other pioneers began to filter into the Pinellas peninsula and establish small farms and orange groves near the stream we now know as Big Bayou. The first house was erected in 1856 by James R. Hay.

The small village suffered disaster during the Civil War. Union troops invaded the peninsula and stole practically all the livestock and crops to be found. Every single house was burned to the ground and the orange trees were wantonly hewn down and left to rot. When the inhabitants returned, they took one look at the devastation and stole away in a rowboat that the troops had left behind.

Dr. James Hackney was the first to settle on the site of St. Petersburg. The good doctor bought six hundred acres of land from the state in 1873 for twenty-five cents an acre.

In 1875 one of the two men credited with being the founders of St. Petersburg arrived. Gen. John C. Williams of Detroit first visited Pinellas in 1875. Over the next four years he acquired some 1,600 acres of land and returned for good in 1879. After an unsuccessful attempt at farming, Williams conceived the idea of establishing a town, complete with rail service. At about the same time, Peter Demens, an emigrant from Russia, had just completed a narrow-gauge railway from Lake Monroe (near the modern city of Sanford) to Lake Apopka. This was the beginning of the famous "Orange Belt Railroad."

Through shrewd business dealings, Williams convinced Demens to extend the railroad to his settlement rather than his next intended choice. Construction was hampered by lack of funds, heavy rains, and yellow fever, but the line was finally completed in 1888. It wasn't long before tons and tons of oranges were being shipped to and from Lake Monroe and Pinellas via this new mode of transportation.

St. Petersburg acquired its present-day name sometime during this period. There have been many stories that purport to tell how the moniker was acquired. The tale usually given the most credence relates the desire of both Williams and Demens to name their new settlement. Agreement seemed to be impossible, so the two played a poker game for the privilege and Demens won. He selected the name of his native Russian city, St. Petersburg.

Citrus cultivation in St. Petersburg received a tremendous boost during the winter of 1894-95. Two hard freezes struck Florida within as many weeks and orange trees all over the state were laid waste. Due to the mitigating effects of the warm Gulf of Mexico, the orange groves in St. Petersburg survived. When word of this reached orange growers in other parts of the state, many moved to St. Petersburg to found new groves.

Since those days the growth of St. Petersburg has been phenomenal, and yet not at the total expense of the natural environment. Perhaps this is because many of St. Petersburg's citizens settled here during the twentieth century for the healthful climate and beautiful waters. An 1885 paper delivered to the New Orleans medical convention stated flatly, "Those who have carefully surveyed the entire state think it (St. Petersburg) offers the best climate in Florida.

The Harborage at Bayboro and Salt Creek Facilities (Various Lats/Lons—see below)

North of Big Bayou, cruisers following the

The Harborage at Bayboro

marked channel along the bay's western shoreline will come upon flashing daybeacon #S. This aid signals the intersection with the important, well-marked, westward-flowing Bayboro Channel, which leads pleasure craft into the charted deep water south of Albert Whitted Airport. Some of the finest facilities in St. Petersburg are accessed through this fortunate cut and adjacent Salt Creek.

The first charted cove on the northern banks serves the St. Petersburg commercial shipping port. While the various oceangoing ships that dock there make for a fascinating sight from the water, there are no services for pleasure craft. The situation is very different just to the west.

Mariners cruising down Bayboro Channel for the first time will be amazed by the huge collection of yachts, which they will spy at the western terminus of the cut. This partially breakwater-enclosed harbor is part of the Harborage at Bayboro (27 45.552 North/082 38.168 West), one of the largest privately owned marinas in western Florida. This writer has always found that the staff and management of the Harborage, unlike many huge marina complexes, are friendly and ready to do all in their power to make your stay a pleasure. A full 500 feet of all-concrete-decked floating docks are set aside for transient vessels. Even so, advance reservations would be a wise precaution. Dockside depths of 11 to 14 feet are ready to serve even the deepest-draft sail craft. The breakwater that fronts the harbor to its eastern side deflects rough water when winds are blowing strongly from this quarter.

Every conceivable power, water, and communication connection, plus waste pump-out service, is readily available dockside. Behind the dockage basin, visitors will discover the dockmaster's building, which contains somewhat small but air-conditioned showers and a Laundromat. There is also an attractive cruisers' lounge, with a color television, VCR, and microwave oven located on the second floor. This is a great place to gather and share cruising stories with your fellow skippers after a long day on the water. If it's a bit warm, don't overlook the marina swimming pool just behind the main dockage basin.

The Old Key West Deli restaurant (727-894-4363) is located behind the dockage basin. This popular dining spot has changed hands repeatedly over the past several years. Only time will tell what the future will hold here. In the past, the sandwiches have been super.

Since 1998 we have been told that the entire landside portion of the Harborage dockage basin is slated for renovation. If these plans should ever come to fruition, it is likely that the building containing the Old Key West Deli will be razed to make room for a far more expansive retail/dining/office complex.

Many other restaurants in downtown St. Petersburg are only a short taxi ride away. Check out our account of this district attached to our review of the large St. Pete Municipal Marina below.

The building that plays host to the Key West Deli is also the current St. Petersburg headquarters for the Steve Colgate Offshore Sailing School (800-221-4326). This is one of the most prestigious organizations of its type in the world.

Would you believe that only covers about half of the Harborage's services? The firm also maintains a mammoth dry-stack storage facility on the western shores of Salt Creek, to the south. Here cruisers will find the marina fuel dock and repair services.

Hard by the Harborage's dry storage on Salty Creek, cruisers will discover the Fish Tale Bar and Grill (727-821-3474). We have not had the good fortune to sample the bill of fare here yet, but we did notice quite a few cruising types enjoying the semi-open-air dining when last we eased our way down Salty Creek.

Shazam! If there is a better-equipped marina operation anywhere, this writer has yet to find it. As an added incentive, the Salvador Dali Museum, described earlier, is next door to the docks.

The Harborage at Bayboro (727) 821-6347
http://www.internationalmarinasll.com

Approach depth—15 feet plus
Dockside depth—11-14 feet
Accepts transients—yes
Transient dockage rate—above average
Floating concrete docks—yes
Dockside power connections—up to 50 amp
Dockside water connections—yes
Waste pump-out—yes
Showers—yes
Laundromat—yes
Gasoline—yes (Salt Creek facility)
Diesel fuel—yes (Salt Creek facility)
Mechanical repairs—yes (Salt Creek facility)
Restaurant—on-site

Deep Salt Creek breaks off from the southwestern corner of the Bayboro Harbor Channel and leads south and southwest through minimum 10-foot depths. Within the last five years, the eastern shores of Salt Creek have become the home of an almost incredible array of pleasure-craft-oriented repair yards and an equally impressive number of yacht brokerages. Some of these firms are highly specialized, while others provide almost everything an ailing vessel might need. This writer will not even guarantee that the catalog of businesses below is complete. New operations on Salt Creek seem to be springing up by leaps and bounds!

Captains and crew cruising into the northern mouth of Salt Creek will first catch sight of a commercial seafood dock to port, followed by Progressive Boat Yard (27 45.422 North/082 37.979 West, 727-822-2886), also on the eastern banks. This outstanding repair firm features a 35-ton travelift, which is outfitted with a crane to facilitate mast stepping and unstepping. Full-service mechanical repairs for gasoline and diesel power plants are offered, as is fiberglass servicing and marine painting. As Joe, the owner, put it to

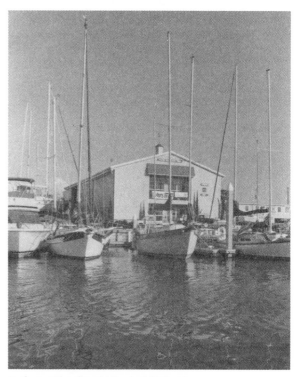

Sailor's Wharf Yacht Yard, Salt Creek

me, "if we can't do it, we know who can." Trust me when I tell you that this yard is truly "full service."

Next up, also to port, are the docks and extensive yards of Sailor's Wharf Yacht Yard (27 45.374 North/082 37.989 West, http://www. sailorswharf.com, 727-823-1155). As its name implies, this firm specializes in haul-out (60-ton travelift) and full service mechanical repairs for sail craft. There is also an on-site ship's and parts store as well as an extensive sail-craft brokerage associated with this operation. If you happen to be in the market for a new boat, give Jopie, Sandy, or one of their fine staff a call. One look at this yard will clue you in to the fact that this is a first-class operation that does quite a business with local sailors.

Sailing Florida with Sunsail (866-894-7245) makes its home at Sailor's Wharf as well. In addition to offering extensive sail-craft charters, this operation includes an ASA-certified sailing school.

Opposite Sailor's Wharf, on the western shores of Salt Creek, passing cruisers will observe the dry-stack storage, fuel dock, and the Fish Tale Bar and Grill associated with the Harborage at Bayboro. As these facilities are extensively described above, we need only note here that you would have to be blind to miss them.

Next up is Salt Creek Marina (27 45.348 North/082 38.018 West, 727-821-5482), overlooking the stream's easterly banks. This firm has a huge repair yard, which offers both full-service and do-it-yourself repairs. This is a real rarity in modern-day Florida. Salt Creek features a 50-metric-ton travelift and full mechanical servicing for both diesel and gasoline engines.

Several other repair firms are located on the Salt Creek Marina site, including Maltrop Marine (727-505-0315), featuring diesel-engine

repairs; Advanced Sails (727-896-7245), and Sunshine Marine Canvas (727-455-9070). The list justs seems to go on and on.

A touch farther to the southwest, yet another impressive facility, the St. Petersburg Marine Center (27 45.318 North/082 38.074 West), also guards the southeasterly banks. Here, mariners will discover a wealth of yacht brokerages, including the notable Massey Yacht Sales and Service (727-828-0090). The repair portion of the St. Pete Marine Center features a 40-ton travelfit, but this yard specializes in repairs and renovation of the Bertram brand of power yachts. As the manager put it to this writer, "We are not a typical haul-out yard."

Finally the docks and travelifts of Embree Marine (27 45.297 North/082 38.141 West, 727-896-0671) will come up on the southeastern shores. Again, complete haul-out (30x-ton travelift) and full-service mechanical services are readily available for both power and sail craft. Clearly, diesel work is the forte of the mechanical-repair department here. These good people have been doing their thing since 1947. How's that for longevity? This writer has always found the Embree Marine management especially friendly and ready to go that extra mile to do the job right.

Salt Creek is blocked by a low-level fixed bridge just upstream from Embree Marine. This is the end of the line for all but very small powercraft.

St. Petersburg Municipal Marina and St. Petersburg Yacht Club (Various Lats/Lons—see below)

You may think that you've seen large, city marinas before, but just wait until you lay eyes upon the St. Petersburg Municipal

Marina. Consisting of two large dockage basins bisected by a parklike tongue of land, this facility frequently plays host to more than one thousand transient cruisers annually. All dockage is at modern, fixed, concrete piers featuring recently modern power, water, cable-television, and telephone connections. Entrance depths range widely from as little as 7 to as much as 20 feet. Soundings at the piers run from 20 feet at the outer slips to 7 feet against the concrete seawall. Transient berths are provided in the central yacht basin (the northernmost of the two municipal harbors). One of the staff of dockmasters will direct you upon arrival. Be sure to call ahead of time on VHF Channel 16 for dockage availability and arrival instructions. Advance reservations are not accepted, but even during the season most boats can usually be accommodated. Note that the dockmaster's office, as well as one set of showers and a welcome cruiser's lounge, are located near 27 46.165 North/082 37.802 West, overlooking the south-side harbor's northerly banks.

Gasoline, diesel fuel, and full mechanical repairs (for both diesel and gasoline engines), are available at the adjacent Marina Point Ship's Store-St. Petersburg Yacht Charters, found at the entrance to the central harbor basin (27 46.314 North/082 37.672 West, 727-823-2555). Marina Point features an expansive ship's store set in ultramodern headquarters. We have always been very impressed with the store's many offerings.

Charters of both sail- and powercraft are available as well. Marina Point also provides first-class mobile marine service, including mechanical and sail-craft rigging repairs.

Waste pump-out service is available in the central dockage basin, just beside the public launching ramps. Make arrangements in advance with the dockmaster for this service, as the pump-out station is not regularly manned.

Adequate, air-conditioned showers and a nice Laundromat are found at the dockmaster's building adjacent to the south basin, side by side with a skipper's lounge, featuring a color television (provided by local cruisers). Other, non-climate-controlled shower buildings are spread about the marina's extensive grounds.

The beautifully restored St. Petersburg downtown section is but a short step away from the municipal piers. Among other attractions, visitors might consider the Bayfront Center and Al Lang Stadium, both quite visible from the south dockage basin. All in all, it's unlikely that you will exhaust the list of things to do, see, and places to dine while docked along the St. Petersburg waterfront.

Downtown St. Petersburg can now lay claim to many more dining attractions than in years past. We only have space to mention three restaurants that are worthy of any cruiser's attention and within an easy step of the municipal marina, the St. Petersburg Yacht Club (see below), and the Renaissance Vinoy Resort Marina (see below). The Moon Under Water (332 Beach Drive, 727-896-6160) is housed in an extremely attractive building overlooking the water. It features an English-style menu, including some notable curry dishes. Indoor and outdoor seating is available. Midtown Sundries (200 First Avenue S, 727-502-0222) has a mixed menu and a sports-bar feel, but it's not too noisy. There are separate no-smoking areas, pool tables, and, most importantly, good food at moderate prices. Finally, Tangelo's Grill (226 First

Avenue N, 727-894-1695) serves outstanding Cuban-style cuisine. The streetside seating is our personal favorite.

So, you prefer to cook up the evening meal in your own galley? Well, downtown St. Petersburg is ready for you too. While you will need to take a taxi to access a full supermarket, don't overlook the Marketplace Express (284 Beach Drive NE, 727-894-3330) gourmet market and deli. Located near the Moon Under Water restaurant, and within walking distance of all the St. Pete waterfront marinas, this is a real find!

To be sure, there are many other places to eat, things to see, and places to go in the downtown St. Petersburg business district. Many more attractions are just a short taxi ride away.

St. Petersburg Municipal Marina (727) 893-7329
(800) 782-8350
http://www.stpete.org/marina.htm

Approach depth—7-20 feet
Dockside depth—7-20 feet
Accepts transients—yes (extensive)
Transient dockage rate—below average
Fixed concrete piers—yes
Dockside power connections—up to 50 amp
Dockside water connections—yes
Waste pump-out—yes
Showers—yes
Laundromat—yes
Gasoline—yes (Marina Point Ship's Store)
Diesel fuel—yes (Marina Point Ship's Store)

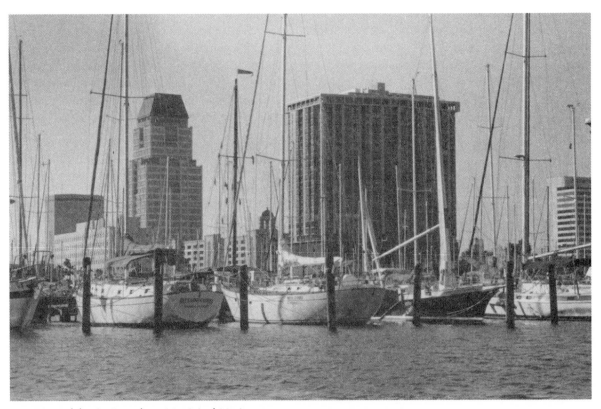

A portion of the St. Petersburg Municipal Marina

Scale 1:20

1. Embree Marine
2. St. Petersburg Marine Center
3. Salt Creek Marina
4. Sailor's Wharf Yacht Yard
5. Progressive Boat Yard
6. The Harborage at Bayboro
7. St. Petersburg Municipal Marina
8. Marina Point Ship's Store /
   St. Petersburg Yacht Centers
9. Renaissance Vinoy Resort Marina
10. St. Petersburg Yacht Club

Mechanical repairs—yes (Marina Point Ship's Store)
Ship's store—yes (Marina Point Ship's Store)
Restaurant—several nearby

Now, just in case you are not quite motivated to check out the municipal dockage basin, let it be known that this harbor is also home to the prestigious St. Petersburg Yacht Club (27 46.290 North/082 37.898 West). This organization maintains its piers in the southwestern corner of the central dockage basin. Cruisers entering the central harbor can quickly identify the docks by the "SPYC" sign at the eastern end of the club's piers. Members of other yacht clubs with reciprocal privileges are accepted for overnight or temporary dockage at fixed piers with power and water connections. Advance reservations with the club dockmaster are required. He (or she) is on duty from 8:30 A.M. to 5:00 P.M., seven days a week. Gasoline and diesel fuel can be purchased, when the dockmaster is on duty, by members and accredited guests only! Showers are also available "on the dock."

St. Petersburg Yacht Club is known as one of the most prestigious organizations of its ilk in the world. Its tres elegant clubhouse overlooks the docks from across the street to the west. Here guests will find full dining services in both formal and informal settings. Bicycles are also available from the yacht club, which certainly facilitates a cycle tour of downtown St. Petersburg. As is true with the city marina, all of downtown St. Petersburg's charms and the Pier are but moments away.

St. Petersburg Yacht Club (727) 822-3873
http://www.spyc.org

Approach depth—7-20 feet
Dockside depth—8-16 feet

Accepts transients—members of clubs with reciprocal privileges (advance reservations required)
Fixed piers—yes
Dockside power connections—yes
Dockside water connections—yes
Showers—yes
Gasoline—yes (members and club guests only)
Diesel fuel—yes (members and club guests only)
Restaurant—on site

The Pier

One of the most exciting attractions on the St. Petersburg waterfront is the retail and dining complex known, appropriately enough, as "the Pier." Look at the inset on chart 11413 for a moment and notice the label "Municipal Pier" north of the city marina. The long finger of land extending to the east serves as means

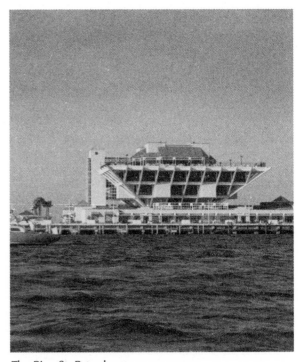

The Pier, St. Petersburg

of access to what will appear from the water to be a huge, inverted pyramid.

It's a long walk from the mainland to the Pier, but trams run regularly from the shoreside parking lot to the outer building for those who are weary of foot. Even before beginning your journey out to the Pier, there is an attraction you should not miss. The St. Petersburg Historical Museum (727-894-1052) guards the northern side of the Pier's entrance. This most worthwhile attraction is open Monday through Saturday, 10:00 A.M. to 5:00 P.M. and on Sundays from 1:00 P.M. to 5:00 P.M.

The Pier's main building, the aforementioned inverted pyramid, contains an incredible collection of retail and gift shops, restaurants, and even an aquarium. This latter attraction features a wide variety of tropical and saltwater fish in large, glass tanks. A visit is almost mandatory.

To visit the Pier, dock at either the St. Petersburg Municipal Marina or the yacht club and walk over. While the Pier was originally designed to have boats dock directly against its sides, this practice has very much fallen out of use, possibly due to the strong winds and wicked waves that sometimes batter the docks. Sea gulls and pelicans seem to be the only current dockside residents.

North Yacht Basin Anchorage and Renaissance Vinoy Resort Marina (27 46.648 North/082 37.735 West)

Refer to the inset on chart 11413 yet again and notice the deep basin north of the Pier, designated as "North Yacht Basin." Most locals call this harbor the Vinoy Basin. Besides making for a wonderfully sheltered overnight anchorage, these waters also play host to one of St. Peterburg's most prestigious marina facility.

The harbor derives its local name from the pink, stuccoed Renaissance Vinoy Resort Hotel which overlooks the northwestern corner of the cove and is noted on 11413 as "Hotel Cupola." This venerably hostelry has been magnificently restored and is now one of the great showplaces in St. Petersburg. If you want to really blow the old wallet, try spending a night or two (that's all most of us could afford) in this unforgettable hotel. I can't think of a better way to take a break from the live-aboard routine.

Along with the Vinoy's renovation a decade ago, a full-service pleasure-craft facility, the sumptuous Renaissance Vinoy Resort Marina, was constructed on the adjoining banks of the basin. Besides offering just about any service you might ever require (except repairs), visiting cruisers can be readily assured of an unusually warm and knowledgeable welcome, somewhat unusual for a marina of this size. Transients are cheerfully accepted at the ultramodern concrete decked floating docks, which feature every conceivable water, power (including some 100-amp hookups), and telephone connection. First-class showers and dry-cleaning/laundry services are available across the street in the resort hotel. Mechanical repairs can be arranged, by the dockmaster or his accommodating staff, with a nearby independent service firm.

Visiting cruisers are given full resort privileges at the Vinoy. These services include access to the health club, with sauna, steam room, and spa with two hot tubs, as well as an on-site swimming pool. Complimentary transportation is provided to an 18-hole golf course a scant one mile away, where visitors may also make use of a clubhouse and a second swimming pool. Still not enough for you?

Well, how about 12 clay-surfaced tennis courts within walking distance of the docks and free ice for all nautical visitors?

Within the elegant arms of the Vinoy Resort, visitors will find five wonderful restaurants. The Terrace Room and Marchand's Bar and Grill specialize in luscious Mediterranean cuisine. Give them a try, but check the price lists first.

As you might have already discerned, transient dockage rates at this sumptuous facility are above average (but *not* ridiculously so). This time, the extra cash may well be worth shelling out!

Renaissance Vinoy Resort Marina
    (727) 824-8022
    http://www.renaissancehotels.com

Approach depth—9-11 feet
Dockside depth—11 feet
Accepts transients—yes
Transient dockage rate—above average
Floating concrete docks—yes
Dockside power connections—up to 100 amp
Dockside water connections—yes
Showers—yes (across street in resort)
Dry-cleaning/laundry service—yes (across street in resort)
Mechanical repairs—independent technicians
Restaurant—five on site and others nearby

Anchorage is still allowed in the Vinoy

Renaissance Vinoy Resort Marina, St. Petersburg

Basin for stays up to one week in duration. After 24 hours, visiting cruisers are required to check in with the dockmaster at the St. Petersburg Municipal Marina. Protection is excellent from all winds save easterly breezes over 20 knots, which would blow directly into the harbor. Even in this circumstance, you could favor the southern shores for some protection.

One good spot to drop the hook will be found near 27 46.538 North/082 37.765 West. Here cruisers can anchor amidst 9-foot minimum depths with tons of swinging room.

The surrounding shores are mostly comprised of a delightful waterside park, with St. Petersburg's usual lush Bermuda grass very much in evidence. This is certainly a great spot to spend an evening or two in pleasant surroundings, just where you might least expect to find such a haven. Of course, you must expect some lights and traffic noise from the main road to the west.

Coffeepot Bayou

If my boat drew no more than 4½ feet, you would find me anchored in Coffeepot Bayou whenever I was in the St. Petersburg region and wanted to spend a night away from the marina docks. This fortunate stream is found north of Vinoy Basin (northwest of flashing buoy #1). Its entrance channel only carries 5 feet of water at MLW, but depths improve considerably on the interior reaches. First-timers should be sure to check out our navigational account of Coffeepot Bayou (below) before attempting entry. The channel can be a bit confusing.

Study chart 11413 for a moment, and notice that a deep offshoot makes off to the north, just short of Coffeepot Bayou's easterly entrance. It's a relatively simple matter to maintain minimum 6-foot depths and cruise

into the interior reaches of this fortunate stream. There, you can anchor near 27 47.494 North/082 37.050 West in a good 10 feet of water. There should be enough elbowroom for a 38-footer. The surrounding shores are guarded by incredibly heavy but elegant residential development.

The channel leading through the entrance to Coffeepot Bayou leads on to the west-northwest. As you pass through the entrance, an absolutely gorgeous home overlooks the northeasterly point, and the houses to the south aren't too shabby either.

Entrance depths on this portion of the channel run between 5½ and 8 feet, with most soundings being on the deeper end of that range. Soon the bayou opens out into a bay-like region, which just begs you to drop the hook. Notice on chart 11413 that a small island is found amidst this wider portion of the stream and the 6-foot fixed bridge. Stay away from this landmass. Between the island and the bridge, captains can anchor in 5½ to 6 feet of water with superb protection from all winds (near 27 47.487 North/082 37.521 West). There is ample room for a 50-footer. It doesn't get much better than this, gang, so put a red circle around Coffeepot Bayou.

Smacks Bayou

The crescent-shaped channel leading to Smacks Bayou makes into Tampa Bay's westerly flank north-northwest of flashing buoy #1, north of Coffeepot Bayou. This sidewater boasts several excellent overnight stops, though it cannot lay claim to the aesthetic qualities of its sister to the south.

The entrance cut is outlined by small, privately maintained (unlighted) daybeacons and carries a good 6 to 7 feet of water. The bayou itself soon splits into two branches. The southerly tier, charted as Snell Island Harbor, eventually leads to a lakelike body of water that is surrounded by very dense residential development.

Captains piloting larger vessels might consider anchoring at the intersection of the northern and southern branches of Smacks Bayou, near 27 47.954 North/082 36.445 West. Good 10+-foot soundings are complemented by enough elbowroom for a 40-footer. There is super shelter from all but fresh southeasterly winds, as is true with all the other havens on Smack Bayou's northerly arm.

Continuing upstream on the northerly branch, you might also consider setting the hook abeam of the small, correctly charted, 6-foot offshoot that cuts to the southwest, near 27 48.030 North/082 36.509 West. Here, mariners will discover impressive soundings of 8 feet or better and room enough for vessels as large as 30 feet.

Skippers whose vessels are 32 feet or (preferably) a bit smaller can also anchor just south of the 11-foot fixed bridge, near 27 48.109 North/082 36.529 West. While this spot is most certainly narrower than its sisters to the south are, there is good protection.

So, you're looking for a foul-weather hidey-hole? Well, look no farther than the southern tier of Smacks Bayou. As alluded to above, the entrance canal soon leads to an almost-enclosed bay, charted as "Snell Island Harbor." Anyone dropping anchor anywhere near the mid-width of this body of water (27 47.692 North/082 36.558 West) will find themselves and their vessels almost totally protected from all winds. Of course, the surrounding banks are flanked by heavy residential development, and there is nary a possibility of dinghying ashore.

Bayou Grande

The marked but indifferently charted channel leading to the interior reaches of Bayou Grande strikes to the west, west of flashing buoy #15J. This aid is found on the charted "Cut J-2 Channel." While the initial passage into Bayou Grande holds minimum depths of 6 feet, soundings quickly rise to the 4- to 4½-foot region as the channel flows into the interior portion of the bayou. There is really not enough room to anchor in the deeper section of the passage. Considering these less-than-desirable characteristics, most cruising captains would be wise to forego exploration of this sidewater.

LOWER TAMPA BAY—WESTERN SHORE NAVIGATION

Navigation on any portion of Tampa Bay cannot be taken for granted. This is a large body of water, and captains used to the more protected confines of the ICW can find the breadth daunting and occasionally downright dangerous. Always plan your cruise on Tampa Bay with an ear to the latest NOAA weather forecasts. With winds above 10 knots, be prepared for chop. If the forecast calls for breezes blowing 25 knots or more, it would be far wiser to stay at the dock and play a few more rounds of checkers.

Successful navigation of lower Tampa Bay's western shoreline is facilitated by the presence of a deep, well-marked channel paralleling the banks. While it is certainly possible for skippers to follow the big ship's channel up the bay, this passage favors the easterly shoreline. Almost all cruisers will want to choose the westerly route. It is convenient to all the various side trips on this portion of the bay, including St. Petersburg's excellent marine facilities.

Note that some of the marked channels leading to the various sidewaters and anchorages off this portion of Tampa Bay can be confusing, particularly for first-timers. This potential difficulty is mostly the result of side channels entering the main passage and either having uncharted markers or being uncharted entirely. It is an all-too-simple process to mistake the aids to navigation on one of these alternate cuts for those on the primary passage. Read the info below carefully to minimize this possibility.

Approaches to the Western Shore
Captains northbound on the Western Florida ICW or those entering from the open Gulf via any of the bay's three entrance cuts will find it convenient to follow the Waterway's official passage through the central span of the Sunshine Skyway bridge. This route was reviewed in the last section of this chapter.

Cut north between flashing buoys #3B and #6B and follow the ICW until you pass between flashing daybeacon #4 and unlighted daybeacon #3. At this point the Waterway route turns sharply to the west, but, to reach the various ports of call along the western shore (except Little Bayou and the Annapolis Sailing School), continue due north, pointing to pass between flashing daybeacon #6 and unlighted can buoy #5.

Conversely, southbound ICW skippers (and northbound cruisers making for the Holiday Inn/Annapolis Sailing School marina or the adjacent anchorage on Little

Bayou) should follow the Waterway to the intersection with the Sunshine Skyway Channel, south of Indian Key at flashing daybeacon #26. You can then turn east and pass north of unlighted daybeacon #13A on your way to 65-foot twin fixed bridges. Once through the span, set course to come abeam of unlighted daybeacon #13 to its northerly quarter. As you approach #13, you will most likely spy a sign advertising the "Holiday Inn Marina Beach Resort." From this marker, skippers may choose to cruise north to this facility or anchor in the lee of the Sunshine Skyway Causeway.

Holiday Inn/Annapolis Sailing School Marina and Sunshine Skyway Anchorage
For best depths continue to follow the Waterway channel east past unlighted daybeacon #13 for 100 yards or so. Then, turn back sharply to the northwest and set course for the water tank-shaped basin at the northwesterly corner of the cove. If you choose to visit the marina, watch for a single unlighted red daybeacon at the entrance. Take this aid to your starboard side, as you would expect from the "red, right, returning" rule. This maneuver will run you hard by the port-side banks, but, believe it or else, this is where the best depths are located. A shoal has built across a goodly portion of the basin's entrance to the east (starboard side).

Those who decide to anchor off in the shelter of the causeway leading to the Sunshine Skyway can drop the hook at any convenient spot short of the marina basin. Good depths run to within 50 yards of shore. Remember, this anchorage is only sheltered in westerly winds and could be a real bear when breezes are blowing from any other direction.

On to Point Pinellas If your destination is found elsewhere on the western shoreline, continue following the well-outlined Waterway channel to the east. Review the preceding section of this chapter outlining the ICW route across Tampa Bay for more details. As you come abeam of flashing daybeacon #6 to its southerly side (south of Point Pinellas), the western shoreline's first good sidewater opportunity beckons to the north.

Little Bayou North of the gap between unlighted day beacon #3 and flashing daybeacon #4, two channels veer in toward Tampa Bay's westerly shoreline. The shorter, southerly cut leads only to a public launching ramp and is of little use to cruising craft.

The northerly passage follows a track covering some 1.4 nautical miles from the ICW to the mouth of Little Bayou. As you are traversing this portion of the channel be ready to discover different aids to navigation than those pictured on chart 11414. During our last visit, we found a new unlighted daybeacon #9. Whatever aids you find, just keep red markers to your starboard side and green beacons to port in the usual pattern. North of unlighted daybeacon #12, watch for unlighted junction daybeacon #A. A series of charted markers leads east from #A and are part of a mostly uncharted channel that hugs the western banks and strikes north to Big Bayou. We specifically recommend against making use of this side cut for cruising-size craft. While it may be fine for local outboarders,

those of us with deeper-draft vessels are all to likely to find the bottom.

The main Little Bayou passage cuts to the northwest from #A. This channel will take you hard by a concrete seawall to starboard and a small mangrove to port. Continue favoring the easterly shoreline as you work your way into the interior reaches of Little Bayou, just as the markers indicate. Be sure to stay east of unlighted daybeacons #17, #19, and #21. Even though chart 11411 shows a sounding of 6 feet west of #17, we recently encountered only 3 feet of water while trying to ease our way west from #17. Either the charted deep water in the middle of the cove has shoaled in, or there is a shallow, uncharted bar between the main channel and these deeper soundings. In any case, smart navigators will keep to the east side of Little Bayou.

Continue following the markers until you come abeam of unlighted daybeacon #17. You can then ease your way to the west ever so slightly and anchor between #17 and #19. As noted above, mariners who venture too far to the west in pursuit of this anchorage will most likely find the bottom.

Good depths continue on the Little Bayou channel to a point southeast of unlighted daybeacon #21. These waters provide another possible anchorage.

All but very small, outboard-powered boats should discontinue their explorations of Little Bayou at #21. Farther upstream, the waters narrow and a fixed bridge with only 9 feet of vertical clearance blocks the passage.

As you prepare to leave Little Bayou, be sure to retrace your steps to the south. The seemingly inviting waters of Tampa Bay to the east are shoal, with depths of as little as 2 feet.

On the Western Shore Channel   To reach the main western shore channel serving lower Tampa Bay, cruise due east for another .2 nautical miles after passing flashing daybeacon #1 (27 41.750 North/ 082 36.834 West). Watch to the south for unlighted daybeacon #3 and flashing daybeacon #4. As these aids come abeam to starboard, swing to the north and point to pass between flashing daybeacon #6 and unlighted can buoy #5. The southerly and northerly approaches join at this point and we need only concern ourselves with a single, well-marked channel as we work our way to the north along the western shoreline.

From a position between #5 and #6, the channel runs almost due north. While the track is well outlined, the various aids to navigation are rather widely placed. It might be a good idea to run compass/GPS courses, particularly as you approach unlighted can buoy #7. Some shoal water is found to the west along this stretch of the channel.

Eventually, navigators will pass to the east of flashing daybeacon #9 and shortly thereafter find themselves abeam of unlighted nun buoy #10 to its westerly side. While the straight course to St. Petersburg's primary marine facilities runs due north from #10, there is a questionable anchorage to the west.

Big Bayou   Please remember that Big Bayou is not the most easily navigated of Tampa Bay's western shore sidewaters. Only experienced captains with a sense of adventure should attempt to drop the hook on this stream.

There are actually two causes for navigational concern on the Big Bayou channel. First, there is yet another side channel, this one making off to the south from unlighted junction daybeacon #B. Some of the aids to navigation outlining this cut are charted, and some are not. Once again, we advise cruising captains to avoid this alternate cut.

The second cause for concern is far more basic. We don't know who placed the markers on the interior reaches of Little Bayou, but some run mariners hard by the correctly charted 1- and 2-foot shoals. Look at chart 11414 and note the 2-foot waters just northwest of unlighted daybeacon #16 and the 1-foot soundings west of #17. There doesn't seem to be much rhyme or reason to all of this. So, we strongly suggest that captains piloting cruising-size craft confine their explorations or anchorage to the waters northeast of unlighted daybeacon #16.

Those who choose to enter Big Bayou should continue on the main channel for some .4 nautical miles north of unlighted nun buoy #10. Then, turn 90 degrees to the west and use your binoculars to pick out the easternmost aids of the Big Bayou channel, unlighted daybeacons #1 and #2, as you cruise toward the stream's mouth.

Past this point, this writer would not begin to try and describe all the channel's twists and turns. Simply pass all red beacons to your starboard side and take green to port as usual and hope for the best. The best place to drop the hook is found southwest of unlighted daybeacon #14.

Only small craft drawing less than 4 feet

should attempt to follow the Big Bayou Channel past unlighted daybeacon #16. Depths become much more uncertain farther to the southwest on the way to the previously mentioned public launching ramp.

On the Western Shore Channel   North of unlighted nun buoy #10, it's a straightforward run to flashing daybeacon #S. Switch to the St. Petersburg inset section of chart 11413 for navigation on these waters. To the west, Bayboro Harbor Channel and Salt Creek offer the first of St. Petersburg's myriad marina facilities.

Bayboro Harbor and Salt Creek   It doesn't get much simpler than this cut. If you run aground here, better break out the old Chapman's and have a refresher course in basic coastal navigation. Come abeam of flashing daybeacon #S to its westerly side and turn almost due west into the Bayboro Harbor entrance channel. As you come abeam of flashing daybeacon #10, look north and you will spot the St. Petersburg Coast Guard station.

West of #10, powercraft should proceed at no-wake speed. Soon you will sight the huge dockage complex of the Harborage at Bayboro dead ahead. Enter this facility by cruising around to the northern side of the harbor.

Enter Salt Creek on its mid-width and, for best depths, continue on the centerline as you work your way upstream toward the low-level fixed bridge.

St. Petersburg Municipal Marina   Again, the channels to the St. Petersburg Municipal Marina and St. Petersburg Yacht Club are deep and obvious. From flashing daybeacon #S continue cruising north by passing well to the west of flashing buoy #3. Watch the western banks for twin stone breakwaters. As the gap between these two barriers comes abeam to the west, cut in straight toward this entrance and pass through its mid-width. Be on guard against the charted spoil area to the south, running northeast then south from Albert Whitted Airport.

Both ends of the breakwaters flanking the marina's entrance are delineated by flashing aids. These are fixed to the jetties themselves and should be avoided. While this is obvious during daylight, it's good to know for nighttime entries.

Once past the breakwater, simply follow the docking instructions you should have already received over your VHF from the municipal dockmaster's office. For best depths, stay away from the banks west of the entrance. Some shoal water runs out from this shoreline. Turn either north or south and head for your assigned slip.

Marina Point Ship's Store and fuel dock are found at the entrance to the central basin. The docks belonging to St. Petersburg Yacht Club are also found in this harbor's southwesterly corner.

North Yacht Basin and Anchorage   While the entrance to North Yacht (or Vinoy) Basin is mostly unmarked, it's still relatively easy to enter. Cruise north past the easterly limits of the Pier and watch to the west for the basin's entrance. As it comes abeam, cut sharply west, pointing to avoid the charted shoals immediately north of the entrance. A

354 CRUISING GUIDE TO WESTERN FLORIDA

sign at the bay's mouth warns powerboats to proceed at idle, no-wake speed.

As you cruise through the entrance to Vinoy Basin, watch for uncharted and unlighted daybeacons #2 and #4. Gee, to what side should we pass these markers? Could it be our starboard side, since we are "returning"?

Once past the entrance, simply select a likely spot anywhere near the mid-width and drop the hook. The pink-stuccoed Renaissance Vinoy Resort Hotel and its marina will be readily visible to the northwest.

North along the Western Shore   From a position to the west of flashing buoy #3, east of the St. Petersburg Municipal Marina basin, consider setting a course to come abeam of flashing buoy #1, east-southeast of Coffeepot Bayou, to its western side. Both Coffeepot and Smacks bayous can be accessed from this aid.

Coffeepot Bayou   To enter Coffeepot Bayou from Tampa Bay, set course to the west-northwest from flashing buoy #1. Use your binoculars to pick out the easternmost pair of small, privately maintained unlighted daybeacons marking the stream's mouth. Cruise between the various aids and do not wander from the marked passage.

Watch for the sharp northeasterly entrance point, which is shown on chart 11413 as an almost-island, joined to the mainland by a narrow neck. At this point, some uncharted markers break off to the east and outline the charted deep water running along the banks north to Smacks

Bayou. While we don't recommend following this cut all the way to Smacks, you might choose to enter the previously described offshoot making off to the north (just east of the "almost-island") and anchor. To access this haven, cut to the northeast. Favor the northerly and northwesterly banks heavily as you work your way into the offshoot. Cruise into the stream's mid-width and anchor anywhere along its mid-line, short of the correctly charted turn to the northwest.

Cruisers continuing on to the inner section of Coffeepot Bayou will soon enter a wide bay, where you will spot the charted marsh island to the northwest. Pass this body of land to your starboard side. Depths fall off to the 5- to 5½-foot region as you pass the small island, but improve to 6-foot soundings a bit farther upstream. Consider dropping the hook some 50 to 100 yards after passing the small island. Farther upstream, passage is barred by a 6-foot fixed bridge.

Smacks Bayou   Successful navigation of Smacks Bayou calls for a traversal of the crescent-shaped channel rounding the hook-shaped point east of Snell Island Harbor. From flashing buoy #1, set a compass course for the charted, easternmost entrance channel aids, unlighted daybeacons #1 and #2. Be sure to avoid the charted fish haven, which you will pass just north of your course.

Follow the various other uncharted marks past #1 and #2 as they curve to the north and eventually cut to the west at the stream's mouth. Remember "red, right, returning," and you should not have any undue difficulty. As you enter the stream, favor the south-side banks slightly.

Shortly after entering the mouth of Smacks Bayou, the stream splits. This is a no-wake zone, and all boats should proceed at idle speed during their explorations of the stream. Larger craft can anchor at the intersection of the two branches in good water.

If you need better shelter, turn south and follow the mid-width of the deep stream into the charted lake known as Snell Island Harbor. Favor the western shores slightly as you enter the lake to avoid the charted underwater wreck. Anchor anywhere you choose. Good water runs to within 100 yards (or sometimes closer) of the banks.

Captains might also choose to continue upstream on Smacks Bayou and anchor either abeam of the charted 6-foot cove running to the southwest or short of the 11-foot fixed bridge. In either case, stay anywhere within shouting distance of the mid-section, and all should be well.

On to Old Tampa Bay Northeast of flashing buoy #1, cruisers should probably rejoin the large ship's channel leading into Old Tampa Bay at flashing buoy #10J. It's a fairly lengthy run of 1.8 nautical miles between #1 and #10J. Use your GPS and/or compass, and watch for excessive leeway.

From #10J, you can follow the Cut G big ship's channel to the east, or turn north for Old Tampa Bay. This latter route will be reviewed later in this chapter.

Those few brave souls who should decide to visit Bayou Grande will find its entrance channel west of flashing buoy #15J, north of #10J. All I can say is, good luck!

Lower Tampa Bay—Eastern Shore

The eastern banks of lower Tampa Bay could not show a greater contrast to their westerly counterpart. For one thing, while deep water often runs almost up to the west-side banks, a considerable shelf of shoal water extends out for a goodly distance from the eastern shores. To reach the various sidewaters along the coast, cruisers usually must traverse dredged channels.

Perhaps even more disparate is the amount of development on this region of Tampa Bay. Large sections of all-natural shoreline are interspaced with small coastal developments backed by tiny towns and villages.

There are several marinas that serve transients, but it is often a long run between stops. Similarly, while you can certainly find some of the most enchanting overnight anchorages available anywhere, these refuges could not exactly be described as numerous.

In spite of these seemingly less-than-ideal characteristics, this writer could not help but like this coastline. The lack of heavy development and the opportunity to drop the hook in an isolated haven, often within a few hour's sail of St. Petersburg, are qualities which should not be dismissed out of hand. I recommend you give lower Tampa Bay's eastern shores a try. Captains and crew who treasure a bit of seclusion now and then may just discover this to be their favorite cruising grounds on Tampa Bay.

Terra Ceia Bay and Anchorage (Various Lats/Lons—see below)

The channel leading from Tampa Bay to Terra Ceia Bay lies east of flashing daybeacon #TC (itself northwest of Snead Island). The marked entrance cut exhibits minimum depths of 5½ to 6 feet, but a navigational error could stick the unfortunate cruiser in 3-foot soundings.

While the main entrance to Terra Ceia Bay, outlined above, makes off from Tampa Bay just north of the Manatee River's westerly mouth, there is, as we learned earlier in this chapter, also a passage directly from the Manatee River, near Bradenton Yacht Club. This small stream is, unfortunately, crossed by a 13-foot fixed bridge and most cruising-size craft must gain access to Terra by the main channel making in directly from Tampa Bay.

Immediately north of the 13-foot fixed bridge, one repair yard, a huge trawler dealer, and a small marina offer some services for cruising craft. Cut's Edge Harbor Marina, in particular, seems to be popular with the do-it-yourself crowd.

The principal Terra Ceia entrance channel is marked but, to be frank, additional beacons would be a welcome improvement. Be sure to read the navigational data on Terra Ceia presented later in this chapter before attempting to visit the bay.

Chief among Terra Ceia Bay's attractions are its generally undeveloped character and the possibility for secluded overnight anchorage. The banks support only a few homes and some portions of the shoreline are well wooded. It can be a very special treat to drop the hook where you are likely to be the only pleasure craft within sight. None of these overnight havens is well sheltered, however. Be sure to keep the weather forecast in mind.

The main body of Terra Ceia Bay is actually far larger than it would appear from a cursory study of chart 11414. Anchoring on the bay's deep mid-width is not a practical possibility except in almost windless conditions. Fortunately, there are at least three more sheltered havens to consider.

The first spot where you might drop the hook is found along the band of deep water south of unlighted daybeacon #9 (near 27 32.644 North/082 36.975 West). Minimum depths of 5½ feet can be carried to within 250 yards of the southerly banks. While there is some protection from southerly and northerly winds, this spot is clearly a good-weather anchorage. Blows of as much as 10 knots from the east or west would make for a very bouncy evening. The surrounding shores are almost completely in their natural state, and a real treat for the eyes. In short, this is a beautiful anchorage with plenty of swinging room. In good weather, with no strong breezes forecast, this is probably the spot that I would choose on Terra Ceia. But wait—there are more sheltered havens on the main portion of the bay.

In northerly (or light to moderate southerly) winds, skippers of most sizes of pleasure craft may well consider dropping the hook on the tongue of deep water north-northeast of Bird Key (north of unlighted daybeacon #13 and near 27 33.403 North/082 35.766 West). Moving west from Beville Point to a point where you are just short of coming abeam of

Bird Key to the south, 5½-foot minimum depths can be held to within 200 yards of the northerly banks. A few homes peep out amidst the tall trees overlooking this shoreline, but these serve to add to the anchorage's appeal, rather than detract from its character.

Finally, for those willing to make a somewhat lengthy trek from Tampa Bay, you can drop anchor on the extreme northwesterly corner of Terra Ceia Bay, short of the charted sunken wreck (near 27 34.004 North/082 34.442 West). Depths of 6 to 8 feet can be held to within 150 yards of the lightly developed banks, and there is fair to good shelter from all winds save southerly breezes. This is the most sheltered refuge on the bay, and it has plenty of elbowroom for a 50-footer.

Turning our attention to the pleasure-craft facilities of southern Terra Ceia Bay, first up is Cut's Edge Harbor Marina (27 31.461 North/082 36.452 West, 941-729-4878). The channel leading to Cut's Edge strikes off to the east, south of unlighted daybeacon #4. Eventually, the passage hooks back around to the west and enters the charted lagoon-shaped body of water almost due south of #4. The harbor is well sheltered but virtually all of the available wet-slip dockage is rented out strictly on a month-to-month basis. Low-water entrance and dockside depths of as little as 4½ feet could be a problem for especially long-legged vessels.

Clearly the forte at Cut's Edge is service work. Boats are hauled out by way of a 40-ton travelift, and full mechanical repairs for both gasoline and diesel engines are offered as well. There is some do-it-yourself work allowed.

While it will never live up to the class of a Snead Island Boat Works, Cut's Edge is clearly popular, as evidenced by the large number of hauled craft we have witnessed during our several visits. So, if you are up for a somewhat offbeat yard, don't fail to give Cut's Edge your consideration.

The face piers and protected harbor of Marlow Marine Sales (941-729-3370) line the charted canal's western flank, south of unlighted daybeacon #4. This firm is a huge trawler dealership. Cruisers will undoubtedly note any number of impressive Grand Banks and other trawlers while passing by. You may also observe several large work barns and other repair facilities. However, my discussion with this facility's management strongly suggests that service work is now confined to vessels sold or awaiting sale at Marlow Marine.

Lastly, low-key Marsh Harbor Marina (941-723-5067) guards the canal's westerly banks immediately north of the 13-foot fixed bridge. We have never found anyone to talk with here save fellow boat owners. It seems as if Marsh Harbor is pretty much relegated to those docking here on a more or less regular basis. During an earlier visit, a fellow captain informed us that the "owner has been gone for three days." Clearly, there's not much in the way of services for visitors at Marsh Harbor.

Bishop Harbor

Bishop Harbor is a rather controversial body of water lying between the Sunshine Skyway and the Port Manatee Channel. Another well-respected guide to anchorages and stops along Western Florida's coastline highly recommends the harbor. Indeed, one of this writer's good friends, who once called Tampa Bay his home waters, asserts that he prefers this anchorage over any other along the bay.

However, despite these rave reviews, all captains should know that the entrance channel is narrow, winding, unmarked, and surrounded by water running as shallow as ½ foot. I think it not only possible, but likely, that any cruising craft visiting Bishop Harbor for the first, second, or possibly even the third time is going to run aground.

So, if you want to visit Bishop Harbor for its natural beauty, fine—but you will have to do it without my help. In spite of all the sentiment to the contrary, this writer recommends that you pass by and continue cruising on to Bahia Beach.

Port Manatee Channel

The deep, well-marked cut leading to Port Manatee breaks off from the main Tampa Bay big ship's channel between flashing buoys #6B and #8B. This channel serves the large commercial vessels which frequently visit the commercial center at Port Manatee. The shipping of phosphate and other agricultural chemicals are a primary concern at this complex. There are no services or anchorage possibilities for pleasure craft, and most cruisers will only want to give a quick wave as they pass.

Little Manatee River (Various Lats/Lons—see below)

The Little Manatee River, just south of Bahia Beach and Mangrove Point, is named, like its bigger sister to the south, for the gentle manatee, or sea cow. The creature's name is apparently derived from a Spanish word that refers to the handlike use of the sea cow's front flippers.

I don't like to make anyone cross with me, but that's what I'm about to do with the marina owners and those mariners who call the Little Manatee River home. The Little Manatee entrance channel has never, ever been a piece of cake, but now, it's even harder to find. The primary charted cut coming in from Tampa Bay, marked by unlighted daybeacon #3, has apparently disappeared entirely, or at least, we couldn't find it. And, by the way, #3 is just not there anymore. The only route we could find into the river's interior reaches involved making use of the channel cutting from the Bahia Beach Island Resort's (see below) fishing pier south to Bahia Del Sol Marina (now renamed Mariner's Club) and then abandoning this cut and trying to follow some very nondescript markers ranging off to the south and east into the interior reaches of Little Manatee River. Yet, when we got to Shell Point Marina (see below) we observed any number of large craft there, including fixed-keel sailboats. Obviously these people know the channel intimately. However, this will not be the case with visiting cruisers, and despite the wrath of the Little Manatee River locals, we suggest that you look elsewhere for dockage or an overnight anchorage. For those who choose to ignore this advice, we will present a quick account of what we found on Little Manatee River during August 2003.

Despite these navigational difficulties, Little Manatee River is known as one of the most unspoiled bodies of water on Tampa Bay. Writing in Del and Marty Marth's *The Rivers of Florida*, Greg Lamm comments, "The area is considered the most important nursery ground for marine life in the bay. River marsh and uplands provide habitats for a number of endangered species, including the American bald eagle." Unfortunately, cruising reality intruded and has led this writer to believe

Little Manatee would be a difficult gunk hole for most cruising-size craft.

Shell Point Marina (27 43.118 North/082 28.755 West) overlooks the river's northern banks between the 6- and 7-foot soundings noted on chart 11414, well north of Whiskey Key. This facility keeps 2 or 3 slips open for transients with freshwater hookups and modern 30-amp power connections. Dockage is mostly found at fixed, wooden piers, though there is also one floating wooden dock as well. One shower is located on the marina

1. Shell Point Marina
2. Mariner's Club
3. Bahia Beach Island Resort and Marina
4. Bahia Beach Marina

grounds. Complete mechanical repair services are offered and haul-outs are accomplished by a 25-ton travelift. Extensive outside dry-stack storage is available for smaller power-craft, as is a well-stocked ship's store, featuring full electronics sales and services. Dockside depths are in the 6- to 8-foot region.

Recently, a restaurant known as Katt's on the River has opened within a very few steps of the marina docks. Screened-porch dining is available in the main building, and a semi-open-air bar overlooks the river. We did not have a chance to dine here.

> **Shell Point Marina (813) 645-1313**
> **http://www.shellpointmarina.com**
>
> **Approach depth—4½-6 feet**
> **Dockside depth—6-8 feet**
> **Accepts transients—yes (2 or 3 slips usually open)**
> **Transient dockage rate—below average**
> **Fixed wooden piers—yes**
> **Dockside power connections—up to 30 amp**
> **Dockside water connections—yes**
> **Showers—outside only**
> **Mechanical repairs—yes**
> **Below-waterline repairs—yes**
> **Ship's store—yes**
> **Restaurant—on site**

Skippers can also feel their way carefully to the south, off the main river channel, a short distance upstream past Shell Point Marina, and drop anchor near 27 43.051 North/082 28.686 West, amidst 6 feet of water. You must be careful to stop before reaching the shallows to the south and drop the hook in such a way as to preclude swinging into these shoals. There should be room enough for a competent 34-footer to perform this feat. Protection is at least adequate for all winds and really superb when breezes are blowing from the north or east. This anchorage does require caution, and the reader is once again advised to review the navigational information on Little Manatee River presented later in this chapter.

Bahia Beach Facilities and Anchorage (Various Lats/Lons—see below)

The largest set of marina facilities on lower Tampa Bay's eastern shoreline and one surprising anchorage are gathered about the resort community of Bahia Beach, well east of flashing buoy #1E on the big ship's channel. Two marinas wait to greet visiting cruisers.

There have always been two very different routes by which mariners can make their way into Crab Creek and gain access to Bahia Beach's two facilities, which are friendly to transients. Both passages now sport far more markers than the scheme of aids to navigation depicted on chart 11416. While it would be nice if all the marks were correctly charted, it's actually not too difficult for strangers to find the good water. Check out our navigational account of these waters in the next section of this chapter!

The first entrance route involves following the charted cut from Tampa Bay east to the head of a fishing pier associated with the Bahia Beach Island Resort (near 27 43.935 North/082 28.606 West). Skippers can then cut north and intersect the direct Crab Creek channel near unlighted daybeacon #6. However, while the channel from Tampa Bay to the fishing pier was dredged recently, the cut from the fishing pier to #6 has not, and low-water soundings of as little as 4½ feet are possible.

Instead, both this writer and the good folks at Bahia Beach Marina (see below) now suggest that captain and crew make use of the direct approach to Crab Creek, beginning at charted, unlighted daybeacon #1 (near 27 43.972 North/082 29.301 West) and running east to the mouth of Crab Creek. Low-water soundings of 6 feet or better can be maintained on this cut. Of course (guess what?), charted unlighted daybeacon #1 is actually not there anymore. May we be so bold as to once again heartily suggest that you be sure to check out our navigational account of the Crab Creek channel below *before* attempting first-time entry?

There is a third marina in this region, but it is now in the process of conversion to a condo and townhouse development, which will be known as the Mariner's Club. Several locals who keep their boat in this basin have told us about a rumor to the effect that they will all be told to leave soon as the development picks up steam. Only time will tell if the new incarnation of this facility boasts any services for visiting cruisers.

In any case, what has up to now been known as Bahia Del Sol Marina (the future Mariner's Club) is located on the upper reaches of the rectangular cove northeast of charted Sand Island (near 27 43.643 North/082 28.464 West). You must follow a twisting channel with some 5-foot depths to reach the facility, but you will find 6 to 8 feet of water dockside.

Returning now to Crab Creek, two marinas and one secluded anchorage are available to cruising craft on this stream. After traversing the marked entrance cut, captains will cruise through a sharp turn to the south on Crab Creek. As you follow this turn in the stream, the large Bahia Beach Island Resort and Marina complex will be very much in evidence on the

western banks (near 27 43.866 North/082 28.490 West). Soon thereafter the resort's wet-slip dockage will come abeam along the western banks near unlighted daybeacon #5. The adjacent motel features excellent lodging, and the marina showers are air conditioned and in good shape. There are also two swimming pools, a Laundromat, five tennis courts, two shuffleboard courts, and a hot tub. Still not enough for you? Well, check out the three on-site restaurants: the Sunset Lounge, the Captain's Quarters, and the Tropics. This latter dining attraction is open for all three meals of the day.

The marina portion of Bahia Beach Island Resort features berths at fixed wooden piers with all power and water connections (including telephone hookups). The dockage basin is well sheltered and makes for a good spot to ride out inclement weather.

Bahia Beach Island Resort and Marina
   (813) 645-9269
   http://www.bahiabeachresort.com

Approach depth—6-8 feet (direct channel)
   4^1/$_2$-8 feet (fishing pier channel)
Dockside depth—6^1/$_2$-8 feet
Accepts transients—yes
Transient dockage rate—below average
Fixed wooden piers—yes
Dockside power connections—up to 50 amp
Dockside water connections—yes
Showers—yes
Laundromat—yes
Restaurant—3 on site

The second Crab Creek, Bahia Beach marina facility is accessed by continuing to follow the course of Crab Creek as it cuts sharply east and then back to the south. Eventually, the stream will take a final turn to the east, and Bahia Beach Marina (27 43.544

North/082 28.235 West) will be sighted dead ahead. This firm's dockage basin is extremely well sheltered, and the management is unusually knowledgeable and friendly.

Transients are readily accepted on a space-available basis. Call ahead of time to check on slip availability. A huge dry-stack storage building guards the harbor's easterly flank, and the adjacent repair yard's haul-out business is quite active. The yard's travelift is rated at 25 tons. We observed literally dozens of pleasure craft on the dry, waiting for various service tasks to be performed. There are few better recommendations for any repair yard. Full mechanical service work for both diesel and gasoline power plants is also offered.

Transient and resident craft alike will find berths at excellent, fixed wooden piers in the ultra-well-sheltered dockage basin. All slips feature full power and water hookups. Gasoline and diesel fuel are readily available dockside. Currently, this is the only facility in Bahia Beach offering fuel.

Shoreside, visiting cruisers will discover three sets of adequate, climate-controlled showers, a Laundromat, a swimming pool (open to transients), and a small but well-stocked ship's store.

Cruisers wanting to dine out can walk the short stretch to any of the three restaurants at Bahia Beach Island Resort (see above). Unfortunately, there is no provisioning stop nearby.

All in all, we heartily recommend a visit to Bahia Beach Marina, whether you are in the market for secure dockage or full-service repairs. Just don't forget to call ahead and check on the latest transient space situation.

Bahia Beach Marina (813) 645-2411
http://www.bahiabeachmarina.com

Approach depth—6-8 feet (direct channel)
   4½-8 feet (fishing pier channel)
Dockside depth—6-7 feet
Accepts transients—yes (space-available basis)
Transient dockage rate—below average
Fixed wooden piers—yes
Dockside power connections—30 amp
Dockside water connections—yes
Showers—yes
Laundromat—yes
Gasoline—yes
Diesel fuel—yes
Mechanical repairs—yes
Below-waterline repairs—yes
Ship's store—yes
Restaurant—nearby

Well, do you prefer to anchor off rather than spend your evening hours whiling away the time at a marina dock? Fear not—Bahia Beach is ready for you. Just where you might least expect to find it, there is a wonderfully isolated anchorage with heavily vegetated, completely undeveloped shores and excellent depths.

Look at 11414 for a moment and notice the stream that comes off Crab Creek just upstream from Bahia Beach Island Resort and Marina, where the main creek takes a 90-degree turn to the south. You can follow this sidewater through a whole series of twists and turns, holding minimum 5½-foot depths, to a lake-like basin (which is pictured on chart 11416, but not 11414). Here you can anchor in 6 to 8 feet of water (near 27 43.804 North/082 27.965 West), with excellent protection from even the heaviest weather and enough swinging room for boats as large as 50 feet. Be warned that the bottom is black, oozy mud, which may require some washing of the anchor rode next morning.

Recently, we received an e-mail from a fellow

cruiser who informed us that after staying at this anchorage for several days he was courteously told by the "owner" to move on. This seemed very curious to this writer, as I have always thought all bottom land was owned by the state of Florida. However, it turns out that this anchorage is a man-made basin, and it is indeed privately owned. In talking with the powers that be, we were told that if a boat only anchors here for a night or two, chances are very good that they will not be hassled. However, longer stays, as was the case with the cruiser who tipped us off, may well bring on a request to leave.

Mangrove Point Channel

Study chart 11414 for a moment and note the obscurely charted cut running north from the Crab Creek (Bahia Beach) Channel. This former passage has now shoaled in entirely and all the markers have been removed. No craft, not even of the outboard variety, should attempt to venture on this lost channel. Your prop or keel is sure to find the bottom in short order.

Apollo Beach (Various Lats/Lons—see below)

North of flashing buoys #7F and #8F, the large ship's channel traversing lower Tampa Bay splits into eastern and western passages. The east-side fork hurries on toward the southern mouth of Hillsborough Bay, but there is one additional stop along the eastern shoreline associated with lower Tampa Bay.

The charted and well-marked entrance channel to Apollo Beach is found well southeast of flashing buoy #8. Even though you must cross a charted spoil to reach the cut, on-site research revealed that minimum 6-foot depths can be carried, with most soundings showing considerably better water.

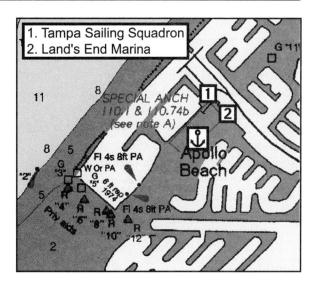

The marked Apollo Beach entrance channel carries minimum low-water soundings of 5 feet. Actually, most of the cut boasts soundings of 6 to 8 feet, but there are one or two 5-foot spots at low tide. Eventually the channel leads to a sheltered bay where one yacht club and a new marina are complemented by anchorage possibilities.

After passing unlighted daybeacon #12, the wide bay sweeps to the northeast. Pleasure boats of almost any size can drop the hook on the bay's mid-section (one good spot is found near 27 46.703 North/082 25.506 West) in 7 to 15 feet of water, with excellent protection from all but gale-force winds. The shores are overlooked by fairly heavy, but not unattractive, residential development. Notice that chart 11413 proclaims the bay's northeastern waters a "Special Anchorage." With this designation, no one should bother you to move on in the near future.

The Tampa Sailing Squadron (a private yacht club) maintains piers on the northwestern corner of the cove, near 27 46.871 North/082

25.451 West. You will readily spy this facility courtesy of the many local sail craft anchored at mooring buoys south of the docks. Visitors who choose to anchor in the bay would do well to avoid the club's anchorage and drop their hook farther to the southwest.

Tampa Sailing Squadron sometimes accepts members of other yacht clubs with reciprocal privileges for overnight or temporary dockage. This is a superfriendly but very informal organization without a full-time dockmaster, so advance arrangements are definitely in order. Good depths of 6 to 10 feet are set against fixed wooden piers with water and simple power connections, though approach soundings can run as thin as 5 feet here and there.

Tampa Sailing Squadron (813) 645-8377
http://www.tampasailingsquadron.org

Approach depth—5-15 feet
Dockside depth—6-10 feet
Accepts transients—limited (open to members
    of other yacht clubs with reciprocal
    privileges with special permission only)
Fixed wooden piers—yes
Dockside power connections—up to 30 amp only
Dockside water connections—yes
Showers—yes
Restaurant—nearby

Just southeast of Tampa Sailing Squadron, Land's End Marina (27 46.829 North/082 25.405 West) overlooks the waters of Apollo Beach. This facility's primary function is as a dry-stack storage facility for smaller powercraft, but they do have a good selection of wet slips as well. Dockside soundings range to an impressive 8 feet or better. Transients are accepted at this facility's (mostly) fixed wooden piers, featuring freshwater hookups and 30- and 50-amp power connections. Gasoline, diesel fuel, and waste pump out services are also available, as are good, air-conditioned, shoreside showers. Some, gasoline-engine only, mechanical repairs are offered.

Circles Bar and Grill is located immediately beside Land's End Marina. This dining spot is open for lunch and dinner seven days a week, though we were a bit pushed for time during our last visit and did not get to sample its offerings. Sigghhh! So many good restaurants, so little time!

Land's End Marina (813) 645-5594

Approach depth—5-15 feet
Dockside depths—8+ feet MLW
Accepts transients—yes
Transient dockage rate—average
Fixed wooden piers—yes
Dockside power connections—30 and 50 amp
Dockside water connections—yes
Waste pump-out—yes
Showers—yes
Gasoline—yes
Diesel fuel—yes
Mechanical repairs—gasoline engines only
Restaurant—on-site

LOWER TAMPA BAY—EASTERN SHORE NAVIGATION

Navigation of lower Tampa Bay's eastern shoreline is facilitated by the relative proximity of the large ship's channel traversing the bay from south to north. Most of the various sidewaters along the way have marked channels knifing through the substantial shelf of shoal water extending well outward from a goodly portion of this coastline. All but one are reasonably simple to follow, though all require caution, particularly Terra Ceia Bay. Take your time, have charts 11414 and 11413 in your hands, study the information presented below, and, in fair weather, you should be all right. Let the wind get up, though, and you could remember this passage for an altogether different reason.

Sailors can easily abandon the ship's channel and follow the mostly deep waters to the north. The few shoals are well charted and larger shallows are marked. Avoid these problem stretches and you should have a wonderful cruise.

Terra Ceia Bay and Anchorages   Mariners traveling north or south on the Western Florida ICW can enter Terra Ceia Bay by abandoning the Waterway some .6 nautical miles south of flashing daybeacon #70 and setting course to come abeam of flashing daybeacon #TC (at the western mouth of Terra Ceia) fairly close to its southerly side.

East of #TC the entrance channel is not nearly so straightforward as you might expect from a casual inspection of chart 11414. The channel wanders a bit, and you cannot always depend on the markers to keep you to the good water.

From #TC, set course to come abeam of and pass unlighted daybeacons #1 and #3 to their fairly immediate southerly sides. East of #3, set course to pass just north of unlighted daybeacon #4, and then point to come abeam of unlighted daybeacon #5 to its southerly quarter. Shallow water encroaches on the south side of the channel between #3 and #5. A straight course

between these two aids could land you in these shallows. Therefore, bend your course slightly to the north after passing #3 and point to favor the Terra Ceia Point side of the channel somewhat. Of course, don't approach the point too closely, as it is surrounded by a thinner strip of shallows. As #4 comes abeam, south of your track, adjust course to come abeam of unlighted daybeacon #5 to its immediate southerly side.

From #5, the channel takes a sharp turn to the southeast and heads for unlighted daybeacon #7. At #7, the cut turns again, this time back to the east. Remember your "red, right, returning" rule and you should be in good shape until coming abeam of unlighted daybeacon #10 to its northerly side.

If you decide to anchor in the deep water south of unlighted daybeacon #9, feel your way carefully due south from this aid with your sounder. Be sure to drop the hook before approaching to within less than 250 yards of the southerly banks. Closer to shore, depths quickly rise to grounding levels.

Past #10, the next aid to the east, unlighted daybeacon #12, guards a patch of very shallow water to the southwest. Set course to come abeam of #12 by about 20 yards to its northerly side. Don't allow leeway or a navigational miscue to lead you south of this course line.

Once abeam of #12, turn sharply to the southeast and follow the wide ribbon of deep water south of Bird Key past unlighted daybeacon #13 into the deeper portion of the bay.

To reach the anchorage on the northwestern corner of the bay, simply follow the deep mid-width of the bay and avoid the shoreline. As you sight the low-level fixed bridge blocking the northeasterly portion of the bay, begin working your way carefully toward the north-northwestern banks. Be sure to drop the hook at least 150 yards from shore. Be on guard against the correctly charted shallows to the east and northeast adjacent to the fixed bridge.

Cruisers desiring to anchor in the haven north of Bird Key should turn off the main body of the bay as the centerline of the waters lying between the key and Beville Point comes abeam to the west. For best depths, favor the northern shores slightly. Good depths continue west to a point just before coming abeam of the eastern tip of Bird Key, to the south. Farther to the west, soundings come up to 4-foot levels. Avoid Bird Key itself. The charted ½-foot shoal building east from the isle is for real.

To access the marine facilities on southern Terra Ceia Bay, follow the centerline south, pointing to eventually come abeam of unlighted daybeacon #4 to its fairly immediate westerly side. From #4, point directly for the mid-width of the canal, which will be obvious to the south-southwest. Just before entering the canal, the marked but uncharted channel to Cut's Edge Harbor Marina will open out to the east. After you enter the canal, Marlow Marine Sales followed by Marsh Harbor Marina will come abeam on the westerly banks.

On Tampa Bay   All other ports of call on lower Tampa Bay's eastern shore can be gained by crossing under the main pass-through of the Sunshine Skyway, east of

flashing buoy #1A. This truly monstrous span has a vertical clearance of 175 feet.

North of the Sunshine Skyway, it is navigationally simple to follow the big ship's channel all the way to either Hillsborough or Old Tampa bays. There are several ranges along the way, but pleasure craft can almost always depend on the prolific flashing buoys to show them the way.

On-site research revealed that 8-foot minimum depths can be found over most of the charted spoil areas adjacent to the main channel on lower Tampa Bay. Many soundings were considerably deeper. The same cannot always be said of the spoil banks bordering some of the side channels, so proceed with caution.

Farther north, some of the spoil banks lining the channel near Hillsborough and Old Tampa bays can be truly shallow. Obviously, mariners must give these hazards considerably more respect on these waters.

Notice that chart 11413 correctly forecasts some depths in the 4- to 6-foot range south of the Gadsden Point and Cut A channels. This branch of the large ship's channel strikes northeast toward Hillsborough Bay. Study chart 11413 carefully and give these hazards the respect they deserve.

As you might well expect, when winds exceed 10 knots, this otherwise easy passage can become more than slightly rough. As always on Tampa Bay, it would be best to choose a day of fair winds for your sojourn.

Bahia Beach Channels   In earlier editions of this guide, I have reviewed the navigational characteristics of Little Manatee

River before those of Bahia Beach. However, as the only approach to the Little Manatee (at least that we could find in August 2003) now uses a portion of the Fishing Pier channel (see below), we are first taking a look at the various Bahia Beach passages this time around.

Newcomers should approach the various Bahia Beach channels with respect. Take your time and read this account thoroughly before making your attempt. Many of the aids to navigation have been changed, added to, or deleted since the last edition of chart 11414 came along. The account below is based on what we saw during our last visit during August 2003. Things could certainly have changed further by the time of your arrival. Take it slow and take it carefully.

Study chart 11414 for a moment, and notice flashing daybeacon #1, marking the southern tip of a long, long shoal making in from the north. This daybeacon has now been replaced with an unlighted sign on several pilings that says, "Danger Shoal." Obviously, you should stay south of the warning marker. There is also a currently uncharted flashing daybeacon #LM (near 27 43.436 North/082 30.008 West), which is a fairway marker, sitting in the heart of the deep water south of the shoal-warning sign. We suggest that you pass close by the northerly side of #LM and then set course to come between the outermost markers on the direct Crab Creek approach channel, unlighted daybeacons #1 and #2. Chart 11414 shows another #2 along the way, but it has apparently been removed.

At this point, navigators bound for Crab Creek must decide whether to take the direct route or run the Fishing Pier channel, a bit farther to the south, and thereby follow a convoluted route to Crab Creek. As mentioned above, the direct passage now holds the best depths and is much to be preferred. Barring some future deterioration of this channel, we suggest that you bypass the Fishing Pier cut, unless your destination is the Mariner's Club or the Little Manatee River.

To continue on directly to Crab Creek, set course to pass unlighted daybeacon #3 to its fairly immediate southerly side. Abeam of #3, you will catch sight of another set of markers just south of your course line. These aids to navigation outline the outer reaches of the Fishing Pier channel and will be further considered below.

From #3, point for the gap between unlighted daybeacons #4 and #5. The channel turns slightly farther to the east at this point, heading directly for the mouth of Crab Creek, while passing between unlighted daybeacons #7 and #8 along the way.

Turn to the south as soon as is practical after entering Crab Creek, and be sure to stay west of unlighted daybeacons #1, #3, and #5. This maneuver will cause you to favor the western shore, which is a very good thing, as shoal waters lie just east of the markers.

Abeam of unlighted daybeacon #5, the dockmaster's headquarters at Bahia Beach Island Resort and Marina will come abeam to the west. If this marina is your intended designation, check here for your slip assignment.

Soon after leaving the Bahia Beach Island Resort and Marina docks behind, the creek swings sharply east and then back to the south. Those cruisers who are headed to Bahia Beach Marina need only follow the stream's centerline all the way there.

If you are inclined to try the Bahia Beach basin anchorage, watch for a sign advertising Bahia Beach Marina just as the creek swings sharply back to the south. You will spy the eastward-running stream leading to the anchorage just beside the sign. Follow the mid-width of the twisting, but deep, creek through its various turns. At one point it may look as if the channel dead ends, but keep the faith—it cuts back to port.

Eventually, you will enter a deep lake. Some sort of concrete storage building and a set of power lines will be spied over the eastern banks. There is also a small marsh island near the entrance into the lake. Leave the marsh island to port and curl around into the open northerly portion of the anchorage. Drop the hook anywhere that will allow your craft to swing clear of the shoreline and settle in for an evening of peace and security. Don't forget that you can probably only stay here for a day or two without being asked to move along.

Moving back to the Fishing Pier channel, this is the route to the Mariner's Club (formerly Bahia Del Sol Marina) and, at least to our way of thinking, the only currently available passage to Little Manatee River. To enter this cut, abandon the direct Crab Creek channel at unlighted daybeacon #3 and pick up the markers just to the south, starting with an unlighted daybeacon #2. This cut runs along to the east in an almost arrow-straight passage. Along the way, you will find far more markers than what are

portrayed on chart 11414. Just remember your good, old "red, right, returning" rule and pass all red, even-numbered aids to navigation to your starboard side and take green markers to port.

East of unlighted daybeacon #6, cruisers will sight the outer face of the Bahia Beach Island Resort fishing pier. It is possible (but don't do it) to cut to the north at this point and follow a currently unmarked channel to unlighted daybeacon #6 on the direct Crab Creek channel. However, as noted earlier, this cut has not been dredged in some time, while the direct approach has. If and until dredging is completed on the waters between the fishing pier and #6, we strongly suggest that all mariners avoid this route.

On the other hand, cruisers bound for the Mariner's Club can cut south from the fishing pier and follow a channel outlined by a whole collection of uncharted daybeacons. Just continue to pass red marks to your starboard side and green to port. Eventually, those following this passage will meet up with unlighted daybeacon #10. Just south of #10, unlighted daybeacon #2 marks the western tip of the channel running east and then north to the Mariner's Club basin. If this is your destination, cut east at #2 and follow the markers to the Mariner's Club harbor.

Little Manatee River   As noted above, the Little Manatee River channel is now more difficult than ever. One of the reasons for this less-than-happy state of affairs is the disappearance of the former entrance channel. Look at chart 11414 and try to pick up unlighted daybeacon #3 (near 27 43.640 North/082 28.769 West). This aid to navigation used to mark the easterly edge of the northern entrance to the Little Manatee River approach channel. However, using a GPS interfaced with a laptop computer, we looked and looked for this old channel during August 2003, and we simply could not find any deep water in this region. Additionally, unlighted daybeacon #3 has been removed entirely—a sure sign that the former entrance cut is no more.

The only way we could find to make good our entry to Little Manatee River was to follow the Fishing Pier channel, outlined above, and then turn south as if we were going to enter the Mariner's Club harbor. At unlighted daybeacon #2 (the westernmost of the markers cutting east to the dockage basin), we abandoned the Mariner's Club channel and felt our way to the south-southwest. We were able to find a few, unnumbered, decrepit daybeacons, which lacked any markings, and some white PVC pipes, which sported hard-to-see red and green colorations on their tops. By keeping the red-topped pipes off our starboard side and the green-topped pipes to port, we finally made our way to Shell Point Marina, but not without plenty of fits and starts along the way.

Gee, wasn't that fun? If all this sounds complicated, that's because it is! Even though the locals could probably do all this with their eyes closed, it's a very different story for visitors. Barring some future improvement of this entire route, we strongly suggest that visiting mariners contact Shell Point Marina for very specific instructions on how best to enter Little Manatee River before deciding on a visit to these waters.

As noted earlier, I'm sure the locals, not to mention the management of Shell Point Marina, will not like my description of this channel one bit. However, my responsibility is to my readers, and the account above expresses exactly what we found during extensive on-site research.

If you are lucky enough to run the entrance cut successfully, Shell Point Marina will eventually be sighted on the northern banks. Cruisers who decide to anchor in the deep water just upstream from the marina should continue following the centerline past Shell Point Marina for a short distance until you are some 150 to 200 yards to the west of the island that flanks the south side of the river. Begin feeling your way off the main track with your sounder for a short distance to the south.

Continued exploration on the river's track to the east past this anchorage is not recommended for cruising craft without very specific local knowledge.

On Tampa Bay   North of flashing buoy #7F, Tampa Bay's large ship's channel (Cut F Channel section) divides. The so-called Cut G Channel flows on to Old Tampa Bay. This route will be considered later in this chapter. Captains and crew making for Apollo Beach, Hillsborough Bay (Tampa), or any other points of interest on the lower bay's eastern banks should cut east-north-east and follow the prolifically marked Gadsden Point and Cut A channels.

Avoid the marked channel north of flashing

buoy #5 (on the Gadsden Point Channel). This small cut makes into the southern shores of Interbay Peninsula and is associated with MacDill Air Force Base.

Apollo Beach   Entry into Apollo Beach is complicated somewhat by the presence of some of the few shoals directly adjacent to Tampa Bay's large ship's channel. To avoid these shallows, cruise south-southwest from flashing buoy #8 for .7 nautical miles. This maneuver will bypass the charted 4- to 6-foot patches south and southeast of #8.

Once the shallows are well behind you, set a new compass/GPS course in order to come abeam of flashing daybeacon #2 to its northeasterly side. This is a long run of 1.9 nautical miles or so. Use your binoculars to help locate #2.

From #2, the channel stretches its well-defined way to the southeast. Pass all red markers to your starboard side (what else?) and take green beacons to port. As you pass unlighted daybeacon #10, the cut runs hard beside the port-side banks. After passing unlighted daybeacon #12, turn northeast into the mid-width of the broad, baylike cove. If you plan to anchor, be sure to drop the hook southwest of the yacht club's special anchorage charted on 11413.

On Tampa Bay   The portion of Cut A Channel that is northeast of flashing buoy #8 borders on some shoals well south of its track. While it would take a whopper of a navigational error to land in these 4- and 5-foot shallows, stranger things have happened, so stay alert.

Northeast of flashing buoys #10 and #11, the large ship's channel takes a sharp swing to the north and enters the foot of Hillsborough Bay.

Hillsborough Bay

Any discussion of Hillsborough Bay is inextricably interwoven with the sprawling metropolitan city known as Tampa. This behemoth community's tall skyline dominates Hillsborough's northerly reaches. The bay's main feeder stream, the Hillsborough River, cuts directly through the heart of Tampa and serves the many commercial vessels which regularly call at the commercial port. For good or ill, the city and Hillsborough Bay are bound together.

We are sorry to report that the pleasure-craft dockage situation in Tampa has all but disappeared. In times past, visiting cruisers could pretty well count on finding a slip at the Harbour Island complex in the heart of Tampa. Sadly, those days are gone. In fact, as this account is being tapped out on the keyboard, there are only two (that's right, two) non-yacht-club transient slips available in all of Tampa. That's not what one could accurately describe as a welcoming state of affairs for the cruising community.

South of Tampa, the bay's shoreline is less developed, though a number of large industrial facilities line the eastern banks. The western shores are a part of the so-called Interbay

Peninsula. The southern half of this land is occupied by MacDill Air Force Base. Several anchorages and one powerboat-oriented marina (and repair yard) are available along the bay's eastern banks and adjacent to the spoil banks lining the large ship's channel.

Hillsborough Bay's shoreline is a study in striking contrasts. It ranges from the incredibly impressive Tampa skyline to the lesser developed lower easterly shores and the glass-and-concrete-shrouded track of the Hillsborough River. Few cruisers will forget their first visit to this fascinating body of water.

The Alafia River (Various Lats/Lons—see below)

The deep, well-buoyed Alafia River (translated as "oleander") channel strikes east to the south of flashing buoy #22 of the "Cut C" (large ship's) channel, well northeast of Gadsden Point. This cut is used regularly by the barges and commercial vessels calling upon the Gardinier Phosphate Plant, which dominates the river's northern banks to the west of the fixed bridge that crosses the stream some 1.1 nautical miles east of its mouth. Indeed, you will unquestionably be able to see a huge hill of waste earth piled up beside this plant, just north of the river, long before the entrance actually comes into sight. During our first visit to the Alafia, we were amazed by this man-made geographical feature and wondered where this mountain had come from.

As Greg Lamm again comments in The Rivers of Florida, "Once a paradise for fishermen and hunters, the Alafia River in recent decades has lost its fishing and recreational significance because of voluminous pollution. Nearby phosphate mining has degraded the Alafia into an industrial stream, but state agencies and private preservation groups are struggling to reestablish the river as a natural attraction."

As you might expect with this sort of commercial traffic coming to and from the Gardinier phosphate facility, the river channel is deep as far as the plant, with at least 20 feet of water. The upstream waters between the commercial wharves and the river's fixed bridge have minimum depths of 5 feet, with soundings of 6 to 8 feet being more the norm.

In spite of the Alafia's commercial character, there are several intriguing anchorage possibilities and one marina facility to consider. One fair-weather haven sometimes employed by local captains lies off the southeastern tip of the large spoil island north of (the Alafia channel's) flashing daybeacon #7 (near 27 51.818 North/082 25.689 West). Skippers piloting craft no more than 45 feet in length can cut off from the channel abeam of flashing daybeacon #7 and cruise through minimum 7-foot depths to within 150 yards of the island's southeastern point. Closer to shore, depths fall off to 4 and 5 feet.

In light airs, or when winds are blowing from the west or northwest, this refuge provides fair shelter. It's not the spot for foul weather, though. During inclement times, I would suggest the anchorage outlined below on the Alafia's interior reaches. The spoil island exhibits low, scrubby growth which is not particularly appealing. To the east, the huge waste earth hill described above is quite prominent.

It is also possible to continue cruising north off the eastern shores of the spoil island, keeping well off the beach. Minimum 7-foot depths can be held to a point some 200 yards

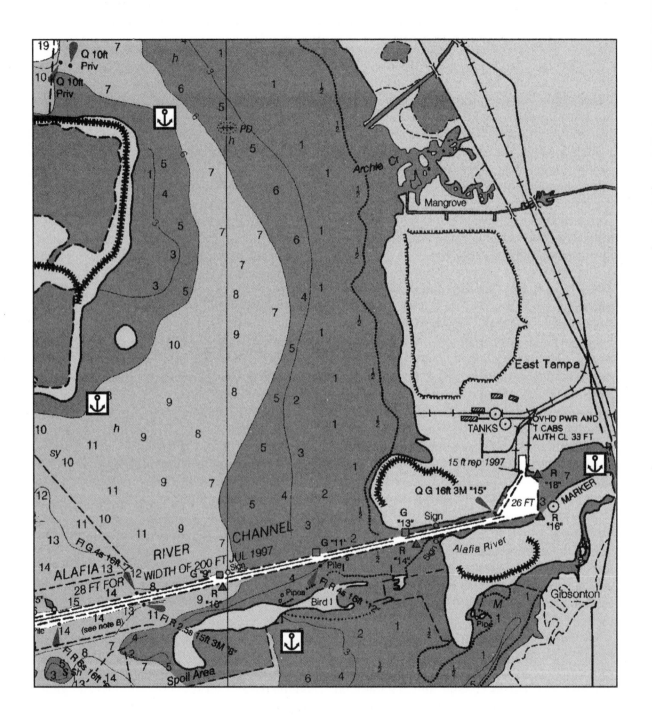

off the spoil island's northeasterly tip. Here you may also drop the hook in appropriate wind conditions (near 27 53.115 North/082 25.395 West). This refuge does provide shelter from southwesterly winds.

Do not try to cruise around the spoil island's northerly tip and rejoin the large ship's/Cut C channel. Unmarked (but charted) shoals with less than 4 feet of depth are waiting for you.

In northerly blows, vessels can find good shelter south of charted Bird Island. To reach this haven, you must abandon the Alafia Channel between flashing daybeacons #6 and #8 and find an unmarked passage leading across the southerly spoil banks. On sunny days when the water is clear, it's often possible to navigate by eye, but at other times, you just have to take your best guess. With this sort of unpredictability, the anchorage can only be recommended for boats drawing less than 4½ feet and piloted by die-hard explorers. Minimum depths of 5½ feet are carried in the unmarked channel until reaching a point south of the charted, narrow neck on Bird Island, near 27 50.756 North/082 24.688 West. Minimum depths of 5 feet are held only to within 100 yards of the beach. Closer in, soundings deteriorate rapidly. This anchorage offers some protection in moderate easterly winds courtesy of the mainland shores. Of course, the body of the island itself provides super shelter from northerly breezes. With winds out of the south or west, head for the river or points north.

This is a particularly attractive anchorage with some special treats. The beautifully undeveloped banks of Bird Island are part of an official Audubon Society sanctuary. While landing is prohibited, there is nothing to stop us cruisers from anchoring and enjoying the many birds usually in view, often including quite a flock of giant, white ibises.

Boats drawing less than 4½ feet can follow the river's interior track past the phosphate plant with minimum 5-foot depths (typically 7 to 8 feet) and anchor short of the fixed bridge, near 27 51.547 North/082 23.123 West. There is excellent protection from all but particularly strong easterly winds. While it is possible to get away from the phosphate plant a bit, there might still be some noise during the evening hours (not to mention the chemical smells), particularly if a barge loading is in progress. The nearby Highway 41 bridge is also apt to throw in its share of automobile lights. Fortunately, the shoreline in this area is more attractive. The northern banks are part of a small park with a public launching ramp, while the southerly counterparts are mostly undeveloped.

Skippers who pilot vessels that can clear the 28-foot fixed bridge (and the charted 33-foot power lines) may consider tracking their way upstream on Alafia River through mostly 5-foot depths to Inter Bay Moorings (27 51.419 North/082 22.893 West). This facility flanks the Alafia's southerly banks a short distance east of the fixed bridge. Inter Bay accepts transients at their fixed wooden slips, with freshwater hookups and 30- to 50-amp power connections. Depths alongside range from 4½ to 8 feet. Gasoline, diesel fuel, and waste pump-out services, plus adequate, non-air-conditioned, shoreside showers and a semi-open-air Laundromat are available as well. Cruisers in need of repair work will find that Inter Bay offers full mechanical servicing (gasoline and diesel engines), welding, and haul-outs. The yard's 70-ton travelift is most impressive. Do-it-yourself work is also allowed. There is even a small ship's and variety store in the complex and a "country store" is within walking distance. All in all, Inter Bay Moorings can be described as a decent facility for cruising craft that can stand some 5-foot depths and clear the 28-foot bridge.

Inter Bay Moorings (813) 677-2739
   http://www.interbaymoorings.com

Approach depth—5-6 feet
Dockside depth—4½-8 feet
Accepts transients—yes
Transient dockage rate—below average
Fixed wooden piers—yes
Dockside power connections—30 and 50 amp
Dockside water connections—yes
Showers—yes
Laundromat—yes
Waste pump-out—yes
Gasoline—yes (planned)
Diesel fuel—yes (planned)
Mechanical repairs—yes
Below-waterline repairs—yes
Ship's and variety store—yes

Tampa Yacht and Country Club (27 53.257 North/082 28.758 West)

Moving south to north, the first facility on Hillsborough Bay comes up on the western banks, well west-northwest of flashing buoy #25. Tampa Yacht and Country Club accepts transients who are members of clubs with appropriate reciprocal agreements. Berths are provided at fixed wooden piers with a full set of power and water connections. The harbor is partially breakwater enclosed and well protected from all winds. There is even a fuel dock offering both diesel and gasoline for members and accredited club guests only. The club docks are attended 24 hours a day, seven days a week. This welcome service is a real

rarity when it comes to private yacht clubs. Call ahead of time to make your slip reservations.

Shoreside amenities include showers, a swimming pool, two dining rooms, tennis courts, and extensive horseback-riding facilities. Lunch and dinner are served seven days a week, while breakfast is offered Saturday and Sunday only. Dining reservations are recommended by the management.

The yacht club's entrance channel holds minimum depths of 7 feet, with soundings of 8 to 11 feet as the norm. The channel skirts north of a small island of concrete riprap set out from the harbor's entrance for extra protection from easterly breezes. While there is nothing complicated about the entrance, first-time visitors may want to read the navigational account of the club channel before their first stopover.

Tampa Yacht and Country Club (813) 831-1621

Approach depth—7-11 feet
Dockside depth—7-10 feet
Accepts transients—members of clubs with
   reciprocal agreements
Fixed wooden piers—yes
Dockside power connections—up to 50 amp
Dockside water connections—yes
Showers—yes
Gasoline—yes (members and accredited guests
   only)
Diesel fuel—yes (members and accredited
   guests only)
Mechanical repairs—independent contractors
Ship's store—small
Restaurant—on site

East Bay/McKay Bay

The Cut C/large ship's channel serving Hillsborough Bay splits at Pendola Point. The passage angling to the northwest, known as the Cut D Channel, allows access to downtown Tampa and the Hillsborough River. The wide cut to the northeast quickly leads to East Bay. This deep bay and its various side passages are perhaps the most commercial bodies of water that you will ever visit. Oceangoing freighters, tankers, and the huge wharves to serve them are everywhere in evidence. All this maritime paraphernalia makes for fascinating viewing from the water. Unfortunately, the rank smell of diesel fumes and other chemicals permeates the air everywhere. There is certainly no place to

anchor, nor are there any real marina facilities on East Bay.

East Bay is eventually blocked by a 40-foot fixed bridge and a power line with 32 feet of vertical clearance. The waters northeast of this span are known as McKay Bay. On-site research revealed that, in spite of soundings shown on chart 11413, minimum 5½-foot depths can be held on a broad band between the fixed bridge and a point just short of the charted overhead power cables. There is little in the way of shelter, but in light airs, it would

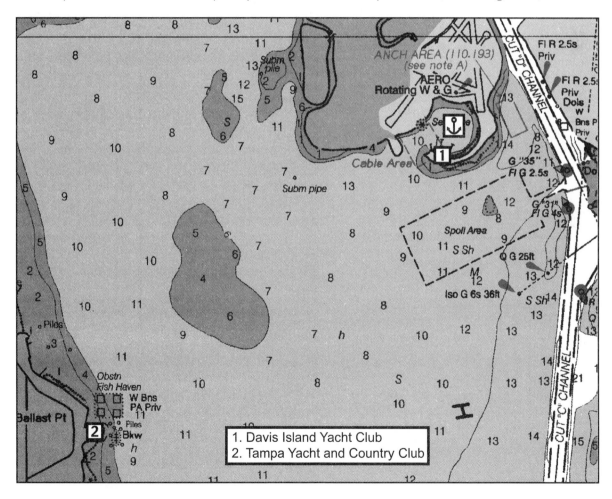

1. Davis Island Yacht Club
2. Tampa Yacht and Country Club

be possible to anchor here (near 27 56.212 North/082 25.694 West). The westerly banks exhibit some low-key residential development, while the shallow easterly shores are guarded by scrub growth. Frankly, I wouldn't anchor here unless there were no other choice. One sniff of the commercial odors wafting on the wind will put you in touch with the reason for my opinion.

Davis Island Yacht Club (27 54.498 North/082 27.059 West)

Study the Tampa area inset on chart 11413 for a moment and notice the "Seaplane Basin" on the southeastern tip of Davis Island. This sheltered harbor, no longer used by pontoon-equipped aircraft, is now the home of Davis Island Yacht Club. This organization has the reputation of being "the sailingest club on the Gulf coast." The club docks are found on the basin's southern shores. This friendly group tries to keep the ends of each pier open for transients. Members of yacht clubs with reciprocal privileges are accepted for overnight or temporary dockage at fixed wooden piers with power and water connections. The club does not have a regular dockmaster, so be sure to make arrangements in advance.

Davis Island Yacht Club has a shoreside swimming pool, showers, and lounge, but no dining room. Visitors can take a taxi into Tampa to sample its multitude of restaurants and shoreside businesses of all descriptions.

Davis Island Yacht Club (813) 251-1158
  http://www.diyc.org

Approach depth—10 feet
Dockside depth—9-10 feet
Accepts transients—members of clubs with
  reciprocal privileges
Fixed wooden piers—yes

Dockside power connections—up to 50 amp
Dockside water connections—yes
Showers—yes

It is also possible for any cruiser to anchor in the basin north of the yacht club docks in 8 to 10 feet of water (anywhere remotely near 27 54.604 North/082 26.990 West). Much of this space is already taken up by boats belonging to members of the Davis Island Yacht Club tied to mooring buoys. You may be able to find enough swinging room amidst this throng, but be sure to set the hook carefully to avoid bumping into your neighbor at night when the wind or tide shifts. The basin bottom is composed of soft mud. Watch for a dragging anchor.

Northwestern Hillsborough Bay

The northwestern lobe of Hillsborough Bay, west of Davis Island, is an area that most cruising skippers should think seriously about avoiding. A broad band of shallows flanks almost all of the surrounding shoreline, and the creeks making into the bay from Davis Island are all small and mostly shallow. Additionally, there are several unmarked shoals in the bay itself to contend with. The charted cut-through between the bay's northernmost reaches and Seddon Channel is spanned by two low-level fixed bridges. One has only 9 feet of vertical clearance. Obviously, cruising-size craft cannot make use of this passage.

So, here is one of the few places where this writer concludes that the cruising effort is not worth the reward. However, for those captains who just have to poke their bow into everything, a brief navigational sketch is provided in the next section of this chapter.

Tampa

The so-called Cut D Channel cuts to the northwest at Pendola Point and soon runs head on into an intersection with the Seddon and Sparkman channels. This former passage quickly runs on toward the Tampa metropolitan area. Let us pause a moment in our waterborne coverage to reflect on this successful city.

Tampa is a city that seems bent on entering the twenty-first century with a real boom. Population-wise, Tampa is now the state's second largest city. New, high-rise development is everywhere in evidence. The tall glass-and-steel towers make for an awe-inspiring site from the water.

High-tech and research development firms have flocked to Tampa since the 1990s. One draw is the Tampa International airport, considered to be one of the finest and safest air terminals in the world. Another good reason for all this business interest is the University of South Florida. Founded in Tampa in just the 1960s, the school has grown to be the state's second largest state-supported university.

Tampa is a city that loves its sports. The NFL Super Bowl came to town in 1984 and 1991. This writer was on hand for the latter event, and I can tell you from personal experience that the place was buzzing! Of course, Tampa has its own NFL football team with the Tampa Bay Buccaneers.

Tampa has a whole bevy of attractions for (mostly) landlubber visitors. Cruisers moving up the Hillsborough River past Harbour Island will be astounded by the Tampa Bay Performing Arts Center (1010 W. C. Macinnes Place, 813-229-7827). The building looks impressive, to say the least. Automobile traffic has been routed directly under the building in an arrangement that this writer has never before witnessed. The center contains three theaters designed to handle specific types of entertainment. Be sure to check on events that may be in progress during your visit.

Franklin Street Mall is found just north of Harbour Island and the Performing Arts Center. This development was part of Tampa's downtown revitalization program, which has been in full swing since the 1990s. Now only pedestrian traffic is allowed on the avenue amidst the many retail shops and frequent sidewalk entertainment.

A few steps farther to the north will bring the interested visitor to the Old Tampa Theater (711 N Franklin, 813-274-8286). Originally opened in 1926 by John Eberson, this facility earned the nickname of "Opera House John." Eberson chose a Hispanic architectural theme for his theater which has survived down through the years and still evokes "oohs" and "ahhs" from first-time patrons with its intricate detail. Some of the world's finest art treasures still grace the lobby and halls. The theater was donated to the city of Tampa in 1976 and since then it has become a cultural center. Shows and exhibitions are constantly in progress.

The Tampa Art Museum (600 N Ashley Drive, 813-274-8130) and the $134 million Curtis Hixon Convention Center overlook the Hillsborough River two blocks west of the Tampa Theater. The center regularly features the country's top talent and the museum houses an impressive collection of paintings and sculpture.

Ybor City, a suburb of Tampa, has been closely linked with the American manufacture of cigars since Don Vicente Martinez moved his factory from Key West to Ybor City in 1886. While only one cigar plant today remains in Ybor City, the industry has left an indelible print on the town.

The unique heritage of the Ybor City cigar workers, an eclectic mix of Cubans, Germans, Spaniards, Italians, and Jews, has been painstakingly preserved in the Ybor City State Museum. Among many fascinating exhibits, four of the original cigar workers homes have been moved to the museum site and restored.

Ybor City itself has been undergoing a tasteful renaissance over the past decade. While there is still much work to do, many of the long-vacant buildings have been restored as both retail businesses and fine restaurants.

Finally, if you are interested in a more modern mode of entertainment, take a taxi or public transportation to the nearby Busch Gardens theme park. Renowned for its exotic birds and animals, the park is a potpourri of rides and demonstrations that will thrill the whole family.

Now for the bad news. Where once transient dockage was available in downtown Tampa at the Harbour Island complex (see below), the waterside portion of this facility is now all but shut down. Adding insult to injury, one of Tampa's downtown hotels that used to be friendly to cruisers no longer offers overnight dockage. In fact, as it now stands, there is virtually no dockage for overnight (or a few days') visitors in or near downtown Tampa. This lack of readily available slip space is a real impediment for cruisers who want to visit the vital, active city that is modern-day Tampa. It is to be hoped that the city, or some private entity, will get on the proverbial ball in the near future and secure far more slip space for overnight cruising visitors. Until that happy occasion comes to pass, those who arrive by water will be forced to visit Tampa strictly by way of motorized land transportation.

Numbers to know in Tampa include

Tampa Bay Cab—(813) 251-5555
United Cab—(813) 253-2424
Yellow Cab—(813) 253-8871
Avis Rental Cars—(800) 331-1212
Budget Rent A Car—(813) 878-2451
West Marine—(813) 348-0521

Henry B. Plant and the Fabulous Tampa Bay Hotel

The silver minarets of the world-famous Tampa Bay Hotel still gaze unwinkingly out over the shores of Hillsborough Bay as they have since 1891. This totally astounding edifice was actually modeled in part after the Alhambra Palace in Granada, Spain. An example of Moorish and Turkish architecture, it cost over $2 million to build and $500,000 to furnish.

Henry Bradley Plant, one of the two most influential men in Florida's history, came to the Sunshine State during the aftermath of the War Between the States. Plant was a great financier and he is often considered to be the father of the modern American railroad system and of Tampa itself. Much as Henry Flagler pushed his railroad down Florida's east coast, bringing tourism to such diverse towns as St. Augustine and Palm Beach, Plant brought his competing west-coast railway line to Tampa, and the city's future as a major port was assured. At the time of the line's completion in 1884, the city had a mere 700 inhabitants. When the hotel was completed a scant seven years later, the city's population was nearly 6,000. Tampa has seemingly never looked back.

Stories persist that Plant's motivation to build the Tampa Bay Hotel in such a grand fashion was to outdo Henry Flagler's Ponce de Leon Hotel in St. Augustine. Both structures still display an opulence the likes of which will probably never be seen again.

Tampa Bay Hotel first opened its doors on January 31, 1891. Fifteen thousand written invitations were extended. The ladies were presented fans and brass crumb trays, and shaving mugs and ash trays were given to the men. Chinese lanterns and candles lit the grounds and the Albert Opera Company performed Faust. The hotel was filled to capacity and guests slept in the public rooms, bunking on tapestried couches.

Over the years famous guests included the Russian ballerina, Anna Pavlova; John Drew, the famous actor uncle of the Barrymores; and Minnie Maddern Fiske, a leading American actress for 60 years. Theodore Roosevelt, Clara Barton, and Stephen Crane were also guests there. Crane, who died at 28, was author of *Red Badge of Courage*. He drafted *The Price of the Harness* while staying at the hotel.

The hotel was a focal point for the invasion of Cuba by American forces during the Spanish-American War in 1898. The war with Spain brought a concentration of 30,000 troops bound for Cuba to Tampa. Theodore Roosevelt camped with his Rough Riders about a mile from the hotel.

Following Mr. Plant's death in 1899, the old hostelry passed through a succession of owners, including the city of Tampa, until it became home to the University of Tampa in 1933. Today, the University of Tampa has become a bustling institution of higher education with almost 3,000 students.

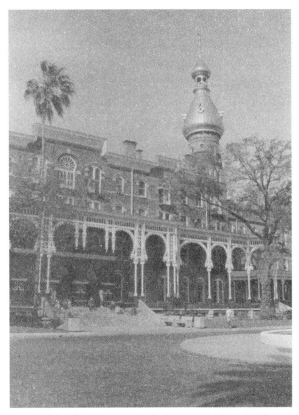

University of Tampa, formerly the Tampa Bay Hotel

The splendor of Tampa Bay Hotel and Mr. Plant's invaluable contribution to the development of Western Florida are remembered in the Henry B. Plant Museum (813-254-1891), which is now housed in the southern wing of the old hotel. The museum is open Tuesday through Saturday from 10:00 A.M. to 4:00 P.M. If you see nothing else in Tampa, be sure to visit this outstanding attraction!

Tampa History The first mention of Tampa is found in the sixteenth-century memoirs of Fountaneda. A shipwrecked Spanish lad, he spent seventeen years among the Indians of Tampa Bay. One of many villages he wrote of was one called "Tanpa." Early mapmakers changed the spelling to "Tampa."

S. T. Walker and C. B. Moore mapped more than 75 mound sites in the Tampa region in 1879. Their map shows Indian mounds present at the time of the DeSoto expedition. These locations are now the neighboring cities of Ruskin, Tarpon Springs, Crystal River, Clearwater, Safety Harbor, St. Petersburg, Pass-a-Grille, Gibsonton, Palmetto, Bradenton, and Terra Ceia.

Robert Hackley, Tampa's first settler, arrived at the mound on the northeast side of the Hillsborough River in 1823. He cleared land around it and started his plantation near it.

In 1824 Col. George Mercer Brooke saw the shell mound near the clearing of Hackley's plantation and confiscated the property and mound for the U.S. Army and his namesake, Fort Brooke. Early drawings of Fort Brooke show the Indian shell mound still intact in the 1840s.

After the army withdrew, early settlers expanded the settlement of Fort Brooke by hauling shells from the mound in ox carts for road beds. The last mound in this area (Bullfrog Creek) was used as a foundation in building the Tampa Bay Hotel (now the University of Tampa).

Sparkman and Ybor Channels

North of the charted Peter O'Knight Municipal Airport on Davis Island, the Sparkman Channel breaks off to the north and runs along its deep way to Ybor Turning Basin and Ybor Channel. All these waters are extremely commercial and are very reminiscent of East Bay, discussed above. Again, while the commercial shipping makes for some unforgettable sights from your cockpit, there are no facilities nor anchorage possibilities for pleasure craft.

Marjorie Park Marina (27 55.837 North/082 27.291 West)

The small marina known as Marjorie Park Marina occupies the tadpole-shaped cove making into the eastern banks of Davis Island off Seddon Channel. Two slips at the fuel dock are sometimes available for transients, and additional space is occasionally offered when resident craft are away from their home slips. Would you believe that this meager ration is now the only non-yacht-club, transient dockage currently available in all of Tampa? Things can sure change in a few years.

Marjorie Park's slips are well sheltered and feature fixed, concrete piers with 7- to 10-foot depths alongside. Most slips for resident craft have freshwater hookups and power connections up to 50 amps, but sometimes power hookups can be a bit hard to come by in the transient spaces. Gasoline (only) can be purchased at the fuel pier.

Shoreside, visiting cruisers will not find any showers or a Laundromat. On the plus side, a whole host of businesses on charming Davis Island is within walking distance. Patrons of these firms will quickly discover that this community has a far more small-town atmosphere than nearby Tampa.

Cruisers interested in dining ashore will find a host of choices. Rick's Italian Cafe (214 E Davis Boulevard, 813-253-3310) is excellent, and Pink Flamingo Cafe (210 E Davis Boulevard, 813-251-2928) is open for breakfast and lunch. Other good choices are Estela's Mexican Restaurant (209 E Davis Boulevard, 813-251-0558) and 220 East (220 E Davis Boulevard, 813-259-1220). Galley restocking is made ever so convenient by the close proximity of Davis Island Farmer's Market (202 East Davis, 813-251-8767). There is also a convenience store nearby.

Marjorie Park Marina (813) 259-1604

Approach depth—8-20 feet
Dockside depth—7-10 feet
Accepts transients—very limited (2 slips usually
    open)
Transient dockage rate—below average
Fixed concrete piers—yes
Dockside power connections—30 and 50 amp
Dockside water connections—yes
Gasoline—yes
Restaurant—several nearby

Harbour Island Marina

Until a few short years ago, transient dockage in downtown Tampa was reasonably easy to come by, courtesy of the huge Harbour Island development. Located at the southeastern corner of the intersection between Seddon and Garrison channels, this complex has clearly fallen on hard times. The dockmaster's office has been closed, all the furniture removed, and the phone disconnected. For all practical purposes, Harbour Island Marina is now closed to transient visitors, and even though there are plenty of open slips, there is no one currently on site who is responsible for this dockage.

It is always sad for us to note the passing of any marina facility, but the demise of Harbour Island is particularly unfortunate. As it now stands, a visit to downtown Tampa by waterborne tourists is really rather difficult. Until the marina portion of the Harbour Island development can enjoy some sort of renaissance, we no longer recommend that visiting cruisers attempt to berth here. Let's hope the future brings on better times.

Garrison Channel

The Garrison Channel cuts north of Harbour Island and spans the gap between the Seddon and Sparkman channels. Unfortunately this deep cut is spanned by two low-level fixed bridges and is unusable by all but very small powercraft.

Upper Hillsborough River

While dockage facilities for visiting craft are nonexistent, and there is no opportunity to anchor, a cruise on the Hillsborough River north of Harbour Island is accessible to boats that can clear a 40-foot fixed bridge. There are also several other spans with restricted opening schedules with which you must contend. The huge skyscrapers are a sight indeed, but you may just think you have been transported back to the times of the Arabian Nights after passing under the John F. Kennedy Boulevard (Highway 60) Bridge. The famed thirteen silver minarets of the Tampa Hotel (now the University of Tampa) overlooking the western banks are a sight you will never forget.

The Radisson Riverside Hotel maintains a face dock between the 15-foot Brorein bascule span and the John F. Kennedy Boulevard Bridge along the eastern shore. Depths at dockside run 5 to 7 feet. No overnight stays are currently allowed, but it is possible to moor here temporarily while dining at one of the hotel's several fine restaurants.

North of the 15-foot bascule bridge, downtown Tampa's skyscrapers are a mammoth presence overlooking the eastern banks. The architecture is striking, to say the very least.

Mariners cruising down the course of the upper Hillsborough River will spy a host of hand-painted college logos along the concrete seawalls. Before long you will divine that these have been painted by crew racing teams from colleges all over the country. Apparently the University of Tampa uses this portion of the river for its crew races. If one of these contests should happen to be scheduled during your visit, you should make every effort to attend this exciting event.

North of the John F. Kennedy Boulevard Bridge, passing cruisers can't miss the minarets of the old Tampa Bay Hotel/ University of Tampa to the west. Of all the sights and attractions in downtown Tampa, this massive building was the most unforgettable for this writer.

This guide's coverage of upper Hillsborough River ends at the railroad bridge upstream from the university. The river is now dammed at 30th Street and all boating traffic is barred from the stream's upper reaches.

HILLSBOROUGH BAY NAVIGATION

As with the eastern shoreline of lower Tampa Bay, successful navigation of Hillsborough Bay is very much facilitated by the presence of the large ship's channel. Pleasure craft of any size and draft can easily follow this waterborne interstate highway to Tampa and the Hillsborough River. Then, it's only a matter of keeping anywhere near the mid-width for good depths.

Outside of the ship's channel, Hillsborough Bay is mostly deep, though some shoals are in evidence. Not all of these shallows are marked and fixed-keel sail craft must keep a current position at all times through electronic navigation, dead-reckoning, or whatever means are available. There are also some shallows abutting the eastern flank of the ship's channel. Most of these are north of the Alafia River. Be sure to keep well away from these hazards.

On to the Alafia River   Follow the Cut C Channel north from its intersection with Cut A. Pass flashing buoy #13 to its easterly quarter and continue north by passing between flashing buoys #15 and #16.

North of #15 and #16, the channel runs near the first of the hollow spoil islands east of the marked track. This body of land will appear much more substantial from the water than you might think from a cursory examination of chart 11413.

After passing unlighted nun buoy #20 to its westerly quarter, the Alafia River Channel makes in from the east.

The Alafia River   The main Alafia River Channel is child's play to navigate as far as the phosphate factory perched on the stream's northerly shores. The 20-plus feet of water and numerous beacons have been erected to guide the considerable commercial shipping that serves the plant. Pleasure cruisers can take advantage of these excellent aids to navigation as well. Shallow water does border a portion of the deep cut, particularly near the river's entrance, so stay alert and follow the markers, unless you intend to make one of the side trips detailed below.

The north-side anchorage behind the large spoil island can be reached by abandoning the river's entrance channel at flashing daybeacon #7. Cut to the north and set course to come abeam of the spoil island's southeasterly tip some 150 yards off the point. Drop anchor well short of the charted circular island to the north. This small land-mass is surrounded by shoal water.

Cruisers who continue cruising north behind the spoil island should stay at least 150 yards to the east of both the large spoil island and the smaller (charted) round island just north of the anchorage reviewed above.

Should you decide to do so, good water can be held all the way to a point abeam of the island's northeastern tip. Don't attempt to cut to the west and rejoin the big ship's channel, north of the spoil island. In spite of some reports you may have heard to the contrary, depths of 4 feet or less block this passage.

Cruisers choosing the delightful Bird Island anchorage should depart the main channel about halfway between flashing daybeacons #6 and #8. Slow to idle speed and feel your way carefully south with your sounder. You will be trying to discover a dredged but unmarked (and uncharted) channel across the bar south of the main cut. On sunny, clear days, the deeper depths can be spotted from the darker color of the water. In low-light or poor visibility conditions, proceed with the greatest caution.

Once past the unmarked bar channel, continue almost due south until you are at least 100 yards past the southwestern tip of Bird Island, well east of your course line. Carefully curve your track around to the east and point to come behind the western half of Bird Island, at least 100 yards to your northerly side. Don't approach the island more closely or proceed too far to the east into the charted 2-foot waters.

Skippers continuing east into the interior reaches of the Alafia River should proceed at slow speed. The river channel east of flashing daybeacon #7 is a manatee zone,

Very shallow water abuts both sides of the main channel east of unlighted daybeacons #9 and #10. Stay strictly in the channel and keep a careful watch over your stern to make sure lateral leeway is not easing you onto the surrounding shoals.

You will enter the westerly mouth of the Alafia River after passing between unlighted daybeacons #13 and #14. Daybeacon #13 is located hard by the northern banks, but depths seem more than adequate.

East of flashing daybeacon #15 your course will take you into the deeply dredged turning basin associated with the phosphate plant. Not that you would, but don't even think about anchoring here.

Instead, look east and find unlighted daybeacons #16 and #18. You will spy #16 almost on the southerly banks. For best depths, pass almost midway between these two aids, favoring #18 slightly. In spite of the 3-foot sounding shown on chart 11413, on-site research revealed that at least 4½ feet of water can be carried over this bar. Farther to the east, the waters deepen to 7- and 9-foot levels. As the small park and public launching ramp come abeam to the north, consider dropping the hook well short of the fixed bridge and the charted power line. It goes almost without saying that this is the end of the line for sail craft.

A stone's throw to the east, Alafia River is spanned by a fixed bridge with 28 feet of vertical clearance. There is also a power line set 33 feet above the water. East of the bridge, expect typical 5-foot depths. Mariners who make it this far will spot Inter Bay Moorings on the southern shoreline.

On Hillsborough Bay Captains cruising north past the Alafia River Channel should pass between flashing buoys #21 and #22. Ignore the charted channel to the west. This cut serves as a crash channel for MacDill Air Force Base. Ponder that for a second as you pass. A second was about as long as this writer could stand to think about it.

Tampa Yacht and Country Club Mariners visiting the Tampa Yacht Club's well-sheltered basin must take into account the presence of a concrete riprap breakwater just east of the harbor's entrance. While this man-made feature serves to blunt sharp chop that might otherwise enter the club's basin, woe to the navigator who tries to go straight into the harbor entrance from Hillsborough Bay. Instead, set course from flashing buoy #25 to bring your craft to a point 100 yards north of the Ballast Point harbor. As you approach the shore, you will see a long pier jutting out into the river. Do not approach this dock. It is founded in shoal water. Instead, look for the yacht club's markers making off to the southwest. These markers will lead you easily into the sheltered basin.

Long Shoal Sailors leaving the large ship's channel and cruising the mostly deep waters to the north and west must take great care to avoid Long Shoal. This clearly charted hazard is located due north of the MacDill crash channel (see above). Its lim-its are outlined by two aids to navigation, unlighted daybeacons #1 and #2. Stay away from #1 at all costs. It is founded in extremely shallow water, with oysters lining the bottom.

Davis Island Yacht Club Captains and crew visiting this fine club and its sheltered basin can depart the ship's channel at flashing buoy #23. Set a careful compass course to pass between Long Shoal to the west and the charted spoil bank west of flashing buoy #31. You must eventually follow a long, slow curve to the northeast to come around the spoil zone and cruise toward the basin's entrance. Enter the "Seaplane Basin" by avoiding the starboard-side point. From here on, you need only avoid the water immediately adjacent to the shoreline for good depths.

Northwestern Hillsborough Bay Remember that cruising on this shoal-plagued stretch of the bay is not particularly recommended for cruising-size craft. If you should choose to ignore this advice, be mindful of the large shoal southwest of Davis Island. On-site research revealed that this hazard is correctly charted on 11413. Also, note the shoals west of Davis Island's southwesterly reaches.

Farther to the north, depths decline to 5-foot levels. While some good water continues to flank Davis Island's western banks, there are a multitude of uncharted shallows farther to the west. Two low-level fixed bridges span the charted passage to Seddon Channel above Davis Island. These bridges have 13 feet and 9 feet of vertical clearance, respectively.

North on Hillsborough Bay As you approach flashing buoy #28 on the Cut C Channel, switch to the Tampa Inset section of chart 11413. The blown-up scale of this inset gives far better details of East Bay and the channels leading north to the Hillsborough River and Tampa.

East Bay North of flashing buoy #28, Tampa's large ship's channel divides. The Port Sutton Channel leads northeast into East Bay. Shallow water abuts Hookers Point to the north. Be sure to stay well south and southeast of flashing daybeacons #1 and #3 to avoid this shoal. Flashing buoy #5 should also be passed well to its southeasterly quarter. Continue to avoid the northwesterly banks as the bay sweeps around to the north. From this point very deep water stretches out almost from shore to shore as far as the 40-foot fixed bridge. Don't forget to hold your nose.

Wild-eyed captains who insist on entering McKay Bay must remember the power lines with only 32 feet of vertical clearance immediately northeast of the fixed spans. If (and only if) you can clear the 40-foot bridge and the lines, cruise straight out into McKay Bay, setting course for the water body's mid-width. Cease your forward progress at least 100 yards short of the second set of charted power lines.

Cut D Channel The Cut D Channel swings to the northwest from its intersection with the Cut C and Port Sutton channels toward Tampa. This channel initially borders on a small park and the Peter O'Knight Municipal Airport along its southwesterly banks. There is a public boat-launching ramp along this track. Larger power vessels should slow to idle speed when passing.

While you would just about have to be asleep at the helm to run aground on Cut D, tidal currents do run quite swiftly through this section. Sail craft should proceed under auxiliary power and single-screw trawlers should be ready for quick course changes.

Cut D soon leads to a fork. The Sparkman Channel strikes to the north and leads to the Ybor turning basin and channel. A small band of shallows flanks the eastern shores of Harbour Island along the Sparkman Channel, but otherwise the waters are quite deep until Ybor Channel comes to a dead end well to the north.

Seddon Channel flows to the northwest and is the straight course to downtown Tampa. No-wake regulations are in effect from the Sparkman Channel intersection to Marjorie Park Marina. This small facility will come up on the southwestern banks of Seddon Channel at the charted "CG" (Coast Guard) station. Cruise into the marina on the centerline of its entrance.

Mariners who continue following the Seddon Channel will soon spy the condos and private docks associated with the Harbour Island development on the northeastern banks. Powercraft must again slow to idle speed.

Garrison Channel Two fixed spans having only 10 feet of vertical clearance cross the Garrison Channel, north of Harbour Island. Only small powercraft can use this cut-through as a short cut between the Harbour Island facilities and Ybor Turning Basin.

Hillsborough River   Those skippers who choose to continue north on the Hillsborough River and visit downtown Tampa must contend with a bevy of bridges. There is also a charted shoal abutting the northeastern corner of Davis Island. Stay away from this point or you could land in three feet of water.

After passing the Garrison Channel intersection, look toward the northeastern shore for a close view of downtown Tampa's performing arts center. You can scarcely ignore its mammoth, columned facade.

The charted channel striking back to the southwest, north of Davis Island, plays host to some slips for resident craft, but no transient services are available. On-site research failed to reveal the charted bubble of 3-foot water on this stream's mid-width. Apparently, dredging has now removed this obstacle. The passage is soon blocked by a fixed bridge with 9 feet of vertical clearance.

Moving north on the Hillsborough River,

the first bridge encountered will be a bascule span with 15 feet of closed vertical clearance. All the non-fixed bridges on the Hillsborough River have the same restrictive opening schedule. From 9:00 A.M.to 4:30 P.M., Monday through Friday, and from 8:00 A.M. to 6:00 P.M., Saturdays, Sundays, and legal holidays the spans open only on the hour and half-hour.

Next up are twin fixed bridges with 40 feet of vertical clearance. These spans are followed closely by a second 15-foot bascule bridge. Past this span, the river crooks to the northwest and moves on toward the 11-foot (closed clearance) John F. Kennedy Boulevard bascule bridge. Once under this bridge, passing cruisers will spy the famous minarets of the old Tampa Bay Hotel to port.

The track is eventually blocked by a 7-foot railway bridge. Our account of the Hillsborough River ends here, though small powercraft can continue upstream for quite some distance.

Old Tampa Bay

Even though it is several times larger than Hillsborough Bay, Old Tampa Bay is certainly the least desirable body of water in the Tampa region for cruising purposes. The upper 75 percent of the bay is spanned by three long, fixed bridges that have vertical clearances ranging from 40 to 44 feet. Obviously, most sail craft will have to forego cruising the majority of Old Tampa Bay due to these height restrictions. While one marina south of the southernmost span does cater to cruising craft,

and a few repair yards are available hard by the Gandy causeway, there are no other significant facilities on the bay. There are very few anchorages to be found on some of the side-waters along the way, but none of these is particularly appealing, at least to this writer. For these reasons, Old Tampa Bay is rarely frequented by visiting cruisers.

It should be noted that the shoreline is, for the most part, less developed than that of upper Hillsborough Bay and, if you can clear the bridges, the bay can make for a good afternoon sail. Nevertheless, one can only conclude that Old Tampa Bay is not Western Florida's most cruising-rich body of water.

Our discussion of Old Tampa Bay will begin with a review of the marinas and anchorages south of Gandy Bridge (the southernmost span), covering both shorelines. We will then begin a travelogue north of Gandy Bridge and follow the western shoreline around to the bay's northerly reaches and descend south again by way of the eastern banks.

Industrial Canal

North of flashing buoy #2K, the large ship's channel running north to Old Tampa Bay splits. The northeasterly fork is known as Cut K Channel and provides the best access for cruising-size craft to the bay's upper reaches.

Cut K leads directly to a deep, charted canal that strikes east into Interbay Peninsula. While this cut has excellent 25-foot-plus depths, it is quite commercial in nature and more than slightly noisy. It might be possible for pleasure craft to anchor here overnight (if you should have enough anchor rode for a proper scope), but this writer does not recommend it.

Power Plant Channel

The well-outlined channel cutting to the northwest north of flashing buoy #2K leads to a coal-fired power plant. The plant can be located by its bevy of charted stacks east of Masters Bayou. While, as you would expect, there are no facilities for pleasure craft, nor even anchorage possibilities, a portion of this cut does make a good approach to South Gandy Channel and Masters Bayou, reviewed below.

South Gandy Channel and Masters Bayou Facilities and Anchorage (Various Lats/Lons—see below)

The South Gandy Channel runs hard by the southern flank of the long causeway leading from the western shores of Old Tampa Bay to Gandy Bridge. This fairly well-marked cut leads to Masters Bayou, home of a couple of repair yards catering to pleasure craft. There is also one sheltered spot to anchor for those cruisers with a bit of risk-taking in their blood.

Gandy Channel holds minimum depths of 6 to 6½ feet, with typical soundings in the 10- to 19-foot range. While most of Masters Bayou is quite shallow, a deep cut (for the most part) follows the western and northern banks well upstream. A series of private markers helps keep you to the good water. Shallow water abounds on both sides of Gandy Channel and the Masters Bayou cut. Caution is certainly called for.

West of unlighted daybeacon #5, the first of Masters Bayou's facilities will come up along the northerly banks. First up is Gandy Bridge Marina (727-576-5117). This is a mostly small-craft facility that does offer bait, tackle, gasoline, and a small variety store. The adjoining docks are rented out on a month-to-month basis and are not appropriate for larger, cruising craft.

Next up is NOA Marine (27 52.227 North/082 36.722 West, 727-576-9315). This repair yard offers mechanical repairs (gasoline and diesel engines) and below-waterline repairs. The firm's travelift is rated at a 60-ton capacity. All wet-slip dockage is reserved for service customers. NOA specializes in the renovation and refitting of wooden-hulled vessels. It is the only yard that we know of in the Tampa Bay region that offer this service as the their principal line.

The Tampa Bay version of the ubiquitous Galati's Marine will next come up along the northerly banks near 27 52.205 North/082 36.796 West. This portion of the Galati's operation is now primarily a yacht-sales dealership, and the on-site repair facilities are almost exclusively geared toward their own new and brokerage vessels.

South of Galati's, the Masters Bayou Channel meanders to the south and eventually cuts back to the west. Soon after you traverse this westward bend, you will see the docks of Viking Boatworks (27 51.796 North/082 36.952 West, 727-576-1094) overlooking the northern shore. Depths alongside run around 8 feet. This friendly yard offers full-service mechanical (gas and diesel), electrical, and below-waterline, haul-out repairs. Twenty-four-hour emergency servicing is also available. Viking's travelift can lift up to 70 tons. There is a large parts department in the yard as well. Talk about a can-do attitude, the management at Viking has informed this writer that there "isn't anything we can't do." All wet-slip dockage is reserved for service customers.

After leaving the Viking yard behind, Masters Bayou opens out into a baylike body of water known as Snug Harbor. Most of the bay's waters are quite shallow, but there is one fortunate exception. Notice the charted bubble of 12-foot water (on 11413) just west of the repair yard. On-site research reveals there is enough swinging room for boats up to 38 feet to anchor in 11-foot depths near 27 51.718 North/082 37.101 West. Protection is superb from all winds except westerly blows exceeding thirty knots. The bay's northern shores are bordered by private docks and attractive homes. You will sight several sunken derelicts sitting on the charted shoals to the south. Be sure to anchor well north of the old wrecks.

Interbay Peninsula Facilities

North of unlighted can buoy #11K (an aid on the Cut K Channel), cruisers can follow a broad band of deep water running roughly parallel to Interbay Peninsula. This passage eventually leads to the Gandy Bridge pass-through, but two facilities of note are found south of the span.

Study chart 11413 for a moment and notice the large Y-shaped canal cutting east into Interbay Peninsula, south of Gandy Bridge.

Tampa Bayside Marina (813-831-5757) over-looks the southerly banks of the peninsula of land south of the Y-shaped creek, near 27 53.118 North/082 32.071 West. This is a large high-dry storage operation that offers no services for cruising craft, other than possibly gasoline.

The northern fork of the Y-shaped stream plays host to Imperial Yacht Center (27 53.490 North/082 31.853 West). This facility boasts row upon row of covered slips in a very well-protected harbor. Obviously, these berths are only suited for powercraft, unless some sailor

1. Tampa Bayside Marina
2. Imperial Yacht Club

were to go through the arduous job of mast removal.

Imperial Yacht Center dredged their harbor some 24 months ago, and for the foreseeable future, dockside soundings are in the 9+-foot region. This deeper water is a welcome improvement indeed.

Call ahead of time to check on transient-slip availability. This marina is very popular, and most of its extensive dockage is now rented out to local craft.

Berths are found at fixed concrete piers, featuring water hookups and 30- and 50-amp power connections. Gasoline, diesel fuel, and waste pump-out are all readily available. As a matter of fact, Imperial claims to have "the cheapest fuel in the area." A well-stocked ship's and parts store is located in the complex, and a convenience-type variety store is found in the dockmaster's office, just behind the dockage basin. There is also a fairly large powercraft-sales operation on the premises, featuring small- to medium-size vessels. Full mechanical and haul-out repairs (75-ton travelift) are offered.

Jimmy Mac's restaurant (813-839-3449) is found just south of the Imperial Yacht Center dockage basin, within easy walking distance. It is set in an old Florida-style building with a metal roof, and outside dining overlooking the water is available on the wraparound porch. The menu is heavy into sandwiches and seafood. You might also consider taking a taxi ride into nearby Tampa for many additional dining options. In short, Imperial Yacht Center is a large, full-service operation that can meet just about any conceivable need of the powercruiser.

Imperial Yacht Center (813) 832-2628
    http://www.yachtworld.com

Approach depth—15 feet minimum
Dockside depth—9+ feet
Accepts transients—call to check on availability
Transient dockage rate—average
Fixed, concrete, covered slips—yes
Dockside power connections—up to 50 amp
Dockside water connections—yes
Waste pump-out—yes
Gasoline—yes
Diesel fuel—yes
Mechanical repairs—yes
Below-waterline repairs—yes
Ship's store—yes
Restaurant—nearby

Cross Bayou Canal

The smallish stream known as Cross Bayou Canal cuts into the southwestern shores of Old Tampa Bay above the W. Howard Franklin Bridge, west of the charted St. Petersburg/Clearwater Airport. This stream once led to a shopping center (seemingly in the middle of nowhere) and a possible anchorage. However, that facility is now gone. It has been swallowed up in the expansion of the nearby St. Petersburg-Clearwater

airport, and we now suggest that cruisers avoid this offshoot entirely.

Allen Creek

The small and winding stream known as Allen Creek makes off from Old Tampa Bay's westernmost reaches northwest of Cross Bayou, and almost due south of the charted "Penthouse," which is actually only one of the many high-rise condos overlooking the banks along this portion of the bay. To reach this body of water, your craft must be able to clear the charted bridge spanning the westerly lobe of Old Tampa Bay west of Cross Bayou. Vertical clearance is set at 47 feet for this fixed bridge.

Allen Creek features some markings and minimum depths of 6 feet, with typical soundings running from 7 to 8 feet. Care is still necessary to keep to the deep water and avoid the surrounding shoals. The stream eventually wanders to the west and meets up with the docks and dry-stack storage building of MarineMax of Clearwater (727-536-2628). This is a boat-sales facility that does not offer any transient dockage. This lack of dockage, plus the absence of room for anchorage, will probably relegate this creek to those captains doing business with MarineMax.

Safety Harbor Anchorage

Only the wild-eyed captains among us will be drawn to the possible anchorage on the northernmost section of Old Tampa Bay known as Safety Harbor. Unmarked shoals are everywhere in evidence, and it's all too easy to wander into 1 to 2 feet of water, even when you are trying to be cautious.

The entrance to Safety Harbor is spanned by a charted power line with 98 feet of vertical clearance. For once, this particular electrical conduit is useful. It can serve as one of the only navigational points of reference on upper Old Tampa Bay.

If you somehow bypass all the shoals, boats of most sizes can anchor off Philippe Point in 7 to 10 feet of water, near 28 00.309 North/082 40.303 West. Depths are shallower than those shown on the current edition of chart 11413, but still more than adequate, at least outside of the shoals. Shelter is good for light to moderate winds only. Strong blows from the north or south would be particularly uncomfortable.

Philippe Point is the site of a park bearing the same name. Its green shores are attractive and restful, and one of the old Indian mounds has been preserved in the park. Its position is actually noted on chart 11413. You may catch sight of a large church from the water, sitting just behind the park. The east-side banks are overlooked by moderate residential development.

North of Philippe Point, depths begin to rise markedly, in spite of the soundings noted on 11413. The stream is soon blocked by a low-level fixed bridge. This writer suggests that cruising mariners discontinue their explorations once abeam of Philippe Point.

Safety Harbor History   Philippe Park is named for Count Philippe, a doctor in the French Navy who was captured during Colonial times by pirates. The outlook for the Count's longevity was dim indeed until an epidemic of yellow fever struck the band of marauders. His ministrations were so appreciated by the pirates that they give him a map of Tampa Bay, describing it as "the most beautiful body of water in the world." Count Philippe established a large plantation on the shores of Safety Harbor on the site of the park

that today bears his name. It is said that he later introduced the first grapefruit to Florida here. This writer has also heard that claim for a plantation on the St. Johns River, however. In any case, it is fitting that the modern-day name of Philippe Park commemorates the name of this early Floridian pioneer.

Culbreath Bayou
The charted U-shaped channel southeast of the W. Howard Franklin Bridge, on the bay's eastern banks, is actually much more obscure than it appears on 11413. On-site research found that many of the charted markers were missing and those that were in place were low and hard to spot. As we have grown to expect, this channel leads only to small canals lined by private homes and docks, with one exception. East of unlighted daybeacon #12, the eastward-flowing creek divides into two northern branches. The westernmost of these two streams hosts a series of docks that are used by local sail craft and are under the management of Imperial Yacht Center. No transient services of any type are available and the docks are unattended. Cruisers would do far better to call on the main site of Imperial Yacht Center south of Gandy Bridge.

Four Finger Creeks
Southwest of charted Sunset Park (on Interbay Peninsula), four creeks comprise what appears to be a four-fingered hand cutting east into the shoreline. Our on-site research discovered two pilings marking an entrance channel into these creeks with minimum 6½-foot depths. Unfortunately even the two middle streams, the largest of the quartet, are too small for anchorage by all but petite power vessels under 28 feet. All four of the

streams are lined by heavy residential development and private docks. So, for all their promise on chart 11413, these four creeks are probably best avoided by the visiting cruiser.

OLD TAMPA BAY NAVIGATION

Navigation of Old Tampa Bay is, shall we say, interesting. North of Gandy Bridge, there are essentially no aids to navigation outlining the preferred channel, or the surrounding shoals, for that matter. While a few side channels display some low-key markers, you must often hunt carefully for these with your binoculars. Captains cruising on Old Tampa Bay must practice sound navigation and keep a running check of their position at all times. This would be another great spot to try out that new chart plotter or a GPS interfaced with a laptop computer.

South of the Gandy span, the situation is very different. Two big ship and barge channels allow pleasure craft reliable access to the marina facilities on Masters Bayou and Interbay Peninsula.

As mentioned at the beginning of this section, skippers who choose to cruise the upper reaches of Old Tampa Bay must be able to clear three fixed bridges with vertical clearances of as little as 40 feet. Transiting southernmost Gandy Bridge is not too complicated, but both the W. Howard Franklin and the Courtney Campbell Parkway spans are quite long and often require a lengthy cruise just to reach the raised pass-throughs.

A broad shelf of shoal water extends out for a goodly distance from most of Old Tampa Bay's shoreline. Navigators who lose track of their current position are all too likely to meet up with this underwater obstruction.

Strong northerly winds that blow for several days can lower water levels on Old Tampa Bay below charted levels and those soundings discussed below. While this is not too likely, it might be best to check on conditions at Imperial Yacht Center if breezes are blowing strongly from the north upon your arrival.

The various creeks and sidewaters reviewed below can only be described as fair to prohibitive. This is quite simply not the place to take your 55-foot Hatteras, or even a 35-foot Pearson.

Entrance into Old Tampa Bay Cruisers following the Cut F, big ship's channel should take the westward-running Cut G Channel north of flashing buoys #7F and #8F. At flashing buoy #10J, the marked passage takes a 90-degree turn to the north and becomes the Cut J Channel. Avoid the charted spoil banks east of the channel between flashing daybeacon #12J and flashing buoy #4K. These are some of the few spoils on Tampa Bay which are shallow. On-site research revealed that depths can run to as little as 4 feet.

North of flashing buoy #2K, the channel splits. The northwesterly fork runs on to a coal-fired power plant and can be used by pleasure craft bound for the facilities or anchorage on Masters Bayou and the South Gandy Channel. The northeasterly passage is known as the Cut K Channel. This passage provides access to Tampa Bayside Marina, Imperial Yacht Center, and the pass-through on Gandy Bridge. This is the route to take if you are bound for the bay's northerly reaches. We shall first review the power plant channel, followed by a discussion of Cut K and points north.

Masters Bayou/South Gandy Channel
From flashing buoy #2K, cut northwest into the power plant channel, pointing to pass between flashing buoys #1 and #2. Continue following the well-marked track until you are just short of passing between flashing buoys #9 and #10. Leave the power plant channel at this point and set a careful course to come abeam of the easternmost aid on the South Gandy Channel, unlighted daybeacon #1, by some 100 yards to its easterly quarter. Be on guard against the correctly charted tongue of 3- and 4-foot water extending south from #1. Also note the shoals well east of #1.

As you make your approach to #1, the two charted radio towers will be quite visible on the causeway leading to Gandy Bridge. These huge antennae make excellent landmarks, but remember that they are well west of #1.

Once abeam of #1, turn sharply west and point to pass #1 by some 15 yards to its northerly side. Past #1 the channel remains well marked to unlighted daybeacon #5. There is shallow water both north and south of the marked cut, so watch your stern in order to quickly note any leeway.

Once abeam of #5 (to its northerly side), there are no further markers short of the Masters Bayou entrance. It is still a fairly lengthy run between #5 and the creek's mouth. This portion of the channel certainly calls for caution. Believe it or else, on-site research revealed that best depths are maintained by favoring the southern side of the channel slightly between #5 and the bayou's entrance. While there is certainly shallow water to the south, there seems to be a broad shelf of shoals extending out from the northern banks.

After coming abeam of the south-side entrance point, begin immediately favoring the northern banks as you head into the stream's interior reaches. You will first pass the small docks of Gandy Bridge Marina, followed by NOA Marine and Galati's Marine. Soon thereafter the creek cuts sharply south.

Moving upstream on Masters Bayou, the channel turns south. The deep water is outlined by pilings with arrow pointers along this stretch of the bayou. For the most part, the good soundings run along the western and then northern banks, though there is one spot where an oyster bank runs off the western shore. A piling with an arrow marker warns cruising craft away from this hazard.

Eventually the stream turns back to the west. You will spot Viking Boatyard at this point. West of the yard, favor the northern banks as the stream is squeezed between an undeveloped island to the south and the mainland to the north. Soon the water opens out into a bay. Continue cruising west for 50 to 75 yards past the island. You should spot several sunken boats just west of the island and south of the channel. Be sure to cruise past (upstream and to the west of) these old wrecks before attempting to anchor. Feel your way carefully south for a very short distance with your sounder. Be sure to drop the hook well before coming abeam of the sunken vessels to your eastern side. The trick is to cruise only as far from the northern banks as is necessary to leave enough swinging room to comfortably anchor. Cruising farther to the south invites a nighttime session on the southern shoals.

Imperial Yacht Center and Passage to Northern Old Tampa Bay   From flashing buoy #2K on the Cut J-2 Channel, bend your course to the northeast and point to pass between flashing buoys #3K and #4K on the Cut K Channel. This passage is easy to follow as far as flashing buoy #10K. At this point, the deep industrial canal runs east into Interbay Peninsula. If you should make the questionable decision to enter this highly commercial area, do so on the stream's mid-width.

To continue north, point to pass unlighted can buoy #11K to its immediate easterly side. You can then set course to pass the forward, lighted Cut K range marker to its fairly immediate westerly side. This maneuver will avoid the shallows to the east. While they do not come too close to your track, be aware of the charted shoals to the west as well.

From the forward range marker, set course to come abeam of the rear lighted range marker by some .3 nautical miles to its westerly quarter. This course will lead you away from the charted "subm piles" (submerged pilings).

Once abeam of the rear range marker,

you can either set course for the mid-width of the eastward-running canal leading to Imperial Yacht Center (on the southeast side of Gandy Bridge), or point for the Gandy twin span pass-through. The Gandy Bridge passage has a vertical clearance of 43 feet. Sometimes sustained northerly winds can increase this clearance, but it's best not to count on more than 43 feet.

On Old Tampa Bay   As there are no real anchorage opportunities or viable gunk holes for cruising-size craft on either shore between Gandy and W. Howard Franklin bridges, most captains will want to set course for the charted pass-through of the Franklin span. This track does not really lead near any water shallower than 10 feet. The closest shoal water is found on the charted tongue of shallows running north-northeast from the northern quadrant of the west-side causeway, leading to Gandy Bridge. It would take a big-time course error to find the bottom here.

The W. Howard Franklin Bridge has a vertical clearance of 44 feet. Sailors who happen to tack a bit to the east or west on the broad bubble of deep water south of this span may be in for a long trek back to the raised section of the bridge.

After leaving the W. Howard Franklin Bridge behind, navigators must begin to concern themselves with the huge tongue of shallow water to the west. Those bound for Safety Harbor can set a direct course for the 40-foot pass-through of the Courtney Campbell Parkway Bridge to the north-northwest. Even small, outboard craft should avoid the charted 10-foot span on this bridge's western reaches. On-site research revealed that depths can run to 2 feet just north of this opening.

Cruisers headed for Allen Creek may want to set course for the privately maintained but charted (16-foot) flashing day-beacon #A. From #A you can cut west to Allen Creek.

Cross Bayou Canal   Please remember that we no longer suggest that any size craft plan a visit to the interior reaches of Cross Bayou. This stream is now well inside the St. Petersburg—Clearwater Airport complex.

Allen Creek   There is one problem in cruising to Allen Creek. The charted tongue of shoal water running south from the westerly limits of Courtney Campbell Causeway is apparently building out. We noticed that it seems to have thrust its way much farther south than you might think. One nondescript pile is the sole aid marking this hazard. Set your course so as to stay well south of these shallows.

Captains must cruise under the fixed, high-rise bridge, east of the creek. Vertical clearance is set at 47 feet.

After leaving the long shoal and the bridge behind, work your way west to the Allen Creek Channel. Approach the entrance carefully, watching for two small, triangular markers. Pass these aids to your starboard side and an unadorned piling to your port. Continue cruising down the centerline of the creek. Soon you will spy an old, semi-sunken barge to port which sports a goodly growth of bushes and small trees.

Eventually the stream takes a hard jog to starboard. The piers and buildings of MarineMax will then be visible dead ahead, while a huge concrete-and-glass office building will be prominent to starboard.

On to Safety Harbor   The entrance to Safety Harbor is flanked by huge shoals to the east and west. The shallows running south from Booth Point, east of the harbor's entrance, are particularly impressive. To avoid these potential grounding zones, slant your course to the northwest after passing through the Courtney Campbell Parkway Bridge and point to eventually pass between unlighted can buoy #1 and unlighted nun buoy #2. Be mindful of the shallows extending well south from Booth Point north of your course track.

Once between #1 and #2 cut back to the north-northeast just a bit and set course to come abeam and pass unlighted nun buoy #4 to its fairly immediate westerly quarter. You can then point for the middle of the five huge power poles marching across Safety Harbor's southerly entrance. These lines have a 98-foot vertical clearance.

Watch the depth finder as you cruise along. If your soundings start to rise above 8 feet, slow down and make corrections before grounding depths are reached.

Cruise past the center power pole and hold scrupulously to the centerline of the bay as you move along to the north. Drop anchor as Philippe Point comes abeam to the west. Farther passage to the north is not particularly recommended in light of the extensive charted but unmarked shoals abutting both shorelines and extending far out into the bay.

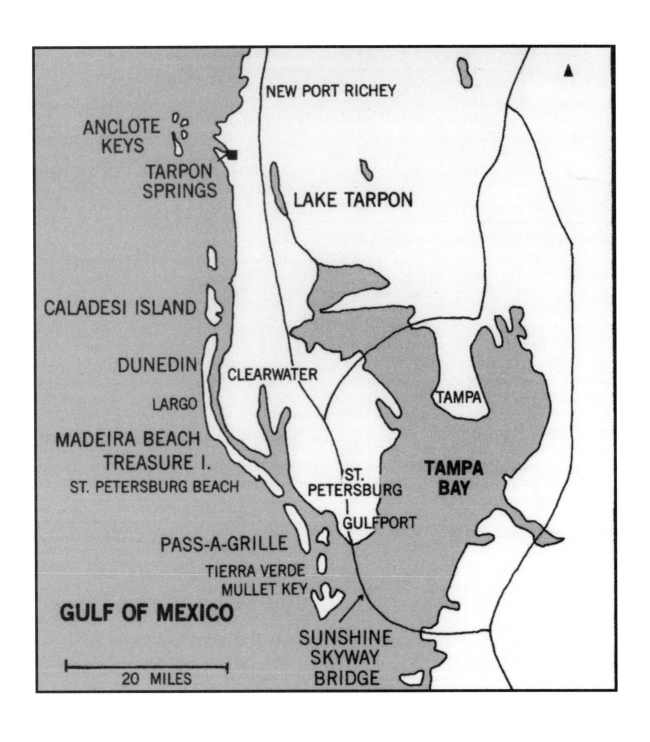

CHAPTER 5

Boca Ciega Bay to Tarpon Springs

Okay, class, now listen up. It's time for your weekly nautical pop quiz. What 36-statute-mile section of the Western Florida ICW plays host to almost 50 marinas and boatyards sitting side by side with more anchorages than you can imagine? Well, if you guessed the extremely, heavily developed section of the Waterway between the northern reaches of Tampa Bay's entrance and Anclote Key, then go to the head of the class.

This is truly an amazing section of the Waterway. If you have not traveled this stretch before, you are in for an unforgettable experience. Never before have we seen such an incredible selection of pleasure craft facilities crowded into such relatively few miles. With the exception of isolation, if you can't find it here, better give up.

The ICW leaves Tampa Bay and the Sunshine Skyway behind and enters the southerly reaches of broad Boca Ciega Bay. Two alternate passages lead cruisers north past the lower bay's complicated islands and peninsulas. To the west, Pass-A-Grille Inlet offers a reliable passage to the Gulf of Mexico.

Farther to the north, the Waterway runs between beach-side barrier islands displaying a level of development which can only be described as a concrete jungle, and the far more attractive mainland St. Petersburg shoreline. A host of marinas waits to greet cruising craft along the St. Petersburg waterfront. Johns Pass Inlet, near the city's northerly limits, provides another dependable seaward access point.

After transiting a canal-like passage known, appropriately enough, as "the Narrows," the ICW spills into broad Clearwater Harbor. Now

the heaviest development shifts to the mainland shores. If there is a more built-up community anywhere than Clearwater, I haven't found it. Of course, the Gulf barrier islands also support a heavy population. Facilities run the full gamut and are available on both shorelines. Yet a third Gulf passage, Clearwater Pass, is reliable and convenient for all types of pleasure craft.

Finally the ICW begins to leave all the heavy development behind as it enters the broad waters of St. Joseph Sound. Some portions of the ICW channel through St. Joseph Sound display low-water depths of as little as 6 feet, or sometimes slightly less. Deep-draft vessels take note.

Anclote Key heralds the northerly terminus of the Western Florida ICW. The nearby Anclote River and the absolutely delightful village of Tarpon Springs make a great jumping-off point or port of arrival from the wide-open waters of the Big Bend to the north.

With the exception of the overnight refuges around Anclote Key and one haven near Tierra Verde, almost all the ICW anchorages north of Tampa Bay are overlooked by a variety of developed shores. While some may yearn for the peace and serenity of Pine Island Sound, there are still plenty of sheltered spots to ride out even the nastiest weather for those who prefer to swing on the hook rather than tie up to the dock.

In short, while those among us who enjoy backwater cruising may not be totally taken with this stretch of the Western Florida ICW, there is no denying that it has more to offer than can be imagined. Take your time, watch out for all the restricted bridges and no-wake zones, and enjoy your cruise.

Charts   Most navigators will need only one chart for the complicated waters between northern Tampa Bay and Tarpon Springs. A few cruisers will also want the offshore chart detailing these waters.

11411—large-scale chart providing excellent detail of the Waterway route and the various inlets along the way from Boca Ciega Bay to Anclote Key; also includes the Anclote River to Tarpon Springs

11412—covers all the offshore waters between Tampa Bay and Anclote Key

Bridges

Isla Del Sol/Alternate Channel Bridge—crosses alternate Boca Ciega Bay channel north-northwest of flashing daybeacon #11 and Frenchman Creek—Fixed—18 feet

Pinellas Bayway southern "E" span—crosses ICW at Standard Mile 113, northwest of unlighted daybeacon #39—Bascule—25 feet (closed)—opens on the hour and every 20 minutes thereafter 9:00 A.M. to 5:00 P.M.—at all other times opens on demand

Pinellas Bayway northern "C" span—crosses ICW at Standard Mile 114, north of unlighted daybeacon #25—Bascule—25 feet (closed)—opens on the hour and every 20 minutes thereafter 7:00 A.M. to 7:00 P.M.

Mud Key Channel Bridge—crosses Mud Key Channel immediately south of the Pass-A-Grille Yacht Club—Fixed—14 feet

Corey Causeway Bridge—crosses ICW at Standard Mile 118, northwest of unlighted daybeacon #39—Bascule—23 feet (closed) —opens on the hour and every 20 minutes thereafter 8:00 A.M. to 7:00 P.M. weekdays and 10:00 A.M. to 7:00 P.M. weekends and holidays

Treasure Island Causeway Bridge—crosses ICW at Standard Mile 119, north of flashing daybeacon #14—Bascule—8 feet (closed)—opens on the hour and every 15 minutes thereafter 7:00 A.M. to 7:00 P.M. seven days a week—11:00 P.M. to 7:00 A.M., only opens with 10 minutes' notice

Long Bayou/Seminole Bridge—crosses Long Bayou north of unlighted daybeacon #31—Fixed—20 feet

Johns Pass Bridge—crosses interior reaches of Johns Pass, west-southwest of flashing daybeacon #6—Bascule—25 feet (closed)—opens on demand

Welch Causeway Bridge—crosses ICW at Standard Mile 123—Bascule—25 feet (closed)—opens on the hour and every 20 minutes thereafter 9:30 A.M. to 6:00 P.M. weekends and holidays—at all other times opens on demand

Park Boulevard Bridge—crosses ICW at Standard Mile 126, north of unlighted daybeacon #12 in the heart of "the Narrows—Bascule—25 feet (closed)—opens on demand

Indian Rocks Beach Bridge—crosses ICW at Standard Mile 129, northwest of flashing daybeacon #33—Bascule—25 feet (closed)—opens on demand

Belleair Bridge—crosses ICW at Standard Mile 132, north-northeast of flashing daybeacon #47—Bascule—21 feet (closed)—opens on the hour and every 15 minutes thereafter noon to 6:00 P.M. weekends and holidays—at all other times opens on demand

Clearwater Pass Bridge—crosses Clearwater Pass west of flashing daybeacon #14—Fixed—74 feet

Clearwater Memorial Causeway Bridge—crosses ICW at Standard Mile 136, north-northeast of unlighted daybeacon #13—Bascule—25 feet (closed)—opens on the hour and every twenty minutes thereafter 9:00 A.M. to 6:00 P.M.

weekdays and on the hour and half-hour 2:00 P.M. to 6:00 P.M. weekends and holidays—at all other times opens on demand—note that new, high-rise bridge currently under construction at this location
Mandalay Channel Bridge—crosses Mandalay

Channel just north of the Clearwater Municipal Marina—Fixed—14 feet
Dunedin/Honeymoon Island Bridge—crosses ICW at Standard Mile 142—Bascule—24 feet (closed)—opens on demand

Boca Ciega Bay to Treasure Island

There are two alternate passages that one might choose to cruise from the northern tip of the causeway leading to the Sunshine Skyway Bridge into the northern reaches of Boca Ciega Bay. This large body of water is split, fractured, and subdivided by bridges, causeways, man-made islands, and islets. It's all too easy to become confused, so take your time and keep chart 11411 at hand.

The mainland shores of Boca Ciega are part of St. Petersburg, while the Gulf-side barrier islands consist of the abundant beach development so typical of the entire run from Tampa Bay to Anclote Key. All this variable landscape is not necessarily bad news for cruisers. Anchorages abound, even if few are of the isolated variety. Marinas are dotted here and there all along the way. Many are large, first-rate operations which cruisers can make use of with full confidence that they will find every imaginable service.

The Split (Standard Mile 111)

At flashing daybeacon #26, skippers northbound on the Western Florida ICW meet a very definite parting of the ways. The Waterway channel cuts west and then northwest through the broad mid-width of southern Boca Ciega Bay. An alternate passage for those boats which can clear an 18-foot fixed bridge swings to the north. Assess your craft's requirements and the

on-the-water conditions carefully before choosing your route.

We shall first review the many cruising opportunities of the alternate channel, followed by the side trips, anchorages, and marinas of the ICW passage via Pass-A-Grille and Tierra Verde. After the two routes rejoin, we will follow the ICW to Treasure Island Causeway.

Alternate Channel (Standard Mile 111, Various Lats/Lons—see below)

Powercraft that can ease under an 18-foot fixed bridge without scraping their flybridge might well choose the alternate route running north, east of Indian Key. Not only is this passage far more sheltered than the Waterway channel, it also offers easy access to several first-rate marinas and two anchorages. Even sailors can take advantage of an anchorage and one marina, as these points of interest are both thankfully located well south of the fixed span.

The first and possibly the best anchorage on the alternate route is found on the correctly charted ribbon of deep water north of unlighted daybeacon #7, near 27 42.524 North/ 082 41.082 West. We have discovered that minimum 7-foot depths run to within 200 yards of the northeasterly shoreline.

Be careful of some of the small sail craft you may see swinging on a mooring buoy in this anchorage. We discovered the hard way that these small vessels are floating in only 4 feet of water.

The banks to the east and northeast afford excellent protection when winds are blowing from this quarter, while Indian Key to the southwest gives some protection from moderate southwesterly breezes. There is even some shelter to the north. A strong southerly wind clearly calls for an ongoing search elsewhere. Swinging room should be sufficient for most sizes and types of pleasure craft. The shores to the north and northeast are only lightly developed, but you may be bothered by traffic entering and leaving the Sunshine Skyway during the night.

The marked passage to O'Neill's Marina (27 42.431 North/082 40.808 West) will be spied on the eastern banks, east of flashing daybeacon #6. This facility accepts transients on a space-available basis. Call ahead of time to check on slip availability. Low-water entrance depths are in the 4- to 5-foot range, while dockside soundings run from 5½ to 7 feet. Berths are provided at fixed, wooden piers, all with freshwater hookups, and some featuring 30-amp power connections. The

harbor is well sheltered from inclement weather. Mechanical repairs are available for gas-powered engines only. Gasoline (no diesel fuel) can be purchased, and there is a combination variety store and bait-and-tackle shop on the premises. The one on-site shower is adequate but not climate controlled.

O'Neill's Marina (727) 867-2585
http://www.oneillsmarina.com

Approach depth—4-5 feet (minimum)
Dockside depth—5½-7 feet
Accepts transients—space-available basis
Transient dockage rate—below average
Fixed wooden piers—yes
Dockside power connections—up to 30 amp (most but not all slips)
Dockside water connections—yes
Shower—yes
Gasoline—yes
Mechanical repairs—gas engines only
Variety store—yes

Frenchman Creek cuts the northeastern banks of the alternate channel between unlighted daybeacons #7 and #8. This stream leads under two fixed bridges with 18 feet of vertical clearance to Huber Yacht Harbor (727-867-2117). Approach depths run some 6½ to 8 feet, with 5½ to 8 feet of water dockside. While this facility does not take transients for overnight dockage, repair and fueling services are available. Haul-outs are accomplished by a 70-ton travelift.

The northern shores of Frenchman Creek below (before reaching) the fixed bridges and Huber Yacht Harbor play host to a collection of docks associated with nearby Eckerd College. While there are no services for visitors, cruisers will be interested to observe the bevy of small craft pulled up on the shore. Powercraft should be alert for small boats in the creek.

Some boats occasionally anchor in the

charted deep water west-southwest of unlighted daybeacon #9. While minimum depths run in the 4½- to 6-foot region, there is absolutely no protection from fresh westerly breezes, and strong easterly winds are none too welcome either. In northerly and southerly breezes, Indian Key to the south and the islets to the north do give some protection, but even so you wouldn't catch this writer here if winds were forecast to exceed 10 knots. If the weather chooses to cooperate, there is plenty of swinging room for most craft. The undeveloped sands of Indian Key to the south make a delightful backdrop.

Returning now to the main track of the alternate channel, north of the 18-foot fixed bridge, the track follows a well-marked passage out into a wide and mostly deep eastward-striking lobe of Boca Ciega Bay. No fewer than two first-class marinas, one yacht club, and a new, much-welcome city dock are found on the easterly reaches of this body of water.

Before we go on to discuss these facilities in depth, let us take a moment to note that southbound cruisers on the ICW can easily reach these marinas via the northern leg of the alternate channel, *without having to suffer the 18-foot bridge*. This portion of the alternate passage leaves the ICW hard by flashing daybeacon #32. Thus, the facilities described below are readily accessible to sail craft as well as to their powered brethren.

It is quite possible to follow the broad path of deep water north and west of flashing daybeacon #15 to a large yacht club guarding the northern shores of Isla del Sol. The passage features minimum 8-foot depths at least as far as the marina, with most soundings being considerably deeper. This facility will be detailed in the discussion of the main Waterway channel later in this chapter.

The charted canal cutting into Boca Ciega's southeastern shores, east-northeast of unlighted daybeacon #14, leads fortunate cruisers to Maximo Marina (27 43.468 North/082 40.931 West). This facility's location can be identified by the "Boathouses" designation on chart 11411. If you are looking for a marina that satisfies most needs that might arise for cruising craft (and who isn't?), then your search is finished. Set your course for Maximo Marina, sit back, and enjoy.

Minimum entrance depths of 8 feet are coupled with very impressive dockside readings of 10 to 15 feet, surely enough for even the longest-legged sail craft. Transients are enthusiastically accepted at both fixed wooden and (somewhat older) floating docks. The harbor is extremely well sheltered and would make an excellent haven in which to ride out heavy weather. The marina features 330 wet slips (with both fixed, wooden, and some new floating wooden decked piers, many of these slips are of the covered variety) and 320 dry-storage slots. The management claims to offer the largest selection of covered slips on the Sunshine State's western coastline. We would certainly not argue with that contention. Every conceivable dockside power and water connection is readily available, as are diesel fuel, gasoline, and waste pump-out service. Full mechanical repairs are featured, and haul-outs are quickly accomplished by a 50-ton travelift. There are three sets of shoreside showers, with the central unit featuring air conditioning. There is also an on-site Laundromat with a small paperback exchange library. Recently, Maximo has added Fathom Bait and Tackle Shop, plus a marine electronics dealer, to their offerings. A West Marine store (727-867-5700) is also found within easy walking distance of the dockage basin.

The adjacent restaurant was closed during

our last visit, in August 2003, but the management informed this writer that they were "talking with several prospective new owners." Only time will tell what, if any, new restaurant may occupy these premises.

All in all Maximo must be rated as a good find for visiting cruisers, and one you will want to check out.

Maximo Marina (727) 867-1102

Approach depth—8-11 feet
Dockside depth—10-15 feet
Accepts transients—yes
Transient dockage rate—average
Fixed wooden and floating docks—yes
Dockside power connections—up to 50 amp
Dockside water connections—yes
Waste pump-out—yes
Showers—yes
Laundromat—yes
Gasoline—yes
Diesel fuel—yes
Mechanical repairs—yes
Below-waterline repairs—yes

Now, just in case that's not quite enough to attract you to Boca Ciega's easterly reaches, there is yet another notable marina and yacht club to be found on the upper reaches of the charted channel entering the bay's northeasterly reaches (near Clam Bayou). As you cruise through the marked channel with minimum depths of 7½ feet, the protected harbor of Boca Ciega Yacht Club will come abeam to port (near 27 44.296 North/082 41.728 West). Believe me, you can't miss it. The clubhouse is also quickly spotted just east of the harbor. We found one 5½- to 6-foot lump at the entrance to the club harbor, but otherwise dockside depths range between 7 and 9 feet. The docks are of the fixed wooden variety and feature modern power and water connections. Groceries, supplies, and several restaurants are found within a

mile of the clubhouse. Many cruisers may want to call a taxi to access these services.

Boca Ciega Yacht Club is glad to accept overnighters if (and only if) prior arrangements have been made. Longer-term dockage is not available. Transient slip space is limited and is usually at a premium during weekends. Be sure to call the club's dockmaster at the number listed below well ahead of time. If there is any way that the club can accommodate you, it will do all in its power to meet your needs.

Boca Ciega Yacht Club (727) 321-7295
http://www.sailbcyc.org

Approach depth—5½-6 feet (minimum)
Dockside depth—7-9 feet
Accepts transients—limited (prior arrangements necessary)
Fixed wooden piers—yes
Dockside power connections—up to 30 amp
Dockside water connections—yes
Restaurant—several within a long walk

Gulfport Municipal Marina (27 44.422 North/082 41.767 West) occupies the well-sheltered dockage basin at the channel's northeasterly limits. This fine and friendly municipal marina welcomes overnighters and provides berths at (mostly) fixed wooden piers. Within two years, all the docks will be of the fixed wooden variety, but for the moment, some of the older, fixed concrete structures remain. Approach and dockside depths are currently in the 6-foot MLW range. The harbor is well sheltered from inclement weather.

The city dockmaster suggests that visiting captains call ahead and make advance arrangements. Cruisers will find the harbor crowded with a beautiful collection of sleek sail craft and a few powerboats to round out the bill.

All berths feature freshwater hookups and

30- and 50-amp power connections. Shoreside amenities include good, air-conditioned showers and a ship's and variety store. Gasoline and diesel fuel can be purchased, waste pump-out service is available, and some mechanical repairs can be arranged through independent local contractors.

Five restaurants are located within a long, long walk of the docks. One of the best choices is La Cote Basque (727-321-6888), a French-style dining spot. We suggest that you call a taxi to visit these local dining attractions. You won't catch this writer walking through the neighborhoods behind the dockage basin after dark.

Gulfport Municipal Marina (727) 893-1071
http://www.ci.gulfport.fl.us.com

Approach depth—6 feet MLW
Dockside depth—6 feet MLW
Accepts transients—yes
Transient dockage rate—below average
Fixed wooden and concrete piers—yes
Dockside power connections—up to 50 amp
Dockside water connections—yes
Waste pump-out—yes
Showers—yes
Gasoline—yes
Diesel fuel—yes
Mechanical repairs—yes (independent local contractors)
Ship's and variety store—yes
Restaurant—long walk or (better yet) short taxi ride

Other Eastern Boca Ciega Bay Facilities

Mariner's Cove Marina (727-321-5792) guards the bay's northern shores as facility designation #9 on chart 11411. This small

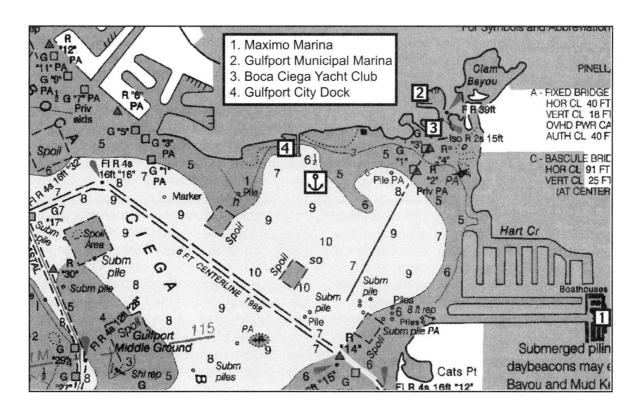

1. Maximo Marina
2. Gulfport Municipal Marina
3. Boca Ciega Yacht Club
4. Gulfport City Dock

operation is engaged exclusively in the dry storage of smaller powercraft, and no facilities except gasoline are available to the cruising craft. Meager entrance depths of only 4 to 4½ feet will restrict even gasoline purchases to small, shallow-draft vessels.

Why in the world would this writer be so excited about a new, fixed wooden city dock that doesn't even allow overnight stays? Well, let me tell you, the Gulfport Town Dock (27 44.202 North/082 42.452 West) *is* something to get the adrenaline pumping.

First, let's note that, while overnight stays are not in the offing, visiting cruisers can anchor overnight (or for a few days) on the waters of Boca Ciega Bay near 27 44.072 North/082 42.316 West. Depths seem to run around from 5 to 7 feet at low tide. Once the hook is down, it's then a simple proposition indeed to dinghy ashore to the new city dock.

This anchorage is not really fit for foul weather. There is some protection to the north, but winds whistling in from any other direction have free rein to spoil your evening. Nevertheless, during fair weather, this is an overnight haven to consider. Read on and discover why!

The Gulfport City Dock features six slips, facing to the south, which are not really appropriate for vessels larger than 45 feet and do not afford sufficient shelter in any but good weather. Depths alongside run in the 5- to 6½-foot region, with most soundings on the deeper end of that scale. No power or water connections are located on the docks, and as stated above, no overnight stays are permitted. *However*, you are welcome to moor here while visiting downtown Gulfport, just to the north.

OK, OK, enough of the big buildup. What makes the Gulfport dock so special is that this community's fascinating downtown district lies within an easy step of the dock. We found this entire region so very charming that I can't believe I missed it during earlier editions of this guidebook. Well, let me make up for those omissions now.

Downtown Gulfport is an enchanting combination of Old Florida and an arts, crafts, and fine-dining bonanza. There is a whole host of art galleries, gift-type shops, and a really fine community theater, which will be of interest to all but the dull witted. If you've arrived with a burgeoning appetite, so much the better. There are many excellent (and surprisingly reasonable) dining attractions in downtown Gulfport waiting to greet you. We particularly recommend the Pierhouse Grill (5401 Shore Boulevard, 727-322-1741). During my last presentation to the Boca Ciega Yacht Club, my hosts brought me to the Pierhouse beforehand. I was in gastronomical heaven with my Black and Blue Steak (a beef filet stuffed with blue cheese), and my companions' seafood dishes appeared ever so appetizing as well. Trust me on this one. Don't miss the Pierhouse Grill!

Let me also strongly recommend a visit to the Peninsula Inn and Spa (2937 Beach Boulevard, 727-346-9800, http://www.inn spa.net). Visitors will find another top-class restaurant on these premises, as well as an inviting bar set in a true Old Floridian atmosphere. This is a super spot to gather with friends over drinks after a long but satisfying day on the water. They also offer top-flight lodging, but hold on to your wallet.

Finally, if you happen to arrive in Gulfport on the first Friday of any month, a lucky star is shining on your cruise. On these evenings, the town holds an "art walk." Many local craftsmen and artists feature their work throughout the downtown district, and the activity goes on well into the nighttime hours. It's an event you will want to check out time and time again.

If, by now, you have detected a certain rampant enthusiasm on this writer's part for the downtown Gulfport business district, you are on the right track. How fortunate that the new city docks allow the cruising community easy access to this wonderful attraction. See you there!

Coming down from cloud nine and returning to the waters of eastern Boca Ciega Bay, the alternate channel eventually cuts to the west and rejoins the principal ICW route at flashing daybeacon #32. Our discussion will now return to the official ICW passage, beginning at the split with the alternate channel on the southerly reaches of Boca Ciega Bay.

ICW to Pass-A-Grille (Various Lats/Lons—see below)

The ICW channel sweeps sharply west from its intersection with the western Tampa Bay and alternate Boca Ciega Bay channels on its way to the Pinellas Bayway "E" Bridge. This is an open passage where fresh winds have more than enough fetch to foster an unwelcome chop.

Shortly after you pass through the Pinellas span, northwest of unlighted daybeacon #22, the extensive piers of Tierra Verde Marina (27 41.560 North/082 43.164 West, Standard Mile 113) will come abeam to the southwest. This marina has an impressive array of convenient dockside and shoreside services. Tierra Verde Marina accepts transients at its modern, fixed wooden piers. There are currently 84 wet slips, and a dry-storage building housing 343 powercraft is also available. Depths alongside are an impressive 9 to 10 feet or better. As you would expect, all dockside power and water connections are provided, as are gasoline, diesel fuel, and waste pump-out service. The pump-out charge is $5. One fair, non-climate-controlled shower

is available shoreside. Full mechanical repairs for both gasoline and diesel engines are available through Tierra Verde Marina. Boats as large as 35 feet can be hauled via the dry-storage facility's forklift.

A large, strip-type shopping center sits just behind the piers. Here you will discover a convenience/variety store, a Sub-Way, a large hardware store, and the Ship Side Café (727-906-9794), open for all three meals, seven days a week. A tiki-style, open-air bar known as the Sandbar overlooks the dockage basin.

About the only negative aspect of Tierra Verde Marina is its relative openness to wind, wave, and strong tidal currents. Strong northerly and southerly blows, in particular, can be a problem at the piers, which lack breakwaters. During normal weather, this aspect of the marina should not be too great a problem.

Tierra Verde Marina (727) 866-0255
    http://www.lakewaymarina.com/tierraverde/

Approach depth—15+ feet
Dockside depth—9-10 feet (10 feet directly
    against seawall)
Accepts transients—yes
Transient dockage rate—above average
Fixed wooden piers—yes
Dockside power connections—up to 50 amp
Dockside water connections—yes
Waste pump-out—yes
Shower—yes
Gasoline—yes
Diesel fuel—yes
Mechanical repairs—yes
Restaurant—on site and several nearby

Pass-A-Grille Inlet and Associated Channels (Standard Mile 113.5)

Southwest of flashing daybeacon #24, a broad swath of deep water leaves the ICW and runs south and west toward reliable Pass-A-Grille Inlet. This cut is used on a regular basis by a host of local pleasure craft, and it can be relied upon to provide reliable access to and from the open waters of the Gulf of Mexico. Most markers are clearly charted, a sure sign of a stable seaward cut.

Some low-key marina and repair yard facilities are available on the tongue of deep water

cutting north from flashing daybeacon #11, and a marina of note is found on the Tierra Verde Canal, south of flashing daybeacon #10.

Pass-A-Grille Beach and Facilities
(Various Lats/Lons—see below)

The southerly tip of the barrier island flanking

1. Tierra Verde Marina
2. Tierra Verde Resort Marina
3. Merry Pier Marina
4. Pass-A-Grille Marina
5. Warren's Marina
6. Pass-A-Grille Yacht Club

Pass-A-Grille Inlet's northerly flank is known as Pass-A-Grille Beach. We felt a noticeable change for the better when visiting this community. A far less frenzied, small-town atmosphere is coupled with these shaded, quiet neighborhoods than that found in boisterous St. Petersburg Beach to the north. Most cruisers will welcome this change and will want to spend some time in this community, which, thankfully, has been overlooked by the minions of concrete and steel.

North of flashing daybeacon #11, deep water runs along the westerly banks to a fixed bridge with 14 feet of vertical clearance. Two small marinas and a boatyard overlook the westerly shores between #11 and the bridge. The first of these is found south of #11.

Merry Pier Marina (27 41.266 North/082 44.173 West) consists of a single fixed wooden T-shaped dock, which sits in an exposed position near Pass-A-Grille Beach Channel's southern foot. Overnighters are occasionally accepted, but if winds are forecast to exceed 10 knots (particularly from the south), this writer advises you to seek shelter elsewhere. During one of our on-site research trips, a moderate southerly breeze was enough to raise a chop that would not only disturb your evening's rest, but also make docking hazardous as well. I suspect that most of the local captains use this pier as a fuel and supply stop and berth their craft at another marina.

Gasoline, diesel fuel, and a medium-size ship's and variety store are available on the pier.

Probably the best reason to tie up to Merry Pier is found just across the street, at the notable Sea Horse Restaurant (727-360-1734). The bill of fare is a bit on the simple side, but we have consistently found everything on the menu to be superb. The grouper sandwiches, by any account, are wonderful.

Merry Pier Marina (727) 360-6606
  http://www.merrypier.com

Approach depth—8-15 feet
Dockside depth—8-16 feet
Accepts transients—limited
Transient dockage rate—below average
Fixed wooden piers—yes
Dockside power and water connections—yes
Gasoline—yes
Diesel fuel—yes
Ship's and variety store—yes
Restaurant—across the street

Next up is the small dockage basin of Pass-A-Grille Marina (27 41.754 North/082 44.135 West, 727-360-0100), located along the westerly banks, some .3 nautical miles north of flashing daybeacon #11. This facility features a large, metal, dry-storage building, which is highly visible from the water. There are also 15 wet slips on site, but the marina management has informed this writer that these berths are filled "99 percent of the time" by resident craft. Besides fuel (gas and diesel) and small-craft mechanical (outboard and I/O) repairs, visitors will find few services here.

Tiny Warren's Marina (727-360-1784, 27 41.818 North/082 44.130 West) flanks the westerly banks, immediately south of the 14-foot fixed bridge. Clearly service work is the forte here. Full mechanical repairs are supplemented by a do-it-yourself or leave it to be done (your choice) haul-out yard. The facility's travelift is rated at a 12-ton capacity. Warren's is a family-owned business, and we found the staff to be in touch with the needs of cruising craft.

Captains cruising north from Warren's are soon greeted by a fixed bridge with only 14 feet of vertical clearance. Pass-A-Grille Yacht Club (27 41.921 North/082 44.120 West) is found north of this span. Sailboats and taller powercraft can reach this facility via Mud Key Channel to the north (reviewed later in this chapter). While this club does not employ a regular dockmaster, members of other clubs with reciprocal agreements are accommodated for a maximum three-day stay. Advance reservations are required. Lunch and dinner are served Tuesday through Sunday (lunch only on Sunday) in the well-appointed dining room (reservations requested).

The docks consist of modern, fixed wooden piers which feature impressive depths of 9 to 10 feet at the outer slips, while 6 to 7 feet of water can be held alongside the inner harbor docks. Power connections up to 50 amps and water outlets are ready at hand. Retail and grocery stores are within walking distance, as are several additional restaurants. The harbor is well sheltered from all but the heaviest weather.

> **Pass-A-Grille Yacht Club (727) 360-1646**
> **http://www.pagyc.com**
> **Approach depth—8-15 feet (via Pass-A-Grille**
> **Beach Channel)**
> **5½-11 feet (via Mud Key Channel)**
> **Dockside depth—6-10 feet (deeper depths on**
> **outer face dock)**
> **Accepts transients—members of clubs with**
> **reciprocal agreements**
> **Fixed wooden piers—yes**
> **Dockside power and water connections—yes**
> **Showers—yes**
> **Restaurant—on site (and several others nearby)**

Tierra Verde Resort Marina and Canal (27 41.363 North/082 43.279 West)

An excellent marina is found on the northeasterly terminus of the Tierra Verde canal, whose entrance cuts the island southeast of flashing daybeacon #10 (on the Pass-A-Grille Inlet channel). This stream can also be accessed by the smaller charted canal south of unlighted daybeacon #14 (near Tierra Verde Island's northwesterly tip), but this passage is crossed by a low-level fixed bridge. Most cruising-size craft will need to make use of the unencumbered stream southeast of #10.

The canal's entrance from the Pass-A-Grille Channel is well marked. Minimum depths at the entrance are some 6-8 feet, improving to 10-19 feet on the stream's interior reaches. Heavy residential development overlooks both shores. This is obviously the high-rent district. Many of the houses have swimming pools and private docks. The huge powercraft usually moored at these piers are incredibly impressive. Yards look as if the yardman lives on the premises. But wait—the best is yet to come.

Northeast of the canal's intersection with its small, northwesterly sister, cruisers will soon catch sight of a mammoth collection of both power and sail yachts ahead. This is your first sight of Tierra Verde Resort Marina.

First of all, it doesn't take a nautical genius to quickly discern that this is one of the most sheltered harbors you will ever find. If really nasty weather is in the forecast, you couldn't do better than quickly coil your lines at this marina and batten down the hatches.

The marina itself is associated with a low-rise condo complex, an on-site restaurant, plus a bar. Transients of every description are accepted for overnight or temporary dockage at fixed concrete (and some wooden) piers set atop wooden pilings. Every conceivable power, water, telephone, and cable-vision connection is to be found at all slips. Dockside depths of 8 to 12 feet are enough for even the deepest-draft sailboat. Gasoline, diesel fuel, and waste pump-out services are readily available, and mechanical repairs for both gasoline and diesel power plants are now available on site. Transients are afforded the use of the large swimming pool, tennis courts, and hot tub. Good, air-conditioned showers are found at two different locations in the marina complex. A Laundromat is, as you would expect, part of the package.

The grounds at Tierra Verde Resort Marina are immaculately manicured. The green,

green grass and waving palms are definitely recommended for those who have seen one too many steep waves.

All of the adjacent condos are now owned on a time-share basis. Sometimes, the owners choose not to use their particular week of scheduled occupancy, and then the rooms are rented out to visitors. If you should want to take a break from the live-aboard routine, ask the dockmaster if any of these temporary shoreside lodgings are available.

The on-site Cocomos Bar and Grill seems very popular with the local crowd. Both indoor and outdoor dining are featured.

Tierra Verde Resort Marina (727) 866-1487
   http://www.tvresortmarina.com

Approach depth—8¹/₂-19 feet
Dockside depth—8-12 feet
Accepts transients—yes
Transient dockage rate—above average
Fixed concrete and wooden piers—yes
Dockside power connections—up to 50 amp
Dockside water connections—yes
Waste pump-out—yes
Showers—yes
Laundromat—yes
Gasoline—yes
Diesel fuel—yes
Mechanical repairs—yes
Ship's and variety store—yes
Restaurant—on site

Mud Key Channel (Standard Mile 114, 27 42.434 North/082 43.692 West)

Let us now return our attention to the principal ICW passage as it begins its approach to the northern leg of the Pinellas Bayway Bridge (also known as the Pinellas Bayway "C" bridge), north of unlighted daybeacon #25. Immediately south of the span, cruisers can easily enter charted Mud Key Channel. While offering an anchorage possibility in its own right, this cut allows access to Pass-A-Grille

Yacht Club for craft which cannot clear the 14-foot fixed bridge at the channel's southern foot.

Minimum depths on the channel are around 6 feet, with typical soundings in the 8- to 11-foot region. The entire passage is surrounded by heavy, but not visually displeasing residential development. There are one or two tricky spots along the way, so be sure to read the navigational information presented later in this chapter before making your first entry.

As you cruise down the main body of Mud Key Channel, the tall, pink tower of the beautifully restored Don CeSar Hotel (727-360-1881) will be readily spotted to the northwest. Recalling the days of Florida's golden age, when only the rich and powerful regularly visited the Sunshine State, this edifice has been a mariner's landmark for many a year. The tall building is noted on chart 11411 as "Hotel." While the Don CeSar does not have any dockage of its own for cruising visitors, a close approach to the structure is described in the next subsection below.

Boats up to 36 feet and drawing no more than 4 feet can drop the hook at the mouth of the first southward-striking canal near Mud Key Channel's entrance from the ICW (near 27 42.434 North/082 43.692 West). As you ease into this sidewater, one patch of 5-foot depths will be encountered, followed by 6- to 11-foot soundings. Farther to the south, the side canal narrows far too much for anchorage, and depths become uncertain. This haven has excellent protection from all winds save exceptionally strong easterly blows.

Big McPherson Bayou (Standard Mile 114, Various Lats/Lons—see below)

For my money, one of the best anchorages short of Clearwater Harbor is found on the channel cutting into the Waterway's western banks, just north of the Pinellas Bayway

Bridge (northern "C" half). Big McPherson Bayou leads to not one, but two magnificent havens with a plenitude of shelter from any weather short of a hurricane.

The entrance portion of the channel is unmarked and somewhat tricky, but elementary caution should see you into the deeper interior reaches with minimum 6½-foot depths.

The first and best spot to anchor is found at the mouth of the first stream that comes abeam to the northeast (near 27 42.645 North/082 43.863 West). Boats as large as 38 feet will find plenty of elbowroom. Just be sure to pick your spot carefully to avoid swinging into the correctly charted shallows to the south and southwest. The starboard shore of this offshoot has fairly heavy, but attractive residential development, while the port-side banks are only sparsely built up at this time. All in all, this is one of the most superb anchorages you will find along this developed portion of the Waterway.

Boats up to 34 feet may also choose to drop the hook in the charted 7- and 9-foot cove farther to the west (near 27 42.747 North/082 43.989 West). This delightful sidewater is surrounded by attractive homes and features almost perfect shelter.

From both anchorages, the tall, pink tower of the Don CeSar Hotel looms over the shallow western banks. No dockage facilities are available for pleasure craft, but if you are of a mind, break out the dinghy and go ashore at one of the undeveloped portions of the western shoreline. Please don't trespass! It would be a memorable experience indeed to dine ashore at the Don CeSar. Reservations are most certainly recommended and this would definitely be the time to dig out the old navy blazer. Just be sure to brush off the mold and mildew first.

Isla del Sol Yacht and Country Club (Standard Mile 114.5)

A side channel runs east from unlighted

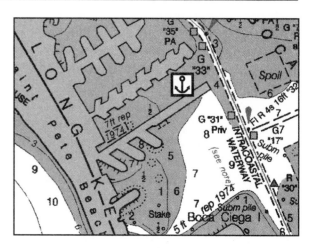

daybeacon #2 (south of flashing daybeacon #26) and skirts the northern shores of artificial Isla del Sol. This cut eventually intersects the alternate ICW channel, discussed earlier in this chapter, near flashing daybeacon #15. While minimum 8-foot depths, with soundings running as deep as 25 feet, can be held all the way from the ICW to the alternate channel, the passage is unmarked and should be run with care.

The extensive piers of Isla del Sol Yacht and Country Club (727-867-3625) will come abeam to the south about halfway between the ICW and flashing daybeacon #15. This facility has reverted to its former status as a private yacht club.

St. Petersburg Beach Anchorage (Standard Mile 116, 27 44.154 North/082 44.079 West)

The charted deep water between the two artificial islets, southwest of unlighted daybeacon #33, offers a sheltered overnight anchorage unless winds of over 15 knots are blowing from the east. Minimum depths of 5 feet can be held by scrupulously holding to the mid-width at the entrance to the cove. East of the charted shallow water at the rear of the cove, typical soundings range from 5½ to 10 feet. There is plenty of swinging room for vessels up to 45 feet. Surprise, surprise—the surrounding shores feature heavy development with barely a space between the various buildings and houses.

Corey Causeway Facilities (Standard Mile 117.5)

Southeast of Corey Causeway Bridge (northwest of unlighted daybeacon #39), a few low-key facilities are available along the westerly banks. The most promising is a branch of Johnny Leverocks Seafood Restaurant (727-367-4588). This dining spot maintains a face dock fronting onto the Waterway's southwestern banks, just southeast of the bridge. There should be room for a boat as large as 50 feet to moor alongside. Dockside depths range from 10 feet at the outer pier to some 6 feet nearer the seawall. Visiting cruisers are welcome to tie up while dining, but no overnight dockage or other marine services are available.

One small hotel offers a few low-level docks on the charted branch of deep water sweeping south, on the western shores of the large cove that is southeast of Corey Causeway. While Bay Palms Motel (727-360-1754) allows guests to dock their boats here, the piers are obviously only appropriate for smaller craft. Cruising captains would do well to look elsewhere.

Blind Pass Marina and Inlet (Standard Mile 118, 27 45.418 North/082 45.619 West)

Blind Pass Marina is screened off from the Waterway by a high-rise condo building southwest of flashing daybeacon #9. It is a simple matter nevertheless to follow the deep water around the northern point of the peninsula southwest of #9 and work your way back toward the low-level fixed bridge to the south. Soon the extensive fixed wooden piers of Blind Pass Marina will come abeam on the eastern banks. This facility offers transient dockage, though there are currently only 3 to 4 slips open for this purpose, and these can only handle certain sizes and drafts of pleasure

boats. The dockmaster suggests calling ahead of time and checking on availability.

Dockside power and water connections are very much in evidence, and the docks are well sheltered from all but strong southerly winds. One adequate, non-climate-controlled shower and an air-conditioned Laundromat with a large paperback exchange library are available shoreside. Waste pump-out service is also offered by way of both fixed and mobile systems.

The on-site restaurant has reopened as Leprechauns Cove Tap Room and Waterfront Grill (727-360-5960). We didn't get a chance to check it out yet. Maybe next visit. You might also consider walking across the street to Groupers Restaurant (9524 Blind Pass Road, 727-367-9000). Our conversation with several fellow cruisers seemed to indicate that the food here "is not half-bad."

Further passage south past the marina to Blind Pass Inlet is blocked by a low-level fixed bridge with only 11 feet of vertical clearance. This is not really objectionable, as the inlet is shoal and quite unsafe.

Blind Pass Marina (727) 360-4281
   http://www.blindpassmarina.com

Approach depth—9-11 feet
Dockside depth—6-8 feet
Accepts transients—yes (somewhat limited)
Transient dockage rate—below average
Fixed wooden piers—yes
Dockside power connections—yes
Dockside water—yes
Waste pump-out—yes
Shower—yes
Laundromat—yes
Restaurant—on site

Waterway Anchorage (Various Lats/Lons—see below)

Mariners in immediate need of getting off the ICW may consider anchoring in the deep water east of flashing daybeacon #14. This is a tricky anchorage for first-timers. Shoal water actually lies almost due east of #14, running out from the charted point of land separating two canals. You must anchor either north (near 27 46.018 North/082 45.086 West) or south (near 27 45.929 North/082 45.115 West) of these shallows. The north-side haven features depths of 8 feet or better, with enough swinging room for a 34-footer, while 6-foot MLW soundings can be expected in the southerly anchorage (where a 38-foot vessel can be comfortably accommodated). Be *sure* to read our navigational account of these waters before trying to access this anchorage for the first time.

You will be exposed to the wake of all passing vessels, and there is minimal shelter from inclement weather in both these anchor-down spots. Frankly, there are much better anchorages not far to the north or south, so these spots should probably be considered strictly for emergencies or in fair weather.

1. Blind Pass Marina

Treasure Island Tennis and Yacht Club (Standard Mile 119, 27 46. 127 North/082 45.370 West)

The docks of Treasure Island Tennis and Yacht Club sit perched on the northern banks of the rectangular cove making into the Waterway's western shoreline between flashing daybeacon #14 and the Treasure Island Causeway bascule bridge. This club accepts transient guests for overnight or temporary dockage if they are members of yacht clubs with appropriate reciprocal privileges. Visitors are required to give at least 24 hours' notice before arrival. The club employs a full-time dockmaster who is very accommodating to visitors. The fixed wooden slips feature full power and water connections, and showers are available in the clubhouse. Minimum entrance and dockside depths are a very impressive 8 to 10 feet. Shoreside, visitors will find a cooling swimming pool, 14 clay tennis courts, a Nautilus room, and full dining facilities. Dinner and lunch are served Tuesday through Saturday. Several other restaurants and a shopping center are found a half-mile from the clubhouse in downtown Treasure Island.

Treasure Island Tennis and Yacht Club
   (727) 367-4511
   http://www.tityc.com

Approach depth—8-10 feet MLW
Dockside depth—10-12 feet
Accepts transients—member of yacht clubs with
   appropriate reciprocal privileges
Fixed wooden piers—yes
Dockside power connections—up to 50 amp
Dockside water connections—yes
Showers—yes
Restaurant—on site

BOCA CIEGA BAY TO TREASURE ISLAND NAVIGATION

Successful navigation of the Western Florida ICW and its various auxiliary channels between the southerly reaches of Boca Ciega Bay and Treasure Island is not a matter to be taken lightly. Dozens of channels crisscross the Waterway as it works its way to the north and the various aids to navigation on these conflicting tracks can be confusing, to say the least. Then, just to make matters a bit more interesting, there are three bridges with restricted opening schedules.

Most sidewaters have unmarked entrances. While many are deep enough for most craft, they do warrant cautious navigation to avoid the surrounding shallows.

Large portions of this run are open to wind and wave. While the islands and causeways give some shelter, winds over fifteen knots (and sometimes less) can make for a spray-filled voyage. If possible, pick a day of fair breezes for your transit across the bay.

So, keep chart 11411 at hand. Read the information below carefully and make advance plans to avoid any likely trouble spots. With these precautions, you should enjoy your cruise and not meet up with Boca Ciega's bottom.

Approaching the Split   As mentioned earlier, the convergence of three channels at flashing daybeacon #26 can bring on more than a spot of confusion. The track to the east runs under the fixed high-rise northerly span of the Sunshine Skyway and allows access to Tampa Bay's western shoreline. This route was covered in the last chapter. The ICW sweeps sharply to the west, while the alternate channel between Isla del Sol and the mainland strikes to the north. This latter route will be reviewed first, followed by a discussion of the ICW and the various side passages along its northward run.

Slow down as you approach flashing daybeacon #26 and use your binoculars to pick out unlighted daybeacon #25 and flashing daybeacon #26. You should pass directly between these two aids. There is shoal water to the east and west, so don't become confused by the various other markers. Be sure to positively identify #25 and #26 before making your final approach to the intersection.

Alternate Channel   Power cruisers not making for the excellent marinas at Pass-A-Grille and Tierra Verde may wisely choose the sheltered alternate passage east of Indian Key and Isla del Sol. Just remember that you must be able to clear a fixed bridge with a scant 18 feet of vertical clearance to rejoin the ICW.

After passing between unlighted daybeacon #25 and flashing daybeacon #26, continue almost straight ahead, pointing to pass unlighted daybeacon #2 to its westerly side. From this point, northbound mariners should take all red aids to their (the cruisers') starboard side and pass all green beacons to port until rejoining the ICW at flashing daybeacon #32.

North of unlighted daybeacon #3, set a course to pass unlighted daybeacon #4 by some 15 yards to its westerly quarter. Don't allow leeway to ease you to the east. As chart 11411 clearly and correctly indicates, there is shoal water with depths rising to a mere ½ foot east of this aid.

Once #4 is behind you, point for the gap between flashing daybeacon #6 and unlighted daybeacon #7. At this point the channel takes a jog to the northwest and hurries on toward a canallike passage between the artificial islands east of Isla del Sol and the mainland banks. First, however, cruisers might decide to check out either the Maximo Point Anchorage or O'Neill's Marina.

Maximo Point Anchorage and O'Neill's Marina   To reach the somewhat open anchorage northeast of Indian Key, depart the alternate channel at unlighted daybeacon #7. Feel your way north with the sounder for about 50 to 75 yards. You will almost certainly spot several other craft anchored on these waters. Just remember that some of the smaller sail craft may actually lie in 4-foot waters. Drop the hook well before reaching the charted shallows to the north and northeast.

Cruisers making for O'Neill's Marina will spot the entrance channel east of flashing daybeacon #6. Be sure to stay to the north of flashing daybeacon #6 as you enter to avoid the charted shallows to the south.

On the Alternate Channel   You will enter this passage immediately after passing flashing daybeacon #11 to its easterly side.

After passing between unlighted daybeacon #7 and flashing daybeacon #6, the alternate channel cuts sharply to the northwest. Several additional markers lead captain and crew into the mouth of a canallike body of

water. Eventually, the charted 18-foot fixed bridge crossing the canal will be spotted dead ahead. Once through this span, point to pass flashing daybeacon #12 to its westerly side. The channel takes a small jog farther to the west at #12 and continues on its well-marked way into the deeper waters of eastern Boca Ciega Bay.

Northwest of unlighted daybeacon #14 and flashing daybeacon #15, good depths spread out in a wide swath before you. It is now a simple matter to visit the marinas to the east.

Eastern Boca Ciega Marinas   To enter the long canal leading to Maximo Marina, continue on the principal alternate channel for several hundred yards past (northwest of) #14 and #15. You can then safely curl back around to the east and set course for the southernmost of the charted canals cutting the bay's easterly limits. A whole series of uncharted markers leads you safely into the canal's mouth. Simply stick to the centerline as you cruise up the canal, and the marina docks will soon appear dead ahead.

Use your binoculars to pick out the bevy of unlighted daybeacons outlining the channel to Gulfport Municipal Marina and Boca Ciega Yacht Club to the northeast. Remember your "red, right, returning" rule.

Cruisers making for the new Gulfport City Dock or its adjacent anchorage will spot this structure guarding the northerly banks, some .55 nautical miles west of the Gulfport Municipal Marina entrance markers. Be advised that the city dock lies just west of a municipal fishing pier that actually juts farther out into the waters of Boca

Ciega Bay than the dock does. Don't even think about trying to tie up to the fishing pier. It has not been designed for this activity.

Passage West to Isla del Sol Yacht and Country Club   Captains traveling the alternate channel who visit the private yacht club on Isla del Sol's northerly shores need not cruise all the way back to the ICW and then follow the Waterway south to this facility. Instead, abandon the alternate channel some 100 yards northwest of unlighted daybeacon #14 and flashing daybeacon #15 and follow the wide channel of deep water to the west-southwest. Simply by staying several hundred yards off the southerly shores and to the south of unlighted daybeacon #3, minimum 8-foot depths should be held all the way to the enclosed harbor.

You may also choose to continue following this channel west to the ICW. Point to pass just south of unlighted daybeacon #2, and minimum 8-foot depths can be maintained into the Waterway's deeper tract.

Alternate Channel to the ICW   After passing between flashing daybeacon #15 and unlighted daybeacon #14, the alternate channel skirts across a wide and deep section of eastern Boca Ciega Bay. No further aids mark the northwest-flowing cut for almost 1.3 nautical miles. Set a careful compass/GPS course to come abeam of flashing daybeacon #16 to its southerly side. From #16, the channel turns west-southwest and heads directly toward an intersection with the ICW at flashing daybeacon #32. Pass between #32 and unlighted daybeacon #17 and then immediately turn either north or south on the Waterway.

Back on the Western Florida ICW   From the infamous split where our discussion of the alternate channel began, the ICW sweeps west through a broad, deep passage on its way to the southern leg of the Pinellas Bayway Bridge. This is an open run with shoal water of 1 and 2 feet flanking the cut to the north and south. While the channel is certainly broad, you must make sure to pick out the somewhat sparsely placed aids to navigation before forging ahead at speed.

Pass between unlighted daybeacon #25 and flashing daybeacon #26 and remain on course for some 50 yards. Then, cut sharply west, pointing to pass flashing daybeacon #15 to its fairly immediate northern side and unlighted daybeacon #16 to its fairly immediate southerly side. Watch out for the charted shallows to the south during this run. Continue on course, pointing to come abeam of flashing daybeacon #17 to its northerly quarter.

Only four aids mark the long, slowly curving run from #17 to the Pinellas Bayway Bridge. Stay at least 50 yards (or even a bit more) to the south of unlighted daybeacons #18 and #20. Past #20, the Waterway begins a slow bend to the northwest. Pass between unlighted daybeacon #22 (well to its southerly side) and flashing daybeacon #21 (to its northerly quarter). Head straight for the central pass-through of the Pinellas Bayway Bridge once these aids are left behind.

If you like bridges with restricted opening schedules, boy, are you in luck. The southern half of the Pinellas Bayway Bridge, also known as the Pinellas Bayway "E" bridge, is the first in a host of restricted spans plaguing cruisers between Boca Ciega Bay and Anclote Key. By the way, don't become confused—there is another bridge north of flashing daybeacon #24 which is referred to as the Pinellas Bayway "C" bridge. Hence my designation of a northern ("C") and southern leg ("E") of the bayway. This particular bridge (closed vertical clearance 25 feet) features a regulated schedule daily, year round. From 9:00 A.M. to 5:00 P.M., the span opens only on the hour and each 20 minutes thereafter. At all other times, the bridge opens on demand.

Northwest of the southern Pinellas Bayway Bridge, the Waterway continues to follow a very broad and deep passage until passing between unlighted daybeacon #14 and flashing daybeacon #24. Don't approach either of these aids closely. The good water lies in the broad mid-width between the two markers.

From #24, the ICW channel swings sharply to the north and heads for Isla del Sol and the northern half of the Pinellas Bayway. To the south and west skippers may choose to put to sea on Pass-A-Grille Inlet or visit one of the several marinas along the way.

Pass-A-Grille Channel and Facilities A wide channel strikes first west (from the ICW), then southwest, and then west again to Pass-A-Grille Inlet. To enter this passage, depart the Waterway some 100 yards south of flashing daybeacon #24 and cut sharply west. Pass unlighted daybeacon #14 well to its northerly side. This aid marks the channel's southeastern limits and sits hard by the northwestern corner of Tierra Verde Island. Study chart 11411 for a moment and you will note the small canal running southeast from #14. Small powercraft can use this stream to reach the principal Tierra Verde canal and Tierra Verde Resort Marina. A low, fixed bridge bars larger craft from this stream.

Continue on the Pass-A-Grille Channel by passing well to the northwest of unlighted daybeacon #12. Follow the channel as it bends to the south past #12. Be prepared to find additional uncharted markers on these waters. As you can imagine, being this close to an inlet, aids to navigation are frequently moved, added to, and deleted. Just remember than you are now "going to sea" and all red marks should be taken to your port side, and green beacons to starboard.

The Pass-A-Grille Inlet channel remains well marked and reasonably easy to run all the way to its westernmost aid, flashing daybeacon #PG. Between unlighted daybeacon #14 and flashing daybeacon #11, avoid the northwestern banks. Similarly, don't encroach upon the shallows abutting the western banks of Tierra Verde between unlighted daybeacon #12 and flashing daybeacon #10. Take your time, and be sure to pick out all aids correctly.

Before reaching the actual seaward cut, skippers can turn north to the facilities at Pass-A-Grille Beach or southeast to Tierra Verde Resort Marina.

Pass-A-Grille Beach Channel and Facilities
Captains making for Pass-A-Grille Beach should continue cruising on the Pass-A-Grille Inlet channel, as if you were putting out to sea, until flashing daybeacon #11 comes abeam to the northwest. Then turn in toward the westerly banks until #11 comes abeam to the north. Continue toward shore for another 50 yards or so and then turn north and parallel the shoreline as you cruise along. Be sure to stay well to the west of flashing daybeacon #11. Very shallow water is found north of this aid, stretching out from the southerly point of charted Vina del Mar. Heed this warning. Strangers sometimes attempt to pass on the wrong side of #11. A hard grounding is the inevitable and potentially expensive result!

Continue cruising north, keeping about the same distance from the westerly banks. You will first sight Merry Pier to the west, followed farther upstream by Pass-A-Grille Marina and Warren's Marina. Another hop to the north will lead you to a fixed bridge with only 14 feet of vertical clearance. The piers of Pass-A-Grille Yacht Club are located just north of this span. If you need more clearance, enter by way of Mud Key Channel, outlined below.

Tierra Verde Resort Marina Knowledgeable captains who choose to visit Tierra Verde Resort Marina, guarding the northern terminus of Tierra Verde canal, should continue cruising south past flashing daybeacon #10. This aid should be passed well east of your course line. Watch to the southeast and you should spy a whole series of unlighted markers leading into the canal's mouth.

Daytime entry is an elementary matter of cruising between the various marks, favoring the northeasterly side of the channel slightly. A nighttime arrival is tricky and calls for caution by strangers.

Once into the canal, good depths stretch out almost from shore to shore. Simply follow the stream as it flows north to the marina complex. The dockmaster's office is found adjacent to the northernmost piers. Try and raise the office on VHF and the attendant will probably meet you on the piers and direct you to your slip.

South Channel In earlier editions of this guide, I used to cautiously recommend an anchorage just off charted "South Channel," south of flashing daybeacon #10. On-site research in August 2003 showed that the charted landscape is now much altered from its depiction on 11411, and shoaling has erased this once-popular anchorage. We now strongly suggest that cruising-size craft avoid South Channel entirely.

On the ICW At flashing daybeacon #24, the Waterway swerves to the north and flows on toward the northern leg of the Pinellas Bayway Bridge, also known as the Pinellas Bayway "C" bridge. This span (closed vertical clearance 25 feet) has an even more severe regulated opening schedule than its southern sister. The bridge opens on the hour and every 20 minutes thereafter from 7:00 A.M. to 7:00 P.M., seven days a week. Just south of this bridge, cruisers can cut west into Mud Key Channel for anchorage or to visit Pass-A-Grille Yacht Club.

Mud Key Channel   Depart the Waterway some 25 yards before reaching the southern face of the Pinellas Bayway "C" bridge (northern leg). Cruise west, favoring the bridge's southerly flank. Soon the entrance to a canal will come abeam to the south. Mariners seeking anchorage close to the ICW can feel their way into the mid-width of this opening and drop the hook. You must pass through some 5- to 6-foot depths, but soundings quickly deepen again to 6 and 11 feet. Anchor well north of the point where the canal begins to narrow.

Eventually Mud Key Channel curves sharply to the southwest and runs through a canal. There are no depth problems on this stream, but the same cannot be said of the wide water beyond. As correctly indicated on chart 11411, a shoal has built out on the northwestern flank of the canal's southwestern limits. As you exit the canal, heavily favor the port (southeastern) shore to avoid this hazard. Continue favoring this bank while passing the points of the first two charted peninsulas to the southeast. Good water again spreads out almost from shore to shore as the shorter, third peninsula comes abeam. The docks of Pass-A-Grille Yacht Club will be spotted a short distance downstream on the western shores.

Big McPherson Bayou Anchorage   The entrance to what would otherwise be one the best anchorages between Tampa Bay and Clearwater Harbor is complicated by the presence of a large patch of shoal water crossing most of Big McPherson Bayou's eastern mouth. As chart 11411 correctly forecasts, the shallows run from the bridge

completely across the entrance's mid-width. In fact, on-site soundings indicate this shoal has built out even farther than shown on the chart.

Fortunately, it is still quite possible to enter the bayou's interior reaches by closely hugging the starboard-side (northwestern) banks. Continue cruising north on the Waterway until the northern portion of the bayou's mouth comes abeam to the west. Then, curl around to the west-southwest and enter the bayou hugging the northwesterly banks.

Soon the bayou takes a sharp turn to the north-northwest. Cruise around this point by heavily favoring the eastern (starboard-side) banks. Shallows abut the western and southern shoreline on this portion of the creek. You may or may not spot a no-wake sign as you make your turn to the north. If this sign is still present by the time you arrive, be sure to pass to its easterly side.

The best anchorage is found abeam of the first charted offshoot striking northeast. Cruise into the mouth of this sidewater far enough for good shelter and settle down for a night of peace and security.

To cruise upstream to the second sidewater, continue to heavily favor the eastern and northern banks. Enter this body of water on its centerline.

Don't attempt to reach the northerly limits of the bayou. Depths become more than suspect past the second cove described above.

Isla del Sol Channel   Skippers desiring to visit Isla del Sol Yacht and Country Club, or even those simply needing a good shortcut to the alternate channel, can follow the deep waters north of Isla del Sol. Depart the

ICW at unlighted daybeacon #2. Keep 100 yards or so from the southern banks as you cruise east-northeast, and the marina harbor will come eventually abeam to the south.

If you continue on to the alternate channel, point to eventually join up with this cut about .1 nautical miles northwest of flashing daybeacon #15. This passage is not recommended for strangers at night.

On the ICW   Shoal water abuts the Waterway's eastern flank between the northern Pinellas Bayway Bridge and unlighted daybeacon #30. Be sure to identify all aids carefully along this stretch and proceed with caution.

As you approach flashing daybeacon #32, another potential trouble spot is encountered. The various aids marking the alternate channel to the east are sometimes mistaken for the Waterway beacons. Be sure to pass west of #32 in order to stay in the ICW channel.

St. Petersburg Beach Anchorage   For best depths, hold scrupulously to the mid-width when entering the cove southwest of unlighted daybeacon #33. Deep water actually extends much farther west than you would expect from studying chart 11411. Nevertheless, depths eventually do rise dramatically. For safety's sake, it would be better to drop the hook on the eastern third of the cove.

On the ICW   Don't attempt to enter the cove west of unlighted daybeacon #35. Depths of 4½ feet or less are encountered soon after leaving the ICW.

At unlighted daybeacon #35 the Waterway begins a lazy turn to the northwest as it runs on toward the Corey Causeway Bridge.

Northwest of unlighted daybeacon #39, the ICW soon exchanges greetings with the Corey Causeway Bridge. Yes, friends, we can all enjoy yet another restricted bridge. What can I say except, "Enjoy the scenery."

The Corey Causeway span has a closed vertical clearance of 23 feet and opens every 20 minutes weekdays from 8:00 A.M. to 7:00 P.M. and from 10:00 A.M. to 7:00 P.M. on weekends and holidays.

North of Corey Causeway, the waters about the ICW begin to narrow and depths outside of the marked cut are very questionable. Take your time and identify the markers as you cruise along.

A huge no-wake zone now extends north from Corey Causeway to the Treasure Island Bridge. This zone encompasses some 1.3 statute miles of the Waterway, and for powercraft skippers, it can seem to go on forever!

Blind Pass Marina   Cruise into the wide channel west of flashing daybeacon #9 by favoring the southerly point slightly. To continue on to the marina, simply follow the good water as it turns sharply south. The docks will be quite obvious on the eastern banks. Apparently some of the piers on the northern side of the complex belong to the high-rise condo overlooking the shoreline. Farther to the south, the channel to virtually impassable Blind Pass Inlet is blocked by a low-level fixed bridge.

Please note that we no longer recommend that any cruising-size craft attempt to enter the passage flowing north-northwest from the main Blind Pass channel. A shoal has now built completely across the entrance to this errant stream.

Waterway Anchorage Successful entry into the twin anchorages east of flashing daybeacon #14 is complicated by the presence of an uncharted shoal between #14 and the point of land lying directly to the east. To avoid this potential trouble spot, depart the waterway a good 20 yards north or south of #14. Captains making for the southerly anchorage should point as if they were going to enter the centerline of the canal, just south of the shallow point of land east of #14. Drop anchor before coming abeam of the (another) charted canal striking south.

Skippers bound for the northerly haven should set course for the mid-width of the canal, north of the shallow point east of #14. Be sure not to impinge too closely on the point of land that you will pass north of your course line. Drop anchor well short of the actual mouth of the canal that will open out dead ahead.

On to Treasure Island on the ICW North of flashing daybeacon #14, northbound cruisers will sight Treasure Island Causeway Bridge. This span, with a meager closed vertical clearance of only 8 feet, also has a regulated opening schedule. It opens on the hour and every quarter of the hour seven days a week from 7:00 A.M. to 7:00 P.M. During the night, between the hours of 11:00 P.M. and 7:00 A.M., the bridge operator requires 10 minutes' notice before an opening.

Treasure Island Causeway to Belleair Causeway

The waters in and about the Gulf Coast ICW between Treasure Island Causeway and the Belleair Bridge continue the trend toward narrower widths that began near Corey Causeway Bridge. From Treasure Island the Waterway follows the northerly reaches of Boca Ciega Bay to a canal-like passage known, appropriately enough, as "the Narrows." This cut leads in turn to Belleair Causeway, the southern boundary of the baylike body of water known as Clearwater Harbor.

The passage from Treasure Island to Belleair is spanned by a few bridges, two of which (surprise, surprise) currently open on demand. Don't rejoice prematurely. This stretch of the ICW also features a host of minimum- and idle-speed zones with which you must contend. This is not a stretch of the Gulf Coast ICW where powercraft can expect to charge through at double-digit speed. Allow plenty of time in your cruising plans to span this gap.

There are several excellent marinas that offer transient dockage between Treasure Island and Belleair. Nevertheless, your choices, at least compared to those in St. Petersburg and Clearwater, are somewhat limited. Conversely, there are many opportunities to anchor for the evening. None of these overnight refuges can be described as undeveloped. Almost invariably, you will be riding the hook in close proximity to prolific residential and sometimes commercial development.

Much of this passage is overlooked by coastal towns and cities rubbing elbows with one another. This is particularly true on the barrier islands to the west. If it were not for the city limits signs, it would be difficult to tell where one community ends and another begins.

A single inlet provides reliable access to and from the open waters of the Gulf along this stretch of the ICW. Johns Pass is uniformly deep, well marked and charted, and relatively easy to run. Currents do run swiftly though, so have an eye for leeway and maneuvering room.

Although it can scarcely be compared to a cruise up the beautifully undeveloped Little Shark River, the run from Treasure Island to Belleair is nevertheless pleasant, with several opportunities for gunk-holing and side trips. While a few sections are best left behind as soon as possible, many mariners will want to take advantage of this region's cruising delights.

Isle of Palms Anchorage (Standard Mile 119.5, 27 46.559 North/082 45.575 West)

Good depths of 6 feet or better are held just south of the two easternmost fingers of land on the charted Isle of Palms, west-northwest of unlighted daybeacon #17. While you must be careful to avoid the charted spoil shoal farther to the south, cautious skippers can break off from the ICW between unlighted daybeacons #17 and #19 and drop the hook off the second tip of land (moving east to west) in 8 to 13 feet of water. Swinging room is sufficient for boats at least as large as 45 feet. Protection from northerly blows is quite good and is acceptable in light to moderate southerly and westerly breezes. Strong winds from the east could make for a most uncomfortable evening. The anchorage is overlooked by heavy residential development on the Isle of Palms. Traffic noise from nearby Treasure Island Causeway Bridge could also be an annoyance on quiet nights.

Long Bayou Facilities (Standard Mile 120.5, Various Lats/Lons—see below)

A long and complex series of privately maintained daybeacons outlines a long channel striking north from the ICW just northwest of unlighted daybeacon #23. This cut leads into the interior reaches of mostly shallow Long Bayou. The marked channel has minimum low-water depths of 5½ feet. However, a trip outside of the buoyed passage can quickly land careless navigators in 4 feet of water or less. Obviously, captains must exercise more than the usual care when running this cut.

Two marinas are found on the shores of Long Bayou. The first guards the eastern banks northeast of unlighted daybeacon #29. Its location is indicated on chart 11411 by facility designation "20E." Lighthouse Point Marina (27 48.681 North/082 45.591 West, 727-384-3625) is primarily a dry-stack, powercraft-storage facility. This marina also features some fixed wooden wet slips, but this writer was informed in the summer of 2003 that overnight transients were no longer accommodated. So, unless you happen to be looking for excellent dry storage, or gasoline, you can keep on trucking past Lighthouse Point.

A visit to the second of Long Bayou's facilities, Bay Pines Marina (27 49.028 North/082 45.982 West, 727-392-4922, http://www.baypinesmarina.com), calls for a cruise under the 20-foot fixed highway bridge north of unlighted daybeacon #31. As this dry-stack-oriented facility does not accept transients, many visiting cruisers will choose to forego this passage. The channel leading north from the bridge to Bay Pines Marina can be confusing to strangers. Be sure to read the navigational information on Long Bayou presented later in this chapter before making the attempt.

Once the troublesome entrance cut is left behind, visitors will find a collection of wet slips associated with Bay Pines on the western shore of the bayou, followed by a large dry-storage building a bit farther to the north.

Bay Pines Marina requires a minimum two-month stay to rent a wet slip. Dry storage, gasoline, and mechanical repairs are available courtesy of an on-site, independent service firm. Boats up to 28 feet can be hauled out by forklift.

The waters of Long Bayou outside of its improved channel are almost universally shallow. Thus, while the shores are less developed than most in this region, there is little opportunity for overnight anchorage by any but the smallest outboard craft. Even skippers of these petite boats had better proceed with caution or a bent prop could be the result.

Johns Pass (Standard Mile 121.5)

Reliable Johns Pass Inlet strikes into the waters of the open Gulf southwest of the ICW's flashing daybeacon #4, itself west of Turtlecrawl Point. While the charted channel leading to the inlet from #4 is the best-marked and most straightforward route to the seaward cut, adventurous skippers can also reach the pass via the charted deep waters north of Capri Isle. The former channel has minimum 7- to 8-foot depths, while the cut skirting Capri Island has some 5-foot soundings, but most readings are in the 6- to 20-foot region.

With one major exception, Johns Pass is about the most easily run inlet that you will ever find in Western Florida. The channel is straightforward, well marked and charted, and reasonably easy to run for most pleasure craft. Minimum depths are currently around 10 feet, with many soundings showing much better water. The only fly in the ointment is the strong tidal current that regularly boils through this cut. Low-powered trawlers and sail craft must be on maximum alert for these swift waters.

Johns Pass is spanned by a bascule bridge with 25 feet of closed vertical clearance. Fortunately, this bridge opens on demand and does not present too much of an obstruction for pleasure boats.

Johns Pass Marina (27 47.021 North/082 46.806 West, 727-360-6907) guards the northeastern tip of the land mass flanking the southeastern side of the inlet. The facility is easily spotted by its large, powder blue dry-storage building. As you might expect, this marina specializes in dry storage of small powercraft and there is no wet-slip dockage available for transients. A fuel pier and a few wooden-decked wet slips front onto the point and all cruisers can readily purchase gasoline and diesel fuel. Dockside depths range from 8 to 10 feet. Mechanical repairs are available for outboard and I/O powercraft. The marina also features a large bait/tackle store and boat sales department.

Johns Pass's northwestern shoreline is overlooked by a huge retail and dining complex known as Johns Pass Village and Boardwalk. Apparently the center was originally designed to have a rustic look but, at least to my eyes, the glitz has overtaken any rural character that might ever have been present. Today, the

1. Johns Pass Marina
2. Snug Harbor Boat Yard
3. Madeira Beach Marina
4. Lighthouse Point Marina
5. Bay Pines Marine

waterborne visitor usually finds a complex teeming with tourists in search of something to do. Several restaurants are found on the grounds and some certainly serve good seafood. However, cruising visitors may be hard put to find a berth which will allow for a ready visit to the complex.

While a tour ship and a boat rental agency grace the village's waterfront, there is practically nothing in the way of dockage for larger pleasure craft. Skippers will spy a small fuel dock at the northeastern (ICW side) end of the complex. Boats up to 34 feet can probably battle the current and tie up for a time and purchase gas, diesel fuel, bait, beer, and ice. You may be able to negotiate a stay while dining at one of the on-site restaurants, but don't count on it.

All in all, Johns Pass Inlet provides reliable access to the open Gulf and features the added bonus of a fuel stop and the village complex. Only one other inlet in this region can lay claim to so many positive attributes.

Madeira Beach Anchorage (27 47.603 North/082 47.273 West)

The large, charted offshoot striking west from flashing daybeacon #7 (on the Johns Pass approach channel) makes an ideal anchorage for boats drawing 4½ feet or (preferably) less. While 5½-foot low-tide depths can be maintained by careful navigators, it's likely that boats swinging on the hook will ease into some 5-foot waters before the night is over. The shores are surrounded by dense residential development and afford excellent protection from all winds. This is not the most attractive overnight anchorage that you will ever encounter, but it would be a good spot to ride out a heavy blow.

Farther to the west, the sidewater splits into

two branches. The spot with, probably, the most swinging room will be found east of this fork in the creek. These waters also afford maximum shelter.

The southern fork leads to the docks of Snug Harbor Boat Yard (27 47.540 North/082 47.389 West, 727-398-7470). This friendly firm offers complete mechanical repairs for both gasoline and diesel engines, and haulout repairs via a 25-ton travelift. Additionally, marine carpentry, electrical, and even canvas service is available. Approach depths run 5 to 8 feet with 8- to 9-foot soundings dockside. This writer found the staff at Snug Harbor to be exceptionally affable and willing to go that extra mile to satisfy all the visiting cruiser's needs. No transient dockage or fuel is available on the premises.

Mitchell Beach Sidewater

Chart 11411 correctly portrays a cove, shaped like a piece of a jigsaw puzzle, cutting into the western banks of the Johns Pass approach channel between flashing daybeacons #6 and #7. In earlier times, this writer used to recommend this sidewater as an anchorage for boats up to 34 feet. Sad to say, but there is now so much residential development and so many private docks that there is no longer enough room for any vessel larger than a runabout to anchor. Oh dear, another overnight haven falls to rampant development.

Veterans Hospital Anchorages (Standard Mile 122, 27 48.321 North/082 46.926 West)

Study chart 11411 for a moment and you will quickly spy the designation "Veterans Hospital" northeast of the ICW's flashing daybeacon #6. The old hospital is a striking edifice and makes for a readily recognized landmark from the water. A good anchorage is available to cruising craft on the charted patch of 6-foot water north and northeast of #6. Careful captains can ease in toward the northeastern banks and drop the hook before reaching the ½-foot shoal clearly shown on 11411. This rather open refuge is only appropriate in light to moderate northerly and southern breezes. A forecast calling for winds from the west or east over 15 knots nixes this spot. You will also be open to any wake raised by passing powercraft. While this is not too likely during the later evening hours, it can make for a rough awakening in the morning if a 55-foot Hatteras should happen by at full bore. The anchorage is overlooked by the old hospital

and the beautifully green grounds surrounding the building.

Boats drawing less than 3½ feet might choose to carefully feel their way into the pondlike body of water, just west of the Veterans Hospital's charted position. Chart 11411 shows only 3½ feet of water at the entrance to the pond, but on-site research revealed soundings of as little as 3 feet.

Those who can stand this very thin water will glide into a beautifully protected anchorage surrounded by mostly undeveloped and, to the southeast, parklike shores. Of course, the old hospital gazing benignly over the water only adds to the haven's appeal. Protection is absolutely super from all winds. Always assuming that you can stand the thin

Veterans Hospital

depths, there is simply not a better foul-weather hidey-hole between Tampa Bay and Anclote Key.

Madeira Beach Facilities (Standard Mile 122.5, 27 48.217 North/082 47.735 West)

Madeira Beach Marina is found on the northwestern banks of the cove southwest of unlighted daybeacon #10, itself just southeast of the Welch Causeway Bridge. Some care must be exercised to avoid the charted shoal southeast of the marina, but several pilings outlining this hazard help visiting cruisers avoid the shallows with minimal difficulty. MLW entrance soundings range from 6 to 9 feet, while 6 to 8 feet of water can be expected dockside.

We are pleased to report that this facility has recently been taken back over by the city of Madeira Beach. That's a very good thing, as the private group that had leased it during the past several years had not exactly kept things in Bristol shape! Now, with the city back in charge, the future of Madeira Beach Marina is definitely looking up.

Future plans call for an entirely new shore-side support building, which will reportedly contain vastly improved showers and a Laundromat. Currently, the one on-site shower and Laundromat could only be accurately described as "minimalist," and not at all climate controlled.

This facility accepts transients at its fixed wooden piers with 30- and 50-amp power hookups and freshwater connections. The city of Madeira Beach had already embarked upon a dock-improvement project during our last visit in August 2003. Gasoline and commercial diesel fuel are at hand, as are free waste pump-out services. Mechanical repairs can occasionally be arranged through local, independent contractors. A small ship's and variety store is located on the premises. Famished cruisers can easily visit the nearby Johnny Leverocks Restaurant or five other restaurants within walking distance. Ask the friendly dockmasters for advice. Both a Publix and a Winn-Dixie supermarket are located within a five-block walk, and a convenience store is only a short step away.

Madeira Beach Marina (727) 399-2631
http://www.cimadeirabeachflus.com

Approach depth—6-9 feet
Dockside depth—6-8 feet
Accepts transients—yes
Transient dockage rate—below average
Fixed wooden piers—yes
Dockside power connections—mostly 30 amp (some 50)
Dockside water connections—yes
Waste pump-out—yes
Showers—yes
Laundromat—yes
Gasoline—yes
Diesel fuel—yes
Mechanical repairs—limited (independent technicians)
Ship's and variety store—yes
Restaurant—several nearby

Another branch of the notable Johnny Leverocks Restaurant (727-393-0459) flanks the ICW's southwestern banks just southeast of the Welch Causeway Bridge. This dining chain seems to be adding more and more locations all up and down the waterfront between Tampa Bay and Dunedin.

This particular Leverocks maintains its own dock fronting directly onto the ICW. While the pier's southeastern side is reserved for a resident charter sportfisherman, visiting cruisers are welcome to tie up while dining on the northwestern face. There should be enough room for one 34-footer. Dockside depths run around 6 to 7 feet.

The small, charted cove cutting into the northeastern banks just northwest of the Welch Causeway Bridge is currently undergoing a radical transformation. As late as the fall of 2003, passing cruisers could spot what appeared to be a giant, landlocked sailing ship of yesteryear. This unique structure played host to the Santa Madeira restaurant. This building is slated for demolition to make way for a new condo project. Of course, Florida is critically short of this sort of development!

Opposite the new condo project, visiting cruisers may be surprised to spy a metal floating dock flying the "McDonald's" flag. Yes, that's right. Captains and crew who yearn for a Big Mac or a Quarter Pounder with cheese and those inimitable French fries can feed their faces after a quick tie-up at the floating pier. Dockside depths of 5 feet can be expected, plenty for most powercraft, although a bit skimpy for particularly deep-draft sailboats. Note that there is a shopping center with a supermarket and large drugstore within walking distance of the McDonald's dock. Cruisers who make it snappy might be able to restock their onboard larders after making a purchase at the restaurant.

Redington Shores Anchorage (Standard Mile 125.5, 27 49.676 North/082 49.705 West)

The charted cove south of unlighted daybeacon #1 at Redington Shores makes for a protected overnight anchorage set amidst a heavily developed shoreline, if and only if you can figure out the complicated entrance

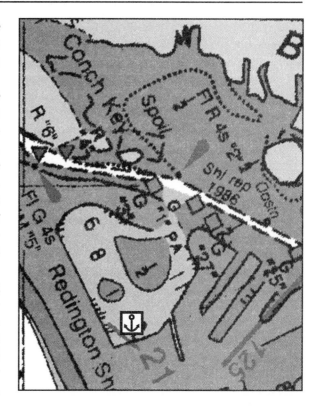

cut. Great care must be exercised to avoid the correctly charted ½-foot shoal occupying the center portion of the cove. Minimum depths of 7 feet are found in the unmarked channel hugging the banks, while soundings range up to as much as 11 feet of water in the southwestern corner of the bay. Be sure to read the navigational information presented in the next section of this chapter before visiting this bay for the first time.

Captains seeking overnight shelter should consider dropping anchor near the cove's southwesterly corner. Chart 11411 currently indicates 18-foot depths on these waters, but on-site research revealed that 11-foot soundings are now the norm. Protection is excellent from all winds, but particularly good for strong blows from the south and west. The nearby highway and residential districts may produce a considerable quantity of light and noise during your evening's rest, but that, unhappily, is the norm along this stretch of Western Florida's coastline.

The Narrows and Associated Facilities (Standard Mile 126, Various Lats/Lons— see below)

Northwest of flashing daybeacon #2, the northbound ICW cruiser enters a long, skinny stretch of the Waterway known as the Narrows. The run from #2 to the southern foot of Clearwater Harbor is plagued by several long, minimum-wake zones. Mariners, particularly those of the powered ilk, should leave plenty of time in their cruising itinerary to legally put this stretch behind them.

Tidal currents can also run swiftly in the Narrows, but at least rough water won't be a problem. It would take near hurricane-force winds to raise a menacing chop in these confined waters. Cruisers will also be happy to learn that the two bridges spanning the Narrows currently both open on demand.

The Narrows is overlooked by heavy residential development dominated by high-rise condos to the west. The mainland shores are surprisingly only lightly developed and provide a refreshing change from the concrete jungle so evident elsewhere.

The Pub Waterfront Restaurant and Lounge (727-595-3172) guards the Waterway's western shores between flashing daybeacon #27 and unlighted daybeacon #27A (near 27 51.989 North/082 50.879 West). This dining attraction boasts an extensive set of floating docks, with soundings alongside running in the 5-foot range. I wouldn't want to try and jockey any vessel larger than 36 feet into these piers. The Pub has been recommended to us by a fellow cruiser, but we have yet to try it for ourselves.

The charted harbor east of flashing daybeacon #31 is home to Indian Springs Marina (Standard Mile 129, 727-595-2956). This writer originally visited the marina in 1989 on a January morning with a temperature of some 50 degrees. Having just left the cold North Carolina winter behind a few days before, the weather was warm to me, and I was decked out in shirt-sleeves for my day of on-the-water research. Upon entering the junk-filled but homey office, I observed the marina owner amongst a group of the yard regulars sitting close-packed around a flaming wood stove. They were all dressed in jackets and looked at me as if they wondered whether I had a screw loose as I strolled up sans warm clothing. Nevertheless, after explaining my mission, I was courteously shown about.

This was a rather comical incident, which will always remain with this writer as a fond memory, but things are now entirely different. The old Indian Springs Marina of the late 1980s has disappeared, having been replaced by a modern, dry-stack-storage-oriented facility. There is now no wet-slip dockage to speak of, and except for gasoline, visiting cruisers will find nothing of interest here. Low-water entrance and dockside depths seem to run between 4½ and 5 feet.

A short hop north of flashing daybeacon #33, first-time cruisers on the Western Florida ICW will be astonished to observe a towering complex on the northwestern shoreline. This was once a combination retail-dining-hotel complex, but the entire space has been occupied by a huge Holiday Inn for many years

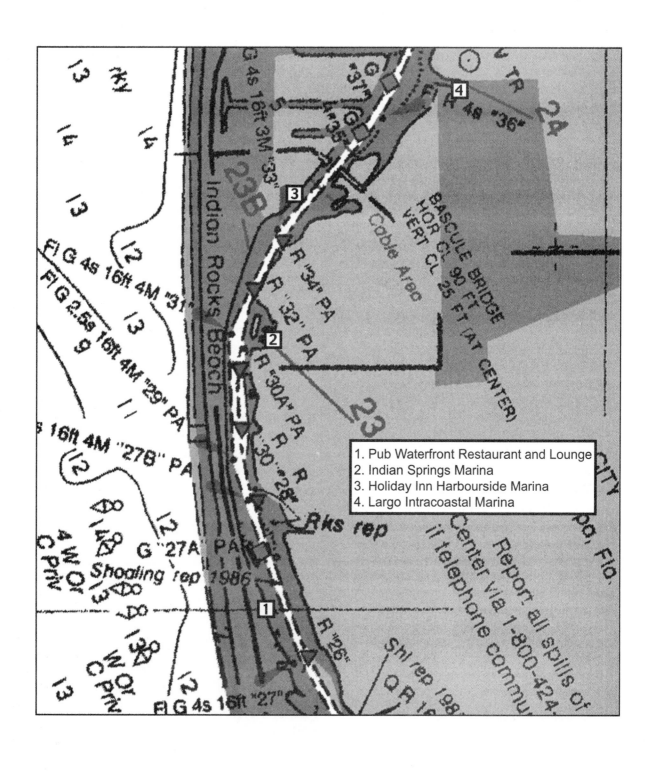

1. Pub Waterfront Restaurant and Lounge
2. Indian Springs Marina
3. Holiday Inn Harbourside Marina
4. Largo Intracoastal Marina

now. The marina portion of the development (Standard Mile 129.5) is known as Holiday Inn Harbourside Marina (27 52.914 North/ 082 50.863 West). Fortunately, this facility is friendly to transients.

Visiting craft are accommodated at the marina's modern, fixed wooden piers with 30- and 50-amp power hookups and freshwater connections. Depths alongside run 4 to 7 feet. Pilots of deep-draft vessels should call ahead and request one of the deeper berths. The docks are sheltered and make a good spot to ride out a heavy blow. As is true all along the Narrows, tidal currents do move swiftly. Practice your best docking technique. Gasoline and diesel fuel are available, and both showers and a Laundromat are located hard by one of the hotel's two swimming pools. It's quite a walk from the docks to these services, and visiting cruisers should take this disadvantage into account.

An on-site variety store is very convenient for light restocking, and both an Eckerd drugstore and another convenience store are found within 1½ blocks of the dockage basin. Ask the dockmaster for directions.

There are several restaurants located within the Holiday Inn Harbourside complex, including Brewmaster's Steak House (727-595-2900). This writer once met with the Florida Offshore Multi-hull Association here to make a presentation about cruising the waters of Western Florida. The meal was quite acceptable.

Holiday Inn Harbourside Marina (727) 595-9484
http://www.hiharbourside.com

Approach depth—9-13 feet
Dockside depth—4-7 feet
Accepts transients—yes
Transient dockage rate—average
Fixed wooden piers—yes

Dockside power connections—30 and 50 amp
Dockside water connections—yes
Showers—yes
Laundromat—yes
Gasoline—yes
Diesel fuel—yes
Variety store—yes
Restaurant—several on site

Largo Intracoastal Marine (27 53.189 North/082 50.406 West, 727-595-3592) guards the easterly banks of the ICW near the northern terminus of the Narrows, east of unlighted daybeacon #37. The marina's entrance channel (4- to 4½-foot depths) is vaguely outlined by white PVC pipes. Soundings alongside run 4½ to 5 feet. This low-key firm is primarily in the business of dry-storing smaller powercraft. Gasoline and mechanical repairs for outboards and I/Os are available, but there are no other services for transients and cruising-size craft.

Sand Key Anchorage (Standard Mile 130, 27 53.631 North/082 50.480 West)

Cruisers who decide to wait for the morning's light before entering Clearwater Harbor, north of Belleair Causeway, can anchor in the charted deep water west of unlighted daybeacon #40. Minimum depths of 6 feet or better can be held from #40 until coming under the shelter of the point of land to the north. Caution must be exercised to avoid several unmarked shoals, and captains piloting vessels drawing more than 4 feet must be sure to discontinue their forward progress before cruising into the shallower waters to the west. Otherwise, this is a fair overnight refuge with good protection in north-ern winds and adequate shelter from easterly or westerly blows. Strong winds from the south could call for a quick cruise to one of the nearby marina facilities.

The entire anchorage is surrounded by heavy residential development. The houses on the northerly banks sport a whole series of private docks, many with their own resident craft. Powercraft should enter and leave the anchorage at idle speed.

TREASURE ISLAND TO BELLEAIR CAUSEWAY NAVIGATION

Successful navigation of the ICW between Treasure Island Causeway and Belleair Bridge is complicated by a number of lengthy minimum-wake zones and several bridges with restricted opening schedules. Add to these impediments the presence of fairly swift tidal currents and mariners can readily understand why it's not the time to take a snooze at the helm.

Most of the various sidewaters along the way are reasonably simple to enter, though safe access is usually gained by favoring one shoreline or another. Make no mistake about it, some shallow water is present, and the unwary navigator could find it without having to work too hard.

During our various on-site research trips we have discovered that all the restrictive bridges now monitor VHF. While channel 13 is the stated working frequency, the operators can sometimes be raised on old, reliable 16.

On the ICW As you leave Treasure Island Causeway behind, set course to come abeam of and pass unlighted daybeacon #15 to its fairly immediate easterly quarter. Chart 11411 correctly indicates shallow water west of this aid.

From #15, it is a quick hop to a position abeam of unlighted daybeacon #17. Northwest of this marker, cruisers have access to the first anchorage north of the Treasure Island bridge.

Isle of Palms Anchorage If you choose to drop the hook in the somewhat open anchorage off the Isle of Palms' southeastern corner, set a course from a position some 100 yards north-northwest of unlighted daybeacon #17 to come abeam of the island's first charted offshoot of land lying to the west-northwest by some 50 yards to your starboard side. Once abeam of this tip of land, alter course to the west-southwest and point to come alongside of the next point of land by about the same distance to starboard. You can drop the hook in about 10 to 13 feet of water once abeam of the second point.

Study chart 11411 for a moment and you

will see that the procedure described above helps to avoid the charted shoal southeast of the anchorage. Depths of less than 2 feet are quickly encountered by cruisers who accidentally encroach upon this hazard. Be mindful of the shallows as you enter and leave the refuge and stay well north and northwest of the shoal.

Do not attempt to cruise west past the Isle of Palms' second offshoot, or toward the southern side of the cove. Shallow water of 4 feet or less waits to greet the foolhardy.

On the ICW   The charted channel striking east from unlighted daybeacon #21 leads to a small-craft launching ramp and is of little interest to passing cruisers.

Two intertwined channels leave the ICW's northeastern flank northwest of unlighted daybeacon #23. The more southerly of these two marked tracks points toward a beautiful private residence that is almost large enough to be a clubhouse. The northerly fork leads captains and crew up a well-buoyed passage into Long Bayou and its two marinas.

Long Bayou   Much of the interior reaches of upper Boca Ciega Bay, leading to Long Bayou, are quite shallow, with depths of less than 4 feet being the norm. The prolifically marked channel has typical minimum depths of 5½, though an occasional lesser sounding might slip in when strong northerly winds have lowered water levels.

To enter the Long Bayou cut, continue cruising on the ICW until the channel leading east, to the northwest of unlighted day-

beacon #23, is directly abeam. Then, cut off the Waterway and point to pass between unlighted daybeacons #1 and #2.

Once these aids are left behind, the markers leading to the shoreside house will be directly in front of you, while the Long Bayou cut will be spotted to the north. Turn sharply north some 25 yards east of #1 and #2 and point to come abeam of Long Bayou's most southerly aid, unlighted daybeacon #1, to its fairly immediate easterly side. You can then follow the numerous beacons into the bay's interior reaches, always remembering your "red, right, returning" rule.

Eventually, unlighted daybeacon #29 will come abeam to your port side. The docks associated with Lighthouse Point Marina will then be spied to the northeast. You can cruise directly from #29 to the marina, but be ready for some 5-foot (or slightly less) depths.

North of #29, upstream navigation on Long Bayou is complicated by the charted channel striking west from unlighted daybeacon #31. This cut serves a public launching area and is best avoided by cruising-size craft. Also, there is an uncharted shoal west of #31.

Many visiting cruisers will wisely choose to discontinue their upstream explorations at #29. Bay Pines Marina, north of the bridge spanning Long Bayou, does not offer any services for transients other than gasoline and limited mechanical repairs.

For those who choose to continue on, set course from #29 to bring unlighted daybeacon #31 abeam to your fairly immediate port side. Do not slip west of #31. Very shallow water waits to greet your keel.

From #31, point for the central pass-through of the fixed bridge dead ahead. This span has a vertical clearance of only 20 feet, much too low for most sail craft.

Once through the bridge, you will be met by a confusing series of privately maintained daybeacons. All the aids, green or red, are rectangular in shape, an unusual arrangement to say the least. The best advice this writer can give cruisers who make it this far without local knowledge is to pass all red beacons to starboard and all green markers to port, as usual. Good luck!

Johns Pass Inlet   Johns Pass Inlet is plagued by swift tidal currents, and it is spanned by a bascule bridge with 25 feet of closed vertical clearance. Fortunately, this span does open on demand but sail craft and single-engine trawlers can still have a few anxious moments while waiting for an opening. Otherwise, Johns Pass is a navigational delight and visiting cruisers can make use of the cut with confidence.

Two routes lead from the Waterway to Johns Pass. The southernmost of the two skirts the northerly reaches of Capri Isle and is marked by only a single aid to navigation, unlighted daybeacon #1. While local captains use this route safely week in and week out, strangers are advised to choose the well-marked entry channel leading south from the ICW's flashing daybeacon #4.

Enter this latter passage by continuing northwest on the ICW until the pass-through between unlighted daybeacons #13 and #14 is immediately abeam to the south. Then, cruise between these aids and point to come abeam of unlighted daybeacon #11 to its

easterly side. Set course to pass the next two red daybeacons to your fairly immediate port side.

South of flashing daybeacon #10, a minimum-wake zone is in effect throughout the remainder of Johns Pass. All boats should proceed at reduced speed until well past the inlet bridge.

At unlighted daybeacon #8, the channel takes a sharp jog to the south-southeast. If your plan is to continue on to the inlet, point to pass flashing daybeacon #7 to its northeasterly quarter. A good anchorage and a repair yard can be found to the west of #7. This haven will be covered below.

Getting back to the inlet channel, skippers should next point to come abeam of flashing daybeacon #6 to its westerly side. Be mindful of the charted shoal waters to the northeast.

At #6 the inlet channel swings to the southwest and becomes a straight shot to the open Gulf. Simply point for the bridge's central pass-through and leave yourself plenty of maneuvering room if you need to wait for an opening.

As you cruise toward the bridge, the fuel dock and powder blue dry-storage building of Johns Pass Marina will be visible to the southeast. Cruisers would have a hard time missing Johns Pass Village and Boardwalk, lining the opposite banks.

Once the pesky 25-foot Johns Pass bascule bridge is behind you, a series of easily followed markers leads you well out into the Gulf's deeper waters. Be prepared to find more and different markers than those shown on chart 11411.

Madeira Beach Anchorage   To enter the

anchorage west of flashing daybeacon #7 (on the Johns Pass entrance channel), continue on the inlet cut past #7 as if you were putting out to sea. After cruising south for some 25 yards from #7, curl back around to the northwest and enter the stream by heavily favoring the port-side shore. By following this procedure, you can expect 5½-foot depths, while a slip to the east will land you in 5-foot soundings. Drop the hook anywhere you choose, but be aware that a southerly wind might swing you into the somewhat shallower water abutting the northerly banks.

To cruise farther upstream, continue favoring the port shore until coming abeam of the third, short cove to the north. Work your way back to the mid-width as you cruise past this point. Soon the wide stream splits into two branches. If Snug Harbor Boat Yard is your destination, cruise down the centerline of the southerly fork. You will spy the yard at the westerly end of the stream.

Veterans Hospital Anchorage   A somewhat open anchorage is available to cruising craft near the ICW's flashing daybeacon #6. You might choose to drop the hook in the charted patch of deep water north and northeast of #6. Those cruisers making use of this anchorage should leave the Waterway abeam of unlighted daybeacon #5 and cruise carefully to the northeast. Be mindful of the shallows to the west that are marked by #6. Stay well away from #6 and avoid the charted ½-foot shoal along the shoreline as well. Pick any likely spot and settle in for the evening.

Shallow-draft cruising vessels (only!) can make use of the poollike bay northwest of

the charted Veterans Hospital. Hold to the centerline of the shallow entrance stream. Be ready for depths as shallow as 3 feet or occasionally less. For best depths, drop anchor well away from the shoreline. Leave plenty of swinging room to avoid any vessels that happen to be tied to the permanent mooring buoys on the little bay.

On the ICW   Northwest of unlighted daybeacon #5, the ICW follows a sharp turn to the west. This change of course is marked by flashing daybeacon #6, which is itself founded in shallow water. Make the turn, pointing to stay well away from #6. Come abeam of unlighted daybeacon #7 to its fairly immediate northerly side. Shallow water of 2 feet or less guards the channel to the north along this stretch.

Northwest of unlighted daybeacon #10, the Waterway hurries on to the Welch Causeway (also known as the Madeira Beach) Bridge. This span has a closed vertical clearance of 25 feet and still opens on demand except on weekends and holidays. During these times, the bridge opens for us annoying pleasurecruisers every 20 minutes from 9:30 A.M. to 6:00 P.M. Weekend sailors must take these hours into account to avoid a long and frustrating delay.

Before you reach Welch Causeway, a marina and a restaurant with dockage are available to all passing cruisers on the southwestern banks.

Madeira Beach Facilities   The docks of Madeira Beach Marina front onto the northwestern banks of the large cove southwest of unlighted daybeacon #10.

Successful entry into this facility is some-what complicated by the large, charted shoal occupying the cove's mid-width, just southeast of the marina.

To avoid this shoal, continue cruising on the Waterway until you are northwest of #10, and the point of land to the southwest is abeam. Depart the ICW and heavily favor the northwesterly banks as you track your way southwest to the marina. As you work your way along the shoreline, you may catch sight of three unsigned pilings to port. These informal aids to navigation mark the shoal water to the southeast. Stay well away from the piles. You will first pass a series of covered slips. Continue on and the marina's principal dockage basin will soon be readily apparent.

On the ICW North of the Welch Causeway (Madeira Beach) Bridge, the ICW follows a dredged channel through a shallow portion of Boca Ciega Bay. Be sure to stick strictly to the marked cut. Depths outside of the Waterway quickly rise to grounding levels.

Do not attempt to enter the charted patch of deep water west of unlighted day-beacon #19. On-site research revealed that the unmarked channel is too obscure and unsafe for larger boats.

At unlighted daybeacon #25, the ICW channel follows a jog to the northwest and moves on toward the last anchorage avail-able to the cruisers short of the Narrows. Northwest of unlighted daybeacon #27, the Waterway markers begin a new series of numbers. The next northerly aid past #27 is unlighted daybeacon #1.

Redington Shores Anchorage In a situation similar to the small bay guarded by Madeira Beach Marina, the cove striking south from unlighted daybeacon #1 features very shoal water on its mid-width, though a good chan-nel hugs the banks. Additionally, there is a smaller 1-foot shoal near the rear of the cove, which can cause problems. This is *not* the most easily entered of the anchorages along this stretch of the Waterway, and it is not rec-ommended for deep-draft vessels.

To enter, depart the Waterway at unlighted daybeacon #1 and heavily favor the westerly shores as you cruise through the bay's mouth. Immediately after entering the bay, cruise quickly over to the south-easterly banks, and favor this shoreline as you work your way to the south and south-west. If depths start to rise, you are proba-bly encroaching on the shoal in the middle of the cove. Hug the shoreline even more tightly and see if soundings improve. Drop the hook anywhere that strikes your fancy as you approach the southwestern corner and settle down for a night of security, even if the nearby automobile traffic does not grant you the most peaceful of evenings.

On the ICW West-northwest of flashing daybeacon #2, the ICW enters the Narrows and rough water drops away. Tidal currents do run quite swiftly; however, so stay alert.

A minimum-wake zone begins at #2 and runs north through the Park Boulevard Bridge to unlighted daybeacon #18. This would be a particularly good zone in which to obey the restrictive regulations. The county sheriff's dock is located on the western shores south of #18.

This would probably be a good time to note that it is *very* difficult to tell where no-wake (and minimum-wake) zones begin and end on the Narrows portion of the Waterway. The limits presented above and below are our best take on the situation, but don't be surprised if these limited-speed sections have been enlarged by the time of your visit. If you want to be dead sure that you are in compliance, proceed at idle speed throughout the whole length of the Narrows.

Just north of unlighted daybeacon #12, cruisers will be greeted by the Park Boulevard Bridge. This fortunate span features a closed vertical clearance of 25 feet and opens on demand—great news indeed for sailors and skippers of single-screw vessels.

North of Park Boulevard, unlighted daybeacon #14 marks a series of semisubmerged stones flanking the easterly banks. Stay well clear of this aid to avoid a rocky experience.

At unlighted daybeacon #21, the Waterway takes a brief northward run through a shallow slough. Stick to the channel. Be sure to watch your stern as well as your progress ahead to quickly note any lateral slippage.

Flashing daybeacon #27 heralds the beginning of a long, long minimum-wake zone stretching north past the Indian Rocks Beach Bridge. Take your time and enjoy the sights.

Unlighted daybeacon #27A marks a small spoil island or shoal fronting onto the western banks. Between unlighted daybeacons #28 and #30, rocks again line the eastern shores. Favor the westerly side of the channel slightly to give this threat a wide margin.

Northwest of flashing daybeacon #33, the ICW extends greetings to the Indian Rocks Beach Bridge. With its closed vertical clearance of 25 feet, sailors will be glad to learn that this span does open on demand.

At unlighted daybeacon #40, northbound cruisers will begin to notice an increase in the breadth of the surrounding water. You are now beginning your approach to Clearwater Harbor and the Belleair Bridge. Daybeacon #40 also heralds the last good anchorage south of Belleair.

Sand Key Anchorage   To enter the Sand Key anchorage, west of unlighted daybeacon #40, depart the Waterway some 75 yards north-northeast of this aid. Set course to come abeam of the north-side entrance point by some 75 yards to your starboard quarter. Avoid the southerly point. It is actually a spoil island and is surrounded by shoal water. Drop the hook after coming under the lee of the peninsula to the north. Farther to the west, depths of 5 feet or possibly less are encountered.

On to Clearwater Harbor   The ICW continues to follow a well-marked, dredged passage set amidst otherwise shoal water to flashing daybeacon #47. The Belleair Bridge spans the Waterway just north of this aid. From this point and for several miles to the north, depths outside of the ICW improve somewhat. There are still shallow spots, however, so depart the marked track only with the greatest care.

The Belleair Bridge has restrictive weekend opening times. With a closed vertical clearance of 21 feet, this span can be another impediment for tall ships. On Saturdays, Sundays, and legal holidays, the bridge opens every 15 minutes, beginning at the top of the hour, from noon to 6:00 P.M. At all other times, it opens on demand.

Clearwater Harbor to Dunedin

Cruisers leaving Belleair Causeway behind are immediately introduced to the oblong, baylike body of water known as Clearwater Harbor. If ever there was a portion of the Western Florida coastline that could be described as overdeveloped, the shores about Clearwater Harbor is it. Yet, even amidst this "progress," there is still at least one opportunity to get off the beaten path and visit lands still in their natural state.

To the east, the mainland ports of call are dominated by the city of Clearwater, which is set atop the highest point of land on the Western Florida coastline. The city's waters spread out in a breathtaking view from the vantage of any of the many high-rise office buildings or condos. Clearwater clearly has its problems, but it is nevertheless a vital, flourishing community which boasts an array of services for cruisers and just about every shoreside business or convenience that can be imagined.

The beach-side barrier islands are a morass of high-rise condos, rubbing shoulders with extensive residential development and commercial shopping centers. The honk of frustrated automobile horns is a far more frequent sound to the visiting ear than the call of the breaker.

North of Clearwater, the eastern shores are graced by the once very Scottish town of Dunedin. Settled in 1870, the city now sports a well-protected harbor. Several outstanding restaurants are located nearby.

Clearwater Pass Inlet, near the midline of Clearwater Bay's north-to-south axis, provides dependable access to the Gulf of Mexico. Clearwater Pass can be used with a fair amount of confidence.

The ICW's passage through Clearwater Harbor is one of the shallowest runs on the entire Western Florida Waterway. Low-water soundings between the Clearwater Causeway and flashing daybeacon #4 (near Dunedin) can run as thin as 6½ feet.

As you might imagine amidst so much development, marina facilities are more than adequate. Both the Clearwater (Beach) and Dunedin Municipal marinas are outstanding. The commercial marina operations in the area are ably supplemented by two yacht clubs.

Anchorages directly off the ICW are somewhat slim, but the same cannot be said of the waters in and around Clearwater Beach. Several excellent overnight refuges are available to most pleasure craft near the charted Mandalay Channel.

So, while, to be frank, they're not really this writer's cup of tea, the waters about Clearwater and its adjacent beach communities offer many services for cruising vessels. My opinion notwithstanding, many Western Florida mariners set their course for the waters of Clearwater Bay year after year with no complaint.

City of Clearwater

The sprawling city of Clearwater lies about the mainland shores of the like-named harbor for almost 10 nautical miles. In times past this city was known as one of the most beautiful in Western Florida. Even its name recalls the crystal clear waters that once lapped its shores.

One night in the early 1990s, this writer had the good fortune to glimpse the beauty that Clearwater can still claim. Due to the vagaries of motel hunting in the city, we found ourselves on the seventh floor of a high-rise condo with a clear view of the harbor. I was able to watch the sun set over the water, and as the golden light slowly faded, we could still pick out the daybeacons and spoil island (backdropped by many high-rise condos). It was easy to understand what drew so many to this land in the first place.

Sadly, it must now be noted that this huge influx of people has led to the worst of heavy, heavy strip-type retail and office development which long ago shrouded much of southeastern Florida. I felt as if the Clearwater of old was not to be found.

However, there is still much to see and do in Clearwater, and with good dockage facilities nearby, visitors can rent a car or take a taxi and explore a number of fascinating attractions.

Many visitors will want to explore the Clearwater Marine Science Aquarium (727-447-0980), located just off the causeway connecting Clearwater and Clearwater Beach. Here you can see "Sunset Sam," an Atlantic bottlenose dolphin who has been in residence since 1984. The staff swears that Sam is actually helpful in acclimating animals new to the facility. Another popular creature is "Big Mo," a 500-pound Loggerhead sea turtle, and Max, a very rare Kemp's Ridley sea turtle. In short, if you are interested in creatures from the sea, then by all means set your course to the Marine Science Center. Cruisers docking at Clearwater Beach Municipal Marina can reach this attraction by foot.

Visiting cruisers interested in architectural history may want to take a ride to the Belleview Biltmore Resort Hotel. Built in 1896, the Belleview is "reputed to be the largest still-occupied wooden structure in the world." In its heyday, it was known as the "White Queen of the Gulf." The grand hostelry played host to millionaires, railroad magnates, and industrial barons.

Among other striking features are the dining room's sunburst windows and priceless skylight of Tiffany stained glass. Completely renovated in 1986, the hotel is open to the public. You need not stay at the hotel to experience the historic structure. Historic tours are offered for non-guests. Call (727) 442-6171 for more information.

The Suncoast Seabird Sanctuary (18328 Gulf Boulevard, 727-391-6211) is a fascinating facility that is dedicated to the rehabilitation and hopefully re-release of injured sea birds. Since its inception in 1971, more than 15,000 patients have been returned to their natural environment, with an average of 20 or more sick birds being brought in every day. Visitors are always welcome and cameras are definitely recommended.

Two Clearwater events are worthy of all visitors' attention. The Clearwater Jazz Festival, held the third weekend in October, is, according to the local Chamber of Commerce, "one of the top 20 events in the southeast . . . the finest and fastest-growing jazz festival in the nation."

November brings on the famous Kahlua Cup Regatta, one of the top events in the Southern Ocean Racing Conference. The race begins just off the Clearwater Beach pier and is a colorful sight indeed as all the tall ships jockey for position near the starting line. Cruisers will be especially interested in watching the various racing skippers' techniques.

Numbers to know in Clearwater include

Payless Cab—(727) -442-9999
Yellow Cab—(727) 799-2222
Avis Rental Cars—(727) 530-1406
Enterprise Rent-A-Car—(727) 796-3442
Hertz Rent A Car—(727) 531-3774
Boat/U S Marine Center—(727) 573-2678
West Marine—(727) 443-2280
Chamber of Commerce—(727) 461-0011

Belleair Anchorage (Standard Mile 132, 27 55.146 North/082 49.573 West)

While it can most certainly not be described as a quiet, isolated haven, captains desiring to drop the hook for the evening near the ICW can follow the charted deep water striking east just north of Belleair Causeway. Automobile traffic and headlights may disturb your evening's peace, and this should be factored into your decision whether to stay or move on. Minimum depths of 6 feet, with some soundings showing much better water, can be held well in toward the rear of the cove by avoiding the southern banks. This shoreline hosts a large public launching ramp facility, and the rearward banks are overlooked by a tall, white office building. The anchorage affords excellent protection from southern and eastern winds. There is also some shelter from northerly breezes courtesy

of the tongue of land east of unlighted daybeacon #2. Strong westerly winds could make for a very bumpy night.

Waterway Anchorage (Standard Mile 133.5)

In easterly winds, captains seeking an overnight refuge near the ICW might consider dropping anchor in the 6-foot charted waters east of unlighted daybeacon #6, itself southwest of Belleview Island. Good water of 5½ to 6 feet extends to within 100 yards of the eastern shore. Swinging room is ample for any size or shape of pleasure boat and there is good shelter from easterly breezes. Belleview Island also affords a break when winds are blowing from the north and northeast. Protection from other winds is minimal and anchored craft will be exposed to the wake of all passing vessels. The easterly banks are overlooked by extremely heavy commercial development (what else?).

Clearwater Pass Inlet (Standard Mile135.5)

I keep waiting for the easily run inlet to be invented. As any skipper who has spent more than a few moments on the water knows, the often-unstable threads between offshore and inland waters can produce more than their share of white-knuckle experiences. Well, the bad news is that the problemless seaward cut has yet to come along, but the good news is that Clearwater Pass is about as close as you are likely to get in Western Florida. While waves can still kick up when wind and tides oppose one another, the channel is well marked, consistently deeper than 10 feet, and the cut is carefully maintained. A 74-foot, fixed, high-rise span crosses the inlet. This bridge is a major improvement over its old bascule predecessor.

The direct route from the ICW to Clearwater Pass departs the Waterway west-northwest of flashing daybeacon #12. A second cut running south from the Clearwater Beach Channel intersects the inlet route near flashing daybeacon #14, just east of the inlet's bridge. This cut will be reviewed in the next section below.

Large, high-rise condos gaze benignly over the northern shores west of the inlet bridge, while the southern banks are delightfully undeveloped and sport a parklike atmosphere.

All in all, if you are planning to put to sea or gain access to the ICW from the Gulf, you could scarcely do better than Clearwater Pass.

Clearwater Beach Channel and Facilities (Standard Mile 136, Various Lats/Lons—see below)

Minimum 7-foot depths lead you northwest off the ICW on the well-marked Clearwater Beach Channel just southwest of the Clearwater Memorial Causeway Bridge. This fortunate cut provides ready access to the largest pleasure-craft facility in the Clearwater region. A short side trip can also lead you to a quality yacht club with reciprocal privileges. Veteran cruisers in Western Florida make the turn time after time to visit Clearwater Beach's notable facilities.

While, as noted above, the Clearwater Beach cut is deep and boasts good markings, there are still a few tricks that could trap the first-time visitor. Be sure to read the navigational information presented later in this chapter before running the cut for the first time.

At unlighted daybeacon #9, a second channel cuts south and eventually runs to Clearwater Pass. Minimum 7- to 9-foot depths make successful navigation of this channel a simple joy. But wait—there's more.

North of unlighted daybeacon #7 (on the channel connecting the Clearwater Beach Channel and the approach passage to Clearwater Pass), the large, westward-running cove leads to the Clearwater Yacht Club (27 58.056 North/082 49.283 West) and anchorage possibilities as well. Three privately maintained daybeacons (only one of which is charted) help you to maintain minimum 6-foot depths as you enter this offshoot. Moving east to west, the yacht club's docks will be spotted about halfway down the cove, guarding the southerly banks. This notable facility offers transient dockage for members of other yacht clubs with appropriate reciprocal privileges at modern, fixed wooden piers featuring 30- and 50-amp power hookups and water connections. Dockside depths are 7-8 feet or thereabouts. The club dockmaster is on duty Tuesday through Sunday, 9:00 A.M. to 4:00

1. Clearwater Yacht Club
2. Clearwater Municipal Marina
3. High and Dry Marina
4. Ross Yacht Service
5. Clearwater Bay Marina

P.M. Advance reservations are strongly suggested. Shoreside amenities include a swimming pool, bar, showers, and a full dining room that serves both lunch and the evening meal Tuesday through Saturday. Reservations are required, and a dress code is in effect. Several additional restaurants, including the notable Heilman's Beachcomber (447 Mandalay Avenue, 727-442-4144), are only a walk away. This writer found the members of Clearwater Yacht to be some of the friendliest souls in Western Florida. This stopover is highly recommended for those who meet the visiting requirements.

In May 2003, this writer was lucky enough to make a presentation on cruising the Florida Keys to the Clearwater Yacht Club. After a rousing get-together, my hosts took me upstairs to "pasta night." May you too be so lucky!

Clearwater Yacht Club (727) 447-6000
   http://www.clwyc.org

Approach depth—6-14 feet
Dockside depth—7-8 feet
Accepts transients—members of clubs with
   reciprocal privileges
Fixed wooden piers—yes
Dockside power connections—30 and 50 amp
Dockside water connections—yes
Showers—yes
Restaurant—on site and several others nearby

Cruisers looking for a secure spot to drop the hook can easily anchor abeam or just to the west of the yacht club docks in 7 to 10 feet of water (near 27 58.093 North/082 49.276 West). There is plenty of swinging room and excellent protection from all winds except strong easterly breezes, which would blow straight up the cove. In fresh westerly winds, you may want to sound your way a bit farther in toward the cove's western terminus for increased shelter. The surrounding shores are lined by heavy residential development but, even so, they are more attractive than those of the two anchorages directly adjacent to the ICW discussed above.

Returning our attention to the primary Clearwater Beach Channel, the cut continues running west-northwest from flashing daybeacon #10 to an intersection with the Mandalay Channel. This passage leads through a fixed bridge to additional facilities and anchorages and will be addressed separately below.

West of unlighted daybeacon #11, mariners may choose to visit Clearwater Municipal Marina (27 58.586 North/082 49.593 West). This city-owned facility offers a host of transient slips for the visiting cruiser. Depths alongside run better than 8 feet. Dockage is at fixed wooden piers with water hookups and ultra-modern power connections up to 50 amps, plus telephone and cable-television hookups as well. Gasoline and diesel fuel are readily available, as is waste pump-out service.

Shoreside showers are available in the main dockmaster's building and at another location on the harbor's southerly quarter. The set (two) in the main structure is climate controlled, while the others are not. There is also a petite but air-conditioned Laundromat in the dockmaster's headquaters.

Clearwater Municipal Marina is one of the few pleasure-craft facilities, to my knowledge, that supply an "ADA"-approved lift device to safely transfer handicapped cruisers to and from their vessels. It is only to be hoped that many more marinas will follow the fine facility's lead in this innovative move.

A host of restaurants is only a short step away. Crabby Bill's Restaurant (727-442-2163), located in the shopping complex lining the harbor's northern shores, is famous for its grouper sandwiches. The Marina Restaurant (727-446-6968), located in the same building, is open for all three meals of the day, seven days a week, and serves an excellent breakfast. Galley chefs looking to restock their onboard stores will find a convenience store known as the Pirate's Pantry within the same dockside complex. For more substantial galley supplies, it is a long 1½-mile walk across Clearwater Memorial Causeway to a Publix Supermarket on the mainland. Many visitors will be able to make use of the Jolley Trolley, a mode of public transportation provided by the city of Clearwater Beach at a mere 50-cent cost. To be succinct, Clearwater Municipal

Marina is a first-rate city-sponsored marina that visiting cruisers can use with confidence.

Clearwater Municipal Marina (727) 462-6954

Approach depth—7-17 feet
Dockside depth—8+ feet
Accepts transients—yes (extensive)
Transient dockage rate—average
Fixed wooden piers—yes
Dockside power connections—30 and 50 amp
Dockside water connections—yes
Waste pump-out—yes
Showers—yes
Laundromat—yes
Gasoline—yes
Diesel fuel—yes
Restaurant—two on site and several others nearby

If the urge strikes to try a meal farther afield

Clearwater Municipal Marina

while docking at Clearwater Municipal Marina, there are two dining spots amid the myriad restaurants within walking distance of the piers that demand your attention. Frenchy's Café (41 Baymont Street, 727-446-3607) and its nearby brother, Frenchy's Saltwater Café (419 Poinsetta, 727-461-6295), are probably places that most first-time visitors would pass by without a single thought. Located on small side streets several blocks north of the municipal dockage basin, these combination bar-and-restaurants attract warm and convivial crowds evening after evening. After you've sampled the stone crab claws, conch fritters, and buffalo shrimp, not to mention the amazing burgers, you won't need to ask from whence comes the attraction. This is a "must taste" spot in Clearwater for all who, like this writer, go looking for new and different dining experiences.

Mandalay Channel and Facilities (Standard Mile 136.5, Various Lats/Lons—see below)

A large side channel strikes northwest from the ICW's flashing daybeacon #15 and eventually cuts into a wide passage running just behind Clearwater Beach known as Mandalay Channel. This cut can lead cruisers to several fine anchorages, a yacht club, and a few other casual pleasure craft facilities. Those power captains who can clear a fixed bridge with 14 feet of vertical clearance can follow the Mandalay Channel all the way south to the Clearwater Municipal Marina.

Minimum depths are 6 feet, with soundings of 7 to a much as 13 feet being more typical on Mandalay Channel. Aids to navigation are well placed, but there are a few gaps which do call for slightly more caution than usual.

West of the Mandalay Channel's unlighted daybeacon #14, cruisers whose craft draw 5 feet or less can curl back around to the northeast and anchor in the lee of Moonshine Island (near 28 00.105 North/082 49.180 West). While it may have served as the one-time location of an illegal still, today the island is a wonderfully undeveloped mangrove. If the fickle wind chooses to cooperate, this is one of the most attractive overnight havens on these waters. Minimum depths of 6 feet can be carried to within 25 yards of the island's southwesterly banks. Swinging room is sufficient for boats as large as 45 feet, but good shelter is only available from winds blowing generally from the north. There is some protection from southerly breezes courtesy of the land mass to the south, but blows of more than 12 knots from the east or west call for another plan.

West of unlighted daybeacon #14, the principal branch of the Mandalay Channel takes a sharp jog to the south. Another marked cut makes off to the north and northwest toward impassable Dunedin Pass. Depths of 7 to 9 feet can be carried as far north as a position abeam of unlighted daybeacon #20. Shortly thereafter, soundings drop off to 4½ feet or less.

Under no circumstances should even small craft attempt to run Dunedin Pass. To say that it is dangerous comprises a mammoth understatement.

West of unlighted daybeacon #20, Carlouel Yacht Club offers one or two minimal guest slips for members of clubs with reciprocal privileges. The adjacent clubhouse features showers, a swimming pool, and tennis courts (reservation only). The on-site dining room offers luncheon and dinner Wednesday through Sunday, and as usual with yacht clubs, reservations are required. The club does not employ a regular dockmaster, so advance mooring reservations are even more important than usual.

Carlouel Yacht Club (727) 446-9162

Approach depth—7-9 feet
Dockside depth—5-7 feet
Accepts transients—members of clubs with
  reciprocal privileges (limited)
Fixed wooden piers—yes (also some dockage
  along seawall)
Dockside power connections—yes
Dockside water connections—yes
Showers—yes
Restaurant—on site

The principal Mandalay Channel runs south from unlighted daybeacon #14 to a fixed bridge with 14 feet of vertical clearance. In anything short of stormy conditions, pleasure craft of any size, type, or draft can easily anchor in the channel itself. Just be sure to drop the hook a bit away from the mid-width and show an anchor light in case any night-time traffic happens along. One good spot is found near 27 59.559 North/082 49.352 West. The surrounding shores sport heavy, but not completely unattractive residential development. High-rise condos are very much in evidence to the south.

Captains and crew cruising south on Mandalay Channel toward the fixed bridge will spot a whole bevy of covered slips to the southeast. This facility is pictured as a black *L* and a straight bar on chart 11411. These piers belong to Island Yacht Club, which is actually a boataminium. No services of any type are available for visitors.

Just behind Island Yacht Club (on the southern shore of the southeastward-running cove), High and Dry Marina (27 58.766 North/082

49.241 West, 727-443-0637) offers dry storage, a small ship's store, and gasoline. No dockage or diesel fuel can be had. Depths on the approach channel are in the 6- to 13-foot range with 7 to 9 feet of water dockside. Some small-scale mechanical repairs are available for outboard- and I/O-powered vessels.

Immediately north of the 14-foot fixed bridge, a deep (7½ to 9 feet) channel strikes southeast and leads to a first-rate boatyard. Cruisers traversing this cut will first spot (on the northeastern banks) some slips rented on a monthly basis to local vessels by the city of Clearwater. These docks are clustered around the Clearwater Marine Science Aquarium. Continue cruising upstream and Ross Yacht Service (727-446-8191, 27 58.590 North/082 49.101 West) will come abeam on the northeastern banks. This facility, which has recently undergone a change in ownership, continues to offer full-service mechanical and haul-out (30-ton travelift), below-waterline repairs to all types of pleasure craft.

The canal leading southeast to Ross Yacht Service actually dead-ends just past this facility. Some local sail craft seem to regularly tie up to mooring buoys near the canal's eastern terminus. There is very little additional room for transients, and visiting cruisers would do well to look elsewhere.

Clearwater Bay Marina (Standard Mile 136.5, 27 58.491 North/082 48.090 West)

Clearwater Bay Marina, found in the charted harbor just east-southeast of the ICW's unlighted daybeacon #16, is a mixed bag for cruisers. On the one hand, a gambling ship still makes its home in this harbor, and that is never a good thing for pleasure craft.

However, transient slips are offered, and the dockage basin is well sheltered from all but strong westerly winds. Berths are provided at fixed wooden piers. Minimum, low-water dockside depths of 5½ feet could be a problem for especially deep-draft vessels. Power hookups of the 30- and 50-amp variety are available slip side, as are freshwater connections. Gasoline and diesel fuel can be purchased at a fuel dock near the harbor's easterly entrance. One, low-key, non-climate-controlled, unisex shower is found on the premises. It is a long walk of 5 to 6 blocks to the nearest restaurant (Pickles Plus Two—727-447-0500, 320 Cleveland Street—a very good deli). Cruisers will need to call a taxi to access a grocery store or other provisioning retailers.

There is an on-site MarineMax dealership (727-466-9700). These good folks provide mechanical repairs for both gasoline and diesel engines and perform haul-outs by way of a 50-ton travelift.

1. Dunedin Marina

Clearwater Bay Marina (727) 443-3207

Approach depth—12 feet
Dockside depth—5½ feet
Accepts transients—yes
Transient dockage rate—average
Fixed wooden slips—yes
Dockside power connections—30 and 50 amp
Dockside water connections—yes
Shower—yes
Gasoline—yes
Diesel fuel—yes
Mechanical repairs—yes

Dunedin and Associated Facilities (Standard Mile 139, 28 00.719 North/082 47.542 West)

Northeast of flashing daybeacon #4, a marked and charted channel leads the fortunate cruiser to Dunedin's enclosed harbor. Of all the various mainland and beach communities between Tampa Bay and the waters south of the Anclote River, Dunedin remains this writer's personal favorite.

Dunedin seems to slumber along at a far more relaxed pace than its robust neighbors to the south. During one visit, we discovered a weekly art and craft show on the harbor park grounds. How many times do you run across an event like that? If you enjoy relaxed, small-town life, then by all means affix a red circle to Dunedin on your chart.

According to locals, this downtown Dunedin's tasteful renaissance began when the former railroad bed was paved over and converted to a hiking trail. Soon, new construction brought a host of quaint and varied shops (not to mention more than a few restaurants) to the downtown business district. The town has obviously not looked back ever since, while still maintaining the atmosphere of a small village.

Visitors to Dunedin should also be acquainted with the local Springfest/Seafood Festival held early in May. This wonderful event features some of the finest seafood you will every enjoy along with street entertainment and arts and crafts exhibitions.

Dunedin's yacht basin is very well sheltered and boasts a city marina, which gladly accepts transients. Currently, 9 slips are usually available for visitors. Low-tide minimum entrance and dockside depths of 5 feet could be a concern for deep-draft, fixed-keel sail craft. Dockage is at fixed wooden piers with water connections and power connections up to 50 amps. Shoreside showers are available, and a Laundromat is located three blocks away. The marina does not offer a fuel dock, but waste pump-out service is available.

A supermarket is found within a 1½-mile taxi or bicycle ride east up Main Street. For taxi service call Yellow Cab at (727) 799-2222.

Meanwhile, the dockmaster's office is found at the northeastern corner of the harbor. Visiting cruisers should check in here for slip assignments. A fresh seafood market offering a wide range of selections is located on the first floor of the dockmaster's building. It doesn't get any more convenient than this.

As for what to do when it comes time to dine ashore, let me assure you that eating out will never be dull in Dunedin. You don't believe it? Well, just read on!

Dunedin Municipal Marina (727) 298-3030
http://www.ci.dunedin.fl.us/dunedin/marina.htm

Approach depth—5-7 feet
Dockside depth—5 feet
Accepts transients—yes
Transient dockage rate—below average
Fixed wooden slips—yes
Dockside power connections—30 and 50 amp
Dockside water connections—yes
Waste pump-out—yes
Showers—yes
Laundromat—within three blocks
Restaurant—many nearby

The Best Western Yacht Harbor Inn (727-733-4121) overlooks the northern corner of Dunedin Harbor's entrance. This facility no longer offers any dockage, but the restaurant is still worth your attention. The inn's Bon Appétit Restaurant is renowned among cruisers who have an acute interest in their palates. This very refined dining establishment has received the coveted four-star rating from the Mobil Travel Guide. We found the dining room to be incredibly impressive, the service exemplary, and the Continental-style cuisine all one could ask for. If you have a tie and sport coat on board, this is certainly one of the few restaurants in Western Florida where you will want to don this attire. Prices cannot be described in any way, shape, or form as inexpensive. Bon Appétit comprises one of those "nights out to remember" that comes along once in a cruise. Reservations are mandatory and should be made at the earliest possible date.

Dunedin's yacht harbor is bordered to the east by an attractive park which is highly recommended for cruisers who have acquired a serious case of sailor's stride. Once you get your land legs back, it's only a short stroll to the downtown section from the park. Supplementing the four-star restaurant directly on the harbor, there are two other dining spots within two blocks which must not be missed.

Marker One Marina

First up is the cleverly named Sea Sea Rider's Restaurant (221 Main Street, 727-734-1445), quickly spotted on the southern side of the street leading almost due east from the dockage basin. Housed in a historic Florida "conch house" and specializing in the best seafood you will ever enjoy, the restaurant delights diners with the broiled catch of the day and fabulous crab claws. When it comes time to finish the meal, their Key Lime Pie will make a memory which will linger on and on.

An additional block farther to the east, and also on the southern side of the street, you will find Kelly's (319 Main Street, 727-736-5284) nestled between several other buildings. This restaurant receives my vote as one of the finest in all of Florida. The atmosphere

is as unexpected as it is delightful. It's like someone dropped a New York-style bistro into Dunedin and added a touch of Florida. The walls are decorated with such diverse touches as old bicycles hung from the ceiling and modern art prints. The pace is unhurried and seems to encourage slow sipping of your last cup of cappuccino or espresso, an attitude that is too rare in these hurried times.

Even if it were not for the atmosphere, Kelly's would still attract an ultraloyal clientele with its food alone. Some of the most imaginative dishes that I have ever enjoyed have been served up in this rarefied atmosphere. Shrimp set amidst cumin-infused olive oil and chicken breast stuffed with provolone cheese, crumbled bacon and chives, and grilled with basil-infused olive oil are only two of the unforgettable entrees. You may be assured that appetizers, desserts, and the cocktails and wine all bear the same unmistakable mark of Kelly's' constant attention to the smallest details of quality and culinary delight.

Incidentally, for those readers interested in learning more about what to see, where to go, and even where to dine in the Tampa, St. Petersburg, Clearwater metropolitan area, this writer highly recommends Tampa Bay Magazine. Its quality level is among the very elite regional magazines that I have reviewed. Subscriptions can be obtained by calling 727-791-4800.

Dunedin History   Seven years after Florida entered the Union in 1845, Richard Leroy Garrison filed the first recorded deed on Curlew Creek. He was given 160 acres under the Bounty Land Act of 1850 for service in the Seminole Indian Wars. Following the Civil War in 1865, settlers came from Europe, the British Isles, and the eastern United States.

John Ogilvie Douglas and Hugh Somerville came to the shores of Sarasota Bay from Edinburgh, Scotland, around 1870 and opened a general store on the waterfront. Ships from Cedar Key, bound for Tampa around Pinellas Point, stopped for items including groceries, hardware, dry goods, saddlebags, and good water.

Rival George L. Jones of Marietta, Georgia, established a general store east across the dirt road, putting up a sign that read "Jonesboro." In 1878 the Scots answered this with a sign reading "Dunedin," which is Gaelic for Edinburgh. Apparently the persistent Scots won out, as they often do.

Dunedin was the trading center of the Pinellas Peninsula into the 1900s. It was also the social center. People came from miles around in horse-drawn buggies for waltzes on Saturday nights at the Dunedin Yacht Club Inn. Tourists viewed 40-foot sailboat races and took picnics to the island.

Pioneers struggled with freezes, hurricanes, mosquitoes, roaches, and poverty. There was no electricity, running water, or ice. The community was literally carved out of a wilderness.

With the coming of the Orange Belt Railroad in 1888, waterborne shipping became obsolete. Dunedin slipped back into the guise of a charming village. Incorporated in 1899, Dunedin was nine blocks long and three blocks wide, with a population of one hundred. The town became the City of Dunedin in 1926. To this day, the community retains its small-town flair as a striking contrast to its southerly neighbors.

Visitors to Dunedin should be sure to experience the Dunedin Historical Museum, housed in the 1888 railway station. It will be found on the southern side of Main Street, one block east of Kelly's.

Additional Clearwater Harbor Facilities (Various Lats/Lons—see below)

One other marina and an expanded park dock beckon for passing cruisers to stop and while away a few hours on the waters north of Dunedin.

The amply marked and easily followed channel flowing east to excellent Marker One Marina (28 02.970 North/082 47.246 West, Standard Mile 142) breaks off from the ICW just south of the Dunedin/Honeymoon Island Bridge. To be succinct, this is a noteworthy marina. Boasting a breakwater-protected harbor, Marker One has some of the finest services between the Anclote River and Tampa Bay.

Excellent entrance and dockside depths of 6 to 8 feet provide plenty of margin for most craft. Transients are readily accepted at the most modern of fixed wooden piers with every conceivable power and water connection. Gasoline, diesel fuel, an adjacent swimming pool, waste pump-out service, and full mechanical repairs are supplemented by climate-controlled, shoreside showers. Mechanical services are provided courtesy of the on-site repair firm known as Chuck Dillon's Marine Repairs (727-733-4047). Marker One boasts an on-site ship's and variety store. The adjacent Jesse's Dockside Restaurant (345 Causeway Boulevard, 727-736-2611) is a large, impressive dining spot that seems to be well frequented by the local crowd. Wow! How's that for services? If you are looking for a large marina with every conceivable amenity, then your search is finished. Coil your lines at Marker One for a memorable stay.

Marker One Marina (727) 733-9324
   http://www.marker1marina.net

Approach depth—6-8 feet
Dockside depth—6-8 feet
Accepts transients—yes
Transient dockage rate—below average
Fixed wooden piers—yes
Dockside power connections—up to 50 amp
Dockside water connections—yes
Waste pump-out—yes
Showers—yes
Gasoline—yes
Diesel fuel—yes
Mechanical repairs—yes
Ship's and variety store—yes
Restaurant—on site

Caladesi Island State Park (Standard Mile 142)

Skippers piloting craft that draw less than 4½ feet can track their way to the west and southwest from the Waterway just south of the Dunedin Bridge (north of unlighted daybeacon #15) to the well-marked and charted Seven Mouth Creek Channel. This cut allows access to the marina at Caladesi Island State Park (28 01.933 North/082 49.175 West, 727-469-5917), one of the few undeveloped barrier islands along the central portion of Western Florida. No bridge connects Caladesi to the mainland and access is only by boat. A park service ferry does provide transportation for landlubbers.

The park features tall sand dunes, exotic shell hunting, and more than 2 miles of snow-white, sandy beaches. The nearby nature trail offers a fascinating glimpse of pine flatwoods, oak hammocks, and mangrove swamps.

Visiting cruisers are welcome at the park service's recently expanded metal-decked, floating docks. No power or water connections are available, but there are bathrooms, showers, and a park service snack bar. Minimum entrance depths are only 4 feet, though you will find soundings of 4½ to 5 feet quite common on the inner part of the channel, with 5 to 8 feet of water on the cut's outer section. Dockside soundings range from 4½ to 6 feet. With the relatively shallow depths, and the channel's twists and turns, this side trip will probably appeal more to the power captain than the sailor, but the swing-keel skipper can also take a crack at it, if he or she so chooses.

Hurricane Pass

Hurricane Pass was formed by a violent hurricane which struck the coast in 1921. The seaward cut divides what is now called Honeymoon Island to the north and Caladesi Island to the south.

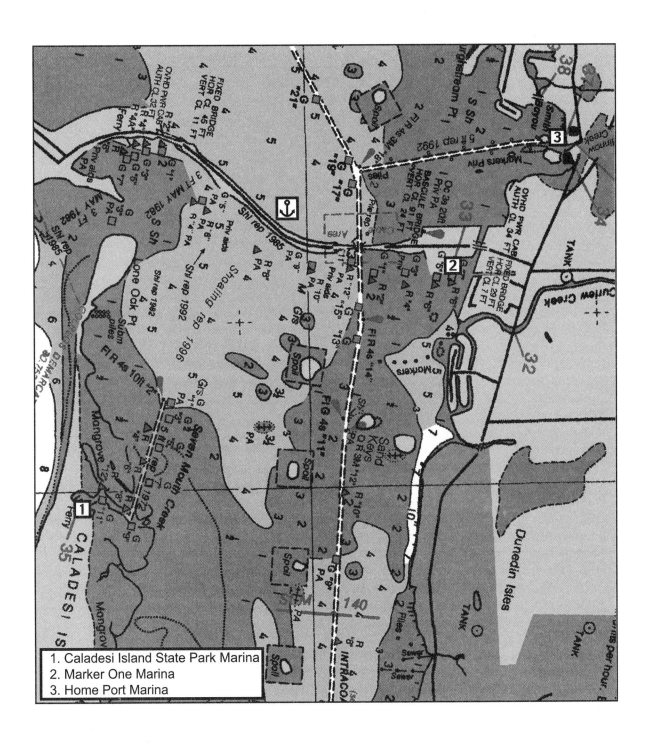

1. Caladesi Island State Park Marina
2. Marker One Marina
3. Home Port Marina

Cruisers studying chart 11411 may note several charted marks leading west from unlighted daybeacon #15 to Hurricane Pass.

Don't be fooled. Depths in this errant seaward cut run to 4 feet or less. All craft should avoid this inlet like the plague.

CLEARWATER HARBOR NAVIGATION

Navigation of the ICW through Clearwater Harbor is an unexpected study in caution. Shallow water (as little as 6½ feet in the ICW channel) and confusing markers are two trademark problems along this stretch of the Waterway. This is clearly not the place to go running along at full throttle. All craft should proceed with caution and keep an eye on the sounder. Always have your binoculars and chart 11411 at hand to help sort out the confusing markers and be ready for quick course changes should the need arise.

Belleair Anchorage   Enter the large pool of deep water to the east, just north of Belleair Causeway, by staying some 100 yards off the southside shore. Watch these banks and you will spot a large, public launching area. Larger, deep-draft vessels should consider dropping the hook before coming abeam of the easternmost portion of this facility. Farther to the east, shoal water extends out for some distance from all the surrounding shores.

Waterway Anchorage   Well, it doesn't get much easier than this. If you choose to drop the hook in the deep water east of unlighted daybeacon #6, simply feel your way east-southeast or northeast from this aid and avoid the narrow strip of shoals abutting the shoreline. Drop the hook and settle in for a secure evening, but remember that a large

powercraft might just happen by and give you a good roll.

Clearwater Pass   The direct route from the ICW to Clearwater Pass departs the Waterway west-northwest of flashing daybeacon #12. An additional channel leading from Clearwater Memorial Causeway will be reviewed in the next section.

While this inlet is consistently deep and well marked, tidal currents do run swiftly. Sail craft and single-screw trawlers should be on guard against excessive leeway. Watch your course over the stern as well as the track ahead to quickly note any slippage.

Leave the Waterway once abeam of #12 and set course to pass between unlighted daybeacons #19 and #20. From a position between #19 and #20 to the bridge spanning the inlet, you need only pass (as you would expect) red, even-numbered aids to your port side and green markers to starboard. This is in marked contrast to the next channel reviewed below.

The fixed high-rise Clearwater Pass Bridge (vertical clearance 74 feet) spans the inlet west of flashing daybeacon #14. This bridge is a welcome replacement for the old 24-foot bascule structure that used to span the pass.

Clearwater Causeway Channel   The channel leading west-northwest from the ICW (just south of the Clearwater Causeway

Bridge pass-through) to Clearwater Municipal Marina is deep and well marked, but the cut is surrounded by shoal water. Some visiting navigators become confused by the profuse markers, and this has led to groundings just where you might least expect such an embarrassing event to occur. Read the information below and watch the sounder as you cruise to the marina. Your overnight stay will be ever so much more peaceful for the extra effort.

Markers on the Clearwater Causeway Channel are the opposite of what you might expect if you were looking at this cut as part of the Clearwater Pass Inlet cut. Moving east to west, red beacons should be taken to your starboard side, while green markers can be waved at to port.

To enter the channel, depart the Waterway as unlighted daybeacon #1 comes abeam to the west. Pass this aid to its northerly side and point to come abeam of the next marker, unlighted daybeacon #2, to its southerly quarter.

From #2 to unlighted daybeacon #6, the cut is reasonably easy to follow, but conditions change between #6 and the next marker, unlighted daybeacon #7. It's all too easy to mistakenly identify the "Sign," obscurely charted on the alternate channel running to Clearwater Pass Inlet, as #7. A quick study of chart 11411 correctly reveals that such an error would land you and yours square on the grassy shoal south of the channel. Use your binoculars to make a positive ID of #7 before proceeding. Point to pass #7 to its fairly immediate northern side, and then continue on for the gap between flashing daybeacon #10 and unlighted daybeacon #9.

At #9, a second channel cuts south to Clearwater Pass. This cut will be reviewed next, but for just a moment, let's push on to Clearwater Municipal Marina. From your position between #9 and #10, point to come abeam of unlighted daybeacon #11 to its northerly side. At this point, the marina docks will be quickly spied to the west. For best water, take a fairly broad turn around #11 before altering course a bit to the west in order to reach the piers.

Returning now to the alternate cut leading to Clearwater Pass, navigators should know that marker colors reverse again. Southbound craft (headed toward the inlet) should take red markers to their (the cruisers') port side and the more prolific green beacons to starboard.

Just before coming between flashing daybeacon #10 and unlighted daybeacon #9 on the main Clearwater Causeway Channel, turn sharply to the south and point to pass unlighted daybeacon #8 to its fairly immediate westerly side. You can then follow the markers to an intersection with Clearwater Pass Channel near flashing daybeacon #14.

To enter the cove northwest of unlighted daybeacon #7, home of Clearwater Yacht Club, depart the north-to-south channel, some 100 yards north of #7, and point to pass privately maintained, and currently uncharted, unlighted daybeacons #1 and #3 to your immediate port side, and take unlighted daybeacon #2 to your starboard quarter. We discovered during our last visit that best depths can be maintained by favoring #1 and #3 over #2. This route will cause you to heavily favor the southern shore, which is exactly as it should be for best depths at the cove's entrance. Do not wander from this track by easing to the north. This is a sure way to land in depths of 5 feet or considerably less.

Once the entrance is some 50 yards behind you, good depths spread out almost from shore to shore. Clearwater Yacht Club is readily visible on the south banks near the midline of the cove's east-to-west axis. Those who choose to anchor off can select any likely spot and settle in for a secure evening.

On the ICW   Mariners cruising north past the ICW's intersection with the Clearwater Causeway Channel will soon approach the Waterway's intersection with the causeway.

As this account is being tapped out on the keyboard, construction is well underway on a new, high-rise bridge to replace the existing bascule span at this location. Until this mammoth project is complete, captains should cruise through these waters at idle speed, with a sharp eye for construction equipment and barges.

The existing Clearwater Memorial Causeway bascule bridge has a closed vertical clearance of 25 feet and, yes (grimace), a restricted opening schedule. For sail craft that need more height (and that's most of us), the span opens weekdays only on the hour and every 20 minutes thereafter from 9:00 A.M. to 6:00 P.M. On weekends and legal holidays the bridge deigns to open on the hour and half-hour from 2:00 P.M. to 6:00 P.M. At all other times, the span supposedly opens on demand.

As is often the case on the entire run from Tampa Bay to Anclote Key, a minimum-wake

zone is in effect on both sides of the bridge. Power captains had best slow down and enjoy the sights.

North of the Clearwater Causeway, cruisers will begin their approach to the first of several confusing sets of markers along the track of the ICW. North of flashing daybeacon #14A all captains should slow to minimal speed and sort out the mess. The outcropping of land you will see ahead shelters Clearwater Bay Marina's dockage basin. Just south of the land, a few charted markers lead east to a public launching ramp. Obviously, this small cut is of little interest to cruising-size craft. Similarly, the Mandalay Approach Channel (detailed below) breaks off to the northwest. All the markers for these various passages, set so close to the Waterway beacons, can be quite confusing. Use your binoculars to pick out flashing daybeacon #15, unlighted daybeacon #15A, and unlighted daybeacon #16. Pass just to the east of #15 and #15A and (you guessed it) close by the western side of #16. This passage will lead you hard by the point of land stretching out from the yacht basin. This is not a cause for worry. If you stay between the proper set of markers, depths remain good. Pick out the wrong aids to navigation and you will most likely make the local prop repair shops very happy.

Mandalay Channel and Approaches   While the Mandalay Channel is well marked and charted, skippers must enter this cut with the understanding that it is surrounded by shoal water. A mistake can quickly lead to that sad sound of a keel crunching along the bottom. So, read the information below carefully, proceed at idle speed, and be sure to positively identify the next marker. Be prepared to find new and different aids to navigation than those pictured on chart 11411, or in the account presented below. This seems to be a changeable area that requires periodic remarking.

Leave the ICW just south of flashing daybeacon #15 and point to pass between the Mandalay Approach Channel's first two aids, unlighted daybeacons #2 and #3. Be sure to pass to the south and west of #2. A sunken wreck sometimes lies partially awash north of this aid to navigation.

Continue on, pointing to pass all green markers to port side until coming between unlighted daybeacons #9 and #8. It is a long run between #8 and #9 and the next marker to the northwest, unlighted daybeacon #10. Both sides of the channel along this stretch border on shallows, but the shoal to the northeast is particularly dangerous, with depths of less than 1 foot. Use your binoculars to pick out #10 and set course to pass this aid by some 15 yards to your starboard side.

Pass unlighted daybeacon #12 by about the same distance to starboard and then break out the binoculars again and pick out unlighted daybeacon #12A to the northwest. This aid marks a westward bend in the channel which allows cruisers to bypass the charted shoal bisecting the Mandalay approach cut. Come abeam of #12A to your immediate starboard side and immediately set a course to come abeam of unlighted daybeacon #14 by some 25 yards to your starboard side. Shallows border both sides of the channel between #12A

and #14. Keep a close watch on the sounder and be vigilant against excessive leeway. Continue on the same course for some 25 yards past #14. Soon good water again extends out on a broad swath before you.

Captains opting for the anchorage adjacent to the southwestern shores of Moonshine Island should depart the marked route leading to Mandalay Channel about halfway between #14 and unlighted daybeacon #16. Cut to the northeast and point directly for the mid-width of the island's shores. Don't stray too close to either #14 or #16, as both aids are somewhat surrounded by shoals. Drop the hook within about 25 yards of shore. Don't attempt to cruise toward the island's southeastern point, where you might see a sign. The placard in question merely warns of a grass shoal (where anchoring is illegal) and is itself founded in shallows.

After passing unlighted daybeacon #14, visiting cruisers must decide whether to continue down the marked cut (to the northwest) to Carlouel Yacht Club or turn sharply south and enter the main body of Mandalay Channel. Remember that Dunedin Pass Inlet is impassable, even for small craft. Thus, only those cruisers heading for Carlouel need enter the northside channel for any but sight-seeing purposes.

If you do decide to enter the northward-flowing cut, point to pass between unlighted daybeacons #15 and #16. Farther to the northwest, you need only pass all red marks to their westerly sides and all green beacons to their easterly quarters until reaching unlighted daybeacon #20. At #20, you will spot the docks of Carlouel Yacht Club on the western banks. Do not attempt to cruise past #20. Depths quickly deteriorate to 4-foot levels or considerably less.

The main body of Mandalay Channel, leading almost due south from its intersection with the Carlouel cut, is easily entered by favoring the western shores slightly. This will help to avoid the clearly charted shoal south of unlighted daybeacon #14. Soon good water envelops the broad channel almost from bank to bank. Skippers can easily follow the cut south to the 14-foot fixed bridge by observing the markers along the way.

On the ICW   The Waterway stretch between flashing daybeacon #18 and (moving north) unlighted daybeacon #2 may just hold the honor of being the shallowest section of the ICW along this coastline of the Sunshine State. During low water, depths of as little as 6½ feet are common. This should not be a problem for boats drawing 6 feet or less, but if you need more, better wait until high water.

Dunedin Harbor   The somewhat indifferently marked channel leading to Dunedin Harbor strikes off to the northeast at flashing daybeacon #4. As you would expect from the "red, right, returning" rule, pass all red markers to your starboard side and all green beacons to port.

Some of the charted aids on the Dunedin harbor channel are not exactly regulation. The first green beacon is denoted by a tiny daymark set atop a sign advertising the Dunedin dockage basin. Similarly, flashing daybeacon #5 is found set atop the Best Western Yacht Harbor Inn dock to port, and flashing daybeacon #4 is actually perched on the rocks just south of the breakwater's entrance. In spite of these vagaries, it's really easy to enter the harbor in daylight and few visiting cruisers will experience any difficulty whatsoever. Just be sure to stay well away from #4. Obviously, visitors should make every effort to arrive before dark and to continue this practice until becoming familiar with the channel.

On the ICW   The ICW channel between unlighted daybeacon #9 and the Dunedin bascule bridge (north of unlighted daybeacon #15) is another problem-plagued stretch of the Waterway. The cut is narrow and closely bordered by shallows with only 2-and 3-foot soundings. Again, these are waters where you can't be in a hurry. Powercraft should slow to nonplaning speed and all captains should keep their binoculars close by. Detail a crew member to keep a watch on the sounder. If depths rise above 6½ feet, you are doing something wrong. Stop and make corrections at once before you give Sea Tow some business.

Cruising north from unlighted daybeacon #9, set course to come abeam of unlighted daybeacon #10 close by its western side. There seems to be a tendency to wander onto the shallows to the west during this run. Watch your course behind as well as ahead to quickly note any lateral slippage.

From #10, point to pass between flashing daybeacons #11 and #12. Flashing #12 is located hard by the western shores of a small spoil island.

The worst part of the passage is found between #12 and the Dunedin (Honeymoon Island) Bridge. While you would never guess it, the Waterway aids just to the north, unlighted daybeacons #13 and #15, and flashing daybeacon #14 are hard to spot from a position between #11 and #12. Just to make matters a bit worse, the charted channel cutting east to Marker One Marina and the markers pointing west toward impassable Hurricane Pass can be easily mistaken for the Waterway daybeacons. Be sure to pick out #13, #14, and #15 before cruising on to the bridge.

As always in changeable waters such as these, captains should be prepared to find different markers than those discussed above. Occasionally the Army Corps of Engineers decides to completely change the configuration of aids to navigation during their yearly maintenance in a channel of this nature. There's no way to know if this will someday happen here, but be ready!

Seven Mouth Creek and Caladesi Island Remember that low-water depths on the channel leading to the marina at Caladesi Island State Park run as skimpy as 4 feet. If you can stand those sorts of depths, depart the Waterway north of unlighted daybeacon #15 and cut west on the marked Hurricane Pass channel, pointing to eventually come abeam of unlighted daybeacon #8 (part of the errant Hurricane Pass Channel) to its fairly immediate northerly side. Continue cruising past #8 for 100 yards or so, and then turn sharply south-southwest, setting course to come between flashing daybeacon #2 and unlighted daybeacon #1, the

northernmost two aids on the Seven Mouth Creek entrance channel. Don't slip to the east between #8 and #2. The charted patch of 2-foot water is a real hazard on this quarter.

Continue tracking your way to the south on the channel, keeping all red markers to your starboard side and all green beacons to port. Stick to the marked cut. Depths outside of the channel immediately rise to 1 foot or less, and some of the shoals are foul with stumps and other underwater obstructions.

After passing unlighted daybeacon #8, the channel cuts hard to starboard, and depths fall off a bit. At unlighted daybeacons #11 and #12, the passage turns back to port a bit and no-wake regulations begin. The park service docks and ranger office will then be obvious dead ahead.

Hurricane Pass Channel A series of mostly uncharted daybeacons that are nevertheless prominent on the water strikes west just north of unlighted daybeacon #15. The first part of this cut carries depths of 7 to 11 feet, but west of unlighted daybeacon #4, depths become all too questionable. While cruising craft may safely use the easterly portion of this channel as an approach to Seven Mouth Creek, this writer strictly advises his fellow mariners to avoid the remainder of the cut and the inlet itself.

On the ICW North of unlighted daybeacon #15, the Waterway soon approaches the Dunedin bascule bridge. South of the span, the well-outlined Marker One Channel cuts east. This passage is easily tracked by simply passing between the sets of prolific markers and remembering your "red, right, return-ing" maxim.

The Dunedin Bridge has a closed vertical clearance of 24 feet and, wonder of won-ders, the span actually opens on demand. A minimum-wake zone is in effect for a short distance both north and south of the

bridge. On-the-water signs clearly outline the restricted area.

Once the bridge is behind, the broad waters of St. Joseph Sound sweep out before you. The delightful cruising about Anclote Key and river is but a short hop to the north.

Honeymoon Island to Anclote Key

The northernmost leg of the Western Florida ICW stretches for some 7 nautical miles from the Dunedin-Honeymoon Island Bridge to Anclote Key and the mouth of the Anclote River. Farther to the north, cruisers face a long and sometimes troublesome voyage of better than 140 nautical miles across Florida's "Big Bend" to the easterly genesis of the Northern Gulf ICW near the village of Carrabelle. This daunting passage will be covered in the last chapter of this guide.

North of Dunedin Bridge the Waterway knifes through the open reaches of St. Joseph Sound. With a channel featuring low-tide depths of as little as 6 to 6½ feet, boats draw-ing 6 feet or better might want to think long and hard, or at least consult the tide tables, before beginning this journey. Fortunately, the shallower water is found mostly on the south-ern leg of this run. If you should decide the depths are too skimpy for your craft, you can always sail into the Gulf's deep waters from Clearwater Pass and then visit Anclote Key and river by reentering the more inland waters via the inlet north of Three Rooker Bar. From this vantage point, you may choose to anchor next to gorgeous Anclote Key or ease up the

Anclote River, with its numerous facilities, and visit the absolutely charming village of Tarpon Springs.

Much of St. Joseph Sound's westerly reaches are wide open to the waters of the Gulf of Mexico. It doesn't require too much nautical prowess to realize that the shallow depths, coupled with a long wind fetch in westerly breezes, can raise a most uncomfortable and occasionally dangerous chop. Small craft in particular had better plan their departure with the latest NOAA weather forecast in mind.

A few marinas line St. Joseph Sound's main-land shores south of the Anclote River, but none offers much in the way of services for transients. Also, all of these facilities require captains to transit long, sometimes rather shal-low channels running east from the ICW. Captains piloting boats that draw more than 5 feet should read the various accounts below carefully before committing themselves to a particular port of call.

The Anclote River itself and Tarpon Springs feature a host of marinas and yards waiting to greet the visiting cruiser. This wonderful cruis-ing ground will be covered in the last section of this chapter.

Anchorages between the Dunedin Bridge and the mouth of the Anclote River are fairly few and far between. Even these are not particularly sheltered and call for an accurate appraisal of the evening winds.

Finally, all mariners who, like this writer, enjoy cruising through less crowded waters will be glad to learn that shoreside development falls away more and more as you cruise to the north. Anclote Key, in particular, is protected from commercial exploitation and is absolutely beautiful. A trip ashore by dinghy is a must!

Dunedin Bridge Anchorage (Standard Mile 142, 28 03.290 North/082 48.120 West)

Some boats occasionally anchor along the Waterway's western flank, just north of the Dunedin bascule bridge. Depths of 5 to 5½ feet can be carried for several hundred yards west of the bridge by staying 75 yards or so north of the causeway shores. Farther to the west, depths rise to 4-foot levels. Protection is good from southerly winds, but minimal for blows exceeding 15 knots from any other direction. The nearby highway could bring on a fair amount of noise and passing headlights during the evening hours.

Home Port Marina and other Minnow Creek Facilities (Standard Mile 142.5, 28 03.542 North/082 46.642 West)

A charted channel leads east from the ICW at flashing daybeacon #18 to three facilities on Minnow Creek. The cut carries typical low-tide depths of 5 to 7 feet and is outlined by pilings with arrow markers, but no daybeacon signs. In strong northerly winds, soundings occasionally rise to 4½-foot levels.

Cruisers nearing the easterly reaches of the Minnow Creek Channel will quickly spy Home Port Marina's large collection of covered slips and dry-storage building ahead and a little to the northeast. At this point, the channel branches out into three different forks. Visiting skippers must take care to properly identify their chosen passage. The northernmost of the three leads to a small boatyard on the creek's northerly banks. This is a tricky run and is best avoided by visitors. The middle channel strikes east-northeast to Home Port, while the most southerly cut leads to two smaller marinas on the southern shores of Minnow Creek.

Home Port Marina (727-784-1443) no longer accepts transients for overnight dockage. The (mostly) fixed wooden piers with water and 30- to 50-amp power connections are now rented out strictly on a month-to-month basis. Many of these slips are covered, ideal for long-term storage of powercraft. Full mechanical repairs of the gasoline variety can be had and your craft can by hauled out via a 35-ton travelift. Strangely enough, though, the management of Home Port has informed this writer that "bottom jobs" are no longer available. Gasoline can be purchased at a floating pier, just north of the main dockage basin. A ship's and variety store is found on the grounds, along with a swimming pool and open-air tiki bar. Dry storage is featured for resident craft. The harbor is a bit open to strong westerly winds, but otherwise is well sheltered.

An additional marina is accessed via the southernmost of the three Minnow Creek channels. Island Harbor Marina (727-784-3014) is almost exclusively a dry-storage facility for smaller powercraft. No fuel is available.

Ozona Channel (Standard Mile 143.5)

The forgettable Ozona Channel strikes east

from the Waterway between flashing daybeacon #23 and unlighted daybeacon #26. This cut eventually leads to two small marinas near its eastern terminus. After having left the last daybeacon behind, this writer has tried, on several widely separated occasions, to reach the docks from any number of separate angles. Each attempt has led to a grounding and occasioned assorted blue language and (once) a jump over the side to push the boat off while wading in chilly January waters. The boats docked at this marina most certainly know where the channel is from trial and error. Cruisers not familiar with this cut would do very well to salute as they continue on by.

Klosterman Bayou

Study chart 11411 for a moment and you will note a marked channel running east-northeast between flashing daybeacon #31 and unlighted daybeacon #34. This minimum-5-foot cut leads to a private condo dock, and there are no services available to visiting craft nor room to anchor. Just keep on trucking up the ICW.

Three Rooker Bar Anchorage (Standard Mile 147, 28 07.535 North/082 50.076 West)

In good weather with winds of less than 10 knots (preferably blowing from the west), local captains often drop the hook in the correctly charted 5- and 6-foot waters near the northern tip of Three Rooker Bar. This body of land is actually now far larger and more substantial than its depiction on chart 11411. This can lead to confusion as you make your approach, so be ready for this anomaly. Not to be repetitive, but this would be an excellent occasion to break out the new chart plotter or GPS and computer.

THREE ROOKER BAR

To reach this haven successfully, you must follow a markerless passage from the ICW's unlighted daybeacon #35 (or #36) and feel your way carefully with the sounder into the sheltered water just behind the sand spit's northern tip. Great care must be exercised to avoid the 1-foot shallows to the south.

If you are lucky enough to catch the weather right and can find the anchorage without meeting up with the bottom, this is an absolutely enchanting spot. The nearby Three Rooker Bar is, as you would expect, completely in its natural state. Landing on this small landmass is now prohibited to help protect the many nesting birds there. Leave the dinghy on the davits.

Route to the Gulf

Cruisers anxious to begin their sail on open

water (and willing to forego the charms of Anclote Key and Tarpon Springs) can put out to sea by using the marked and charted channel running between Anclote Key and Three Rooker Bar, west of unlighted daybeacon #37. This seaward cut currently carries minimum depths of 7 feet, with typical soundings in the 8- to 11-foot region. Of course, with these depths, the chop can be wicked when winds and tide oppose but, then again, when isn't that true of inlets?

Anclote Key and Associated Anchorages (Standard Mile 150, Various Lats/Lons—see below)

Northbound cruisers will spy the proud Anclote Key Lighthouse topping the horizon by the time they reach flashing daybeacon #39. This now abandoned sentinel heralds one of the most beautiful barrier islands in Western Florida. Roughly translated, Anclote means "fair harbor." The Spaniards, who originally gave this designation to the isle, knew whereof they spoke. Whether by good fortune or careful planning, Anclote Key has remained almost completely undeveloped. You will have to experience for yourself its virgin maritime forests, white sand beaches, and clear waters to understand what a special place this really is for visitors. Every single cruiser should set aside a day or so in his or her travel itinerary to enjoy Anclote as one of the last, vanishing reminders of what barrier islands were once all like in Western Florida.

Unfortunately, Anclote Key is surrounded by a broad shelf of shoal water on all sides. The anchorages described below all require a long dinghy trip ashore over very shoal water.

During the winter months, the prevailing winds blow from the north through most of

Western Florida. With the passage of bad weather fronts, these blows can reach alarming proportions. None of the Anclote anchorages offer any real protection from these

winds. Be sure to check the latest NOAA forecast before committing to an overnight stay.

Do not attempt to enter the channel noted on chart 11411, south and west of unlighted daybeacon #7X (near the island's southerly tip). This cut has shoaled in completely and even a small outboard is likely to match prop against sand.

If you are careful to avoid the shoal water just north and northwest of #7X, you can anchor in 7- to 10-foot depths in the charted tongue of deep water some .3 nautical miles northwest of #7X, near 28 10.426 North/082 50.386 West. Holding ground is good and the key gives some protection from westerly winds.

Another possible anchorage lies on the charted 8-foot waters, east of Dutchman Key's southern tip, near 28 11.351 North/082 50.335 West. You can approach to within .2 nautical miles of this smaller island and stay in good water. This relatively tight access renders this anchorage the closest to Anclote Key, which, of course, also heralds the best shelter in brisk western breezes. Offsetting this advantage to some extent is the longer dinghy ride necessary to reach the main body of Anclote Key. It would also be a prodigious walk to the lighthouse from this locale.

Wherever you choose to anchor, Anclote Key is well worth your time. Pause for a moment and, if you look with your mind's eye, you may still see an old, sail-powered sponge boat headed for Tarpon Springs, or a sprightly clipper bound for the bustling port of Tampa. Few places in all of Florida can give the sensitive visitor such a sense of this state's bygone days.

HONEYMOON ISLAND TO ANCLOTE KEY NAVIGATION

While it is a feast for the eyes, cruising the ICW through St. Joseph Sound to Anclote Key is certainly no navigational walk in the park. Low-tide depths of as little as 6 (occasionally 5½) feet on the southern portion of this run are a real concern for skippers piloting sail craft with deep, fixed keels. If you draw better than 5½ feet, it would be far wiser to either put out into the Gulf and cruise back into St. Joseph Sound via the marked inlet between Anclote Key and Three Rooker Bar, or (at the least) cruise through on a rising tide.

As if that weren't cause enough for worry, most of the passage through St. Joseph Sound is very much open to wind and wave from the deeper Gulf waters to the west. Winds over 10, and certainly 15

knots, can be uncomfortable and stronger blows are sometimes downright dangerous. Be sure to schedule your cruise only after consultation with the latest NOAA prognostication.

The Waterway route is well marked all the way to Anclote Key. The side channels are another affair entirely. All these cuts call for caution and a steady hand on the helm.

Cruisers studying chart 11411 will note a series of spoil islands marking the easterly side of the ICW between the Minnow Creek Channel and flashing daybeacon #36. These bodies of land seemed a bit larger on the water to this writer than they appear on the chart. Most are covered with scrub growth and a few even have some low-lying trees. All are surrounded by shoal water, but shallow-draft vessels can usually anchor some 50 to 75 yards offshore in 4 to 5 feet of water and dinghy in for a closer look. This is a popular weekend pastime for small-craft skippers plying these waters.

On a day of fair weather, most mariners will thoroughly enjoy their passage north to Anclote Key. Those forced to make the trip in less than ideal conditions may have a different story to tell.

Dunedin Bridge Anchorage   To access the anchorage north of the Dunedin/ Honeymoon Island bascule bridge, depart the Waterway channel immediately after coming abeam of unlighted daybeacon #17. Set course to stay at least 75 yards north of the causeway to the west. Consider dropping anchor soon after coming under the lee of the land (causeway) west of the bridge

Minnow Creek Channel   Remember that the channel leading east from flashing daybeacon #18 to Home Port Marina and the other facilities on Minnow Creek is outlined by a profuse, often-confusing collection of low-level, privately maintained aids. Some consist of pilings with arrow markers, while others are nothing more than white PVC pipes stuck in the water. These markers lack any daybeacon signs and could be more than slightly difficult for strangers to locate at night

As the large dry-storage buildings of Home Port come into sight, watch for an uncharted split in the channel. The center passage provides access to central dockage basin and fuel dock at Home Port Marina, while the southern branch escorts vessels to Island Harbor Marina.

Be sure to stay within the channel markers. Depths outside of the marked passage are 3 feet or less. If you become confused by the numerous beacons, be sure to stop and sort out the situation before moving ahead. Your keel will be ever so much happier for the extra effort.

On the ICW   The Waterway channel between Dunedin Bridge and flashing daybeacon #31 is the shallowest portion of the entire Western Florida ICW. Mean low-water depths of only 6 feet are common and if tides are below normal levels, soundings can rise to 5½ feet. Stick strictly to the marked cut and watch your course astern as well as the track ahead to quickly note any leeway.

Ozona Channel   The charted cut leading to the two small marinas at Ozona strikes east between flashing daybeacon #23 and unlighted daybeacon #26. This writer suggests that visiting cruisers pass this channel by with hardly a thought. The unmarked easterly reaches of this cut are rife with shoal water.

On the ICW   Between flashing daybeacon #31 and unlighted daybeacon #34, the channel markers outlining the passage to Klosterman Bayou flank the easterly portion of the Waterway. The close proximity of unlighted daybeacons #1 and #2 (the westernmost aids of the Klosterman cut) allows these aids to be easily misidentified as the Waterway markers, particularly for southbound cruisers. Such a mistake could land you in the shallower water east of the ICW.

As you approach this intersection, break out the spyglass and be sure to pick out the correct markers.

The Klosterman Bayou channel leads only to a private condo dock. Passing cruisers should keep on trucking up or down the ICW.

Three Rooker Bar Anchorage   To visit this popular anchor-down spot, leave the Waterway at either unlighted daybeacon #35 or #36. Set a careful compass course for the northerly tip of Three Rooker Bar. Expect some 5-foot soundings as you approach the land.

Remember that Three Rooker Bar is now actually larger and more substantial than what is depicted on chart 11411. Don't let this increased size throw you. Just point to anchor inside the northerly hook, keeping at least 75 yards offshore.

All captains must be mindful of the 1-foot shallows south of this anchorage. Also, note the correctly charted patch of 3-foot shoals northwest of Three Rooker Bar. It would also be a good idea to avoid the sunken wreck to the north-northeast.

Seaward Cut   Those who can't wait to sail those beautifully blue offshore waters may depart the ICW by using the marked passage between Three Rooker Bar and Anclote Key. To make use of this cut, depart the Waterway at unlighted daybeacon #37 and set course to come abeam of flashing daybeacon #7 by some 25 yards or so to its southerly side. Set a new course to come abeam of and pass flashing daybeacon #1 to the same quarter. To the west, the deeper Gulf waters now spread out before you.

On the ICW   Once between unlighted daybeacons #42 and #41, the old, reliable magenta line vanishes. We must bid a fond goodbye to the Western Florida ICW in our passage to the north. From #42, cruisers must choose whether to continue north and visit the anchorages adjacent to Anclote Key or cut northeast into beautiful Anclote River, home of many marina facilities and the wonderful village of Tarpon Springs.

Anclote Key   Remember that the charted channel south and west of unlighted daybeacon #7X no longer exists. Take my bent prop's word for it, even small craft should desist from trying to find this wayward cut.

To access the anchorage on the patch of deep water north and west of #7X, cruise north, passing #7X by at least 200 yards to your westerly side. This maneuver will allow you to avoid the clearly charted 2- to 4-foot shoal water north and northwest of #7X. Continue on course to the north for .4 nautical miles and then turn 90 degrees to the west and slow to idle speed. Use your sounder to feel your way in toward the shore. As #7X comes abeam to the south, you can continue cruising west toward the banks for another .1 nautical miles in good water. Closer in, depths rise markedly.

If you should choose to anchor abeam of Dutchman Key instead, follow the deep water north of #7X. Be on guard against the charted tongue of 2-foot water southeast of Dutchman Key. Use your binoculars to identify the smaller island. Once the southern tip of the key is abeam to the west, continue on for some 50 yards to the north. Then, cut sharply west and use your sounder to feel your way in. Be sure to drop the hook before approaching to within less than .2 nautical miles of shore.

Out through Anclote Anchorage Cruisers anchoring along Anclote Key or leaving Tarpon Springs bound for points north can easily use the northerly reaches of the waters around the island to reach the Gulf.

Simply follow the broad tongue of deep water as it sweeps to the northeast. Stay well to the west and northwest of unlighted daybeacon #3 and well to the east of flashing daybeacon #6. These two aids mark the outer limits of the shallows bordering Anclote Anchorage to the east and west. Typical depths will be 7 to 10 feet along this run. Next stop—the Big Bend!

Anclote River and Tarpon Springs

What would you call a river with an absolutely enchanting shoreline interspaced with all-natural stretches and light, attractive residential development? Don't answer yet—we still need to throw in one of the most unique and colorful villages in all of Florida. How about if we also add at least one super anchorage, a whole host of marina facilities, and minimum 8-foot channel depths, with most soundings being deeper? Well, I don't know what you call it, but I term this body of water the Anclote River, with the town of Tarpon Springs perched along its banks to the east. It's not going too far to say that those few mariners who have not experienced the climes of the Anclote River will have missed what are undoubtedly some of the finest cruising waters between Flamingo and Carrabelle.

Besides all of the Anclote's many fortunate qualities described above, the river is also well positioned for those ready to make the jump across the Big Bend, or those just arriving from the open waters to the north. Captains can wait for good weather or rest from their travels at the many transient slips available along the stream's course. When it comes time for dinner, the fabled Tarpon Springs restaurants could make you forget to come home.

On the negative side, depths outside of the marked Anclote River Channel rise quickly and dramatically. This is not the place to go exploring off the beaten path. With the sole exception of the anchorage described below, cruising craft are pretty much restricted to the marked track and the various marina channels.

It's not too hard to understand why the Anclote River and Tarpon Springs have become one of the most popular ports of call in northwestern Florida. These cruising grounds certainly deserve a heavy, red circle on every cruiser's chart. Read on and discover why for yourself.

Power Plant Anchorage (28 10.608 North/082 47.318 West)

North of unlighted daybeacon #18, cruisers will find the Anclote River's only deep, well-sheltered anchorage that lacks heavy local traffic. The charted stream skirts to the west of a small park (with multiple small-craft launching ramps) and eventually leads to the huge power plant readily visible to the northwest. A floating barrier crossing this sidewater several hundred yards north of its intersection with the Anclote River blocks upstream passage for all vessels. There is plenty of room for boats up to 45 feet in length to drop the hook south of this obstruction. Minimum depths are 5½ to 6 feet, with some 7-foot soundings also in evidence. During our many visits to the cove, we have often observed multiple vessels anchored here. There are even a few permanent mooring buoys, but not so many as to obstruct anchorage by visitors.

Be warned! Strong tidal currents flow through this anchorage. Be sure the anchor is well set before heading below for a toddy!

The nearby park makes a nice landside stop for those cruisers willing to break out the dinghy. Picnic tables are well shaded by tall pines, and restroom facilities are available. You might be able to phone for a taxi from nearby Tarpon Springs and motor in to this village's many dining spots.

Lower Anclote River Marinas (Various Lats/Lons—see below)

A host of marinas and boatyards lines the banks of the Anclote River below Tarpon Springs and offers a wide variety of services.

Newly minted Anclote Village Marina guards the Anclote River's northeasterly banks between unlighted daybeacons #19 and #21, near 28 10.346 North/082 47.160 West. This facility is easy to spot, courtesy of its large, dry-stack storage building. Low-water depths in the marked entry channel and alongside run about 5 to 5½ feet. Currently, two slips are usually open for transients. Berths consist of concrete-decked, floating docks with very

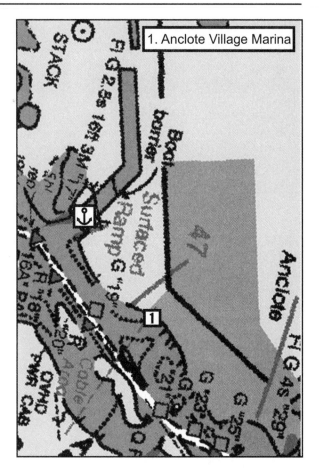

1. Anclote Village Marina

modern, 30- and 50-amp power hookups and water connections. Gasoline and diesel fuel are available, and some light repairs can be arranged through local, independent technicians. No showers or Laundromat are available, and there are no provisioning facilities within walking distance. Hungry cruisers could take a pretty good walk to Marker 25 Marina (see below), but otherwise, dinner will be a "fixed in the galley" phenomenon here.

Anclote Village Marina (727) 937-9737

Approach depth—5-5½ feet MLW
Dockside depth—5-5½ feet MLW

1. MAR-Marina
2. Port Tarpon Marina
3. Anclote Harbors Marina
4. Sail Harbor Marina
5. Anclote Isles Marina
6. Gulf Marine Ways
7. F&Y, Inc.
8. Tarpon Springs City Marina
9. Landings at Tarpon Springs

Accepts transients—yes (two slips usually open)
Transient dockage rate—average
Floating concrete slips—yes
Dockside power connections—30 and 50 amp
Dockside water connections—yes
Gasoline—yes
Diesel fuel—yes
Mechanical repairs—local, independent
    technicians

Mariners cruising east of unlighted daybeacon #25 will quickly spot the docks of Marker 25 Marina (727-934-4474) to the north. This firm is now comprised of a dockside cafe and semi-open-air bar with a few fixed, wooden wet slips fronting the facility. No repairs or transient dockage are now available. Enterprising captains and crew might be able to find a berth for tying off temporarily while sampling the restaurant's bill of fare.

Between unlighted daybeacons #32 and #34, visiting cruisers will find MAR-Marina (formerly Flaherty Marine) near 28 09.790

North/082 46.561 West. This facility is currently in transition. The original owners have taken the property back over from a leased outfit and are in the process of upgrading the entire physical plant. The new incarnation of MAR-Marina is clean and neat as a proverbial pin. Future plans call for all new, floating docks to be installed, but currently, fixed wooden piers are still in place. By the way, when construction begins on the new piers, the old docks will be removed, and no wet-slip space will be available for several months, until the project is completed. Depths alongside run 5½ feet or better. Transients are welcome, and all berths feature 30- and 50-amp power hookups and freshwater connections. Mechanical repairs are offered for both gasoline and diesel engines. MAR-Marina's travelift is rated at 35 tons. You will need to take a taxi in Tarpon Springs for dinner ashore or supplies.

We were most impressed with the friendly welcome at MAR-Marina, but, again, this place is undergoing a transformation. A call ahead to check on slip availability and current services would be a wise precaution.

MAR-Marina (727) 698-6021

Approach depth—6-9 feet
Dockside depth—5½ feet minimum MLW
**Accepts transients—yes (call to check on current
    slip availability)**
Transient dockage rate—above average
Fixed wooden piers—yes
Dockside power connections—30 and 50 amp
Dockside water connections—yes
Mechanical repairs—yes (gas and diesel)
Below-waterline repairs—yes

A no-wake sign attached to unlighted daybeacon #38 heralds one of the densest concentrations of marina facilities on the whole of the Anclote River. No fewer than three large marinas, two of which cater to transient craft, line the northern and northeastern banks as the river follows a slow turn to the south. While shoreside restaurants within walking distance of these three are minimal, transportation to downtown Tarpon Springs, with its sponge markets and many fine restaurants, can usually be arranged.

The first of the three is Port Tarpon Marina (28 09.690 North/082 46.178 West), easily recognized by its large, metal, dry-storage buildings. Port Tarpon is the largest facility on the Anclote River, and the structures of its associated repair firms testify to the wide array of services available. The marina itself offers transient dockage (though advance reservations are definitely recommended) at fixed concrete piers perched atop wooden pilings. Every conceivable power, water, and communication connection is at hand, as is a fuel dock dispensing gasoline and diesel fuel. Many of the slips are covered and would only be appropriate for powercraft, but there are plenty of open berths as well for sailboats. Showers are available shoreside.

Captains of deep-draft vessels should be on guard against an underwater rock ledge, with low-water depths of 5½ feet or so, stretching from the Port Tarpon fuel dock toward the eastern side of the harbor. Skippers whose craft draws more than 5 feet should take careful note of this obstruction. Call Port Tarpon Marina on VHF 16 before approaching the docks and ask for instructions about how to avoid the ledge while entering the harbor. During our last visit to Port Tarpon, in August 2003, we noticed that the rock ledge's position seemed to be marked by some floating, red, ball-type buoys. Otherwise, (except for the ledge) Port Tarpon's outer docks have impressive depths of 8 to 9 feet, while the innermost slips exhibit soundings of 6½ to 7 feet.

If you are in need of service, you've certainly come to the right place. Port Tarpon leases out its repair facilities, and the list is impressive indeed. Cleveland's Diesel and Yacht Services (727-942-2967) provides full mechanical repairs (gasoline and diesel engines) and below-waterline, haul-out services courtesy of a 50-ton travelift. Cleveland's also boasts a well-stocked parts department. Brown's Marine Service (727-938-3322) features a ship's store and repairs to smaller powercraft. Seebird Canvas (727-938-7152) offers the most up-to-date marine canvas fabrication and repair. The on-site Pelican Landing Restaurant serves breakfast and lunch, but it closes at 3:00 P.M. weekdays and 4:00 P.M. weekends. A small dock adjacent to the restaurant allows cruisers (with craft up to 35 feet) to dock temporarily while dining. Visiting mariners wishing to dine out during the evening will find it necessary to take a taxi into nearby Tarpon Springs (call Yellow Cab at 727-848-1707). There you will find a host of dining choices.

Port Tarpon Marina (727) 937-2200
   http://www.porttarponmarina.com

Approach depth—5-10 feet
Dockside depth—6½-9 feet
Accepts transients—yes
Transient dockage rate—average
Fixed concrete-decked piers—yes
Dockside power connections—30 and 50 amp
Dockside water connections—yes
Showers—yes
Gasoline—yes
Diesel fuel—yes

Mechanical repairs—yes
Below-waterline repairs—yes
Ship's store—yes
Restaurant—on site (breakfast and lunch only)

Sandwiched between its two sisters, genial Anclote Harbors Marina (28 09.681 North/082 46.136 West) also offers transient dockage at fixed wooden piers with water hookups and twin 30-amp power connections. Dockside depths at the outer piers are an impressive 7 to 8 feet, with some 6½ feet of water alongside the inner docks. Live-aboards are also welcomed at Anclote Harbors. Shoreside amenities include good, air-conditioned showers and an adjacent Laundromat. No fuel is available. Breakfast and lunch can be eaten at the restaurant associated with Port Tarpon Marina next door. Otherwise, you will have to find ground transportation into Tarpon Springs (call Yellow Cab at 727-848-1707).

Anclote Harbors Marina offers a new dry-stack storage building, but the extensive repair and servicing capabilities that this firm used to offer are now a thing of the past. Some mechanical repairs can be arranged through local, independent technicians, but there are no more haul-outs or other on-site service capabilities.

Anclote Harbors Marina (727) 934-7616
   http://www.ancloteharbors.com

Approach depth—8-10 feet
Dockside depth—6½-8 feet
Accepts transients—yes
Transient dockage rate—average
Fixed wooden piers—yes
Dockside power connections—yes (dual 30 amp)
Dockside water connections—yes
Showers—yes
Laundromat—yes

Mechanical repairs—independent technicians
Restaurant—nearby (breakfast and lunch only)

Easternmost of the three related facilities, Sail Harbor Marina (727-945-1056) is something of an enigma to this writer. The gambling ship that once made its home at this marina is apparently gone (hallelujah), but we have found the docks completely unattended during a couple of visits, and we have been equally unsuccessful in getting anyone on the telephone. We therefore tentatively conclude that Sail Harbor Marina has become a month-to-month dockage facility for live-aboards and other local craft.

One of the most exciting marinas on the Anclote River guards the stream's northerly banks, opposite unlighted daybeacon #50 (near 28 09.519 North/082 45.870 West). Anclote Isles Marina offers a super welcome for visiting cruisers. The dockage basin features excellent shelter from foul weather with first-class, fixed wooden piers. Mean, low-water approach and dockside depths run 6 feet or better. Transients are eagerly accepted, and visitors will discover modern power (30- and 50-amp), freshwater, cable-television, and telephone hookups. How's that for a well-wired marina?

Waste pump-out service is offered, but the marina does not have a fuel dock. Some mechanical repairs can be arranged through local, independent technicians. Ask the friendly dockmaster or any of his staff for assistance.

Anclote Isles' shoreside showers are first rate and completely air conditioned. No Laundromat is readily available, however.

It's a quick taxi ride into Tarpon Springs for some really first-class dining and intriguing attractions (see below). Call Yellow Cab at (727) 848-1707. If you happen to be cruising with bicycles aboard, it's an enjoyable ride into Tarpon Springs as well.

Anclote Isles Marina (727) 939-0100

Approach depth—6+ feet (MLW)
Dockside depth—6+ feet (MLW)
Accepts transients—yes
Transient dockage rate—below average
Fixed wooden piers—yes
Dockside power connections—30 and 50 amp
Dockside water connections—yes
Waste pump-out—yes
Showers—yes
Mechanical repairs—independent technicians
Restaurant—taxi ride needed

Tarpon Springs

When I was originally researching *Cruising Guide to Eastern Florida*, my first travels through the Okeechobee Waterway were nothing short of amazing. The huge ranches, thousands upon thousands of grazing cattle, the cowboys, and tiny towns caused me to wonder if this could really be the same state which hosts the condo caverns of Fort Lauderdale, Hollywood, and Clearwater. Well, the village of Tarpon Springs is no less unexpected than the backwaters of Okeechobee. As you cruise up the Anclote River, your arrival at Tarpon Springs will be heralded by a fleet of incredibly colorful sponge boats spread along the town waterfront. These docks, along with numerous sponge markets and a vast array of wonderful restaurants, are set amidst a small-town atmosphere which would be very much at home in New England or along the North Carolina coastline. Tarpon Springs, quite simply, is charming.

Among Tarpon Springs' many and varied attractions are its annual festivals. Nowhere outside the country of Greece is the Feast of Epiphany, a Greek Holy Day, celebrated as elaborately as it is in Tarpon Springs. January 6, one of the oldest festival days of the Christian Church, commemorates the baptism of Christ and marks the end of the Christmas season. Originating in the Eastern Orthodox Church as early as the third century, it is still known in the Greek Orthodox Church by its ancient name, Theophany (manifestation of God).

Each year the Epiphany ceremony begins at the Greek Orthodox Church of St. Nicholas. Mass is performed at an altar surrounded by a half circle of striking, gold-framed icons. When the last chants of liturgy subside, the archbishop performs the traditional custom of the Blessing of the Waters, praying for calm seas and the safety of all sailors.

Ecclesiastics from archbishop to altar boy, resplendently gowned in embroidered robes of crimson and gold and carrying jeweled crosses and croziers, lead the procession to the beautiful waters of Spring Bayou. The archbishop casts a white cross into the waters at the edge of the bayou, and some fifty youths dive from a semicircle of small boats to retrieve it. The one who can retrieve the cross will be blessed with good luck for one year.

Every year, the Chamber of Commerce hosts the annual "Seafood Festival," where visitors can sample everything from alligator and oysters to shrimp and squid. Check with the Greater Tarpon Springs Chamber of Commerce (727-937-6109) about the dates. It has been held in May of each year in the past, but that date may change.

Modern-day Tarpon Springs really began in 1890, when diving for natural sponges came to be the dominant local industry. The technology and technique for this colorful enterprise was imported from Greece and the Mediterranean isles. As the industry grew, many a native Helene emigrated to Florida to seek his fortune in the sponge-rich Gulf waters off Anclote Key. To this very day, you are just as likely to hear Greek as English spoken along the quiet streets of Tarpon Springs or in the streetside sponge markets. The bonhomie is often a tangible quality. Few, if any, other ports of call can lay claim to such a friendly atmosphere in such unexpected surroundings.

If you happen to be in the market for a natural sponge or two, then you have certainly set your course for the right port of call. Far more durable and economical than their synthetic counterparts, natural sponges are enjoying a modern-day renaissance and are very much in demand. You will find no better prices anywhere. Even if you don't need a sponge, please take the time to stroll through the markets. They are like nothing you will see anywhere else in all of Florida.

Of course, people of Greek extraction are known for something besides sponges—namely, wonderful food. Tarpon Springs sports an incredible collection of wonderful restaurants serving everything from authentic Greek fare to the freshest in American-style fried seafood. You can certainly suit your own palate, but this writer recommends the so-called combination dishes that seem to mix the best of both Greek and American cuisine. The "Greek-style shrimp" served at many of the town's best dining spots is a shining example of this cuisine.

It would probably require a short book on

its own to adequately review all the many Tarpon Springs restaurants. It's really hard to go wrong. For now, let's just mention a few standouts among the crowd.

Any discussion of dining in Tarpon Springs simply must begin with Louis Pappas' Riverside Restaurant (10 Dodecanese Boulevard, 727-937-5101). This mammoth dining institution is a three-story affair which overlooks the Anclote River's southeastern banks just upstream from the Tarpon Springs city marina. Louis Pappas and his brothers have been serving seafood—Greek, American, and mixed styles—for many

a year along with a multitude of other fare. Be sure to make reservations ahead of time to avoid a long wait.

Some dockage used to be available at Louis Pappas' for its waterborne patrons. At the present time, all the available wet-slip space is pretty much filled by local craft.

Diners seeking a more informal menu will want to check out Mr. Souvlaki Restaurant (510 Dodecanese Boulevard, 727-937-2795). The Greek-style sandwiches and salads are to die for.

Don't overlook visits to the Hellas Restaurant

Louis Pappas' Riverside Restaurant, Tarpon Springs

(785 Dodecanese Boulevard, 727-943-2400), Mykonos Restaurant (628 Dodecanese Boulevard, 727-934-4306), and/or Santorini Restaurant (698 Dodecanese Boulevard, 727-945-9400). All serve outstanding Greek/American cuisine. You simply can't go wrong with any of these choices.

If the current special in "sea creatures" trips your culinary trigger, check out Paul's Shrimp House (530 Athens, 727-937-1239). The "peel and eat" steamed shrimp and Paul's famous potatoes are not to be missed.

For something entirely different, pay a visit to Ballyhoo Grill (900 Pinellas Avenue N, 727-944-2252). The forte here is Key West style seafood, just where you would least expect to find it.

To break your morning fast, find your way to either the Plaka Restaurant (769 Dodecanese Boulevard W, 727-934-4752) or Taste of Greece (709 Dodecanese Boulevard, 727-938-0088). Try the feta cheese omelets at either dining attraction. Yuuummm!

Numbers to know in Tarpon Springs include

Golden Nugget Taxi—(727) 938-5353
T. S. Yellow Cab—(727) 799-2222
Yellow Cab—(727) 848-1707
Avis Rental Cars—(727) 367-2847
Enterprise Rent-A-Car—(727) 942-3155
West Marine—(727) 846-1903

Tarpon Springs History Tarpon Springs was first settled by A. W. Ormond and his daughter,

Tarpon Springs waterfront

Mary. Coming to Florida from Ninety-Six, South Carolina, in 1876, they built a cabin near Spring Bayou when there were still no other homes in sight. A year later, J. C. Boyer, an adventurer from Nassau, sailed into the bayou. He and Mary were married and started the first family where Tarpon Springs now stands.

In 1877 George Inness, a foremost American artist, discovered the scenic beauty of the Anclote River, which he and his son, George, Jr., would depict in their famous paintings.

Mary found her new home to be a never-ending wonder. Thinking that the fish she saw inhabiting the bayou were tarpon, she named the small settlement Tarpon Springs in 1879. (The fish she saw were in fact mullet and not tarpon.)

The village of Tarpon Springs was founded in 1882 by Anson P. K. Safford, the first territorial governor of Arizona. In the meantime, John K. Cheyney from Philadelphia was building a development concern called the Lake Butler Villa Company and, after Safford's death, Cheyney began promoting the region as an exclusive winter resort. This early Tarpon Springs land boom was to see its share of wealthy and famous customers. Lake Tarpon (formerly Lake Butler) still looks much as it did when the Duke of Sutherland fell in love with its lush vegetation, bought 30 acres, and built an estate overlooking the water where he could peacefully fish and hunt.

The Tarpon Springs town site was laid out by Mayor W. J. Marks and surveyed by John C. Jones. In 1884, a post office was established, and the railroad was soon to follow. Eleven years after it was first settled, Tarpon Springs was incorporated on February 12, 1887.

Sponge harvesting soon became the community's most important industry. In 1890, Cheyney discovered money could be made by harvesting sponges growing in the waters of the Gulf. John Cocoris, the first Greek to settle in Tarpon Springs, brought sponge divers from the islands of Greece to harvest the beds. Tarpon Springs still maintains its reputation as the largest natural sponge market in the world, with an annual revenue in excess of $5,000,000.

Sponges can be found in every ocean of the world, from the tropics to the arctic. Although there are some 5,000 varieties, only a few are suitable for commerce, and four of these are found in the Gulf of Mexico.

The part of the sponge that is used is the skeleton. This is a network of connecting passages built up of a unique fiber called spongin. Tough, compressible, and resilient, it can absorb twenty-five times its own weight in water, and be quickly squeezed almost dry. Sponges vary in size from less than an inch to over three feet in diameter.

When alive, the sponges are covered with a black, fleshy, rubbery skin, and filled with soft, gray matter called gurry. To be used the sponge skeleton must be freed from all organic matter and foreign bodies. It must be thoroughly cleaned, dried, and usually trimmed.

The sponge markets are still very much in evidence amidst modern-day Tarpon Springs. As you stroll the quiet streets of this enchanting village, take a few moments to reflect on all those who have gone before you, as well as on the city leaders who have had the foresight to preserve their vision of Tarpon Springs.

Tarpon Springs Marina Facilities

Anchorages are all but nonexistent on the Anclote River upstream of the power plant haven described earlier in this chapter. Cruisers preferring to spend the evening swinging on the hook would do well to make use of this haven.

Transient dockage in downtown Tarpon Springs is now a bit easier to come by, courtesy of the five slips usually set aside for visitors at the Tarpon Springs City Marina (28 09.338 North/082 45.494 West). You simply can't pick a better spot to coil your lines to experience the color and character of the unique village that is Tarpon Springs. This fortunate facility is found on the principal town waterfront, south of unlighted daybeacon #51, in the heart of the friendly hustle and bustle of the business district and its sponge markets.

Tarpon Springs City Marina is ready, eager, and waiting to serve visiting cruisers. Transient dockage is afforded at fixed wooden piers. There are usually four to five slips kept open just for visitors. Call ahead for reservations during the winter season.

The dockage basin is well sheltered and features mean low-water soundings of 6+ feet. Dockside power connections of the 30- and 50-amp variety are offered, as are freshwater hookups at each slip. Good but somewhat petite (one per sex), air-conditioned showers are available in the dockmaster building immediately adjacent to the piers. It's a long walk of some 1½ miles to the nearest Laundromat. Many cruisers may want to take a taxi (see above).

It's a very quick step from the municipal marina to the restaurants described above (plus many additional choices) and the colorful sponge markets.

A convenience store is found within walking distance, but it's a 1½-mile hike to the nearest supermarket. Fortunately, another grocery store (some 2 miles from the marina) is accessible by way of the city bus service. Ask the city dockmaster or his fine staff for directions and assistance.

So, with the exception of repairs and fuel, I'm sure you will agree that the Tarpon Springs City Marina has just about everything a visiting cruiser could desire. We suggest you pay dockmaster Roy a visit. You won't be sorry!

Tarpon Springs City Marina (727) 937-9165

Approach depth—6 to 10 feet
Dockside depth—6+ feet (MLW)
Accepts transients—yes
Transient dockage rate—below average
Fixed wooden piers—yes
Dockside power connections—30 and 50 amp
Dockside water connections—yes
Showers—yes
Laundromat—1½ miles away
Restaurant—many nearby

One additional, privately owned marina is located upstream of the city marina, northeast of unlighted daybeacon #53. The Landings at Tarpon Springs (28 09.480 North/082 45.438 West) is worth a look. Of course, dry-stack storage is the primary emphasis here, but currently, there are two wet slips available to visitors. Dockage is found at both fixed wooden and floating wooden piers. Entrance depths run as thin as 5 feet at MLW, with 6 to 8 feet of water alongside. Freshwater connections and 30- and 50-amp power hookups are in the offing. Gasoline, diesel fuel, and some minimal shoreside showers are also available. There is an on-site restaurant known as Captain Jacks (727-944-3346), and you can also walk across the Alt. 19 bridge into downtown Tarpon Springs with its many, many dining attractions. The nearest grocery supplies are a good mile away.

So, you want to cruise the waters of

northwestern Florida but don't have your own boat. Well, don't waste any time calling Seacoast Yacht Charters (727-934-5503, 800-322-6070, http://www.seacoastcharters.com), now located at the Landings. Seacoast offers an outstanding fleet of power- and sail craft. Bareboat and captained charters are available. To be succinct, these people simply can't seem to do enough for their customers. We feel confident that anyone wanting to charter a boat in these waters can't possibly do himself a bigger favor than calling Seacoast Yacht Charters. Tell them we sent you!

The Landings at Tarpon Springs (727) 937-1100

Approach depth—5 feet MLW
Dockside depth—6-8 MLW
Accepts transients—yes (two slips usually
    available)
Transient dockage rate—average
Fixed wooden docks—yes
Floating wooden docks—yes
Dockside power connections—30 and 50 amp
Dockside water connections—yes
Gasoline—yes
Diesel—yes
Showers—yes
Mechanical repairs—yes
Ship's store—yes (includes marine electronics
    and bait and tackle)
Restaurant—on-site

Gulf Marine Ways (28 09.359 North/082 45.859 West, 727-937-4401) occupies the Anclote River's southern banks near the heart of Tarpon Springs, east of unlighted daybeacon #50. This friendly yard features full haul-out repairs (via a marine railway), while mechanical services can be arranged through independent local contractors.

Set amidst the sponge boat docks between Gulf Marine Ways and Tarpon Springs City Marina, the large fueling pier of F&Y, Inc. (28

09.361 North/082 45.809 West, 727-937-4351) guards the southern banks. This firm wholesales gasoline and diesel fuel to local retail outlets. Direct fuel sales to pleasure craft are usually confined to larger vessels who need a prodigious load of fuel. We did find the management very friendly, so if you need to fill up your Hatteras, don't fail to stop by and say hello to the manager, John Young (surely one of this writer's long-lost cousins).

Spring Bayou and Tarpon Springs Yacht Club

The small but affable Tarpon Springs Yacht Club is found at the southeastern terminus of the charted channel leading from the main Anclote River track into Spring Bayou. However, captains should not run the marked cut. Instead, navigators must follow the charted but mostly unmarked cut-through just south of Gulf Marine Ways. Even so, depths run as thin as 4 feet on this cut. Be sure to read the navigational information on this questionable passage presented below before attempting to reach the yacht club docks.

Tarpon Springs Yacht Club occasionally accepts members of other yacht clubs with appropriate reciprocal privileges for temporary dockage. Be sure to call ahead of time and reserve space with the dockmaster. The club does not usually have anyone in attendance at the docks unless advance arrangements have been made.

This club is open only on Wednesday, Friday, and Saturday from noon into the evening hours, when dining and bar facilities are available. Dockage is at rather smallish fixed wooden slips with only 20-amp power and water connections. As you might expect, no fuel or repairs are to be had.

Tarpon Springs Yacht Club (727) 934-2136

Approach depth—4 feet
Dockside depth—4-5 feet
Accepts transients—members of clubs with
    reciprocal privileges (advance arrangements
    necessary, *limited* guest dockage)

Fixed wooden piers—yes
Dockside power connections—20 amp
Dockside water connections—yes
Restaurant—on site (open Wednesday, Friday,
    and Saturday only) and many others nearby

ANCLOTE RIVER NAVIGATION

Successful navigation of the Anclote River Channel could almost be summed up by saying, "Stay in the marked channel and remember 'red-right-returning.'" The few exceptions to this general rule will be noted below.

To facilitate passage through Tarpon Springs by deep-draft commercial fishing vessels, the entire Anclote River channel is dredged on a regular basis.

Depths outside of the buoyed Anclote River channel quickly rise to grounding levels. Stay in the marked passage and do not attempt to explore any likely looking coves. The noted anchorage near the power station is the only truly safe haven on the river.

Entrance from Anclote Key The entrance channel into Anclote River from the deeper water of St. Joseph Sound and the Anclote Anchorage lies east of Anclote Key. A huge power plant with the charted stack guards the river's northern mouth and makes an excellent landmark. The channel is sandwiched between very shoal water to the north and south. At unusually low tide, these shallows bare completely and it can look as if the mud flats stretch on forever. You may be getting tired of me saying it, but

stick to the marked cut and you should find nothing less than 6 feet of water, with many soundings substantially deeper.

Cruise into the entrance channel by passing between flashing daybeacon #1 to its southerly quarter and unlighted daybeacon #2 to its northerly side. After passing between #1 and #2, continue cruising on the same course to the east-northeast, passing between three additional pairs of markers along the way. Eventually, you will come abeam of unlighted daybeacon #8 to its northerly side. Upstream of #8, the passage turns to the east-southeast. Point to pass south of flashing daybeacon #9 and north of unlighted daybeacon #10.

Do not attempt to enter the charted channel north-northwest of unlighted daybeacon #8. This errant cut is mostly unmarked and is much too tricky for cruising-size craft.

East-southeast of unlighted daybeacon #10, the channel continues on an arrow-straight course to flashing daybeacon #17. From #17 the channel follows another bend, this time to the southeast. Between #17 and unlighted daybeacon #18, the river's best anchorage will come abeam to the northeast.

Power Plant Anchorage Enter this broad sidewater northeast of flashing daybeacon #17 on its mid-width and continue upstream past the public launching ramp, which will be passed to starboard. Drop the hook anywhere short of the floating barrier.

Tidal currents do run swiftly in this anchorage, so be sure the anchor is well set. It would be a good idea to stay topside and watch a fixed point on shore for at least 10 minutes before beginning your galley preparations.

On the Anclote River No wake regulations are in effect as you cruise past the anchorage and its adjacent public launching ramps, described above. Upstream of flashing daybeacon #29, a no-wake zone stretches all the way to Tarpon Springs. Powercraft skippers had better slow down and spend the extra time enjoying the sights.

As you approach unlighted daybeacon #21, the channel hugs the southern banks. Depths seem to be more than adequate.

After passing unlighted daybeacon #30, watch for a significant shoal off to the north side of the channel. During our last visit, it was covered with pelicans and smaller waterfowl.

East of unlighted daybeacon #38, the three marinas described above line the northern banks. Be *sure* to pass at idle speed.

As you leave the easternmost of these three marinas and follow the river through its turn to the south, watch the eastern banks for a beautiful house overlooking the water. It's one of the most magnificent homes on the river.

Don't attempt to enter the charted Chesapeake Point Channel, which cuts to the south between flashing daybeacons #39 and #43. This cut is now shoal and even outboard craft can find the bottom.

The entrance to Anclote Isles Marina lies north of unlighted daybeacon #50. Cruise straight into the dockage basin on the mid-width of the approach passage. Avoid the starboard-side shores after cruising into the tadpole-shaped harbor. During out last visit, we noted some warning beacons on these waters, possibly marking a sunken wreck.

The Anclote River Channel remains easy to follow all the way upstream to Tarpon Springs City Marina. Be sure to proceed at idle speed along the town waterfront.

To continue on to the Landing at Tarpon Springs, pass just south of unlighted daybeacons #51 and #53. Don't stray to the south. Shoal water shelves out from this shoreline for a surprising distance. East of #53, watch for some private markers leading in toward the marina docks.

Tarpon Springs Yacht Club Channel Remember that the mostly unmarked channel to Tarpon Springs Yacht Club carries low-tide depths of a meager 4 feet, or sometimes less. If your boat can stand these soundings, leave the main Anclote River Channel at unlighted daybeacon #50. Turn due south and heavily favor the easterly banks as you work your way carefully along. Your course will lead you under the stern of the boats docked along the waterfront.

As you leave the moored boats behind, point directly for the small opening dead ahead. As you pass out into the main body of Spring Bayou, head directly for the red, unlighted daybeacon you will see ahead. Shortly before reaching this aid, cut sharply to port and point for the low-level bridge which you will sight ahead. Be on guard against some uncharted shoal water to the east. Soon the yacht club's docks will come abeam to port.

CHAPTER 6

The Big Bend

What can one say about the coastline of Florida's Big Bend? Frankly, this writer has always found himself rather perplexed as to whether the lands and waters between Anclote Key and the St. Marks River are a cruising and nature lover's paradise, a region beginning to undergo destructive development, or a whole collection of shoaly, sometimes rocky waters lying in wait for your keel, lacking any protected intracoastal waterway. The reality is that the Big Bend is probably some of all these and much more.

Perhaps the first thing we should note is that most of the Big Bend's immediate coastline has been preserved in its natural state for the foreseeable future thanks to timely and prolific land purchases by the Nature Conservancy. (As you may have noticed, we try to avoid blatant plugging of any organization other than restaurants and the occasional marina, but if you are looking for a worthy recipient of those tax-deductible dollars, this group is a goodie!) Much of the Nature Conservancy's land has been turned over to the U.S. Fish and Wildlife Service and set up as official wildlife refuges. Writing in the April 1988 issue of *Southern Living* magazine, Harry Middleton gives a haunting portrait of these lands and their waters:

> The Nature Conservancy has really saved . . . the wild pine and hardwood hammocks . . . the miles and miles of clear, clear estuarine creeks; the rich fishing and oyster beds . . . the cool, shady ravines . . . deep blue rivers; . . . unspoiled islands; . . . everywhere the sound of birds . . .

the simple, unpretentious traditions and culture of the old mullet fishing villages and hard luck timber towns; and the oyster men in their armada of small boats, working the bay from dawn till dusk, scraping the oyster beds with their long-handled tongs. . . . And this is a crude sketch, a hasty outline of the Big Bend's seemingly limitless beauty and abundance. There is so much more.

Mr. Middleton's description is entirely apt for the westerly reaches of the many rivers and bays indenting the Big Bend here and there. Indeed, the beauty of the Big Bend's rivers and streams is at times almost dreamlike. The fortunate cruiser in these climes can still experience the same sort of landscape that must have greeted Native Americans hundreds of years ago.

Unfortunately, however, the Nature Conservancy does not have the power to preserve the small towns and villages which lie a few miles to the east along the various streams. While, to be sure, some of these communities remain as quaint and delightful as ever, others have been "discovered." New, sometimes garish construction can only be a grief to those who value the unique character of this region. Yet, other communities remain very much as they have been for the past fifty years. The sensitive visitor must now pick and choose his or her ports of call with care to experience the Big Bend of yesterday.

From a navigator's point of view, the one colossal word which comes to mind when discussing the Big Bend is "shallow." There is no other section of Florida's eastern, western, or panhandle coastline which sports such consistently shallow depths. Except for the marked river channels, the shores can only be approached by small, flat-bottomed craft. Adding insult to injury, many of the buoyed approaches to the Big Bend rivers are themselves rather shallow. Low-water soundings of 4 feet might even be considered the norm. While there are several fortunate exceptions to this rule, skippers piloting craft that draw 5 feet or better may well consider setting course directly from Anclote Key to the St. Marks River or Carrabelle and Dog Island. Sailors with fixed keels who yearn for an uninterrupted offshore passage may want to opt for this plan in any case, but perhaps you should think twice.

In spite of our reservations about recent development, we really can't recommend that you bypass the Big Bend rivers. Their natural beauty will be a part of your cruising stories for many years to come. If time allows, this writer highly recommends that you give them a try. Just read the information presented in this chapter completely and critically, and make your selection of stops along the way accordingly.

By the way, there is an excellent, new source for information about cruising the upper reaches of all the Big Bend River. We simply can't recommend Capt. Rick Rhodes' new volume, *Cruising Guide to Florida's Big Bend*, too highly. Call (800) 803-0809 to order your copy today!

As mentioned in the last chapter, there is no protected intracoastal waterway north of Anclote Key. Mariners will be cruising the waters of the open Gulf all the way to Carrabelle and St. George Sound before picking up the sheltered reaches of the Northern Gulf ICW. This is a run of better than 140 nautical miles in a straight line. If you decide to follow the Big Bend buoyage system, the track is considerably longer. Obviously, this is not the sort of passage to be undertaken lightly. Fuel, supplies, and, of course, the weather forecast must all be planned for and taken into account in order to ensure a safe voyage.

Two fundamentally different strategies are available to cruising captains journeying north or south across the Big Bend's waters. Those who choose to forego the delights of the region's rivers or who are in a hurry can set a straight course from Anclote Key to the St. Marks River or Dog Island (bordering St. George Sound and the village of Carrabelle). This is a wide-open passage which will appeal to many sailors, particularly during times of fair weather with good winds. Powercraft had better be sure their fuel supply is up to the task before undertaking this route. A well-functioning chart plotter or a GPS interfaced with a laptop computer would be a real advantage for navigators following this passage.

The real disadvantage of this offshore cruising plan is that you will often be as much as 40 to 60 miles from the nearest coastline, far too great a distance to run for cover if an unexpected storm should come running up the Gulf. Of course, visits to the Big Bend rivers are also impractical for those following the offshore route. On the other hand, this is clearly the fastest and most direct approach to crossing the Big Bend.

Cruisers of a more conservative bent can

follow the series of offshore markers known as the Big Bend buoy system. These aids to navigation will lead you up the coastline, keeping some 5 to 10 nautical miles offshore. Because of the bend in the land, this route is lengthier, but the buoys and daybeacons along the way will serve to fix your position and keep you on course. The various river channels are readily accessible via this route, though, again, you will have to pick and choose (not to mention consult the tide tables) to make sure a particular passage is deep enough for you.

So there it is, with all its glory and faults. Florida's Big Bend is something different for everyone who visits its singular shores. And just in case we haven't quite yet enticed you to include these unique cruising grounds in your travel plans, let's listen to a bit more of Harry Middleton's description of the Big Bend:

> Just below the water's surface, oyster bars glow white as bone, appearing to snake through the shallow water like enormous sea snakes, even though they are fixed in time and place. In the diminishing light, beds of aquatic grass and wetlands give off a startling range of colors: yellows and golds and soft browns. The wetlands look like a work of art: an etching on stained glass.

Charts Cruisers will need quite a few charts to cover the Big Bend. All but the southernmost and northernmost charts are large-format cartographical aids, which are not always the easiest to use on the water. Unfortunately, short of using digitized, computer charts, there is no choice in the matter.

11411—small-format ICW chart that provides good detail of the coastline from Anclote Key to the Pithlachascotee River

11409—the first of the small-scale, large-format Big Bend charts; covers the coast and offshore waters from Anclote Anchorage to the Crystal River; also includes Gulf Harbors, the Pithlachascotee River, Hudson, Hernando Beach, and the Homosassa River

11408—details the Big Bend from just north of the Crystal River to Horseshoe Point; includes the Withlacoochee River, Cedar Key, and the Suwannee River

11407—yet another large-format chart; details the waters from Horseshoe Point to Rock Islands; includes the Steinhatchee River

11405—an important large chart, showing the waters of the northernmost section of the Big Bend and the easterly reaches of the Florida Panhandle; it is valuable for navigating the St. Marks River, Shell Point, Alligator Harbor, and the easterly entrance into St. George Sound

11406—ultradetailed chart of the St. Marks and Wakulla rivers

11404—detailed, small-format chart showing the easterly tip of the Northern Gulf ICW; also gives good detail of the anchorages on Dog Island and the village of Carrabelle and its like-named river

Bridges
Pithlachascotee River/Highway 19 Bridge— crosses Pithlachascotee River southeast of unlighted daybeacon #41—Fixed—12 feet

Steinhatchee River Bridge—crosses Steinhatchee River well east of unlighted daybeacon #24—Fixed—officially 25 feet but local reports say 30

Anclote Key to the Homosassa River

The southernmost 20 nautical miles of the Big Bend shoreline between Anclote Anchorage and the Homosassa River is perhaps the shallowest portion of the entire passage south of the St. Marks River. With one important exception, the entrance channels at Gulf Harbors, Hudson, Aripeka, Hernando Beach, Bayport, and the Homosassa River have low-water depths of 4 feet, or sometimes less. The Pithlachascotee (locally known as the Cotee) River boasts a 6-foot entrance channel. While almost all of these streams feature some marina facilities, they are mostly oriented to smaller, outboard and I/O craft. As depths rise quickly and dramatically outside of the marked channels, anchorages are practically nonexistent.

Frankly, with the possible exception of the Pithlachascotee River, this is a portion of the Big Bend that many skippers of larger cruising craft will choose to put behind them. If you should need shelter, of course, and catch the tide high enough, it is possible to duck inside and visit with the few marinas catering to cruising craft.

Gulf Harbors Channel

The two marked channels serving the resort community of Gulf Harbors lie almost due east from flashing daybeacon #4, north of Anclote Key. Both these cuts have shoaled severely over the past several years, and low-water depths of 3 feet or so are now common.

The dredging of the two Gulf Harbors channels is an issue of great interest to the local cruising community in this region. There is considerable agitation to get these passages deepened. Only time will tell whether these

local efforts will be successful. Barring the completion of some future dredging project, we now recommend that mariners piloting cruising-size craft bypass both these cuts.

The Pithlachascotee River

Let's get this cleared up right away. Don't even try to pronounce the name of this river. Even the locals don't make the attempt. Rather, they call this stream the "Cotee River," and that is how we shall refer to it hereafter.

The Cotee is one of the deepest rivers on Florida's Big Bend. Its well-marked entrance channel will be spied some 2.5 nautical miles north of the (northern) Gulf Harbors passage. Minimum low-tide entrance and interior depths of 6 feet drop to 12-foot soundings in a few spots. The river flows east to the town of Port Richey and two small marinas, both of which lack transient dockage. In fact, with the demise of Joshua's Landing Marina (see below), there is currently no wet-slip space for visitors on the Cotee. Good anchorages are also totally lacking. Thus, cruising craft need only enter the Pithlachascotee for sightseeing.

Even before entering the river's mouth, cruisers are in for a real visual treat. Study chart 11411 for a moment and note all the charted "Shacks" north and south of the Cotee entrance channel. These houses are actually far more prolific than the chart would lead you to believe. On the water, they dot the seascape like spots on a leopard.

In a situation very similar to the one we encountered to the south on Pine Island Sound, these so-called shacks, or houses built on stilts, were originally constructed to serve

1. American Marina
2. Sunset Landing Marina

commercial fishermen. As this salty trade dropped off during the 1950s, many of these structures were bought and redone as private weekend residences. Larry Korman of Sunset Landing once informed this writer that by the mid-1990s the Who's Who of Port Richey owned the old stilt houses. It was obvious from our on-the-water inspection that these weekend homes were universally well cared for and highly prized. Don't attempt too close an approach, however, as they are all founded in shoal water.

The first of the Cotee's facilities comes up on the southern shores between unlighted daybeacons #25 and #26. A well-marked channel leads through minimum 5-foot entrance depths to the well-sheltered fixed wooden and metal decked floating piers of American Marina (727-842-4065). Low-tide soundings at the docks run from 4½ to 5 feet. This medium-size facility is obviously most interested in the dry-stack storage of smaller powercraft. The available wet slips are pretty much rented out on an annual basis. Don't look for anything in the way of transient dockage here. In fact, except for gasoline, a tiny ship's store, and mechanical repairs for outboards and I/Os, there is very little to interest visitors at this facility.

Sunset Landing marina (727-849-5092) will be spotted, also on the southern banks, between unlighted daybeacon #33 and flashing daybeacon #35. This ultrafriendly establishment does not have the facilities to accommodate overnight transients, but if you need any advice about the Cotee or about cruising the Big Bend in general, be sure to stop and ask for Larry or his son Buddy. They are some of the nicest and most helpful individuals you will ever find under the Florida sun. Sunset Landing offers gasoline and a fine ship's and variety store. Some mechanical repairs to outboards and I/Os are also available.

The Port Richey version of the infamous Hooters Restaurant (727-841-0801) gazes out over the Cotee's eastern banks opposite flashing daybeacon #35. This dining spot offers dockage for its clients and features open-air dining overlooking the river. Of course, interior tables are also available in air-conditioned comfort. Entrance depths can easily run as thin as 4½ feet of water, while 5- to 6-foot depths will be encountered dockside.

Until a few years ago, Joshua's Landing Marina guarded the charted cove north of flashing daybeacon #35. This facility is now closed and will probably be redeveloped as residential property soon.

Southeast of unlighted daybeacon #41, the Cotee is crossed by the fixed Highway 19 Bridge. Just before you reach the span, the small Port Richey city pier overlooks the southwestern bank. This quaint dock is obviously designed for fishermen and it is seldom frequented by boats of any description.

This guide's coverage of the Cotee River ends at the Highway 19 Bridge. Boats that can clear the span may continue cruising east for some distance in good depths, but there are no more marinas nor opportunities to anchor.

Hudson

The three channels serving the resort community of Hudson lie 9 to 10 nautical miles southeast of flashing daybeacon #10, designated as "St. Martins" on chart 11409. The town's location can be readily spotted from the water, courtesy of the three snow-white, high-rise condos overlooking the point just south of the middle channel. The southernmost cut serves several private dockage basins and is mostly uninteresting to visiting cruisers.

The middle channel leads to two marinas that have some services for visitors, but low-water depths on the entrance cut have now shoaled to 3 feet or even slightly less in a few spots. Cruisers piloting craft that draw 3 feet or more may want to look elsewhere, at least for the moment, for an overnight stop. At the very least, you should time your entry and egress for high tide.

We have been told that the Hudson channel is slated for dredging during the late fall of 2003. I always believe that a dredging will actually take place when and only when the dredge appears over the horizon and drops anchor. Let's hope in this instance that all these good plans really come to pass.

At unlighted daybeacon #22, a side channel cuts to the south and curls around the adjacent point. This passage provides access to the sheltered harbor serving Skeleton Key Marina. The owner of this facility informed this writer that few transients have heretofore visited his marina, but he certainly would not turn them down. Berths consist of tiny, floating wooden-decked finger piers stretching out from a concrete seawall. Larger cruising craft will find these finger docks to be of minimal use. Dockside depths are a nice 12+ feet. Freshwater connections and 30- and 50-amp power hookups are available at all slips. Mechanical repairs for gasoline and diesel engines are complemented by gasoline, open-air dry-stack storage, clean but non-climate-controlled showers, and a minimal ship's and variety store. Two restaurants are close by. Sam's Hudson Beach Snack Bar (727-868-1971) is an open-air, sandwich-type establishment whose patrons dine while looking out onto the Hudson Channel. Many cruisers will prefer the restaurant at Inn on the Gulf (727-868-5623); the grouper sandwiches are outstanding. Ask the friendly marina owner or his staff for directions.

Skeleton Key Marina (727) 868-3411

Approach depth—3 feet (low water)

Dockside depth—12+ feet
Accepts transients—yes
Transient dockage rate—below average
Floating wooden finger piers—yes
Dockside power connections—30 and 50 amp
Dockside water connections—yes
Showers—yes
Gasoline—yes
Mechanical repairs—yes (gasoline and diesel engines)
Ship's and variety store—small
Restaurant—two nearby

A second marina now makes its home to the northeast, off the central Hudson channel. As this account is being tapped out on the keyboard, this facility is undergoing serious expansion and rebuilding of their docks and wet slips. While this construction is underway, transients are not being accepted, and this situation will probably continue into late 2003. It is very likely that when the project is complete, all available dockage will be considerably upgraded, as will the power and water hookups. A fuel dock is slated for addition as well. In keeping with our long-standing policy of not reviewing a facility until we can see its eventual outcome for ourselves, we will not say anything further about dockage at Port Hudson Marina in this edition of *Cruising Guide to Western Florida*. However, be sure to subscribe to our free, on-line quarterly newsletter, the *Salty Southeast*, for updates.

Port Hudson Marina does offer a ship's store, dry-stack storage, and mechanical repairs for both gasoline and diesel engines. Smaller cruising craft (up to 30 feet) can be hauled out by a travelift.

Two restaurants, Mike's Dockside Bar and Grill plus the Blackbeard Raw Bar, make their homes at Port Hudson Marina. We have not had the chance to sample either dining spot.

The northernmost of the three charted Hudson channels, like its southernmost counterpart, serves local craft and is of virtually no interest to cruising visitors. We suggest you bypass it entirely.

Aripeka

It's a shame that the channel leading to the old fishing village of Aripeka (4 nautical miles north of the northernmost Hudson Channel) is so shallow. There may be no better preserved example of a tiny fishing community in all of the Big Bend. Unfortunately, low-tide depths rising to as little as 2 feet relegate this cut to flat-bottomed, outboard-powered craft exclusively.

Hernando Beach

The shallow channel leading to Hernando Beach lies some 4.5 nautical miles north of the Aripeka cut. Clearly Hernando Beach is a questionable stop that will only interest those cruisers who are willing to risk an arduous channel and some thin water. On the plus side, two marinas of medium size wait to greet visiting cruisers with some services. On the negative side (are you tired of hearing this?), the entrance channel carries a bare 3 to 4 feet of water at low tide. Additionally, the access cut is surrounded by shoals which sport a few thousand rocks. A member of the local Coast Guard Auxiliary warned this writer to stay "strictly in the middle of the channel." He related that boats deviating just slightly from the midline have been known to have a rocky encounter, and we don't mean a meeting with a boxer from Philadelphia. Of course, depths at high water are a good 6 feet or better.

There are many more aids to navigation in the Hernando Channel than those shown on the current edition of chart 11409. The pru-

dent and cautious mariner may be able to run the channel during daylight without problems, always assuming that you can stand those low-tide depths. You will simply have to evaluate your draft, the weather, and the time of day to decide whether to try this cut or move on to the Homosassa River.

The town of Hernando Beach is delightfully still more of a fishing village than a resort town. No high-rise condos mar the landscape and, particularly during weekends, the local anglers are out in force. While it may lack some of the old, quaint homes of Apalachicola, there is no denying that Hernando Beach will appeal to those who cherish small-town America.

At unlighted daybeacon #24, a somewhat confusing channel cuts south, then east, and eventually leads up a long canal to two marinas. First up is Gulfstar Marine, overlooking the eastern banks just as the canal takes a sharp turn to the south. This operation struck us as being a bit on the rough side.

Gulfstar is very much into haul-out repairs. There are two on-site travelifts that can haul up to 50 tons. A host of boats was sitting on cradles during our last visit. Mechanical repairs for both gasoline and diesel power plants are also available.

A couple of the fixed wooden slips (with low-key power and water connections) are usually open for transients, with low-tide depths of 5½ to 7½ feet. There is also an on-site ship's and variety store. The nearby Gators restaurant (352-596-7160) is highly recommended by the locals.

Gulfstar Marine (352) 596-5079
    http://www.gulfstarmarine.com

Approach depth—3-4 feet (low tide)
Dockside depth—5½-7½ feet

Accepts transients—limited
Transient dockage rate—below average
Fixed wooden piers—yes
Dockside power connections—up to 30 amp
Dockside water connections—yes
Mechanical repairs—yes
Below-waterline repairs—yes
Ship's and variety store—yes
Restaurant—one nearby

Hernando Beach Yacht Club maintains a few docks with 7 feet or so of depths just south of Gulfstar. This is a small club that probably does not have room enough for cruising visitors.

Snappers Marina (352-596-2952) sits just south of the yacht club. We were told in the summer of 2003 that this facility no longer offers transient dockage. Resident craft are tied up to wooden-decked floating piers featuring good depths of 5 to 8 feet. Dockside power and water connections are available, as is one unisex, non-climate-controlled shower, gasoline, full mechanical repairs, and a 25-ton travelift for haul-outs. There is also a small ship's and variety store on the premises. Gators restaurant (352-596-7160) is a short step away.

The Homosassa River

Since the time when Europeans first began exploring the shores of la Florida, or "the land of flowers," the Homosassa River has had the reputation of being one of the loveliest streams in the Sunshine State. Happily, that air of beauty continues to this day on the river's lower reaches. Indeed, the Homosassa's banks, west of unlighted daybeacon #57, are idyllic. Here the hardwoods so reminiscent of the Big Bend begin to appear and often stretch right down to the water's edge.

In the 1930s Babe Ruth used to come here for the quail hunting. The river's waters were some of Pres. Grover Cleveland's favorite fishing grounds. In 1880 he built a hunting and fishing lodge, which used to occupy the site of present-day Riverhaven Marina. The painter Winslow Homer came to Homosassa in 1904 and completed some of his most noted works here. Obviously, this lovely river has been attracting admirers for some time.

On a far less happy note, the river's winding, sometimes hard-to-follow channel has shoaled to low-water depths of only 3 feet in several places. Obviously, cruising-size craft will have to enter and exit the Homosassa at high tide only.

An equally unfortunate note is sounded in the town of Homosassa, east of unlighted daybeacon #74. This small community has begun to develop as a tourist and fishing center. On weekends, small craft dot the river's waters in a passable imitation of a swarm of killer bees. A host of private homes and low-level town houses now overlooks the banks here and there. The local marina facilities are clearly pointed toward outboard and I/O-powered runabouts. Overnight dockage for transient-size craft is very hard to come by.

Homosassa does boast its own state historic site, the Yulee Sugar Mill Ruins. This 5,100-acre sugar plantation on the Homosassa River became productive about 1851. In those early days, the manufacture of sugarcane products was an exacting and expensive business, requiring a boiler, steam engine, horizontal mill, and kettles.

Operating for thirteen years, the mill supplied sugar products for Southern troops during the Civil War. In May 1864, a Union naval force captured ammunition and supplies at the plantation and burned it to the ground.

Made of native limestone, the mill has been partially restored. It consists of a large chimney about nine feet square with an extending structure about forty feet long that housed the boiler. Beside the mill are parts of the grinding machinery.

In this 2003 edition of *Cruising Guide to Western Florida*, I am going out on the proverbial limb and recommending that mariners piloting cruising-size craft (30 feet and larger) bypass the Homosassa River entirely. Despite the natural beauty along its lower reaches, the shoaly depths, coupled with the lack of marinas catering to larger vessels (not to mention the huge population of small powercraft), all lead to the conclusion that this stream is not really suited for larger boats. For those who choose to ignore this advice, we present a sketch of the Homosassa below, but to be clear about all of this, we suggest you keep on trucking north to the Crystal River.

Homosassa River Facilities

Flashing daybeacon #2, the southwesternmost aid on the Homosassa entrance channel, is found better than 10 nautical miles south-

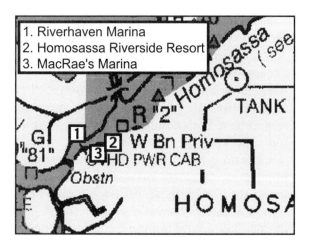

1. Riverhaven Marina
2. Homosassa Riverside Resort
3. MacRae's Marina

east of flashing buoy #2, itself many miles west of St. Martins Keys. The channel is more than slightly twisty and turny. Depths outside of the marked cut, even on the river's interior reaches, rise dramatically. This is not the place to go exploring. Stick to the buoyed route.

Unlighted daybeacons #37 and #38 mark the Homosassa's westerly entrance. Northeast of these aids, there was once a very neat, water-access-only restaurant known as the Crow's Nest. Sad to say, this restaurant is gone now, and the buildings that remain are a private fishing club.

A heavy concentration of small-craft facilities lines the river along the town waterfront farther to the east. Cruising-size craft may find a few available slips, but clearly the emphasis here is again on smaller outboard- and I/O-powered vessels. Dry-stack storage of runabouts seems to be big business.

West of unlighted daybeacon #81, Riverhaven Marina will come up on the northern banks, near 28 47.096 North/082 37.211 West. This facility offers limited overnight transient dockage. As minimal as it is, Riverhaven has pretty much the only transient dockage in Homosassa for vessels larger than 30 feet. Berths are provided (sometimes) at floating, wooden-decked piers with 5 feet of water alongside at low tide. Some electrical connections up to 30 amps and freshwater hookups are provided. There are adequate, on-site showers, but strangely enough, they are locked and not available after the marina closes in the evening. Gasoline can be purchased dockside, and there is a small ship's store on site.

Riverhaven Marina (352-628-5545)
  http://www.riverhavenmarina.com

Approach depth—3 feet (minimum)
Dockside depth—5 feet

Atlantic Fishing Club, Homosassa River

Accepts transients—limited
Transient dockage rate—below average
Floating wooden piers—yes
Dockside power connections—30 amp
Dockside water connections—yes
Gasoline—yes
Showers—yes (closed during the evening hours)
Ship's store—yes
Restaurant—next door

A bit farther upstream, passing cruisers will be amazed by K. C. Crump Restaurant (352-628-1500) on the northern banks. This establishment consists of a huge restaurant, featuring outdoor dining, built to resemble an antebellum plantation house. A wide swath of green grass runs down to the river and the restaurant's extensive fixed wooden piers.

While no overnight dockage is allowed and no other marine services are offered, dining patrons are welcome to tie up while feeding their faces. Depths alongside run 6 to 9 feet.

Opposite K. C. Crump, MacRae's Marina (352-628-2602) consists of a host of smaller, fixed wooden (covered) slips, a waterside variety, bait, and tackle store, and a motel set back from the water. No transient dockage is available, but gasoline can be purchased in front of the dockside bait and tackle store. Of course, the rustic motel would be a good bet for taking a break from the live-aboard routine, and the notable Charlie Brown's Crab House restaurant is immediately adjacent.

Homosassa Riverside Resort (28 47.103 North/082 37.057 West, 352-628-2474) graces the southern banks of the Homosassa River a short distance upstream from MacRae's. This combination marina, motel, and restaurant has changed their dockage policies since the last edition of this guide went to press. Overnighters are no longer provided for. Sometimes, you can tie up briefly while catching a meal at the on-site restaurant, Charlies Browns' Craft House restaurant (352-621-5080), but dining patrons must depart when their meal is complete. We have been told that this entire complex is in the process of being "condoized."

A bit farther upstream, almost abeam of Riverside Resort, a small body of land that has come to be known as Monkey Island will be spotted in the river. Here, passing boats can watch three black monkeys playing. Go figure!

East of Riverside, the Homosassa becomes somewhat shallower and a new series of markings begins. Magic Manatee Marina (352-628-7334) flanks the northern banks opposite unlighted daybeacon #5. This facility is strictly concerned with the dry-stack storage of smaller powercraft. Gasoline and some mechanical repairs to outboards and I/Os, as well as a small ship's and variety store, are the only marine services available.

The Homosassa continues upstream for many miles, often frequented by canoes and smaller powercraft. The zoo up at the main spring features an underwater viewing room where visitors can watch the fish and manatees that frequent the locale. Depths become much too unreliable for cruising craft long before reaching this point.

ANCLOTE KEY TO HOMOSASSA RIVER NAVIGATION

If you have opted for the direct route from Anclote Key to Carrabelle, St. George Sound, and Dog Island, there's not a whole lot more that we can add except set the GPS and keep a careful DR plot. Obviously, the various ports of call and channels discussed below will be of minimal interest to mariners choosing this straight path.

Cruisers following the Big Bend buoyage system and remaining within 5 nautical miles or so of shore can pick and choose among the passages outlined below. Just remember that most of these cuts are shallow and several have the added benefit of adjacent rocks! On the other hand, almost all of the cuts have many more markings than those shown on the charts. Always remember your faithful "red, right, returning" rule,

take your time, and, if your draft allows, you may come through with nothing more than a few jangled nerves.

North from Anclote Flashing daybeacon #6 marks the northerly exit from Anclote Anchorage. This aid can actually be passed on either side, but for best depths, leave it off your westerly flank (its easterly quarter). From #6, consider setting a course for flashing daybeacon #4, north of Anclote Key. Come abeam of this aid to its easterly quarter. Once abeam of #4, the Gulf Harbors channel lies to the east.

Gulf Harbors Channel Remember that we no longer recommend that cruising-size craft try to enter either of the Gulf Harbors channels until dredging has improved soundings on these waters. We'll keep you up to date in our free, quarterly, on-line newsletter, the *Salty Southeast*.

The Pithlachascotee River   Captains can also cruise northeast from flashing daybeacon #4 to flashing daybeacon #1 and unlighted daybeacon #2, marking the western tip of the Pithlachascotee (Cotee) River Channel. For best depths, we suggest that you do not cruise directly from #4 to #1 and #2. Rather, set your course farther to the north and come abeam of #1 and #2 by some .5 nautical miles to their westerly quarter. You can then turn directly into the channel, passing between flashing daybeacon #1 and unlighted daybeacon #2.

The Cotee River channel remains well outlined and reasonably easy to follow as far as unlighted daybeacon #12 and flashing daybeacon #13. At this point, the cut takes a hard jog to the south. Point to come abeam of flashing daybeacon #16 to its immediate easterly side. Once abeam of #16, immediately cut hard to the east again, and point to pass between unlighted daybeacons #17 and #18. Take your time through this stretch of the channel and identify all your markers carefully. Hapless navigators who miss the channel will be in 4 feet of water.

The marked channel to American Marina cuts to the south between unlighted daybeacons #25 and #26. Sunset Landing is readily accessible south of flashing daybeacon #35.

Cruisers bound for the docks of Hooters Restaurant should watch for a white-PVC-pipe-outlined channel cutting east, just before reaching flashing daybeacon #35. Enter this small channel on its mid-width. Soon it will lead you toward a commercial dockage area. Break off to starboard some 20 yards before reaching the commercial craft and cruise to Hooters' docks.

Southeast of unlighted daybeacon #41, the fixed Highway 19 Bridge soon spans the river. The city fishing pier will be spotted on the southwestern shores. Our coverage of the Cotee ends at the fixed bridge.

On to Hudson   North of the Cotee Channel, cruisers must bid good-bye to their old friend chart 11411 and switch to 11409. Throughout the remainder of the Big Bend, navigators must contend with large-format charts. The more detailed, small-craft charts do not resume until reaching St. George Sound, Dog Island, and Carrabelle.

The charted channel leading to Double Hammock Creek, just north of the Cotee River cut, is quite shallow and does not lead to any marina facilities or anchorages. It is highly recommended that you keep on trucking.

The next possible ports of call are Skeleton Key Marina and Port Hudson Marina at the village of Hudson. Remember that these facilities are accessed via the center of the three channels serving the Hudson waterfront. The charted channels to the south and north are two more of those passages serving local boats and are best avoided by visiting cruisers.

It is tempting to set a direct course from flashing daybeacon #4 for flashing daybeacon #2, the first aid to navigation of the center Hudson Channel. Notice, however, that such a course would lead you perilously close to the shallow water northwest of the Cotee Channel and the 1-foot depths off South St. Martins Reef. Be sure to pass both these shoals well to their westerly sides.

While it is a bit longer, cautious navigators might consider setting course from #4 for flashing daybeacon #10 off St. Martins reef. After traveling 7.4 nautical miles along this route, you can break off due east and cruise some 6.9 nautical miles to the center Hudson Channel's westerly genesis. Granted, this is the longer way to do it, but it's certainly the safest.

Hudson Channel   The center Hudson Channel is exceedingly well marked and easy to run in daylight for most boats that can stand the thin 3-foot low-water depths. As is usually the case along this section of the Big Bend, you will find many more markers than what is shown on the current edition of chart 11409.

The only tricky spot on the Hudson Channel is found as you approach its easterly limits. After passing between unlighted daybeacons #22 and #23, cruisers bound for Skeleton Key Marina should curl their course around to the south and point for the gap between unlighted daybeacons #1 and #2, the first two aids to navigation on the marina entrance channel. After passing between unlighted daybeacons #6 and #7, turn back to the east and round the northside entrance point. Soon the marina docks will come abeam to starboard, perched on the western shores.

If, on the other hand, you are bound for Port Hudson Marina, break off to port at #22 and #23, and follow the green markers into the marina's harbor.

North along the Big Bend   Cruisers interested in following the Big Bend buoyage system will want to set a course from flashing daybeacon #4 to flashing daybeacon #10 off St. Martins reef. It is a lengthy run of 12.2 nautical miles between #4 and #10. Be sure to come abeam of #10 to its westerly side. East of this daybeacon, depths run to as little as 5 feet on the reef.

Of course, captains who are confident of their navigation can cut north inside of the reef and save several miles of cruising. Should you follow this adventurous strategy, let me again remind you of the 1-foot depths of South St. Martins Reef, west-southwest of the Hudson channels.

Captains bound for the Homosassa River may want to consider setting course from #10 for flashing daybeacon #2, well southwest of the river's entrance. Some 16.6 nautical miles of open water separate #10 and #2. Minimum depths on this straight run are about 6 feet, with most soundings ranging from 8 to 10 feet.

Cruisers choosing to enter the relatively shallow channel leading to Hernando Beach should set course from #10 for flashing daybeacon #2, but break off from this run after cruising about 5.9 nautical miles from #10. You can then set a new course for flashing daybeacon #HB at the head of the Hernando Beach Channel, to the east-southeast. Be sure to pass north of the charted "Ruins" clearly noted on 11409.

Those bypassing both Hernando Beach and Homosassa will probably want to ignore flashing daybeacon #2 and make the 21.5-nautical-mile run to flashing buoy #2, well west of Homosassa Bay.

Hernando Beach   The Hernando Beach Channel is one of the shallowest and trickiest of the passable cuts between Anclote Key and the Homosassa River. It is quite well marked, though, and in fair weather during daylight, boats up to 38 feet (with appropriate draft and tide) may be able to make a successful but cautious approach.

Be warned, however, that the passage is very twisty in places, and it is flanked to the north by rocky islets. There are even a few reports of rocks impinging upon the channel's edge. Fortunately, our keel has never met up with any of these obstructions, but it is certain that you will want to hold strictly to the middle of the channel.

As you approach tripod-shaped flashing daybeacon #HB, two signs designating "Shoal" water will be observed to the north and south. Don't approach either of these makers. Incidentally, while #HB is labeled properly, there is also a sign on the markers designating it as the "Bill Watts Tripod."

Pass #HB to its fairly immediate northerly side and continue following the various markers east, always remembering your "red, right, returning."

Contrary to what you might expect from studying chart 11409, rocky shoal water lines the northern flank of the channel all the way in to shore. More shallows lie to the south, so stay to the channel's centerline.

During low water, the rocky shoals to the north uncover and appear as small, oblong islets. Believe it or else, it's actually easier to cruise this cut during low tide. The shallows are far more obvious.

Follow the marked cut carefully as it twists and turns around the various rocky islands. If you meet another craft, stay as close to the channel's center as possible when passing.

As you approach the channel's easterly end, the situation is confused by a side channel running south to the marina facilities. Just to make matters a little more juicy, there are two unlighted daybeacon #40s in close proximity to each other.

Our best advice is to carefully stay on the main cut as it runs on to the northeast past the first #40 and then continue on to unlighted daybeacon #38. Only after coming abeam of #38 should you curl around to the south and enter the south-running passage by passing the second unlighted daybeacon #40 to your starboard side. If all this sounds confusing, it is, and we can only advise you to take extra care.

Anyway, once you are on the southerly side cut, continue following the prolific markers on to the south until the channel leads you around a point and you enter an eastward-running canal. Don't be tempted to enter any of the canals to the east short of the turn around the point. While they have somewhat respectable depths, they do not lead to any facilities.

Once on the canal that you have been led to by the markers, cruise to the east until the stream dead ends. Turn to starboard. Both marinas and the Hernando Beach Yacht Club will then be quite obvious on the eastern banks.

The Homosassa River   It is an unfortunate reality that low-water depths of 3 feet have built across the main Homosassa River channel in the vicinity of unlighted daybeacons

#57A and #58. Clearly, the vast majority of cruising-size vessels will need to navigate the Homosassa channel strictly at high water. Even then, boats drawing more than 3½ feet should pick another port of call.

The long Homosassa Channel begins at flashing daybeacon #4 and winds its way to the northeast for some 4.2 nautical miles before turning more to the east at unlighted daybeacon #28. The waters abeam of #28 exhibit low-tide depths of only 4 feet or so.

At unlighted daybeacon #30, the channel takes a turn to starboard and rounds unlighted daybeacon #31. A whole bevy of markers leads into the river's mouth and tidal currents begin to pick up.

A manatee, slow-speed zone begins near #31 and runs upstream to unlighted daybeacon #44. On the water, this seems such an unlikely place for a manatee speed-restricted area, but the Florida DEP must know something I don't.

Unlighted daybeacons #37 and #38 usher mariners into the mouth of the Homosassa River. To the northeast, passing cruisers will note the old location of Crow's Nest Restaurant. This is now the site of a private fishing club.

East of #38, the undeveloped portion of the Homosassa will open out before you. The shores are absolutely beautiful, particularly around unlighted daybeacon #45.

The interior reaches of the Homosassa River channel wind this way and that, with many, many markers (most of which are unlighted) outlining the correct path. Miss just one of these, and your keel will almost certainly meet up with the rocky bottom.

Take your time, sort out all the many, sometimes-confusing aids to navigation, and have your four-leaf clover ready!

As mentioned repeatedly above, the Homosassa River channel has shoaled badly between unlighted daybeacons #57A and #58. This region is known locally, and charted on 11409, as "Hell Gate." Low-water depths run as thin as 3 feet. Our only advice is to wait for high water before attempting this portion of the channel.

Yet another manatee no-wake zone begins at unlighted daybeacon #70 and stretches upriver all the way to the village waterfront. Power captains have no other choice than to slow down and take in the sights.

At unlighted daybeacon #74 development picks up, and the marked cut takes a sharp jog to starboard and then cuts back to port at unlighted daybeacon #75. By the time you reach unlighted daybeacon #81, the riverbanks will become lined with private homes. A bit farther upstream, the marina facilities described earlier will be obvious on both shorelines.

After passing Homosassa Riverside Resort on the southerly banks, watch for a small island near the southern shoreline sporting a miniature lighthouse. This small body of land plays host to the marooned monkeys described earlier in this chapter.

East of Monkey Island, the numbering system on the Homosassa begins anew with unlighted daybeacon #2. This portion of the river is far shallower than its westerly counterpart; it's probably best left to smaller craft.

Should you decide to visit Magic Manatee Marina anyway, the dry-storage building and docks will be obvious to port as you come abeam of unlighted daybeacon #5.

Crystal River to Cedar Key

The central section of Florida's Big Bend is a real study in striking contrasts. To the south, Crystal River boasts beautiful scenery and some of the clearest water to be found anywhere in the world. Yet the stream is overlooked by a huge nuclear power plant to the north. The Withlacoochee River lies a few miles north of its sister stream, but it sports a different character. This is really the first of the beautifully undeveloped rivers of the Big Bend, and visiting cruisers will come away with haunting memories of the stream's loveliness. Cedar Key, another 14 nautical miles or so to the north, was once one of the quaintest villages in all of Florida. While much of the historic downtown section remains, Cedar Key has clearly (and most unfortunately) been "discovered." New construction is very much in evidence and two modern restaurants overlooking the principal waterfront stick out like proverbial sore thumbs.

From the cruiser's point of view, the three ports of call along the central Big Bend have quite a bit to offer. All have deeper entrance channels than most of the streams to the south. The Crystal and Withlacoochee rivers have good marina facilities, while Cedar Key can at least boast one of the few good anchorages along the Big Bend.

So, perhaps there's something for everyone and you may just find waters that demand a return time and time again. By all means, you should give both the Crystal and the Withlacoochee rivers your most careful attention.

The Crystal River

The crystal-clear waters of Crystal River are fed by more than 30 natural springs, pumping in 300 million gallons of water each day. The river is considered by many to be the most important manatee refuge in Western Florida. Biologists have identified some 200 of the gentle beasts, or about 17 percent of the entire state's manatee population, living along the river. For all these reasons and more, Crystal River is one of the most popular bodies of water for diving and snorkeling in all of Florida.

The lower, undeveloped portion of the Crystal River shoreline is quite appealing to the eye. This area is part of the Chassahowitzka Wildlife Refuge and is protected from strip malls and T-shirt shops. Here the landscape begins to change in response to your northward movement along Western Florida's coastline. Increasingly, visiting cruisers will observe oaks, cedars, and other hardwoods.

Today, the modern age is being felt along the banks of this pristine stream. A huge nuclear power plant overlooks the river to the north, near its westerly mouth. Everywhere you go on land, the nuclear-accident warning sirens are very much in evidence.

The town of Crystal River sits sprawled about the upper cruising limits of the stream. This community is much frequented by fisher folk and tourists during the weekend.

Crystal River's channel can usually be relied upon to hold minimum depths of 5½ to 6 feet as far upstream as the charted "Indian Mound." To be on the safe side, skippers piloting vessels drawing better than 5 feet might want to wait for a rising tide. Some low-water soundings between the Indian mound and Pete's Pier Marina at Crystal City run to 5, possibly 4½ feet. Chart 11409 also notes several rocks along the river's course. These hazards can be avoided by sticking to the river's centerline.

Two marinas provide transient dockage on Crystal River. The best of the two is found in the town of Crystal River itself. There are also several anchorages of note along the course of

Crystal River. This is a real rarity among the Big Bend rivers.

The western limit of the Crystal River entrance channel lies a good 14 nautical miles northeast of flashing buoy #2. The entrance passage here is far easier to run that its counterpart on the Homosassa, which we considered above. Basically, the passage consists of two straight stretches, which are amply marked. Daylight entrance should not be too much of a problem for cruisers piloting boats drawing less than 5 feet. Even sail craft can and do run this passage successfully. Just east of unlighted daybeacon #21, the marked cut enters the mouth of Crystal River.

Lower Crystal River Anchorage (28 55.509 North/082 41.463 West)

Boats with as much as 4 feet of draft can anchor in some 5 feet of water, or slightly less, in the lee of undeveloped Shell Island, southwest of unlighted daybeacon #23, near 28 55.509 North/082 41.463 West. Soundings of 5 feet (MLW) hold to within some 75 yards of the Shell Island shoreline. Closer in, soundings rise dramatically. Approach the island shores only by dinghy. Protection is good for all winds, but swinging room is probably only sufficient for boats as large as 34 feet.

Between #25 and the stretch of river charted as "the Rocks," good depths of 6 feet or better stretch out in a broad band along the river's track. It is possible to ease a bit off the river's mid-width and set the hook with excellent protection from all winds. Just be aware that commercial fishing traffic is possible, and even likely, during the evening hours. A bright anchor light is your best defense against a rude awakening.

One good spot to set the hook along this stretch will be discovered east of unlighted daybeacon #8 (near 28 54.790 North/082 39.218 West). In August 2003, we sounded excellent low-water depths of 6½ feet to within 50 yards of the southerly banks. Protection is good from all but particularly strong eastern and western breezes. Of course, you will be exposed to the wake of all passing vessels, but hey, nothing's perfect.

Twin Rivers Marina and the Infamous Power Line (28 54.242 North/082 38.456 West)

Twin Rivers Marina guards the southern banks of the Salt River, east of charted Coon Gap. This stream intersects its larger sister (Crystal River) between unlighted daybeacons #12 and #18. A marked channel carrying 3½ to 4½ feet at MLW leads from the juncture with Crystal River to the marina. Most of this

cut exhibits soundings of at least 4½ feet, but a rock shelf just off Twin Rivers Marina may only be covered by 3½ feet of water at dead low tide.

Before going on to consider the merits of Twin Rivers Marina itself, we must first call your *immediate* attention to the charted 47-foot power line that crosses Salt River and the marina approach channel. This line was (at least supposedly) raised to its charted height a couple of years ago. However, in the spring of 2003, this writer received a worried e-mail from a fellow sailor who had struck this line with a 35-foot mast. Fortunately, no one was hurt, but the cruiser's electronics were fried, and everyone aboard was quite, understandably, shaken up. Both this writer and Jim Flannery, regional editor for *Soundings* magazine, immediately began to investigate this *dangerous* situation.

1. Twin Rivers Marina

Since that time, I've heard a lot of explanations as to why this power line is now considerably lower than its charted clearance of 47 feet. Many people simply don't want to talk about this situation, and getting correct information has been a bit like pulling teeth. While I still can't say definitely what happened, a persistent story holds that the line was knocked down earlier by a sail craft with a mast height well in excess of 47 feet. Apparently, when the power company restrung the line, it was set *below* the charted clearance. Let me emphasize that I have *not* been above to completely verify this story, but it seems a likely explanation.

However, since the line was lowered (and no one can now tell us what its current height actually is), **we now firmly suggest that all sail craft, no matter what their mast height, avoid Salt River like the Black Plague!** Let's be crystal clear about this one. Any sail-craft skipper who enters Salt River is risking *death* and severe damage to his vessel. Enough said!

Twin Rivers offers well-sheltered transient dockage at fixed wooden piers. Most of the slips are set in a man-made cove cutting back from the riverbanks. Freshwater hookups and power connections up to 30 amps are available. Low-tide dockside depths run between 4½ and 6 feet. Twin Rivers features full mechanical repair services and haul-outs via a 35-ton travelift. There is also a fuel dock offering both gasoline and diesel fuel and an on-site ship's and variety store. There is no restaurant or any provisioning possibilities for miles around. Be sure your galley is well stocked before committing to an overnight stay at Twin Rivers.

Twin Rivers Marina (352) 795-3552

Approach depth—3½-5 feet (low water)

Dockside depth—4½-6 feet (low water)
Accepts transients—yes
Transient dockage rate—above average
Fixed wooden piers—yes
Dockside power connections—up to 30 amp
Dockside water connections—yes
Gasoline—yes
Diesel fuel—yes
Mechanical repairs—yes
Below-waterline repairs—yes
Ship's store—yes

Historic Indian Mound

Take a quick gander at chart 11409 and notice the charted "Indian Mound" north of unlighted daybeacon #17. This historical point of interest is for real and easily visible from the water. This awesome, man-made accomplishment reminds us of how very long Native Americans lived in Florida before the first European explorer touched these shores.

Kings Bay Facilities and Anchorages (Various Lats/Lons—see below)

Farther upstream, the Crystal River flows into Kings Bay, source of many of its freshwater springs. Cruisers have access to one good marina, a deep-water anchorage, and a shallow-draft-only overnight haven on the waters of Kings Bay.

South of the gap between unlighted daybeacons #29 and #30, a charted island bisects the bay. During our last visit here, we discovered several sailboats anchored some 150 yards north of this isle's northerly tip, near 28 53.486 North/082 36.202 West. Soundings are in the 6-foot realms, and there is good shelter from all but truly nasty weather. There should be ample elbowroom for a 42-footer. This anchorage also has the considerable side benefit of being surrounded by the crystal-clear waters of Kings Bay. What more could you ask?

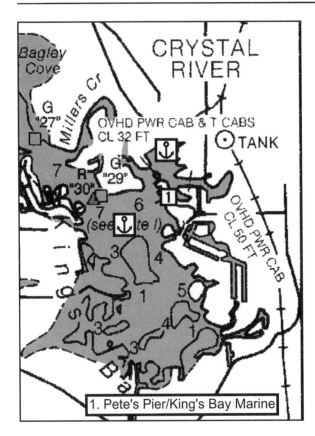

1. Pete's Pier/King's Bay Marine

powercraft, but there are a dozen open berths fit for sail craft. Clean, air-conditioned showers are readily available, as are gasoline, diesel fuel, and free waste pump-out service (for dockage patrons). An on-site bait, tackle, and variety store adds to the marina's offerings.

If it's dinnertime, ask any of the marina staff for directions to either Cravings on the Water (614 NW Highway 19, 352-795-2027) or Charlie's Fish House Restaurant (352-795-3949). Both these dining spots are accessible by foot and dinghy! We were particularly impressed with Charlie's Fish House. The combination platters are *outstanding!*

Pete's Pier/Kings Bay Marine (352) 795-3302

Approach depth—4½-5 feet (low water)
Dockside depth—4½-6 feet
Accepts transients—yes
Transient dockage rate—below average
Fixed wooden piers—yes
Dockside power connections—up to 50 amp
Dockside water connections—yes
Waste pump-out—yes (for dockage patrons)
Showers—yes
Gasoline—yes
Diesel fuel—yes
Mechanical repairs—yes
Ship's and variety store—yes
Restaurant—several nearby

If, and only if, your vessel draws 3 feet or (preferably) less, you can drop anchor on the small, charted bay just north of Pete's Pier, near 28 53.862 North/082 35.874 West. Low-water depths run to 4 feet if you are lucky. Make a wrong swerve, and you could end up in 3-foot soundings (or even a bit less). First-timers should be *sure* to read our navigational account of this anchorage below *before* attempting entry.

Besides offering almost perfect shelter from

Vessels that can stand some 4½-foot low-tide depths can make use of Pete's Pier/Kings Bay Marine (28 53.639 North/082 35.883 West), located on the bay's northeastern quadrant, east of unlighted daybeacon #29. This facility sits almost in the heart of the town of Crystal River. A host of restaurants, motels, and retail establishments of all descriptions is a short walk away.

Pete's Pier is glad to accept transients for overnight berths at fixed wooden piers with water hookups and 30- and 50-amp power connections. The 50-amp hookups are only available in certain slips. Many of the piers are covered and therefore only appropriate for all wind directions, this anchorage has the considerable advantage of being within sight of Charlie's Fish House Restaurant (352-795-3949). As noted above, this dining attraction receives our vote as the *best* restaurant in Crystal River.

The Withlacoochee River (Various Lats/Lons—see below)

Okay, no quibbling this time. The Withlacoochee River has almost everything going for it you can possibly imagine. It used to be that the Withlacoochee had minimum entrance depths of 8 feet, making it the deepest of the Big Bend Rivers short of St. Marks. Following the awesome March 1993 "Storm of the Century," typical minimum, low-water depths in the entrance channel rose to some 5½

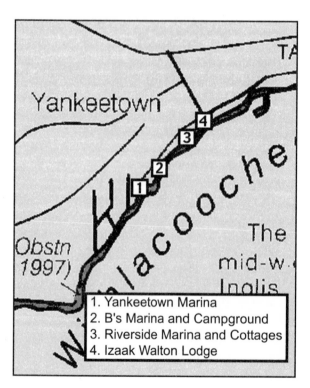

1. Yankeetown Marina
2. B's Marina and Campground
3. Riverside Marina and Cottages
4. Izaak Walton Lodge

feet and have stayed pretty much at that level to the present day. Fortunately much of the channel yields considerably better water. Vessels drawing more than 5 feet might wait to plan their entrance and egress of the Withlacoochee to correspond with a rising tide.

The Withlacoochee's banks are a celebration of deep, almost secret cypress swamps. Yet, in spite of this natural character, the stream's marina facilities are more than adequate. Still not convinced? Well, consider Rex Henderson's unforgettable description of the Withlacoochee as he writes in Del and Marty Marth's *The Rivers of Florida:*

> The river's name comes from an Indian word meaning "little great water," a contradiction that speaks eloquently of the Withlacoochee.
>
> On a quiet canoe trip, the Florida that the Seminoles knew unfolds. The river's flat, glassy surface mirrors thick green tangles of cypress, oak, ash, and cedar boughs overhanging the banks. . . . Turtles sun themselves on logs. An alligator's eyes and snout poke out above the water in the shallows, then sink quietly beneath the surface. . . . The skies are an aviary of beautiful birds. A bird watcher who spies an osprey may then find his attention claimed by great blue and great white herons.

Well, both Mr. Henderson and this writer could go on and on, and have, but perhaps by now you are getting the picture. If you visit only one river between Anclote Key and St. Marks, let it be the Withlacoochee. In an experience similar to the one above, we once came motoring quietly along the river on a foggy morning in October. The primeval landscape of tall cypress and cottonwood trees that opened reluctantly before us was absolutely awesome and completely unforgettable. That same experience waits for any fortunate cruiser who makes the Withlacoochee a port of call.

Getting down off cloud nine for a moment, the Withlacoochee's entrance channel lies some 19.5 nautical miles east-northeast of flashing buoy #2, just north of the never-completed Cross-Florida Barge Canal channel. Minimum entrance and interior depths are some 5½ feet, though 6 feet or better can still be carried along the vast majority of the track. The river is somewhat narrow, and this writer would be reluctant to send any craft larger than 50 feet upstream.

Powercraft skippers will want to make note of the fact that pretty much the entire inner section of the Withlacoochee (east and northeast of unlighted daybeacon #40A) is now a slow-speed, manatee zone. Some of these restrictions are only in effect from March 1 to August 31. However, on the waters of the river's upper reaches, where the private homes associated with Yankeetown begin to border the northwestern banks, no-wake restrictions are in effect year round.

East of unlighted daybeacon #40, the river channel passes into the Withlacoochee's interior reaches. At unlighted daybeacon #40A, passing cruisers will be surprised by the now-rotten hulk of a huge, combination sail- and powercraft moldering away on a small offshoot to the south. Believe it or else, this is actually a German World War I spy ship that was brought to America following the close of the conflict. It sank a decade ago off the Eastern Florida coast. A new owner raised the vessel and had it towed to the Withlacoochee, where he planned to restore it. Obviously, that plan never came to fruition, and the only

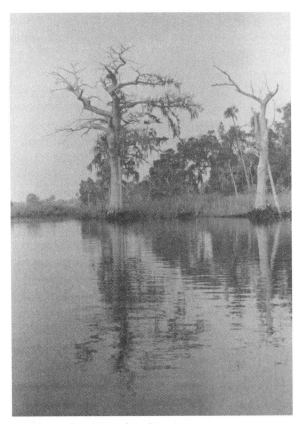

Withlacoochee River shoreline

part left intact these days is the pilothouse.

While depths are certainly adequate for anchorage along the course of the Withlacoochee, this is a fairly narrow river, and swinging room is somewhat skimpy. It could become even tighter if one of the river's commercial fishing fleet happens along during the night and fouls your rode.

The Withlacoochee's marina facilities are small but accommodating. All three are located at the charted location of "Yankeetown" on the river's northwestern banks. First up is Yankeetown Marina (29 01.403 North/082 43.346 West). Most of this facility's docks are tucked away in a small cove indenting the banks, while a few piers front directly onto the river. There is a definite flavor of commercial fishing at Yankeetown Marina, but the superfriendly staff and management are glad to take transient pleasure craft for overnight or temporary dockage. The marina features fixed wooden piers with good dockside depths of 6 to 9 feet. Many of the slips are covered, but there are usually a few open slots available for sail craft. Freshwater connections and 30- and 50-amp power hookups are now available at all the marina's slips. Gasoline and diesel fuel are on hand (with good prices), as are mechanical repairs. Shoreside cruisers will find a small ship's and variety store.

It's an easy walk to Izaak Walton Lodge Restaurant (see below). However, there are no grocery stores within walking distance.

Yankeetown Marina has the added attraction of a resident pair of otters. These loveable creatures can often be seen sporting around the docks. Feel free to look or even take pictures, but don't try to touch the otters. They are, after all, wild creatures with sharp teeth.

Yankeetown Marina (352) 447-2529
http://www.yankeetownmarina.com

Approach depth—5½-20 feet
Dockside depth—6-9 feet
Accepts transients—yes
Transient dockage rate—below average
Fixed wooden piers—yes (many covered)
Dockside power connections—up to 50 amp
Dockside water connections—yes
Gasoline—yes
Diesel fuel—yes
Mechanical repairs—yes
Ship's and variety store—yes
Restaurant—nearby

B's Marina and Campground (29 01.496 North/082 43.236 West) guards the northwesterly banks a bit farther upstream. This facility is a bit, well, low key. During our last visit, we found the bathroom facilities a bit on the scuzzy side. However, transients are accepted at fixed wooden piers, and 20- and 30-amp power connections and freshwater hookups are offered. Depths alongside run around 7 feet. Again, the Izaak Walton Lodge is within walking distance but there are no provisioning facilities.

B's Marina and Campground (352) 447-5888
http://www.bmarinacampground.net

Approach depth—5½-20 feet
Dockside depth—7 feet (MLW)
Accepts transients—yes
Transient dockage rate—below average
Fixed wooden piers—yes
Dockside power connections—up to 30 amp
Dockside water connections—yes
Showers—yes
Restaurant—nearby

A few more upriver twists and turns will bring you abeam of the wooden face dock of friendly Riverside Marina and Cottages on the northwestern banks (near 29 01.652 North/ 082 43.097 West). Some additional slips are located in a small cove cutting into the banks. One glance at Riverside will convince you that this is the spot where most of the resident and visiting sail craft plying the waters of the Withlacoochee find their berths. This facility exudes good management, and the whole ambiance simply cries out, "Stay here!" During our times on the river, we inevitably spot no less than a dozen sailors moored to the piers.

Riverside Marina is happy to accept overnight transients at its fixed wooden piers featuring water hookups and 30-amp power connections. Depths along the pier fronting onto the river run between 6 and 10 feet, while 4 to 6 feet of low-tide soundings are encountered alongside the cove slips. Considering the popularity of this facility, advance dockage reservations are definitely recommended. Shoreside, cruisers will find a single unisex shower, a Laundromat (with ironing board), and, of course, the adjacent rental cottages. Recently, the management has added mechanical, sail, electronic, and refrigeration repairs to their offerings. All service work is done by independent, local technicians.

Don't miss the on-site gift shop. Their selection of handmade "presentation boxes" must be seen to be believed.

Once again, the Izaak Walton Lodge restaurant is within an easy step. As we will discover just below, it's all any culinary desirer could ask for.

Riverside Marina and Cottages (352) 447-2980
http://www.riversidemarinacottages.com

Approach depth—5-20 feet
Dockside depth—6-10 feet (outer dock)
4-6 feet (inner cove slips)
Accepts transients—yes
Transient dockage rate—below average
Fixed wooden piers—yes
Dockside power connections—up to 30 amp
Dockside water connections—yes
Shower—yes
Laundromat—yes

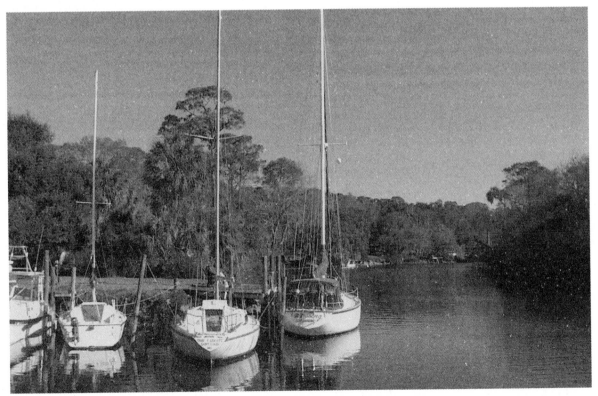

Riverside Marina and Cottages, Withlacoochee River

Mechanical repairs—yes (independent
   technicians)
Restaurant—nearby

Izaak Walton Lodge (29 01.692 North/082 43.004 West)

Just a short hop farther upstream, visiting cruisers will discover the Withlacoochee's most venerable hostelry and restaurant, the Izaak Walton Lodge, coupled with the Compleat Angler Restaurant (352-447-2311). The lodge is surrounded by the delightful residential community of Yankeetown. Quiet lanes shrouded with pines and hardwoods are lined by a pleasant collection of quaint private homes. There is no downtown, and the community seems to center around the lodge.

That is only as it should be. For many years the story of Izaak Walton Lodge was synonymous with the history of Yankeetown. For those of you who don't know, Izaak Walton was a famous English outdoors writer of the 1600s whose classic book, *The Compleat Angler*, extolled the virtues and peace of sport fishing as opposed to the violence of hunting. By 1922 a group known as the Izaak Walton League had been formed in America. The members were dedicated to the "preservation of clean water and natural resources." One of the league's members, A. F. Knotts, came to the Withlacoochee during this time to try his luck with the river's angling opportunities. He immediately fell in love with the natural splendor of the Withlacoochee and its wonderful banks. Before many months had passed, he had purchased an old Civil War sugar landing site along the river and begun clearing land for a lodge. With this hostelry, he hoped to lure his friends from the northeast to share in the great outdoor beauty that he had discovered.

During the 1920s, the Knotts family ran the lodge and lived there during the winter and spring months. The local mail carrier was often heard to say that he had to trudge miles down the river to deliver the mail to those "damn Yankees." Somehow this designation stuck, and that is how Yankeetown came by its name.

The lodge survived the Great Depression and was later used as a health retreat and a private residence. After falling on hard times, the old structure was purchased in the 1980s by Linda and Wayne Harrington. They undertook a magnificent restoration. In addition to the lodge rooms and river cabins, Izaak Walton's featured what was surely one of the most outstanding restaurants in all of Florida.

Then, in the spring of 1999, tragedy struck. A fire destroyed the historic lodge and restaurant. We first learned about the conflagration at the 1999 St. Petersburg Sail Expo, and it was a lowly day in this writer's life. We are happy to report that reconstruction was completed several years ago. The new inn resembles the historic structure as much as possible, but guestrooms are no longer located in the main building. Instead, there are currently two nearby duplex apartments for rent, and eventually, the owners hope to construct a separate but connected building that will house additional guestrooms.

The new incarnation of the on-site restaurant is known as the Compleat Angler. It is open for business Tuesday through Saturday, 5:00 P.M. to 9:00 P.M., and Sundays from 3:00 P.M. to 8:00 P.M. Ever single item on the menu is simply outstanding. If you are up for something different, try the blackened venison or the smoked grilled boar with rosemary sauce.

For us cruisers, the Walton lodge features a

small pier fronting onto the river. You can certainly tie up here, while enjoying the shoreside bill of fare. It may even be possible to stay overnight, but no power connections, water connections, or other marine services are offered. We think it would be best to dock at one of the marinas described above and then walk the short, pleasant distance to Izaak Walton Lodge. Of course, if you're only in for a quick visit to the Withlacoochee, then the inn dock may well be of benefit. Dockside depths run about 8 feet and there should be room for two cruising-size craft at the fixed wooden pier.

Less than a mile up from Izaak Walton's, a U.S. Coast Guard Base guards the northern banks. This headquarters serves mariners along the entire Big Bend.

Our coverage of the Withlacoochee sadly ends at the Coast Guard base. While good depths continue for many miles upstream, the river narrows further, and this portion of the timeless river is better left to our canoeing brethren.

The Waccasassa River

The extremely shallow entrance channel of the Waccasassa River makes into the Big Bend shoreline about halfway between the Withlacoochee and Cedar Key. Unfortunately, low-water depths of 3 feet, or occasionally less, relegate this beautifully unspoiled stream to small, outboard-powered craft. If you should ever find yourself piloting one of these shallow-draft boats, then by all means consider giving the Waccasassa a try. If you enjoy nature, your time will be more than well spent.

Cedar Key (Various Lats/Lons—see below)

The main Seahorse Key Channel, leading to

the old port town of Cedar Key, cuts into the Gulf's clear waters 10.8 nautical miles northeast of flashing buoy #2. A second passage known as the Northwest channel allows ready access to and from the Suwannee River and points north from the town waterfront. The Sea Horse Key Channel holds minimum 8-foot depths, and the Northwest passage has similar soundings except for one 6½- to 7-foot lump. Both cuts wind and turn quite a bit. The Sea Horse Key passage has an amazing S turn that has to be seen to be believed. Be sure to read the Cedar Key navigation section later in this chapter before making your first entry attempt.

The downtown section of Cedar Key is a very mixed bag for visitors. Dock Street flanks the town waterfront. This road is a menagerie of gaudy tourist shops, less-than-spectacular

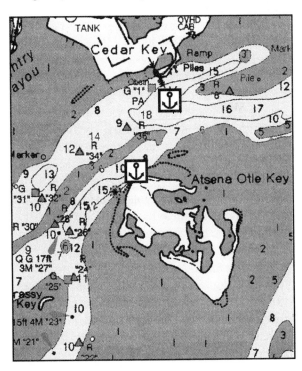

restaurants, noisy bars, and precious little automobile parking. To be blunt, this is Florida at its worst!

On the other hand, a stroll along Second Street, the main passage through the historic downtown section, is absolutely delightful. Be sure to visit the Cedar Key Historical Museum (352-543-5549) at the corner of Second Street and Florida 24. There is also a host of art galleries, which we found to be absolutely delightful.

When it comes time to slake a healthy appetite in Cedar Key, you have to pick and choose carefully. There is a host of bad choices. One of your best bets is a place called Pat's Red Luck Café (390 Dock Street, 352-543-6840). My ace research assistant Morgan Stinemetz reports that the food here is "excellent." He particularly recommends the fried shrimp, oysters, and "home potatoes."

It goes almost without saying that Cedar Key is becoming increasingly popular with landlubber tourists, particularly on weekends. On every one of our visits here, parking spaces have been about as rare as an easily run inlet.

Cedar Key has very little in the way of real dockage facilities for passing cruisers. The often rebuilt city pier is located in the heart of the downtown waterfront. It does have five slips, with some 6 feet of water alongside. There are no power or water connections, and the adjacent bathrooms would probably be avoided even by buzzards. The Cedar Key pier is not very sheltered either. This fact is verified by the frequent reconstruction necessary to keep this dock from falling into the water. By all accounts, you don't want to be caught dead here in foul weather. Adding insult to injury, fellow cruisers report that boats docking at the city pier are often at odds with local fishermen who seem to think that the pier is their private domain. Are you starting to get the picture?

Perhaps your best bet, if you should choose to ignore this writer's advice and berth at the city pier (and not make use of the good anchorages described below), is to carefully tie off your boat, and then spend the night ashore. Those following this plan should check out either the Dockside Motel (491 Dock Street, 352-543-5432), directly across the street from the city pier, or the Island Hotel (373 Second Street, 352-543-5111). This latter hostelry is a wonderful bed and breakfast inn listed on the National Register of historic buildings. Its walls, constructed of seashell tabby with oak supports, have withstood the vagaries of storms since the mid-1800s. The inn has 13 guestrooms, all of which are outstanding. It should also be noted that the Island Hotel has its own dining room, at which the food has been reported to be a "knockout."

Thankfully, there are at least two good anchor-down spots within sight of the Cedar Key waterfront. One is located adjacent to historic Atsena Otie Key. While it may look as if you can cruise directly to the key from the town waterfront, an intervening shoal makes this a tricky proposition indeed. Most skippers should enter this anchorage by cruising northeast from unlighted daybeacon #26 to a point near 29 07.656 North/083 02.030 West. Minimum 10-foot depths are held to a point abeam of Atsena Key's northwesterly point. Farther to the east, depths may look good on the chart, but they begin to deteriorate to 5 feet or so. Nevertheless, boats drawing 4 feet or less may consider easing around the point for better shelter in fresh winds.

This anchorage is well protected from

southerly blows and shelter is fair from northerly winds. Strong westerlies or easterly winds over 15 knots call for another plan.

During fair weather, skippers can anchor south of the city pier, between unlighted day-beacons #36 and #8 (near 29 07.957 North/083 01.825 West). Depths run 12 to 18 feet and there is plenty of swinging room. Show an anchor light to identify yourself to nighttime traffic. Winds blowing over 15 knots from any quarter would bring on a very bumpy evening.

Cedar Key History   Cedar Key, established in the 1840s, played a significant role in the Seminole Indian Wars, the development of the first railroad to cross the state of Florida, Gulf coast shipping and trading, fishing, and the manufacture of cedar for America's major pencil companies. Still largely preserved, the town affords an insight into the development of coastal Florida's towns and architecture of yesteryear.

Rich archaeological artifacts remaining in the form of shell middens and mounds certainly indicate that occupancy of the Cedar Keys predates the coming of Europeans to the New World. The first residents may have arrived as early as a.d. 1500.

In 1834 and 1835 John Gilleland and Edmund Bird were searching for sources of cedar for lumbering. They explored the Santa Fe and Suwannee rivers and discovered the Cedar Keys and their associated harbor. Gilleland was killed during the Seminole Indian War in 1837 and Bird returned to Georgia without pursuing plans for settlements on the Suwannee.

It was between 1842 and 1844 that five settlers established homesteads and obtained

Cedar Key waterfront

permits in the region. Thomas H. Parsons and Henry Crane built houses on Way Key, which was probably the first occupation of the present-day site of Cedar Key. In 1843 Augustus Steele secured a permit to settle on Depot Key (now known as Atsena Otie Key). The 168-acre key, which contained a military depot and hospital left over from the Seminole Indian Wars, was purchased for $227. Steele secured the designation of Cedar Key as a new customs district and helped to establish the abandoned military post as a major seaport on the Florida Gulf Coast. Cotton production and lumbering up the Suwannee and the interior of Florida contributed to the emerging role of Cedar Key as a port.

In 1845, the Florida legislature petitioned the U.S. government for the establishment of a lighthouse on Seahorse Key. The petition noted that the Cedar Keys area was the "depot for all the trade and communication up and down" the Suwannee River.

The steamboat business expanded in the 1850s at Cedar Key. In 1854, 3,000 to 4,000 bales of cotton, sugar, tobacco, and lumber were shipped from Depot Key.

A major event for Cedar Key was the establishment of the Eberhard Faber Mill for the production of cedar pencil blanks and pen holders. It was located on Atsena Otie Key (formerly Depot Key) and soon became the major industry in the area.

Between 1851 and 1852 a charter was granted to the Florida Railroad Company for the establishment of a railroad from Fernandina to Cedar Key. This was a joint venture of Augustus Steel and David Levy Yulee, who was also interested in the Keys' shipping potential.

The outbreak of the Civil War created a lull in the development of Cedar Key and the surrounding lands. The Florida Railroad was in financial difficulty and the establishment of a Federal blockade along the Gulf Coast severely limited the use of the port. Following the destructive war, work began anew at the sawmills which had been established before the Civil War and business began to steadily improve. By September of 1868 there were seven steamer lines running out of Cedar Key, touching at Mobile, New Orleans, and Galveston.

In 1869 Way Key was incorporated as the City of Cedar Key. The town continued to improve and grow and by 1870 had a population of 400. The fishing and lumber industries were going great guns.

By 1884 Cedar Key had an impressive main street and several large commercial establishments. A huge wharf was built out over the water with warehouses nearby and the railroad ended there. Hotels and residential structures were begun west of the town high on a large Indian midden.

When the South Florida Railroad was completed to Tampa in 1884 the deep-water port there began to draw shipping interests away from Cedar Key. This had a devastating effect on the economy and mills began to shut down. The last nail in the coffin was the hurricane of 1896. The destruction was so severe that Cedar Key was abandoned for all intents and purposes.

The turn of the century posed a new challenge to the community's survival. All the major industries had relocated from the island and a report in 1913 indicated no waterborne traffic entering the port. The population was reported at 1,000, and the pier was dilapidated. The only industry in the town was fishing, which survives today as part of the local economy. The significant period in the town's history was over around 1900. The 20th century would see a gradual discovery by tourists of the special qualities of the town and the establishment of a rather important artists' colony and resort atmosphere.

CRYSTAL RIVER TO CEDAR KEY NAVIGATION

Successful navigation of the rivers along the central section of the Big Bend from the Crystal River to Cedar Key is generally simpler than that found on the streams to the south. These channels are somewhat deeper and the passages are exceedingly well buoyed. This does not preclude a few interesting and unexpected twists and turns along the way, so read the information presented below carefully.

Passage along the offshore Big Bend buoyage system now becomes comprised of runs of 10 to 20 nautical miles or better. Just to make life a bit more interesting, the Coast Guard has seen fit to label two of the most important aids to navigation both as #2. Study both chart 11408 and 11409 carefully to be sure you understand the different locations of these two flashing buoy #2s.

As with all passages along the Big Bend, fair-weather voyages are pleasant and often memorable, while foul winds can bring about decidedly different memories. Always plan any cruise along the Big Bend with a ready ear to the NOAA weather forecast.

North to Crystal River   Well, this subhead should really read "northeast." From the flashing buoy #2, well west of Homosassa Bay, that we met in the last section of this chapter, cruisers bound for the Crystal River should set course for flashing daybeacon #1 and unlighted daybeacon #2, the westernmost aids to navigation on the Crystal River entrance channel. It is a lengthy run of 14 nautical miles between flashing buoy #2 and #1. Run a careful compass/GPS course and watch for leeway. Don't allow any slippage to the south. An error of this nature could possibly land you in the charted 5-foot depths ranging west from Crystal Bay, south of the river's entrance.

From #1 and #2 the Crystal River channel runs first to the northeast, then cuts east into the mouth of the Crystal River. Remember "red, right, returning" and proceed with caution, making sure to carefully identify each marker correctly as you move along.

After passing between unlighted daybeacons #21 and #22, you will enter the river's interior reaches. The huge nuclear power plant to the north will be prominently visible. The channel cuts a bit to the southeast at this point and skirts around the northeastern tip of Shell Island.

A short, slow-speed, manatee zone begins at unlighted daybeacon #21 and continues only to unlighted daybeacon #23. Slowing down is not a bad idea anyway, in case a vessel happens to be anchored near Shell Island, as described below.

Shell Island Anchorage   If you choose to try the anchorage east of Shell Island, continue on the main channel for some 25 yards east of unlighted daybeacon #23. You can then carefully curl around to the west and feel your way along with the sounder for some 25 to 30 yards, keeping at least 75 yards off the small beach on Shell Island. Drop the hook before proceeding any farther to the west.

On Crystal River   Cruisers bound upstream on the Crystal River will have no trouble identifying unlighted daybeacon #24. However, we noticed that this marker can be hard to spot when you are voyaging downriver toward the Gulf. Use your binoculars, if necessary, to pick it out from the dark background of trees.

Moving upstream, a newly numbered set of aids to navigation begins east of unlighted daybeacon #25. Pass between unlighted daybeacons #1 and #2, and continue upstream by passing all subsequent red, even-numbered aids to navigation to your starboard side while taking green markers to port.

To access the anchorage east of unlighted daybeacon #8, continue cruising upstream (east) for some 25 yards past #8, and then turn in toward the southerly banks. Feel your way to within 75 yards of the banks and drop the hook.

Hold strictly to the river's centerline as you cruise through "the Rocks," east of unlighted daybeacons #11 and #12. Careful and repeated soundings in 2003 seemed to indicate that you could safely avoid any rocky underwater obstructions by holding to this plan of action. Local reports also speak of other scattered rocks along the river's path. Again, your best defense is to hold to the mid-width.

Soon after leaving "the Rocks" behind, the intersection with the Salt River, home of Twin Rivers Marina, will come up along the southern banks. Please remember, *no sail craft of any size should attempt to enter the Salt River*. As described earlier, the power line crossing the river's entrance is now lower than charted height. This *deadly obstruction must be avoided by sailors at all costs!*

If you decide to frequent Twin Rivers Marina, turn into the Salt River, favoring the northwestern shores a bit. Watch for a whole series of uncharted and unlighted daybeacons that will lead you to the dockage basin. Just as you would expect, pass all red markers to your starboard side, and take green markers to port.

On Crystal River   Depths begin to rise on the Crystal River upstream from the Salt River intersection. The charted "Indian Mound" will appear as a tall hill on the northern banks soon after you leave the Salt River behind. Soundings become somewhat suspect east of this point. We found that 5-foot depths could be carried into the westerly reaches of Kings Bay. Thereafter, low-tide soundings of 4½ feet were sometimes encountered.

To enter Kings Bay, cruise between unlighted daybeacons #29 and #30. To the south-southeast, cruisers will discover a good anchorage, while a turn to the east will lead to Pete's Pier.

Kings Bay Anchorage and Facilities Captain and crew making for the anchorage south-southeast of unlighted daybeacons #29 and #30 should head for the center of the island, which will be spotted to the south-southeast. Drop the hook well short of the banks, and settle down for a beautiful night of peace and security.

Boats continuing on to Pete's Pier should make a lazy turn to the east after passing between unlighted daybeacons #29 and #30. Watch ahead, and you should spy the docks and slips associated with Pete's Pier/Kings Bay Marine. Don't cruise too close to the northerly banks along this stretch. Some rocks apparently shelve out from this shoreline.

If you pilot a shallow craft and want to make a try at the shoaly anchorage on the waters of northeastern Kings Bay, watch for two small islands indenting the northern banks. Turn north as the gap between these isles and the mainland come abeam to the north, and enter the basin just to the north, favoring the two island's shorelines slightly. Anchor along the mid-section of the wider waters, which will open out before you.

North along the Big Bend Cruisers continuing north from flashing buoy #2, well west of Homosassa Bay, must make a fundamental choice. If you opt for the enchanting Withlacoochee River, set course almost due north for the westerly limits of the huge Cross-Florida Barge Canal channel. This passage covers a distance of 7.9 nautical miles. It's then a straightforward matter to cruise east to the Withlacoochee Channel.

Cruisers continuing on to the north will want to set course for another flashing buoy #2, this one south of charted Seahorse Reef. It is a lengthy run of 14.3 nautical miles between the two #2s.

Before moving on to a discussion of the Withlacoochee's navigational characteristics, let's briefly mention the two large, charted channels lying north of the Crystal River. The southern of the two serves the nuclear power plant north of the Crystal. Need we say more? All cruisers are advised to keep clear, unless you fancy glowing in the dark.

The second cut is a bit more interesting. It was to be part of a long, long canal allowing for easy movement of barge traffic between the two coastlines of Florida. Plans for this waterway stretch back to 1935 and Franklin Roosevelt's "New Deal." Actual construction did not begin until 1964. Several miles of the canal were completed on both its eastern and western ends before fervent objections by environmentalists and cost-conscious legislators put a stop to this boondoggle in 1971. Now the channel and a few miles of canal sit idly in mute testament to a project that never should have been begun.

The Withlacoochee River Navigation of the Withlacoochee is generally straightforward. After the March 1993 "Storm of the Century," minimum depths rose to some 5 to 5½ feet at typical low water. Skippers whose craft need more than 5 feet of water to stay off the bottom may want to consult the tide tables and time their arrival and departure with the high water mark.

Be warned that the outer portion of the

Withlacoochee entrance channel is flanked by a whole collection of semisubmerged rocks. Stay in the marked cut.

While it is possible to track your way east-northeast directly to flashing daybeacon #1, the westernmost aid to navigation on the Withlacoochee entrance cut, most navigators would be well advised to make use of the prolifically marked "Barge Canal" entrance passage to unlighted daybeacon #25. At #25, you can cut north through minimum 7-foot depths to flashing daybeacon #1, and then swing east and eventually northeast into the river's well-marked entrance passage.

Begin following the prolific markers through the 3.8-nautical-mile channel leading to the Withlacoochee's westerly entrance. Rocks line this channel along much of its run from the Gulf to the river's mouth. Take extra care to keep strictly to the marked passage. Some of the more obvious rocks are noted below.

Take careful note of the long rock ledge that flanks the northern side of the channel from unlighted daybeacon #7 to unlighted daybeacon #15. Obviously, you need to stay south of this rocky obstruction. Even more worrisome, the charted "Warning Beacon" north of flashing daybeacon #9 sits *north* of the rocky ledge. Boy, talk about bad placement of an "aid" to navigation. Ignore the "Warning Beacon" and pass south of #9.

More rocks line the channel's northwesterly side near unlighted daybeacon #23A. Be certain to pass southeast of this additional hazard.

At unlighted daybeacon #40, mariners can breathe a sigh of contentment as they enter the Withlacoochee's mouth. The channel passes between a small island with a launching ramp to the north and an even smaller islet to the south. Continue straight ahead down the marked cut into the river. Pass the launching ramp area at idle speed.

Watch for the old derelict described earlier along the southerly shoreline, immediately west of unlighted daybeacon #40A. The pilothouse is pretty much the only recognizable part of this sad, old vessel at this point.

Upstream (east and northeast) of unlighted daybeacon #40A, all the way to the Yankeetown waterfront, a slow-speed manatee zone is in effect from March 1 to August 31. No-wake regulations are enforced year round in the Yankeetown portion of the river.

Visiting cruisers might be tempted to try their luck outside of the channel on the wider stretches of the river between unlighted daybeacons #40A and #44. Don't do it. Waters with only 4 feet of depth or less will be immediately encountered.

Between unlighted daybeacons #42 and #43, watch out for a rocky outcropping on the southerly banks. Favor the north side of the channel slightly when passing to avoid this hazard.

Unlighted daybeacon #46 is the last aid to navigation you will see on the Withlacoochee moving upstream. Simply hold to the mid-width as you cruise upstream past #46 and enjoy the scenery.

Eventually, you will spy the first house associated with Yankeetown on the northwestern banks as well as the offshoot where smaller cruising craft might consider anchoring. Powercraft should come down to idle speed as you cruise past the Yankeetown waterfront. All the facilities described earlier will be found on the northwestern banks. Eventually, if you continue upstream, the Coast Guard docks will be prominent to your port side. This guide's coverage of Withlacoochee River reluctantly ends at this point.

On to Cedar Key   Probably the easiest way to find the main Cedar Key—Seahorse Key Channel (also known as the "Main Ship Channel") is to set course from flashing daybeacon #3, at the western terminus of the Cross-Florida Barge Canal channel, to a point some .6 nautical miles southwest of flashing daybeacon #1, south of Seahorse Key. A distance of 10.2 nautical miles separates these two aids. Of course, there are several more imaginative and less straightforward, but perhaps shorter, ways to reach #1, but I'll leave that up to you and your GPS chart plotter.

Cedar Key Channels   Cruisers arriving from points south will find it most convenient to enter Cedar Key by way of the Main Ship Channel, south of Seahorse Key. Skippers cruising south along the Big Bend will probably want to make use of the Northwest Channel. We will first review the Main Ship Channel, followed by a discussion of Cedar Key's anchorages, and finally outline the Northwest Channel.

Notice in the discussion of the approaches to the Seahorse Key—Main Ship Channel above that this writer advised navigators to set course to come abeam of flashing daybeacon #1, the first aid on this cut, by some .6 nautical miles to its southwesterly side. Only when #1 is directly abeam should you cut northeast into the channel. This set of maneuvers will avoid the correctly charted spoil and dump area southeast of #1.

No mariner that this writer knows of would call the Cedar Key Main Ship Channel a piece of cake. Some of the markers are set a bit far apart for comfort, and there is one S turn that you will have to see to believe. Read the account below carefully, and sort out all the markers with care before moving ahead. Be sure to use the "Cedar Keys" inset of chart 11408 for navigating the Main Ship Channel. Its detail is essential.

From #1, point to pass between unlighted daybeacons #3 and #4. Continue on to flashing daybeacon #7, pointing to come abeam of this marker to its southeasterly quarter. We discovered that on the water, the run between #3 and #7 is a bit longer than you might think. You may want to set a compass/GPS course between these two aids. Very shallow water abuts the northwestern side of the channel at #7. Come abeam of this aid by at least 20 yards to its southeasterly side.

As you approach flashing daybeacon #9, look northwest to Seahorse Key for a good view of its old lighthouse. This structure seems to be in excellent repair and it makes for a truly memorable sight from the water.

At unlighted daybeacon #12, the cut begins a sharp jog to the northeast. Set course so as to pass flashing daybeacon #14 and unlighted daybeacon #16 to their northwesterly sides.

Continue following the markers to the gap between unlighted daybeacons #24 and #25. At this point, all cruisers not intimately familiar with the Main Ship Channel should come to a virtual stop and begin sorting out the markers. The confusing array before you is enough to make any navigator lose his or her religion. Before we try to find our way through this mess, let's take a moment to first consider the anchorage on nearby Atsena Otie Key.

To reach this excellent haven, continue cruising north from #24 and #25, pointing to pass between flashing daybeacon #27 and unlighted daybeacon #26. Continue north for another 20 yards or so toward unlighted daybeacon #28. Break off sharply to the northeast before reaching #28 and point to come abeam of Atsena Otie Key's northwesterly tip by some 25 to 30 yards to your starboard side. Avoid the island's shoreline to bypass the charted rock. For best depths, drop the hook as the northwesterly point comes abeam. Boats drawing 4 feet or less can continue around the point for another 100 yards and anchor some 25 yards off the island's northern beach. Farther to the east, depths rise quickly to grounding levels. Caution—this channel is completely unmarked and borders on shallow (and rocky) waters. Proceed at maximum alert!

Let us now return to the more than confusing Seahorse Key entrance channel. North of unlighted daybeacons #24 and #25, the Main Ship Channel passes through a mind-boggling S turn. From the gap between #24 and #25, set course to pass between flashing daybeacon #27 and unlighted daybeacon #26. Continue past #26 and #27 for a short distance and then turn sharply southwest, pointing to pass between #27 and unlighted daybeacon #28. Continue following this track until flashing daybeacon #30 comes abeam to the north of your course. Cruise past #30 a bit and then curl 180 degrees back around #30's southwesterly side until your course is set to the northeast. From here, point to pass between unlighted daybeacons #31 and #32.

If all this sounds more than slightly harried, it is. Study the inset on chart 11408 and compare it to the information above. Take your time, sort out the markers, and with luck you'll come through with only a half-dozen curses aimed at the designers of this channel.

East of unlighted daybeacon #36, the Cedar Key pier will come abeam on the northern shore. If the weather is good, anchor abeam of this dock and consider dinghying ashore. Do not approach unlighted daybeacon #8 (to the east) too closely. It is founded in shoal water.

Northwest Channel   Northbound cruisers leaving Cedar Key or southbound mariners bound for this port of call will find the charted Northwest Channel far simpler than the run in from the Gulf by way of the Seahorse Key—Main Ship Channel. However, Northwest Channel's approach to the Cedar Key waterfront brings up a very confusing array of markers. Read on, lest this situation comes to be a real on-the-water problem.

Cruisers heading into Cedar Key via the Northwest Channel should slow down after passing between unlighted daybeacons #21 and #22. Continue east for 50 yards or so after leaving these aids behind. Use your binoculars to pick out unlighted daybeacons #31 and #32 to the northeast. Ignore the other markers to the east; they are part of the Main Ship Channel and can cause nothing but grief for those entering Cedar Key from this quarter. However, be sure to pass to the northwest of flashing daybeacon #30.

Set course to pass between #31 and #32. You can then follow unlighted daybeacons #34 and #36 (pass them well to your starboard side) to the town waterfront.

Cruising craft departing Cedar Key through the Northwest Channel should conversely set course to pass between unlighted daybeacons #31 and #32 and then point for the gap between unlighted daybeacons #21 and #22. Be sure to pass to the northwest of flashing daybeacon #30 as you make your run between the two sets of unlighted daybeacons.

Once between #21 and #22, turn almost due west and point to pass between flashing daybeacon #19 and unlighted daybeacon #20. From this point, northbound craft should pass all red, even-numbered aids to their (the cruisers') port side and take all green markers to starboard. Of course, skippers bound south on the channel will employ the opposite strategy.

This southernmost portion of the Northwest Channel is the shallowest stretch of the passage. Expect some 6½- to 7-foot soundings.

At flashing daybeacon #16, the Northwest Channel cuts sharply north and then curves more slowly back to the west between flashing daybeacons #11 and #9.

North Key will come abeam south of your course near flashing daybeacon #6. Avoid this islet. It is surrounded by shoals. Flashing daybeacon #2 is the westernmost aid to navigation on the Northwest Channel.

The Suwannee River to St. George Sound

North of Cedar Key, the waters of the Big Bend begin to spread out far and wide before you with increasing distances between the various ports of call. Consider these mileage figures based upon the marked Big Bend offshore route: From flashing daybeacon #2, at the western extreme of Cedar Key's Northwest Channel, it is a cruise of some 11 nautical miles to the Suwannee River. The Steinhatchee Channel is found some 37 nautical miles from

#2, while the entrance to the St. Marks River is a prodigious 77 nautical miles from the same aid. Should you choose to follow the markers and bypass the St. Marks River, heading directly for St. George Sound, you will be dealing with a cruise of slightly better than 100 nautical miles.

Of course, these distances can be shortened considerably by abandoning the Big Bend coastline and setting a direct course for your destination. Over the past several years, several of the so-called Big Bend aids to navigation have been remove from this stretch of remote waters (for who knows what reason), and it now makes more sense than ever to make directly for your goal from Cedar Key.

However you slice it, the trek across the wide-open waters of the northern Big Bend to the Florida Panhandle is not something to be taken lightly. Powercraft, in particular, had better take a long look at their fuel state before beginning their passage from the Steinhatchee to either the St. Marks River or St. George Sound.

The rivers and other ports of call along the northern Big Bend are absolutely fascinating. The Suwannee River vies with the Withlacoochee for the honor of being the most beautiful stream in Florida. The Suwannee is far broader than the Withlacoochee and has a charm of its own that is not easily quantified. The Steinhatchee leads to a fishing village, with much improved dockage for transients. By the time you see the snow-white St. Marks Lighthouse peeping over the horizon, marking the river of the same name, you will have completed your passage across the Big Bend. The St. Marks is, for all intents and purposes, a river of the Florida Panhandle with corresponding deeper depths and heavily wooded shores. At the St. Marks, your passage will turn west toward St. George Sound and the delightful village of Carrabelle, not to mention the anchorages on Dog Island and the easterly genesis of the Northern Gulf ICW.

It has been said by many others, but it bears repeating here, that the Big Bend's northernmost waters hold something for every true cruiser. Just don't forget those long passages through open water, and plan accordingly.

The Suwannee River (Various Lats/Lons—see below)

> Way down upon the Suwannee River
> Far, far away
> That's where my heart is yearning ever
> That's where the old folks stay

It is to the good fortune of every cruising skipper that the sentiments expressed above in the first verse of Stephen Collins Foster's immortal "Old Folks at Home," now the official song for the state of Florida, are as true today as when he penned the tune so many years ago. Indeed, the vast majority of the Suwannee River shores are part of a huge wildlife refuge and are protected from any development. The deep, densely wooded and overgrown banks set against the wide, light-brown waters simply must be experienced to be understood. Words are not supposed to fail a writer, but we found it difficult to put this river's almost dreamlike charm into simple phrases and sentences. Perhaps we should turn to the words of an unknown earlier writer who observed, "The Suwannee River rises in the highest mountains of the human soul and is fed by the deepest springs in the human heart."

Adding to, rather than detracting from, the Suwannee's enchantments, is the small village of the same name guarding the northerly shoreline at the river's mouth. If you want to see what a fishing village on Florida's Big Bend of yesteryear was like, then by all means visit Suwannee. If you took away the automobiles, electric lights, and a few other modern conveniences, it would be quite easy to believe that you had somehow traveled back to simpler times. The village offers one marina

THE BIG BEND 519

friendly to visiting cruisers and one restaurant of note.

The marina facilities at the village of Suwannee offer the only dockage for cruising-size craft along the first twenty miles or so of the Suwannee. Anchoring off, though, is a very real option. In fair weather, you can often pitch out the hook just off the river's centerline. When more shelter is needed, the Suwannee offers the largest selection of sheltered coves and refuges of any river along the Big Bend.

Now for the bad news! Study chart 11408 for a moment and note the two marked channels leading from the Gulf of Mexico to the Suwannee River. Both are now quite shallow. In fact, the southerly of the two, known alternately as West Pass and Alligator Pass, is impassable by any vessel larger than a canoe. As the owner of Miller's Marina put it to me recently, "You'll need a set of roller skates to navigate Alligator Pass at low tide."

Obviously, cruising skippers must make use of the northerly passage. This cut, known locally as the McGriff Channel, darts south of charted "Boiler Gap" and skirts the southern shores of Bradford Island. Even this channel has low-tide depths of 3 to 3½ feet.

The incredibly friendly staff at nearby Miller's Marina is a great help to cruisers trying to run the McGrill channel into the interior reaches of the Suwannee. Call them up on VHF channel 16, and they will be glad to advise you about current channel conditions and the state of the tide. It is our experience that these fine people can get most any boat drawing less than 5 feet into the river during an appropriate tide level. Just listen to what they say! Incidentally, the tidal range on the Suwannee seems to maintain the Big Bend average of 3 feet.

After leaving the pesky entrance cut behind, depths improve markedly upstream of Bradford Island. Minimum soundings on the river's interior reaches seem to be about 6 feet, with typical depths ranging from 8 to as much as 20 feet.

After traversing the Suwannee's entrance passage, you will meet up with a northward-running side cut northeast of unlighted daybeacon #16. This channel runs first north and then northeast to Salt Creek and a portion of the Suwannee village waterfront. With one major exception, this route serves only local docks, and if it were not for Salt Creek Shellfish Company (29 19.702 North/083 09.031 West), cruising captains would probably want to bypass it entirely. Skippers whose craft can't stand this side channel's low-tide depths of 3 feet may choose to enter at a higher tide to visit the shellfish company. This facility offers a laid-back, informal seafood restaurant that serves some of the best fried shrimp, oysters, scallops, and fish in all of Florida, or anywhere else for that matter. This writer particularly recommends the "Salt Creek Fisherman's Platter." This bounteous combination of softshell crab, shrimp, oysters, and Salt Creek crab roll (and more) is sure to bring a look of glee into the eyes of any true lover of good seafood. Low-tide depths at the restaurant's fixed wooden face pier run 3½ to 4 feet with, of course, more water during high tide. Take note that the Salt Creek Shellfish Company (352-542-7072) is closed Mondays and Tuesdays and open all other days of the week from 11:00 A.M. to 10:00 P.M.

Markings on the Suwannee River cease east of unlighted daybeacons #30 and #31. Depths soon improve markedly and the Suwannee's first and best marina facility will soon come abeam on the northwestern shoreline. Watch the banks for two yellow signs advertising Miller's Marina (entrance—29 19.433 North/083 08.511 West, marina—29 19.536 North/083 08.668 West). Allow me to pause for a moment to say a special word about the reception you will find at this facility. In all our travels up and down the Western Florida coastline, seldom have we ever encountered any other marina that took as much time and trouble to give this writer all the information that might ever be needed. Visiting cruisers will find a warm welcome upon arriving at this medium-size, family-operated marina. If you want to know anything about the river, its history, or its people, this is the place to be. The Miller's can relate all you care to know, and then some. As far as I'm concerned, Miller's is the place to dock on the Suwannee River, and it is the last word in friendly service.

Miller's Marina is located along the banks of a well-sheltered harbor that is accessed through a small canal leading northwest from the river's banks. Minimum low-tide entrance and dockside depths run around 4½ and occasionally 4 feet. In addition to the amiable reception, Miller's also offers a good array of services. Transients are accepted for overnight or temporary berths at a combination of floating and fixed wooden piers. The available slip space is limited, so call ahead to check on availability. Freshwater connections and 30-amp power hookups are available at all slips. The showers are squeaky clean, but not climate controlled. Gasoline, diesel fuel, and waste pump-out service are also offered. There is an adjacent ship's store as well a complete campground with clubhouse. The Salt Creek Shellfish Company, mentioned above, is a moderate walk away and is highly recommended.

Miller's Marina (352) 542-7349
   http://www.Suwanneehouseboats.com

Approach depth—4-4½ feet (low tide)
Dockside depth—4-4½ feet (low tide)
Accepts transients—yes
Transient dockage rate—below average
Fixed and floating wooden piers—yes
Dockside power connections—30 amp
Dockside water connections—yes
Waste pump-out—yes
Showers—yes
Gasoline—yes
Diesel fuel—yes
Ship's and variety store—yes
Restaurant—nearby

Suwannee Anchorages (Various Lats/Lons—see below)

Glance at the Suwannee's outline on chart 11408 again for just a moment. Note the location of Hog Island, lining the river's southern banks, just past the village waterfront. From this point, it is an upriver cruise of 20 statute miles to Manatee Springs State Park, the limit of this guide's coverage. In many instances, mariners can simply pitch out the hook on a likely looking part of the river, being sure to show an anchor light. Those wanting a little bit more of an out-of-the-way haven, or seeking better shelter in inclement weather, will want to consider one of the havens outlined below.

First up are the waters off the western tip of the unnamed island (westernmost of two) north of charted Hog Island (29 19.396 North/083 08.301 West). Minimum depths of 7 feet can be carried to within 50 yards of the island's northwesterly tip. There should be enough swinging room for boats as large as

1. Miller's Marina
2. Salt Creek Shellfish Company

38 feet, with plenty of protection from even the heaviest blows. The surrounding shores are the usual extravaganza of natural beauty that is so typical of the Suwannee.

Similarly, cruising craft up to 45 feet should have enough elbowroom in 8+-foot waters off the westerly tip of the second (moving west to east) unnamed island, north of Hog Island (near 29 19.311 North/083 07.811 West). This body of land lines the Suwannee's northern banks, with the river channel passing to the south of the island. Again, the protection and surrounding shores are all anyone could ask

for. Boats as large as 36 feet should find enough swing room.

Well, gang, I've saved the best till last. Note the entry of "East Pass" into the southerly banks of the Suwannee River on chart 11408. Captains can choose from at least four anchorage possibilities on this sidewater, and the southernmost haven is about as good as it gets.

Mariners with larger craft might want to anchor on the northern mouth of this offshoot, near 29 18.903 North/083 07.155 West. Boats as large as 48 feet should find enough swinging room just north of the entrance, amidst at least 10 feet of water.

Forget about chart 11408's 4-foot sounding shown on East Pass's interior reaches. We sounded nothing less than 8 feet on the stream's mid-width, with depths running up to as much as 15 feet. We did note a few snags along the way, so watch out for them.

Next up are the waters in the first, charted knucklelike bend to the east, where chart 11408 shows a sounding of 17 feet (near 29 18.485 North/083 06.999 West). This spot features good soundings of 15 feet or more, enough space for boats as large as 42 feet and superb shelter from foul weather. Oh yes, did I fail to mention the hauntingly beautiful, primeval shores? Of course, all the other anchor-down spots on East Pass share this same advantage.

Those cruising on slightly smaller vessels (up to 34 feet) might also consider dropping the trusty hook on the straight stretch of the creek, just south of the anchorage described above, where chart 11408 notes a small, unnamed creek cutting off to the east (near 29 18.326 North/083 06.927 West). Again, depths run better than 10 feet, and the scenery plus shelter from foul weather are all any mariner could ever ask for.

Finally, captains piloting boats as large as 40 feet may consider tracking their way south on East Pass to the charted knuckle curve where chart 11408 shows a 13-foot sounding (near 29 18.153 North/083 07.034 West). We found 10-foot minimum depths along the centerline of this turn. This is, to my mind at least, the best and most beautiful anchorage on the Big Bend. The deep green shores of this isolated haven have an almost mysterious air as one gazes at their brooding cypress and

hardwoods. Shelter is sufficient for anything short of a hurricane. Be sure to show an anchor light just in case some commercial fishing vessels happen along during the night.

Upper Suwannee River

Intrepid cruisers can continue tracking their way upstream on Suwannee for the 20 statute miles to Manatee Springs State Park. Depths remain good and the shoreline remains idyllic. Eventually, you will sight Turkey Island (see map) flanking the southeastern shores. You might possibly anchor off the southwesterly tip of this land body in 6-foot depths with plenty of swinging room. Don't approach the island's northeasterly reaches, however, as shoal water is soon encountered.

You will sight a single house at the charted location of Vista, while a series of fish-camp-type homes overlooks the western banks at Fowlers Bluff. Otherwise, the natural character of the river is undisturbed all the way to Manatee Springs State Park.

As the park comes abeam on the southeastern bank, captains will find a fixed wooden dock fit only for small powercraft. Mariners piloting cruising-size vessels would do well to anchor off and dinghy ashore. Here you will find an amazing fishbowl where crystal-clear waters boil up from springs 50 or more feet below the surface. The waters are so spectacularly clear that you can see all the way to the bottom. As you can imagine, the springs are a very popular site for scuba diving. The surrounding park features a large campground.

Our coverage of the Suwannee River ends at the state park. The river continues to wind its way north and east for better than 200 miles until finding its source in Georgia's great Okefenokee Swamp. Small craft and canoes can continue their upstream journey into this amazing paradise.

The Steinhatchee River

The Steinhatchee is one of the shorter rivers of the Big Bend, but it has very respectable minimum entrance and interior depths of 6 feet. After traversing the well-marked entrance channel, captains and crew will soon find themselves cruising beside the waterfront of the town of Steinhatchee along the river's northern banks. This undiscovered and unspoiled fishing community is one of the most laid-back towns that this writer visited in Western Florida. The chief topic of conversation at all the local gathering places is almost certainly to be about what's been biting lately, rather than the latest world news event. While Steinhatchee cannot lay claim to any quaint buildings or architecture, the town's relaxed

atmosphere is most certainly welcome amidst the hustle and bustle of our modern lifestyle.

The Steinhatchee does not boast any deep sidewaters, so the only opportunity to drop the hook is found on the river itself. While the stream is certainly wide enough for plenty of swinging room, and protection is quite good, commercial fishing traffic from the village is likely to pass by during the night. Should you attempt to anchor anyway, squeeze as far off the mid-width as is practical and consider setting two or more anchor lights.

Pleasure-craft facilities along the Steinhatchee have improved markedly compared to what they were a few short years ago. However, note that all but one of the marinas detailed below are still mostly oriented to smaller powercraft and sportfishing vessels.

First up is Wood's Gulf Breeze Marina. This small facility guards the Steinhatchee's northerly banks opposite unlighted daybeacon #36, near 29 40.465 North/083 23.960 West. Woods struck us as far more of a fish camp than a real marina. The marina's floating wooden docks are quite low and clearly intended for smaller vessels.

Nevertheless, some cruising transients are occasionally accepted at Wood's Gulf's fixed wooden piers, but no power or freshwater connections are to be had. Approach depths run around 7 feet at MLW with minimum dockside soundings of 4 feet or so. Shoreside, primitive, non-climate-controlled showers and an equally rustic Laundromat sit beside a small ship's and variety store. Gasoline can be purchased pier side. There are eight adjacent guestrooms that are quite convenient for those who want to take a break from the live-aboard routine. The local restaurants (see below) are all within walking distance, and Mason's Market (corner of First Avenue S and Ninth Street E, 352-498-3028), the only grocery in town, is only some three blocks away.

Wood's Gulf Breeze Marina (352) 498-3948
http://www.woodsgulfbreeze.com

Approach depth—7-20 feet (MLW)
Dockside depth—4 feet (MLW)
Accepts transients—limited
Transient dockage rate—below average
Floating wooden piers—yes (very low level)
Showers—yes
Laundromat—yes
Gasoline—yes
Ship's and variety store—yes
Restaurant—two nearby

Ideal Marina and Fish Camp (352-498-3877) also overlooks the Steinhatchee's northerly shoreline a short hop farther upstream. Low-water entrance and dockside depths of a very scant 1 to 2 feet render this facility unusable by almost all cruising-size craft. Therefore, it is not further reviewed here.

Sea Hag Marina, a far better choice for cruising craft, lies north of flashing daybeacon #47, near 29 40.252 North/083 23.320 West. This facility has improved markedly since we were here last. The friendly folks at Sea Hag facility have put some serious bucks into the place. It shows.

From the water, one can see the large name painted in red on the side of a white building. If you cannot find Sea Hag on the north bank of the Steinhatchee River, get thee to an ophthalmologist.

Sea Hag currently boasts 45 wet slips, with 16 of these reserved for transients. Dockside, there are 30- and 50-amp power connections and freshwater hookups. Depths alongside run 4½ to 6 feet at MLW. The dockage basin is reasonably well sheltered from foul weather. Gasoline and diesel fuel can be pumped dockside. The marina ship's store is well stocked with all manner of stuff you might need or want. Here you will discover a 24-hour marine-weather television broadcast. Oddly, because Steinhatchee is not in a population center—or even near one—this is one of only a handful of marinas in Florida that offers such complete weather information. It includes Doppler radar and forecast winds.

Sea Hag has a complete, on-site dive shop, so if you want to go out in the Gulf to dive for fun or meat, this is the place to stop for tank fill-ups or for more equipment. There's a marine electronics sales and repair shop on site, too.

The marina showers are located "across the street" in a motel. That may sound a bit inconvenient, but the people who run this operation are sincere and purposeful, so you can assume that it will be worth the trip.

For larger cruising craft, this is "the" place to stop in Steinhatchee. While there is another marina upriver, you need to have a boat short-masted enough to get under a bridge with 26 feet of vertical clearance.

Sea Hag now features a dockside tiki bar, where a good time was being had by all during our last visit. For serious dining, the local restaurants are close by and so is provisioning at Mason's Market (corner of First Avenue S and Ninth Street E, 352-498-3028). Three riverfront rooms are available for rent, two with kitchens, while the third has a Jacuzzi.

Sea Hag Marina (352) 498-3008
   http://www.seahag.com

Approach depth—10+ feet
Dockside depth—4½-6 feet (MLW)
Accepts transients—yes
Transient dockage rate—average
Floating wooden docks—yes
Dockside power connections—30 and 50 amp
Dockside water connections—yes
Showers—yes
Gasoline—yes
Diesel fuel—yes
Mechanical repairs—gasoline engines only
Ship's and variety store—yes
Restaurant—two nearby

A new facility going by the moniker of Gulfstream Marina and Motel guards the Steinhatchee's southerly banks just upstream from Sea Hag, near 29 40.146 North/083 23.275 West. This is a bit more like a fish camp than like a standard marina, though it has some of the trappings of a modern marina, including an outside restaurant of at least 50 seats. There's a bar and plenty of seating on patio furniture arranged around tables at the restaurant. We cannot vouch for the food here, because the kitchen was closed down, awaiting the arrival of a new entity to operate it. That kind of news always makes one wonder what happened to the previous operator. Was he so wildly successful that he bought a string of Burger King franchises and retired to Key Biscayne, or was there just not enough business to make it? You'll have to decide.

There is plenty of water on the approaches to Gulfstream Marina. Closest to land, at dockside, there is less, about 4 to 7 feet, depending on the tide. Sailboats should get outside slips. For the rest of the craft, it doesn't make any difference.

Yes, transients are accepted for overnight or temporary dockage at Gulfstream's floating wooden piers. Happily, freshwater hookups and 30-amp power connections are in attendance.

The proximity of the restaurant/bar to the marina could cause concern. Teetotalers could get a bit peeved if late-night weekend partying at the bar caused the noise level to rise in the marina. On the other hand, marina guests who managed to get overserved at the bar would have only a short way to stagger to get back to their boats.

There are no transient showers here. If you are dying for a shower, then you'll need to get a motel room. The transient bathrooms, in a separate building, are modest but adequate. They were clean. They also serve the restaurant.

It is a good idea to call ahead for docking arrangements. Weekends could get crowded. On the debit side of the ledger, the only market is across the river in Steinhatchee. It is a good hike and not one of those trips that promotes bringing back ice cream to your boat on a hot summer's day.

Gulfstream Marina and Motel (352) 498-8088
   http://www.gulfstreammotelmarina.com
Approach depth—14+ feet
Dockside depth—4-7 feet at MLW

Accepts transients—yes
Floating wooden piers—yes
Dockside power connections—30 amp
Dockside water connections—yes
Gasoline—yes
Diesel—yes
Variety store—yes
Restaurant—on site (closed)

East of the charted 25-foot fixed bridge (which the locals swear has a typical vertical clearance of 30 feet), River Haven Marina overlooks the Steinhatchee's northerly banks near 29 40.050 North/083 22.536 West. After passing under the bridge (whatever its height may really be), the 6-foot MLW channel used to be outlined by red and green Clorox bottles. Now, red and green 55-gallon drums have been substituted. Progress reaches Steinhatchee.

The nice folks who are the owner/operators of River Haven have made some large improvements in recent years. There are now 51 slips here, with freshwater connections at every berth. Electricity, on the other hand, was in short supply during our last visit. Only one slip had 50-amp service, and another had 30-amp service. You can, however, look for more electrical hookups in the near future.

Transients are accepted at the floating wooden piers, with low-water, alongside soundings of 7½ to 8 feet at the outer slips and at least 4½ to 5 feet on the innermost berths. Some slips are covered, while a second set of berths is to be found on an uncovered *L*-shaped pier.

River Haven now offers waste pump-out and both gasoline and diesel fuel at the head (south side) of their piers. There is a small ship's store just behind the docks. Mechanical repairs for both gasoline and diesel engines can be arranged through a local, independent technician, and some smaller vessels can be hauled out by way of a 15-ton sling lift.

The showers that were under construction the last time we were here have been finished. Just to the west side of the marine store, they are modest but spotless. If cleanliness is next to godliness, the people who run this marina have an inside track to heaven.

When it comes time to visit one of the local restaurants (see below) or stock up the galley at Mason's Market (corner of First Avenue S and Ninth Street E, 352-498-3028), River Haven has an electric golf cart, which they are glad to lend to cruising visitors. How's that for full service?

River Haven Marina (352) 498-0709
    http://www.steinhatchee.com/riverhaven

Approach depth—6-20 feet
Dockside depth—7½ to 8 feet outer slips (MLW)
    4½ to 5 feet inner berths (MLW)
Accepts transients—yes
Transient dockage rate—below average
Floating wooden piers—yes
Dockside power connections—limited (see
    above)
Dockside water connections—yes
Showers—yes
Waste pump-out—yes
Gasoline—yes
Diesel fuel—yes
Mechanical repairs—yes (independent
    technicians)
Ship's and variety store—yes
Restaurant—two nearby

The village of Steinhatchee has (at least) two dining choices that visiting cruisers can patronize with confidence. Bridge End Café (352-498-2002) is located on the Steinhatchee side of the fixed bridge. This dining spot is open for all three meals of the day. It is located in a homey cottage that somehow seems to reflect the friendly character of Steinhatchee village. The selection of omelets for breakfast is outstanding, and there are seven different styles of burgers to pick from for the midday meal.

Roy's Restaurant (on Highway 51, 352-498-5000), right on the Steinhatchee, features a superb view of the water. Seafood is the specialty here. Satisfied diners pick and choose from a selection of flounder, grouper, catfish, scallops, shrimp, and deviled crab. Prices are bit steeper here than at Bridge End.

St. Marks River (Various Lats/Lons—see below)

The snow-white crown of the St. Marks Lighthouse signals the end to your passage across Florida's Big Bend. This old sentinel marks the entrance to the St. Marks River. You will only need a quick glance at the marsh grass shores, backed by pines and a few hardwoods, not to mention the good depths shown on your sounder, to know that you have now arrived at the Florida Panhandle, with all its rich cruising opportunities.

Before going on to look at the St. Marks River itself, let's pause for a moment to consider its beautiful lighthouse. Floridians like to say the first lighthouse in North America stood on the banks of the St. Marks River near where Florida begins to bend westward into its panhandle. Local historians claim the Spanish raised a light at the mouth of the river during their early explorations in the 1600s. There's no real evidence to support this claim, and the Boston Harbor Light, built in 1716, remains recognized as America's first lighthouse.

1. Shields Marina
2. Lynn's Riverside Marina

The old Spanish light, if it ever did exist, was gone by the early nineteenth century when control of the area passed from Spain to the United States. Commercial importance of the Spanish settlement at St. Marks was recognized in Washington and in 1828 Congress appropriated $6,000 for a light to mark the harbor's entrance. Unfortunately, builders scrimped on materials so much that the walls were actually left hollow, and the tower had to be demolished.

A new, solid-walled tower erected in its place was well constructed, but the river quickly undercut its foundations. The government was forced to pull it down and rebuild on another, safer location.

This third tower was built much better and raised the lantern to a point seventy-three feet above sea level. Fifteen lamps and fifteen-inch reflectors allowed the light to be seen by ships more than a dozen miles at sea under ideal conditions. The brick-and-mortar tower has endured and still stands proudly to this very day.

Having survived the Seminole Indian Wars, the tower was almost blown up by Confederate soldiers during the Civil War to prevent its use by the Union navy. The blast knocked out a third of its circumference, but the stubborn tower refused to fall. Shortly after the war, the Lighthouse Board managed to repair the lighthouse and, by early 1867, had it back in service.

No longer in use, this old sentinel of the sea still gazes proudly over the waters of the northeastern Gulf of Mexico as a constant reminder of the days of wind, wood, rope, and canvas. The light is often rated as one of the most picturesque sights on the Gulf Coast. Located in a pristine refuge, it's alive with sea birds and other wildlife. Although not open to the public, it is well worth a few moments of gazing time as you enter the river.

The St. Marks River Channel boasts minimum depths of 10 feet, with many soundings showing 15 feet or more of water. The passage is extremely well marked, but it twists and winds first one way and then another. Numerous conversations with local captains, as well as our own soundings and observations, point up the important fact that, while the channel itself is deep, you must keep to the marked cut. Outside of the buoys and other aids to navigation, depths quickly rise to grounding levels.

During daylight, most careful cruisers will be able to run the St. Marks entrance channel with few problems. Be advised that it is a long run of almost 8 nautical miles from the outermost marker, flashing buoy #1, to the intersection of the St. Marks and Wakulla rivers. Then it's another mile or so up the former stream to the two regional marinas serving cruising vessels. Sail-craft and slow-moving trawlers should factor these distances into their plans if a late arrival seems to be in the cards. We do not recommend strangers running the long and winding entrance channel after dark.

The St. Marks is an absolutely enchanting river. The riverbanks are almost completely undeveloped as far as the intersection with the Wakulla River. The prevailing marsh grass is backdropped by densely wooded shores, which seem to have changed little since Spanish conquistadors first visited this timeless stream. The village of St. Marks sits at the forks of the St. Marks and Wakulla rivers. Holding to the same theme as the river for which it is named, St. Marks is a delightful, unspoiled fishing town. A stroll along the village's quiet lanes is definitely recommended after a rough Big Bend crossing.

After traversing the entrance channel, cruisers will find themselves at the intersection of the St. Marks and Wakulla rivers near flashing daybeacon #63. Most mariners will want to cut northeast and follow the track of the St. Marks River. While 5-foot depths continue for a mile or so up the Wakulla, unmarked shoals are soon encountered. Our own cruise of this stream taught us that it's easy to wander onto these shallows, even when trying scrupulously to follow the centerline.

One happy exception to the Wakulla's cruising problems is found on its southernmost reaches, well short of the troublesome shoals described above. St. Marks Yacht Club (850-925-6606) flanks the Wakulla's eastern banks just above the St. Marks intersection. This private club is obviously centered around powercraft, as evidenced by its covered slips. Dockside depths are an impressive 8 to 10 feet.

Fort San Marcos De Apalache State Park (850-925-6216) occupies the point of land separating the St. Marks and Wakulla rivers. This must-see point of interest (see history below) features a natural trail, museum, and interpretive outdoor signage. It is a quick walk away from either of the two St. Marks marinas and is highly recommended for all visiting cruisers.

After turning up the St. Marks River past the state historic site, leaving the Wakulla behind, the village waterfront will come abeam on the northern banks. First of the area facilities is Shields Marina (30 09.369 North/084 12.039 West), which will come up to the north in the heart of the St. Marks village waterfront. This writer votes Shields the nicest marina in the Big Bend. Finally, cruisers of all descriptions will feel as if they have found an absolutely first-class marina more interested in boats of their size, rather than smaller powercraft. Shields Marina is closed on Mondays, so make your plans accordingly. Shields gladly accepts overnight transients at a well-maintained and well-sheltered collection of newly rebuilt, fixed concrete piers. Depths alongside run from 4 to 7 feet at mean low water. Long-legged craft drawing more than 4½ feet should check with the marina staff for the deepest slips before tying up. Dockside power connections run the full gamut up to 50 amps, and water connections are also on hand. Gasoline, diesel fuel, waste pump-out service, and full mechanical repairs are available, as is one of the nicest ship's and variety stores on the Big Bend. Cruisers will also find nice, air-conditioned, controlled showers, a small Laundromat, and expanded dry-stack storage for smaller powercraft. Come mealtime, you are in luck. All the St. Marks village restaurants, reviewed below, are within easy walking distance. You can reprovision at nearby St. Marks Country Store (859 Port Leon Drive, 850-925-9908).

Are you beginning to get the picture? You simply can't do wrong by coiling your lines at Shields Marina, whether it's just overnight or a weeklong stay. This is a family operation, and Chuck and Brett Shields (father and son) simply can't seem to do enough for both visitors and their resident cruisers. Stop by and spend some time with them, and, oh yes, tell them we sent you!

Shields Marina (850) 925-6158
   http://www.shieldsmarina.com

Approach depth—9-15 feet
Dockside depth—4-7 feet (low water)
Accepts transients—yes
Transient dockage rate—below average
Fixed and floating concrete piers—yes
Dockside power connections—up to 50 amp
Dockside water connections—yes
Waste pump-out—yes
Showers—yes
Laundromat—yes
Gasoline—yes
Diesel fuel—yes
Mechanical repairs—yes
Ship's and variety store—yes
Restaurant—several within walking distance

A short cruise upriver will bring the floating piers of Lynn's Riverside Marina abeam to the northwest, near 30 09.365 North/084 11.960 West. This friendly firm features dockage for transients at several ranks of floating and fixed piers facing onto the river. A surprisingly large collection of covered slips housing resident powercraft is found on a sheltered canal cutting into the marina's banks just southwest of the marine store and fuel dock. Depths at the outer slips run from 5 to 6 feet at low water, while soundings of 6 to 7 feet of water are found at the fuel pier and inner docks. Lynn's also accepts overnighters and offers full power hookups and water connections, complemented by gasoline, diesel fuel, and full mechanical repairs. The marina features a nice ship's and variety store. The village restaurants and the local grocery are still only minutes away from the docks.

Lynn's Riverside Marina (850) 925-6157

Approach depth—9-15 feet
Dockside depth—5-6 feet (outer slips—low water)
**   6-7 feet (fuel pier and inner slips)**
Accepts transients—yes
Transient dockage rate—below average
Fixed and floating piers—yes
Dockside power connections—up to 50 amp
Dockside water connections—yes
Gasoline—yes
Diesel fuel—yes
Mechanical repairs—yes
Ship's and variety store—yes
Restaurant—several nearby

As my *Cruising the Florida Keys* coauthor, Morgan Stinemetz, put it so succinctly, dining in St. Marks village is "looking up." All the locals swear by Two Rivers Restaurant (785 Port Leon Drive, 850-925-6732). We have not yet had a chance to check out the bill of fare here, but we keep hearing phrases that are some variation of "the best food in town."

Riverside Café (69 Riverside Drive, 850-925-5668) is open seven days a week (for all three meals of the day) and located right on the St. Marks River. The menu features sandwiches, full dinner entrees, veggie specials, and salads. During the winter months, breakfast is served from 10:30 11:00 A.M.; during the summer from 9:00 to 11:00 A.M. This place has a casual, friendly atmosphere, which most cruisers will cozy right up to.

Posey's Oyster House (55 Riverside Drive, 850-925-6172) has been around forever. It is a large, ultraclean operation with a full bar out back. Posey's is famous for their "topless oysters." If you like raw oysters, be sure to give them a try. Posey's host more than a few "parties," particularly on weekends. Be sure to check out the unique wallpaper composed of genuine one-dollar bills.

As mentioned above, those in search of galley supplies should make their way to the St. Marks Country Store (859 Port Leon Drive, 850-925-9908). Besides basic foodstuffs, the country store also features a bar, deli sandwiches, pizza, and the largest collection of (shall we say) female-oriented beer-company posters that I have ever seen (and I don't want to see any more after this).

St. Marks History For two centuries the St. Marks River has been the site of struggle by Indians, Spanish, British, Spanish again, and Confederate troops.

In 1528, the Spanish explorer Narvaez marched overland with his troops to join ships at Apalachee Bay. His ships never showed, so Narvaez and his men rigged makeshift vessels and set sail, only to perish in a Gulf storm.

Spaniards in 1679 constructed Fort San Marcos de Apalache at the point of land where the Wakulla and St. Marks rivers join. The Spanish were forced to yield the fort to pirates and Indians in the 1700s. The British took San Marcos in 1763, and ceded it back to Spain 20 years later. It is now a state historic site and open to the public.

An international crisis in 1818 was nearly created when Andrew Jackson seized the fort.

Ol' Hickory court-martialled two British citizens for aiding Indians and executed them. Fort San Marcos became known from Washington to London to Madrid. The U.S. Congress spent 27 days debating Jackson's conduct, with the House of Representatives voting for censure.

Three years later, Tallahassee became a territorial capital and, to solidify the region's new status, the St. Marks River became a valued transportation route for cotton, slaves, timber, furs, hides, tobacco, alcohol, and mosquito netting. In 1828 the U.S. government built a lighthouse at the St. Marks entrance.

That beacon signaled the channel at which a fourteen-ship flotilla in 1865 disembarked more than 800 Federal soldiers. They marched north to capture Newport, then St. Marks in a rear attack. The ultimate goal was Tallahassee.

Forced to cross the St. Marks River at Natural Bridge because a railroad bridge had burned down, the Union troops were driven back by the Confederates, and Tallahassee was saved. Florida's Confederate capital was the only one east of the Mississippi never captured by the Union.

Today the river is bounded by the St. Marks National Wildlife Refuge, which was founded in 1931. It's the only large parcel of publicly owned land along the St. Marks. An estimated 300 species of birds, including migrating geese, bald eagles, osprey, heron, and egret, inhabit the refuge.

Hunters on the upper St. Marks can still sight bear and wild turkey. Native Wakullan Tony Ward recalls days down on the river's lower end when the town of St. Marks echoed with more than hunters' gunshots. "I had kin who wouldn't dare let the sun set on 'em if they were in St. Marks. During the 1930s it was like 'Gunsmoke' around here. On a Friday or Saturday night you'd see two or three good fights and shootings."

Additional Facilities

Cruisers bypassing the St. Marks River face a voyage of an additional 40.8 nautical miles to St. George Sound's easterly entrance. Another run of 5.5 nautical miles will bring you to the easterly beginnings of the Northern Gulf ICW. There is but one marina along this lengthy trek to which cruisers might turn for shelter.

In earlier editions of this guide, I used to always review a marina some 5.7 nautical miles west-northwest of the St. Marks River's flashing buoy #1 (the St. Marks' outermost marker), near the charted village of Shell Point. Well, Shell Point Marina is currently closed, though there are boats still docked at its wet slips. This facility seems to be embroiled in some sort of legal harangue, and its future, if any, is uncertain. Until this situation resolves itself, we suggest you avoid the complicated Shell Point channel.

Finally, cruisers have one last chance to stop short of St. George Sound at Alligator Harbor, north of flashing daybeacon #1, itself hard by the northeastern tip of Dog Island Reef. The marked Alligator Point Yacht Basin entrance channel leads around the northwesterly tip of the shoal guarding the harbor's western reaches. The passage then cuts back to the southeast and leads through 4-foot MLW depths to the marina's collection of both floating and fixed wooden piers lining the southern banks. The fixed wooden docks are in fair shape, but the floating piers rate a C- in our book. Transients are accepted, and most berths feature freshwater connections and 30- and

50-amp power hookups. Depths alongside are also in the 4-foot region. Dockage services are complemented by gasoline, diesel fuel, some mechanical repairs, haul-outs via a 40-ton travelift, and a modest bait-and-tackle shop. The one on-site shower can only be rated as inadequate. The adjacent restaurant has erratic hours of operation, and there are no other restaurants or provisioning depots nearby. Quite frankly, we believe that unless you are in a need of immediate dockage, it might be best to continue cruising west to the good marina facilities at Carrabelle.

Alligator Point Yacht Basin (850) 349-2511

Approach depth—4 feet
Dockside depth—4 feet
Accepts transients—yes
Transient dockage rate—below average
Fixed and floating wooden piers—yes
Dockside power connections—up to 50 amp
Dockside water connections—yes
Shower—minimal
Gasoline—yes
Diesel fuel—yes
Mechanical repairs—yes
Below-waterline repairs—yes
Variety store—yes

St. George Sound and the Northern Gulf ICW

West of Alligator Harbor, weary cruisers can track their way through a marked channel to the easterly reaches of St. George Sound. The eastern tip of the Northern Gulf ICW lies just a few miles to the west, while Dog Island to the south offers wonderful anchorage and the village of Carrabelle to the north features delightful marina facilities set amidst a wonderfully unspoiled village. Cruisers wanting to know more about this region and the Northern Gulf ICW between Carrabelle and New Orleans should consult this writer's *Cruising Guide to the Northern Gulf Coast.*

SUWANNEE RIVER TO ST. GEORGE SOUND NAVIGATION

Two terms describe navigation along the northern section of Florida's Big Bend—"wide-open" and "long." Runs between the various aids to navigation become 20 to 30 nautical miles or better, necessitating careful compass courses, good DR tracks, and frequent reference to the GPS (if you're lucky enough to have one).

This task has been made even more difficult as of late by the seeming removal (at least they've disappeared from the charts) of several key Big Bend aids to navigation. Personally, I wouldn't tackle this stretch anymore without a well-functioning GPS aboard (at a minimum), and, preferably, a chart plotter or GPS interfaced with a laptop computer.

The passage from the Steinhatchee to the St. Marks River is a cause for special concern. Averaging better than 40 nautical miles, this can be as much as an eight-hour run for sailors through wide-open water. Powercraft had better make sure their tanks are topped off before beginning this lengthy run and all skippers should consult the latest NOAA weather forecast.

The three side channels along this portion of the Big Bend run the full range from fairly complicated (the Suwannee cut) to basically simple (the St. Marks River). The

Steinhatchee Channel falls somewhere in the middle.

The offshore passages along the northerly Big Bend are really ideal for sailors and trawlers in good weather. Planing powercraft may look at it very differently, particularly if there is a good chop. However you travel it, lay out a good plan, keep a constant update on weather conditions as you go along, and you'll soon be admiring the white serenity of the St. Marks Lighthouse peeping over the horizon.

The Suwannee River Remember that entry into the Suwannee River is possible only by way of the northernmost of the two marked and charted channels (known as the McGriff Channel). In fact, the southerly cut, called alternately West and Alligator Pass, is not really a channel anymore. According to the good people at Miller's Marina, "You need roller skates to traverse this channel at low tide."

Even the McGriff Channel is none too deep, with low-water soundings of 3 to 3½ feet. Stay strictly to the marked channel. Skippers wandering outside of this passage may well find themselves in but a few inches of water.

Up until now, I've always recommended that cruisers set course from flashing daybeacon #12 off Cedar Key's Northwest Channel to unlighted daybeacons #1 and #2, the westernmost aids to navigation on the McGriff entrance channel. Sadly, it seems as if #12 has been removed. At least it's not showing up on the latest edition of chart 11408. So, now you must keep a very good DR plot and/or make use of your GPS

(or your new, flashy, GPS chart plotter) to find your way to a point abeam of #1 and #2.

Fortunately, this passage does not stray near any shallow water, but for maximum safety, set your course so as to come abeam of #1 and #2 a bit to their westerly sides. This plan will ensure a wide berth around the shoal waters south and east of these two aids.

Once #1 and #2 are abeam, cut directly between the pair and begin tracking your way east on the channel. Switch to the Suwannee River inset on chart 11408 for additional detail. East of #1 and #2, pass all subsequent red, even-numbered markers to your starboard side and take green beacons to port. Most of the channel markers are not charted, even on the inset, but they are fairly numerous and reasonably easy to pick up during daylight. Nighttime entry would be fraught with peril.

Extremely shallow water abuts the entrance channel north of unlighted daybeacon #6. Favor the south side of the cut slightly for additional security.

At unlighted daybeacon #15, the channel ducks to the northeast and begins to pass into the river's interior reaches. Northeast of unlighted daybeacon #16, the alternate Salt Creek Channel makes in from the north. The first two aids to navigation on this side cut, unlighted daybeacons #1 and #2, can be confusing to first-timers. Unless you happen to be visiting the Salt Creek Shellfish Company restaurant by way of the side passage, ignore #1 and #2 and point to pass unlighted daybeacon #24, the next upstream marker on the Suwannee, by some 15 yards to its northerly side.

Salt Creek Channel If you decide to visit Salt Creek and its delightful dining spot, continue on the main channel until the mid-width of the gap between unlighted daybeacons #1 and #2 is directly abeam to the north. Then, cut 90 degrees to port and begin tracking your way north on the cut by keeping red aids to your starboard side and green to port.

Note that as of August 2003, unlighted daybeacon #1 at the southern head of the Salty Creek channel was missing. Hopefully, it will be restored soon, but if it's not there when you stick your bow into this cut, be sure to pass unlighted daybeacon #2 to its fairly immediate westerly side.

Unlighted daybeacon #9 is a source of potential confusion on the Salt Creek channel. Remembering "red, right, returning," one can quickly see that you should pass unlighted daybeacon #9 to your port side. However, this will run your craft hard by the shores of Goodson Island. It's tempting to pass #9 to its westerly side, and if you aren't paying close attention (as we weren't during our last sojourn on these waters), this may well be just what you do. Trust my bent prop's word for it, this is a bad idea. Though it's far from obvious on the water, the good depths do abut the shores of Goodson Island. Pass #9 strictly to its northeastern side.

At #9, the channel cuts to the northwest. Unlighted daybeacon #12 marks a sharp turn in the channel to the northeast on its way directly into Salt Creek's southwestern mouth. Pass #12 to its fairly immediate northwesterly side and immediately set a new course to cruise between unlighted daybeacons #15 and #16.

The docks of Salt Creek Shellfish Company will come abeam on the southern banks east of unlighted daybeacon #29. Get ready for a gut buster.

Back on the Suwannee The current edition of chart 11408 shows two aids to navigation, unlighted daybeacons #30 and #31, as the innermost markers on the eastern-flowing channel into the Suwannee River. The waters in and around #30 and #31 are some of the shallowest in the Suwannee (McGriff) entrance channel. At low tide, expect depths as thin as 3 to 3½ feet.

East of #30 and #31, simply follow the mid-width of the deepening channel upstream to the Suwannee village waterfront. Watch for two yellow signs along the northwestern banks marking the entrance to Miller's Marina. This entrance will be found near 29 19.435 North/083 08.511 West.

Soon, the river flows through a sharp bend to the east-southeast. Recently, shoaling has begun to encroach on the southern flank of the Suwannee's path along this stretch. The shallows seem to be shelving out from the northerly banks of the charted but unnamed island that lies just north of Hog Island. Favor the northerly shores slightly as you cruise upstream on the main river channel. After passing this isle's south-easterly tip, head back for the centerline.

Suwannee Anchorages After turning to the east-southeast, as described just above, two islands flank the main river channel to the north and south. Captains choosing to anchor northwest of the westernmost island (lining the river's southerly banks) should ease their way off the river's centerline toward the entrance to the small passage running south of this body of land. Stop at least 50 yards short of the entrance and throw out the hook. Don't attempt to actually cruise into the waters behind the island. Depths of 3 feet or less are lurking there for you.

You may also anchor west of the second small island, found just east-southeast of charted Lock Creek, by setting course from the main channel as if you intended to enter the small stream that runs behind the island. Drop anchor some 25 yards before coming abeam of Lock Creek's mouth on the river's northern banks. Farther to the east, depths rise markedly behind the island.

Soon the deep mouth of East Pass will come abeam on the Suwannee's southern shore. You can anchor easily at this stream's northerly mouth or cruise downstream, holding to the mid-width, to all three additional anchorages described earlier. There's nothing remotely hard about this. Just stay within shouting distance of the centerline, and all will be well, at least as far as the southernmost recommended anchorage on the waters of the charted "13 foot" knuckle. South of this point, the stream narrows a bit and may become a bit too tight for larger cruising vessels.

Upstream on the Suwannee   It's a delightful run of some 20 statute miles upstream on the Suwannee River from Hog Island to Manatee Springs State Park. Simply hold to the mid-width. You need only worry with two shoals, which are indicated on the map pictured on page 477.

Mariners may also anchor southwest of Turkey Island (southwest of the charted location of Vista), but don't attempt to approach the island's northeastern tip or cruise the small creek running behind this body of land. Both plans will land you in shallow water.

Eventually, Manatee Springs State Park will come abeam on the starboard shores (moving upriver). Watch for a fixed wooden pier.

Our coverage of this wonderful river ends at the state park. Cruisers continuing farther upriver should consult Capt. Rick Rhodes' excellent book *Cruising Guide to Florida's Big Bend*.

North on the Big Bend   Captains and crew continuing their northerly trek must contend with yet another seemingly removed aid to navigation. Heretofore, we've always recommended setting course to flashing daybeacon #14, well southwest of Horseshoe Point. Guess what? Daybeacon #14 no longer makes its appearance on chart 11408 either. Again, not to be repetitive, but let us remind you to keep an accurate DR plot and have a well-functioning GPS aboard.

By the way, if anyone who reads this account discovers that #12 and #14 are really still out there, even though they've disappeared from the charts, we would very much like to hear from you. Please send an e-mail to opcom@cruising guide.com. Thanks in advance.

Vessels bound out from the Suwannee River for points north will have to contend with the charted shallows of Red Bank and Hedemon reefs. Set a series of careful compass/GPS courses to avoid these hazards.

Steinhatchee River Cruisers northbound on the Big Bend must find their way to flashing daybeacon #1, the first (western-most) aid to navigation on the Steinhatchee entrance channel.

Don't approach any of the aids to navigation on the westerly section of the Steinhatchee's entrance channel too closely. Local captains suggest that shoaling is beginning to encroach on the various aids. Instead, hold to the channel's centerline when passing between the various markers.

From #1 the channel continues on a straight run east-northeast to the gap between flashing daybeacon #22 and unlighted daybeacon #21. I bet you've already guessed that you should pass all red, even-numbered markers to your starboard side and take green markers to port.

After passing between #22 and #21, the channel cuts a bit farther to the northeast and runs past unlighted daybeacon #23 and on to flashing daybeacon #29.

At flashing daybeacon #32, no-wake restrictions begin and remain in effect throughout the Steinhatchee waterfront. Soon after passing #32, you will see the village's various houses and docks, mostly along the northern banks.

A sign along the channel warns of shoaling along the cut's northerly flank near unlighted daybeacon #46. Favor the southerly side of the passage slightly through this stretch.

The 25-foot fixed bridge spans the Steinhatchee just upstream from unlighted

daybeacon #25. Any number of locals have informed us that this bridge typically carries 30 feet of vertical clearance. Short of getting out the old measuring tape, however, vistiors had better be prepared for only 25 feet of clearance.

Those boats that successfully cruise under the bridge will immediately spot River Haven Marina to port. Cruise between the red and green drums that will be quickly spied just east of the span, and wait to turn into River Haven's dockage basin until it is immediately abeam to the north.

Farther upstream, the river cuts to the north. This portion of the stream is not recommended, as the waters soon narrow and depths become quite suspect.

North to the St. Marks River It is a lengthy run of some 40 nautical miles from the waters lying west of the Steinhatchee River to the southern genesis of the St. Marks River entrance channel. Using DR and/or electronic navigation, cruisers must make their way to flashing buoy #SM, the southernmost aid to navigation on the lengthy St. Marks approach passage.

St. Marks River The St. Marks River is one of the few bodies of water that is graced with its own special nautical chart, #11406. While this cartographical aid is certainly the last word in detail on the river's passage, many cruisers will be able to follow the prolific markers safely. In case of entry during bad weather, darkness, or other less-than-ideal conditions, 11406 would be invaluable.

The St. Marks Channel is quite deep and most portions of the cut are outlined by a bevy of aids to navigation. Be warned, however, that depths outside of the channel are usually quite shoal.

Quite a few of the St. Marks aids to navigation are small, unlighted, floating buoys. While these show up fairly well during daylight, they are certainly far easier to miss than daybeacons, and finding them at night could be a study in frustration. If possible, time your arrival before dusk.

Take a moment to glance at either chart 11405 or 11406 and notice the unnumbered flashing marker north of unlighted nun buoy #4. Believe it or not, this aid acts as a forward range marker, paired with the white St. Marks lighthouse to the north. The unnumbered flashing daybeacon does not mark the channel and it should be ignored except as part of the range.

From the gap between flashing buoy #1 and unlighted nun buoy #2, at the southern genesis of the St. Marks entrance channel, to the passage between #4 and unlighted can buoy #3A, you can follow the above-described range. From #3A and #4, cut your course a bit to the northwest and point to pass between unlighted can buoy #5 and unlighted nun buoy #4A.

The run from #5 and #4A to the next set of markers, flashing daybeacon #7 and unlighted nun buoy #6, is a rather lengthy gap of better than 1 nautical mile. One set of markers can be hard to spot from the other. Use your compass and/or GPS to keep you on course.

By the time you reach unlighted nun buoy #8, you will have a wonderful view of the snow-white St. Marks Lighthouse on the point to the northeast. Look all you want, but don't try to approach the light. The waters about the foot of the tower have depths of only 1 to 2 feet.

A charted, semisunken wreck flanks the channel to the east just short of unlighted nun buoy #12. We discovered that a portion of this old derelict is visible during low tide, while it is completely covered at high water.

Northwest of flashing daybeacon #14 the channel remains exceedingly well marked to the intersection with the Wakulla River. The cut does wind quite a bit, so take your time and follow the beacons and buoys carefully.

The intersection of the two rivers is encountered soon after passing between flashing daybeacon #63 and unlighted daybeacon #62. Unless you are visiting the St. Marks Yacht Club, this writer suggests turning up the St. Marks and leaving the Wakulla for small, shallow-draft vessels.

Pass unlighted nun buoy #64 to your starboard side as you enter the St. Marks side of the fork. The old fort and state park will be visible on the northwestern banks. There are no dockage facilities, but there is a launching ramp. Slow to idle speed as you pass.

Soon the village waterfront will become obvious, also on the northerly shoreline. You will soon sight Shields Marina to port. Lynn's Riverside Marina will be spotted on the same side soon after the stream takes a small jog to the north.

Channel to Shell Point Please recall our earlier account of the marina's closing at Shell Point, to the west of the St. Marks entrance channel. Considering the navigational difficulty of this approach, we suggest that cruisers not already familiar with these waters bypass this passage until (and if) the marina reopens. As such, we will not present any other navigational data about this route in this edition.

On to St. George Sound Cruisers bound for Dog Island, Carrabelle, and/or St. George Sound should set course to come abeam of flashing buoy #24, southeast of Ochlockonee Shoal, well to its southern side. Be sure to stay south of #24 to avoid the shallows.

From #24, those who have not studied chart 11405 might think it possible to track a direct course west to St. George Sound. Such plans would not take into account the long "South Shoal" running (you guessed it) south from Alligator Harbor. To bypass this hazard, set your course from #24 to come abeam of flashing buoy #26, south of South Shoal, by some .2 nautical miles to its southerly side. A distance of 9.7 nautical miles separates #24 and #26.

Continue on the same course for 1.8 nautical miles southwest of #26, and then turn sharply northwest and set a new course to come abeam of flashing daybeacon #1, northeast of Dog Island Reef, by several hundred yards to its northeastern side. Don't slip southwest of #1. The shoal water of Dog Island Reef is waiting for a skipper careless enough to make this mistake.

Cruisers bound for Alligator Point Yacht Basin can make their way north from #1 to flashing daybeacon #2, the first aid on this facility's entrance channel. Follow the red markers around Bay Mouth Bar shoal stretching west and northwest from Alligator Point. Stay close to the markers as you pass unlighted daybeacons #4 and #8. There is shallow water to the east and west.

From #8, you can begin to bend your course back to the southeast. The red markers will eventually lead you to the marina docks on the southern banks.

Cruisers continuing directly to St. George Sound can set course from flashing daybeacon #1 to come abeam of unlighted daybeacon #2, southeast of Lanark Village, by .5 nautical miles to its southerly side. A closer approach might put you in the charted 3-foot waters shelving out from Turkey Point Shoal, northeast of #2.

From #2, a slight adjustment of your course will bring you abeam of flashing daybeacon #3 to its northern side. From #3, point to pass flashing daybeacon #5 by about 200 yards to its northerly side. Now, bend your course to the southwest, and work your way to a point some 200 to 300 yards west of flashing daybeacon #7.

Now the waters of St. George Sound, Dog Island, and Carrabelle lie before you. For more information concerning these delightful waters, please see my *Cruising Guide to the Northern Gulf Coast*.

Well, we made it. It's been quite a journey from Cape Sable and Flamingo to St. George Sound. I hope you will agree that we've seen some wonderful sights and more than interesting waters along the way. I also hope you've had as much fun cruising these waters yourself as this writer has had in bringing them to you. Good luck and good cruising!

Bibliography

Alger, Daniel B. *Two If by Sea: A Guide to Waterway Dining*. Sarasota, Fla.: Siesta Publishing, 1989.

Howard, Robert J. *The Best Small Towns Under the Sun*. McLean, Va.: EPM Publications, Inc., 1989.

Jahoda, Gloria. *Florida: A History*. New York, N.Y.: W. W. Norton and Company, 1984.

Johnson, Capt. Carey. *Boca Grande—The Early Days: Memoirs of an Island Son*. Placida, Fla.: Barrier Island Parks Society, 1990.

Marth, Del and Martha Marth, eds. *The Rivers of Florida*. Sarasota, Fla.: Pineapple Press, 1990.

McCarthy, Kevin, ed. *Florida Stories*. Gainesville, Fla.: University of Florida Press, 1989.

McIver, Stuart. *True Tales of the Everglades*. Miami, Fla.: Florida Flair Books, 1989.

——. *Glimpses of South Florida History*. Miami, Fla.: Florida Flair Books, 1988.

Mulder, Kenneth W. *Tampa Historical Guide*. Tampa, Fla.: Tampa Historical Society, 1983.

Mullen, Harris H. *A History of the Tampa Bay Hotel*. Tampa, Fla.: The University of Tampa Foundation.

Oppel, Frank and Tony Meisel, eds. *Tales of Old Florida*. Secaucus, N.J.: Castle, 1987.

Rinhart, Floyd and Marion Rinhart. *Victorian Florida*. Atlanta, Ga.: Peachtree Publishers, Ltd., 1986.

Roberts, Bruce and Ray Jones. *Southern Lighthouses*. Chester, Ct.: Globe Pequot Press, 1989.

Schueler, Donald G. *Adventuring Along the Gulf of Mexico*. San Francisco, Ca.: Sierra Club Books, 1986.

Sokoloff, Nancy. *Walking Tours on Boca Grande*. Akron, Ohio: Tarpon Press, Inc., 1986.

Stewart, Laura and Susanne Hupp. *Florida Historic Homes*. Orlando, Fla.: The Orlando Sentinel, Sentinel Communications Company, 1988.

Stone, Calvin R. *Forty Years in the Everglades*. Tabor City, N.C.: Atlantic Publishing Company, Inc., 1979.

Tebeau, Charlton W. *A History of Florida*. Coral Gables, Fla.: University of Miami Press, 1971.

——. *The Story of the Chokoloskee Bay Country*. Miami, Fla.: Florida Flair Books, 1991.

Wright, Sara Bird. *Islands of the Southeastern United States*. Atlanta, Ga.: Peachtree Publishers, Ltd., 1989.

Index

POWER CRUISING
The Complete Guide to Selecting, Outfitting, and Maintaining Your Power Boat, Second Edition
By Claiborne S. Young

Boating enthusiast Claiborne S. Young offers sportsmen a complete guide to the selection, outfitting, and maintenance of a power boat. Young has assembled his firsthand experience with power boats into a step-by-step manual, designed particularly with beginners in mind.

Young's guide saves beginners and seasoned captains, who are stepping up to a larger boat both time and money. It contains a wealth of research as well as valuable inside tips for avoiding common pitfalls. Young begins with preliminary advice to navigators who are buying their first thirty- to forty-five-foot boat. Explaining how different types of hulls and designs can affect a boat's on-the-water performance, he helps determine the skipper's needs of size, power, and style.

While waiting for the boat to be delivered, Young suggests that captains take care of details such as acquiring appropriate insurance, choosing a marina, and taking preliminary courses on navigation or safety. Once the boat has arrived, the most exciting part—outfitting—begins. Young lists the basic necessities as well as practical and optional accessories that can facilitate on-board tasks. His emphasis is on safety as he discusses flotation devices, communication and navigation systems, and the dual importance of reading charts and heeding the warnings of offshore navigational aids.

ABOUT THE AUTHOR
Claiborne S. Young is the author of six books on cruising, including *Cruising Guide to Eastern Florida* ($32.00 pb), *Cruising Guide to the Northern Gulf Coast* ($32.00 pb), *Cruising Guide to Western Florida* ($32.00), and *Coastal Charts for Cruising Guide to Western Florida* ($65.00 sp), all published by Pelican.

240 pp. 6 x 9
Illus. Photos Glossary Index 2nd ed.
ISBN: 1-56554-635-0 $17.95 pb

Readers may order toll free from Pelican at 1-800-843-1724 or 1-888-5-PELICAN.

CRUISING GUIDE TO THE NORTHERN GULF COAST
Florida, Alabama, Mississippi, Louisiana, Fourth Edition
By Claiborne S. Young

"A fine, new guidebook, a bona fide keeper."
—Sailing

"Young's warm and conversational writing style gives even a landlubber a comfortable trip through the navigational intricacies of sailing the coastal waters enroute to the shoreside attractions that beckon all travelers."
—Touring America

For the boating enthusiast, this volume is invaluable as an interesting, unique, and thorough guide to the uncommon waters that stretch from Florida to Louisiana.

Captains will be interested in the Pensacola Lighthouse, both for its value as a tourist attraction and as a navigational reference. Unique restaurants, including Tin Lizzie's on the Tickfaw River, will delight weary, hungry skippers, while thorough marina information will make any scheduled stop a pleasant one with few surprises.

ABOUT THE AUTHOR
Claiborne S. Young is the author of six books on cruising, including *Power Cruising* ($17.95 pb), *Cruising Guide to Eastern Florida* ($32.00 pb), *Cruising Guide to Western Florida* ($32.00 pb), and *Coastal Charts for Cruising Guide to Western Florida* ($65.00 sp). The newest entry in this series is *Cruising Guide to New York Waterways and Lake Champlain* ($32.00 pb) by Chris W. Brown III. All are published by Pelican.

576 pp. 8 x 9¼
118 photos 99 maps Index 4th ed.
ISBN: 1-58980-093-1 $32.00 pb

Readers may order toll free from Pelican at 1-800-843-1724 or 1-888-5-PELICAN.

CRUISING GUIDE TO EASTERN FLORIDA
Fourth Edition
By Claiborne S. Young

Boating enthusiasts will welcome this thoroughly researched and comprehensive guide. *Cruising Guide to Eastern Florida: Fourth Edition* is the most accurate source of details on the facilities and waters of the Sunshine State's eastern shore. In this updated edition, the reader will discover an overview of bridges at the beginning of each chapter. There is also firsthand information on current navigation data, anchorage locales along the entire shore, marinas, shoreside dining, and other attractions.

These waters are the most diverse of any U.S. state's coastline. From the broad path of St. John's River to the secret streams of the Okeechobee Waterway to the "condo caverns" of Hollywood and Miami, Florida offers challenges and excitement. As with his other books, Claiborne S. Young furnishes dozens of invaluable maps, photographs, and chart references. Intriguing historical profiles and coastal folklore give visitors a flavor of the region, while sections on unsafe areas help captains avoid dangerous waters.

ABOUT THE AUTHOR
Claiborne Young's guides have become the gold standard of cruising guides. The author and his navigator wife, Karen, are avid, experienced skippers who have logged countless hours exploring eastern Florida to ensure the accuracy of their descriptions and recommendations. Young also is the author of *Cruising Guide to Western Florida* ($32.00 pb), *Cruising Guide to the Northern Gulf Coast: Florida, Alabama, Mississippi, Louisiana* ($32.00 pb), and *Power Cruising: The Complete Guide to Selecting, Outfitting, and Maintaining Your Power Boat* ($17.95 pb). Additionally, he is the editor of *Cruising Guide to New York Waterways and Lake Champlain* ($32.00 pb). All are published by Pelican.

544 pp. 8 x 9¼ 122 photos 71 maps Index 4th ed.
ISBN: 1-56554-736-5 $32.00 pb

Readers may order toll free from Pelican at 1-800-843-1724 or 1-888-5-PELICAN.

CRUISING GUIDE TO NEW YORK WATERWAYS AND LAKE CHAMPLAIN

By Chris W. Brown, III
Edited by Claiborne S. Young

"One of the most complete boating guides to the eastern waterways I have ever seen . . . a top-notch, well-conceived and wonderfully produced book. . . . This one's a winner!"
—*Great Lakes Cruiser*

No serious captain planning a cruise in the area would want to be without *Cruising Guide to New York Waterways and Lake Champlain,* written in the same format as Pelican's other famous cruising guides.

This firsthand account covers everything from more than 1,000 miles of popular waterways (including Lake Champlain, the Hudson River, the Erie Canal, Lake Erie, and Lake Ontario) to less-traveled waters. The Thousand Islands are also explored. The author's personal knowledge perfectly complements the data on the NOAA charts that he suggests for each area. Among the many useful topics covered are

- current navigational data
- water depths
- anchorage locales
- detailed marina evaluations

- shoreside dining and other attractions
- dozens of invaluable maps, photos, and tables
- intriguing historical profiles

ABOUT THE AUTHOR

Chris W. Brown, III, a native of Albany, New York, has owned thirty-seven boats in more than thirty-five years of boating. His most recent adventure was a five-month, 3,300-mile cruise from Miami to the Great Lakes.

Also available in Pelican's cruising-guide series are *Cruising Guide to the Northern Gulf Coast* ($32.00 pb), *Cruising Guide to Western Florida* ($32.00 pb), *Coastal Charts for Cruising Guide to Western Florida* ($65.00 sp), and *Cruising Guide to Eastern Florida* ($32.00 pb), all written by Claiborne S. Young.

480 pp. 8 x 9¼
116 photos 63 maps Appendixes Biblio. Index
ISBN: 1-56554-250-9 $32.00 pb

Readers may order toll free from Pelican at 1-800-843-1724 or 1-888-5-PELICAN.

FLORIDA ALMANAC: 2004-2005

By Del Marth and Martha J. Marth
Edited by Bernie McGovern

This is a complete update of the previous edition. Thousands of fascinating facts on Florida are available at your fingertips. A first-rate activities guide, reference manual, atlas, directory, and history book, the *Florida Almanac* contains useful information on everything from government in 1875 to how to get a driver's license. This edition also features a hurricane-survival guide.

For those interested in the history and settlement of the Sunshine State, this book covers
- Native American cultures;
- national memorials and monuments;
- landmarks on the national registry;
- the state constitution; and more.

Anyone considering moving to Florida will find
- information on schools;
- descriptions of each county;
- facts on utilities, such as bill comparisons;
- tax and government information; and more.

For the tourist or the Floridian, there are
- maps of each county;
- lists of major festivals, attractions, and art museums;
- charts of rivers and waterways;
- regulations for boating, fishing, and hunting; and more.

496 pp. 5½ x 8½ 27 illus. 155 maps
2 charts Index 16th ed.
ISBN: 1-58980-135-0 $15.95 pb

Readers may order toll free from Pelican at 1-800-843-1724 or 1-888-5-PELICAN.

THE GARDENS OF FLORIDA

By Steven Brooke and Laura Cerwinske

Florida's environment produces a breathtaking variety of plant life, and nineteen of its most famous and most fabulous gardens are featured in this coffee-table book.

Vivid color photographs—almost two hundred of them—showcase these lovely sanctuaries, small and large. Each garden's focus and history is discussed.

Readers can visit well-known places such as Cypress Gardens and Busch Gardens, tropical fantasies like the Parrot Jungle, and quiet retreats such as the Morikami Japanese Garden. Floral fans, weekend gardeners, and anyone who appreciates beauty will love this book. A list of annual events at Florida gardens is included.

ABOUT THE AUTHORS

Steven Brooke, an internationally acclaimed architectural photographer, was awarded the Rome Prize in 1991 and is a Fellow of the American Academy in Rome and the Albright Institute in Jerusalem. He received the National Honor Award from the American Institute of Architects and two Graham Foundation grants. Brooke is the author of *Seaside* ($29.95 /$19.95 pb) and *Seaside Picket Fences* ($12.95 pb), published by Pelican, and *Views of Rome*. A graduate of the University of Michigan, Brooke lives in Miami with his wife, architect Suzanne Martinson, and their son, Miles.

Laura Cerwinske, a native of Miami, was the founding editor of *Florida Home & Garden* magazine and writes articles on garden design for numerous magazines, including *Garden Design, Southern Accents,* and *Veranda.* She is the author of *The Book of the Rose* and *A Passion for Roses,* as well as a long list of books on architecture and design. This is her first book with Pelican. She describes her own garden—a wooded acre of exaggerated botany—as a subtropical Giverny.

128 pp. 11 x 8½
199 color photos
ISBN: 1-56554-184-7 $29.95
ISBN: 1-56554-179-0 $19.95 pb

Readers may order toll free from Pelican at 1-800-843-1724 or 1-888-5-PELICAN.

VIC KNIGHT'S FLORIDA

By Victor M. Knight

Drawing upon the lore of the true cracker, **Vic Knight's Florida** points out everything you *thought* you knew about the state. Sit back with the wit and wisdom of a tenth-generation native as he tells the real history of the Sunshine State that you didn't learn in school. Covering five centuries of people and events, plus speculations on the next century as well, **Vic Knight's Florida** spins the yarns that give Florida its unique character.

Knight dispels many historical myths, starting with how the state's name was chosen. Most people, Floridians and foreigners alike, would claim that "Florida" came from a Spanish word for flowers. Actually, Florida is named for *Pascua de Flores,* the Spanish name for Easter Sunday, the day Ponce de Leon first set foot on Cape Canaveral's sandy shore. Another historical piece of lore describes how the Johnson administration nearly removed five hundred years of history in just thirty minutes when it tried to change the name of Cape Canaveral to Cape Kennedy.

Other points of trivia include the story of the hotel run by the Duchess of Windsor; a single bud of a Japanese plant that created a nightmarish choking of the major waterways; the land boom towns that failed and those that survived when railroads came through; and how, for a brief period in time, Florida was its own country.

ABOUT THE AUTHOR

Vic Knight has compiled his stories from a variety of respected sources, but the telling is all his. He brings a stylish humor to each story with a flair for highlighting the funny, but true, folklore of the state. Knight has owned and operated four radio stations throughout Florida and currently produces his own nationally syndicated Big Band program from his studio at WDBF in Delray Beach. A native of St. Petersburg, he comes from a long line of crackers. Many of Knight's forefathers are the same pioneer settlers who started some of Florida's towns and his grandfather was a state senator. When not on the air, his voice carries across banquet halls, meeting rooms, and sundry locations, where he has entertained thousands with his popular storytelling and particular view of history.

240 pp. 6 x 9¼
48 photos 4 illus. 2 maps Biblio.
ISBN: 0-88289-964-3 $16.95

Readers may order toll free from Pelican at 1-800-843-1724 or 1-888-5-PELICAN.

FLORIDA SCAMS

By Victor M. Knight

We all know about Florida's sun, surf, and senior-citizen population, but what do we know about its seedy underbelly? It is a fact that Florida's loophole-laden tax laws and laissez-faire attitude have attracted all kinds of swindlers, from the garden variety con man to criminals as infamous as Al Capone. It is also a fact that Vic Knight knows virtually all there is to know about every one of them.

As a tenth-generation Floridian, Knight has abundant personal knowledge of Florida history, which augments his wealth of research on scams. Taking the immortal words of his Papa Johnson and Papa Knight, he has compiled a set of Grandaddy's Rules that can help a person see through the "smooth-talking jaspers" who, over the years, have bamboozled victims out of billions of dollars.

Witty, informal, and sprinkled with down-home Florida vernacular, Knight's tales of the strange educate as they delight. Shady characters like mayor/preacher/convicted felon Oyster King Willie Popham, the fictitious Prince Michael of Austria, and "the mysterious fifty-dollar tipper" carry off a potpourri of scams involving everything from luxury cars to ostrich eggs to phony tax returns. Knight explains how Boca Raton is a city based on the scam, like Treasure Island, whose very name comes from the scam that put it on the map. These cons attract scores of people because they seem fool-proof, but remember Grandaddy's Rule #3: "Nobody ever pulled a rabbit out of a hat without carefully puttin' one in there first."

Victor M. Knight, a successful radio-station owner turned Florida guru, is a busy lecturer and television-show host. His first book, **Vic Knight's Florida** ($16.95), is also published by Pelican.

176 pp. 5½ x 8½
Appendix Biblio.
ISBN: 1-56554-190-1 $9.95 pb

Readers may order toll free from Pelican at 1-800-843-1724 or 1-888-5-PELICAN.

A CONCISE NATURAL HISTORY
OF EAST AND WEST FLORIDA
By Bernard Romans

Covering everything from Acadians to Yellow Fever, Bernard Romans exhaustively addresses daily life in Florida and describes its natural features—but he also does much more. He copiously conveys the manners and customs of the native Chickasaw, Choctaw, and Creek Indians, including, despite their bad traits, one common outstanding virtue: hospitality. Romans also notes the habits and character of the colonists and comments on the prevalence of drinking. By focusing his attention on even the most minute detail, Romans has given us a fascinating, true account of early Florida.

According to the Library of Congress, "the variety of natural, aboriginal, historic, and miscellaneous information which [the book] graphically gives is far more original than a great many pioneer histories." Originally published in 1775, this rare work was first reprinted by Pelican in 1961.

ABOUT THE AUTHOR
Bernard Romans was sent by the British government to America in 1755 as a civil engineer. He has been called a universal genius, distinguished not only as an engineer, but also as a surveyor, botanist, writer, and cartographer. His great and extensive map of the Floridas is one of the finest pieces of cartography of the region.

A CONCISE NATURAL HISTORY OF EAST AND WEST FLORIDA
By Bernard Romans
316 pp. 5½ x 8½
9 illus. 3 maps Table Appendix
ISBN: 1-56554-613-X $30.00 pb (F)

Readers may order toll free from Pelican at 1-800-843-1724 or 1-888-5-PELICAN.